THE NEW
Salmagundi
READER

THE NEW
Salmagundi
READER

Edited by

Robert Boyers *and* Peggy Boyers

SYRACUSE UNIVERSITY PRESS

First Edition 1996

96   97   98   99   00   01   6   5   4   3   2   1

The paper used in this publication meets the minimum requirements
of American National Standard for Information Sciences—Permanence
of Paper for Printed Library Materials, ANSI Z39.48-1984. ∞™

Library of Congress Cataloging-in-Publication Data
The New Salmagundi Reader.
p.   cm.
ISBN 0-8156-2704-1 (alk. paper). — ISBN 0-8156-0384-3 (pbk. : alk.
paper)
1. Social sciences. 2. Humanities.
H35.N49   1996
300—dc20   96-8965

Manufactured in the United States of America

In memory of Christopher Lasch

Contents

Contents

Foreword

BY STANLEY KAUFFMANN

This book, like every anthology drawn from one magazine, will have two kinds of readers. First, those who have not often or at all read the magazine in the years covered, which here are 1982 to 1995, and will respond to the book without any proprietary or temporal sense. Second, probably the larger group, those who have been reading the magazine with at least some regularity and feel affiliated with it.

This second group of readers may also feel, as I did, a peculiar sense of surprise. When the originating magazine is as extraordinary as *Salmagundi*, and even though we are quite aware of this fact, the book nonetheless surprises us by its high quality. Humanly porous, we have forgotten how much of it we have forgotten. To read this Reader as a *Salmagundi* regular is to feel at once guilty and desperate. It seems imperative to reread every issue of the magazine at once from cover to cover because this anthology is clearly not presented as the best of *Salmagundi*, only as a substantial sampler. How much more there must be that has stupidly slipped through the cracks of memory. This impulse is quickly checked by hopelessness: there simply isn't enough time, enough cranial space, to keep all the valuable reading one has done fresh in the forefront of one's mind. Indexes are not much more than a tease: they only remind us that we haven't time enough. (Besides, we need first of all to remember what it is we want to look up.)

So this anthology simultaneously brings pleasure, including several majestic kinds, and pain—pain that is provocative and deviously enlightening. Also, whatever one's age, it is a reminder of the passage of time.

I had these mixed feelings in the 1940s when I read the anthology drawn from Cyril Connolly's *Horizon*.

For writers, and for those with empathy for writers (how could *Salmagundi* readers be bereft of it?), this anthology has a correlated purpose and pathos. It is an attempt to stay oblivion. Anyone who writes for journals knows the flush of gratification at seeing his or her work appear relatively soon after completion. (Even publication in a quarterly is swifter than book publication.) And that writer also knows the price paid for this swift gratification. His essay, or whatever it is, is part of a steadily flowing stream that roars over a cliff into a pool so far beneath that one cannot even hear the splash. Often, often, often we read in journals pieces of writing whose fineness of thought and elegance of expression are virtually being consigned to darkness as we read. Sometimes the writing is preserved in the author's books. Even though books are hardly a solid guarantee against the dark, still we can feel that material in book form is at least partially protected—by library preservation, anyway. With journals, we wave at the treasures as they purl past.

So an anthology of this quality is a solace, a partial redemption. As with the first *Salmagundi Reader*, published in 1983, and as with other anthologies drawn from distinguished journals, this book fights the very essence of its place of origin. The word "journal" derives from the Latin for "day." (The word "magazine" derives from the Arabic for "storehouse"—a white lie if there ever was one.) *Diurnalis*, the origin of "journal," gives us "diurnalness," which this anthology strives to counter. The journal as such, the very idea, is invaluable. To speak only of the English language, it was the product of a burgeoning society in the early eighteenth century that, along with Addison and Steele, surged with appetites—for comment on topical matters, on thought as it was being broached and considered, on life as it was being lived. But—we can all breathe "alas" here—some of the comment, like some of the fiction and poetry in journals, is too good to be lost: and yet is lost.

Welcome to (at least partial) recovery.

The New Salmagundi Reader blazons truth about its authors: they have one sense in common. Certainly they disagree on issues and certainly are not interchangeable. Certainly, too, they share a special impatience. This impatience is defined by Bernard Shaw in the preface to *The Doctor's Dilemma.*

> I have always despised Adam because he had to be tempted by the woman, as she was by the serpent, before he could be induced to pluck the apple from the tree of Knowledge. I should have swallowed every apple on the tree the moment the owner's back was turned.

The contributors to this book don't need praise for their fearlessness, but it's cheering to note that, whether or not they would put it that way, they all share Shaw's contempt for Adam's hesitation. The word "intellectual" is possibly the most frequently defined word in our language; so one more definition can't do much harm. An intellectual is someone who thinks that order, of every kind, exists to be challenged: thus to be confirmed, altered, or destroyed. Intellectuals are by definition—by this one, anyway—actively and permanently dissatisfied.

Herewith is a company of such people.

A few comments on the articles that follow, but only a few. I generally dislike the "master of ceremonies" introduction, in which the introducer offers a line or two about each of the pieces to come, like an m.c. presenting acts at a benefit. Still, some comments press forward, about themes common to several authors.

One salient concern is the relation of intellectuals to power. Leszek Kolakowski, Elizabeth Fox-Genovese, and Cornelius Castoriadis (though he dislikes the term "intellectual") are concerned, in their ways, with this matter. Kolakowski, particularly, speaks about the intellectual's itch for power as a kind of quest for legitimacy.

> After all, nobody asks what the plumbers are for or what the physicians are for, but the question what are intellectuals for is quite natural and understandable. And it is intellectuals who put this question incessantly. They hope eventually to find a kind of social legitimacy which they feel they lack.

Kolakowski's immediate concern—presumably he is thinking of Heidegger—is to comprehend how intellectuals sometimes become "court philosophers in a totalitarian system," but this craving for legitimization through power has numerous different guises.

In 1946 Lionel Trilling wrote the introduction to a *Partisan Review* anthology, a memorable essay in which he regretted that the "power of the word," the "power of the idea" had declined. "It is now more than twenty years since a literary movement in this country has had what I have called power." Not since the social criticism in 1920s literature, he said, has there been any writing "to advance our civilization."

In 1983 Denis Donoghue wrote the foreword to the first *Salmagundi Reader*, cited Trilling's essay, and noted the lack of improvement— worse, a decline.

> The status of ideas is not what it was in 1946. Some people still live part of their lives with serious ideas, but their sense of such ideas is likely to be far more rueful, more dispirited, than it was for their parents.

In 1996 few of us would argue that the decline has been arrested, fewer that the importance of ideas, as part of people's lives, has grown. Yet, paradoxically, as the intensity of discussion indicates in the following pages, the debate over intellectuals' power persists. For me, this debate has always had a slightly comic side. Philosophers and historians and political scientists and artists argue the matter vociferously, often brilliantly, while the people who really have power, whose lives have meaning only in the environment of power, people in governments and armies, push forward with their programs, usually oblivious of journals like *Salmagundi*. (I've been told that there was once a meeting in New York between the prime minister of a large Asian country and a group of American intellectuals. After the prime minister had presented some of his plans and policies, a literary critic asked: "Tell me, sir, what can we in the West do to help?")

Nonetheless, despite the slightly comic aspect, the Trilling-Donoghue concern is authentic: because two truths are visible in the intellectuals-and-power subject. First, only great chunks of time can disclose to what extent an idea has permeated the world of praxis. Second, the health of thought itself is at stake: the thinking of others is as necessary as oxygen to those who think. The thinker, like misery, loves company.

Besides, the influence of an idea in the practical world is only one measure of its importance, and not even that measure is always pertinent. Lately I read a line by an early German film critic that seems to me piercingly relevant to this matter of the pragmatics of intellect. In 1909 Gustav Melcher said: "Criticism is as powerless against cinematographic presentations as philosophy is about life." Glossed, this might read: "Film criticism has about as much effect on film-making as philosophy has on life." Who would therefore argue against criticism of the arts or against philosophy?

Criticism of the arts is, of course a large part of this Reader. (*Salmagundi* has sometimes concentrated an entire issue on an artist—Vermeer and Robert Lowell, for instance, or Nadine Gordimer and V. S. Naipaul— which could almost constitute an anthology in itself.) Here, among many enlightenments, Seamus Heaney discusses the past as "a quality of feeling" in selected twentieth-century poets; J. M. Coetzee considers the "rhetorical violence" done to "nuanced readings" by works opposed to censorship but invested in "a metaphorics of battle;" Richard Howard makes a case for Marguerite Yourcenar, Charles Molesworth for the painter Anselm Kiefer.

However, discussion of art in our day must entail discussion of the (possibly transitory?) question of political correctness. On this matter, Daniel Harris says:

> As a writer and gay activist, my contact with pc over the years has led me again and again to the disturbing realization, not only that its cliquishness demands rigid, totalitarian conformity of opinion, but that it is funda-mentally *disrespectful* of cultural differences within society at large.

This rigidity, this crypto-puritanism, has been noted by liberal writers in other fields—in the "discourses" of feminism and racial relations, for example. One residual solemnity of all these observations is a dreadful fact. Totalitarianism is a chameleon. The totalitarian impulse, huge, hungry, is always lurking just outside, looking for one polemical crevice or another through which to slip inside. This Reader cannot represent the full range of voices brought together by *Salmagundi* in recent issues devoted to "The New Puritanism in America" or "Race and Racism." But it amply demonstrates the magazines's will to intervene and have its say in disputes bearing on the culture wars.

In the beginning of *The Pilgrim's Progress*, John Bunyan sees a man, who turns out to be Christian, his protagonist, walking in the fields, reading. "And as he read, he burst out. . . crying, 'What shall I do to be saved?'" For those who pick up this Reader, Christian or not, thinking of salvation by divinity or not, the question is likely to resound. Even those convinced that they have found an answer, of whatever kind, know that the question surrounds them. Phrased variously, differently hoped about and despaired of, considered psychologically or politically or spiritually or however, it is the fundamental question for serious people. Therefore it is present in this book.

The self that is to be saved is probably no longer as unitary as Christian's. Says J. M. Coetzee:

> No one believes any longer that the self is the monadic unit described by classical rationalism. On the contrary, we picture the self as multiple and in many ways divided against itself.

David Rieff, possessed of a comparable view, carries it ruthlessly to his own conclusions:

> It is not just a matter of our having neither Marx nor Jesus to turn to. The great discovery of our time is that the rapid fracturing of identity, the dissolution of confidence in any single purpose or account either of ourselves or our societies, means that we may really have nowhere to turn . . . Cut off from our ancestors . . . by the sheer pace of change—technological, material and cultural—we stare into the void and pretend that we are looking at something intelligible.

This bleakness (it is not too sanguine to say) is itself a manifest of courage. Rieff induces us to summon up yet again a familiar line from a Keats letter, a line that is frequently misquoted or misapplied: "*Negative capability*, that is when a man is capable of being in uncertainties, Mysteries, doubts, without any irritable reaching after fact & reason." The person with the strength to recognize this state of being, and to continue, has a chance.[1]

* * *

To close, a possibly discomfiting but absolutely essential note. The authors included here, and all others who have contributed to *Salmagundi*, will surely be glad to see the Reader. This book, like the magazine from which it is drawn, would not exist without the devotion to ideas and art, to social inquiry, that marks the editor of *Salmagundi*, Robert Boyers, who founded it in 1965: a devotion shared by his co-editor, Peggy Boyers, who joined him in 1975. I could say much more, but the editors would delete it.

Note

[1] One sees evidence of this negative capability in many essays included in the Reader and a great deal more evidence in the Salmagundi interviews with writers scheduled for publication in a companion volume next year. Included will be interviews with Saul Bellow, Nadine Gordimer, Carlos Fuentes, Don DeLillo, V. S. Naipaul, Milan Kundera, G. Cabrera Infante, Seamus Heaney and Czeslaw Milosz.

I
The Sense of the Past

The Order of Battle at Trafalgar

BY JOHN BAYLEY

Some years ago, Lionel Trilling was writing in *Partisan Review* about the "unargued assumption" of our time that the one true object of the intellectual's imaginative life was the modern world and its preoccupations. He expressed a certain nostalgia—even though rather diffidently—for "a quiet place" in which today's intellectual "can be silent, in which he can *know* something—in what year the Parthenon was begun, the order of battle at Trafalgar, how Linear B was deciphered: almost anything that has nothing to do with the talkative and attitudinizing present." Things have changed a bit since then of course. I do not know whether the intellectual at the time was at all heedful of Trilling's point, but I suspect that for his successor in the next generation—the present—the status of facts as facts has been still further diminished. *Knowing* something, in the sense Lionel Trilling had in mind, may seem to him more naive than ever.

The climate of structuralism has something to do with this, particularly where the study of literature is concerned. Rejecting "the metaphysic of presence" we study "self-consuming artifacts"; codes and strategies have replaced facts and objects. The past, in literature, no longer consists of events and things. There may be at least one elementary and grim reason for this shift of attitude towards the past, the negating of any cherished sense of it, and this is that so much in the immediate past will hardly bear thinking about. The Germans for many years resolutely refused to think about it at all. The railway timetables that dispatched trains to Auschwitz do not bear contemplating with the same sense of

3

knowledge—the same "fond participation" in Henry James's phrase—as does, say, the order of battle at Trafalgar.

In his Charles Eliot Norton Lectures, published as *The Witness of Poetry*, the Nobel prize-winner Czeslaw Milosz talked about the implications of this, and how Polish poets like Zbigniew Herbert, Alexander Wat, and Anna Swirszczynska, had reacted to it. A poem of Herbert's implicitly rejects the nightmare of memory in favour of contemplating a pebble:

I feel a heavy remorse
when I hold it in my hand

and its noble body
is permeated by false warmth

and he foretells of such stones that

to the end they will look at us
with a calm and very clear eye

"The Pebble" does without the past in an honourable sense, not the sense in which the past has been rejected by today's critics on the ground that there can be nothing outside the area they control. Reductive as it may be, the poem does not seek to escape from human events or to deny that they ever take place. "The fact," for Roland Barthes, "can only exist linguistically, as a term of discourse," so that the statement: 'Napoleon died at St Helena on May 5th 1821' merely shows that there is an item called "historical truth" in our culture codes. The fact that Poland was occupied by the Germans from 1939 to 1945, and that millions of Poles and Jews died as a result, strike poets who were close to and intimate with these events in a rather different light.

Herbert and the other poets had come up against the fact—for that is what it seems to be—that certain other facts are not susceptible to being dealt with either by our culture codes or by our capacity for human feelings. They remain outside us, like the pebble in the hand, "permeated by false warmth." Much has been written, often histrionically, about the inability of language to confront Auschwitz, but it is not language which is at fault—language as description will do all that is asked of it—but our awareness of facts which remain outside the possibility of feeling. Milosz remarks that many poets tried to bring these events, and their proper feelings about them, into poetry. Such attempts were honourable but a complete failure. Herbert's pebble, looking at us with a calm and very clear eye, shows us why this is the case. Poetry, in such cases, must respect what has happened by acknowledging that it cannot feel it. Paradoxically it will then be in accord with that other sense of the past which Lionel Trilling was thinking of. In both cases the mind reaches out to facts outside itself: in the one case, facts in which the mind can participate just because they are outside; in the other, those in which it cannot participate for the same reason. It is the externality of the past, as of the pebble, which makes art possible in some cases and impossible in others.

The question we have to ask when Barthes tells us that "the fact can only exist linguistically, as a term of discourse," is "why does he want to say that?" The answer may be that history and the past, where so called facts are, have come to repel him, and that he wishes to seal off the language of art and our response to it. That would be in effect a kind of higher escapism, an intellectual elaboration of the theory of art for art's sake. But the more probable explanation has to do with the necessary division between the past and ourselves, between works of art and literature and ourselves. We abolish this division by refusing to admit that the past exists or that the facts of literature are anywhere but in our own codes of discourse. The technique is to insist that what is self-evidently true is therefore comprehensively so. Barthes might have said: "I can only exist biologically, as a function of cellular activity," and thus taken for granted that he cannot think, suffer or recognize the external world for what it is and has been.

Herbert's pebble is irreducible for his consciousness, bringing its own kind of comfort, giving its own kind of feeling. It is "the feel of not to feel it," as in Keats's poem "In A Drear-Nighted December," which concerns the difference between natural objects which have no memory, and therefore feel no pain, and human subjects which do. Comfort? Certainly; any honest poem is comforting, because it tells the truth about our feelings, or lack of them, our powers, or lack of them, in face of externality. The sort of poem which Milosz mentions, one in willed pursuit of "proper" responses to the Holocaust, to the scale and terror of the death camps, has to construct its message in codes which are familiar without being really felt. Faced with Herbert's pebble, on the other hand, we catch a glimmering of what the horror is really all about. The poet did not know he was doing this, did not understand what he was doing. In the phrase of Valery, he only knew what he had said when he had said it. The sense of the past revealed itself to him in an unexpected way.

Barthes and the structural analysts would scarcely find a way of understanding this, because their methods do not recognize the absolute existence of the past or of the fact outside ourselves. Wittgenstein's reasons for saying "the limits of my language are the limits of my world" were strictly and intently philosophical: his statement has had an unfortunate effect, none the less, on the software of literary theory. Dr. Johnson broke the Berkleian hypothesis, to his own satisfaction, by kicking a stone, and common sense is always trying to disenmesh itself from literary theory in the same way. Richard Wilbur, like Wittgenstein, may have been expressing a certain kind of truth when he protested:

> Kick on, Sam Johnson, till you break your bones,
> But cloudy, cloudy, is the stuff of stones

but in using stones as a "term of discourse" he was not saying that was the end of the fact of them. For the structural analyst, however, literature and the past have no existence outside his own analysis of them. One result of this is that he cannot understand why a poem cannot be written "about" a concentration camp.

Such a poem would revolt us by its attempt to merge and be with its subject, by its inability to realize that any feeling it concocts is wholly alien to the fact it describes. This is an extreme case of what structural analysis does to literature itself, and to the past and the events on which literature depends. The common critic, like the common reader, has always been conscious that whatever he thought about the works he read, whatever the degree of his fond participation in them, they remained outside himself, their existence was different from his own and would remain unchanged by it. I am now myself trying to say something about the relation of literature and the past, their relation and their externality;

trying, like all critics, to make a point. Whatever its validity, however, I know that what I think about it has no significance whatever in contrast with literature itself, and the past in which it lives. The ingenuities of structural analysis—and they can be very ingenious indeed—rest on the premise that the facts in literature are themselves as transparent as the critic's words, into which they merge and are reconstituted.

Again it is necessary to ask the simple question: why do the new analysts want to look at things in this light? The answer too seems simple. They are dissatisfied with the traditional position of critics and teachers as on the sidelines of the real, watching the actual ball-game, so to speak, and commenting on it as spectators. They wish to seem, by their processes, to be manufacturing the stuff itself, to manipulate and metamorphose it into endless new shapes, so that it becomes a cloudy constituent of the climate of the modern world. The process needs no facts and truths—the death of Napoleon or the battle of Trafalgar: these have only a relative existence, if any, in the new discourse.

The neo-classic critics and the old rhetoricians were, to be sure, almost equally and confidently dogmatic, and their exercises were often judged not by how much truth they revealed but by how much ingenuity they displayed. Day could be darker than night if the virtuoso produced enough ingenious tropes to prove it so. But the paradox of such ingenuity was that its liveliness depended on a deep belief in the truths and facts available to common sense. It would have been pointless otherwise. Novels today are often written under the influence of the modern critical climate, but it is noticeable that the liveliest ones often resemble old rhetorical practice in that they involuntarily underline the significance of fact even while modishly engaged in calling it in question. Thus in Julian Barnes's novel, *Flaubert's Parrot,* the narrator becomes obsessed with finding the stuffed parrot which Flaubert had on his desk while he wrote *Un Coeur Simple*, a story about a woman who is, among other things, devoted to her parrot. He finds what purports to be the real stuffed parrot in a museum, but then finds a rival parrot in another shrine devoted to Flaubert relics. Flaubert's writings, and what the narrator makes of them, mingle with a sense of unreality presided over by the ambiguous legend of Flaubert, the disappearance of things under close scrutiny, the impossibility of the past itself.

These are the modish notions canvassed by the novel, but the impression it makes on the reader is rather different. The past, the parrot, and Flaubert himself all come most vividly to life, as if to confirm that there *was* a parrot, however now unverifiable, just as there was a real moment (among many others) when Flaubert sat down one afternoon to write *Madame Bovary*, the novel which neither he then, nor its readers now, have ever been quite sure about. The conscious implication of *Flaubert's Parrot* is that since we cannot know everything about the past we cannot know anything; but its actual effect—and its success—is to suggest something different: that the relative confirms the idea of truth instead of dissipating it, that the difficulty of finding out how things were does not disprove those things but authenticates them. It may be that few things happened as they are supposed to, and many things did not happen at all, but why should this be a reason for abandoning traditional conceptions of history, of art, of human character? All three depend upon our sense of the past, and are confirmed by the unknowability of the past. Is it the influence of science, a horror of the past, or a passing fashion of defeatism, which makes us reluctant today to speculate in Lionel Trilling's "quiet place," to assemble the materials of creation and participation?

Our conception of character depends on our conception of history, and can either be seen to be dissolved in the dissolution of history, or actually confirmed by the impossibility of knowing what things and people were like. In the case of Hamlet the uncertainty produced by the brilliance, or perhaps the inadvertency, of Shakespeare's art makes the Prince more of a character, not less of one. He has all the magnificence and the despair, the familiarity and the hauteur, which history suggests about the character of the renaissance ruler. The contradictions make the man. It is significant that historical novels which try to recreate the past, particularly the distant past, seem unable to make use of the uncertainty which marks the idea of a character at any point in history. Novels about ancient Greece, say, construct a Theseus or an Alcibiades who is held together by the fatal assumption, on the novelist's part, that he must be coherent, recognizable, just like one of us. The element of mystery which determines the possibility of a true character is sacrificed to the attempt to produce a convincing and consistent historical picture—"what it must have been like." This is even more marked in science fiction and fantasy, where the Lord of the Rings, or whoever, is a flat figure without any of the queries and incongruities which history supplies. Such fictions are the abdication of that consciousness of the past which was once second nature to all novelists, who instinctively set their period thirty or forty years before the time they wrote, in order that it might become part of the memory and retrospection of the reader, who was unconsciously creating himself and his own past through the medium of the novel.

That instinct of the novel comes to its full and conscious fruition in Proust, who reconstitutes himself from the past and becomes his own novel in the process. Hamlet is a figure of mystery because he lives in the unknowable past, but this does not stop us from having, like Coleridge, a lot of Hamlet in us. What we do not have in us is a character fixed in a historical role decreed by the writer—Tito Melema, say, in George Eliot's *Romola*. The author spent laborious years getting the background of the novel right, and putting Tito—the man who is a complete self, living only in and for the self—into it. The result is that Tito is neither alive in history nor in the present, nor can we be alive in him. He resembles one of those sad statues on the Albert Memorial in London, in a stony limbo of art which has neither the truth of a photograph album, nor the mystery that continues life and joins past with present.

Trilling's "quiet place" is not quiet in the sense of being fixed and definitive. It is, on the contrary, a place of perpetual speculation, contemplation calmed by an awareness of fact, the fact that lies behind history, art, and human character, and makes them one and indivisible. The line of battle at Trafalgar is well known, amply documented. We know the moment of the day and the look of the calm sea when the *Victory's* bowsprit surged into the gap between the *Redoubtable* and the *Bucentaure*. All else beyond the fact is mysterious, given over to the possibilities of historical personality. Did Nelson say "Kiss me, Hardy," as he lay dying that evening in the flagship's cockpit? How much it reveals about him if he did, as about his flag-captain, the big bluff invulnerable Captain Hardy, who was not to die for a generation later, full of years and honours. By the end of the century expectations of behaviour had radically altered, and his admirers had elected to forget what seems to have been Nelson's feminine, histrionic, emotional nature. What might a man with a stiff upper lip say as he lay dying, something that sounded like "Kiss me, Hardy"? Perhaps, "Kismet, Hardy"? Nelson had been in the Middle East, after all, and had dealings with the followers of Islam. For the contemporaries of Sherlock Holmes it seemed the kind of thing that a naval or military man might utter, with a slight smile, a notional shrug of the shoulders.

The example is comic, certainly, but at the heart of the comedy is the stuff of true fiction, as it is the stuff of the past. It is because fiction cannot deal in fact that it absorbs us in the nature and reward of fact. In disqualifying the category of fact from text and discourse the modern critic often shows a curious naiveté about its historical relation to fiction. In an essay on how we should read novels today David Lodge notices the moment in Arnold Bennett's *The Old Wives' Tale* when Sophia, foreseeing difficulties in the future, decides to relieve her drunken new husband of his money and secrete it about her own person. His wallet she hides at the back of the cupboard in their hotel bedroom, "where for all I know," writes the author, "it is there to this day." It would be a very naive reader, comments Lodge, who might wonder if the wallet really was still there, in that hotel in the French provincial town. This comment seems to me to miss the point in a potentially disastrous manner. The reader does not need to be reminded that he is reading fiction: but the author has just shown him how clear, how close, how unmistakable is fiction's relation to fact. How peculiar as well. "There to this day . . . " Sophia and her experience are abruptly brought out of the past where, in an obvious sense, all fiction resides, and into the present. The interchange shows art's simultaneous dependence on its relations with the concepts of past and present, the invented and the real.

Those relations form a criss-cross pattern. Hamlet the character is a literary invention, but he carries his own personal reality both into our sense of history and into our contemporary experience of life. Was he in love with Ophelia? The play gives us no answer: the idea that he might have been increases none the less his potential as a fictional character because it is precisely the same kind of possibility which attends our experience of other people in life. Fiction and life are, so to speak, continually changing places, each under the scrutiny that produces art. In theory we can know everything in a fiction, and about a character in fiction, and very little in life, or about the people we meet in life. In practice fiction avails itself of the disablements of life, and under the guidance of a master hand is enriched by them. In *The Princess Casamassima* James gave up the completely rounded fictional form which defined the character of Christina Light in *Roderick Hudson*. As the Princess Casamassima Christina has become, as it were, an "unsatisfactory" character, the sort of person often met with in real experience who calls forth our curiosity without in any way satisfying it. Christina simply continues through her "life." In his later preface to Roderick Hudson James was to write that "relations stop nowhere," and that the artist's problem was "to draw, by a geometry of his own, the circle within which they shall happily *appear* to do so." He may have been reflecting, at least in part, on the way in which the circle drawn in the earlier novel was ruptured by the reappearance of Christina in *The Princess Casamassima*. She disappears as the completed concept of a character and comes back in a secondary role, seen differently because she is now free to carry on living in an ordinary untidy way. James has washed his hands of her; she is no longer determined by the resolution of the plot and by a completed role in fictional history. The "fond participation" he was to write of in the New York preface to *The Princess Casamassima* hardly includes her, and this reminds us that characters, although they have to be regarded from the standpoint of art, whether we are reading about them or experiencing them in life, have also their own unshaped existence which we cannot enter, and about which speculation is wasted.

A singular instance of the writer removing a character from the flux of events in order to perpetuate him for the "inward eye," occurs in the original version of the *Lyrical Ballads*. In 1797 Wordsworth saw an old man travelling, and composed a sketch on the subject, subtitled "Animal Tranquillity and Decay." What struck Wordsworth, and makes the crux of his description, is the fact that the old man does not seem conscious of the impression he most makes on others—that of patience and "settled quiet." He doesn't seem to "need" the tranquillity his outward form exhibits, and "the young behold / With envy, what the old man hardly feels." Wordsworth observes appearances with the keenest possible eye,

and from them draws conclusions familiar to himself, and with their own sort of comfort for himself and his readers. In the poet's eye the old man does indeed, in some sense, "exist linguistically, as a term of discourse." We are impressed by our own conception of him rather than by the man himself, as is evident from Wordsworth's peroration.

> He is by nature led
> To peace so perfect, that the young behold
> With envy, what the old man hardly feels.

But this view of the matter is completely blown away by the last few lines of the original poem, which Wordsworth dropped in the 1800 edition of the *Lyrical Ballads* and never afterwards restored.

> —I asked him whither he was bound, and what
> The object of his journey; he replied
> Sir! I am going many miles to take
> 'A last leave of my son, a mariner,
> Who from a sea-fight has been brought to Falmouth,
> And there is dying in an hospital.'

Even the original punctuation, with the speech commas at the beginning of the lines, indicates the totality of the contrast with what has gone before. The old man shows that he is neither led by nature to peace so perfect, nor that he is indifferent to the calm about him which is the envy of the bystander. So far from being subdued to settled quiet he is concerned with one overriding purpose, to see his wounded son before he dies, the son who has been present in a battle at sea.

This collision of fact with appearance was first presented by Wordsworth with complete fidelity, as if he were unconscious—as perhaps he was—of the contrast between his view of the old man and the old man's real preoccupations and place in things. The poem has stubbed its toe on a fact which has brought it to an end; but because it is a poem, and a very successful poem, a remarkably fitting end. There is no incongruity between the old man's speech and the impression that he made on the poet, but Wordsworth later became sensitive about such things, and by removing the end of the poem spoilt the wonderful interplay in it between character, fact and history, the interplay which was not "subdued" to poetic discourse, but left in what can only be described as its natural state, the state where our sense of these things is most receptive.

Wordsworth's original poem is both close to Herbert's poem on the pebble, and opposite to it. It is close in the involuntary way it opens itself to history and the fact, to what is going on. Both poems contain a great weight of implication of things the poet knows about but lets only look over his shoulder. Herbert's pebble knows nothing of what has been happening, of all miseries since the world began, and it lets its "noble body" be permeated by the "false warmth" of the poet's and reader's vision of it, and the comfort it brings. Poetry cannot take over the pebble, and this is an obscure earnest of the dire truth that poetry also cannot approach or explain the recent past and its horrors, the massacres and concentration camps.

"Old Man Travelling" takes over its subject, the old man, but is then forced to relinquish him when he opens his mouth and speaks, stating things which the poem cannot handle and take over, which can only be dealt with by their removal and suppression in all subsequent editions. His poetry can deal with "old unhappy far-off things," as Wordsworth did in his poem "The Highland Reaper," where subject and vision remained wholly in his mind. But these instances all emphasize the way in which the recalcitrance of the past, its separation from us, confronts art as firmly as does the individual character, and in the same way. Art must both use and respect them; the reader himself feel their presence as separate entities, and speculate on their several realities, as he does in that quiet place where he can learn in what year the Parthenon was begun, and what ships formed the battle line at Trafalgar.

Place, Pastness, Poems:
A Triptych

I

The sense of the past constitutes what William Wordsworth might have called a "primary law of our nature," a fundamental human gift, as potentially civilizing as our gift for love. It is a common, nonliterary faculty, embodied very simply in Thomas Hardy's poem, "The Garden Seat":

> Its former green is blue and thin,
> And its once firm legs sink in and in;
> Soon it will break down unaware,
> Soon it will break down unaware.
>
> At night when reddest flowers are black
> Those who once sat thereon come back;
> Quite a row of them sitting there,
> Quite a row of them sitting there.
>
> With them the seat does not break down,
> Nor winter freeze them, nor floods drown,
> For they are as light as upper air,
> They are as light as upper air!

The poem is about the ghost-life that hovers over some of the furniture of our lives, about the way objects can become temples of the spirit. This garden seat is not just an *objet*, a decorous antique; it has become a point of entry into a common emotional ground of memory and belonging. It

14

transmits the climate of a lost world and keeps alive a domestic intimacy with a reality which might otherwise have vanished. The more we are surrounded by such things, the more feelingly we dwell in our own lives. The air which our imaginations inhale in their presence is not musty but bracing.

It could even be maintained that objects thus seasoned by human contact possess a kind of moral force. They insist upon human solidarity and suggest obligations to the generations who have been silenced, drawing us into some covenant with them. In this passage by Pablo Neruda, for example, although the poet is not explicitly concerned with the object as capsule of time past, he is nevertheless testifying to the power of the inanimate, its aura of persuasiveness:

> It is well, at certain hours of the day and night, to look closely at the world of objects at rest. Wheels that have crossed long, dustydistances with their mineral and vegetable burdens, sacks from the coalbins, barrels and baskets, handles and hafts for the carpenter's tool chest. From them flow the contacts of man with the earth . . . The used surfaces of things, the wear that the hands give to things, the air, tragic at times, pathetic at others, of such things—all lend a curious attractiveness to the reality of the world that should not be underprized.

Neruda's declaration that "the reality of the world. . . should not be underprized" implies that we can and often do underprize it. We grow away from our primary relish of the phenomena. The rooms where we come to consciousness, the cupboards we open as toddlers, the shelves we climb up to, the boxes and albums we explore in reserved places in the house, the spots we discover for ourselves in those first solitudes out of doors, the haunts of those explorations at the verge of our security—in such places and at such moments "the reality of the world" first wakens in us. It is also at such moments that we have our first inkling of pastness and find our physical surroundings invested with a wider and deeper dimension than we can, just then, account for.

What I am talking about is at the time an unconscious process. It is neither sentimental nor literary, since it happens during the prereflective stage of our existence. It has to do with an almost biological need to situate ourselves in our instinctual lives as creatures of the race and of the planet, to learn the relationship between what is self and what is non-self. It has to do with feeling towards, sniffing out, settling in and shaping up.

In my own case, the top of the dresser in the kitchen of the house where I lived for the first twelve years of my life was like a time machine. This was where much of the bric-a-brac of the farmyard would end up, broken whetstones, old nails, putty, screwdrivers, lampwicks. Its mystery had to do with its inaccessibility, yet when I did manage to hoist myself up there, the dusty newspaper round the putty, the worn down grains of the whetstone, the bent nails, the singed wicks, all that dust and rust and stillness suggested that these objects were living some kind of afterlife. Something previous was vestigially alive in them. They were not just inert rubbish but dormant energies, meanings that could not be quite deciphered. Naturally, I did not think this to myself at the time. It was all sensation, tingling with an amplification of inner space, subtly and indelibly linked with the word "old."

"Old" was not an idea. It was an atmosphere, a smell almost, a quality of feeling. It brought you out of yourself and close to yourself all at once. "Old" drifted in the mind and senses when you came upon mossed-over bits of delph or fragments of a clay pipe plugged up with mould. You took such things for granted yet they swam with a strangeness. And the strangeness deepened when you actually dug such things out of the ground for yourself. My first archaeological tremor occurred when I was making holes for goalposts in one of our fields which had always been kept as grazing and was therefore always pure surface, pure present. When I dug down about a foot into the tightpacked ground, I came upon a hoard of soft red brick and white crumbly mortar, an unexpected cache that even to a six year old meant foundations, meant house, a living but obliterated past. I pestered my father to tell me who might have lived there and found that he did not remember any house on the site. Then I heard him questioning a neighbour about whose place it might have been, who was supposed to have owned that land in the old days, and the hole for the goal-post began to open down and back to a visionary field, a phantom whitewashed cottage with its yard and puddles and hens. The world had been amplified; looking and seeing began to take on aspects of imagining and remembering.

Another example: I knew more from overhearing and piecing together than from being told directly that a number of my father's family had died in their teens and twenties from "the decline," as tuberculosis had been called in rural Ulster in those days. Names of uncles and aunts who might have been floated through the conversation. Johnny and Jamie and Maggie and Agnes. Agnes, I knew, had died young and her invalid pallor which I had never seen was intuitively present to me, again because of her association with an object. This was a little trinket which was kept wrapped in tissue paper and laid away with other specially conserved knick-knacks in the bottom of a sideboard in my parents' bedroom. I knew there was something slightly taboo about rummaging in those shelves but I was drawn again and again to unwrap the thing because I knew that it had belonged to Agnes. It had obviously been bought at the seaside as a present for her. A little grotto about four or five inches tall, like a toy sentry box, all covered with tiny shells, a whitish gleaming secret deposited in the family sideboard like grave-goods in the tomb of a princess. To this day, I cannot imagine the ravages of disease in pre-inoculation rural Ireland except in relation to the slight white fact of that trinket.

In such ways we read ourselves into a personal past, but it is not a past which is chronologically determined by calendar dates or any clear time-scale. Rather it is a dream time, a beforehand, a long ago. We learn it without deliberate instruction, and the result of our learning is a sense of belonging to a domestic and at the same time planetary world of pure human being.

But there is another past which is not just inhaled unconsciously but which is to some extent imposed and to some extent chosen. This gives us our cultural markings, contributes to our status as creatures conditioned by language and history. It is posited upon images which have a definite meaning and implication, unlike images of the bricks and grotto sort whose meanings are accidental and familial.

Take the fairytales we were told at home and at school: these also conjure up a potent sense of the long ago and can endow the world with a sort of legendary history. There is, for example, a story which I can now recall only in the vaguest way about a hen that panics when a nut drops down upon her out of a tree and causes her to think that the end of the world is coming. That tale gave a marvelous status to the corner of our yard where the fowl used to mould themselves in the roots of an old hawthorn. I kept looking there to make sure that the sky was still in position, that no crack was appearing in the dome and that the hens were going about their business free from the hens' version of the nuclear terror. Another story about the man—or maybe it was a widow—who grazed a cow on the grass growing up on the thatched roof of a cabin invested certain old houses and wallsteads in the district with an aura of the fantastic; and the story of the traveller shut beneath the hill with the fairy queen populated certain local slopes with rare possibilities as well.

This fairytale glamour was real enough, but it was dispersed and impalpable. It had nothing to do with the sense of history which began to be derived from books and pictures at around the same time, but which could also be derived from objects in the everyday surroundings. There was in our house an old, cock-hammer, double-barrelled pistol, like a duelling piece, fixed on a bracket above a door in the kitchen. It was a completely exotic item in our world of dressers, churns, buckets, statues and Sacred Heart lamps. It did not belong and it was never explained. Yet when I began to get comics and to read adventure stories, this pistol linked the kitchen with highwaymen, stage-coaches, women in crinoline skirts, men in ruffs and duels at dawn in the woodlands of great estates. Not that this involved any great reverence for the thing itself. When my brothers and I grew up a bit, we got our hands on it and broke it into pieces, inevitably, accidentally and, in truth, not very regretfully.

More significantly influential than exotic items like the pistol, however, are those images and objects which signify common loyalties and are recognized as emblems of a symbolic past which also claims to be the historical past. These guarantee our own way of feeling about ourselves as a group and as such have a potent influence upon our everyday attitudes. I am thinking, for example, of a picture dear to the Irish Catholic heart in years gone by. This was an oleograph of the outlawed priest in red vestments, raising the host above a massrock in a secluded corner of the hills. The hills are covered in snow, the congregation huddles around in shawls and frieze coats under a frosty sky, a band of redcoats is coming into view over a distant crest and in between, a man is running wild over ditches to alert the congregation. Nothing I have learned or could ever learn about penal laws against Catholics in eighteenth century Ireland could altogether displace the emotional drama of that picture. The century will remain in some corner of the mind technicolour, panicky, humble and heroic. Just as Wolfe Tone, our enlightenment revolutionary and founding father of Irish Republicanism, will never quite escape from his reincarnation as the figure in tight-fitting white trousers and braided green coat whose large profiled nose stared out over the audience in our local hall. There he was, a given figure with a strange name, a man called wolf.

He was to come up again, this time as an illustration in an old *Wolfe Tone Annual* that I came across some time in the late forties; now he was dressed in an open shirt and dark breeches, his arms folded, staring into a shaft of light that struck into his prison cell from a high barred window. Again, this image of a noble nature stoically enduring had a deeply formative effect on my notion of the United Irishmen, the 1798 rebellion and the whole tradition of Irish separatism. I do not mean that I closed my mind to other notions but it offered a dream against which all further learning took place. Tone's eloquent profile, for example, was not entirely eroded when I read Sir Joshuah Barrington's description of him: "His person was unfavourable—his countenance thin and sallow; and he had in his speech a hard guttural pronunciation of the letter R."

In Ireland we have been properly taught to be wary of these idealized images of the political past because of the righteousness and simplifications implicit in them and the dangerous messianic arrogance which can flow from them. Less ideologically conditioning, more humanly accurate are those objects and documents which survive from the historical moment. No image of Hugh O'Neill, the last Gaelic Earl of Tyrone—to take another powerful figure from the pantheon—no portrait of him with his strong Ulster face and Elizabethan clothes can get as close to our feelings and be as acutely suggestive of the conditions of his life in the hill fort at Tullyhogue as this list of his abandoned possessions, compiled after his defeat at the Battle of Kinsale. I can almost feel the wind press the quill in the English secretary's hand as his cold Tudor gaze falls upon the debris of a world:

> 2 long tables, 2 long forms, an old bedstead, an old trunk, a long stool .
> . . 5 pewter dishes, a basket, a comb and a comb case, 2 dozen trenchers
> and a basket . . . one pair of taffeta curtains, an other pair of green satin
> curtains, a brass kettle, 2 baskets with certain broken earthen dishes and
> some waste spices, a vessel with two gallons of vinegar, 2 glass bottles,
> 2 stone jugs whereof one broken, a little iron pot and a great spit.

We have entered the realm of the museum where pastness is conjured as we run the tips of our sympathy and understanding over the braille of the exhibits. When we gaze at an ancient cooking pot or the shoe of a Viking child or a gaming board from the rubble of a Norman keep, we are exercising a primary part of our nature. It is the part which cherishes human contact and trust, which responds with gratitude to a lighted window in the countryside at night, is consoled when it finds on a mountainside a path worn out by previous feet, and is well pleased to discover old initials carved on the range-wall of a bridge or in the bark of a tree.

The contemplation of such things emphasizes the truth of that stunningly simple definition of our human neighbor offered by the old school catechism. "My neighbor," the catechism declared, "is all mankind." So I think of my mesolithic Ulster neighbor, and of his flint flakes, flint spears and arrowheads which were found in abundance at New Ferry on the River Bann during the drainage of the river in the early part of the century. Seeing these on display in the Ulster Museum in Belfast once gave me a vision of those first hunters among the reeds and bushes at the lower end of our parish, and I thought of them not as having disappeared but as being at one with the farmers and clayworkers and fishermen and duck-shooters who were the geniuses of the place when I first got to know it. And that time scale, that double sense of great closeness and great distance, subtly called into question the factual and sectarian divisions which are and have long been pervasive in that part of the country. I do not say that a sense of the mesolithic ancestor could solve the religio-political conflicts of the Bann Valley but I do say that it could significantly widen the terms of the answer which each side could give to the question, "Who do you think you are?"

Similarly with that magnificent hoard of gold objects found in my native County Derry and now held in the National Museum in Dublin as

"The Broighter Hoard": to gaze at those arm-bands and gorgets and lunulae, so silent and solid and patiently beyond one, is to be displaced from one's ordinary sense of what it means to be a County Derry person. For the moment, the gazer is carried out of himself, is transported into a redemptive mood of openness and readiness. He has, in fact, crossed the line that divides instinctive apprehension from artistic experience.

II

It is tempting to slip from this personal experience and inflate it by analogy, recalling Keats's rapt vigils in the British Museum and the way his entrancement with the Elgin Marbles supplied some of the dreamcharge for his "Ode on a Grecian Urn." Yet in that poem Keats's gaze emanated not from any desire to savour the local and domestic world but from a thoroughly self-aware literary imagination. His response was not dictated by his sense of belonging to a particular place, nor was it especially afflicted by the burden of a particular history. His was a gaze that pined to found itself upon a trust in the reality of art in time. Historical Greece may have provided images for his daydream but transfigured Greece, under the aspect of the urn, awakened his imaginative and intellectual appetites—although not in the same way as Neruda's imagination was awakened in the presence of human artifacts. Neruda's words come from a piece called "Towards an Impure Poetry" and they are anti-idealist and anti-aesthetic, strongly reminiscent of Moneta's indignation (in "The Fall of Hyperion") against "dreamers," and her urgent preference for "those to whom the miseries of the world / Are misery, and will not let them rest." Neruda, we might say, is tormented by the injustice of history and his past is accusatory, whereas Keats's past is closer to the long-ago of fairy-tale and functions in his mind as a source of possibility, a launch-pad for transcendence.

For all poets, Neruda included, pastness is to a greater or lesser degree enabling. The word poetry itself is an orb on the horizon of time, simultaneously rising and setting, imbued with the sunset blaze of master-works from the tradition yet dawning on every poet like hope or challenge. It is very hard to conceive of an imagination which creates without the benefit of inherited forms, modes of expression historically evolved

yet universally available, and that benefit itself is an unconscious perspective backward.

Language, too, is a time-charged medium. No matter how much the
poetic mind may wish to rid itself of temporal attachment and observe
only its own pristine operations, its very employment of words draws it
into the "backward and abysm" of common human experience. Indeed,
even though one of the results of the Symbolist experience was to educate
us in a language that abandons its referential tasks and revels in the echo-
chamber of its own inner memory, this liberation placed upon reader and
writer alike an obligation to be responsive, at some level, to literary
history, to the cultural and phonetic heartbeat of words themselves. The
idea that each vocable, each phonetic signal, contains a transmission from
some ur-speech and at the same time is wafted to us across centuries of
speaking and writing, that the auditory imagination unites the most
ancient and most civilized mentalities, this has been one of the most
influential refinements of poetic theory during the last century and it is
deeply underwritten by an implied identification of the literary imagination *with* a sense of the past.

Take Wallace Stevens's "The Irish Cliffs of Moher," a poem which
originated when Stevens received a postcard from a friend in Ireland. It
carried a photograph of the cliffs, a prospect of sheer dark promontories
dropping hundreds of feet to the Atlantic Ocean, distant from Stevens by
three thousand miles, but nevertheless reaching and compelling him to
this:

Who is my father in this world, in this house,
At the spirit's base?

My father's father, his father's father, his—
Shadows like winds

Go back to a parent before thought, before speech,
At the head of the past.

They go back to the cliffs of Moher rising out of the mist,
Above the real,

Rising out of present time and place, above
The wet green grass.

This is not landscape, full of the somnambulations
Of poetry

And the sea. This is my father or, maybe,
It is as he was,

A likeness, one of the race of fathers: earth
And sea and air.

The argument of the poem could be reduced to something like this: the black mass of these cliffs loom before us rather as the father's presence first looms above the infant; they also affect us as the memory of a father and the idea of forefathers affect our adult imagining. Their plumb implacable bulk suggests foundation and origin and a security in the world. Yet they appear strangely insubstantial when shawled in mist, and this hallucinatory aspect also suggests that our natural father may only be an accidental incarnation of an archetypal form, of a dream father previous to all our biographies and potentially present when the world was earth and sea and air. Hence our sense of being at home upon the planet may depend as much upon our mental and imaginative powers—seen in action here as they search out a sense of God the Father—as upon any physical evolution or biological adaptability.

Whether this would be every reader's paraphrase of the poem does not really matter. What does matter is the sorry deprivation that occurs when any conjectural meaning is divorced from the poem's body of sound. The stateliness, the pomp of its progress, the solemn march established in three-time at the beginning—"in this world, in this house, / At the spirit's base," "My father's father, his father's father, his—," "before thought, before speech, / At the head of the past"—all this contributes to a deep horn music, the rounded-out, lengthened-back note of the *cor au fond du bois*; and it is this musical amplitude that persuades the ear of the reality of an inner space where the dimension of time has been precipitated out of the dimension of space, where density streams towards origin. Yet for all its shadowy effectiveness, the poem is not a mere "somnambulation." It is rather a definite matter of sensation, arising from the cliffiness not of the cliffs themselves but of the word-cliffs in the poem, the vowel-caverns of "house," "father," "shadows," "Moher."

"The Irish Cliffs of Moher," then, is a poem which discovers "at the head of the past" a haven for the imagination itself, yet we would never want to claim that "a sense of the past," in any of its pathetic or emotionally conditioning manifestations, is an attribute of Stevens's subjects or a part of his intonation. Rather, by its independence of all such affective machinery, the poem emphasizes the idea that the primary laws of our nature are organically linked, that "pastness" and "language" and "imagination" are grafted together at some radical level and that, to quote the conclusion of Eliot's great encyclical upon the subject, the poet "is not likely to know what is to be done . . . unless he is conscious not of what is dead, but of what is already living." ("Tradition and the Individual Talent")

III

The actual poetic task is to find a way of melding the intuitive and affection-steeped word-world of personal memory with the form-hungry and projecting imagination, to find an idiom at once affective and objectified, as individual as handwriting and as given as the conventions of writing itself. This happens most naturally when the poet inherits a coherent place and a language imbued with the climate and love and history of that place. In this way we can see that Thomas Hardy was lucky and John Crowe Ransom, say, was needy. Hardy had a natural sense of his past, Ransom had a perfected literary imagination. Hardy could be busy, Ransom had to be adept; Hardy could speak, Ransom had to write; Hardy could follow his nose, Ransom had to mind his step.

Think of Hardy's "Channel Firing." A touch of the grotesque. A hint of the blasphemous—God tells men that the "rest eternal" which they need may well be an unresurrected sleep in the earth. A parson called Thirdly. A church mouse. A God who calls men "mad as hatters" and goes on to rhyme "hatters" with "matters." Who exclaims with an iamb—surely it is not a spondee—"Ha, ha." By this account it should be a rickety performance, yet Hardy gets away with it, in fact, triumphs with it:

That night your great guns, unawares,
Shook all our coffins as we lay,

And broke the chancel window-squares,
We thought it was the judgment-day

And sat upright. While drearisome
Arose the howl of wakened hounds:
The mouse let fall the altar-crumb,
The worms drew back into the mounds.

The glebe cow drooled.
Till God called, 'No;
It's gunnery practice out at sea
Just as before you went below;
The world is as it used to be:

'All nations striving strong to make
Red war yet redder. Mad as hatters
They do no more for Christes sake
Than you who are helpless in such matters.

'That this is not the judgment-hour
For some of them's a blessed thing,
For if it were they'd have to scour
Hell's floor for so much threatening. . . .

'Ha, ha. It will be warmer when
I blow the trumpet (if indeed
I ever do; for you are men
And rest eternal sorely need).'

So down we lay again. 'I wonder,
Will the world ever saner be,'
Said one, 'than when he sent us under
In our indifferent century!'

And many a skeleton shook his head.
'Instead of preaching forty year,'
My neighbour Parson Thirdly said,
'I wish I had stuck to pipes and beer.'

Again the guns disturbed the hour,
Roaring their readiness to avenge,
As far inland as Stourton Tower,
And Camelot, and starlit Stonehenge.

—April 1914

When the first line talks of "your great guns," who is the "you"? Hard to say until the second line when "our coffins" give the answer. The speakers are the dead addressing "you"—us—the living. And it is speakers, not a speaker; a communal rather than an individual voice enunciates the poem. Already a continuum of past and present has been created and immediately after that a site, indeed sacred site with its "chancel window-squares," is also established.

We are at the tribe's centre of feeling and belonging, where the spirits of the ancestors are pressing actively in upon the consciousness of the living. The withdrawing worms, like the astonished mouse, may be an image of the shock that all life must sustain in an age of naval gunnery, but the mounds into which they withdraw remind us not just of graves and churchyards and the Christian culture of England. The associations of the word "mounds" itself reach back to the hill-forts and earth-works of Celtic Britain and infuse the atmosphere of the poem with a feeling of ancient belonging.

The settled world of glebe and hound-pack is menaced, yet in the perspective of folk memory the gunnery is recognized both as a new danger and as a part of the old pattern of war and destruction. The length and reliability of this perspective is enforced when God speaks in an idiom completely at one with the dialect usage ("forty year") of the head-shaking skeletons. God's speech is not particularly solemn or oracular; it is more a voice from a local pulpit, colored by the liturgical and biblical drone of official religion—"the judgment hour," "the trumpet," "rest eternal"—and by the echo of a medieval popular pageant—"for Christes sake," "to scour / Hell's floor"—these latter terms putting us in touch with an age when Christ was crucified and hell was harrowed by the tradesmen of the parish. The mixture of eternal verity and domestic expression lodges us firmly in a world of continuity, yet the continuity is neither offered as a rebuke to a more fragmented world nor patronized as Philip Larkin's "ruin-bibber, randy for antique" might patronize it. It is simply the natural climate of Hardy's imagination.

The "Channel" of the title, for example, while it may not be endowed with the big patriotic legends of "Camelot and starlit Stonehenge," is nevertheless more than a name on a map. It is deeply ingrained with

England's island history, with crossings by Julius Caesar and William the Conqueror, the defeat of the Armada, the threat of Napoleon's invasion. It is a word that somewhat mutely sweeps the string of Englishness, yet an English person would not dwell on it for a second. It enters the common consciousness much as the garden seat entered Hardy's personal awareness, as a fume of affection and ordinariness. It contains the folk world of neighbors and parsons and assumes it into a bigger unity of historical achievement and cultural unity.

A crucial fact about the poem is the date of its composition which Hardy deliberately appends, "April 1914." By now this constitutes part of our own sense of the past, a marker of the critical point when for the last time war might be contemplated as part of the natural cycle of human life and could still be contained within a half-admiring cliché as "red war." That patient God's eye view of all things, war included, as a cyclic pattern, a pattern seemingly demonstrated by history to be inevitable like seasonal labor or young love—Hardy could still envisage it like that in 1915 in his poem "In Time of 'The Breaking of Nations' "—that view was no longer tenable after the First World War. In "Channel Firing," however, while the word "gunnery" does rumble with danger and modernity, it still manages to harmonize with the hymn tune swell of the quatrains. The music of continuity could still absorb the vocabulary of danger, and one of the pleasures of the poem (which we both relish and suspect) is this deeply founded security. We recognize that the land of England with its legendary placenames, its yeoman tillage and its "pipes and beer" has here found its equivalent "in the farming of a verse."

So Edward Thomas could lift a handful of earth and declare that that was what he was fighting for. Yet the fight itself changed all that. Hardy's England became a matter of elegy. Auden and Larkin, two of his natural heirs, are much more at a remove from their emotions when they come to feel about a past which they know to be, among other things, a construction of the literary imagination. They may well recognize a connectedness within the past and feel themselves connected to it, but the posture of their writing selves is different from Hardy's. They have crossed a divide that opened when hostilities opened in 1914 and which had its repercussions in the big push of modernism in the subsequent years, a divide blasted into consciousness by a work like Pound's *Mauberley* where the quatrain operated not, as in "Channel Firing," like an aural shock-absorber but more like a chiselled niche packed with explosive.

Pound's past was neither parochial nor patriotic, but literary. His myriad dead went under the earth not for any Thomas-like love of the earth, but "For two gross of broken statues / For a few thousand battered books." He could perceive and lament the patriotism which produced "fortitude as never before," but his relationship to it was critical: a stance interposed itself in the tooling of the stanzas, the poem is driven forward by a ferocity of present-tense intelligence rather than by any drumroll of loss. The resulting idiom is stretched between rage and elegance, a style won out of despair at "styles," a palimpsest of literary modes and allusions which derives from his necessary passionate love of literature and a simultaneous scepticism about that very love.

Hardy's poetic ear was to the ground, Pound's was tuned to the airwaves. Hardy naturally heard a kind of indigenous background murmur which his voice took up, Pound was assailed by transmissions from foreign stations and messages from the old dispersed centers of civilization. Hardy holds, as it were, the string of a single persisting tradition while Pound gathers the fallen beads of many traditions. Pound's imagining had its first impulse in the excitement of encountering classical and medieval poetry at university; it is historical, eclectic, prescriptive, a project of retrieval and design. Hardy's imagining is not as intellectually fired nor as academically ratified; it has a smallholder's grip upon its territory rather than a developer's ambition; and it is not exactly historical since it never goes beyond its own ken but subdues everything within its unifying mythic scope.

For Hardy, place, pastness and poems were all aspects of a single mind-stuff. Even his seeming bookishness was the result of a naturalness, a readiness to bring the common word of the district out of the mouth and ear, straight on to the page. The same is true, in a more anxious and scholastically self justifying way, of Hopkins, whose linguistic experiments were part of a patriotic urge to keep all of English hard at work. There may be more of the lexicographer in Hopkins but there is still earth under the nails of his hand turning the dictionary pages. His poetry does not spacewalk in the ether of literary associations but is grounded in the insular landscape which, in the month of May, blooms and greens in a way that is still Marian, sacramental, medieval English Catholic.

The early Auden style, too, for all the ellipses and disjunctions and angularities which, at the time, seemed so fast and up to date, can be recognized half a century later as a mode of English belonging. Its skaldic abruptness is the natural marking of a voice from the Danelaw, a runic disposition as ancestral to the English language as it is to his own nordic surname. Fells, kestrels, dooms, dingles, snows, crossroads—they are not simply "effects" but passports to a locale, a sensibility and an inheritance. Unlike Hardy, however, Auden could neither settle for the inheritance nor settle into it. For him, "channel" could not be a word that secured the mind within a moat of national triumph: it was a strip of water under "the new European air / On the edge of a sky that makes England of minor importance." ("Dover") The southern cliffs of the country were similarly diminished to "the small field's ending pause." ("On This Island") On a summer night, "in this English house," he could feel

> Soon, soon, through dykes of our content
> The crumpling flood will force a rent
> And, taller than a tree,
> Hold sudden death before our eyes
> Whose river dreams long hid the size
> And vigours of the sea.
>
> —"A Summer Night"

Auden certainly owns a past yet he also owns up to a present where past attitudes are both inadequate and inefficacious. Impatience with a nostalgic and politically wobbly England is countered by a natural reflex of love for it as it comes under threat. He performs brilliantly in verse partly in order to distract himself from the sombreness of his recognitions. Auden's contemporaneity was most evident in his sensitivity to current dangers but his ironical affection for the surviving and apparently imperturbable surfaces and rituals of English life guaranteed that the poetry was as emotionally ballasted as it was brilliantly admonitory. It was domestic and it was a *tour de force*, the work of a lonely mind made lonelier by a critical attitude to what it prized, a victim of the new conditions as inevitably as Hardy was a beneficiary of the old ones.

So, to come back to John Crowe Ransom: when I contrasted him with Hardy, I was thinking of a poem like "Captain Carpenter," of the way it is a performance, a set piece, a system of diction and rhyme and enjambement that is never for a moment unaware of itself as a set of variations upon well known lyric tunes. Like Auden, Ransom was at a detached angle to what he cherished. He was in two, maybe three places at once: in the parochial south, within the imposed Union, and inside the literary "mind of Europe." He was in place and displaced and consequently his poetic challenges and their resolutions were tactical, venturesome and provisional. His plight was symptomatic of the double focus which the poet from a regional culture is now likely to experience, caught between a need to affirm the centrality of the local experience to his own being and a recognition that this experience is likely to be peripheral to the usual life of his age. In this situation, the literary tradition is what links the periphery to the centre—wherever that imaginary point may be—and to other peripheries. It is a kind of pseudo-past which can absorb the prescribed local present and which allows each writer—by way of parody, allusion, inflection, parallelism—equal access to its resources. No wonder that it—the literary past, the tradition—became a category of our thinking at precisely that moment when, politically and culturally, the centre could not hold, when one place could no longer be proved more than another place, when St. Louis and Dublin and Wnycote, Pennsylvania could each affirm its rights to it all and Paterson, New Jersey could, with equal and opposite confidence, proclaim an independence of it.

A quarter of a century after he had thought it all out in "Tradition and the Individual Talent," Eliot with equal authority but new and mind-sweetening simplicity, summed it all up:

> This is the use of memory:
> For liberation—not less of love but expanding
> Of love beyond desire, and so liberation
> From the future as well as the past. Thus love of a country
> Begins as attachment to our own field of action
> And comes to find that action of little importance

Though never indifferent. History may be servitude,
History may be freedom. See, now they vanish,
The faces and places, with the self which, as it could, loved them,
To become renewed, transfigured, in another pattern.

—"Little Gidding"

Remember the Future

BY CARLOS FUENTES

As a young law student, I used to walk every morning at a quarter to eight across the Zócalo, the central plaza of Mexico City, my terrifying and wonderful city. The collective taxi took me from my home near the Paseo de la Réforma to the corner of Madero Avenue at the Majestic Hotel. Then I would walk the breadth of the square into the narrow colonial quarter leading to the School of Law of the National University on San Ildefonso Street.

Every day, as I crossed the Zócalo, another scene hurried, violent, in flight, across my eyes. I could see, to the south, men and women in white tunics riding on flat-bottomed canoes in a flowing dark canal. On the north, there was a corner where stone broke into shapes of flaming shafts and red skulls and still butterflies: a wall of snakes beneath the twin roofs of the temples of rain and fire.

Both images, that of the ancient city and that of the modern city, dissolved back and forth in my eyes, each the mirror without background for the reappearance of the other. The palace of the Spanish viceroys had been erected on the very site of the temple to the god of war, Huitzilopochtli, and in the same plaza that had been the seat of Aztec power. A vast Catholic cathedral had grown upon the ruins of the *coatepantli*, the wall of serpents. The houses of the conquistadores had been built on the emplacement of the *tzompantti*, the walls of skulls. And the foundations of the municipal palace had been laid upon the vanquished palace of the emperor Moctezuma, with its courtyards of birds and beasts, its chambers for albinos, hunchbacks and dwarfs, and its rooms filled with silver and gold.

Today, the Zócalo is a cracked shell covering the slime of a dead lagoon. This was once an Indian Venice. As I walked over the enormous square of broken stone, I knew that my feet were trampling on the graveyard of a civilization. I knew that all these things that I imagined had existed there and existed no more. I was walking on the ashes of the capital city of Tenochtitlan, never to be seen again. That was in 1951.

But Mexico is instant Fellini. Almost thirty years later, the works for the Mexico City subway led to archaeological excavations in this, the heart of Mexico ancient and modern. The former Templo Mayor of the Aztec metropolis reappeared, practically intact, with its temples to water and fire, its stones of sacrifices, its red angry gods reclining forever in the posture of a Henry Moore statue. Its humble offerings were to be seen there, burnt and dry, but mysteriously clinging to the shapes of life. And the platform of serpents and the altar of frogs serving as the stage for the centerpiece of this underground museum: the gigantic disc of Coyolxauhqui, the moon-goddess.

And so we found out that what had been dead had come alive; that what I had imagined was really there; that the things I thought belonged to a past synonymous with death were things of a living present; or, rather, they had become, surprisingly, a part of my future.

For as we advance towards the end of the twentieth century–the end of our modern age, the age of the instant and short-lived millenia–Henry Luce's American Century became, in Felix Rohatyn's words, the Twenty-Year Century; Hitler's Two Thousand Year Reich lasted only thirteen; Mussolini could resurrect the Roman Empire in movies about Scipio the African but not on the shores of Tripoli; and Nikita Khruschev did not only not bury capitalism: his 1960 forecasts for Communist paradise in the 1980's have not become true; everywhere, the future seems to have come short of its promise.

I know few phrases as ominous as those of Lincoln Steffens on his return from Russia in the early years of the Bolshevik Revolution: "I have seen the future and it works." My friend the writer Fletcher Knebel, who every year sends me a happy conception-day card–remembering that I was one day a distant future–visited East Germany recently and came back saying: "I have seen the Future, and it looks like Perth Amboy."

Yet no single concept has been as overpowering since the eighteenth century as this of the Future: not any Future, but a Future synonymous with Happiness. The Pursuit of Happiness is inscribed as a right, but perhaps even more so as a Duty, in your Declaration of Independence. No longer as a right, only as a duty, it is also inscribed in blood on the back of Kafka's prisoner in the penal colony. This obligation to happiness is the surest guarantee of an unhappy future: in the East, it means the suppression of any doubts or criticism about the state of things, which then cease to move dialectically and end in historical stagnation. In the West, it means the dulling of the senses by a pounding image of cheer, beauty and eternal youth at the fingertips of him or her who acquires this look, applies that cosmetic, drinks this sugar-free poison, or never leaves home without it. The image, as C. Wright Mills called it, of the cheerful robot, who is caught in the paradox of being obliged to be happy: the future is at his instant command, but it never satisfies him, so he must have more and more, and so the future is never attainable—the economy would stop functioning if it were truly satisfactory, if it truly gave us the Future—its promise, its joy—in an everlasting now.

The comparison of these travesties of happiness with the actual pain of the world accentuates despair, which no longer finds the normal outlet of tragic art. We must all be happy, or else . . . we are not good Communists, we are not good Americans, we are not good Revolutionaries, we are not good Conservatives. We must all stand tall and smile, smile, smile.

Pollyanna with a Whip: the future is rosy; you had better put on your glasses. The Future, in this optic, is governed, East and West, North and South, by the beatific Dr. Pangloss.

But the reaction against futuristic beatitude is inevitable in a world where the screen of the future-as-happiness has vainly hidden the scenery of the present as terror, violence and madness, more cruel than ever, because less expected than ever. How could the Holocaust of the Innocent be unleashed by the armed children of Bach, Beethoven and Brahms? How could the marvelous dream of socialist liberation end in the Stalinist Gulag? How could the democracy of Thomas Jefferson and Franklin Roosevelt exterminate whole Vietnamese villages and its own fighting men with Agent Orange and napalm? How, indeed, finally, have we managed not only to demonstrate over and over that behind the mask of progress the future wears the face of death, but that we are for the first time capable not only of exterminating ourselves, while at least leaving nature to contemplate our folly, but that, now, we are capable of exterminating nature herself, so that there shall be no further witnesses: no further future?

Onto this terrifying sceno-graphy two lonely hobos, Vladimir and Estragon, wander in, led by the noose of power. The voice we hear, filling the stage, is from Krapp's Last Tape, and it says:

"This earth could be uninhabited."

Vladimir and Estragon, looking for Godot, have arrived at the written territory of Kafka's skin, a stage of flesh and blood desperately trying to avoid the final knowledge of this future: that flesh and blood are now dust, that the sacrament is rubble and that Beckett's Winnie is buried up to her neck in garbage, singing against all evidence:

"Oh, les beaux jours!"

So the future has become this basic solitude, this unsheltered terror: we have been born faceless in the land of the dead.

Progress has ended in mass extermination.

We have screamed that God is dead because we want him to admit that his creature, Man, is also dead and then have him join us in the comradeship of sadness.

As in Kafka's novels and Beckett's plays, God joins the "unhappy consciousness" of the world and is invited to share death as a joy–for it is life that we shall blame on the Gods, if life becomes a future indistinguishable from death, echoing Milton's unhappy Adam:

Did I request thee, Maker, from my Clay
To mould me Man, did I sollicitte thee
From darkness to promote me . . .?

These are the fruits of the huckstering of the future which has been the biggest con-game of modernity. They are dead fruits, rotten, born from barren grounds and trees that shine black and naked: beautiful, perhaps, but deadly.

Can we achieve a less despairing, more modest and reasonable sense of the future, without falling into despair or beatitude once more? I am sure that as we think about the future today, we are all worried by this question. The future no longer seems irrevocably destined to happiness; indeed, the future, at times, does not seem possible at all.

But the problem with the future as either despair or beatitude is that it is a future considered in the abstract: loosened from its historical bearings, separated from its cultural context and, thus, easily kidnapped by a paramount philosophy manipulated by a paramount political or military power. Both the United States and the Soviet Union have claimed, more or less constantly throughout their histories, to represent the future, a good future which they then consider it their duty to offer and, if rejected, to impose on the rest of us. Kipling's "white man's burden" is once more being carried in Afghanistan, where the Soviets declare that they are saving a few goatherds from feudalism and bringing them into a progressive future, or in El Salvador, where the American government is supposed to know better than the Salvadorans how their civil war should turn out in order to become an instant democracy: a New Hampshire in the tropics.

When the Nazis came to power, Dr. Goebbels called in the great German film-maker, Fritz Lang, and asked him to produce several motion pictures for the regime.

"But, Herr Doctor, I am a Jew," Lang said, and Goebbels answered, "From now on, we decide who is a Jew."

From now on, we decide who is authoritarian, democratic, totalitarian, reactionary, feudalistic, progressive: this arrogant privilege is the result of power as the monopoly of the future.

Beyond beatitude, beyond despair, beyond Pollyanna and Pangloss, beyond Krapp and crap: what can we reasonably expect?

I would like to answer this question from a paradoxical position—by reminding everyone, and myself, that we must also remember the past if we are to have a future which shall be more than an ever-receding illusion, leaving in its tide vast empty shores of rotten slime and dead scales. The future has no more powerful anchor than the past because the past is the only certifiable future we have: the past is the only proof we now have that the future did, in effect, once exist.

We live today. Tomorrow we shall have an image of today. We cannot ignore this, as we cannot ignore that the past was lived, that the origin of the past is the present: we remember here, today.

But we also imagine here, today. And we should not separate what we are able to imagine from what we are able to remember.

Remember the future; imagine the past: I believe that this is the truthful articulation of time as it is lived, inevitably, in the present:

Remember the future:

Imagine the past: you can only do so in this present we share.

Only this interlocking activity permits me, for one, to understand my position and my work, as a Mexican national and as a Latin-American writer, bound to a tradition and a hope inseparable from a history and a language, and as a writer convinced that there is no new creation without a living tradition, in the same way that there is no living present, or possible future, without a living past.

So let me take a quick look, as a Mexican and as a writer, at two aspects of this remembrance of the future: history and literature. My historical example has to do with a world that first totally conceived and then totally met and exhausted its future: the world of the Aztecs in Mexico. Paul Valery warned us, between the two world wars, that civilizations knew themselves to be mortal. But perhaps the Indian world of Mexico did not have to be warned: it was so obsessed with its own demise that it actually transformed its foreseeable death into a constant part of its life. In doing so, it manipulated its past for purposes of power, until it lost its past. The Aztec world offers a terrifying example of a civilization that lost its future because it lost its past. Let us go back to Mexico City, where I was writing in the fifties, in sadness, about a world gone forever; I was to see that world, resurrected, in the eighties. In the past I had written about the past not knowing it was hidden in my future: let us imagine the future as that city lived it in the past. The Year of the Reed, Ce Acatl, 1519, rose ominously over the Aztec Capital, Tenochtitlan.

Comets streaked for long hours across the sky.

The waters on which the city was built churned up gigantic waves, toppling down houses and towers.

The mirrors of the kingdom reflected starry skies at noon.

Strange women roamed the streets at midnight, sobbing over the death of the children and the loss of the empire.

Dreamers, as they are wont to, dreamt of apocalypse. The Aztec emperor, Moctezuma, then had all the dreamers brought to his court, there to repeat their dreams aloud.

Once they had done so, they were all violently put to death before the assembled court.

If the dreamers were killed, the dreams would not take place: by killing the dreamers, Moctezuma hoped to kill the future.

For all the Indian peoples of the Americas, the world had not existed once, but several times. These successive worlds were called Suns. Under the Fifth Sun, present humanity was created by a benevolent God, Quetzalcoatl, the Plumed Serpent, whom the envious demons one day visited, offering him a gift that was also a temptation: a mirror.

The Divinity, who had never seen his face, thinking that Gods were faceless, saw himself in the mirror and feared that, because he had a face, he could no longer be a God: the face of men had a destiny, a future; not that of the God, which was timeless.

When he discovered that he had a human face, Quetzalcoatl feared that he must also have a human destiny: a historical fate. He accepted this fate in fear and trembling, and that night he slept with his sister, Quetzaltepatl, and drank himself into a stupor. He had seen his own face. It was frightening: pale, bearded, blond.

The *Annals* of Cuautitlian, recovered by the most patient disciples of the most patient scribe of the conquered culture, the Franciscan friar Bernardino de Sahagún, say that the next day Quetzalcoatl fled on a raft of serpents, to the East, to the faraway seas and the rising sun, traveling towards an unknown destiny and an unknown identity.

But the voices of the myth also said that one day he would return to see if the men and women to whom he had given physical birth and moral identity, by identifying in the Divinity both the act of creation and the act of the fall—the God as protagonist of both Genesis and Eden—had learned how to be morally free.

This meant that Quetzalcoatl would return in peace, if his children had peacefully cared for the earth; and in war, if they had devastated the land and oppressed other human beings. For the *Annals* recalled that the earth had been given to men by the Gods; men were not the owners of this earth, but its gardeners.

Quetzalcoatl promised to return on a precise year: the Year of the Reed, Ce Acatl.

The history of ancient Mexico—perhaps also the history of modern Mexico—is the history of its faces and its masks. The link between the solar calendar and the calendar of personal destiny was five days, the five *Nemontani* or Masked days, when it is convenient to stay at home, keep quiet and avoid taking chances. The destiny of the creative God, Quetzalcoatl, was shaped by the discovery of his face: his future was to have a face in the mirror. And the Aztecs were late-comers in the waves of migrant civilizations from the North; the peoples who preceded them into the Central Valley of Mexico called them "the last people to come"; "every one persecuted them"; "no one wished to receive them"; "they had no face."

Tragically at war with themselves, the Aztec people had to choose their future by choosing either the face of Quetzalcoatl, which was the face of the Toltec moral heritage they required in order to achieve ethical and political legitimation, or the mask of the ferocious war-god, Huitzilopochtli, which they needed in order to conquer and subdue the other Indian nations.

In other words, the Aztecs had to conciliate the need for identity (they had no face) with the need for legitimation (they had no past). They had to live both in the time of morality (the past) and in the time of necessity (the present) in order to have an imperial future.

They solved their dilemma by burning all the ancient writings of the older people that they defeated, because in them the Aztecs appeared as barbarians of no consequence. "History was burnt—the informants told Sahagún—because the Aztec lords said it was not convenient for all the people to know the papers"—that is, to know the truth about the past.

Through this bit of Orwellian travesty, the Aztecs believed they could have a future by denying a past. This was to prove impossible. They needed the past if they were to be seen as heirs to the prestigious Toltec tradition; but their actions in the present flaunted this same heritage. They created a schizophrenic society, divided between the demands of the past and the demands of the future, a world divided between the Pyramid and the Raft: the pyramid of the God of War, his death squadrons and his ritual sacrifices; or the raft of the plumed serpent, its humane values and its appeal, once more, to the face, this time the true face, of men and women:

"I shall speak to your face" (says the Aztec poet)
"I shall speak to your heart."

These beliefs and values were not only an evocation of the moral past of the Indian world; they were a developing set of ideas, caught in living movements, and then stunted, but not killed, by the conquest of Mexico.

We now understand that the culture of the past reappears as part of our present future because it was only the political power of the past—the power most interested in monopolizing the future—that was killed in the past: the sceptre of Moctezuma dissolved, but not the stone of the artist.

For the future so feared by the rulers of the Aztec world posed a moral question: it is the question of Quetzalcoatl in which the future is seen as the responsibility of the past and the present.

Have you taken care of this earth?
Have you healed it or polluted it; have you tended or razed
    it?
Have you given your hand to those in need, or have you
    refused it?
Have you given songs or have you given orders?
Have you remembered, or have you forgotten?

The masked world of Moctezuma had to answer negatively and hide from these questions, masking its own mask: in its heart, the world of despotism, sacrifices and ritual fear knew it could not admit the scrutiny of its past by a future suddenly made present; a future punctually arriving on the foreseen date.

For to know the future minutely—its calendar, its face—is to know your own death: life becomes impossible, and this is what happened to the Aztec world. The blond and bearded gods were here, sailing in from the East on the raft of Quetzalcoatl, belching fire and riding mythological, four-legged beasts: The Fearful Future Had Arrived.

Moctezuma imposed upon the Spanish conqueror, Hernan Cortés, the mask of the returning god, Quetzalcoatl. But the Aztec emperor lost, in so doing, the same mask he had usurped.

What was Moctezuma to think?

The auguries had foretold the arrival, and this occurred in perfect synchronization with a calendar that ruled people's lives and destinies to a formidable degree. Moctezuma knew that the world had been born of catastrophe and would end in catastrophe. But the final cataclysm would be the work of the gods, as promised in all the eschatologies of the Indian world. Moctezuma could accept his fate at the hands of the Gods. He refused a historical destiny for himself because he wished to elevate history itself to the faceless dialogue of the Gods. The Spaniards had to be Gods so that Moctezuma could continue to be the masked Emperor.

The people themselves came to understand that they were fighting men, not gods, and the final resistance of the young emperor, Cuauhtiemoc, as well as the courage and intensity of the final battle of the Aztecs against the Europeans, now seen as foreign invaders and colonizers, make one wonder if the people really believed that the Spaniards were acting out the destiny of Quetzalcoatl, or if this was a charade, a passion play of legitimacy and doubt and fear in which the Aztec monarchy and priest-hood maintained a myth in order to maintain their power. Whatever the truth, they could not avoid a short empire and a quick death, which came on their Bicentennial.

So a state which had predicted its Future saw it come true and could then, from its ashes, at least sigh: I told you so; I always knew this would happen.

Seldom has the form of the Future, almost a hard, sculptured form, been so clearly and terribly seen. The sadness of the event, and the consciousness of the same, is told by the poets in rags of the defeated Indian world:

Where shall we go now, oh my friends?
The smoke is rising, the fog is spreading.
Cry, my friends.
The waters are red.
Cry, oh cry, for we have lost the Aztec nation.

The Aztecs lived to know and then, conclude, their future. Or did they? The Aztec Empire destroyed the past of others in order to possess the future for itself: it burned the papers, the codexes, the memory of other peoples. It wanted it to be believed that history was theirs: The Aztec Century. The future belonged to them. It arrived on their Bicentennial, and it spelled Death.

By disregarding the living past of others or disfiguring it for their own political purposes, the Aztecs courted a future similar to the one they had imposed on others: they were repaid in kind by the Spanish, who attempted to obliterate the Indian past.

But the Indian world was able to reconquer itself through the power of its moral heritage and its artistic creations: all that had survived Aztec political necessity then went on to survive Spanish political necessity. The past thus became the future, through the living present of culture. What the Aztecs had manipulated, disregarded or hidden from view—what it had appropriated for purposes of theoretic power—is the only time that survived it in the ongoing future beyond the fall of the Empire—the art, the literature, the ethics.

The conquest, at this level, was conquered too, and, through the bias of Syncretism, the Baroque and the sheer necessity of survival, a Spanish American, a Latin American culture began to emerge.

This possibility of the Past becoming the true Future again, when a fearful Future has occurred and threatened to drive the whole world to death with it, is exemplified in the conquest of Mexico by the role of Words and Woman.

The official title of the Aztec monarch was the Heutlatoani, literally He of the Great Voice, He who Speaks. Cortes availed himself of a captive Princess from Tabasco, Malintzin—La Malinche—to translate his words to the Indians and the Indian words to the Spanish. Cortes conquered the gods by talking to men through a woman. He called her "m*i lengua*," my tongue. The tongue of a woman defeated the tongue of an emperor disguised as a God. The emperor wanted the monopoly of speech. The woman wanted words for all. She defeated the Indian monarch; she also defeated the Spanish conquistador by giving birth to his child, the first Mestizo, the first Latin American, who would speak Spanish with an Indian accent and cover his brown face with the mask of Christ and his white face with the mask of Quetzalcoatl.

Yes, a new future had appeared.

But on the condition that it be understood as a living present.

This is, indeed, the source of our modern Latin American culture. We thought for a long time that we had no future except the one determined by the linear promise of the West: progress, wealth, technology–equal happiness. The tragic history of the twentieth century has made us stop and understand that we must remember our past in order to have our future: that to remember the past is to remember the future.

Parallels, analogies: history is never the same, but we do share a historical destiny, or at least the memory of experience and the resonance of fate.

That is why we cannot dismiss the art and life of Pre-Columbian antiquity as irrelevant to our deeper cultural and political search today. Art, power and death come together in the images of the past which were once the images of the future, and which we consign to a dead past only at the risk of having them reappear, one day, as a surprising, uncontrollable or unrecognizable future.

The art—the stone, the sculpture, the form, the poetry—have outlived death, power, and religion, and are still with us, in the hushed respect of museums, in the clamorous throb of the marketplace, but also in the faces and the hearts of all of us in Latin America.

If we cannot have a future without a past, how are we to integrate that past into our future? The answer is: by giving both of them the time of the present.

Let me offer a response based on how the Indian past came to be rescued from genocide.

One of the first attempts to organize the knowledge of American antiquity was the work of an acute Italian observer, the gentleman

Lorenzo Boturini, who in the mid-eighteenth century toured the Caribbean, Mexico and Central America, publishing in 1746 his commentaries in a book titled *Idea for a New General History of North America*. In effect, what Boturini did in this remarkable book was to apply the system of his compatriot Gianbattista Vico, the founder of modern historiography, to the Indian cosmos of the Americas north of the Isthmus of Panama.

Vico, as you all know, conceived history as having a basic rhythm of *corsi* and *ricorsi,* a cyclical scheme by which civilizations succeed themselves, never identical to each other, but always bearing the memory of the previous stage, its accomplishments as well as its failures, its unfinished business as well as its assimilated values: its time lost, and its recovered time.

The *corsi* and *ricorsi* ascend as a spiral; they are not properly the circular time beloved by Jorge Luis Borges or the eternal return evoked by Alejo Carpentier, but the present-in-the-instant favored by the poetry of Octavio Paz and the fiction of Julio Cortazar. Vico's philosophy of history is an inclusive conception, but first it is a human conception: we can only know what we have made; history is our own fabrication; we must know it because it is ours and because we must continue making it and remembering it: if we are the makers of history, then maintaining history is our duty.

Seen as the omni-comprehensive task of humankind, history is for Vico the history of culture, since only culture binds all the multiple facets of human existence into an understandable whole, but not an abstract whole: Vico was despised by the Enlightenment because he properly saw through the ethnocentrist pretension to a universality on purely European terms. Or as Isaiah Berlin puts it—I quote Sir Isaiah— "The notion of absolute standards, moral, aesthetic, social, in terms of which the entire human past is largely a story of mistakes, crimes, deception—the very cornerstone of the outlook of the Enlightenment— is the absurd corollary of the fallacious belief in a fixed, ultimate, unchanging human nature."

Human nature for Vico is a historically determined, various, eternally changing reality: constantly on the move, but carrying the baggage of the cultural realizations of its own making. Men and women make their own history and what they make is first of all language and then myths and then works of art and then customs, laws, table manners, fashions, political organizations, sexual mores, systems of education, sports, all of it, says Vico, in perpetual flux, always coming into being. This is the proper perspective from which to judge a past as distant as that of the aboriginal cultures of the Americas. Let me quote Vico in *La Scienza Nuova* (The New Science) posthumously published in 1744:

> In the night of thick darkness enveloping the earliest antiquities, so remote from ourselves, there shines the eternal and never failing light of a truth beyond all question: that the world of civil society has certainly been made by men, and that its principles are, therefore, to be found within the modifications of our own human mind.

The knowledge of the past is thus, if I read Vico correctly, the possibility of shaping an imperfect but reasonable future. If we understand that we made the past, we will not permit a future made without us–or against us.

This is, I think, a valid statement for the work of the novelist as he evokes the past or imagines the future from the present in which all writing actually takes place.

For a writer does but conjugate the tenses and the tensions of time through verbal means, and his scope is dismally reduced if he too, in order to synchronize with the ruling philosophy of modernity, must keep step with the indiscriminate rush towards the future, disregarding the only fullness in time: the present where we remember and where we imagine.

Modernity feels itself to be modern because it believes that happiness on earth is possible thanks to human perfectibility in an unending avenue of progress.

But this central highway of modernity–the way to paradise on earth– must coexist with a subterranean path, obscure and demanding: Modernity is also modern because it must constantly admit the critique of itself. In rebellion against dogma, it cannot be dogmatic; in opposition to absolutes, it must be relative.

If happiness—its identification, its pursuit, its possession—was the objective—the future-horizon—of the revolutionary freedoms gained in the eighteenth century, then it was inevitable that the image of freedom for evil and for unhappiness would immediately stake its claims to a contradictory presence in the culture.

Literature, both political and poetic, gives abundant proof of this presence.

Condorcet says that human history is a constant progress towards final perfection.

Blake reminds him that cruelty has a human heart.

Montesquieu calls economics the science of human happiness.

Carlyle calls it the dismal science.

Fourier dreams of a phalangstery of perfect social harmony.

De Sade has already dreamed of the phalangstery of perfect erotic cruelty—or of perfect erotic synchronization, which amounts to the same.

Adam Smith says that, if left to himself, man will always pursue his own happiness and thus the happiness of all.

Dostoyevsky answers from the underground that man ferociously seeks his own advantage not in what is good but in what is bad for him.

Voltaire condemns the past as barbaric. Tom Paine praises a future that begins freed from the chains of the past. But Schiller, in his famous conference at Iena in 1789, demands the future *now*.

Hegel summed it all up as the "unhappy consciousness" by which we discover, in history, the enemy self—but then he also thought that the future would overcome, dialectically, this tragic knowledge. Nietzsche answered that "there is no pre-ordained harmony between the development of truth and the happiness of humanity": the Future is not necessarily joyful or rewarding; we must be prepared to face it through the multiple affirmations of the tragic life.

Two heroes bear the signs of two different destinies in time. Oedipus, the tragic hero, accomplishes a double trajectory (according to the French philosopher Jean-Marie Domenach): he walks toward his future—his destiny—in order to resolve the enigma of his past; his past is his future. Napoleon, the modern hero, and with him Rastignac, Julien Sorel, Becky Sharp, Barry Lyndon, Mr. Pip, Raskolnikov, only walk towards the future until he-they-we exhaust an existence identical to the possibilities of futurization.

A rush to the future, the empire of money, success and middle-class compensation: nothing can compensate King Lear for his solitude and the ingratitude of his daughters; whereas Pere Goriot can be compensated by monthly payments from his equally ungrateful daughters. The middle class has the virtues of the middle ground and it transforms ends into means: *classes meyennes*, the middle class is the class of means. Means are thus the future and the future is a happy one.

This notion of time is linearly expressed in consonance with a limited rational experience and with the identification of material progress and the strait and narrow road. But the theory of Vico—the past—became the literature of James Joyce—the future—and through them we can attempt to recover a fuller sense of participation in time. This is my second literary example of the memory of the future.

Three great categories can guide us here: Myth, Epic and Tragedy, as they were originally conceived in the spirit of the Mediterranean world.

Epic was seen by Hegel as an act, a human act, an act of man as he ambiguously tears himself away from the aboriginal land of myth, the land of his primary identification with the Gods as Actors.

Now, Man himself is the Actor. And his Action is self-conscious: it disturbs the peace of the substance, says Hegel, the peace of Being identical to itself. Epic is an accident, a rupture of the simple unity which now, epically, divided and opens itself up to the variable world of natural powers and moral forces.

Epic is born as individuals displace themselves and defy the Gods: are you traveling with me to Troy, or are you going to stay near the tombs of the ancestors here in Argos or Tanagra?

The first victory of Men and Women over the Gods is to oblige them to come with them to Troy: to force them to travel. Epic is born of the *peripaetia*, this movement from the familiar land to the foreign land. Myth remains next to the tombs, in the land of the dead, protecting the ancestors, seeing to it that they remain quiet. No one has understood this better in Latin American fiction than Juan Rulfo.

But because of its very nature as pilgrimage, epic is the literary form of transit and displacement, the bridge between myth and tragedy.

Nothing exists in isolation in the original conceptions of the universe, and Hegel, in the *Phenomenology of the Spirit*, sees in epic an act which is a violation of the peaceful earth—that is, a violation of the peace of the cemetery; the epic transforms tomb into trench, it vivifies it with the blood of the living and in so doing it calls forth the spirit of the dead, who feel the thirst for life and receive it with an alert knowledge of epic transmuted into tragedy, self-knowledge, consciousness of the personal fallibility and error which have struck the collective values of the city, the *polis*.

In order to restore those values, the tragic hero—the former epic hero—returns home, to the land of the dead, and closes the circle in the re-encounter with the myth of the origin: Ulysses in Ithaca, Orestes in Argos.

So: in the Mediterranean world, myth precedes everything, and epic transcends myth but also prolongs it in the hero's actions.

But as it demonstrates heroic fallibility, epic reveals itself as a passage towards the tragic. The several forms of mankind end up by constantly nurturing one another.

The infinite pain of the defeated hero, says Nietzsche, exercises a beneficial influence on his society: the epic hero, transformed into the tragic man, furthers with his actions "a circle of superior consequences, capable of founding a new world on the ruins of the world," writes Nietzsche in *The Birth of Tragedy*.

Christianism first, and mercantile individualism later—cresochristianity—broke this great wheel of fire of Antiquity and substituted for it a string of gold and excrement (since both elements are always confused in the dark recesses of the human mind, where gold is the excrement of the gods). This rust-colored line, then, points toward the following truth: there is no reason to look back towards the cities of the past unless you wish to become a pillar of salt; salvation is not in the origin but in the future—the transcendental future of religion, or the secular paradise of social engineering.

The novel, in some measure, is the historical product of a loss: that of medieval unity—and of a gain: that of the displaced astonishment and curiosity of humanism. It becomes the first literary form to transcend epic form in a linear manner, not circularly through the tragic form which reintegrates epic to the original myth.

A succession, indeed, but also a rebellion within the succession: ever since its modern birth, the novel, as if it had an intuition of the pain of absence, the pain of half its missing being, has desperately searched for a new alliance with myth–from Emily Bronte to Franz Kafka—or with tragedy—from Dostoyevsky to Faulkner. But it has refused its epic parenthood, transforming it, from *Don Quixote* to *Ulysses*, into an object of parodic fun.

Why?

Perhaps because the novel, being the result of a critical operation of the Renaissance which secularized, relativized and contradicted its own critical foundations, first felt the need to criticize the epic form from which it emerged and on which it supported itself, denying it. But then, it suffered the nostalgia of myth and tragedy, this time as a critical nostalgia: a child of the faith in progress and the future, the novel sensed that it would degrade its function if it was not capable of criticizing its own ideology. To achieve this critical aim, it needed, again, both myth and tragedy. It had to become the future by remembering the past: the novel, novella, bearer of news, had to bring to us the supreme novelty of the future remembered: that is, a future inconceivable without its past.

Don Quixote looks for the arms of myth in the depths of the Cave of Montesinos; Dostoyevsky for the seeds of tragedy in the sediment of Holy Russia; and Kafka for both myth and tragedy in the basements of the Germanic and Hebrew fables. But Dostoyevsky, Kafka, Faulkner and Beckett also break the futurizing line of succession: the destinies of Ivan Karamazov, K the Land Surveyor, Miss Rosa Coldfield or Malone are not, like those of Julien Sorel, David Copperfield or Eugene de Rastignac, shot towards the future. Their destiny now has the face of simultaneous times. The form of all times is the here and now, said Thomas Mann in *Jacob*; and Jorge Luis Borges gave these words a Latin American echo in *The Garden of Forking Paths*:

> He believed in the infinite series of times, in a growing and dizzying web of divergent and convergent and parallel times.

But a plurality of times means a plurality of truth, a plurality of points of view, a plurality of groupings and, with all of this, a plurality of cultures and, with the plurality of cultures, a plurality of polities.

If this is true, then no time–past, present or future–belongs to any one man, any one nation or any one culture. We have all suffered from a futurization which is only an abstraction, cut off from the cultural plurality of the faces of mankind and arrogantly believing it can impose its version of the future on others who do not share it.

Nations that kidnap the future for themselves refuse others both a future and a past. The future can only be a creative community if it belongs to a shared past: remember the future, it happened once. It is happening all the time, your future is in the rediscovery of an Aztec temple, in the persistence of a Hebrew legend, in the sound of the rain on the uneven pavements of Venice: you cannot have a future without these.

This concert of the history of concrete, varied cultures and their past is the only guarantee we have of a reasonable, modest, humane future.

If we are to have a future, it will depend on the growing presence of cultures long relegated to insignificance because they did not participate in the truths proper to the triumphalist West; it will depend on the emergence of a plurality of times and their organization as valid presences in a multipolar world no longer dominated by only two world powers.

It will have these infinitely practical consequences:

The contribution of untapped political, diplomatic, material and cultural resources to the solution of our vast international problems.

The growing security of each nation that comes from self-respect and self-assurance as its culture manifests itself freely, in benefit of all.

The reflection of a veritable, pluralistic internationalism on the internal levels of democratic participation within each nation: no one can give anything to others that he does not also give to himself.

A multipolar, internationalist world, polycultural and pluralistic, will signify the affirmation of life by those who do not have the power of death.

Remember the Future:

It shall be multiple, it shall be shared, it shall be historically and culturally diverse.

Remember the Future:

It shall have a future because it has had a past.

Remember the Future:

It is the value we all give to our present, where the times of mankind, being many, are one.

Puritans and Prigs:
An Anatomy of Zealotry

BY MARILYNNE ROBINSON

Puritanism was a highly elaborated moral, religious, intellectual and political tradition which had its origins in the writing and social experimentation of John Calvin and those he influenced. While it flourished on this continent—it appears to me to have died early in this century—it established great universities and cultural institutions and an enlightened political order. It encouraged simplicity in dress and manner and an esthetic interest in the functional which became bone and marrow of what we consider modern. Certainly the idea that a distaste for the mannered and elaborated should be taken to indicate joylessness or an indifference to beauty is an artifact of an old polemic. No acquaintance with New England portrait or decorative art encourages the idea that Puritan tastes were somber. Even their famous headstones display a marked equanimity beside headstones in Church of England graveyards in Britain, with their naturalistic skulls with bones in their teeth and so on. Puritan civilization in North America quickly achieved unprecedented levels of literacy, longevity and mass prosperity, or happiness, as it was called in those days. To isolate its special character we need only compare colonial New England and Pennsylvania—Quakers as well as Congregationalists and Presbyterians were Puritans—with the colonial South.

Or let us compare them with ourselves. When crops failed in Northampton, Massachusetts in 1743, Jonathan Edwards of course told his congregation that they had their own wickedness to blame for it. They had failed to do justice (his word) to the poor. He said, "Christian people are to give to others not only so as to lift him above extremity but liberally to furnish him." No one bothers us now with the notion that our own failures in this line might be called sinful, though we fall far short of the standard that in Edwards' view invited divine wrath. Nor does anyone suggest that punishment might follow such failures, though the case could easily be made that our whole community is punished for them every day. In one respect at least we have rid ourselves entirely of Puritanism.

My reading of Puritan texts is neither inconsiderable nor exhaustive, so while I cannot say they yield no evidence of Puritanism as we understand the word, I can say they are by no means characterized by, for example, fear or hatred of the body, anxiety about sex, or denigration of women. This is not true of Christian tradition in general, yet for some reason Puritanism is uniquely synonymous with these preoccupations. Puritans are thought to have taken a lurid pleasure in the notion of Hell, and certainly Hell seems to have been much in their thoughts, though not more than it was in the thoughts of Dante, for example. We speak as though John Calvin invented the Fall of Man, when that was an article of faith universal in Christian culture.

For Europeans, our Puritans showed remarkably little tendency to hunt witches, yet one lapse, repented of by those who had a part in it, has stigmatized them as uniquely inclined to this practice. They are condemned for their dealings with the Indians, quite justly, and yet it is important to point out that contact between native people anywhere and Europeans of whatever sort was disastrous, through the whole colonial period and after. It is pointless to speak as if Puritanism were the factor that caused the disasters in New England, when Anglicans and Catholics elsewhere made no better account of themselves. Cortez was no Puritan, but William Penn was one. By the standards of the period in which they flourished, American Puritans were not harsh or intolerant in the ordering of their own societies. Look a little way into contemporary British law—

Dr. Johnson would never have seen a woman flayed in New England, yet it is Old England we think of as having avoided repressive extremes. As for religious intolerance, one must again consider the standards of the period. The Inquisition was not officially ended until 1837. Quakers living in Britain were deprived of their civil rights well into the 19th Century, as were Catholics and Jews. It seems fair to note that such tolerance as there was in Europe was to be found in Calvinist enclaves such as Holland.

What does it matter if a tradition no one identifies with any longer is unjustly disparaged? If history does not precisely authorize the use we make of the word Puritanism, we all know what we mean by it, so what harm is done? Well, for one thing we make ourselves ignorant and contemptuous of the first two or three hundred years of one major strain of our own civilization. I am eager to concede that in our cataclysmic world this is a little misfortune, arousing even in me only the kind of indignation that could be thoroughly vented in a long footnote somewhere. In fact it is by no means proved to my satisfaction that a society is happier or safer or more humane for having an intense interest in its own past.

Yet the way we speak and think of the Puritans seems to me a serviceable model for important aspects of the phenomenon we here are calling Puritanism. Very simply, it is a great example of our collective eagerness to disparage without knowledge or information about the thing disparaged, when the reward is the pleasure of sharing an attitude one knows is socially approved. And it demonstrates how effectively such consensus can close off a subject from inquiry. I know from experience that if one says the Puritans were a more impressive and ingratiating culture than they are assumed to have been, one will be heard to say that one finds repressiveness and intolerance ingratiating. Unauthorized views are in effect punished by incomprehension, not intentionally and not to anyone's benefit, but simply as a consequence of a hypertrophic instinct for consensus. This instinct is so powerful that I would suspect it had survival value, if history or current events gave me the least encouragement to believe we are equipped to survive.

To spare myself the discomfort of reinforcing the same negative associations I have just deplored, and for weightier reasons, I will introduce another name in the place of "Puritanism" to indicate the phenomenon we are here to discuss. I choose the word "priggishness." This fine old English word, of no known etymology and therefore fetched from the deep anonymous heart of English generations, is a virtual poem in the precision with which it expresses pent irritation. One imagines the word being spat, never shouted, which suggests it is a trait most commonly found among people at some kind of advantage. *Webster's Third New International Dictionary* defines "priggish" as "marked by overvaluing oneself or one's ideas, habits, notions, by precise or inhibited adherence to them, and by small disparagement of others." In adopting this word I hope to make the point that the very important phenomenon it describes transcends culture and history. I believe we have all heard accounts of unbridled priggishness during the Cultural Revolution in China, for example, or in Spain under the dictatorship of Franco.

Americans never think of themselves as sharing fully in the human condition, and therefore beset as all humankind is beset. Rather they imagine that their defects result from their being uniquely the products of a crude system of social engineering. They believe this is a quirk of their brief and peculiar history, a contraption knocked together out of ramshackle utilitarianism and fueled by devotion to the main chance. This engineering is performed by them and upon them negligently or brutally, or with shrewd cynicism or mindless acquiescence, all tending to the same result: shallowness, materialism, a merely ersatz humanity.

Clearly there is an element of truth in this. The error comes in the belief that they are in any degree exceptional, that there is a more human world in which they may earn a place if only they can rid themselves of the deficiencies induced by life in an invented nation and a manufactured culture. They have one story they tell themselves over and over, which is: *once we were crude and benighted, and in fact the vast majority of us remain so, but I and perhaps certain of my friends have escaped this brute condition by turning our backs on our origins with contempt, with contempt and derision.* When anything goes wrong, the thinkers among us turn once again to the old conversion narrative: *This is a resurgence of former brutishness, which we will spurn and scorn till we have exorcised it, or at least until those whose approval we covet know this old spirit no longer has power over us, personally—though we cannot of course speak for all our friends.* In great things as in small, we are forever in a process of recovery from a past that is always being re-interpreted to account for present pathologies. When things went wrong in Calvinist America, the minister or mayor or governor or president, including of course Lincoln, would declare a Day of Fasting and Humiliation, during which businesses and offices closed and the population went to their various churches to figure out what they were doing wrong and how to repent of it.

The assumption of present responsibility for the present state of things was a ritual feature of life in this culture for two and a half centuries, and is entirely forgotten by us now. Though I cannot take time to make the argument for it here, it is my belief that a civilization can trivialize itself to death, that we have set our foot in that path, and that our relation to the issue of responsibility is one measure of our progress. No matter, it is a self-limiting misfortune—by the time the end comes the loss to the world will be very small. My point here is simply that there is a reflex in this culture of generalized disapproval, of small or great disparagement, of eagerness to be perceived as better than one's kind, which is itself priggish, and which creates the atmosphere in which these exotic new varieties of priggishness can flower.

The Calvinist doctrine of total depravity—depravity means warping or distortion—was directed against casuistical enumerations of sins, against the attempt to assign them different degrees of seriousness. For Calvinism we are all absolutely, that is equally, unworthy of, and dependent upon, the free intervention of grace. This is a harsh doctrine, but no harsher than others, since Christian tradition has always assumed that rather few would be saved, and has differed only in describing the form election would take. It might be said in defense of Christianity that it is unusual in a religion to agonize much over these issues of ultimate justice, though in one form or another every religion seems to have an elect. The Calvinist model at least allows for the mysteriousness of life. For in fact life makes goodness much easier for some people than for others, and it is rich with varieties of cautious or bland or malign goodness, in the Bible referred to generally as self-righteousness, and inveighed against as grievous offenses in their own right. The belief that we are all sinners gives us excellent grounds for forgiveness and self-forgiveness, and is kindlier than any expectation that we might be saints, even while it affirms the standards all of us fail to attain.

A Puritan confronted by failure and ambivalence could find his faith justified by the experience, could feel that the world had answered his expectations. We have replaced this and other religious visions with an unsystematic, uncritical and in fact unconscious perfectionism, which may have taken root among us while Stalinism still seemed full of promise, and to have been refreshed by the palmy days of National Socialism in Germany, by Castro and by Mao—the idea that society can and should produce good people, that is, people suited to life in whatever imagined optimum society, who then stabilize the society in its goodness so that it produces more good people, and so on. First the bad ideas must be weeded out and socially useful ones put in their place. Then the bad people must be identified, especially those that are carriers of bad ideas. Societies have done exactly the same thing from motives they considered religious, of course. But people of advanced views believe they are beyond that kind of error, because they have not paused to worry about the provenance or history of these advanced views. Gross error survives every attempt at perfection, and flourishes. No Calvinist could be surprised. No reader of history could be surprised.

Disallowing factors of disruption and recalcitrance called by names like sin, what conclusion can be drawn? If human beings are wholly the products of societies, and societies are accessible to reform, what other recourse is there than to attempt to reform one and the other? The question seems pressing now that the community increasingly fails its individual members, and as it is more and more feared, abused or abandoned by them.

I depend here on the general sense that we are suffering a radical moral decline which is destroying the fabric of society, seriously threatening our sense of safety as well as of mutual respect and shared interest. Such anxieties can be dangerous and irrational—perhaps they are in most cases. But the evidence is impressive that we are now looking at real decay, so I will accept the notion for the purposes of this discussion. I take on faith Tocqueville's lapidary remark that we were great because we were good, when he knew us. Let us say, as history would encourage us to do, that one great difference between then and now is the sense of sin which then flourished, the belief that mortals are born in a state of sin, that no one is or is likely to be perfected. One implication of that belief is certainly that neither social engineering nor intellectual eugenics could produce a good society full of good people. Americans studied the example of biblical Israel, for whom God himself had legislated, and who sinned and strayed very much in the manner of people less favored. The teaching that surrounded the biblical history of Israel suggested that to do justice and love mercy made the community good, but never that the community could be so ordered as to create a population conditioned always to do justice and love mercy. The community never ceased to struggle against contrary impulses, which it did not induce in itself and from which it could not free itself. Christian individualism enforced the awareness that exactly the same impulses are always at work in one's own soul.

The Stalinist vision is much more optimistic. It can propose a solution. Society is simply other people, useful or not, capable of contributing to the general good, or not. Creatures of society, they are also the reasons for the continuing failure and suffering of society. At the same time, since society is the only possible agent of its own transformation, the victim stands revealed as the enemy, the obstacle to reform, the problem to be eliminated. Freed of those it has maimed, it might at last be perfect. This is a great solipsism, a tautology, based on a model of human being-in-the-world which, curiously, has long seemed scientific to people because it is so extremely narrow and simple and has no basis in history or experience.

It has also an attraction that Puritanism never had, Puritanism with its grand assertion and concession, In Adam's Fall / We sinned all. It creates clear distinctions among people, and not only justifies the disparagement of others but positively requires it. Its adherents are overwhelmingly those who feel secure in their own reasonableness, worth and goodness, and are filled with a generous zeal to establish their virtues through the whole of society, and with an inspiring hope that this transformation can be accomplished. It would seem to me unfair and extreme to liken our new zealots to Stalinists, if I did not do so with the understanding that the whole of the culture is very much influenced by these assumptions, and that in this as in other ways the zealots differ from the rest of us only as an epitome differs from a norm.

Optimists of any kind are rare among us now. Rather than entertaining visions, we think in terms of stop-gaps and improvisations. A great many of us, in the face of recent experience, have arrived with a jolt at the archaic-sounding conclusion that morality was the glue holding society together, just when we were in the middle of proving that it was a repressive system to be blamed for all our ills. It is not easy at this point for us to decide just what morality is or how to apply it to our circumstances. But we have priggishness at hand, up to date and eager to go to work, and it does a fine imitation of morality, self-persuaded as a method actor. It looks like it and it feels like it, both to those who wield it and to those who taste its lash.

(Since I am already dependent on one, I will attempt a definition of authentic morality, based on common usage. When we say someone is moral, we mean that she is loyal in her life and behavior to an understanding of what is right and good, and will honor it even at considerable cost to herself. We would never say she was not moral because she did not urge or enforce her own standards on other people. Nor would we say she was more moral for attempting to impose her standards than she would be if she made no such attempt. Similarly, we say someone is immoral because she does not govern her behavior to answer to any standard of right or good. That being true of her, we would never say she was not immoral because she tried to enforce a standard of virtue on the people around her, nor even that she was less immoral for making such an attempt. Nor would we say someone was moral because her society had one way or another so restricted her behavior that she could not, in its terms, do anything wrong.)

Though etymologically morality means something like social custom, as we use it it means the desire to govern oneself, expressed as behavior. People who attempt this fail, and learn in the course of failing that to act well, even to know what it is to act well, is a great struggle and a mystery. Rather than trying to reform others, moral people seem to me especially eager to offer pardon in the hope of receiving pardon, to forego judgment in the hope of escaping judgment.

So perhaps what I have called priggishness is useful in the absence of true morality, which requires years of development, perhaps thousands of years, and cannot simply be summoned as needed. Its inwardness and quietism make its presence difficult to sense, let alone quantify, and they make its expression often idiosyncratic and hard to control. But priggishness makes its presence felt. And it is highly predictable because it is nothing else than a consuming loyalty to ideals and beliefs which are in general so widely shared that the spectacle of zealous adherence to them is reassuring. The prig's formidable leverage comes from the fact that his or her ideas, notions or habits are always fine variations on the commonplace. A prig with original ideas is a contradiction in terms, because he or she is a creature of consensus who can usually appeal to one's better nature, if only in order to embarrass dissent. A prig in good form can make one ashamed to hold a conviction so lightly, and, at the same time, ashamed to hold it at all.

I will offer an example of the kind of thing I mean. Our modern zealots have dietary laws. Puritans did not, Calvin having merely urged moderation. For him many things were "things indifferent," that is, he considered it wrong to attach importance to them. This is a concept alien to the new zealotry.

There has been much attention in recent years to diet as a factor in determining the length and quality of life. That is, the idea together with all sorts of supporting information and speculation has been more than commonplace for a very long time. So here priggishness has a natural stronghold. One codicil of these dietary laws: It is good to eat fish. It is good to eat fish because it is bad to eat beef, an inefficient way to package protein, as Ralph Nader told us years ago, and a destructive presence in the world ecology, and a source of fat and cholesterol. It is good to eat fish because breast cancer is relatively rare in Japanese women and the Japanese life expectancy is imposing and beef was associated somewhere by someone with aggressive behavior in men. Also, steers are warm and breathy and have melting eyes, while fish are merely fish.

A shift in American tastes is a shift in global ecology. The sea has been raided and ransacked to oblige our new scruple, till even some species of shark are threatened with extinction. I myself am inclined to believe that no ecology is so crucial as the sea, or so impossible to monitor or to repair. Until we have some evidence that that great icon the whale can learn to live on municipal refuse and petroleum spills, we might try a little to respect the intricate and delicate system of dependencies necessary to its survival, and already profoundly disturbed. Fish is a terribly inefficient way to package protein, if it is provided on a scale that diminishes the productivity of the sea. And consider: the sea is traditionally the great resource of the poor. We are ashamed to eat beef because only a very wealthy country could sustain such a food source. And it makes us fat, parodies of ourselves. So what is any self-respecting people to do? Why, take away the food of the poor. Then at last we will be virtuous as they are.

As for the matter of the health benefits of eating fish. I think that person is a poor excuse for an ecologist who would tax a crucial and faltering natural system to extend her life a few years, assuming so much can be hoped. People in poor countries whose coasts and fishing grounds have been ruined will give up many years for the sake of the few she will gain, losing children to lengthen her old age. But certain of us have persuaded ourselves that a life lived in accordance with sound principles will be long, so longevity is as solemnly aspired to as goodness would have been in another time.

It is not hard to raise questions about the virtue of eating fish, or about the ecological consequences of mining quartz for those crystals that make us feel so at one with the earth. Is it really worth the petroleum, the pollution, the environmental wear and tear, to import drinking water? Such questions would be inevitable, if these were not the tastes of people who are strongly identified in their own minds as virtuous, and if these were not in fact signs by which they make themselves recognizeable to others and to themselves as virtuous. For a very long time this country has figured in the world as a great appetite, suddenly voracious, as suddenly sated, disastrous in either case. The second worst thing that can be said about these virtuous people is, they have not at all escaped the sins of their kind. The worst thing that can be said is, they believe they have escaped them.

People who are blind to the consequences of their own behavior no doubt feel for that reason particularly suited to the work of reforming other people. To them morality seems almost as easy as breathing. Fish-eating water-drinkers who confront their geriatric disorders in long anticipation—we could all be like them. But if there is, as I wish to suggest, little to choose between the best of us and the worst of us in terms of our ecological impact, how do the zealots command the attention they do? Why do they have no real critics?

First of all, as I have said, they are arch-defenders of the obvious, for example, of the proposition that the planet needs looking after, and that one's health needs looking after—and while their diligence may in fact be as destructive as the general lethargy, it is reassuring to all of us to think that there is a radical vanguard, girded with purpose, armed with fact, etc.

Second, there is simple snobbery. Here I am, reaching yet again into the lexicon of British dialect—no language of flatterers, in fact a reservoir of painful truth. Our zealots adopt what are in effect class markers. Recently I saw a woman correct a man in public—an older man whom she did not know well—for a remark of his she chose to interpret as ethnocentric. What he said could easily have been defended, but he accepted the rebuke and was saddened and embarrassed. This was not a scene from some guerrilla war against unenlightened thinking. The woman had simply made a demonstration of the fact that her education was more recent, more fashionable and more extensive than his, with the implication, which he seemed to accept, that right thinking was a property or attainment of hers in a way it never could be of his. To be able to defend magnanimity while asserting class advantage! And with an audience already entirely persuaded of the evils of ethnocentricity, therefore more than ready to admire! This is why the true prig so often has a spring in his step. Morality could never offer such heady satisfactions.

The woman's objection was a quibble, of course. In six months the language she provided in place of his will no doubt be objectionable—no doubt in certain quarters it is already. And that is the genius of it. In six months she will know the new language, while he is still reminding himself to use the words she told him he must prefer. To insist that thinking worthy of respect can be transmitted in a special verbal code only is to claim it for the class that can concern itself with inventing and acquiring these codes and is so situated in life as to be able, or compelled,

to learn them. The more tortuous our locutions the more blood in our
streets. I do not think these phenomena are unrelated, or that they are
related in the sense that the thought-reforms we attempt are not extensive
enough or have not taken hold. I think they are related as two manifestations of one phenomenon of social polarization.

There is more to this little incident. In fact, I must back up a
considerable distance, widen the scene a little, if I am to do it any sort of
justice. First of all, where did the idea come from that society should be
without strain and conflict, that it could be satisfying, stable and harmonious? This is the assumption that has made most of the barbarity of our
century seem to a great many people a higher philanthropy. The idea
came from Plato, I suppose. Our social thought has been profoundly
influenced by a categorical rejection of Periclean Athens. No point
brooding over that.

Let us look at the matter scientifically. The best evidence must lead
us to conclude that we are one remote and marginal consequence of a
cosmic explosion. Out of this long cataclysm arose certain elements and
atmospheres, which in combination and over time produced, shall we say,
New York City, with all it embraces and implies. Well, all right. Imagine
accident upon coincidence upon freak, heightened by mysterious phenomena of order and replication, and there you have it. That natural
process should have produced complicated animals who exist in vast
aggregations is conceivable. But, I submit, that they should be suited to
living happily—in vast aggregations or in farming villages or as hermits
on the tops of mountains—is a stroke of thinking so remarkable in a
supposedly non-theological context that it takes my breath away. Scientifically speaking, we are weird, soft, big-headed things because we
adapted to the mutable world by keeping a great many options open.
Biologically speaking, we are without loyalties, as ready to claim an
isthmus as a steppe. In our bodies we are utterly more ancient than Hittites
and Scythians, survivors of the last swarm of locusts, nerved for the next
glaciation. We have left how many cities standing empty? That any
condition of life should be natural and satisfactory to us is an idea
obviously at odds with our nature as a species, and as clearly at odds with
our history. Would not mass contentment be maladaptive? Yet so much

of modern life has been taken up with this nightmare project of fitting people to society, in extreme cases hewing and lopping away whole classes and categories. Humankind has adopted and discarded civilization after civilization and remained itself. We have done the worst harm we have ever suffered by acting as if society can or should be stable and fixed, and humankind transformed by whatever means to assure that it will be.

I am making this argument in terms not natural to me. My heart is with the Puritans. I would never suggest that history, whatever that is, should be left to take its natural course, whatever that is. I accept what Jonathan Edwards might have called the 'arbitrary constitution' of behests and obligations. I draw conclusions from the fact that we cannot reason our way to a code of behavior that is consistent with our survival, not to mention our dignity or our self-love. But, even in the terms of this argument, what could have been more brutal than these schemes to create happy and virtuous societies? Might we not all have been kinder and saner if we had said that discontent is our natural condition, that we are the Ishmael of species, that, while we belong in the world, we have no place in the world? And that this is true not because something went wrong, but because of the peculiar terms of our rescue from extinction? Our *angst* and our *anomie* have meant to us that society has gone wrong, which means that other people have harmed us. The corollary of this notion, that our unhappiness is caused by society, is that society can make us happy, or remove the conditions that prevent us from being happy. And if the obstacle to collective happiness is believed to be other people, terrible things seem justified.

When the woman in the episode I described rebuked and embarrassed someone for using the wrong language, she was acting on an assumption that is now very common and respectable, which is that vice, shall we call it, is perpetuated in society in words, images, narratives and so on, that when these things are weeded out vice is attacked, that where they still appear vice is flourishing. Now the cruelest words and the most disturbing images have normally been discountenanced in this society, and have been cherished by those who love forbidden things, just as they are now.

Formerly the society was more tolerant of racial slurs and vastly less tolerant of depictions of violence, especially against women. It was also more racist and less violent. I cannot speculate which is cause and which effect, or even if it is meaningful to describe the phenomena in those terms. In any case, the 'vice' in this instance was on the order of saying Mohammedan for Muslim, Oriental for Asian. Neither of the forbidden words has a hint of aspersion in it. They are simply associated with old attitudes, which they are taken to contain and reveal. No matter that the man who mis-spoke is known to be a very generous-spirited man, who would never intend an aspersion against anyone. Social methods that have been used to restrict the expression of obscenity or aggression, shaming, for example, are slurring over to control many other forms of language (and therefore, on the short-blanket principle that is always a factor in moral progress, no longer obscenity and aggression). This is done on the grounds that they are socially destructive, as indeed in varying degrees and circumstances they may sometimes be. This would be no fit subject for an analysis of priggishness if it did not have at least one foot in safe moral territory.

But, needless to say, there are problems. One is in the binary assumption that ideas equal words and that words carry ideas in them. If the relationship between words and ideas were indeed that close, no one would be paid for writing. Words would not be transformed by use. New ideas would depend on new coinages. This is thinking of the kind I call Stalinist, because it derives moral confidence and authority from its incredible simplicity. Now, if anything in the world is complex, language is complex. But the point is not really to characterize language but to characterize society by implying that certain things are true about language. A great mythic world rests on the back of this small conceptual turtle.

Very early on I proposed that priggishness is so available to us, and that where we do not subscribe to it we are nevertheless so helpless against it, because we cherish a myth of conversion in which we throw off the character our society gives us and put on a new one in all ways vastly superior. Normally this great change is achieved by education, enhanced by travel, refined by reading certain publications, manifested in the approved array of scruples and concerns, observed ritually in the drinking of water, the eating of fish, the driving of Volvos, and otherwise. (I think to myself, if we must be so very imitative, why can we never imitate a grace or an elegance? But that is outside the range of the present discussion. Though I do note that priggishness has never shown any aptitude for such things, any more than elegance or grace have claimed an affinity with priggishness.) Among us salvation is proved by a certain fluency of disparagement and disavowal. The prig in us could not enjoy all this, or believe in it, if the distinctions made were only economic and social. They must also, first of all, be moral.

Here I will divulge a bitter thought. I will say, by way of preparation, that much of the behavior I observe in these people looks like the operations of simple fashion. Phrases and sensitivities change continuously, perhaps as a function of evolving consciousness, perhaps as a feature of intense and active peer group identification. Clearly as economic subset our zealots experience the same frissons of consumer optimism we all do, though they might be focused on fetish bears rather than video cameras, one desideratum supplanting another in the ordinary way. Traffic in moral relics is an ancient practice, and while it is not harmless, neither is much else.

But I think there might be another impetus behind all this mutation. I think because our zealots subscribe to the conversion myth, they can only experience virtuousness as difference. They do not really want to enlist or persuade—they want to maintain difference. I am not the first to note their contempt for the art of suasion. Certainly they are not open to other points of view. If it is true that the shaping impulse behind all this stylized language and all this pietistic behavior is the desire to maintain social distinctions, then the moral high ground that in other generations was held by actual reformers, activists and organizers trying to provoke debate and build consensus, is now held by people with no such intentions, no notion of what progress would be, no impulse to test their ideas against public reaction as people do who want to accomplish reform. It is my bitter thought that they may have made a fetish of responsibility, a fetish of concern, of criticism, of indignation.

More bitter still is the thought that those who are, in Edwards' terms, in need of justice, are, in contemporary terms, damaged, imperfectly humanized, across the divide. The fact is that in this generation change in the lives of the poor and the undefended is change for the worse, again for the worse, always for the worse. If serious efforts at rectification were being made, would this be true? If serious solutions were being attempted, would not someone hold them to the standard of their effect, and suggest a reconsideration?

While Calvinists spoke of an elect, Leninists and such like have spoken of an elite. The two words come from the same root and mean the same thing. Their elect were unknowable, chosen by God in a manner assumed to be consistent with his tendency to scorn the hierarchies and overturn the judgments of this world. Our elites are simply, one way or another, advantaged. Those of us who have shared advantage know how little it assures, or that it assures nothing, or that it is a positive threat to one's moral soundness, attended as it is with so many encouragements to complacency and insensitivity. I have not yet found a Puritan whose Calvinism was so decayed or so poorly comprehended that he or she would say to another soul, I am within the circle of the elect and you are outside it. But translated into the terms of contemporary understanding, and into the terms of my narrative, that is what that woman said to that man.

A small thing, foolishness, bad manners. I run the risk of being ungenerous in taking this woman so much to task, and there is a whiff of snobbery in my own scorn for her pretentions. I accept the justice of all this, yet I persist.

The American salvation myth and the Stalinist salvation myth have in common the idea that the great body of the culture is a vast repository of destructive notions and impulses, that certain people rise out of the mass in the process of understanding and rejecting all that is retrograde, and that, for those people, there is never any use for, nor even any possibility of, conversation on equal terms with those who remain behind. The history of elites is brutal and terrible. When the impact of scientific and industrial and political elites finally becomes clear—and it has been devastating in every part of the world—it will become clear also that people picked at random off the street would probably have made better decisions. It would be wonderful if there were a visible elect, a true elite, who could lead us out of our bondage, out of our wilderness. But we are not so favored. Our zealots seem to assume they do provide such leadership—that if one cannot embrace their solutions it is surely because one is indifferent to great problems, or complicit in them. This is a manifestation of their presumption of legitimacy that I find especially disturbing, not least because their solutions then become the issue while the reality of the problems is forgotten, except by the police, the courts, the coroners.

If there is any descriptive value in the definition of morality I offered above, its great feature is autonomy. Tacitus admired the morality of the Germans, Calvin admired the morality of Seneca and Cicero—anyone who considers the question knows that morality can take any number of forms, that it can exist in many degrees of refinement and so on. We all distinguish instantly between a moral lapse and a difference of standards. Whatever else it is, morality is a covenant with oneself, which can only be imposed and enforced by oneself. Society can honor these covenants or not. Historically it seems that repression often encourages them. The great antidote to morality is cynicism, which is nothing more than an understanding of how arbitrary morality is, how unpredictable and unenforceable, how insecurely grounded in self-interest. It appears to me that even very thoughtful people discover what terms they have made with themselves only as they live, which prohibitions are conditional, which absolute, and so on. So in this great matter of moral soundness or rigor or whatever, we are as great mysteries to ourselves as we are to one another. It should not be that way, of course. The human condition has an amazing wrongness about it. But if it is agreed that we are in this respect mysterious, then we should certainly abandon easy formulas of judgment. If it is true that morality is a form of autonomy, then social conditioning is more likely to discourage than to enhance it.

If, putting out of consideration the inwardness of people, and putting aside the uniqueness of the terms in which everyone's relations with the world are negotiated, and excluding the very prevalent desire of people to align themselves with what they take to be right, and ignoring the fact that people have ideas and convictions for which they cannot find words, we choose to believe all the errors of our past are stored in the minds of those who use language we have declared to embody those errors, then we make the less sophisticated tiers of the society the problem and the enemy, and effectively exonerate ourselves. We know what they mean better than they do, so we only listen to hear them condemn themselves. In the name of justice we commit a very crude injustice. We alienate a majority of our people, and exclude them from a conversation of the most pressing importance to them, having nothing but our smugness to justify the presumption. We must find a better model to proceed from.

This is John Calvin glossing the text "Love thy neighbor":

> Here, therefore, let us stand fast: our life shall best conform to God's will and the prescriptions of the law when it is in every respect most fruitful for our brethren . . . It is very clear that we keep the commandments not by loving ourselves but by loving God and neighbor; that he lives the best and holiest life who lives and strives for himself as little as he can, and that no one lives in a worse or more evil manner than he who lives and strives for himself alone, and thinks about and seeks only his own advantage . . .

Here is John Calvin answering the question "Who is our neighbor?"

> It is the common habit of mankind that the more closely men are bound together by the ties of kinship, of acquaintanceship, or of neighborhood, the more responsibilities for one another they share. This does not offend God; for his providence, as it were, leads us to it. But I say: we ought to embrace the whole human race without exception in a single feeling of love; here there is no distinction beween barbarian and Greek, worthy and unworthy, friend and enemy, since all should be contemplated in God, not in themselves. When we turn aside from such contemplation, it is no wonder we become entangled in many errors. Therefore, if we rightly direct our love, we must first turn our eyes not to man, the sight of whom would more often engender hate than love, but to God, who bids us extend to all men the love we bear to him, that this may be an unchanging principle: Whatever the character of the man, we must yet love him because we love God.

Here is John Calvin explaining how we are to determine our obligation to others:

Say, "He is contemptible and worthless"; but the Lord shows him to be one to whom he has deigned to give the beauty of his image. Say that you owe nothing for any service of his; but God, as it were, has put him in his own place in order that you may recognize toward him the many and great benefits with which God has bound you to himself. Say that he does not deserve even your least effort for his sake; but the image of God, which recommends him to you, is worthy of your giving yourself and all your possessions. Now if he has not only deserved no good at your hand, but has also provoked you by unjust acts and curses, not even this is just reason why you should cease to embrace him in love and to perform the duties of love on his behalf . . . Assuredly there is but one way in which to achieve what is not merely difficult but utterly against human nature: to love those who hate us, to repay their evil deeds with benefits, to return blessings for reproaches. It is that we remember not to consider men's evil intention but to look upon the image of God in them, which cancels and effaces their transgressions, and with its dignity allures us to love and embrace them.

This is the theological basis for Jonathan Edwards' wonderful definition of "justice."

Whatever confronts us, it is not a resurgence of Puritanism. If we must look to our past to account for our present circumstances, perhaps we might ponder the impulse long established in it to disparage, to cheapen and deface, and to falsify, which has made a valuable inheritance worthless. Anyone who considers the profound wealth and continuing good fortune of this country must wonder, how do we make so little of so much? Now, I think, we are making little of the language of social conscience and of the traditions of activism and reform. We are losing and destroying what means we have had to do justice to one another, to confer benefit upon one another, to assure one another a worthy condition of life. If Jonathan Edwards were here, he would certainly call that a sin. I am hard pressed to think of a better word.

Revolutions, Universals and Sexual Categories

BY JOHN BOSWELL

The twentieth century has witnessed three revolutions in the study of history. The first was the sudden triumph of what is now loosely called the "Annales school,"[1] which laid the ground work for the scientific study of social history. *Annaliste* history radically and permanently changed the course of historical studies in the West. No serious challenge to its authority has emerged, and almost all modern works of European history depend to some extent on its methodologies and assumptions.

The second revolution followed on the first: the introduction of statistical techniques to assess and organize historical data. Statistical history has enjoyed considerable success, but will probably have less permanent effect than *annaliste* techniques, because its application is necessarily limited, and it is open to reasonable criticism for the distorting effect it can have on the direction of historical inquiry. A German joke depicts a drunk searching for his keys under a streetlamp on a dark night. Observing his unsuccessful search, a policeman asks him if he's sure he dropped them there. "No," the drunk answers, "I dropped them there under that tree, but the light is better here." Many historians are suspicious—that statistical approaches attract researchers to hunt where the light is best rather than where the answers are most likely to be found.

The third revolution might be called "minority history": the effort to recover the histories of groups previously overlooked or excluded from mainstream historiography. Minority history has provoked predictable skepticism on the part of some traditional historians, partly because of its novelty—which will, of course, inevitably wear off— and partly because the attitudes which previously induced neglect or distortion of minority history still prevail in many quarters. The most reasonable criticism of minority history (aside from the objection that it is sometimes very poor scholarship, against which no discipline is proof) is that it lends itself to political use which may distort scholarly integrity. As a point about minority history as a genre this is not cogent: since the exclusion of minorities from much historiography prior to the twentieth century was related to or caused by concerns other than purely scholarly interest, their inclusion now, even for purely political ends, not only corrects a previous "political" distortion, but provides a more complete data base for judgments about the historical issues involved. Such truth as is yielded by historical analysis generally emerges from the broadest possible synthesis of the greatest number of viewpoints and vantages: the addition of minority history and viewpoints to twentieth-century historiography is a net gain for all concerned.

But at a more particular level political struggles can cause serious problems for scholars, and a curious debate now taking place among those interested in the history of gay people provides a relevant and timely example of a type of difficulty which could subvert minority history altogether if not addressed intelligently. To avoid contributing further to the undue political freight the issue has lately been forced to bear, I propose to approach it by way of another historical controversy, one which was—in its day—no less heated or urgent, but which is now sufficiently distant to be viewed with dispassion by all sides.

The conflict in question is as old as Plato and as modern as cladism, and although the most violent struggles over it took place in the twelfth and thirteenth centuries, the arguments of the ancients on the subject are still in use today. Stated as briefly and baldly as possible, the issues are these: do categories exist because humans recognize real distinctions in the world around them, or are categories arbitrary conventions, simply names for things which have categorical force because humans agree to use them in certain ways? The two traditional sides in this controversy, which is called "the problem of universals," are "realists" and "nominalists." Realists consider categories to be the footprints of reality ("universals"): they exist because humans perceive a real order in the universe and name it. The order is present without human observation, according to realists; the human contribution is simply the naming and describing of it. Most scientists operate—tacitly— in a realist mode, on the assumption that they are discovering, not inventing, the relationships within the physical world. The scientific method is, in fact, predicated on realist attitudes. On the other hand, the philosophical structure of the modern West is closer to nominalism: the belief that categories are only the names (Latin: nomina) of things agreed upon by humans, and that the "order" people see is their creation rather than their perception. Most modern philosophy and language theory is essentially nominalist, and even the more theoretical sciences are nominalist to some degree: in biology, for example, taxonomists disagree strongly about whether they are discovering (realists) or inventing (nominalists) distinctions among phyla, genera, species, etc. (When, for example, a biologist announces that bats, being mammals, are "more closely related to" humans than to birds, is he expressing some real relationship, present in nature and detected by humans, or is he employing an arbitrary convention, something which helps humans organize and sort information but which bears no "truth" or significance beyond this utility?)

This seemingly arcane struggle now underlies an epistemological controversy raging among those studying the history of gay people. The "universals" in this case are categories of sexual preference or orientation (the difference is crucial). "Nominalists" in the matter aver that categories of sexual preference and behavior are created by humans and human societies. Whatever reality they have is the consequence of the power they exert in those societies and the socialization processes which make them seem real to persons influenced by them. People consider themselves "homosexual" or "heterosexual" because they are induced to believe that humans are either "homosexual" or "heterosexual." Left to their own devices, without such processes of socialization, people would simply be sexual. The category "heterosexuality," in other words, does not so much describe a pattern of behavior inherent in human beings as it creates and establishes it.

Realists hold that this is not the case. Humans are, they insist, differentiated sexually. Many categories might be devised to characterize human sexual taxonomy, some more or less apt than others, but the accuracy of human perceptions does not affect reality. The heterosexual/ homosexual dichotomy exists in speech and thought because it exists in reality: it was not invented by sexual taxonomists, but observed by them.[2]

Neither of these positions is usually held absolutely: most nominalists would be willing to admit that some aspects of sexuality are present, and might be distinguished, without direction from society. And most realists are happy to admit that the same real phenomenon might be described by various systems of categorization, some more accurate and helpful than others. One might suppose that "moderate nominalists" and "moderate realists" could therefore engage in a useful dialogue on those areas where they agree and, by careful analysis of their differences, promote discussion and understanding of these issues.

Political ramifications hinder this. Realism has historically been viewed by the nominalist camp as conservative, if not reactionary, in its implicit recognition of the value and/or immutability of the status quo; and nominalism has generally been regarded by realists as an obscurantist radical ideology designed more to undercut and subvert human values than to clarify them. Precisely these political overtones can be seen to operate today in scholarly debate over issues of sexuality. The efforts of sociobiology to demonstrate an evolutionary etiology of homosexuality have been vehemently denounced by many who regard the enterprise as reactionary realism, an effort to persuade people that social categories are fixed and unchangeable, while on the other side, psychiatric "cures" of homosexuality are bitterly resented by many as the cynical folly of nominalist pseudo-science: convince someone he shouldn't want to be a homosexual, persuade him to think of himself as a "heterosexual," and— presto!—he is a heterosexual. The category is the person.

Whether or not there are "homosexual" and "heterosexual" persons, as opposed to persons called "homosexual" or "heterosexual" by society, is obviously a matter of substantial import to the gay community, since it brings into question the nature and even the existence of such a community. It is, moreover, of substantial epistemological urgency to nearly all of society[3] and the gravity and extent of this can be seen in the case of the problems it creates for history and historians.

The history of minorities poses ferocious difficulties: censorship and distortion, absence or destruction of records, the difficulty of writing about essentially personal and private aspects of human feelings and behavior, problems of definition, political dangers attendant on choosing certain subjects, etc. But if the nominalists are correct and the realists wrong, the problems in regard to the history of gay people are of an entirely different order: if the categories "homosexual/heterosexual" and "gay/straight" are the inventions of particular societies rather than real aspects of the human psyche, there is no gay history.[4] If "homosexuality" exists only when and where people are persuaded to believe in it, "homosexual" persons will have a "history" only in those particular societies and cultures.

In its most extreme form, this nominalist view has argued that only early modern and contemporary industrial societies have produced "homosexuality," and it is futile and misguided to look for "homosexuality" in earlier human history.

> What we call "homosexuality" (in the sense of the distinguishing traits of "homosexuals"), for example, was not considered a unified set of acts, much less a set of qualities defining particular persons, in pre-capitalist societies. . . . Heterosexuals and homosexuals are involved in social "roles" and attitudes which pertain to a particular society, modern capitalism.[5]

If this position is sustained, it will permanently alter, for better or worse, the nature and extent of minority history.

Clearly it has much to recommend it. No characteristics interact with the society around them uniformly through time. Perceptions of, reactions to, and social response regarding blackness, blindness, lefthandedness, Jewishness, or any other distinguishing (or distinguished) aspect of persons or peoples must necessarily vary as widely as the social circumstances in which they occur, and for this reason alone it could be reasonably argued that being Jewish, black, blind, left-handed, etc. is essentially different from one age and place to another. In some cultures, for example, Jews are categorized chiefly as an ethnic minority; in others they are not or are not perceived to be ethnically distinct from the peoples around them, and are distinguished solely by their religious beliefs. Similarly, in some societies anyone darker than average is considered "black"; in others, a complex and highly technical system of racial categorization classes some persons as black even when they are lighter in color than many "whites." In both cases, moreover, the differences in attitudes held by the majority must affect profoundly the self-perception of the minority itself, and its patterns of life and behavior are in all probability notably different from those of "black" or "Jewish" people in other circumstances.

There can be no question that if minority history is to merit respect it must carefully weigh such fundamental subtleties of context: merely cataloguing references to "Jews" or to "Blacks" may distort more than it reveals of human history if due attention is not paid to the meaning, in their historical setting, of such words and the concepts to which they apply. Do such reservations, on the other hand, uphold the claim that categories such as "Jew," "black," or "gay" are not diachronic and can not, even with apposite qualification, be applied to ages and times other than those in which the terms themselves were used in precisely their modern sense? Extreme realists, without posing the question, have assumed the answer was "no"; extreme nominalists seem to be saying, "yes."

The question can not be addressed intelligently without first noting three points. First, the positions are not in fact as clearly separable as this schema implies. It could be well argued, for example, that Padgug, Weeks et al., are in fact extreme realists in assuming that modern homosexuality is not simply one of a series of conventions designated under the same rubric, but is instead a "real" phenomenon which has no "real" antecedent in human history. Demonstrate to us the "reality" of this homosexuality, their opponents might legitimately demand, and prove to us that it has a unity and cohesiveness which justifies your considering it a single, unparalleled entity rather than a loose congeries of behaviors. Modern scientific literature increasingly assumes that what is at issue is not "homosexuality" but "homosexualities"; if these disparate patterns of sexuality can be grouped together under a single heading in the present, why make such a fuss about a diachronic grouping?

Second, adherents of both schools fall prey to anachronism. Nearly all of the most prominent nominalists are historians of the modern U.S., modern Britain, or modern Europe, and it is difficult to eschew the suspicion that they are concentrating their search where the light is best rather than where the answers are to be found, and formulating a theoretical position to justify their approach. On the other hand, nominalist objections are in part a response to an extreme realist position which has been predicated on the unquestioned, unproven, and overwhelmingly unlikely assumption that exactly the same categories and patterns of sexuality have always existed, pure and unchanged by the systems of thought and behavior in which they were enmeshed.

Third, both extremes appear to be paralyzed by words. The nominalists are determined that the same word can not apply to a wide range of meaning and still be used productively in scholarly discourse: in order to have meaning, "gay," e.g., must be applied only as the speaker would apply it, with all the precise ramifications he associates with it. This insistence follows understandably from the implicit assumption that the speaker is generating the category himself, or in concert with certain contemporaries, rather than receiving it from a human experience of great longevity and adjusting it to fit his own understanding. Realist extremists, conversely, assume that lexical equivalence betokens experiential equality, and that the occurrence of a word which "means" "homosexual" demonstrates the existence of "homosexuality," as the modern realist understands it, at the time the text was composed.

It is my aim to circumvent these difficulties as far as possible in the following remarks, and my hope that in so doing I may reduce the rhetorical struggle over "universals" in these matters and promote thereby more useful dialogue among the partisans. Let it be agreed at the outset that something can be discussed, by modern historians or ancient writers, without being named or defined. (Ten people in a room might argue endlessly about proper definitions of "blue" and "red," but could probably agree instantly whether a given object was one or the other [or a combination of both].) "Gravity" offers a useful historical example. A nominalist position would be that gravity did not exist before Newton invented it, and a nominalist historian might be able to mount a convincing case that there is no mention of gravity in any texts before Newton. "Nonsense," realists would object. "The Latin *gravitas*, which is common in Roman literature, describes the very properties of matter Newton called 'gravity'. Of course gravity existed before Newton discovered it."

Both, of course, are wrong. Lack of attention to something in historical sources can in no wise be taken as evidence of its nonexistence, and discovery can not be equated with creation or invention. But *gravitas* does not mean "gravity"; it means "heaviness," and the two are not at all the same thing. Noting that objects have heaviness is entirely different from understanding the nature and operations of gravity. For adherents of these two positions to understand each other each would have to abandon specific nomenclature, and agree instead on questions to be asked of the sources. If the proper questions were addressed, the nominalist could easily be persuaded that the sources prove that gravity existed before Newton, in the sense that the operations of the force now designated gravity are well chronicled in nearly all ancient literature. And the realist could be persuaded that despite this fact the nature of gravity was not clearly articulated—whether or not it was apprehended—before Newton.

The problem is rendered more difficult in the present case by the fact that the equivalent of gravity has not yet been discovered: there is still no essential agreement in the scientific community about the nature of human sexuality. Whether humans are "homosexual" or "heterosexual" or "bisexual" by birth, by training, by choice, or at all is still an open question.[6] Neither realists nor nominalists can, therefore, establish any clear correlation—positive or negative—between modern sexuality and its ancient counterparts. But it is still possible to discuss whether modern conceptualizations of sexuality are novel and completely socially relative, or correspond to constants of human epistemology which can be documented in the past.

To simplify discussion, three broad types of sexual taxonomy are abbreviated here as Types A, B and C. According to Type A theories, all humans are polymorphously sexual, i.e., capable of erotic and sexual interaction with either gender. External accidents, such as social pressure, legal sanctions, religious beliefs, historical or personal circumstances determine the actual expression of each person's sexual feelings. Type B theories posit two or more sexual categories, usually but not always based on sexual object choice, to which all humans belong, though external pressures or circumstance may induce individuals in a given society to pretend (or even to believe) that they belong to a category other than their native one. The most common form of Type B taxonomy assumes that humans are heterosexual, homosexual and bisexual, but that not all societies allow expression of all varieties of erotic disposition. Subsets or other versions of Type B categorize on the basis of other characteristics, e.g., a predilection for a particular role in intercourse. Type C theories consider one type of sexual response normal (or "natural" or "moral" or all three) and all other variants abnormal ("unnatural," "immoral").

It will be seen that Type A theories are nominalist to the extent that they regard categorizations like 'homosexual' and 'heterosexual' as arbitrary conventions applied to a sexual reality which is at bottom undifferentiated. Type B theories are conversely realist in predicating categories which underlie human sexual experience even when obscured by social constraints or particular circumstances. Type C theories are essentially normative rather than epistemological, but borrow from both sides of the universals question in assuming, by and large, that people are born into the normal category but become members of a deviant grouping by an act of the will, although some Type C adherents regard 'deviants' as inculpably belonging to an 'abnormal' category through mental or physical illness or defect.

That no two social structures are identical should require no proof; and since sexual categories are inevitably conditioned by social structure, no two systems of sexual taxonomy should be expected to be identical. A slight chronological or geographical shift would render one Type A system quite different from another one. But to state this is not to demonstrate that there are no constants in human sexual epistemology. The frequency with which these theories or variations on them appear in Western history is striking.

The apparent gender blindness of the ancient world has often been adduced as proof that Type B theories were unknown before comparatively recent times. In Plutarch's Dialogue on Love it is asserted that

> the noble lover of beauty engages in love wherever he sees excellence and splendid natural endowment without regard for any difference in physiological detail. The lover of human beauty [will] be fairly and equably disposed toward both sexes, instead of supposing that males and females are as different in the matter of love as they are in their clothes.[7]

Such statements are commonplaces of ancient lore about love and eroticism, to the extent that one is inclined to believe that much of the ancient world was completely unaware of differentiation among humans in sexual object choice, as I have myself pointed out at length elsewhere.[8] But my statements and the evidence on which they rest can easily be misapprehended. Their purport is that ancient *societies* did not distinguish heterosexuality from homosexuality, not that all, or even most, individuals failed to make such a distinction.

A distinction can be present and generally recognized in a society without forming any part of its social structure. In some cultures skin color is a major determinant of social status; in others it is irrelevant. But it would be fatuous to assume that societies which did not "discriminate on the basis of" [i.e., make invidious distinctions concerning] skin color could not "discriminate" [distinguish] such differences. This same paranomastic subtlety must be understood in regard to ancient views of sexuality: city-states of the ancient world did not, for the most part, discriminate on the basis of sexual orientation, and, as societies, appear to have been blind to the issue of sexual object choice, but it is not clear that individuals were unaware of distinctions in the matter.

It should be obvious, for instance, that in the passage cited above Plutarch is arguing against precisely that notion which Padgug claims had not existed in "pre-capitalist" societies, i.e., Type B theories. Plutarch believes that a normal human being is susceptible to attraction to either gender, but his comments are manifestly directed against the contrary view. Which attitude was more common in his day is not apparent, but it is clearly inaccurate to use his comments as demonstration that there was only one view. The polemical tone of his remarks, in fact, seems good evidence that the position he opposes was of considerable importance. The whole genre of debates about the types of love of which this dialogue is a representative[9] cuts both ways on the issue: on the one hand, arguing about the matter and adducing reasons for preferring one gender to the other suggests a kind of polymorphous sexuality which is not predirected by heredity or experience toward one gender or the other. On the other, in each of the debates there are factions which are clearly on one side or the other of the dichotomy not supposed to have existed before modern times: some disputants argue for attraction to males only; some for attraction to females only. Each side derogates the preference of the other side as distasteful. Sometimes bisexuality is admitted, but as a third preference, not as the general nature of human sexuality:

> Zeus came as an eagle to god-like Ganymede, as a swan came he to the fair-haired mother of Helen. So there is no comparison between the two things: one person likes one, another likes the other; I like both.[10]

This formulation of the range of human sexuality is almost identical to popular modern conceptions of Type B: some people prefer their own gender; some the opposite; some both. Similar distinctions abound in ancient literature. The myth of Aristophanes in Plato's *Symposium* is perhaps the most familiar example: its manifest and stated purpose is to explain why humans are divided into groups of predominantly homosexual or heterosexual interest. It is strongly implied that these interests are both exclusive and innate; this is stated outright by Longus, who describes a character as "homosexual by nature *[physei]*."[11]

It is true that there were no terms in common use in Greece or Rome to describe categories of sexual preference, but it does not follow that such terms were wholly unknown: Plato, Athenaeus, and other writers who dealt with the subject at length developed terms to describe predominant or exclusive interest in the apposite gender.[12] Many writers, moreover, found it possible to characterize homosexuality as a distinct mode of erotic expression without naming it. Plautus, e.g., characterized homosexual activity as the "mores of Marseilles," suggesting that he considered it a variant on ordinary human sexuality.[13] Martial found it possible to describe an exclusively heterosexual male, even though he had no terminology available to do so and was himself apparently interested in both genders.[14]

One even finds expressions of solidarity among adherents of one preference or another in ancient literature, as when Clodius Albinus, noted for his exclusively heterosexual interest, persecutes those involved in homosexual behavior[15] or when a character who has spoken on behalf of love between men in one of the debates bursts out, "we are like strangers cut off in a foreign land . . . ; nevertheless, we shall not be overcome by fear and betray the truth";[16] or when Propertius writes, "Let him who would be our enemy love girls; he who would be our friend enjoy boys."[17] That there is a jocular tone to some of these statements, especially the last, is certainly attributable to the fact that the distinctions involved in no way affected the wellbeing, happiness or social status of the individuals, owing to the extreme sexual tolerance of ancient societies; but it does not cast doubt on the existence of the distinctions. Even when preferences are attributed ironically, as is likely the case in Plato's placing the myth of sexual etiology in the mouth of Aristophanes, the joke depends on the familiarity of the distinction.

Subtler indications of Type B taxonomies can also be found. In the *Ephesiaca*, a Hellenistic love novel by Xenophon of Ephesus, sexual categories are never discussed, and are clearly not absolute, but they do seem to be well understood and constitute an organizing principle of individual lives. Habrocomes is involved throughout only with women, and when, after his long separation from his true love Anthia, she desires to know if he has been faithful to her, she inquires only if he has slept with other women, although she knows that men have been interested in him, and it is clear that sex with a man would also constitute infidelity (as with Corymbus). It seems clear that Habrocomes is, in fact, heterosexual, at least in Anthia's opinion. Another character, Hippothoos, had been married to an older woman and attracted to Anthia, but is apparently mostly gay: the two great loves of his life are males (Hyperanthes and Habrocomes); he left all to follow each of these, and at the end of the story he erects a statue to the former and establishes his residence near that of the latter. The author tidies up all the couples at the end by reuniting Anthia and Habrocomes and introducing a new male lover (Clisthenes) for Hippothoos. This entire scenario corresponds almost exactly to modern conceptualizations; some people are heterosexual, some homosexual, some bisexual; the categories are not absolute, but they are important and make a substantial difference in people's lives.

Almost the very same constellation of opinions can be found in many other pre-industrial societies. In medieval Islam one encounters an even more overwhelming emphasis on homosexual eroticism than in classical Greek or Roman writing. It is probably fair to say that most pre-modern Arabic poetry is ostensibly homosexual, and it is clear that this is more than a literary convention. When Saadia Gaon, a Jew living in Muslim society in the tenth century, discusses the desirability of "passionate love,"[18] he apparently refers only to homosexual passion. There is the sort of love men have for their wives, which is good but not passionate; and there is the sort of love men have for each other, which is passionate but not good. (And what of the wives' loves? We are not told.) That Saadia assumes the ubiquity of homosexual passion is the more striking because he is familiar with Plato's discussion of homosexual and heterosexual varieties of love in the *Symposium*.[19]

Does this mean that classical Islamic society uniformly entertained Type A theories of human sexuality and regarded eroticism as inherently pansexual? No. There is much evidence in Arabic literature for the very same Type B dichotomies known in other cultures. Saadia himself cites various theories about the determination of particular erotic interests (e.g., astrological lore),[20] and in the ninth century Jahiz wrote a debate involving partisans of homosexual and heterosexual desire, in which each disputant, like his Hellenistic counterpart, expresses distaste for the preference of the other.[21] Three debates of this sort occur in the *Thousand and One Nights*, a classic of Arabic popular literature.[22] "Homosexuals" are frequently (and neutrally) mentioned in classical Arabic writings as a distinct type of human being. That the "type" referred to involves predominant or exclusive preference is often suggested: in Tale 142 of the Nights, for example, it is mentioned as noteworthy that a male homosexual does not dislike women; in Night 419 a woman observes a man staring longingly at some boys and remarks to him, "I perceive that you are among those who prefer men to women."

A ninth-century text of human psychology by Qusta ibn Luqa treats twenty areas in which humans may be distinguished psychologically.[23] One area is sexual object choice: some men, Qusta explains, are "disposed towards" (*yamilu ilā*) women, some towards other men, and some towards both.[24] Qusta has no terminology at hand for these categories; indeed, for the second category he employs the euphemism that such men are disposed towards "sexual partners other than women";[25] obviously lack of terminology for the homosexual/heterosexual dichotomy should not be taken as a sign of ignorance of it. Qusta, in fact, believed that homosexuality was often inherited, as did ar-Razi and many other Muslim scientific writers.[26] It has been claimed that 'homosexuality' was viewed in medieval Europe "not as a particular attribute of a certain type of person but as a potential in all sinful creatures."[27] It is certainly true that some medieval writers evinced Type A attitudes of this sort: patristic authors often address to their audiences warnings concerning homosexual attraction predicated on the assumption that any male might be attracted to another.[28] The Anglo-Saxon life of St Eufrasia[29] recounts the saint's efforts to live in a monastery disguised as a monk and the turmoil which ensued: the other monks were greatly attracted by Agapitus (the name she took as a monk), and reproached the abbot for bringing "so beautiful a man into their minster" ["forbam swa wlitigne man into heora mynstre gelaedde," p. 344]. Although it is in fact a woman to whom the monks are drawn, the account evinces no surprise on anyone's part that the monks should experience intense sexual attraction toward a person ostensibly of their own gender.

Some theologians clearly regarded homosexual activity as a vice open to all rather than as the peculiar sexual outlet of a portion of the population, but this attitude was not universal and was often ambiguously or inconsistently held even by those who did most to promulgate it. Albertus Magnus and Thomas Aquinas both wrote of homosexual acts as sins which presumably anyone might commit, but both also recognized that it was somewhat more complex than this: Aquinas, following Aristotle, believed that some men were "naturally inclined" to desire sexual relations with other men—clearly a theory of Type B—and Albertus Magnus considered homosexual desire to be a manifestation of a contagious disease, particularly common among the wealthy, and curable through the application of medicine.[30] This attitude is highly reminiscent of psychiatric opinion in late Victorian times, and a far cry from categorizing homosexuality simply as a vice.

"Sodomy" was defined by many clerics as the improper emission of semen—the gender of the parties and their sexual appetites being irrelevant—but many others understood *sodomita* to apply specifically to men who preferred sexual contact with other men, generally or exclusively, and *sodomia* to apply only to the sexual acts performed in this context.[31]

Medieval literature abounds in suggestions that there is something special about homosexuality, that it is not simply an ordinary sin. Many writers view it as the special characteristic of certain peoples; others argue that it is completely unknown among their own kind. There are constant associations of homosexual preference with certain occupations or social positions, clearly indicating that it is linked in some way to personality or experience. The modern association of homosexuality with the arts had as its medieval counterpart a regular link with the religious life: when Bernard of Clairvaux was asked to restore life to the dead son of a Marquess of Burgundy he had the boy taken to a private room and lay down upon him. No cure transpired; the boy remained lifeless. The chronicler, who had been present, nonetheless found humor in the incident and remarked, "That was the unhappiest monk of all. For I've never heard of any monk who lay down upon a boy that did not straightaway rise up after him. The abbot blushed and they went out as many laughed."[32]

Chaucer's pardoner, also a cleric, appears to be innately sexually atypical, and his association with the hare has led many to suppose that it is homosexuality which distinguishes him.[33] Even non-Christians linked the Christian clergy with homosexuality.[34]

Much of the literature of the High Middle Ages which deals with sexual object choice assumes distinct dispositions, most often exclusive. A long passage in the *Roman d 'Eneas* characterizes homosexual males as devoid of interest in women and notable in regard to dress, habits, decorum and behavior.[35] Debates of the period characterize homosexual preference as innate or God-given, and in the well-known poem "Ganymede and Helen" it is made pellucidly clear that Ganymede is exclusively gay (before the intervention of the gods): It is Helen's frustration at his inability to respond properly to her advances which prompts the debate.[36] In a similar poem, "Ganymede and Hebe," homosexual relations are characterized as "decreed by fate," suggesting something quite different from an occasional vice.[37] Indeed, the mere existence of debates of this sort suggests very strongly a general conceptualization of sexuality as bifurcated into two camps distinguished by sexual object choice. Popular terminology of the period corroborates this: as opposed to words like *sodomita* which might designate indulgence in a specific activity by any human, writers of the High Middle Ages were inclined to use designations like "Ganymede," whose associations were exclusively homosexual, and to draw analogies with animals like the hare and the hyena which were thought to be naturally inclined to sexual relations with their own gender.

Allain of Lille invokes precisely the taxonomy of sexual orientation used in the modern West in writing about sexuality among his twelfth century contemporaries: "Of those men who employ the grammar of Venus there are some who embrace the masculine, others who embrace the feminine, and some who embrace both . . . ."[38]

Clearly, all three types of taxonomy were known in Western Europe and the Middle East before the advent of modern capitalist societies. It is, on the other hand, equally clear that in different times and places one type of theory has often predominated over the others, and for long periods in many areas one or two of the three may have been quite rare. Does the prevalence of one theory over another in given times and places reveal something about human sexuality? Possibly, but many factors other than sexuality itself may influence, deform, alter or transform conceptualizations of sexuality among peoples and individuals, and much attention must be devoted to analysing such factors and their effects before it will be possible to use them effectively in analyzing the bedrock of sexuality beneath them.

Nearly all societies, for example, regulate sexual behavior in some way; most sophisticated cultures articulate rationalizations for their restrictions. The nature of such rationalizations will inevitably affect sexual taxonomy. If "the good" in matters sexual is equated with procreation, homosexual relations may be categorically distinguished from heterosexual ones as necessarily excluding the chief good of sexuality. Such a moral taxonomy might create a homosexual/heterosexual dichotomy in and of itself, independent of underlying personal attitudes. This appears, in fact, to have played some role in the Christian West. That some heterosexual relations also exclude procreation is less significant (though much heterosexual eroticism has been restricted in the West), because there is not an easily demonstrable generic incompatibility with procreative purpose. (Compare the association of chest hair with maleness: not all men have hairy chests, but only men have chest hair; hence, chest hair is thought of as essentially masculine; though not all heterosexual couplings are procreative, only heterosexual acts could be procreative, so heterosexuality seems essentially procreative and homosexuality essentially not.)

In a society where pleasure or the enjoyment of beauty are recognized as legitimate aims of sexual activity, this dichotomy should seem less urgent. And in the Hellenistic and Islamic worlds, where sexuality has traditionally been restricted on the basis of standards of decorum and propriety[39] rather than procreative purpose, the homosexual/heterosexual dichotomy has been largely absent from public discourse. Just as the presence of the dichotomy might be traceable to aspects of social organization unrelated to sexual preference, however, its absence must likewise be seen as a moot datum: as has been shown, individual Greek and Muslim writers were often acutely conscious of such a taxonomy. The prevalence of either Type A or Type B concepts at the social level, in other words, may be related more to other social structures than to personal perceptions of or beliefs about the nature of sexuality.

Another factor, wholly overlooked in previous literature on this subject, is the triangular relationship of mediated desire, beauty, and sexual stereotypes. It seems safe enough to assume that most humans are influenced to some degree by the values of the society in which they live. Many desires are "mediated" by the valorization accorded things by surrounding society, rather than generated exclusively by the desiring individual. If one posits for the sake of argument two opposed sets of social values regarding beauty and sex roles, it is easy to see how conceptualizations of sexual desire might be transformed to fit "mediated desire" resulting from either pole. At one extreme, beauty is conceived as a male attribute: standards and ideals of beauty are predicated on male models, art emphasizes male beauty, and males take pride in their own physical attractions. Greece and the Muslim world approach this extreme: Greek legend abounds in examples of males pursued for their beauty, standards of beauty are often predicated on male archetypes (Adonis, Apollo, Ganymede, Antinous), and beauty in males is considered a major good, for the individual and for his society. Likewise, in the Muslim world, archetypes of beauty are more often seen in masculine than in feminine terms, beauty is thought to be a great asset to a man, and the universal archetype of beauty, to which even beautiful women are compared, is Joseph.

This pole can be contrasted with societies in which "maleness" and beauty are thought unrelated or even contradictory, and beauty is generally predicated only of females. In such societies "maleness" is generally idealized in terms of social roles, as comprising, e.g., forcefulness, strength, the exercise of power, aggression, etc. In the latter type of society, which the modern West approaches, "beauty" would generally seem inappropriate, perhaps even embarrassing in males, and males possessing it would be regarded as "effeminate" or sexually suspect to some degree.

In nearly all cultures some linkage is expressed between eroticism and beauty, and it should not therefore be surprising that in societies of the former type there will be greater emphasis on males as sex objects than in those of the latter type. Since beauty is conceptualized as a good, and since it is recognized to subsist on a large scale—perhaps even primarily—among men, men can be admired even by other men for their beauty, and this admiration is often indistinguishable (at the literary level, if not in reality) from erotic interest. In cultures of the latter type, however, men are not admired for their beauty; sexual interest is generally imagined to be applied by men (who are strong, forceful, powerful, etc., but not beautiful) to women, whose beauty may be considered their chief—or even sole—asset. In the latter case, expressions of admiration for male beauty will be rare, even among women, who will prize other attributes in men they desire.

These descriptions are deliberate oversimplifications to make a point: in fact, no society is exclusively one or the other, and elements of both are present in all Western cultures. But it would be easy to show that many societies tend more toward one extreme than the other, and it is not hard to see how this might affect the prominence of the homosexual/heterosexual dichotomy: in a culture where male beauty was generally a source of admiration, the dividing line between what some taxonomies would define as homosexual and heterosexual interest would be considerably blurred by common usage and expression. Expressions of admiration and even attraction to male beauty would be so familiar that they would not provoke surprise or require designation as a peculiar category. Persons in such a society might be uninterested in genital interaction with persons of their own sex, might even disapprove of it, but they would tend not to see romantic interest in male beauty—by males or females—as bizarre or odd or as necessitating special categorization.

In cultures which de-emphasize male beauty, however, expressions of interest in it by men or women might be suspect. In a society which has established no place for such interest in its esthetic structures, mere admiration for a man's physical attractiveness, without genital acts, could be sharply stigmatized, and a strict division between homosexual and heterosexual desire would be easy to promulgate and maintain.

Female roles would also be affected by such differences: if women are thought of as moved by beauty, even if it is chiefly male beauty, the adoption of the role of admirer by a woman will not seem odd or peculiar. If women are viewed, however, as the beautiful but passive objects of a sexual interest largely limited to men, their expressing sexual interest—in men or women— may be disapproved.[40] George Chauncey[41] has documented precisely this sort of disapproval in Victorian medical literature on "homosexuality": at the outset sexual deviance is perceived only in women who violate the sex role expected of them by playing an active part in a female-female romantic relationship. The "passive" female, who does not violate expectations of sex role by receiving, as females are thought naturally to do, the attentions of her "husband," is not considered abnormal. Gradually, as attitudes and the needs of society to define more precisely the limits of approved sexuality change, attention is transferred from the role the female "husband" plays to the sexual object choice of both women, and both come to be categorized as "homosexual" on the basis of the gender to which they are attracted.

Shifts of this sort, relating to conceptions of beauty, rationalization of sexual limitations, etc., are supported, affected and overlaid by more specific elements of social organization. These include patterns of sexual interaction (between men and women, the old and young, the rich and the poor, etc.), specific sexual taboos, and what might be called 'secondary' sexual behavior. Close attention must be devoted to such factors in their historical context in assessing sexualconceptualizations of any type.

Ancient "pederasty," e.g., seems to many to constitute a form of sexual organization entirely unrelated to modern homosexuality. Possibly this is so, but the differences seem much less pronounced when one takes into account the sexual context in which "pederasty" occurs. The age-differential idealized in descriptions of relations between the "lover" and the "beloved" is less than the disparity in age between heterosexual lovers as recommended, e.g., by Aristotle (19 years). "Pederasty" may often represent no more than the homosexual side of a general pattern of cross-generation romance.[42] Issues of subordination and power likewise offer parallel structures which must be collated before any arguments about ancient 'homosexuality' or 'heterosexuality' can be mounted. Artemidorus Daldianus aptly encapsulates the conflation of sexual and social roles of his contemporaries in the second century A.D. in his discussion of the significance of sexual dreams:

> For a man to be penetrated [in a dream] by a richer and older man is good: for it is customary to receive from such men. To be penetrated by a younger and poorer is bad: for it is the custom to give to such persons. It signifies the same [i.e., is bad] if the penetrator is older and poor.[43]

Note that these comments do not presuppose either Type A or Type B theories: they might be applied to persons who regard either gender as sexually apposite, or to persons who feel a predisposition to one or the other. But they do suggest the social matrix of a system of sexual distinctions which might override, alter or disguise other taxonomies.

The special position of passive homosexual behavior, involving the most common premodern form of Type C theory, deserves a separate study, but it might be noted briefly that its effect on sexual taxonomies is related not only to status considerations about penetration, as indicated above, but also to specific sexual taboos which may be highly culturally variable. Among Romans, for instance, two roles were decorous for a free adult male, expressed by the verbs *irrumo,* to offer the penis for sucking, and *futuo,* to penetrate a female, or *pedico,* to penetrate a male.[44] Indecorous roles for citizen males, permissible for anyone else, were expressed in particular by the verbs *fello,* to fellate, and *ceveo,* not translatable into English.[45] The distinction between roles approved for male citizens and others appears to center on the giving of seed (as opposed to the receiving of it) rather than on the more familiar modern active/passive division. (American prison slang expresses a similar dichotomy with the terms "catchers" and "pitchers.") It will be seen that this division obviates to a large degree both the active/passive split—since both the irrumator and the Negator are conceptually active[46]—and the homosexual/ heterosexual one, since individuals are categorized not according to the gender to which they are drawn but to the role they play in activities which could take place between persons of either gender. It is not clear that Romans had no interest in the gender of sexual partners, only that the division of labor, as it were, was a more pressing concern and attracted more analytical attention.

Artemidorus, on the other hand, considered both 'active' and 'passive' fellatio to be categorically distinct from other forms of sexuality. He divided his treatment of sexuality into three sections— the natural and legal, the illegal, and the unnatural—and he placed fellatio, in any form, among illegal activities, along with incest. In the ninth-century translation of his work by Hunain ibn Ishaq (the major transmitter of Aristotelian learning to the West), a further shift is evident: Hunain created a separate chapter for fellatio, which he called "that vileness of which it is not decent even to speak."[47]

In both the Greek and the Arabic versions of this work the fellatio which is objurgated is both homosexual and heterosexual, and in both anal intercourse between men is spoken of with indifference or approval.

Yet in the Christian West the most hostile legislation regarding sexual behavior has been directed specifically against homosexual anal intercourse: fellatio has generally received milder treatment. Is this because fellatio is more widely practiced among heterosexuals in the West, and therefore seems less bizarre (i.e., less distinctly homosexual)? Or is it because passivity and the adoption of what seems a female role in anal intercourse is particularly objectionable in societies dominated by rigid ideals of "masculine" behavior? It may be revealing, in this context, that many modern languages, including English, have skewed the donor/recipient dichotomy by introducing a chiastic active/passive division: the recipient (i.e., of semen) in anal intercourse is "passive"; in oral intercourse he is "active." Could the blurring of the active/passive division in the case of fellatio render it less obnoxious to legislative sensibilities?

Fuller understanding of shifts in attitudes toward specific activities of this sort may contribute much to future efforts to analyze human sexual taxonomies. They must be correlated with attitudes toward what might be deemed "secondary" sexual behavior. Recent studies have indicated that gay men recall having been less gregarious as boys than their heterosexual counterparts, and that they played more often alone or with girls than with other boys.[48] Both realists and nominalists have reacted negatively to this finding: the former because it suggests to them something about the "real" nature of homosexuality they would rather not believe (i.e., that gay men are not just like straight men in all respects save one); the latter because it suggests that "homosexuality" is a deepseated disposition apparent in childhood behavior patterns rather than a lifestyle or political stance consciously chosen by adults. For future historians these reactions are more revealing than the data which provoke them (and which may well turn out to be false or insignificant). In fact, an explanation for this behavior is already provided by the dominant culture: it is generally recognized that young boys display an aversion to playing with girls. This is taken to be entirely normal and, by accepted irony, assumed to be a harbinger of the attraction which will someday draw the two groups, as adults, together. The most obvious interpretation of a similar disinclination of some boys to play with other boys would run along the same lines:

it, too, is a portent of attraction to come. The subconscious sexual tension—or whatever it may be—which causes some boys to disdain as playmates the girls they will someday pursue as lovers causes other boys to avoid the boys they will someday seek as mates.

The failure of both sides of the universals controversy to recognize the cultural niche already prepared for the finding in question (which, I repeat, may well turn out to be entirely erroneous) discloses more than they intend to reveal about their own awareness of social concepts of sexuality, and illuminates the problems facing research in the area. Not until the full panoply of sexual taxonomy is appreciated—including related but not overtly sexual patterns of behavior such as gender avoidance in childhood, modes of conceptualizing acts as well as preferences, and the social structures which limit sexual behavior regardless of orientation or preference—will there be hope of matching concepts of sexuality to sexuality itself.

Beliefs about sexual categories in the modern West vary widely, from the notion that sexual behavior is entirely a matter of conscious choice to the conviction that all sexual behavior is determined by heredity or environment. The same individual may, in fact, entertain with apparent equanimity contradictory ideas on the subject. It is striking that many ardent proponents of Type C etiological theories who regard homosexual behavior as pathological and/or depraved nonetheless imply in their statements about the necessity of legal repression of homosexual behavior that it is potentially ubiquitous in the human population, and that if legal sanctions are not maintained everyone may suddenly become homosexual.

Humans of previous ages were probably not, as a whole, more logical or consistent than their modern descendants. To pretend that a single system of sexual categorization obtained at any previous moment in Western history is to maintain the unlikely in the face of substantial evidence to the contrary. Most of the current spectrum of belief appears to have been represented in previous societies. What that spectrum reveals about the inner nature of human sexuality remains, for the time being, moot and susceptible of many divergent interpretations. But if the third revolution in modern historical writing—and the recovery of whatever past the "gay community" may be said to have—is not to be stillborn, the problem of universals must be sidestepped or at least approached with fewer doctrinaire assumptions. Both realists and nominalists must lower their voices. Reconstructing the monuments of the past from the rubble of the present requires quiet concentration.

Notes

[1] So called after *Annales, Économies, Sociétés, Civilisations,* the journal which popularized the type of studies and techniques now designated by the name.

[2] For particularly articulate examples of "nominalist" history, see Robert A. Padgug, "Sexual Matters: On Conceptualizing Sexuality in History," *Radical History Review* 20 (1979), 3-33; and Jeffrey Weeks, *Coming Out: Homosexual Politics in Britain from the Nineteenth Century to the Present* (London, 1977). Most older studies of homosexuality in the past are essentially realist; see bibliography in John Boswell,*Christianity, Social Tolerance and Homosexuality* (Chicago, 1980), p.4 n.3.

[3] It is of substantial import to several moral traditions, e.g., whether or not homosexuality is a "condition"—an essentially "realist" position—or a "lifestyle"—basically a "nominalist" point of view. For a summary of shifting attitudes on these points within the Christian tradition, see Peter Coleman, *Christian Attitudes to Homosexuality* (London, 1980), or Edward Batchelor, *Homosexuality and Ethics* (New York, 1980).

[4] Note that at this level the debate is to some extent concerned with the degree of convention which can be sustained without loss of accuracy. It is conventional, for instance, to include in a history of the United States treatment of the period before the inauguration of the system of government which bears that title, and even to speak of the "colonial U.S.," although while they were colonies they were not the United States. A history of Greece would likewise, by convention, concern itself with all the states which would someday constitute what is today called "Greece," although those states may have recognized no connection with each other (or even have been at war) at various points in the past. It is difficult to see why such conventions should not be allowed in the case of minority histories, so long as sufficient indication is provided as to the actual relationship of earlier forms to later ones.

[5] Padgug, "Sexual Matters," p.l3.

[6] For the variety of etiological explanations to date see the brief bibliography in Boswell,*Christianity* p.9 n.9. To this list should now be added (in addition to many articles)two major studies: Alan Bell and M.S. Weinberg , *Homosexualities: A Study of Diversity Among Men and Women* (New York, 1978) and idem, *Sexual Preference:Its Development in Men and Women* (Bloomington, Indiana, 1981). An ingenious and highly revealing approach to the development of modern medical literature on the subject of homosexuality is proposed by George Chauncey, "From Gender Roles to Sexual Desire," in *Salmagundi,* no. 58-59, special issue on *Homosexuality.*

[7] Moralia 767: *Amatorius,* trans. W.C. Helmhold (Cambridge, Mass., 1961), p.415.

[8] *Christianity,* Part I *passim* esp. pp.50-59.

[9] See Boswell, *Christianity,* pp . l 25-27 .

[10] *Greek Anthology,* trans. W.R. Paton (Cambridge, Mass., 1918), 1.65.

[11] Daphnis and Chloe, 4.11. The term *paiderastes* here can not be understood as a reference to what is now called paedophilia, since Daphnis—the object of Gnatho's interest—is full grown and on the point of marriage. It is obviously a conventional term for "homosexual."

[12] For Plato and Pollianus, see Boswell, *Christianity*, p.30 n.56; Athenaeus uses *philomeirax* of Sophocles and *philogynes* of Euripides, apparently intending to indicate that the former was predominantly (if not exclusively) interested in males and the latter in females. Cf. *Scriptores physiognomici*, ed. R. Foerster (Leipzig, 1893), 1:29, p.36, where the word *philogynaioi*, "woman lover," occurs.

[13] Casina V.4.1 957.

[14] Epigrams, 2.47.

[15] Capitolinus, 11.7.

[16] Boswell, *Christianity*, p.127.

[17] 2.4: Hostis si quis erit nobis, amet ille puellas: gaudeat in puero si quis amicus erit.

[18] Saadia Gaon, *Kitab āl- 'Amanāt wa 'I-lctikhadat*, ed. S. Landauer (Leyden, 1880), 10.7, pp.294-97 (English translation by S. Rosenblatt in *Yale Judaica Series*, Vol. 1: *The Book of Beliefs and Opinions*).

[19] *Kitāb*, p.295.

[20] Ibid.

[21] *Kitab mufakharat al-jawari wa'l-ghilman*, ed. Charles Pellat (Beirut, 1957).

[22] See discussion in Boswell, *Christianity*, pp.257-58.

[23] "Le Livre des caracteres de Qusta ibn Louqa," ed. and trans. Paul Sbath, *Bulletin de l'Institute d 'Egypte* 23 (1940-41), 103-39. Sbath's translation is loose and misleading, and must be read with caution.

[24] See p. 112.

[25] ". . . waminhim man yamilu ila ghairihinna mini 'Ighilmani . . .," ibid. A treatment of the fascinating term *ghulam* (pl. ghilman), whose meanings range from "son" to "sexual partner" is beyond the scope of this essay.

[26] Qusta discusses this at some length, pp. 133-36. Cf. F. Rosenthal, "ar-Razi on the Hidden Illness," *Bulletin of the History of Medicine* 52, 1 (1978), 45-60, and the authorities cited there. Treating "passive sexual behavior" (i.e. the reception of semen in anal intercourse) in men as a hereditary condition generally implies a conflation of Types A and C taxonomies in which the role of insertor with either men or women is thought "normal," but the position of the "insertee" is regarded as bizarre or even pathological. Attitudes toward ubnah should be taken as a special aspect of Muslim sexual taxonomy rather than as indicative of attitudes toward "homosexuality." A comparable case is that of Caelius Aurelianus: see Boswell, *Christianity*, p.53; cf. remarks on Roman sexual taboos, below.

[27] Weeks, *Coming Out*, p. 12.

[28] See Boswell, *Christianity*, pp. 159-61.

[29] *Aelfric's Lives of Saints*, ed. and trans. W.W. Skeat (London, 1881), 33.

[30] Discussed in Boswell, *Christianity*, pp. 316 ff.

[31] "Sodomia" and "sodomita" are used so often and in so many competing senses in the High Middle Ages that a separate study would be required to present even a summary of this material. Note that in the modern West the terms still have overlapping senses, even in law: in some American states "sodomy" applies to any inherently non-procreative sex act (fellatio between husband and wife, e.g.), in others to all homosexual behavior, and in still others only to anal intercourse. Several "sodomy" statutes have in fact been overturned on grounds of unconstitutional vagueness. See, in addition to the material cited in Boswell, *Christianity*, pp.52, 183-84, Giraldus Cambrensis, *Descriptio Cambriae*, 2.7; J. J. Tierney, "The Celtic Ethnography of Posidonius," *Proceedings of the Royal Irish Academy*, 60 (1960), 252; and *Carmina Burana:Die Lieder er Benediktbeurer Handschrift. Zweisprachige Ausgabe* (Munich, 1979),95.4, p.334 ("Pura semper ab hac infamia / nostra fuit minor Brittania"; the ms. has *Bricciavia*).

[32] Walter Map, *De nugis curialium*, 1.23, trans. John Mundy, *Europe in the High Middle Ages*, 1150-1309 (New York, 1973), p. 302. Cf. discussion of this theme in Boswell,

Christianity, Chapter 8.

[33] Prologue, 669 ff. Of several works on this issue now in print see especially Monica McAlpine, "The Pardoner's Homosexuality and How it Matters," *PMLA,* January 1980, 8-22 and Edward Schweitzer, "Chaucer's Pardoner and the Hare," *English Language Notes 4,* 4 (1967), 247-250 (not cited by McAlpine).

[34] See Boswell, *Christianity,* p.233.

[35] 8565 ff; cf. *La Roman de la Rose,* 2169-74, and Gerald Herman, "The 'Sin Against Nature' and its Echoes in Medieval French Literature," *Annuale Mediaevale* 17 (1976), 70-87.

[36] Ed. Rolf Lenzen, "Altercatio Ganimedis et Helene: Kritische Edition mit Kommentar," *Mittellateinisches Jahrbuch* 7 (1972), 161-86; English trans. in Boswell, *Christianity,* pp.381-89.

[37] Ibid., pp.392-98.

[38] Ed. Thomas Wright, *The Anglo-Latin Satirical Poets and Epigrammatists* (London,1872), 2:463.

[39] The relationship between the words "propriety" and "property" is not coincidental, and in this connection is highly revealing. Although social attitudes toward sexual propriety in pre-Christian Europe are often touted as more humane and liberal than those which followed upon the triumph of the Christian religion, it is often overlooked that the comparative sexual freedom of adult free males in the ancient world stemmed largely from the fact that all the members of their household were either legally or effectively their *property,* and hence could be used by them as they saw fit. For other members of society what has seemed to some in the modern West to have been sexual "freedom" might be more aptly viewed as "abt se" or "exploitation," although it is of course silly to assume that the ability to coerce necessarily results in coercion.

[40] Lesbianism is often regarded as peculiar or even pathological in cultures which accept male homosexuality with equanimity. In the largely gay romance *Affairs of the Heart* (see Boswell, *Christianity,* pp.126-27) Lesbianism is characterized as "the tribadic disease" [tes tribakes aselgeiasl (s.28). A detailed analysis of the relationship of attitudes toward male and female homosexuality will comprise a portion of a study I am preparing on the phenomenology of homosexual behavior in ancient and medieval Europe.

[41] Cf. n.6, above.

[42] Since the publication of my remarks on this issue in *Christianity,* pp.28-30, several detailed studies of Greek homosexuality have appeared, most notably those of Felix Buffiere, *Eros adolescent: la pe'derastie dans la Crece antique* (Paris, 1980) and K. J. Dover, *Greek Homosexuality* (Cambridge, Mass., 1978). Neither work has persuaded me to revise my estimate of the degree to which Greek fascination with "youth" was more than a romantic convention. A detailed assessment of both works and their relation to my own findings will appear in the study mentioned above, n.40.

[43] Artemidorus Daldianus, *Onirocriticon libri quinque,* ed. R. Park (Leipzig, 1963), 1.78, pp.88-89. (An English translation of this work is available: *The Interpretation of Dreams,* trans. R. J. White [Park Ridge, N.J., 1975]).

[44] "Non est pedico maitus:/ quae faciat duo sunt: irrumat aut futuit." Martial 2:47 (cf. n.14, above: *pedico* is apparently Martial's own coinage).

[45] *Ceveo* is, i.e., to *futuo* or *pedico* what *fello* is to *irrumo*: it describes the activity of the party being entered. The vulgar English "put out" may be the closest equivalent, but nothing in English captures the actual meaning of the Latin.

[46] *Futuo/pedico* and *ceveo* are likewise both active.

[47] Hunayn ibn Ishaq, trans., *Kitab Tacbir ar-Ru'ya,* ed. Toufic Fahd (Damascus, 1964),pp. 175-76.

[48] E.g., Weinberg et al., *Sexual Preference,* as cited in note 6, above.

II
Homelands

Our Homeland, the Text

BY GEORGE STEINER

Successive, often polemic interpretations, citations in a context of
sacred doctrine or of political-historical opportunity, construe, around the
archaic, cardinal words in the Hebrew canon, a resonant field. An aura of
vital paraphrase and definition extends around the word-core; or of
dubious definition and misunderstanding, no less dynamic (misunderstanding can yield the more urgent reading, the more compelling attention). Meaning vibrates as does a crystal, out of whose hidden clarity
pulsate fragmentation and interference.

To the word *mikra* scholars of Biblical and Talmudic Hebrew attach
a network of meanings. They question its literal roots—*kof, resh, alef,* and
the consonantal *mi.* The definitions put forward are polysemic, they
delineate a semantic field (again, literally, *a la lettre*). The *mikra* may, at
the outset, have been the place of summoning, of vocation and con-
vocation. To experience the Torah and Talmud as *mikra*, to apprehend
these texts in cognitive and emotional plenitude, is to hear and accept a
summons. It is to gather oneself and the (inseparable) community in a
place of calling. This summons to responsible response, to answerability
in the most rigorous intellectual and ethical sense, is simultaneously
private and public, individual and collective. The concepts and association that attach to *mikra* make of the reading of the canon and its
commentaries the literal-spiritual locus of self-recognition and of communal identification for the Jew.

It follows, proclaim a number of rabbinic masters, that the supreme
commandment to Judaism, supreme precisely in that it comprises and

animates all others, is given in *Joshua*, 1, 8: "The book of the law shall not depart out of thy mouth; but thou shalt meditate therein day and night." Observe the implicit prohibition or critique of sleep. *Hypnos* is a Greek god, and enemy to reading.

In post-exilic Judaism, but perhaps earlier, active reading, answerability to the text on both the meditative-interpretative and the behavioral levels, is the central motion of personal and national homecoming. The Torah is met at the place of summons and in the time of calling (which is night and day). The dwelling assigned, ascribed to Israel is the House of the Book. Heine's phrase is exactly right: *das aufgeschriebene Vaterland*. The 'land of his fathers', the *patrimoine*, is the script. In its doomed immanence, in its attempt to immobilize the text in a substantive, architectural space, the Davidic and Solomonic Temple may have been an erratum, a misreading of the transcendent mobility of the text.

At the same time, doubtless, the centrality of the book does coincide with and enact the condition of exile. There are radical senses in which even the Torah is a place of privileged banishment from the tautological immediacy of Adamic speech, of God's direct, unwritten address to man. Reading, textual exegesis, are an exile from action, from the existential innocence of *praxis*, even where the text is aiming at practical and political consequence. The reader is one who (day and night) is absent from action. The 'textuality' of the Jewish condition, from the destruction of the Temple to the foundation of the modern state of Israel, can be seen, has been seen by Zionism, as one of tragic impotence. The text was the instrument of exilic survival; that survival came within a breath of annihilation. To endure at all, the 'people of the Book' had, once again, to be a nation.

The tensions, the dialectical relations between an unhoused at-homeness in the text, between the dwelling-place of the script on the one hand (wherever in the world a Jew reads and meditates Torah is the true Israel), and the territorial mystery of the native ground, of the promised strip of land on the other, divide Jewish consciousness.

Hegel's analysis is ominous. By leaving his native land of Ur, Abraham deliberately "breaks the ties of love." He breaks the natural bonds which unite a human person to his ancestors and their places of burial (the 'Antigone' theme obsesses Hegel); he abandons his neighbors and culture. Such bonds, says Hegel, transcend the human and the secular sphere. They constitute man's legitimate presence in nature, in the organic totality of the actual world. Specifically, argues Hegel, Abraham repudiates the works and days of his childhood and youth. No less than for Rousseau and the romantics, such repudiation seemed to Hegel the most corrosive of alienations, of estrangements both from the rest of mankind and the harmonious integration of the self. (Hegel's polemic calls to mind the severance from childhood, the prematurity in the bent shoulders and somnambular mien of the very young Yeshiva students, old readers in the muffled bones of children.)

Abraham, to Hegel, is a wanderer on the earth, a passer-by severed from the familial, communal and organic context of love and of trust. He is a shepherd of the winds, traversing each land with indifferent lightness of foot. He is incapable of love in the unreflexive, instinctual (Greek) sense. Seeking only God and a singular, almost autistic, intimacy with God, Hegel's Abraham is radically uninterested in or even hostile to other men, to those outside the covenant of his search. Abraham objectifies, masters and uses physical nature; contrary to the Hellenic, the Hebraic perceives in the natural and pragmatic order no animate mystery. Thus the Judaic relations between the finite and the infinite, the natural and the supernatural which inspire Greek religiosity and its creative at-homeness in the variousness and beauty of the real world. In its extreme commitment to abstraction, to word and text, Hebraism comes to scorn the natural sphere. As Hegel's dialectic would have it, Abraham and his seed are enmeshed in a tragic contradiction. More than any other people, Jews claim, indeed they seem to achieve, nearness to the concept of God. They do so at the suicidal cost of mundane renunciation, of self ostracism from the earth and its family of nations. But the God to whom the Jew would stand so near is, by virtue of the implacable abstraction, of the unfathomable elevation attributed to Him, furthest from man.

Mosaic law, the Jewish addiction to minutiae of archaic observance, the atrophy of the Jewish tradition through legalism and literalism of reiteration and ritual represent, for Hegel, a logical but also desperate endeavor to keep the world at bay and to remain in God's neighborhood.

The descendant of rootless Abraham has no other place to go. For even the land promised him was not his. He could seize upon it only by cunning and conquest. Driven out of this land by subsequent conquerors, the Jew is, strictly speaking, merely restored to his nativity of dispersal, to his chosen foreignness. According to Hegel, this 'foreignness' becomes ontological. The sensibility of the Jew is, *par excellence,* the medium of the bitter struggle between life and thought, between spontaneous immediacy and analytic reflection, between man's unison with his body and environment and man's estrangement from them. (Levi-Strauss's tragic anthropology, itself a chapter in the critiques of the messianic by emancipated Judaism, is, here, profoundly Hegelian.) To Hegel, 'the people of the Book' are as a cancer— deepseated, vital, enigmatically regenerative. Their Book is not that of life. Their arts and energies of reading, like analytic thought at its most intense, laser-sharp pitch, consume and deconstruct the living object of their questioning.

What is to Hegel an awesome pathology, a tragic, arrested stage in the advance of human consciousness towards a liberated homecoming from alienation, is, to others, the open secret of the Jewish genius and of its survival. The text is home; each commentary a return. When he reads, when, by virtue of commentary, he makes of his reading a dialogue and life-giving echo, the Jew is, to purloin Heidegger's image, "the shepherd of being." The seeming nomad in truth carries the world within him, as does language itself, as does Leibniz's *monad* (the play on, the illicit congruence between the two words are, one senses, unsettling to Hegel, and suggestive).

But whether they are seen as positive or negative, the 'textual' fabric, the interpretative practices in Judaism are ontologically and historically at the heart of Jewish identity.

This is obviously so in a formal sense. The Torah is the pivot of the weave and cross-weave of reference, elucidation, hermeneutic debate which organize, which inform organically, the daily and the historical life of the community. The community can be defined as a concentric tradition of reading. The *Gemara*, the commentary on the *Mishna*, the collection of oral laws and prescriptions which make up the *Talmud*, the *Midrash*, which is that part of the commentary pertaining particularly to the interpretation of the scriptural canon, express and activate the continuum of Jewish being. The incessant readings of the primary texts, the exegetic, disputatious, elaborative readings of these readings (the process is formally and pragmatically endless), define temporality. They manifest the presence of the determinant past; they seek to elicit present application; they aim at the futurities always latent in the original act of revelation. Thus neither Israel's physical scattering, nor the passage of millennia, can abrogate the authority (the *auctoritas* of authorship) or the pressure of meaning in the holy books, so long as these are read and surrounded by a constancy of secondary, satellite texts. By virtue of metaphoric, allegoric, esoteric explication and challenge, these secondary texts rescue the canon from the ebbing motion of the past tense, from that which would draw live meaning into inert or merely liturgical monumentality. Via magisterial commentary, the given passage will, in places and times as yet unknown, yield existential applications and illuminations of spirit yet unperceived.

The Adamic circumstance is one of linguistic tautology and of a lasting present. Things were as Adam named and said them to be. Word and world were one. Where there is perfect contentment, there is no summons to remembrance. The present tense of the verb is also that of the perfect tomorrow. It was the Fall of Man that added to human speech its ambiguities, its necessary secrecies, its power (the counterfactuals, the 'if' constructions) to dissent speculatively from the opaque coercions of reality. After the Fall, memories and dreams, which are so often messianic recollections of futurity, become the store-house of experience and of hope. Hence the need to re-read, to re-call (revocation) those texts in which the mystery of a beginning, in which the vestiges of a lost self-evidence—God's "I am that I am"—are current.

Ideally, such recall should be oral. In Hebraic sensibility, no less than in that of Plato, a distrust of the written word, a critical regret at the passing of orality, are evident. The written is always a shadow after the fact, a post-script, in the material sense of the term. Its decay from the primary moment of meaning is exemplified, obscurely, in the destruction of the Tables of the Law on Sinai, in the making of a second set or facsimile. The letters of fire, of that fire which *spoke* in the burning bush, have been extinguished in the graven silence of the stone. On the other hand, assuredly, writing has been the indestructible guarantor, the 'under-writer', of the identity of the Jew: across the frontiers of his harrying, across the centuries, across the languages of which he has been a forced borrower and frequent master. Like a snail, his antennae towards menace, the Jew has carried the house of the text on his back. What other domicile has been allowed him?

But the destiny and history of Judaism are 'bookish' in a far deeper sense; and in one that does virtually set them apart.

In the relation to God which defines the Jew, the concepts of contract and of covenant are not metaphoric. A narrative charter, a *magna carta* and document of instauration in narrative form, setting out reciprocal rights and obligations as between God and man, is explicit in *Genesis* and in *Exodus*. The foundation of elect identity is textual. In Hobbes and Rousseau, the invocation of an original contract between individuals founding civic society or between the sovereign and those who delegate their powers to him, is a methodological fiction. In Judaism, it is a literal instrument, a spoken-written deed of trust, subject not only to constant personal and communal ratification, but to close probing. Even after the promise to Noah, even after the transcendent redaction at Sinai, and doubly so after each visitation of disaster on the Jewish people, the God-pact, the covenant and its innumerable legal-ritual codicils, are the focus of reexamination. The latter is moral, legalistic and textual. There has been too much agony in the fine print.

The millennial dialogue with God, of which the *Book of Job* is only the most pointed protocol, is that of a 'bookkeeper'. This image can be pressed closely. God 'keeps book' on His people, who are, everlastingly, the debtors to His initial advance—which is, past all repayment, creation, which is survival after the Flood, the covenant at Sinai and the deed of title to the promised land. At all times, for such is the compounding of God's interest, His partner and client Israel is in arrears, even in default. Where it is allowed, a moratorium is an act of grace. The cancellation of the debt, the revaluation of all currency, as proclaimed in Christ, is, to the Jew, an empty fantasy.

Concomitantly, there is a sense in which the Jew 'keeps book' on God. Do the accounts, and note the semantic overlap and interference as between 'account' and 'narration', ever balance? Is there an intelligible balance-sheet to be drawn between merit and recompense (Job's attempt to inspect and certify the book of life), between suffering and happiness? Has God met the obligations He contracted with man, more precisely, with those first advocates and negotiators of being, the Jews? Antisemitism has always denounced in Judaism and its relations to God, *vide* Shylock and his bond, a contractual, litigious economy, an inheritance of sharp practices and barter. Is there not, in the moralistic-didactic epilogue to the *mysterium tremendum* of *Job*, a twofold restitution, payment for damages incurred?

But the 'bookkeeper' is also, and inextricably, a 'keeper of the Book', an archivist of the revealed. The accountant is, by virtue of this custody, accountable to God as is no other tribe. In *Ezekiel*, 3, this 'keeping of books', this clerkship to eternity, takes on a grotesque physical vehemence. God's emissary holds out a scroll to His servant, "and it was written all over on both sides." Ezekiel is bidden "eat this scroll" (Ben Jonson tells of the 'ingestion' of classical texts). "Swallow this scroll." Ezekiel does so "and it tasted as sweet as honey"—we speak still of "honeyed words", of the links between language and that haunting savor which Middle Eastern and Attic mythology associate both with the sun and the gardens of the dead.

It is the contractual, promissory foundation and core of Judaism which have entailed the singularity (the pathology *contra naturam?*) of survival. The 'books have been kept' and kept up to date. The 'keepers' make new entries at every moment in their individual and historical existence. But consider the determinants of terror in the script. Consider the overwhelmingly manifest yet metaphysically and rationally scandalous adherence of Jewish experience to the *pre*-script set down for it in the books which are its card of identity, in the books it has so proudly and contentiously kept. Rigorously viewed, the fate of Judaism is a post-script to the penalty clauses in God's contract (that fine print, again). It is a sequence of demonstrative foot-notes, of marginalia, to the text of God's (non-)reply to Job and to the texts of the Prophets. Everything is there, spelt-out from the start. The rest has been unbearable fulfillment. No other nation, no other culture on this earth has been so *pre*scribed. No other men have had to bear like witness to the cognate meanings of *prescription* and of *proscription*, which signify denunciation, ostracism, and a written designation for death.

What is there to add to *Amos*, which scholars take to be the oldest of prophetic books, dating it c. 750 B.C. when the Northern Kingdom of Israel was heading for ruin? God's promise is unequivocal:

> I will send a fire upon Judah, and it shall devour the palace of Jerusalem.
>
> . . .
> As the shepherd takes out of the mouth of
> the lion two legs or a piece of an ear, so
> shall the children of Israel be taken out . . .
>
> . . .
> The city that went out by a thousand shall
> have a remnant of a hundred, of that which
> went out by a hundred, ten shall remain.

The long terror of the Diaspora is precisely promised: the songs of worship "shall be howlings," Israel "shall wander from sea to sea, and from the north even to the east" seeking sanctuary in vain. Because God's words are of fire, those who hear and who read them are to be made ash.

The oracular is open-ended. Its duplicities and triplicities—*three* roads meet at that crossing near Delphi—are those of human freedom. Prophecies are the contrary of oracles: they answer before they are asked. How has it been possible for the Jewish people to endure without going more or less collectively mad, without yielding to more or less willed self-destruction (the impulse to both do run deep in Judaic sensibility) knowing, reading and retreading the binding foresight of its Prophets? Where did Judaism find the resolve, the life-tenacity, when an apocalyptic writ had been served on it by its own seers of darkness and when the predictions set out in this writ have been realized, to the hideous letter, time and time and time again? This strikes me as *the* 'Jewish question'.

Part of the answer lies, of course, in the antinomian, pendular motion of the Mosaic and prophetic prescripts themselves. Catastrophe is never unconditional. In God's sentence on Israel there are redeeming clauses. The just, be they but a handful, may be saved; the repentant restored. The dialectic of possible rehabilitation springs from the heart of terror. It is eloquent at the close of *Amos*: the captive, wind-scattered remnant of Israel shall be brought back to the promised land, "and they shall rebuild the waste cities, and inhabit them. They shall plant vineyards and drink the wine thereof. They shall make gardens and eat of their fruit." The entire Zionist dream and purpose, the manner of miracle in which these have been realized, are 'programmed' in this fourteenth verse of this ninth chapter of Amos's script.[1] Throughout the Torah, throughout the prophetic books which dictate the future of Israel, the note of compensation, of the messianic horizon, is set against that of interminable suffering.

But this twofold truth in holy writ only complicates the phenomenological and the psychological question. The deterministic imperative of the promise of selective or ultimate rescue is as binding, as coercive a blueprint, as are the previsions of persecution, dispersal and martyrdom. Amos's clairvoyance as to Zionism is as prescriptive as is his foresight of Jewish agony. No other community in the evolution and social history of man has, from its outset, read, re-read without cease, learnt by heart or by rote, and expounded without end the texts which spell out its whole destiny. These texts, moreover, are felt to be of transcendent authorship and authority, infallible in their *pre*-diction, as oracles in the pagan world, notoriously, are not. The script, therefore, is a contract with the inevitable. God has, in the dual sense of utterance and of binding affirmation, 'given His word', His *Logos* and His bond, to Israel. It cannot be broken or refuted.

Again one asks: what abstentions or strengths of spirit, what genius for servitude and what pride, are required of a people called upon to act out a primal pre-script, to, as it were, take dictation of itself? Light blinds us when it is too clear. Yet the Jew has had to inhabit the literal text of his foreseen being. Canetti has written a play which turns on the conceit of a society in which every man knows, in advance and ineluctably, the date of his own death. The parable on Judaism is unmistakable. It is because he lives, enacts privately and historically, a written writ, a promissory note served on him when God sought out Abraham and Moses, it is because the 'Book of Life' is, in Judaism, literally textual, that the Jew dwells apart. (It was just this suffocating *déjà-vu*, this servile immunity from the unknown in the Jewish condition, which both fascinated and repelled Hegel.)

Though the psychological mechanism remains obscure, the fact is a commonplace: prophecies are, to a degree, self-fulfilling. The stronger the prophecy, the more often it is proclaimed, the greater its inertial thrust towards realization. In his dread history, the Jew would seem to have been intent to certify the accuracy of the road mapped for him by the Prophets. The script has been 'acted', first across that valley of the shadow and of the night of dispersal and massacre which climaxed in the "whirlwind" of the 1940s, in the *Shoah* (the noble Greek word, 'holocaust', signifying a solemn burnt offering, has no legitimate place in this matter); more recently in the foretold, contractually underwritten return to Israel.

Does this mean that the utopian pre-vision of homecoming and of peace which, in the settlement with Abraham and in the coda to the prophetic books, follows on millennial suffering, will also be realized? Not *now*, not necessarily in secular time. The print is too fine for that. The messianic is an escape-clause for both parties. It is on the advent of the messianic order that the prevision of blessedness hinges. Till then, even the in-gathering at Zion is, in the exact Latin etymological sense, *provisional*, it is a prevision the nature and temporality of whose certain accomplishment remains uncertain.

But the crux is this: neither the Jewish endurance, indeed traditional acceptance of a continuum of ostracism and persecution across history, nor the rationally, geopolitically absurd, return of a modern ethnic group to a largely barren strip of earth in the Middle East, to a strip of earth long occupied by others and whose frontiers could only be those of hatred, can be understood outside the metaphysics and psychology of the pre-scribed. The canonic texts had to be shown to be true.

The price for this 'keeping of the books' (for this 'going by the book') has been, literally, monstrous. The notion that the night-vision of the Jew has, somehow, in some secret measure, brought on itself the torments foreseen, is irrational, but haunting none the less.

It is compelling in our reading of Kafka. The practices of literary criticism and study are more or less helpless before *The Trial* and *The Castle* with their minutely faithful prevision of the clerical inhumanities of life in our time. Explication, reference to stylistic means or literary context, merely trivialize Kafka's blueprint of the concentration-camp world, of the coming obscenities of intimacy between torturer and victim, as these are spelt out, in October 1914, in "In The Penal Colony"; or consider Kafka's use of the word "vermin" in "The Metamorphosis" of 1912 in precisely the sense and connotations that would be given to it by the Nazis a generation later. In Kafka's writings there is a revealed literalism *avant la lettre* which renders almost wholly worthless the spate of commentaries which they have provoked. Even the masterly exchange on Kafka's religiosity in the Walter Benjamin-Gershom Scholem letters, which may, together with Mandelstam's essay on reading Dante, be the best that the arts of modern literary criticism have to show, avoid the urgent conundrum of the prophetic. As no other speaker or scribe after the Prophets, Kafka *knew*. In him, as in them, imagination was second sight and invention a pedantic notation of clairvoyance. Kafka's misery as one coerced into writing, his almost hysterical diffidence before mundane authorship, are the facsimile, perhaps consciously arrived at, of the attempts of the Prophets to evade the intolerable burden of their seeing, to shake off the commandment of utterance. Jeremiah's "I do not know how to speak," Jonah's flight from foretelling, have their literal parallel in Kafka's "impossibility of writing, impossibility of not writing." Having the unspeakable future so lit to his sight, Kafka was, not only in his writings but also in his personal existence, knowingly posthumous to himself. It is some notation of this scarcely conceivable condition which, I suspect, informs the profoundest allegory produced by western man after Scripture, that of the parable "In Front of the Law" composed in November or December 1914.

In Kafka's credo of reading, the Jewish experience of the imperative terror of the text is manifest:

> If the book we are reading does not wake us, as with a fist hammering on our skull, why then do we read it? So that it shall make us happy? Good God, we would also be happy if we had not books, and such books as make us happy we could, if need be, write ourselves. But what we must have are those books which come upon us like ill fortune, and distress us deeply, like the death of one we love better than ourselves, like suicide.

How much could be said (inadequately) of that mesmeric opposition between "one we love better than ourselves" and "suicide", about Kafka's

implicit finding that suicide is always the killing of the 'other', of the one
'loved better than ourselves' within us. What is pellucid in this famous
dictum is the paradoxical need, the self-testing to destruction, in the
Jewish vision and experience of the book.

The indispensable books, those whose coming upon us is more
powerful even than the death of the beloved, are the syllabus of the Judaic.
What they have in common, what relates the rare secular examples to the
canonic, is, indeed, their status as a *mikra*, a summons and *subpoena* to
mankind. They call and call upon us. The fist hammering on our skull
forces us to keep our eyes open.

> Nothing can erase this night
> but there's still light with you.
> At Jerusalem's gate
> a black sun has risen.

> The yellow one frightens me more.
> Lullaby, lullaby, Israelites
> have buried my mother
> in the bright temple.

> Somewhere outside grace,
> with no priests to lead them,
> Israelites have sung the requiem over her
> in the bright temple.

> The voices of Israelites
> rang out over my mother.
> I woke in the cradle, dazzled
> by the black sun.

This poem by Mandelstam is entitled "Black Sun." Lacking Russian—
the translation is by Clarence Brown and W.S. Merwin—I can say very
little about it, about the sources of its spell. Moreover, there may be in
these four quatrains esoteric echoes of Russian apocalyptic and
eschatological symbolism accessible only to the informed. This happens
to be the case, quite often, in both the great voices of Russian Judaeo-
Orthodoxy (the baptized but remembering Jews), Mandelstam and
Pasternak. Yet the strength and universality of the poem's summons are
such that we must listen as best we can.

Certain motifs declare themselves. In Russian poetry and fiction, in the incomparable articulation of the 'strangeness' of the Russian political and psychological tradition by Pushkin and Dostoevsky, the "white nights," particularly in St. Petersburg, are emblematic. The "black sun" of Mandelstam's lyric, with its precedent in Baudelaire and Nerval, reverses the febrile white nights. The black sunrise answers to the white nightfall. But more ominous to the poet than either is the light of common day—"The yellow one frightens me more." In Paul Celan's poetry on the destruction of European Jewry, a poetry which, by incessant echo and allusion, often incorporates that of Osip Mandelstam, the 'yellow sun' will have become (remaining, in actual reference, the same) the yellow star of the condemned.

As does so much of elegiac and philosophic poetry after *Proverbs* and *Ecclesiastes*—it is the latter text which seems subtly active in Mandelstam's lines—there is in the "Black Sun" an interplay of the cradle and the grave. Lullaby interweaves with requiem. The birth of the child is always, in a banal sense, the end of maternity. On the other hand, a mother's death is a son's re-birth, but a re-birth into adult aloneness, into the most definite of exiles from shared identity and remembrance. From this psychic and somatic exile, there can be no return.

Exile would seem to be at the hammering heart of Mandelstam's poem. Israelites bury the speaker's mother "in the bright temple," a ritual absurdity or scandal. They do so "Somewhere outside grace, / With no priests to lead them." The allusion to burial in unconsecrated ground, a pagan or Christian rather than a Jewish motif, is evident. But, in a larger sense, the statement is one of ostracism. No *kaddish*, but a requiem. In the Diaspora, a Jew is made homeless even in death. The child is woken by the exiled voices of Israel, woken to apocalyptic terror. The sun which dazzles him is a black sun, and it rises "At Jerusalem's gate." We can read this image in at least two ways. That gate is shut to the outcast and/or a blackness at noon shall enter through it into the city.

Mandelstam's poem is dated 1916. Russian Jewry had known the pogroms of the fairly recent past, and the so-called civilized world was at war. But neither the Bolshevik-Stalinist nightmare nor the Whirlwind out of Hitler were in any way visible. Yet Mandelstam wakes, and wakes his

reader, to the clear vision of the night-dawn ahead. He already *knows*—
a knowledge to be fulfilled in his own appalling suffering and death.
As in Kafka, so there is here an inextricable intimacy between the
imagined and the foreseen. Not only Amos, but numerous rabbinic
masters, have conjectured that every Jew, when he is wholly present to
God's word, to the living summons of the Torah, is in a condition of
prophecy and pre-vision. He is, at some level, made a party to the fact that
God remembers the future.

Again the question nags. Where prophecy is so penetratively acute,
does it not prepare for, indeed provoke, fulfillment? Could there be some
(incomprehensible) guilt in annunciation? (In the Brussels museum
hangs an anonymous 'primitive' depicting the Annunciation; behind
Mary's bowed, overwhelmed head, hangs a small painting of the Cruci-
fixion.) In Judaism, has the text come to lord it over life? Does the fact
follow humbly, but also murderously, after the commanding word? At its
greatest, Jewish secular writing when, at last, it springs from the liturgical, exegetical textuality and monopoly of the ghetto, carries with it, from
Heine to Celan, an enforced clairvoyance and guilt of accomplishment.

The bookkeeper is not only the custodian and, in his racked bone and
flesh, the certifier of prophecy. He is a cleric. The mystery and the
practices of clerisy are fundamental to Judaism. No other tradition or
culture has ascribed a comparable aura to the conservation and transcription of texts. In no other has there been an equivalent mystique of the
philological. This is true of orthodox praxis, in which a single erratum, the
wrong transcription of a single letter, entails the permanent removal of the
relevant scroll or page from the holy books. It is true, to the same pitch of
literalist intensity, in the whole theory and techniques of the Kabbala, in
the kabbalist's exhaustive scrutiny of the single Hebrew letter in whose
graphic form and denomination manifold energies of meaning are in-
cised.

The quarrel with Hellenism and with Christian gnosis is stark. In
Judaism, the letter is the life of the spirit, indeed to the kabbalist, it is the
spirit. Hence the clerical ideals, the clerical code of scribal observance
and conveyance in the exilic history of the Jews. Hence the clerisy of the
rabbinic caste in the ghetto and *Stattle*. To say of this ecstatic textuality

and clerkship—both are totally instrumental in Kafka's profession and in Kafka's calling—that they were a surrogate for the political, social acts barred to the Jews, to say of the 'scribal' nature of Jewish survivance that it was an inhibiting substitute for the production of secular intellect and art, is a facile cliché. The point is that the sometimes hallucinatory techniques and disciplines of attention to the text, the mystique of fidelity to the written word, the reverence bestowed on its expositors and transmitters, concentrated within Judaic sensibility unique strengths and purities of disinterested purpose.

It is these which have made so many Jewish men and, more recently, women most native to modern intelligence. It is these that have generated the provocative pre-eminence of the Jew in modernity, be it humanistic or scientific. The 'bookish' genius of Marx and of Freud, of Wittgenstein and of Levi-Strauss, is a secular deployment of the long schooling in abstract, speculative commentary and clerkship in the exegetic legacy (while being at the same time a psychological-sociological revolt against it). The Jewish presence, often overwhelming, in modern mathematics, physics, economic and social theory, is direct heir to that abstinence from the approximate, from the mundane, which constitutes the ethos of the cleric.

Under Roman persecution, Akiba made of his refuge a 'place' or 'house of the book'. A secularized but closely derived system of values was to make of Central European Jewry and its American after-glow the intellectual-spiritual heartland of modernity. Prague, Budapest, Vienna, Leningrad, Frankfurt and New York have been the Jewish capitals of our age, but also the capitals *tout court*. In them, the clerks, the addicts of the word and of the theorem, the exact dreamers after Einstein, have led, have danced the life of the mind; for that motion of the dance before the ark in which the text of the Law is housed, lies at the ancient core of Jewish consciousness.

A kabbalistic and hassidic intimation has it that evil seeped into our world through the hair-line crack of a single erroneous letter, that man's suffering, and that of the Jew especially, came of the false transcription of a single letter or word when God dictated the Torah to his elect scribe. This grim fantastication is utterly expressive of a scholar's code. It points to the definition of a Jew as one who always has a pencil or pen in hand when he reads, of one who will in the deathcamps (and this came to pass) correct a printing error, emend a doubtful text, on his way to extinction. But the morality and metaphysics of the clerk are not only, nor indeed primarily, those of pedantic, mandarin abstraction. We need only look to Spinoza to know otherwise. What is at stake is a *politics of truth*. Such politics are, in essence, Socratic—and Socrates is the one gentile of whom a thinking Jew has the never-ending obligation to be jealous.

The Socratic moment for modern Jewry is the Dreyfus Affair. It compelled on the Jew the question of whether he could, even in an emancipated and assimilationist garb, ever obtain a secure citizenship in the city of the gentile, which is the post-Napoleonic nation-state. With cruel edge, the Dreyfus Affair confronted ideals of justice and of personal conscience with the claims of the nation-state to transcendent loyalty. The case threw the sharpest possible light on the inherently anarchic genius of abstract thought and the search for absolute truth. Imperatives of reason and of conscience clashed, metaphysically and ethically, with those conventions of expediency, of moral approximation and irresolution without which the fabric of society cannot hang together. As does the trial of Socrates, so the Dreyfus Affair passes judgment on the *polis*. The resulting schism, the contested victory of individual justice over patriotism and reasons of state, lamed not only France—the Vichy regime, the rhetoric and tactics of civil war perennial to French politics are a direct legacy—but the very concept of nationalism. *Fiat iustitia, pereat mundus.*

Both the occasion and the logic of the conflict came out of Judaism. They came from the ambiguous entry into the territorial, fundamentally Roman polities of the modern nation of a people at home in exile, of a pilgrim tribe housed not in place but in time, not rooted but millennially equipped with legs. Whether he knew it or not, whether he wished it or not—indeed, he desperately hoped otherwise and did much to deceive himself—the Jew, when given nationality by his adopted gentile hosts, remained in transit. Judaism defines itself as a visa to the messianic 'other land'.

For the cleric, for the ideal of clerisy in Jewishness, this house of the future tense need not be Israel. Or rather, it is an 'Israel' of truthseeking. Each seeking out of a moral, philosophic, positive verity, each text rightly established and expounded, is an *aliyah*, a homecoming of Judaism to itself and to its keeping of the books. The impositions and glory of this trusteeship, as they modulate from the religious to the secular domain, are formulated in Julien Benda's *The Treason of the Clerics*, an inescapably Jewish book which came of the Dreyfus case.

Heir to Spinoza, Benda defines and himself instances the fanaticism of disinterested vision, the ecstatic exactions and exactitudes, which underlie major thought and scholarship. On the Sabbath, the benedictions spoken in the synagogue extend explicitly to the scholar. There is, or ought to be sadness in a Jewish household if there is no scholar or future scholar among its children. Benda goes further. He takes for his own a dictate by a now-forgotten *savant* of the nineteenth century:

> Whoever, for whatever motives—patriotic, political, religious and even moral—allows himself even the slightest manipulation or adjustment of the truth, must be stricken from the roll of scholars.

The tranquil enormity of this commandment must be felt. Observe the ascending order in which the condemned apologias are listed. Patriotism, the love and defense of the homeland—of the Third Republic under threat of German invasion—is the lowest non-excuse. Next come political loyalty, efficiency, those practicalities of civic compromise and herd-instinct which a Socrates and a Spinoza refuse. Let the city and the nation perish before the cleric commits "even the slightest" mendacity. They are not the native ground of his being, which is truth. Where it cannot afford truth a natural habitation, even religion must yield. 'Morality' is the crown of motives. Yet it too is set aside. The injunction to do so is a fearful edict (Kierkegaard will repudiate it utterly). Where Kant postulated a transcendent coincidence between the ethical and the cognitive, Benda knew that there may be cases of irreconcilable conflict between ethics and the pursuit of knowledge—in nuclear physics, in genetics, in the psychologist's and the writer's findings in man. The cleric betrays his calling, he is absent from the *mikra*, if he flinches from, if he muffles or deflects the pure hunt for truth—Plato records the hunter's halloo when a truth is cornered—even if this hunt should lead to his own destruction or that of his community.

It is here that the creed of Spinoza and of Kafka meets with the conduct of Socrates. A true thinker, a truth-thinker, a scholar, must know that no nation, no body politic, no creed, no moral ideal and necessity, be it that of human survival, is worth a falsehood, a willed self-deception or the manipulation of a text. This knowledge and observance *are* his homeland. It is the false reading, the erratum that make him homeless.

A Jew enters on manhood, he is admitted to the history of Judaism, on the day on which he is, for the first time, called, literally, to the text, on the day on which he is asked and allowed to read correctly a passage from the Torah. This summons entails, to a greater or lesser degree of intensity, to a greater or lesser degree of self-awareness, a commitment to the clerisy of truth, of truth-seeking. The prophetic and the speculative addiction to insight are the nationhood of Judaism. In the humblest of clerks as in the greatest of thinkers, the acceptance of this calling, of this 'calling up' in the full sense of a perilous enlistment and promotion, must have practical (impractical) consequences.

How can a thinking man, a native of the word, be anything but the most wary and provisional of patriots? The nation-state is founded on myths of instauration and of militant glory. It perpetuates itself by lies and half-truths (machine guns and sub-machine guns). In his model of the social contract, Rousseau declared unequivocally that there is a contradiction between humanity and citizenship: "Force de combattre la nature ou les institutions sociales, il faut opter entre faire un homme ou un citoyen; car on ne peut pas faire a la fois l'un et l'autre." The consequence is stark: "a patriot is hard on strangers, for they are but men."

The 'patriotism' of the truth-seeker is antithetical to Rousseau's civic option. The sole citizenship of the cleric is that of a critical humanism. He knows not only that nationalism is a sort of madness, a virulent infection edging the species towards mutual massacre. He knows that it signifies an abstention from free and clear thought and from the disinterested pursuit of justice. The man or woman at home in the text is, by definition, a conscientious objector: to the vulgar mystique of the flag and the anthem, to the sleep of reason which proclaims "my country, right or wrong," to the pathos and eloquence of collective mendacities on which the nation-state—be it a mass-consumer mercantile technocracy or a totalitarian oligarchy—builds its power and aggressions. The locus of truth is always extraterritorial; its diffusion is made clandestine by the barbed wire and watch-towers of national dogma.

The quarrel is as ancient as Israel. It is that between priest and prophet, between the claims of nationhood and those of universality. It speaks to us irreconcilably out of *Amos* and *Jeremiah*. The mortal clash between politics and verity, between an immanent homeland and the space of the transcendent, is spelt out in *Jeremiah* 36-9. King Jahoiakim seizes the scroll dictated by God's clerk and bookkeeper. He cuts out the offending columns and casts the entire text into the consuming flame (governments, political censors, patriotic vigilantes burn books). God instructs the prophet: "Take thee again another scroll and write on it all the words that were written on the first."The truth will out. Somewhere there is a pencil-stub, a mimeograph machine, a hand-press which the king's men have overlooked. "So Jeremiah abode in the court of the prison till the day that Jerusalem was taken; and he was *there* when Jerusalem was taken." The formulaic specification is magnificent in meaning. The royal city, the nation are laid waste; the text and its transmitter endure, *there* and *now*. The Temple may be destroyed; the texts which it housed sing in the winds that scatter them.

Pauline universalism was an inspired amalgam of the transcendent, immaterial textuality of the Prophets in Judaism and of Hellenic syncretism. It proved to be the most serious challenge ever to Jewish survival, precisely in so far as it sprang from within the utopian elements in the Jewish tradition (and *utopia* means "no-where"). Paul of Tarsus set prophecy against priesthood, ecumenism against territoriality. It is altogether possible that Judaism would have lost its identity, would have diffused itself in Christianity, if the latter had been true to its Judaic catholicity. Instead, Christendom became, itself, a political-territorial structure, prepared, on all practical counts, to serve, to hallow, the genesis and militancy of secular states. Ideological imperialism is inseparable from the Constantine adoption of Christianity; modern nationalism bears the stamp of the Lutheran programme. Truth was, again, made homeless; or, more exactly, it was left in the (un)safekeeping of the pariah and the exile.

* * *

In the founding secular manifesto of Zionism, Herzel's *Judenstaat,* the language and the vision are proudly mimetic of Bismarckian nationalism. Israel is a nation-state to the utmost degree. It lives armed to the teeth. It has been compelled to make other men homeless, servile, disinherited, in order to survive from day to day (it was, during two millennia, the dignity of the Jew that he was too weak to make any other human being as unhoused, as wretched as himself). The virtues of Israel are those of beleaguered Sparta. Its propaganda, its rhetoric of self-deception, are as desperate as any contrived in the history of nationalism. Under external and internal stress, loyalty has been atrophied to patriotism, and patriotism made chauvinism. What place, what license is there in that garrison for the 'treason' of the Prophet, for Spinoza's refusal of the tribe? Humanism, said Rousseau, is "a theft committed on *la patrie.*" Quite so.

There is no singular vice in the practices of the State of Israel. These follow ineluctably on the simple institution of the modern nation-state, on the political-military necessities by which it exists with and against its nationalist competitors. It is by empirical need that a nation-state sups on lies. Where it has traded its homeland in the text for one of the Golan Heights or in Gaza—"eyeless" was the clairvoyant epithet of that great Hebraist, Milton—Judaism has become homeless to itself.

But this, of course, is only a part of the truth.

To many among the few survivors, the interminable pilgrimage through persecution, the interminable defenselessness of the Jew in the face of bestiality and derision, were no longer endurable. A refuge *had* to be found, a place of physical gathering in which a Jewish parent could give to his child some hope of a future. The return to Zion, the fantastic courage and labor which have made the desert flower, the survival of the 'Old Newland' (Herzel's famous phrase) against crazy political and military odds, have made a wonder of necessity. The overwhelming majority of Jews in Israel, of Jews in the Diaspora, seek neither to be prophets nor clerics deranged by some autistic, otherworldly addiction to speculative abstractions and the elixir of truth. They hunger, desperately, for the common condition of man among men. They would, like all other men and nations, vanquish their enemies rather than be oppressed and scattered by them; if harsh reality dictates, they would rather occupy, censor, even torture than be occupied and censored and tortured as they have been for so long. What mandarin fantasy, what ivory-tower nonsense, is it to suppose that alone among men, and after the unspeakable horrors of destruction lavished upon him, the Jew should not have a land of his own, a shelter in the night?

I know all this. It would be shallow impertinence not to see the psychological, the empirical force of the argument. Moreover, is the return to Israel not foreseen, indeed ordained, in the very texts I have cited? Is Zionism not as integral a part of the 'prescribed' mystery and condition of Judaism as were the terrible times of sufferance (Shylock's word) and dispersal?

The Orthodox answer is clear. Both currents of prevision are to be accomplished. The prescriptions of suffering have long been made manifest. And so shall be the homecoming to the promised land. But not before the messianic hour. The imperilled brutalized condition of the present State of Israel, the failure of Israel to be Zion, prove the spurious, the purely expedient temporality of its re-establishment in 1948. There were, then, armed men about and politicians. The Messiah was nowhere in sight. Thus the State of Israel, as it stands today, neither fulfills nor disproves the Mosaic and prophetic covenant of return. The time is not yet.

Personally, I have no right to this answer. I have no part in the beliefs and ritual practices which underwrite it. But its intuitive and evidential strength can be felt to be real.

The survival of the Jews has no authentic parallel in history. Ancient ethnic communities and civilizations no less gifted, no less self-conscious, have perished, many without trace. It is, on the most rational, existential level, difficult to believe that this unique phenomenon of unbroken life, in the face of every destructive agency, is unconnected with the exilic circumstance. Judaism has drawn its uncanny vitality from dispersal, from the adaptive demands made on it by mobility. Ironically, the threat of that 'final solution' might prove to be the greatest yet if the Jews were now to be compacted in Israel.

But there is a more central intimation. One need be neither a religious fundamentalist nor a mystic to believe that there is some exemplary meaning to the singularity of Judaic endurance, that there is some sense beyond contingent or demographic interest to the interlocking constancy of Jewish pain and of Jewish preservation. The notion that the appalling road of Jewish life and the ever-renewed miracle of survival should have as their end, as their justification, the setting up of a small nation-state in the Middle East, crushed by military burdens, petty and even corrupt in its politics, shrill in its parochialism, is implausible.

I cannot shake off the conviction that the torment and the mystery of resilience in Judaism exemplify, enact, an arduous truth: that human beings must learn to be each other's guests on this small planet, even as they must learn to be guests of being itself and of the natural world. This is a truth humbly immediate, to our breath, to our skin, to the passing shadow we cast on a ground inconceivably more ancient than our visitation, and it is also a terribly abstract, morally and psychologically exigent truth. Man will have to learn it or he will be made extinct in suicidal waste and violence.

The State of Israel is an endeavor—wholly understandable, in many aspects admirable, perhaps historically inescapable—to normalize the condition, the meaning of Judaism. It would make the Jew level with the common denominator of modern 'belonging'. It is, at the same time, an attempt to eradicate the deeper truth of unhousedness, of an at-homeness in the word, which are the legacy of the Prophets and of the keepers of the text.

In Jerusalem today, the visitor is taken to the "Shrine of the Scrolls" or, as it is also known, "House of the Sacred Books". In this exquisite building are kept some of the Dead Sea scrolls and priceless biblical papyri. It is a place of poignant, if somewhat sepulchral, radiance. One's guide explains the hidden hydraulic mechanism whereby the entire edifice can, in the event of shelling or bombardment, be made to sink safely below ground. Such precautions are indispensable. Because nation-states live by the sword. But such precautions are also a metaphysical and ethical barbarism. Words cannot be broken by artillery, nor thought live in bomb-shelters.

Locked materially in a material homeland, the text may, in fact, lose its life-force, and its truth values may be betrayed. But when the text *is* the homeland, even when it is rooted only in the exact remembrance and seeking of a handful of wanderers, nomads of the word, it cannot be extinguished. Time is truth's passport and its native ground. What better lodging for the Jew?

Note

[1] If this is Amos's script, for it is precisely this promissory passage which many scholars regard as a much later insertion.

Ancestral Voices[1]

BY K. ANTHONY APPIAH

I

At least since Herder—you can tell I am not a historian, such grandly vague formulations being anathema to Ranke's heirs—ideas about the connection between a people and the majestic projects of philosophy, literature and the arts, have been central, in a familiar way, to *nationalist* argument. Herder taught us to think that the minimum condition for being the sort of collectivity—a nation—that required and deserved a state for its historical realization, was the possession of a shared *Sprachgeist* : and at the heart of the culture of the Volk, the folk-culture embodied in the language, were certain principles, a certain *Weltanschauung*, that we should naturally call a philosophy.

For Herder, the history of nations is above all the history of cultures, of civilizations. In the *Reflections on the Philosophy of the History of Mankind*, Herder's history of Greece is the history of "the Grecian language. . . the most refined of any in the world; the Grecian mythology, the richest and most beautiful upon Earth; the Grecian poetry, perhaps the most perfect of its kind, when considered with respect to time and place"; as well as the history of the Arts, Religion, "moral and political wisdom" and "scientific arguments."[2] Each person inherited the conceptual materials and the philosophical principles that defined the spirit of her nation. This idea, which was so original in Herder, became part of the common sense of Euro-American high culture in the nineteenth century; a common sense that W. E. B. Du Bois expressed in 1897 in the observation that like "[t]he English nation. . . the German nation. . . [and] the Romance nations. . . the other race groups are striving, each in its own way, to develop for civilization its particular message, its particular ideal. . ."[3] What is attractive, always, in Du Bois's rendering of the issue (as here in the "Conversation of Races,") is that the message of his race is always seen (in a way that is, I think, more fully realized than in Herder's talk of *humanitat*)[4] in the perspective of humanity: for Du Bois it is as one voice in the chorus of races that the negro sings.[5]

DuBois's attachment to this Herderian principle is evident, too, in his definition of a "race" as "a vast family of human beings generally of common blood and language. . . who are both voluntarily and involuntarily striving together for the accomplishment of certain more or less vividly conceived ideals of life."[6] But we shall find the same claim in Edward Blyden—who wrote in 1883: "Among the conclusions to which study and research are conducting philosophers, none is clearer than this—that each of the races of mankind has a specific character and specific work."[7]   And, for example, in Alexander Crummel and in Martin Robinson Delany;[8] in short in most, perhaps all, of those black intellectuals in the anglophone New World who articulated the beginnings of the Pan Africanist vision.

African-American intellectuals mobilized a rhetoric of race, rather than one of nation, and thus, in an age when race was increasingly understood through the sciences of biology and physical anthropology, the connection was made, at least implicitly, not to a *Sprachgeist*, expressed and transmitted through the institutions of language, but to the more material substrate of physical inheritance.

Imposing the Herderian identification of the core of the nation with its national literature on top of the racial conception of the nation, we arrive at the racial understanding of literature that flourished from the mid-nineteenth century in the work of the first modern literary historians. Hippolyte Taine's monumental *History of English Literature*, published in France in the 1860's—perhaps the first modern literary history of English—begins with these words:

> History has been transformed, within a hundred years in Germany, within sixty in France, and that by the study of their literatures.

But he is soon telling us that:

> a race, like the Old Aryans, scattered from the Ganges as far as the
> Hebrides, settled in every clime, and every stage of civilization, trans-
> formed by thirty centuries of revolutions, nevertheless manifests in its
> languages, religions, literatures, philosophies, the community of blood
> and of intellect which to this day binds its offshoots together.

What is revealed, in short, by the study of literature that has transformed
the discipline of history is the "moral state" of the race whose literature
it is. It is because of this conception that Taine finds it proper to start his
study of English literature with a chapter on the Saxons; so that Chapter
1, Book 1 of Taine's *History* begins not in England at all, but in Holland:

> As you coast the North Sea from Scheldt to Jutland, you will mark in the
> first place that the characteristic feature is the want of slope: marsh,
> waster, shoal; the rivers hardly drag themselves along, swollen and
> sluggish, with long, black-looking waves.

The "Saxons, Angles, Jutes, Frisians. . . [and] Danes" who occupied this
region of Holland at the beginning of the first millennium are, according
to Taine, the ancestors of the English; but since they, themselves, are of
German descent, Taine also refers, in describing this "race" a few pages
later, to some of their traits reported in Tacitus.

It is this conception of the binding core of the English nation as the
Anglo-Saxon race that accounts for Taine's decision to identify the
origins of English literature not in its antecedents in the Greek and Roman
classics that provided the models and themes of so much of the best-
known works of English "poesy"; not in the Italian models that influenced
the drama of Marlowe and Shakespeare; but in *Beowulf*, a poem in the
Anglo-Saxon tongue, a poem that was unknown to Chaucer and Spenser
and Shakespeare, the first poets to write in a version of the English
language that we can still almost understand.

Yet this decision is quite representative. When the teaching of English
literature is institutionalized in the English universities in the nineteenth
century, students are required to learn Anglo-Saxon in order to study
Beowulf. Anglo-Saxonism thus plays a major role in the establishment of

the canon of literary works that are to be studied in both British and American colleges; and the teachers who came from these colleges to the high-schools brought the Anglo-Saxon canon with them.

II

This tradition has been much studied recently: and it is clear that the traces of racism in shaping the structure of social sciences and humanistic studies in our universities are legion. It may be irritating for liberal-minded academics who themselves are not racist to be taken to task for a structuring they did not create. That there is this much truth to the claim that the substance of what we teach in the academy is structured by a racist history is one of the facts that we must now study and teach; but it does not make us racists. Indeed, by and large, literary academics at least have responded pretty well to facing this history, seeking to include what was excluded for racist reasons, even to explore genres and notions of literature that history refused to consider. Sometimes, I think, they have gone too far, responding not by rejecting the whole notion of a mapping between races and high cultures, as one should, but by simply insisting that in a multiracial society each race should have an equal place in our histories of that high culture. This seems to me, as I say, to miss the point. To take the example of the analogous point for feminism: one of the reasons why women are underrepresented in high culture has to do with the history of sexism. We cannot now make it true that women writers structured the picaresque novel; what we can do is notice—and notice the consequences of—the fact that they were not permitted to do so. We cannot make it true now that African-Americans contributed their fair share to 18th century American portraiture, either; though we can notice their sometimes neglected contributions and consider the consequences, insofar as they matter to the history of portraiture, of their exclusion.

But the role of a race-culture-literature nexus in structuring the great tradition we were raised in, should, I think, help us to understand something of its contemporary resurgence among African-American intellectuals; just as, at the same time, the critique we have conducted of this older racism should prepare us to resist these anti-racist racisms that are, in some ways, a response to it. These days when proponents of Afro-centricity assert the significance of something called "African philosophy" for the projects of today's African-American education and culture, I take it that it is something like the familiar Herderian argument that they have in mind. Jahnheinz Jahn's *Muntu-African cultures and the Western World*—a work that specifically seeks to give a unified account of African and African-American cultures rooted in an African philosophy—is among the texts most influential, with a new introduction by Calvin Hernton, who tells us "I got my first understanding of what it means to be an African when I read Jahnheinz Jahn's remarkable book."[9]

Among the ideas that made Africa so happily available is the concept of NTU—this is the stem of the Kinyaruanda-Bantu words "Muntu" (Person), "Kintu" (thing), "Hantu" (place and time) and "Kuntu" (modality) and it is a morpheme that does not occur unprefixed in Kinyaruanda. "NTU," Jahn writes with the gravitas of revelation, "is the universal force as such."[10]

Reading this I found myself irresistibly drawn towards fantasizing an African scholar, returning to her home in Lagos or Nairobi, with the important news that she has uncovered the key to Western culture. Soon to be published, *THING: Western Culture and the African World*, a work that exposes the philosophy of ING, written so clearly on the face of the English language. For ING, in the Euro-American view, is the inner dynamic essence of the world. In the very structure of the terms do*ing* and mak*ing* and mean*ing*, the English (and thus, by extension all Westerners) express their deep commitment to this conception: but the secret heart of the matter is captured in their primary ontological category of th-*ing*; every th-*ing* (or be*ing* as their sages express the matter in the more specialized vocabulary of one of their secret societies) is not stable but ceaselessly changing. Here we see the fundamental explanation for the extraordinary neophilia of Western culture, its sense that reality is change.

Muntu is often cited as an Afro-centric source-book in the media. It is important that Jahn explicitly and firmly repudiates (as a German scholar working in the 1950's emphatically would) any notion that (as he puts it) "culture is tied to the chromosomes."[11] And in so doing he seeks to escape the racialization of culture that Du Bois inherited in the general intellectual climate of nineteenth century theorizing about difference. Still the appeal of an account of African philosophy of this sort for many African-Americans surely lies in exactly the sort of nationalist search for identity that is common to the discourse of race and of nation.

Jahn's own argument for the relevance of an African philosophy to the black cultures of the New World is based on historical claims (of the sort made familiar in America by Herskovits) as to the survival of mainly Dahomeyan, Yoruba and Kongo cosmology, ritual and aesthetic notions in Haiti and Cuba. Indeed what I believe is best in Jahn's book—the account of *voodoo* and of *santeria* at the start—shows how an intelligent reading of the cultural meaning of African "survivals" requires a knowledge of the ethnophilosophy of the slaves' cultures of origin. That, at least, is a modest contribution that an African ethnophilosophy can make to African-American studies; and we can hope that it will be carried out with more care in the future, as our scholarly understanding deepens, and without Jahn's insistence on a continental unanimity.[12]

Given the continuing role of *Muntu* and the like even in recent discussions of Afro-centricity, it may be useful to insist on the implausibility of that assumption of what Paulin Hountonji, the Beninois philosopher, has called "unanimism": the factual assumption that there is some key body of ideas that is shared by black Africans quite generally. Consider a representative passage from *Muntu*, which has the advantage over other more recent texts that follow in its train, of being by an author who is no more among us.

> Adebayo Adesanya, a Yoruba writer, has found a pretty formulation to characterize briefly the harmony of African conceptions.
> ... *Philosophy, theology, politics, social theory, land law, medicine, psychology, birth and burial, all find themselves logically concatenated in a system so tight that to subtract one is to weaken the structure of the whole.*
> The unity of which Adesanya is speaking here holds not only for Yoruba thought, but presumably also for the whole of traditional thinking in Africa, for African philosophy as such.[13]

What a heavy burden is borne by that "presumably." Why should the Zulu, the Azande, the Hausa and the Asante have the same concepts or the same beliefs about those matters which the concepts are used to think about and discuss? Indeed, it seems they do not. Nor is it reassuring that Jahn asserts at one point that "[s]ince African culture appears as a unity, it makes no difference from which African language a term is derived."[14] Or that his only observation in defence of his procedure is that "the question of whether or not a plurality is understood as a unity is to a great extent one of interpretation." For the issue is not whether Africa is to be understood as a unity but whether it is to be seen as united in these highly specific philosophical doctrines. Skepticism on this point is hardly met by Jahn's observation that, since Egon Friedell has stated that "[a]ll history is saga and myth," the "neo-African intelligence" whose work Jahn is reporting is "entitled to declare authentic" whatever in its past it believes to be so.[15]

It is even more astonishing to find it being claimed in *Muntu* that highly abstract philosophical notions, originally identified in the structure of some Bantu languages, are the folk-philosophy also of people who speak languages in West Africa as remote from Kinyaruanda as German is from Hindi. (I am aware that such comparisons lack clear sense but you will gather my general drift.) Alexis Kagamé himself, from whom these claims are borrowed, like his teacher the Belgian priest, Placide Tempels, made claims only about the ideas implicit in Bantu *languages*. If there is a case to be made for the relevance of African ethnophilosophy to African-American life, the tradition (transmitted by Jahn) of Father Tempels' *La Philosophie Bantoue* is, on these grounds alone, a poor place to start.

Not that the other starting points currently on offer are much more appealing. In the recent discourse of Afro-centricity it has often been argued that "classical Egyptian philosophy" provides a solid foundation for an Afro-centric education. A similar debate has gone on in Africa, where the importance of ancient Egyptian philosophy for contemporary African intellectual life has been argued with most vigor in the writings of the Senegalese man of letters, Cheikh Anta Diop. Diop's work makes clear, I think, the primary motivations of the school. In *The African Origins of Civilization*, Diop summarizes his claims: "Ancient Egypt was a Negro civilization ... The moral fruit of their civilization is to be counted among the assets of the Black world . . . " Because "[a]nthropologically and culturally speaking, the Semitic world was born during protohistoric times from the mixture of white-skinned and dark skinned people in Western Asia . . . [and] all races descended from the Black race . . ."[16] it followed that the first great human civilization—one from which the Greeks, amongst others, borrowed much—was a black civilization. Since he had also argued in *L'Unité culturelle de l'Afrique Noire* for the existence of "features common to Negro African civilization,"[17] Diop exhibits, in our own day, the essential elements of the romantic racialism of Crummell and Blyden and Du Bois: and he makes quite explicit the connections between claims about Egyptian philosophy and the projects of Pan-African nationalism. For it is the historical depth of the alleged tradition, along with its putative négritude, that makes Egyptian thought a suitable vehicle for contemporary racial pride; and since philosophers have succeeded in persuading many in the West that philosophical ideas are central to any culture—a trick which depends on an equivocation between "philosophy," the formal discipline, and "folk philosophy"— and since these are Western-trained intellectuals, it is natural that they should see in Egyptian philosophy the continent's proudest achievement.

Yet it seems to me that Diop—whose work is clearly the best in this tradition—offers little evidence that Egyptian philosophy is more than a systematized but fairly uncritical folk-philosophy, makes no persuasive argument that the Egyptian problematic is that of the contemporary African, and allows for a hovering, if inexplicit, suggestion that the Egyptians are important just because the originators of the earliest dynasty were black.[18]

I will admit (at the risk of being thought to be just another philistine analytic philosopher) that I have never seen any particular point in *requiring* European and American philosophers—*qua* philosophers—to study the pre-Socratics: their work is a mixture of early "science," poetry and myth, and if it is important for modern philosophy at all it is important partly because it creates the world of texts in which Plato began—or, should we say, took the first faltering step towards—the business of systematically reflecting on and arguing about the concepts of folk-philosophy; and partly because it has been the subject of sustained attention from philosophers in the Western tradition. No analogous argument exists for the study of ancient Egyptian thought in contemporary Africa: there are no founding texts, there is no direct or continuous tradition.[19]

In the appeal to Egypt there is something important to be diagnosed in the urge to find an authentically Negro point of departure. I myself detect here the magical power of a "reverse discourse." We have been lead to think that this philosophy, this history that flows from Plato to Frege, is theirs, that it belongs to Europe and to her New World diaspora. The wrong reaction is to accept this claim and run off after a philosophy of our own. The right reaction is surely Du Bois's: to master and claim what is useful in that tradition, to chide it for its errors, to offer it the insights of the other traditions one has inherited.

If ethnophilosophy is not much like what is practiced in the American academy; if there is nothing that stands to African intellectual life as Greece allegedly stands to the high culture of Heidegger; why can we not simply accept that there is no more reason to suppose that every intellectual activity in the West should have had an African twin, than there is to suppose that there must have been African harpsichords or African sonnets?

Our textbook histories of Western culture may insist that Plato and Aristotle are at the root of its pivotal insights, but if we ask ourselves what is most valuable in Euro-American culture, we shall surely want to mention, for example, democracy, to which Plato and Aristotle—and, for that matter, Kant and Hegel—were opposed; applied science and technology, to which Plato contributed nothing and Aristotle provided a long false start whose overthrow in the Renaissance finally made possible the scientific revolution; and a literary culture that refers back to Plato and Aristotle almost exclusively in moments of Christian religiosity (which they would have repudiated) or snobbism or hocus-pocus. The point is not that these are authors we should not read—reading them has provided me, as it has provided many others, with some of the greatest pleasures of my reading life—but rather that we should not read them as repositories of forgotten truth or sources of timeless value. Plato and Aristotle are often interesting because they are wicked and wrong; because they provide us with access to worlds of thought that are alien, stretching our conception of the range of human thought; because we can trace, in tracing the history of reflection on their work, a single fascinating strand in the history of the mental life of our species. I should add, for the record, that the Afro-centrist's appeal to Africa is often conducted at the price of ignoring the views of Africans.

Molefi Asante in *The Afro-centric Idea* discusses at some length Akan ideas about the self, about naming and about society: his one reference is to an unpublished SUNY Buffalo dissertation.[20] But every major Ghanaian philosopher—J. B. Danquah, William Abraham, Kwasi Wiredu, Kwame Gyeke, Ben Oguah (and many less well know Ghanaian philosophers such as myself) have written a great deal on these topics, and the material Asante offers is a good deal less helpful than it might have been if it had acknowledged this material.[21]

I should add, too, that what is most striking in much of this material is the extraordinary replication of the historic 19th century errors in race science. The *Roots of Soul*, a work of the early eighties written by a member of the faculty of Hunter College and a colleague from Southern University in Baton Rouge (one to which I have heard "Afro-centric" references from time to time recently) spends six or seven pages (following obligatory references to Jahn) taking seriously the idea that the character of African-American culture derives from the presence of melanin both in the skin and in the embryonic tissues from which the brain differentiates. A plausible speculative contribution to science in 1880, perhaps even in 1910, but not in the 1990s.[22]

These works raise an issue that it will be worth our while, I think, to face squarely, which is a question of academic racial etiquette. My impression is that many well-intentioned non-racist academics in this country who are not black, feel that in criticizing such work, they risk contributing to racism (or exposing themselves, dare I suggest, to the risk of being accused of it themselves). The tactic of crying racism when anyone criticizes the work of a black person, including a black scholar, is not, to put it mildly, in the best interests of learning, or of black scholars.

Not only is this refusal to criticize bad for scholarship and for black scholars, in particular, it is also, often, condescending. And part of what makes it possible is a refusal to think seriously about racism and about what is wrong with it. If I had to pick one contribution that a philosopher like myself working in African-American Studies can most usefully make, it is to thinking about what racism is, and why it is wrong, so that it becomes possible both to distinguish racism from other things, and to understand what harm it does and does not do.

III

Our universities are now multi-ethnic and international. The other day I sat on a panel with members of the Harvard faculty who were, apart from my Anglo-Ghanaian self, two people who were born Canadian and Polish, and the son of European Jewish immigrants: I refer to John Kenneth Galbraith, Adam Ulam, and Nathan Glazer. The only person on the panel who could not identify a single ancestor born outside the United States was African-American, my friend and colleague Skip Gates. In these circumstances, the distinctive task of courses on African-American history and culture is not to talk to Afro-American students or build their morale (though neither of these is something we can or should shy away from—it is part of the task of the teacher) but to address the undergraduate and graduate student community of all national and ethnic origins (along with our colleagues in many fields) and to lead them into an understanding of other traditions and cultures and thus into a deepened understanding of their own.

If we had to identify an element that is common to the ideology of Anglo-Saxonism and contemporary Afro-centrism (Jacob to its Esau if not Abel to its Cain) it is that, in the names of difference they make it impossible to understand differences. They erect tidy partitions and divisions in the place of necessary exchange and overlap, they subordinate what was once called the life of the mind—or, more exaltedly yet, the life of the spirit—to the narrower purposes of national or ethnic affirmation, to a politics of authenticity. As a rootless cosmopolitan myself, I have learned to understand these impulses, though I do not share them. And it can hardly be denied that at many times in the last few centuries, nationalism of one kind and another has been a force for human liberation. But *within* the American nation the celebration of differences is dangerous unless it is a shared celebration: and, from the perspective of the world, it may sometimes be more important to remind Americans of what they share.

Notes

[1] For a more extended discussion of these issues see my article on "Race," in *Critical Terms for Literary Study*, Frank Lentricchia & Tom McLaughlin (eds.) (Chicago University Press, 1989), pp. 274-87; and also *In My Father's House: Africa in the Philosophy of Culture* (New York: Oxford University Press, 1992).

[2] Johann Gottfried von Herder, *Reflections on the Philosophy of the History of Mankind*, abridged with an introduction by Frank E. Manuel (Chicago: University of Chicago Press, 1968), pp. 172; 186; 195.

[3] *Du Bois: Writings*, selected and annotated by Nathan Huggins (New York: Library of America, 1986), p. 819.

[4] What I have in mind here is the discussion of "humanity as the end of human nature" in Book XV of Johann Gottfried von Herder, *Reflections on the Philosophy of the History of Mankind*, op. cit.

[5] There are equally benign echoes of this same idea in the shibboleths of multiculturalism: we'll provide the rhythm, you'll bring the discipline, they'll contribute the curry powder.

[6] Du Bois, "The Conservation of Races," American Negro Academy Occasional Papers, No. 2, 1987, reprinted in *W.E.B. Du Bois Speaks. Speeches and Addresses 1890-1919*, edited by Philip S. Foner (New York: Pathfinders Press, 1970), pp. 75-76.

[7] E.W. Blyden, *Christianity, Islam and the Negro Race (1887)*, reprinted (Edinburgh: Edinburgh University Press, 1967), p. 94; from an address to the American Colonization Society given in 1883.

[8] In Brotz, p. 104; 110. "Africa to become regenerated must have a national character. . . Our policy must be—and I hazard nothing in promulgating it; nay, without this design, there would be a great deficiency of self-respect, pride of race, and love of country, and we might never expect to challenge the respect of nations—*Africa for the Africans and black men to rule them*. By black men I mean, men of African descent who claim identity with the race." See also the paragraph at pp. 84-85.

[9] Jahnheinz Jahn, *Muntu: African Culture and the Western World* (translated from the German by Marjorie Grene, with an introduction by Calvin Hernton) (New York: Grove Weidenfield, 1989), p. xix.

[10] Jahn, op. cit. ,p. 101.

[11] Jahn, op. cit., p. 233.

[12] I think, however, we should be careful to proceed with a realistic sense of the relationship between the ideas and practices of religion in the cultures from which the slaves came and their syncretisms with Christianity in the New World. In bringing together in Haiti or Cuba or Brazil ideas from a variety of African cultures and mobilizing them together in the languages developed in the New World, and in working them into new practices, it is obvious that those ideas change their meaning. We understand the practices better as we see them grow out of these older practices in response to new circumstances: but it is as well to remember (to take an analogy that is to hand) that when I explain the rituals of the Black Sabbath by beginning with an explanation of the Eucharist, I do not thereby show that the Black Sabbath is "really" Christian. Nor, to pursue the point a step further, does the Christian origin of the symbolism settle in the affirmative for a Christian the question whether she should adopt it.

[13] Jahn, op. cit., pp. 96-97.

[14] Jahn, op. cit., p. 27.

[15] Jahn, op. cit., p. 17.

[16] Cheikh Anta Diop, *The African Origin of Civilization: Myth or Reality* (New York, Westport: Lawrence Hill and Company, 1974), pp. xiv-xv.

[17] Diop,op. cit., p. xvi.

[18] The work of Diop challenges the claim to Greek originality, to the autocthony of the "Greek miracle": unlike some other claims, this one seems to me plausible and worth examining; and the best case for it, so far as I know, is in Martin Bernal's recent *Black Athena, Vol I: The Fabrication of Ancient Greece 1785-1985* (New Brunswick, N.J.: Rutgers University Press, 1987). I think one of the most important lessons of Bernal's work is that it makes a strong case for the centrality of racism—directed against both "Negroes" and "Semites"—in the rewriting of the official history of the Greek miracle that occurred in the European Enlightenment; a rewriting that rejected the ancient commonplace that the Greeks learned much from Egypt.

[19] Even what we might call the historicist view that understanding a concept involves understanding its history does not justify the study of either Greek or Egyptian "philosophy": for the transformations that the conceptual world of Africa and Europe have undergone since, respectively, the fifth century B. C. and the eighteenth dynasty are so great, and our forms of life so different, that the level of understanding to be gleaned by historical research is surely very limited. (There is, incidentally, something paradoxical about the insistence that we must work with the great *written* texts of philosophy in Africa. For if we are trying to get away from Euro-centrism, then surely the view that all interesting conceptual work is written and the property of an individual, and that all interesting analysis has to be of written texts is one that we should discard faster than many others.)

[20] Since this dissertation is by a Michael Appiah, I should perhaps say that the author is, to the best of my knowledge and belief, no relation of mine.

[21] See Ben Oguah, "African and Western Philosophy: a Comparative Study," in Richard Wright, *African Philosophy: An Introduction* (2nd ed.) (Washington: University Press of America, 1979); Kwasi Wiredu, *Philosophy and an African Culture* (London: Cambridge University Press, 1980); Kwame Gyeke, "Akan Language and the Materialism Thesis", *Studies in Language I*, no. 1., 1977, pp 237-44 and *African Philosophical Thought* (Cambridge: Cambridge University Press, 1962); J. B. Danquah, *The Akan Doctrine of God*, 2nd ed. (London: Frank Cass and Co., 1968).

[22] *The Roots of Soul: The Psychology of Black Expressiveness* by Alfred B. Pasteur, PH.D., and Ivory L. Toldson, ED.D. (Garden City, NY: Anchor Press/Doubleday, 1982.)

Three Columns

BY DAVID RIEFF

European Time

On June 13th, 1940, as the German army marched into Paris, Simone Weil confided a startling and seemingly perverse observation to her journal. "This is," she wrote, "a great day for the people of Indochina."

Few remarks could have been more ill-timed. Indeed, when it is remembered at all, Weil's phrase is usually dismissed as one particularly outrageous example of her unslakeable thirst for self-abnegation, an intellectual analogue to that tragic disdain for her own physical well-being that not only made her an invalid in life but led to what was in reality a self-imposed death from malnutrition in 1942. It is hardly very difficult to make the case, as even her admirers have tended to do, that Weil carried loyalty to abstract principle beyond humane limits, and, in doing so, shirked that most primordial of all moral claims, a proper respect for oneself and an appropriate measure of loyalty and love for one's family and community. After all, what other French Jew, or, for that matter, what other French citizen of any confession who was not pro-German, would have chosen at that instant of catastrophe to stand off at such a distant remove from her own interests, intently carving out the moral space to muse impartially over the repercussions her country's defeat would have upon one of its more remote overseas possessions? If Weil was not quite simply mad, the argument runs, then her gesture at least constituted an act of self-hatred (Jewish, French, European all at once) in the truest and most restrictive sense of that much overused term.

135

And it probably was. Among other things, anyway. Certainly, the intractable, relentless lover of abstract principle is hard to separate from the woman whose discomfort with all things physical bordered on the pathological. Few people since the Cathars, over whose fate she agonized, have so desperately wished to be freed from all indebtedness to the corporeal or so loathed themselves as carnal entities. As a child, Weil confidently informed her brother, Andre, that when he grew up and, as they both expected, became a famous scientist, he would invent a pill that would reprieve her at last from the disgusting necessity of having to eat solid food. Many more examples of this type can be adduced easily enough, and like Sylvia Plath, Weil makes a splendid target of opportunity for the psychobiographer. Usually, the unhappy lives of these women (and of other talented women besides them) are taken to provide the deepest truth about what they did. Weil was a great thinker but unlike, say, Nietzsche (or most any other man: there is a feminist side to this story), her ideas were rigidly linked to her biography, and the effect is that the tale was drowned out by the story of the teller. In reality, it is thought alone that matters: it endures when the person who entertained it has ceased to be. The life is just the dirty underwear, and the question that should really be asked is this: If Weil found it easier, as she undoubtedly did, to sympathize unstintingly with the suffering peasants of Cochin China than to look after even her most immediate and justifiable interests, does this mean that she was wrong about Vietnam?

The truth is that Weil was stunningly, self-evidently right. June 13th, 1940 *was* a great day for the Indochinese people. The empire that France had succeeded in holding together after the First World War (during which French generals spoke contemptuously of the lack of fighting spirit among the Annamese levies on the Western front) would not long survive 1945 despite the best efforts of the colonial powers. The enemy of my enemy is my friend, the old adage goes, which is why the Vietnamese had every reason to welcome a French defeat, just as Bengali nationalists like Subhas Chandra Bose supported the Japanese in their war against the British empire. The fact that there is no reason to suppose that the Japanese would have treated Bengal any better than the Raj did is beside the point. What mattered at the time for Vietnamese and Indian anticolonialists alike was that the empires that had subjugated them were being defeated, and the established order—which is to say the established oppression—was being turned upside down.

In 1903, General von Trotta arrived in German Southwest Africa with the mission of quite simply wiping out the Herero tribe that had rebelled against German colonial authority. This he did. Thus, it is unlikely that the fall of Imperial Germany in 1918, catastrophic as that event was held to be for culture and civilization not only by brutes and militarists but by such epigones of the West as Thomas Mann, can have been received with wails and rent garments along the dusty plains of Ovamboland. The point only seems self-evident because Americans were on the other side during World War I and are thus disposed to believe that the defeat of Germany (though not, perhaps, the Versailles treaty) was good for everyone. The hard moment comes when we ask Weil's question about the defeat of France in 1940, an event that was as absolute a defeat for humanity as it is possible to imagine. And yet in point of fact, it is unlikely that the British or French empires would have ended when they did had they not been leached of will and treasure by that Civil War that engrossed Europe—eleven years of war bisected by twenty years of truce and artistic creativity—during the first half of this century. By the middle of the war, even the lowliest British subaltern must have understood that the Raj was just about over. And though the French tried, after 1945, with British and then with American connivance, to restore their dominion over Vietnam, Simone Weil's intuition was borne out. The battle of Dienbienphu had been lost that morning the Panzers rolled down the Champs-Elysees. As is so often the case, a quarrel between landlords is nothing but good news for the tenants.

This does not mean that June 13th, 1940 was less tragic a day for the peoples of Europe—especially for the Jews and the inhabitants of Eastern Europe and of the Soviet Union—or for the world itself because of this other significance. Indeed, at the deepest level, people recoil from Weil's remark because, understandably, they feel that it somehow taints or impeaches the suffering the Nazis visited on Europe. They also feel that there is something immoral about Weil's impartiality. Perhaps they are right. But it is not the whole story, for what Weil did was to open to question our entire notion of history, its crevices and fault lines, as Ernst Bloch called them, or, to put it another way, the sense in which different people are occupying the same space but living through different historical epochs. In one ruthless, Olympian sentence, Weil reminded us that the history we in the West care about, and over which we rightly grieve or rejoice, is neither the history of everywhere nor of everyone. She invites us to undertake that most uncomfortable act of reasoning, the realization that an event which for us is cause for mourning may be celebrated by other people every bit as decent as ourselves at the moment when hope first dawned.

Pick up a date at random. Make it a famous date, say October 12th, 1492, the day Columbus's fleet reaches the Americas for the first time. What greater day could there have been for Europe, and not only for the Europe of power and money? The problem is not so easily reducible as that. For centuries, probably until as recently as twenty-five years ago for most Western Europeans and right up to the present moment for the subjects of the Soviet empire, America beckoned as the last hope to the Europe of the disenfranchised. And yet from an Amerindian perspective it was the first day of the end of the world. Europeans largely ignore this question (the degree to which Latin America, as Carlos Fuentes has pointed out, is absent from all discussion of the Europe of 1992 is only one sign of this refusal to see) as do North Americans who might, given their history, be expected to raise it. And yet the relation with Latin America and, for that matter, with the rest of the world should be an urgent one for Europeans. Not that the history is clear. The Argentine filmmaker, Edgardo Cozarinsky (the name itself could serve as an illustration), tells the story of visiting the port of Palos, from which Columbus sailed, in the company of a Colombian friend. As they stared West, Cozarinsky found himself strangely moved. "Here," said this Jew from the Pampas, "began our salvation." He found himself fixed by a hard stare and a copper-hued grimace. "Here," the Colombian retorted acidly, "began *our* enslavement."

For Cozarinsky, the notion of America as a haven, an escape route for his ancestors from the Europe of inquisitors and pogroms was so deeply ingrained that it never occurred to him that his Colombian friend would see the same event in a diametrically opposing light. To see it through his mestizo friend's brown eyes rather than through his own steel-blue ones was like entering another world. It was not necessary to see things only in this new way, but once Cozarinsky had looked from this vantage point the world was, he reports, unalterably changed for him. It was precisely this transformation that Weil was trying to effect with her remark, her reminder to herself and to us that, as J. M. Cameron once summarized her view, to think about what was just was to think about the place of impartiality and disinterestedness. It was this notion of justice that Weil extended to politics and to history. And while it would have been preposterous to hear Weil's remark from General de Gaulle or from the Chief Rabbi of Paris, whose obligations were to their own constituencies, and, more profoundly, to their own time, it was precisely the right remark for a thinker to make. That after all was her job, just as De Gaulle's was war and the Chief Rabbi's the welfare of his people.

That day in 1940, that day that announced the European calamity, was the worst possible moment to tell foreign truths. For Europeans needed their strength to save themselves. In 1989, Europeans are strong and growing stronger. The year has been one of celebration as freedom is restored to the peoples of Eastern and Central Europe. That Czech culture which Milan Kundera, to his eternal discredit, self-servingly described as having been destroyed forever has bobbed up alive and well, and Havel in his jeans is in the Castle. Honecker gone, Kadar gone, Zhivkov gone, and even Europe's Idi Amin, Ceausescu, 'the genius of the Carpathians,' also, finally, gone. It does not seem likely that the Red army will be staying either. What better news, in short, could there be for humanity than this collapse of the Soviet empire? American neo-conservatives give the credit to the Cold War, other, saner people overpraise Gorbachev, while Europe exults and the spirit of Masaryk is vindicated. What better news could there be?

Not so fast. Is this great news for Europe also to be welcomed by the rest of the world which, no offence intended, is most of the world? The truth is that not only is this question not being answered, it is scarcely being asked outside of a few radical magazines in the west like the *New Left Review* and a few organizations in the East, particularly New Forum in the DDR. No wonder the responses to the democratization of Eastern Europe are as glum in the Third World as, earlier, they were to the prospect of EC '92. Beyond sheer altruism, is there really any reason for a Nigerian or a Peruvian to be pleased that Europe will be even richer, even more self-sufficient in labor, raw materials, and food than it was before? Or are they not likely to be seized with the legitimate fear that Europe will simply pay less attention? It's happening already, this European *je m'en foutisme* toward the ex-colonial world. "There is no document of civilization," Benjamin wrote, "that is not at the same time a document of barbarism." No people could be more civilized than the democratic Czechs; the question is whether their freedom will be bought at a barbarous price, whether their loans will be forgiven while credit is cut off to Africa, their products favored, their struggles underwritten while the non-European peoples of the world get on with the very bad time they have been having or, arguably, have an even worse time of it?

There is no fault in Europe's self-absorption. Even Weil recognized that preferential love was no sin. But it is no mark of civilization either. Let Europe have its euphoria. It is, after all, an honor to live in 1989. But afterward, when the celebrating subsides, and the playwright in his jeans no longer sits in the castle and has gone home to write—when, in short, states have again become states, with all their great, ingrained wicked-ness, their petty venalities—then let Europe decide what kind of docu-ment its freedom really is and how the rest of the world should react to the good news. If Europe decides to help the colonial world it once pillaged, if Europe remembers not only the enslavement visited upon it by foreign powers, but also the enslavement it visited for so long upon the colored peoples of the earth, when Europeans were lords of the earth, then 1989 in Prague and Sofia, East Berlin and Budapest, Bucharest and of course Moscow, this 1989 of miracles will turn out to have been a great day for the entire world. If not, if instead of at last attempting to help in a serious, committed manner people whose societies Europeans themselves frac-tured and drained, Europeans ignore their obligations, close ranks, and get ready, both metaphorically and actually, to repel boarders, and cover their ears against the harsh, hysterical, and finally just claims of the poor of the world, then 1989, while a great day for Europe, will turn out to have been a very different kind of day for—let's use Simone Weil's modest example—the people of Indochina.

Information and Modernity

From the vantage point of the majority who live in the poor four fifths of the world, the amazing variety of goods possessed by citizens of the rich one-fifth is far more peculiar than the sheer brute fact of their having accumulated so much. After all, the poor have more than enough bitter first-hand knowledge of how well their own elite live, and perhaps the most striking difference between a supermarket somewhere in suburban America and, say, one in the affluent Lima suburb of Miraflores is the extent to which the shelves of the former are stocked with so many different brands of the same product. A privileged inhabitant of the Third World usually is only intent on owning the best version of any particular thing, whether it be a Rolex wristwatch, a Mercedes car, or a jar of English marmalade. But a prosperous North American or Western European takes for granted the ability, no matter what the product in question is, from condoms to cassette players, to select from a 'menu' of different versions. It is the difference between wanting to live in a palace, an ancient ambition, and wanting to go out to dinner every night, which has a decidedly more modern provenance.

What has become true with regard to possessions has become equally relevant to the possessing of information. There, too, a 'North/South' divide looms. And one does not have to be a supporter of the "New Information Order," that excuse for censorship that was being put forward at the United Nations at the height of its silly season during the nineteen seventies, to accept its framers' contention that Westerners possess and control the dissemination of most information that is available in the world. One can even go further, and say that the West possesses it differently than people do elsewhere. For whatever the quality of what can be seen on the dozens of stations that a television with a cable hook-up receives, there is more of it than can be found on all the telecommunications and mass media of several of the world's continents.

Moreover, there has been an exponential increase in the uses to which television, home computers, and, now, fax machines and increasingly sophisticated phone mail systems, can be put to—and at exactly the moment when parts of the Third World, notably Africa, have experienced a radical deterioration of their technological infrastructure. This means that the technological dichotomy between the everyday experience of life in the rich world and in the poor one is likely to increase. In France, which is one of the more electronically 'plugged in' developed countries, it is now quite normal to transact virtually every kind of business from a PC, communicating with others who sit at their own keyboards. In contrast, cholera is appearing in Central America for the first time in a century, the harbinger, many doctors believe, of a new worldwide epidemic in poor regions which will be the direct result of the breakdown of public sanitation.

Westerners tend, whatever their bad conscience and public hypocrisy, to believe that their relative success is a function of their superior political and economic system. But, as in the great age of the European imperial powers, the real advantage they enjoy is technological. "Thank God that we got," ran Hilaire Belloc's tough-minded doggerel written on the occasion of Lord Kitchener's victory over the Sudanese, "the Maxim Gun and they have not." In the nineteen-nineties, what the West has got and the Third World is lacking is, most of all, information.

There is even a sense in which it has become almost impossible to properly describe what is going on in developed societies without first talking, at whatever risk of restating the obvious, about the context of all the informational background noise that somehow must be navigated. The fact that the gravest events must compete for attention with the most trivial, that all information is, to use the term favored by marketing executives at most broadcast companies, "narrowcasted," i.e. presented in a form thought likely to appeal to a specific (and constricted) target audience, means that people are always in some nagging doubt about any particular event's importance. Certainly, we in the West have no analogue to the habit that used to prevail in the Soviet Union of, in effect, stopping the informational flow when a particularly noteworthy thing happened and, in the case of television, presenting the viewer with a blank screen and the music of Beethoven.

Paradoxically, this modern experience of information more closely approximates the real relation most people have to the world than the pious claims they tend to make about their interest in it. There is no particular reason, after all, why a race riot in Brooklyn, New York, should concern an average child in Minneapolis, or even in nearby Long Island. The fact that the dire event in question is being chronicled, often—as they say—'live' is no reason why the kid in question should stop watching Saturday morning cartoons a few clicks down the television dial; no more does our knowing that, at any given moment, every imaginable act is being carried out somewhere in the world really affect the way we live. Such knowledge is as unreal to us as, if historians are to be believed, the great battles of the Middle Ages were largely unknown to peasants living only thirty or forty miles away from where they occurred.

Of course, that specific gap would be inconceivable today. Had there been television in the aftermath of the battle of Agincourt in the way that there was in the aftermath of Operation Desert Storm, doubtless television reporters from CNN, NHK, and the BBC, would have been reporting from that French village, walking with their camera crews amidst the carcasses of fallen French knights and their horses, interviewing the stolid English bowmen, and crowding around the tent in which Prince Hal had come to accept the surrender of the French Seneschal. People's ignorance today is not based on a deficit of information but on a surfeit of it. And even when one wants to know what is going on, the difficulty is often of having to cut through all the other information with which one is being loaded down, of finding a receptive part of oneself still capable of taking in a serious piece of news and excluding, at least temporarily, everything else.

An illustration : On August 19th , 1991, I went to sleep in the room of sons of friends in Miami, Florida, my own possessions sharing drawer and floor space with such things as Miami Marlins T-Shirts, baseball cards, and swimsuits in lurid tropical colors. A few hours later, I was awakened by my hostess, who, in her turn, had just gotten a phone call from an elderly relative much addicted to late-night CNN watching, with the news that Gorbachov had been overthrown and that the 'Right' (how few of us seem to have enough language these days to keep up with our times) was back in power. Blearily, I looked up at my friend. Behind her, I could just make out the image—it was a poster on the far wall, behind the childfriendly Macintosh PC—of the basketball player, Michael Jordan, going up for a slam dunk. After a few moments, I fumbled for the remote control television clicker that I had left on the night table and turned the set on. A screech of sound and then the image of a game show. . . in Spanish. I had been ready for the astonishing news from Moscow, not for information overload from Miami. It took only a few seconds, of course, to move past the other stations on the way to CNN, where, indeed, there was the awful sight of tanks and armored personnel carriers making their way along the wide boulevards of Moscow toward the Russian Parliament building. But on the way, I saw split second bits of the game show, a Disney movie, a televangelist, an exercise show, and a film noir from the nineteen forties. For a coup in the Soviet Union I suspect that few viewers would have lingered, but what about an earthquake in Mexico? A peace treaty in Cambodia? Famine in the Sahel? For most of us, there would have been no disturbing call, so little are such events regarded in America; even in my case it is unlikely, news addict that I am, that had I woken up on my own I would have tuned into CNN. The film noir, after all, was "Double Indemnity," with Fred MacMurray, Barbara Stanwyck, and Edward G. Robinson. Good stuff.

The French expression, 'an embarrassment of riches,' that always seems so appropriate upon returning to the United States or Western Europe from almost anywhere else in the world, is, equally, 'an embarrassment of information.' In this particular case, I had gone to sleep in Miami, my belly stuffed with pork, plantains, yucca, and the other delicacies of the bourgeois Cuban kitchen, and my head stuffed with the dinnertime debate concerning how long Fidel Castro was likely to hold on to power, only to awaken to the noise of another people's history. I do not mean that I awoke to tragedy—that was the unhappy privilege of the people of Russia—only to its news, which, however sobering, was hardly the same thing.

For what I had flicked to I could as easily have flicked away from (not off, at least not in Miami, where, once they are turned on, televisions are rarely turned off while the household is still awake). The news from Moscow no more conformed to any reality that I could see or touch or smell than news of Agincourt might have done in some other part of Europe. Not only were the streets of the pleasant Miami neighborhood where I was staying green, fragrant, and peaceful, but had I been trying to exercise a social conscience there were indisputably plenty of tragic events closer to hand with which I could have legitimately concerned myself. Indeed, it could even be argued that the fact that I, and people like me, have been so concerned about the Soviet Union throughout our lives has meant that we have not paid the kind of attention we should have to the sufferings of so many of our neighbors.

In mitigation, it should be added that this situation is caused as much by the way in which people get their information as by what they do with it. Most of the American media practices a form of serial monogamy where political and social crises are concerned. When the gulf war breaks out, or there is a hardline putsch in the Soviet Union, it is as if nothing else in the world is taking place, as if the dramas that were getting most of the attention when these events occurred had somehow disappeared or been put on hold for the duration. In the case of a prolonged event like the Gulf War, there was even the ancillary phenomenon of viewers getting hooked on the news from the desert and having to reacclimate themselves, almost as if they had served there themselves, after the fighting was over. Similarly, news organizations that had been gearing up to cover the Yugoslav Civil War all but dropped this story during the period when the outcome in Russia was in doubt, and it came as something of a surprise to many to discover that, in the interim, the fighting had intensified.

It could hardly be otherwise. At a time when the morning newspapers summarize the dramas of the previous day and the evening news is often in a position to offer footage of carnage only a few hours old, deformations of consciousness are hard to avoid (for anyone except a genius or a monomaniac). The problem, of course, is not that the tragic and the trivial are conflated (or, rather, that is another problem), but that the notion of tragedy itself gets leeched of its meaning. It is unlikely, for example, that anyone who did not already harbor a passionate, broad interest in world affairs—a viewpoint that is becoming rarer and rarer as specialization engulfs the intellectuals almost as fast as the Sahara is engulfing the African continent—could possibly know all that much about, simultaneously, Sunnis and Shias in Iraq, Buddhist fundamentalism in Sri Lanka, and the resurgence of Peronism in Argentina. Why should they? With a few commendable exceptions, even the reporters who cover these events don't know half as much as they ought to, whatever the accomplished air of authority they do their best to project. Anyone in any doubt about the truth of this would do well to compare a show like the BBC's World Service's "News Hour" with even the best of the television coverage that is available.

With these thin, diverse sources, small wonder that most people in the rich world have taken refuge either in a diffused indifference, or, in the case of the young and the idealistic, in a diffused indignation that is strong on millennial hope but weak and self-referential in most other respects. It is a variant of what international aid workers call 'donor burnout,' something that often happens when there are so many disasters in such a short space of time that each individual catastrophe loses its power to shock and sadden. There are exceptions, of course, national emergencies like the Gulf War (the orchestration of which can be deemed as an accomplishment almost as masterful as the progress of American arms on the battlefield), or perennial causes like that of the Palestinians that, for all the good it has done them, has long commanded the attachment of many Western Europeans, but fewer of them than might be supposed. These days, the only people whose commitment, whether of money, of sympathy, or of attention, can be relied upon are those who feel that their interests are directly affected—Russian immigrants in Brighton Beach, Brooklyn watching the August coup in Moscow, say—or those who have chosen a cause in much the way that others choose a profession, or, more trivially, a sports team to root for, and whether it is AIDS, Salvadoran refugees in Greater Los Angeles, or Western European democracy, attend to it almost to the exclusion of every other concern.

But those who rail against the apathy of citizens of the rich world are in the paradoxical position of denouncing the information revolution that allows them to know anything at all about all these events that are taking place far away and without whose institutions and technologies the rest of the earth would be a blank, as it was a blank for most people during most of the time human beings have made their predatory way in the world. Perhaps it is impossible to care about so many things, or, at least, to care profoundly. But whether this is true or not, there can be little doubt that, like the ecological bill, the informational bill is coming due. Information is expanding, but so is specialization, and so are the peoples of the world, who know of each other more completely than they ever did in the past but are in many ways less able to come to terms with this knowledge. It is one thing to try to be one's brother's keeper; but what happens when every evening the news of all the cousins twice and three-times removed booms its broadcast into the living room? No wonder the trend seems all about fleeing information, or, rather, refusing to differentiate between the various informational stimuli that are available—news, advertising, entertainment, sports, and the rest.

To travel in the Third World is, predictably enough, to be freed of this particular burden. In Sri Lanka, people are talking mostly of Sri Lanka, in Cuba mostly of Cuba. Far from being places where there is information available in paralyzing excess, the poor world is a place where one goes on an informational diet, and a three day old copy of Asian Wall Street journal or last week's edition of Time magazine can seem like almost too much to assimilate. But such places are becoming rarer, and to arrive in Columbo or Havana increasingly feels like an arduous journey through time as well as through space. When Fidel Castro falls, as he will, though probably far later than people in the United States have been predicting, one of the biggest transformations, in many ways more lasting than the demise of communism, will be the arrival of cable television. And it will not be an unmixed blessing.

What it will be is unavoidable. The information revolution is Promethean knowledge. Destructive of national borders, philosophical and moral certainties, and of regional cultures, it is even now having its way with peoples from India to the Dominican Republic. People who do not have access to reliable supplies of potable water usually have seen a music video or two, just as in many poor countries people whose parents had probably never heard of the United States of America now press eagerly at the embassy gate for a visa to emigrate here. These sounds and these queues are harbingers of encroaching modernity. And it does no good to rail at history or murmur 'caveat emptor.' The only question that remains is what kind of modernity, which is to say what kind of Westernization, we will have, and whether the plugged-in future will be humane or brutal. The blandishments of choice are simply too great to resist, and though, for the moment, there are still large parts of the world where information is scarce, it is increasing as vertiginously as the world's population.

The poor will, indeed, always be with us, but the information-poor will not. And when the moment comes—it has not arrived yet, but it is not so far distant—when the distinction between plugged-in societies and technologically innocent ones becomes impossible to draw, then the culture of entropic modernity will finally have triumphed. Whether that world is one most people in the rich world will be happy living in, and whether the transformation will be so great that, as it were, our past will have no future in our future, is of course another matter. The poor world infiltrates the rich one with its people, even as the rich world infiltrates the poor one with its machines, and even the recent past quickly assumes the aspect of a musty, bygone era.

Citizens?

At the French school in New York to which I was sent in the early nineteen-sixties, the second grade history textbook contained the bluff assertion that, "our ancestors, the Gauls, were blond and courageous." We upon whom the task devolved to repeat this astonishing sentence, in the classrooms of what, to be fair, was even by the standards of the time a particularly conservative outcropping of Overseas France, saw nothing incongruous about the act. We recited dutifully enough, though few of us were blonds. In the main, we were the sons and daughters of Francophile Americans, or else the children of businessmen and diplomats from the Francophone regions of Southeast Asia, Africa, and the island republics of the Indian Ocean. Those who could legitimately claim any real biological link with Vercingetorix or the pig-tailed axemen of his tribe were thin on the schoolyard grounds.

Of course, in any self-confidently authoritarian forcing-house like a *Lycée Français*, such discrepancies between rhetoric and reality are more likely to be viewed as evidence of fidelity to high standards than evidence of hypocrisy. For our history teacher to inform us—mixed bag of Americans, Laotians, Senegalese, Séychellois, Belgians, and little French Frenchmen that we were—about our distant kin whom Caesar had conquered was of a piece with the announcements our gym teachers dependably issued at the beginning of every trimester that although people in everyday life walked like *so*—here the instructor would essay a few normally-gaited steps—we would *march* to and from the playing fields of nearby Central Park.

However, the fact that we saw nothing strange about a history class in which people with names like Diop and Ratsophong (I exclude people with names like Rosenblatt and Rieff; the Jews have long been good at mastering the histories of the countries in which they have settled) spent the bulk of their school hours reciting bits of Caesar's *Gallic Wars*, declaiming Lamartine, or tracing maps that marked out the mineralogical resources of Alsace-Lorraine, did not mean that such a curriculum *was* normal. By the same token, the fact of its passing—even in the Lycée Français these days there is, it seems, less '*omnia Gallia*' and more

Khmer history—does not mean, for all the easy talk of diversity and multiculturalism, that anything coherent has arisen to take its place. What we have in abundance are paradoxes of identity. In the nineteenth century and for most of the twentieth as well, it was possible to say that one was French or Spanish or German and know what one meant. This idea of the nation would have had little meaning before the nineteenth century, but such was its success that we tend to think of it as a natural order of consciousness. Imperialism and immigration put paid to all that, and, in retrospect, the triumph of the European nation-states was also the beginning of their undoing. In Africa, for all their competition, Germans and Frenchmen become Europeans or Whites. And later, in our own time, the mass migration of peoples from this colonized world toward the great cities of the colonizers (and we, their American successors) would make identity even in the center of the rich world a subject of debate and anxiety rather than a fixed certitude.

The little black Frenchmen, the Caribbean islanders Derek Walcott once described as "we Afro-Greeks," and the rest are pouring into the metropolis. Did our teachers—did prosperous white people in general—really imagine that they were alone in the world, or that their armies, their ideas, and their commodities, could be exported abroad without there being any chance of those to whom they were destined booking a return passage of their own? If they did, they were kidding themselves. And the ironic coda to the history of European imperialism and of the American century has turned out to be the steady movement of the African diaspora back, not to Africa but to London, Paris, and Miami, of the people of Mexico, the Isthmus, and the Caribbean, toward L.A. and New York, and of the Maghreb toward Rome, Barcelona, and Marseilles.

This movement has had many consequences already, and will have still more, but one of the first and deepest has been to all but extinguish the European notion of citizenship as it has been understood since the nineteenth century. For what can this idea, this civic distillation of shared membership in a group where common racial origins, a common language, and a delimitable geography are assured, mean to people whose everyday experience is not of the familiarity but of the alien-ness of their neighbors? Try asking an Arab in Paris' eighteenth arrondissement about

Léon Blum and the Popular Front or a Turk in Berlin's Kreuzberg district
about Konrad Adenauer. Such references, which are, after all, to figures
and events within the living memory of many French and German people,
might as well be to Vercingetorix or Otto the Fowler. 'Our ancestors . . .
what ancestors?'

And it is not simply a question of information. As the German Jews
learned, circa 1933-1945, a knowledge of German culture, and a talent for
it, did not make so many Germans hate them any less. For the Turkish
immigrant in Berlin or Frankfurt, the situation is less dire, but, if anything,
more confusing. For such people are arriving in the capitals of the modern
world when the whole trajectory of contemporary life is veering away
from any interest in the past—except, that is, the past as seamless idyll—
and in which even those whose ancestors served the Bourbons or the
Prussian kings are more likely to care about the latest soccer scores, to
have opinions about the new line of Mercedes, or be able to recite the
lyrics from the latest American or British pop hit, than they are in
conserving what access they still retain to their threadbare European folk
memories of Hohenzollern military prowess or Spanish imperial splen-
dor. The spectacle of the billboard directly opposite the Spanish Ministry
of Defense building in Madrid advertising, in English, the 'United Colors
of Benetton,' the Italian clothing manufacturer, or the sight of Jack Lang,
the French Minister of Culture, conferring the Order of Arts and Letters
on the American rocker, Lou Reed, provides a more accurate barometer
of what is going on in Europe these days.

It's true that certain emblems of the past still retain their power. But
a controversy like the one that erupted in the United States in 1989 over
the citizen's right to burn the American flag was more instructive as an
example of how fragile and endangered such symbols of national unity
were now perceived to be than as proof of the rightward drift of American
political life. In Europe, the mood is, if anything, even rawer than it is in
the United States. It is commonplace to see another flag, that of the
Imperial German army, brandished at neo-fascist rallies in Berlin and
Leipzig. But even that fraught banner is better construed as an emblem of
present-day German disenchantments and resentments—especially anti-
Immigrant feeling—than any deep nostalgia for Prussian civilization. If the

stubbly-headed standard bearers in question really were rooted in a specifically German past, it is unlikely they would deck themselves out in the latest youth fashion—American football letter jackets and Doc Martens shoes. But they are not interested in the past at all. It is just a pretext, a flag of convenience in the literal sense of the word. What is really going on is that every inhabitant of the developed world is coming to participate in an American style polity. Some will end up living in versions of Park Avenue or Beverly Hills, while others will find themselves in Europe's Harlems or East L.A.s. Of course the pace of this Americanization is proceeding differently in different parts of the world, including some parts of North America itself. But the result is a foregone conclusion. World capital has begun a radical restructuring of the global economy that makes the nation state at best an anachronism and at worst an impediment. By opting for various supra-national confederations (the EC, the North American Free Trade Agreement, the budding East Asian economic zone), the political leadership has created structures more suitable for this refitted world economy. In an age of immigration the American model is really the only one that will serve.

Citizenship in the United States, as Americans and visitors have known since the time of Crèvecoeur, has always been an affair of shared aspirations rather than shared memories. This American idea even encompassed the mixing of peoples—that was what so astonished Europeans in the eighteenth and nineteenth century, this interbreeding of Dutch and French, German and English—though not, self-evidently, of races. But miscegenation too is one of our millenial destinies, and though people tend not to talk about it too much, that process as well is further advanced in America than was conceivable even a quarter of a century ago. Europe will follow, and, for that matter, so will Japan, which, despite being to eugenicist and racialist fantasies what Paraguay once was to S.S. veterans on the lam, has begun to acclimate itself, if not to intermarriage, already to the presence of large numbers of illegal foreign workers. The rest of the process is predictable: the past begins to fade, and the future, which is to say the notional, seems like the last hopeful space.

This does not mean that such hope is well-founded. The quiddity of the past is definable; that of the future is not. To say that, like it or not, we are destined to live in multicultural societies—a statement that, far from being the incendiary, consensus-fracturing provocation that certain cultural conservatives take it to be, represents little more than an acknowledgment, the sketchiest of bows toward the brute facts of demography and the global economy—is not the same as asserting that we will soon learn how to live in them, or navigate the period of transformation without going mad. For if the previous consensus, based as it was on being 'fully-vested' in a particular nation state, seems more and more irrelevant to the way we live now, no alternate system of belief with anywhere near the same degree of interpretive power shows any sign of arising to take its place.

And that is the real novelty of our contemporary situation. Crises of belief are nothing new. We can find examples in all continents and in most periods of history. But when, say, Cortez destroyed the Aztec world, he brought with him a replacement. Over the Aztec temple in what is now the Zocalo Square in Mexico City, the Spanish conquerors built a cathedral. Nor did Muhammad make war on the pagan tribes of Arabia to inform them, after his forces had carried the day, 'that's it, you're on your own.' Even the Enlightenment prescribed reason as the antidote to Christianity. But we are more radically alone than people have been since Fourth century Rome, and, unlike that period, it is by no means clear that new Gods will eventually be conjured up to resolve our crisis of unbelief. Modern physics, chemistry, neurobiology, and, above all, the demotion into insignificance that astronomy and the geologic record have bequeathed humanity have seen to that.

Of course, there is always the possibility of denying both our immediate cultural predicament and our ultimate teleological one altogether. This course is visible in the rise of Islamic fundamentalism, and, to a lesser extent, the faddish enthusiasms throughout the rich world for varieties of religious experience old and new. At the moment, this backlash seems to sweep all before it, from Algeria to Southern California, but it would be a mistake to overestimate either its staying power or its prospects. That the secular American Jew suddenly drawn to Hassidism or the discombobulated Presbyterian who turns to Charismatic Christianity will not long remain devout is a foregone conclusion. But even the

Islamic revival itself, so dreaded in the West, is unlikely to endure. However awful the imposition of Sharia has been in places like Iran and the Sudan, however much the success of fundamentalism has been a disaster for women's rights in particular and humanity in general, we are more likely to be witnessing the traditional world's last coherent effort to defend itself against the encroachments of secularism and science than the rebirth of religious faith.

The Khomeinis, and, for that matter, the John Paul IIs, will fail to stem the tide just as surely as the Jesuits failed to erase the Reformation and the Mahdi failed to stem the tide of British imperialism. It is true that were Catholicism or Shi'ism to triumph everywhere, the world might indeed be transformed, just as it would have been had Trotsky's world revolution really taken place. But the only world revolution that we are witnessing is the revolution of the world market. That is the system, multicultural and supra-national, that is carrying everything else before it. If anything, Christianity and Islam are even less able to compete with capitalism—as opposed to their quarrels with nations, like the former Soviet Union in the case of the Church or the U.S. in that of the ayatollahs—than Communism was. In a battle between Qum or the Vatican and Mitsubishi and Siemens, the multinationals invariably win.

This outcome is inevitable because there is no coherent Christian or Islamic economic worldview—none at any rate that is supple enough to account for the economic activity in the late twentieth century. All that the clerics can bring to the table is a conception of justice that occasionally masquerades as an economic program but is in reality nothing more than a millenarian prediction that one day the last will be first and the first last. The sympathy of some religious leaders with the sufferings of the poor (and it is a selective sympathy at that, as witness the attitudes toward women of both Islam and Christianity) can produce political explosions and explosions of faith, but in truth, for all the noise, capital is rarely listening. John Paul II was feted for his anti-Communism during the nineteen-eighties. When he now speaks about the obligations of the rich world toward the world of misery beyond its gates, the powerful are hard-pressed to mask their indifference. Meanwhile in Teheran, where the rhetoric can still be as fierce as it was in the immediate aftermath of the overthrow of Reza Pahlavi, much the same picture emerges. Not only have the mullahs made peace with the multinationals they once denounced, but at OPEC meetings it is scarcely possible to distinguish the voices of their representatives from those from secular Venezuela.

It is not just a matter of our having neither Marx nor Jesus to turn to. The great discovery of our time is that the rapid fracturing of identity, the dissolution of confidence in any single purpose or account either of ourselves or our societies, means that we may really have nowhere to turn. Subjects without objects, problems without solutions, we see aliens on every streetcorner, and in the mirror as well. And in the midst of this radical disorientation, an untuning of the world that sometimes seems to have taken place overnight, we look desperately for shelter—in fantasies of tribal virtue, in an aggrieved sense of victimization, and in a befuddled desire for more commodities, more amusements, more *distraction*. Cut off from our ancestors, Gauls or otherwise, by the sheer pace of change— technological, material, and cultural—we stare into the void and pretend we are looking at something intelligible.

Memories of Unhousement: A Memoir

BY CLARK BLAISE

I

Before the Interstate system obliterated the old America, you used to come upon them at country cross-roads: clusters of white arrows tipped in black, pointing in every direction. Somewhere on the Plains you would see it, slow down, and be thrilled: *Denver 885*, it would say, or *New Orleans 1045*, or better yet, *Los Angeles 2000*. How they got there, who decided on the city and the mileage, I'll never know. Perhaps they had taken over from the whitewashed rocks, the dabs of tar, left by earlier waves of lost, impatient travelers, when twenty or thirty miles a day was more than fair measure. Nowadays, the green mirror-studded billboards conspire to keep our minds on the effortlessly attainable, the inevitable. No more than two destinations, they seem to say, don't tease us with prospects greater than our immediate ambition. *Glens Falls,* the one nearest to me now says. *Saratoga Springs 18.*

We are deprived of that special thrill when our destination, our crazy, private destination, made its first appearance in one of those black-tipped clusters. No reason at all that on a road between Chicago and Madison, just outside Beloit, Wisconsin, WINNIPEG should miraculously appear. Yet in 1949 when I was nine and guiding my father on our longest trip home, it did. Nine hundred miles in a '47 Chevy, with its split windshield, high fenders and curved chrome bars over the dashboard radio, for my salesman-father was a typical, fifteen-hour long haul. But for old-times' sake he'd break journey in Detroit Lakes, he said. Detroit Lakes, in northern Minnesota, was where they'd honeymooned in 1939. Up there in the headwaters of the Mississippi is where I was conceived, I suppose. I was born in Fargo, North Dakota, in 1940. Along with Roger Maris and William Gass and Larry Woiwode. In that *Ragtime* spirit that haunts us all, I sometimes think of my mother pushing the pram, of Mrs. Woiwode pushing hers, of little Roger Maris, then six, dashing past us, bat on shoulder. Billy Gass, a bifocular teen-ager, squints a moment at these figures of life, then returns to the ice castle of his imagination. "The Pedersen Kid" crystallizing even then. *Beyond the Bedroom Wall* gurgles in his stroller. Babe Ruth's assassin takes a few mean cuts. I am the only Canadian writer born in Fargo, North Dakota.

There is nothing obscure, really, about Fargo. In 1977, at a cocktail party in New Delhi, India, I found myself talking to an agreeable, white-haired American with a professional manner, the U.S. Agricultural attaché. My India-born wife was serving that year as the director of a Canadian academic-exchange program. She was a quasi - diplomat.

"I consider myself half a Canadian, really," he said.

"I'm more than half American myself," I replied.

We shared a smile, wondering who would explain himself first. "I was born in North Dakota," I said. Then, covering my tracks, I added, "My parents had just emigrated."

"I was about to say almost the same thing. Where in North Dakota? "

"Fargo."

"Amazing."

He was the first North Dakotan I had ever met. "What year would that have been," he asked. "Forty, forty-one?"

"April, 1940."

"I was just finishing my M.A. at North Dakota State that spring. My wife was an O.B. nurse."

Parallel lives were beginning to converge, as though a collision course, plotted by children on separate planets, had suddenly become inevitable. We said together, "St. John's Hospital."

I added, "Dr. Hanna."

He called his wife over. As she put her drink down and turned to join us, he said, "How would you like to meet the first person you ever saw?"

We always returned to Winnipeg whenever my father ran out of work. Or when unmentionable things occurred. We had left Pittsburgh in 1945, Cincinnati in 1943, Fargo in 1942, and—a week before—Leesburg, Florida. Everytime we left, we headed back to Winnipeg, my mother's city.

My father was from the village of Lac Megantic, a few mountain ridges north of Maine, directly south of Quebec City. Winnipeg must have been a torture to him. I remember him, slicing luncheon meats in an upstairs bedroom in my grandmother's house, sipping beer and smoking Canadian cigarettes whose cork-tips inflamed his lips, next to a leaking window; he never spoke of his dislikes. He never warned us. He merely acted without apology. He was probably not entirely sane.

Once in Pittsburgh, in an outburst that still lies blottered somewhere, he'd discovered a fellow-salesman sneaking back to the floor just minutes after ducking out for lunch. While my father supposedly ate—he had a weakness for restaurants, for sitting at a table and being served, a leisurely lunch bespoke respectability—the other salesman let himself out of the men's room cubicle, where he'd downed a sandwich, and let himself back on the floor. He'd intended a clear hour to himself, writing up every sale and crediting himself with every commission. Even customers who "belonged" by earlier effort to my father. The rules dictate full credit to the lone name on the final bill. It discourages lunch-hours, among other things.

My father was hiding in the other cubicle. He came back and found the scab writing up one of his juicier sales. My father, even at his most sociopathic, could be a charming man. I came to fear those eruptions of charm. Frenchmen, as Quebeckers of his generation were usually called ("Hey, Frenchie!") are often very charming. Especially to Americans. My father looked more Jewish than French, more gypsy than Jew. He spoke furniture-yiddish and ring-Italian. I am his genetic miscue. Though always impeccably dressed—his code was as inflexible as an autodidact's stiff vocabulary—he appears to me now, two years dead, in a bandana and earrings, a billowing black shirt and dark, baggy pants, tucked into his greasy boots. There should be a tribe, somewhere, that combines all his somber talents.

My father possessed—or, rather, it possessed him—a murderous temper. He had pounded out twenty victories in three weight-divisions, in two countries, under various names that served him like flaps of convenience, until finally being hammered himself by an eventual champion. Thereafter he'd confined his skills to Canada's most successful export industry, helping assure the delivery of Montreal's finest whiskey to parched, Prohibition-dry New York. I learned all this later from his last wife, a cautious woman with police connections in Pittsfield, Massachusetts. She'd had his record routinely checked, after marrying him and growing suspicious. Fifty years ago, or longer now, he'd "been known" to every policeforce between Troy and Burlington. No gesture in the universe is ever lost. They never pinned murder on him, but there had been assault and manslaughter and even an accessory charge, later dropped. He was in the hospital by then, bounced between surgery and intensive care; legs gone, lungs clotted, a face reduced to that sloping nose and fleshy, slightly-folded ears.

The charm and the sledge-hammer. It is 1945, a year I cannot believe I've lived through. We are on the fifth floor of the Pittsburgh Sears, during the putative lunch-break of two very hungry salesmen. My father called his colleague over. He asked him to bring the order book. He smiled so graciously at the customers, his customers from a missed supper the night before, that they were reassured. *No, no*, he grinned, *quite all right*.

The order book was long and narrow and thick. Gripped at its bound end and then snapped against a flat object, it emitted a sharp, satisfying crack, like a solid jab or a clean base hit. The flat, astonished cheek of the salesman was such a surface and my father tattooed each cheek as though they'd been the alternate sides of a small punching bag, until, even with slaps, a cheek like a leather bag can gradually unravel .

That finished him with Sears and, for a while, banished him from the States. We crossed into Canada at Niagara Falls that midnight and were in Winnipeg three days later. That was the earlier time, 1945. Canada was still at War, the same war that (I was told) had sent us to North Dakota in

1939. Canada, part of Britain's war effort, would be on the front lines as soon as the Luftwaffe finished mopping up. German U-Boats already controlled the Gulf of St. Lawrence. The French islands of St. Pierre and Miguelon, off the coast of Newfoundland, were rebelling against the Vichy regime; no one knew how long that would last, a fog-bound Casablanca. Newfoundland and Labrador, British crown colonies and still ten years away from joining Canada, would of course be ceded to the Nazis, just like the Channel Islands. The Frenchies in Quebec refused to fight an English War; Adrien Arcand and his brownshirts were poised for a *putsch*, whenever Hitler ordered it. Which left Ontario, in 1939 and '40, feeling itself in the probable front-line of combat, with Lindbergh-style collaborationists controlling the States, the *Bunds* of Buffalo stirring up border-hate. I'd never been in a War. In Pittsburgh of 1945, I didn't feel part of a War, not like Winnipeg.

My father, a French-Canadian, never even considered fighting an English war. By his lights, justly so. He was barely over-age for the American draft. Brawny, steel-making Pittsburgh had been a good place for a salesman to sit out the hostilities. But for that unprincipled salesman and my father's temper, we might have stayed; no gesture in the universe escapes consequence.

This is my first memory: the soldiers at Canadian customs, their jaunty berets. The smell of a different tobacco in the air. My uncle in his Colonel's khaki, the Passchendaele medals on his chest, smoking thick pieces of glass for me and my cousins. The scientists of the free world had gathered in Winnipeg in 1945 for a spectacular view of a solar eclipse. I remember my twin cousins, limber girls of eight, doing backward flips all around my grandmother's house.

II

For most Canadians the differences between their country and the United States are minimal. The majority of English-speaking Canadians cross the border without papers, taking their places in the United States (we like to think) as nobler sorts of Americans. More respectful, less bumptious, better educated. Lofty types, a touch disdainful; Galbreaths all. We queue up, we don't litter. Compare any large Canadian city with an American counterpart: the difference is obvious and public pride is deeply layered. If we saw anything drop from a car window, or onto the sidewalk, my mother would mutter, "Americans!" There is something to it. Most public facilities in the United States resemble relics from a combat zone. It's hard for Canadians to avoid a little smugness, even those who emigrate.

But there is another kind of Canadian; smaller in number but infinitely richer in influence, who pounces upon every distinction, magnifies it and cherishes the disparity. It might be said that he keeps alive a certain Confederation Flame, for without his voice, Canada would certainly yield to profit and convenience and become, officially, a clean and prosperous corner of the United States. It might be said they are the reason Canada was created and the reason it still exists: to draw fine distinctions, to show that individual liberty and the pursuit of happiness is not the only reason for existing as a nation. To many Canadians, the American is a person who doesn't hesitate shooting a stranger for running over his lawn, for honking at a red light. These Canadians prefer their quiet, more authoritarian country, the sovereignty of parliament and not the litigious individual. They read Canadian magazines and sometimes British, they go only to movies listed as "Canadian or Foreign"; thus acknowledging the peculiar status of things American, they watch (and listen) exclusively to the CBC. Mention "the States" to them and you might pull a blank. "I was in Fargo once," a cousin might say. "Small town. Ugly."

"New York? God, no thanks. You can get killed there."

The only Canadians I know who genuinely like the United States are of course the French-speakers. And for good reason. The French-Canadian, when he leaves home on this continent, is tolerated only in the United States. In Toronto, I have heard the familiar retort, "Speak White!" I've seen my (one-time) fellow Torontonians demand of young Quebec tourists, chatting away on the immaculate Toronto subway, to *please* remember where they are; that so much jabbering in French is giving everyone a headache and no matter what Trudeau is trying to do to the country it won't work because it was settled when Wolfe defeated Montcalm and affirmed when they hanged Louis Riel and they ought to hang Rene Levesque too. On Prince Edward Island, in a tourist home modelled on Anne of Green Gables, the landlady, in showing us our rooms and remarking on my Quebec license plates (but not on my French name) confided in me, "the white man built this country! What are the French trying to do?"

At Old Orchard Beach, *l'etat Maine*, or in many parts of south Florida, America has capitulated to the French fact. Commercial greed, a tradition of tolerance, or simple confidence conspire to make French a conquering language. And all winter long, the tanned Quebecois flock back to Dorval Airport in the most outrageous motley of straw hats and Palm Beach T-shirts, straw bags stuffed with grapefruit. The last Americans. Levesque said as much, appealing to Americans for support: I am the George Washington of my people. I hear more *joual* on the streets of New York than in Toronto.

When my father quit the liquor-escorting business, after deserting his first two wives, he found himself in depression-cold Montreal, thirty-seven, unskilled though not untalented. He'd always sold things, apart from special services, and now he offered his salesmanship to the T. Eaton Company, then considered the world's largest department store. Montreal was Canada's most important city. If wealth had been preserved in those desperate years, it was to be found in the English community of Montreal, a minority of the population with a corner on nearly all its commercial holdings.

My father spoke good English. After all, he'd been up and down the Hudson Valley both as a fighter and as a smuggler and most of his family, by this time, had settled in Manchester, New Hampshire and Fall River, Massachusetts. It was fluent English, the way Trudeau's and Levesque's is fluent, but it was different from his French. A little coarser, with damns and hells when he didn't need them, and other words inappropriate to their context. In English he could be emphatic but not always convincing. At the same time, his childhood and adolescent French had deserted him. He had underworld French, but in truth he had no language, no voice; only expletives. It came as a shock to me, towards the very end of his life, when in a wheelchair he visited us in Paris and confided, "If I went back to Montreal I could speak French again. A couple of months and I could speak it as good as you."

The point is this. First, by unstated rules, and then by directive, he was not permitted to serve English-speaking customers. For him, it would be the priests and nuns, the spinsters with anglicized taste, the maids and charladies of Cote-des-Neiges and Westmount wealth. Whenever the blustery, regimental sorts with their Great War medals still on their blazer pockets came in, my father was instructed to call Mr. Fraser to come over and help, and eventually, write up the sale. I enter this story only because of the interior decorator, to whom he once complained, spoke to the manager. She seemed to be a fair-minded woman, educated, European-trained, and from the West. In 1939 she became his third wife, and they headed off to Winnipeg, and from Winnipeg my father wrote letters and Sears of Fargo gave him a chance. They went to Detroit Lakes to celebrate.

My first long exposure to Canada took place ten years later, following one of my father's failures in the southern part of the United States. Oh, I know what drives a Canadian, especially a French-speaking one, farther and farther south, until he can go no further! Warmth. Heat. *Look, Son, how it shimmers!* Light as thick as syrup bouncing off our car. Seat leather that sizzles. *Ouch* ! my mother cried. Oh, give me a home where the highway ahead looks wet twelve months a year! He was made for swimming trunks: a dark man with an hourglass build who could sleep all day in the sun and glow like walnut at night. Mosquitoes found him unappealing. Women did not. There were so many I lost count, once I learned how to measure them. The only truth I have to go on is that *any* woman he talked to outside of the strictest necessity: any waitress, any bank-teller, any secretary, any neighbor—any woman whose first name he knew (or denied knowing)—was also his part-time companion. Otherwise, he avoided women all together. What could he possibly talk about?

We'd driven up from Florida. Those clustered signposts served us well: *Atlanta 605. New Orleans 590.* We were tearing around America, rolling double-sixes around the old Monopoly board. One day for Florida, another for Georgia. Then they came fast: Tennessee, Kentucky, Indiana, Illinois, and before the half-week was out, that sign in Beloit: *Winnipeg 945.* We were in the green and watery states now, in the lee of Canada: Wisconsin and Minnesota. We were in Fargo for an afternoon and I wandered down the main street of my, and Roger's hometown. He was fifteen now; prime for scouting. We drove past the house we'd lived in, that spring of 1940: Fifth Street, S. E.

They identified the next door neighbor's house for me; we knocked but no one was home. Their name was Hinckle. Mr. Hinckle, back in the summer and fall of 1940, had loved to hold me (my father did not); the only infant-pictures I have were taken by Mr. Hinckle, or by his wife while I was in his arms. A great many years later, in 1973, I published a book of short stories in Canada which, by luck, was reviewed in the Minneapolis *Tribune*. A line in the review moved me, and I repeat it here: "by opening himself to us, he makes it possible for us to better know ourselves." And a few weeks later I received, forwarded by my publisher, a letter from a nursing home in St. Paul, from Mrs. Hinckle, writing in a firm hand, asking if I had possibly been born in Fargo in 1940. She'd never had children, but she'd always thought herself a mother to me. Mr. Hinckle would have been so happy to read this marvelous review. It was in one of those stories that I had written, *no gesture in the universe is ever lost*, in a context that I had tried to make absurd. Now I know that it is the core of all my beliefs.

III

That afternoon in Fargo as I walked on Fifth Street, S.E., feeling attached to the concrete that had possibly supported my pram and to the trees that had, years earlier, bloomed in Mrs. Hinckle's lens, a car slowed down and a window unrolled. Those were Manitoba windows, with their inside sheets of frost-free plastic, and I responded to them as emblems of an even earlier, purer hometown than Fargo. Winnipeg was where all my mother's memories came to rest, where my grandparents and all my relatives lived, and it being only five hours away, it was the city where I would be spending that night and, for all I knew, the rest of my life.

"Sonny?" the driver asked. A resonant, kindly, crinkly, northern voice. He had sandy hair and a reddish moustache. No Americans wore moustaches in those days, except cads and lovers in Hollywood movies. Thirty years ago, Canadians really looked and sounded different, surrogates of Britain, even in border-state situations. (I realize now that *of course*, especially in border confrontations with the United States, Canadians enjoy their only dominance: the might of Vancouver, Calgary, Winnipeg, Toronto and Montreal, exerted against the puny, unpeopled northern fringes of Washington, Montana, North Dakota, and upstate New England. The only exceptions were Detroit and Buffalo, and even there Canadians felt a moral smugness.) I knew which side of this particular border I belonged on.

"Sonny?"

"Yessir?" I answered, still the obedient, drawling Southern boy.

"You from around here?"

Judging from the way my cousins were about to receive me, pretending (I thought) not to understand a word I said, I must have answered, "*Ah wuz boned raht cheach* ."

"Then pardon my French but where the Hell is the Moorhead Bridge?"

Moorhead, Minnesota, faces Fargo from across the Red River. My mother had had her first labor pains on that bridge, where she walked every day. She'd made it sound (as she always did, in all her stories) an exciting chase, which side got an agent to her first. I'd felt myself competed for: the underpopulated hunger of North Dakota against the progressive Sky Blue Waters of Minnesota. A North Dakota birth was just right for me: manageably modest, yet special. Minnesota was too important, too American, it mattered too much in the American scheme of things. If I had to be born an American, let it be North Dakota.

And then it just spilled out. "Y'all lookin for St. Boniface, aincha?"

The driver's head sort of rested, rolling slightly, on the edge of the window, unable to compute, precisely, what had just been heard. St. Boniface was the French-speaking twin city of Winnipeg, just across this same Red River. The river only divided states in America; in Canada it symbolized infinitely more. My cousins in Winnipeg had never crossed the river except to skim far eastward, into the fishing waters of the Whiteshell, near Kenora. Whenever my father visited Winnipeg, he found many reasons to go over to St. Boniface and he often took me with him. Winnipeg was that kind of city to me; a macrocosm of my family, a microcosm of the country, achingly close yet out of reach from the town of my birth.

"Did you *hear* that?" the man was asking, turning to his wife and elderly passengers in the back seat. I heard *St.Boniface* and snorts of laughter. "Yes, son. How do I get to your *St. Boniface?*" Of course I didn't have the slightest notion. If we were on Fifth, I reasoned, the numbers probably got smaller as they approached the water. My own street ran slightly downhill; I pointed the car straight ahead. My parents came along shortly. We drove down the main street, visited Sears—the agent of our Americanization—and then we were gone again, following the river north to Grand Forks, and eventually, Pembina, the border, and Emerson, where Canada started. Like many children, I suppose, I held my breath till we crossed the border and inhaled deeply of Canadian air, convinced it was something purer than the stuff I'd just expelled.

Of all the distinctions I have invented in my life (and come to believe in, with the force of myth), the differences between Canada and the United States—so frail in reality, so inconsequential in the consciousness of America or the world or even most Canadians—is still my last, my most important illusion. It matters, or it mattered until very recently, that a border exists. That people so similar should be formed in different ways. That because I inherited those differences, I should have something special to say on both sides of the border. Through my childhood and adolescence and well into my adulthood, to the ragged fringe of middle age, the faith in a Canada being of a different order of history, experience and humanity, granted me an identity. It was never easy to claim it, but I never doubted it was there, and that I belonged to it. And because of having an identity there, it seemed that I had a prior understanding of Canadian temperament. My humor was Canadian humor. Even with an absurd, rural Florida accent, things I said in Canada, to Canadians, were invariably appreciated, understood on several levels, inflated beyond my own understanding. Canada cultivated an unused part of me that America had never touched. The significant blob of otherness in my life has always been Canada; it sits like a helmet over the United States, but I was the only person who felt its weight.

North, North, North: that glorious direction. The provincial bison-shield of Manitoba, the narrow highway that cut through the wheatfields on the left and the French-speaking hamlets along the river on our right, their lone church-steeples gleaming (to my mother's disgust) higher than the bluffs that hid the rest of the town, and seeming even taller than the wheat elevators that stretched westward, each of them announcing a calloused, sun-reddened Protestant town. And then, the highway divided, trolley tracks appeared, and we were in Winnipeg.

I think often of the compass points. Like the arrow-clusters at cramped country crossroads, the cardinal directions all move me; I dream restless dreams of that *setting out* feeling, of entering a highway for what you know to be a long drive, and reading that first, firm, challenge to the continent. *East*. And I would see fishing boats and a pounding rocky surf and the great cities and I would think (in my southern, and mid-western days) *yes*, that's the best direction. East for me. Culture, history, people, excitement, sophistication. But then, on my only trip to California, undertaken with a group of high school seniors from Pittsburgh, I thrilled to those days of unbroken signposts: *West, West, West*, and even when the land was flat or Appalachian-rolling, I'd be thinking of buttes and mesas and sawtooth mountains and I'd think of getting properly lost in all that space, and feeling free. Well, this was *North* : this was just about as far North as anyone could imagine: watery and glistening and cold, as though the sign itself should be read under a stream of icy water; I think of North and I think of Hamm's Beer and Land o'Lakes butter and of the lakes and pure forests of the Canadian shield, that area that stops just a few hours east of Winnipeg, where town names again turn French and people along the highway are unmistakably Indian. Most of my life has been spent on the southern fringes of the shield and though my opinion of its charms has changed—it is time again for heat—it is still the direction that defines me. North. Northern. I like the northern winter not because of sportiness in me or delight in the bracing qualities of a stern climate, but merely for its obliging me to stay indoors. North gives justification for the torpid side of my personality (that I'm on best terms with) to take over.

I think that is why SOUTH has no charm for me at all; it is the only cardinal point that fails to conjure an unreal, dreamlike essence of itself. When I think of the north Florida and south Georgia I knew, I remember only walls of leggy pine with slash marks on their trunks, hung with resin buckets, and I remember the Coke machines in country gas stations where for a nickel I could lift a heavy metal lid (I can remember the first whiff of that cold, moist air, I remember the pleasure of trailing my fingers in that iced water), spot a bottle cap in one of the metal tracks and glide it along to the spring-catch my nickel had released. And I can remember draining those stubby little Coke bottles with their raised, roughened letters on the side, always checking the bottom to see where it had been bottled, how far it had come, though nearly all were good ol' bottles from Plant City and Orlando. Well, all I remember of *South* is sand and heat and thirst and skies and the color of sweaty undershirts, spotted with buzzards.

IV

On Wolseley Drive in Winnipeg, on the banks of the Assiniboine, my grandparents had their house. Three houses away, my aunt and uncle had an even larger home, with a basement full of hunting rifles, decoys, canoes and kayaks, and a special room for a billiards table. Since my uncle was in those days a writer and commercial artist as well as president of the Wheat Pool—and was soon to become Winnipeg's best-known television personality—and my aunt was a broadcaster, they had studios and libraries on their second floor. The third floor held guest rooms and an attic full of bundled magazines going back to the beginnings of *National Geographic* and *Readers' Digest*, as well as the splashy American weeklies like *Life* and *Saturday Evening Post*. They kept the hunting and fishing magazines, and everything Canadian, particularly everything relating to the Prairies and especially Manitoba. Nothing important had ever been thrown out. The house was virtually a computer, although means of retrieval were still a little primitive.

That house, and their lives, represented something to me called Canada, that was more than merely attractive; it was compelling. In the various towns and cities of my first ten years, we had always lived in small apartments carved out of old servants' quarters, on the fringe of other people's families, and we always seemed to be sharing some vital function of other people's lives. Kitchens, bathrooms, entrances, hallways, washing facilities. Maybe that's why, in years to come when we finally rented our own duplexes, my father celebrated by roaming around in his boxer shorts all day Sunday and from the moment he returned home. I used to wonder about that. In my favorite TV show, "Father Knows Best", Robert Young ("Jim Anderson") always came home in a suit and changed to an elbow-patched tweed or corduroy jacket. Whatever it was, Canada, by virtue of its cool, English houses and its politeness and its streetcars and its formalities and its formidable understanding of everything going on in the world, as well as in the city, was a more interesting place to live than America. It was certainly more complicated, with French instructions running down the sides and backs of every food package. My parents had moved back to Canada at a time when its differences from the United States were unforced but extreme; whatever seemed foreign to me on a perceptual level was nevertheless perfectly comprehensible on a level of precognition. Or, to put it in the terms I would later live by, Canada was a novel that others found dull and difficult, but that I found interesting and accessible from the beginning. You could say that my life was a dissertation on the subject of Canada and the United States, and what it is like, being a part of both.

I visited my aunt and uncle every day and shot pool in the basement by myself or with my cousin. My parents and I stayed at my grandmother's, and between the houses and the school, I became a Canadian.

My grandmother was a classic of the grandmother type; too old to have a life of her own, but young enough to manage the lives of several others. She was small but sturdy, she had wit and a deadpan delivery that was the first to ever "get me going" as she put it—the first person subtler than my comprehension. She had taken up driving and a wee bit of smoking and drinking (the sign of an amateur in these matters: she kept her cigarettes loose in an old sugarbowl in the kitchen cupboard, and she would smoke a cigarette only at predictable times of the morning and evening and when the dough was rising after a first good punch-down).

My grandfather, when awake, was the focus of our awareness, though not of our attention. While he was up, we all kept an eye on him. He was classically senile: a bald, tall, stooped old patriarch, a one-time doctor, a breeder of flowers and fruit trees and an importer of draft horses, the consolidator of an insurance group—a man of great substance in Western Canada. Up on the second floor, in the room occupied by my parents and me, I would read the volumes of *Who's Who in Western Canada* that told my grandfather's tale ("The Luther Burbank of Canada"), and I never tired of reading the biographies of him in the Canadian *Readers' Digest*, the *Who's Who* and all the profiles in the various medical and insurance journals. Canada's best-known novelist of that time and place, Frederick Philip Grove, had even based a novel on him. From those biographies I learned the name of the various prize-winning peaches and apples he'd introduced, the prize-winning horses he'd bred and I learned to feel a touch of family pride whenever we passed an office of the Wawanesa Mutual, the insurance company he had headed. *Everyone* in Winnipeg seemed to be famous, all of my relatives had wealth and power and visibility; casual visitors to my uncle's house turned out to be cabinet ministers, American governors, authors. When I walked down the street with my aunt or uncle, people stopped and often turned around to watch as they walked by. After the bruised, violent, anonymous lives we'd lived in those mildewed Southern towns, Winnipeg was like a jolt of pure, cold oxygen, the only place left in the world that conformed to the notions of reality I'd gotten from reading and from my own intense imagining.

At the age of seventy-five, my grandfather was merely a disturbing presence. He was strong and stern and he kept himself busy through a ten-hour workday in his old study and sometimes in the living room, underlining every sentence in every book and magazine in the house. He did not know his name, or that of his wife and daughters (he'd had nine daughters and one son, and all five of the survivors visited regularly except the son in Toronto, and my mother). His memory had deserted him while he was still in his early fifties, and as a doctor he'd recognized it— it had been his father's fate as well —and had gotten out of medicine, and cut back on the insurance. He'd retired, physically exhausted, with a heart condition. The insurance company had treated him generously. His faculties continued to fail. He was apparently alert enough, in 1940, when my mother brought me up from Fargo for my first visit, to feel the bumps on my head and declare, "Don't worry, Annie, this boy will never be a fighter." So far as I can determine, he never spoke to me, or of me, again.

His heart repaired itself, as it often does in bodies suddenly relieved of stress, and he had his work, the underlining of every word in the *Free Press* and *Tribune*, and all those stacks of magazines. That was my Canada and that was my grandfather's house: a place where everything was intact and even madness could be quietly accommodated. There was, in fact, only one thing that could not be housed, because he was not organically a part of it, and that was my father.

"See what *he* wants," my grandmother would ask, not unkindly. She was as afraid of giving offense as my father was; therefore they worked out elaborate systems of mutual avoidance. He rarely came downstairs. Whenever he did, an aroma of tobacco preceded him by at least a minute, and my grandfather would lay his pencil down, carefully marking his place in the work still before him, stand, and— high, quivering voice fierce with rage—order him out. "How dare you, sir, walk across my carpet with your dirty workman's boots? Out, Out, I say!" My father, in Winnipeg, never went outside in the winter, and was always in slippers. My grandfather was furious, muttering, "the cheek, the gall ! I will report this insolence to Stewart, don't think I won't!" That would be the sign for my mother, first, to interpose herself. "It's all right, daddy, he's Leo, your son-in-law." Stewart had been a stable-hand, imported from Scotland like all the Clydesdales. Now my grandfather was in a proper Victorian rage, throwing my mother aside, "I don't know why you're shielding him, Lillie, but I'm getting to the bottom of this. I won't rest—" by which time my father had sneaked back up the stairs, cursing to himself and my grandfather would be left standing, hands clenched, undecided over the next challenge. All the women in his life were "Lillie," my grandmother's name, except my grandmother, who was usually just "mother." After he died, at the age of eighty-two, my grandmother had her own few bad years, heaping invectives on her husband, not for those last twenty inglorious years, but for the years of his magnificent achievement, the *Who's Who* years. Who, or what, to believe? Even as I write this, my own mother is close to enacting the dramas of her parents, and as I reach back into these events of thirty years ago, I'm aware that truth is simply a matter of framing and reframing. I've chosen to believe certain versions, I've rejected others. I too was blessed with a gifted memory and I've worn it down by now to something dull and ordinary and I fear that the family disease awaits me.

When my grandfather's fists unclenched he'd go back to the chair and begin the assault on a new column of print.

The winter of 1950 was one of the snowiest in Winnipeg history. It would lead to a flood that is still remembered, to sandbags in my aunt's and grandmother's backyards, to those canoes and kayaks pushing off directly from the driveway and bringing relief a few blocks downstream. And, as the head of the Red Cross, it would be my aunt's finest hour: in the pictures we were sent (by that time we too had pushed off; they caught up with us in Cleveland, in a rooming house on Euclid Avenue), my aunt and uncle would be bundled in their parkas, under helmets with the Red Cross painted on the sides, and it would remind me of British Air Raid wardens. The pictures were grainy, black and white, some of them smeared from rainwater on the lenses (a beautiful, accidental effect; what would be its equivalent in language?). I should like that talent — to capture activity, strain, sleeplessness, peril, the direction of a thousand lives and millions of dollars, and the muddy, ice-choked river racing by the fixed point of my grandmother's backyard, tossing boulders of ice, houses, trucks, with the fury of a horizontal Niagara.

That would be the spring. Right now, it is still a hard, Siberian winter day. Winnipeg exists, paradoxically, by virtue of its relative mildness, its southern latitude. Southern only for Canada; America had abandoned any attempt to colonize the lands north of the Twin Cities. Winnipeg should not exist, except as an urban planner's act of defiance, an experiment on the heartless Russian model. But it does exist, as Edmonton exists, as Montreal exists, and the effects of that anomaly—the intense self-consciousness, the isolation, the pride, the shame and absurdity of carrying on normal life at forty below zero—creates a population that fills the studios and boardrooms and lecture halls of Canada with so much talent that old Winnipeggers form a kind of talent-Mafia in Toronto. Some drained south, the Monty Halls and David Steinbergs and Erving Goffmans, but most defied the dominant pulls of the continent and headed East. Winnipeg, meaning "muddy water," is built on one of the very few north-flowing rivers in North America. Maybe there's more of a social component to geology than we had ever suspected.

The people of the city are proud of their winters, proud of their simple survival. They were afraid of softness, at least in my mother's family, and they were constantly headed deeper North, as though to test themselves, as though Winnipeg represented some degenerate, sub-tropical fringe of sybaritic abandonment. My cousins began their kayaking at ten or so, portaging to rivers and lakes right to the shores of Hudson's Bay. They had a farm in the Sand Hills in the western part of the province, where they grew flax and ran trap lines, and in the fall I went with them— Florida child that I was then, accent and all—and learned to shoot at an early enough age to avoid the normal hesitancies and sentimentalities of the urban academic. I learned to hunt like a farmer, like a competitor and protector; I concentrated on gophers and red-winged blackbirds.

V

One Saturday deep in the winter of 1949-50, my grandmother asked me to go up to Portage Avenue to see Mr. McArdle and to bring back the meat-order, which she was phoning in. I was given directions to find the shop, but no money. From what I could see, no money ever entered or left my grandmother's house. Accounts were rendered, usually in person, by well-dressed men who waited in the parlor. Tea and biscuits would be served. My grandfather would be on good behavior, looking from face to face, following conversations, or so it seemed, laughing when others laughed. Sundays would bring visits of an elderly threesome of spinster sisters, "The Bonnycastle Girls," who dressed in sybillant black satins, who exuded the kinds of perfume associated with toilet waters and colognes, something closer to a "scent" than a "fragrance," like a liquified powder. They had visited my grandmother every Sunday for the past forty years, although no one (on our side, at least) was quite prepared to explain to me if they were friends from a different time and place, or relatives, or perhaps, inherited obligations, the weekly visit a form of interest on an unpayable capital. I joined the group enthusiastically, smiling and following faces much like my grandfather, until one day when I got too close and detected odors under the cologne and realized something disagreeable was being hidden; there was, in fact, no attempt being made to attract. I walked up Stiles to McArdle's. The street was packed with white-frame houses behind their deeply snowy yards. I am reminded now, in their winter settings, of a street like an occluded lower jaw, all the way up to Portage Avenue. One long block under the winter sun, in the winds of thirty-five below. "It's nippy outside. Bundle up. Don't tarry," said my grandmother.

I have seen most of the world's major cities by now, but Portage Avenue in the early Fifties remains for me something special, like a Russian movie, molded on a scale of epic tedium that nevertheless achieves a certain indifferent weight. If we could rid our minds of notions of charm and beauty and still be receptive to urban grandeur, then Portage Avenue, the east-west axis of Winnipeg and half the province of Manitoba, would stand as a model. It was conceived on a scale of spaciousness in keeping with the open fields and possibly in revenge for the two thousand miles of crabbed forest at its back. It was wide, straight, and flat, and down its middle in its own private *maidan* , rolled the endless herd of rumbling streetcars. Standing at Stiles, I could look a couple of miles to the west, the buildings showing not a single variation in height and not a single uniformity of design, and spot, *in embryo* as it were, the line of streetcars that would be passing me in the next half hour. Since no one could stand outside more than ten minutes anyway, it was most compassionate of the transport commission to flood the rails with more cars than any city had a right to expect. That was my Winnipeg; a city of prompt and endless convenience.

I presented my request to the aproned, blood-stained, gray-haired man with the scholarly glasses. "What would it be, now?" he asked, the voice foreign yet attractive to me, able to squeeze out twice as many words per second as my slow, hateful speech. I was working on reducing my accent, for I knew from overhearing my parents in their bed that we were finished in the South anyway. I hoped we'd never leave Winnipeg. I was getting more "ays" and fewer "uhs" into every line, though I still couldn't force myself into Canadian pronunciations of *zed* and *shedule*. Canadian spellings all looked right to me; "honour" seemed a graver concept with its extra vowel intact.

"I've come for the meat order," I said.

"I can see that."

"My grandmother called you."

He squinted. Obviously he was expected to know every child in his square mile. "And who might she be, now?"

I gave the name.

His face broke into a *Saturday Evening Post* cover of recognition. The bushy white eyebrows shot up, the rimless glasses slipped, the lips formed an "Oh!" and fell, arms outstretched, against his countertop, as though doing a cheating, standing push-up.

"Why, it's the wee bairn! Why dinja say, lad? You're the wee American bairn she's been talking about. What's your name again?"

"Clark ."

"Clar-r-r-k." he rolled the name like a large, succulent, chocolate-covered cherry. "Now isn't that fine! Clarrrk is music to my ears, it is."

It was a name I despised, and had paid for repeatedly in Southern schools. Clark Bars and Clark Kent and Clark Gable were the extent of my visibility in the American world, and to be named after any of them, as they all assumed I had, was an assault on the rituals of Southern dignity. I realize now that a name like Clark, in those years, was a tribal name— there were two Clarks (first names) and innumerable Clarkes (last name) in the school I now attended, including a teacher, and some of them conformed to my notion of what Clarks inevitably were like. Clarks in America had all been wounded, and they bore their wounds with minimal grace. In Canada they competed with Icelandics for places on the hockey team.

I was, however, even in Winnipeg, a little uneasy with my last name, which was clearly unique — Blais — and which added unpronouncibility to the earlier charge of exploitativeness. I couldn't understand why we didn't spell it "Blaze" since that was the way it usually came out, though I'd heard through my father that it was really an unpleasant little burp of a name, a little like "Bligh" and sometimes "Blay", so that there was no consistency to it, not even a spelling that conformed in any way to its sound. It didn't help matters that I couldn't pronounce my own name; it seemed a minimal expectation in one who took some pride in his academic achievements. My first name outweighed my second name, with its crispness and neat, hard bracketing of a single vowel with two of the most forceful consonant-clusters in the English language. That first name of mine was like an ice-cube; the last name was a head-cold. It had seemed to me, at eight and nine and ten, that the greatest mystery in the world, and the greatest potential for terror, were locked in the letters of my two names. I spent hours in my grandfather's old study, now a laundry room, using his old doctor's fountain pen-set and his old stacks of prescription pads, practicing signatures that would eliminate that last sound from my name.

"How is the old gentleman?" asked Mr. McArdle.

"Just fine."

"A bit of a handful now and then, I reckon. He likes to go for his strolls, y'know. In the summer, of course."

"He's fine."

"But a great man, in his time."

I deposited the "wee gift" that my grandmother had bundled for me: two thick slices of her fresh cracked-wheat bread, separated by waxed paper from a savory, crusty meat. These were unknown foods to me.

"Steak and kidney pie, ay, laddie?" In my previous life as a Southerner, carrying gifts to tradesmen was unthinkable (so was the idea of a special butchershop in those small Florida towns we'd inhabited; my mother had gone to the town's lone chain-store outlet, around back where the black people had their service-window opening onto the alley by the garbage cans, to ask for items that were our meat-staples but which were cat-food or "nigger food" down there— liver, kidneys, sweetbreads, and above all, tongue, her favorite, and my lunch-time sandwich, which could make my classmates retch as I bit into it).

"I have the order," he told me. "I was going to drop it off myself later on, when Cam comes in. My son, Campbell."

I nodded.

"How are your cousins? Fine lads. Clar-r-r-k's my name, too. Clarrrk McArrrdle. Clark's historically a MacArthur, you know. Like that Yankee general. The MacArthur tartan is one we can wear. What's your last name? I don't believe they ever told me."

I told him.

He frowned, screwed up his jolly old elf's face, as though preparing for some ultimate test of strength. But his voice came out muted, almost choked.

"You're an American lad, you say."

"Yes, sir."

"I've never in all my born days heard a name like that. You don't look a Chink. Are you sure you got it right?"

I told him it was my name as best I could pronounce it. He took it, as I half-intended, as approximating "Bligh."

"That's a very sorry name, if you ask me," he said. He stabbed at a piece of my grandmother's pie. "English to boot."

"No sir," I charged. "It's Canadian. French-Canadian, actually."

And here, in a butcher shop on Portage Avenue, I stepped ever so briefly behind the veil, out of the tribal tent, into the special solitude of Canadian life. The butcher's face was simply blank. It registered nothing; as though I'd not even come in or had not been seen. I had meant to say, *naw, it's not one of those foreign British things . . .* it's Canadian. My relatives maintained a discreet silence on things American, but for British institutions they manifested a keen dislike. Whenever the BBC news came on, every day at noon, beginning as it always did with an upper-class twit intoning news of the Royal Family, such as "The King today . . ." my cousin would pipe up, ". . . cut a long, wet one in the Royal Crapper," or some such; it was still an era when Canadian nationalists looked to America for a counter-weight to the British presence. And definitely I was not an American, if you could overlook my accent. I am grandma's boy, and the Old Gentleman's grandson, and I've come to take my place here, trading steak and kidney pie for a few hand-picked lobes of glistening calves' liver. And I can prove I belong; I've got a Canadian name. The only words I knew with "Canadian" in them had "French-" in front of them. It went with "Canadian" the way "early" and "All-" went with "American," as a completion, an intensification of an otherwise ungraspable concept.

"No one ever said that," said the butcher. He moved behind the counter as though the floor were spread with coals; he jabbed out liver from a porcelain tray with a normal dinner fork, and then let it slide off the fork onto waxed paper, with a look that hovered on disgust.

"Understand me, Master Clarrrk," he said. "I have nothing in the world against you parrsonally. But I canna abide the French, as a race. They should stay in St. Bonny and not go mucking with the white races. That's my final warrd on the subject." He wrapped the liver in a purplish, brown paper and tied it neatly with cords. "Good day, lad," he said. "My best to the old folks."

VI

Up on the second floor, in the bedroom we had converted to an apartment, with a hotplate for my father's coffee and a small skillet for my mother's eggs—the smoke-filled haven of my father—a small drama was being enacted that would alter all our lives. My mother had reactivated her old teacher's permit and was, by now, substituting on a near-daily basis in various parts of the city. I was in school, struggling to overcome the deficiencies of a rural Southern background; thanks to family connections, I was not routinely demoted two grades (as was the case with American transfers), and was managing, with after school tutoring, to make a successful transition to the world of ink and nibs, formulas, and long compositions. I was singing British folk songs instead of Military Service Hymns: no one sang "O Canada!" louder than I, every morning in the hall. And for the first time, I was enjoying my classmates. In Florida, students were to be tolerated or avoided while pursuing the fugitive pleasures of the text. Here, there was no schoolyard fighting, despite the tempting target I must have offered. The captains of the various team-sports—most of them imposing Icelandic boys with names like Thordarson and Thorlakson—would choose me first, simply because I was obviously the worst. Selections were made in ascending order of competence. They took time to teach me the unfamiliar games, British Bulldog and broom hockey, and would even stop the action if they saw I was too hopelessly out of place.

No one could have been more displaced than my father. He'd ask me when it was safe to go downstairs and to slip outside (this necessitated checking on my grandfather and enduring his scolding for having snuck into the house from "the stables"). Whenever I'm sitting on a bus these days and see a passenger still outside, devouring the stub of a cigarette and then filling his lungs with a final drag before stepping aboard—to let it out all over the bus—I think back to my father and the way he transformed that house into a Saturday night tavern simply by coming downstairs. My grandmother smoked her cigarettes with barely any smoke, let alone after-smell.

He had been going to St. Boniface, and to the furniture stores in the Jewish North End of Winnipeg, the parts of town rich in contacts for the life he knew. Like my mother, he had a transferable skill. He worked a few days, and decided things were too slow, too old-fashioned. He didn't know the Canadian furniture scene anymore, and the American brands, when carried, were far too expensive. Of course he didn't mention anything to us about working or about looking for other work. That wouldn't be his style.

One day after school I went upstairs to read old magazines and the *Who's Who*. My father was there (he rarely was), at his place by the window, looking out on the snowy roof, up Stiles Street to Portage, in the distance. On his knees was a letter. On the window ledge were some notebook pages he must have stolen from me. When he saw me, he folded the letter back in the envelope. I tried to show I wasn't interested, but a small suitcase on the bed was packed.

I went over to my cousin's to shoot pool. My grandfather was sleeping; my father would have no trouble. I couldn't imagine where we'd be going next, but *West*, I remember, excited me. I felt ready for it now.

I played pool till the phone rang. My aunt called me from the head of the stairs, "Clark, your mother."

No, I said, I hadn't seen him. I didn't know anything about it. She was crying. What can I *tell* them? she cried. I was looking for an apartment for us, she said. *We agreed; we'd try to settle down.*

He was gone, all right. Shirts, suits, shoes, and car: the salesman's clearing-out. My mother was already reframing it for her mother's and sister's sake: "Leo decided he could do better in the States. He's following a lead in . . . (I made it up: Denver) . . . Denver. He'll send for us when he locates an apartment." I even believed in Denver; I looked up a city-map and tried to memorize the grid. Years later, pursuing my own studies of another Franco-American whose life— given a different dominance in our family—I might have crossed, I again encountered those heroic late-forties and 1950 Denver streets of Neal Cassady and Jack Kerouac; madness to push this further, though a message to me seems to linger. Kerouac and Cassady were my father's world, the one he never escaped, and he died back inside it, in New Hampshire, as desolately as Kerouac had in his mother's house in Lowell. His father's name was Leo.

On the sheet of notebook paper, I found drafts of a letter to us that was never, finally, left. It said more or less what we expected; he'd gotten a lead, it looked good, and he trusted himself to make a better personal impression than he could in a letter mailed from Winnipeg. If he got it, we'd live better than we ever had. My mother, too, gazed out over the roof, down Stiles, at that one; no need to say the obvious.

She didn't notice the rest of the page, which wasn't a proper letter at all. It was a page of signatures. His signature. *Lee Blaise*, it said, up and down several rows. Then, Lee R. Blaise, up and down many more.

"Lee Blaise," I said to myself. Yes, Yes. Clark Blaise. It looked right. It balanced. It was anchored.

III
Writers

Yourcenar Composed

BY RICHARD HOWARD

In 1909, the possibility of electing a woman to membership in the Academie Française was for the first time discussed in serious, in plausible terms. Of course the notion of such an exploit had frequently occurred, in the crypto-feminism of the *belle époque*, to many men and to many women as well, but serious discussion could supervene only when adversaries and partisans could acknowledge an inevitable choice. If the police rubric was *cherchez la femme*, the literary motto was *choisessez-la*!

And in the first decade of the new century, such a choice appeared inevitable. If the Forty were ever to open their exalted ranks to a member of the sex, the poet Anna de Noailles (by no means forgotten in France today, where she figures prominently in the Proust Follies, but by no means a consensually admired *writer*) was surely the designated candidate: for the first third of this century it appeared beyond dispute that her poems of an *innumerable heart*, her diffusely sensuous novels, her memorial reflexions on an aristocratic and solitary adolescence (by birth a princess, by marriage a countess, by inclination a conversational imperialist), her essays in tribute to distinguished contemporaries with whom, as in the case of Maurice Barres, she had been notoriously intimate—all these productions seemed not only to warrant but to require elevation to what would be a no more than acknowledged Immortality. Discussion of the issue was indeed serious, yet the election did not occur, and as the years passed and the suffrage passed her by, the nature of the Countess's achievement appeared increasingly nugatory—the productions were found to be no more than effusions—the Countess breathed, she talked, she wrote: it was all quite natural. She was not so much an authority as that unwarrantable entity, a mere if memorable . . . authoress.

During the next seven decades, parallel or analogous qualifications were adduced to support the candidacy of Colette (who like Mme de Noailles and, in 1970 like Yourcenar herself, had already been inducted into the more gynophiliac Belgian Academy), of Simone de Beauvoir, of Nathalie Sarraute, even of Louise de Vilmorin; but it was Marguerite Yourcenar (born *de Crayencour*, a distinguished family name of northern France, which the young writer transformed into the curious anagram so characteristic of her self-invention in every department) who turned out to be the first woman inducted, in 1981, into this holiest and hoariest bastion of French literary and intellectual eminence, regarded for three hundred years as the ultimate redoubt of masculine privilege, though she was shortly and shadowily followed there by the classical scholar Jacqueline de Romilly. No women have subsequently been elected to membership.

Like that of the Countess de Noailles, Marguerite Yourcenar's standing is not uncontested. She is, indeed, one of those French writers whose authentic distinction is frequently indiscernible to anglophone readers dependent upon translation for a fair representation of literary authority. And here is one of the indications of our modernity, and the difference it makes in our apprehension; for whereas Goethe had famously—and to us, almost incredibly—declared to Eckermann that the crucial virtues and values of any writer are inveterately apparent in translation, it is Robert Frost who gains *our* credence by quite as famously remarking that the poetry is just what is lost in translation. Since I myself have translated into English Yourcenar's first volume of discursive prose, I am evidently in no position to decide the issue either way, but I should like to loiter over the *invidium* of this author's remarkable case—over, that is, the reluctance of many American readers to acknowledge her *grandeur* (or perhaps it is just *grandeur* and only *grandeur* they *will* acknowledge, the kind of ceremonial distinction that got the lady into the Academy in the first place).

Perhaps some analysis of our frequently noted recalcitrance with regard to Yourcenar will convince us of more than merely her own virtues or vitiations—perhaps by some consideration of this kind of problematic fame (even more problematic than the erstwhile celebrity of Mme de Noailles, whose fall from a widely acknowledged salon vogue was no more than a matter, like that of Edmond Rostand, of a waning period manner) I can identify the difficulty some of us have with a writer so evidently comfortable with being *official*; perhaps by breathing on it a little I can clear the lens through which we regard (or are prevented from regarding) literary stature beyond provincial applications of celebrity and neglect, of sanction and subversion.

Well then; now that the froth is out of the bottle ... In this country Yourcenar's most widely praised, indeed most nearly popular achievement is a sort of historical novel, *Memoirs of Hadrian* (1951), purporting to be that emperor's recollections bequeathed as a sort of experiential enchiridion to the nephew who was to become Marcus Aurelius; learned and lapidary though it is, this text is often compared—in merit as in accessibility—to the explicitly "entertaining" *Claudius* books by Robert Graves and to Thornton Wilder's *Ides of March*, though as a marker of popularity it might be noted that two of Yourcenar's many other fictions, one antecedent, one subsequent to *Hadrian's Memoirs*, have been made into interesting films, always a register of a writer's vitality in our era. Yet even *Hadrian's Memoirs*, a quasi best-seller translated into 25 languages and, more significantly, still in print in most of them over 40 years later, has its detractors, who in this instance as in so many other productions of her *oeuvre*, find the classicizing prose ponderous, the historicizing psychology portentous, and the homosexual preoccupations pestilential.

They are wrong, I believe, but it is certainly evident that the virtues of Yourcenar's finest books (there are many virtues and many books— novels, tales, poems, essays, plays, translations, autobiographies) have been realized, so to speak, not by plethoric talent and overwhelming appeal, but by pervasive and strenuous effort, by a sometimes rebarbative concentration of will, an application perceived to operate against the very grain of a demanding, even a distressing temperament. Yourcenar is a writer who has composed her career as carefully as any of the works which constitute it; she has revised, rejected, and revived various components of the *oeuvre* until they have established, to her by no means concealed satisfaction, an harmonious image of impulses which were once entertained on entirely different, and latterly despised, premises.

We tend to call such writers "conflicted," and it is they who constitute the subjects of engrossing biographies, even when their careers are apparently serene in terms of incident, for there is a constant agon in the life as in the work, an evidenced struggle to emerge from mere authorship into some kind of apprehended peace, an Olympian perspective granted by the structure of the collected works, an ultimate poetry, so to speak, of reappraisal. There is not a moment of humor in the trajectory formed by such insistant reassessment, and no more than a modicum of grace, but there is passion, and wisdom, and, against all odds, truth to the demands of art.

In the interests of a different truth, a truth to the demands of life, Yourcenar's biographers and critics have often been obliged to contradict, even to upbraid their subject; they have found it necessary to remark such chinks in the ostentatiously donned intellectual armor as her youthful efforts at versification, so reminiscent of George Eliot's clumsy poems (though Yourcenar's later translations of classical and demotic Greek and of American poetry and African-American spirituals into French verse and French prose are another thing: hers was the gift to learn from her mistakes, or rather from her *maladresse*), or to deprecate her improbable musicianship in those insipid essays on Mozart or on Beethoven which resemble nothing so much as the mundanities of Mme Verdurin—or of Mme de Noailles; these are the readily remarked liabilities of a writer determined to present herself as totally equipped to contend with—indeed to overcome—all the challenges of culture. Moreover, in the seven years since Yourcenar's death, we have been made aware of the damages done to her own character and to the confidence of her intimates, the blows dealt out, round an embattled figure, by a felt need to present herself not sympathetically but heroically (as in the case of Katherine Anne Porter, whose biographers have similarly revelled in their discovery of like discrepancies between the velvet glove and the iron fist)—the need, in short, to produce an image of triumphant prowess.

I once had in my hands a copy of Miss Porter's collected stories which belonged to her friend Donald Windham. In the blank spaces between the end of one story and the beginning of the next, as a kind of exultant gloss, Katherine Anne Porter had written brief accounts not of the anecdotal genesis of her fictions, but of how long it took to create, say, *Noon Wine* or *Pale Horse, Pale Rider*. "I wrote *Flowering Judas* early one morning in 1937"—that kind of thing. If we were to believe her (and of course we are not), none of the famous tales was the work of more than a few hours. In Yourcenar we discover a similar, or perhaps a converse impulse, for the desire to heroize the *made thing*—the fiction, the poem, both words mean the same—applies not, as in the American author's case, to a virtually clandestine instancing of the claims of spontaneity, of creative immediacy, but rather to a mythology of will, arduous, extended, and not inscribed somewhere in the margins but printed on the back of every copy, an indication that what had been published initially was merely a trial run, a rescindable enterprise, not to be regarded as part of the final design, the ultimate structure.

Indeed, when I first began reading Yourcenar in 1953, I was struck by the fact that most of the works she had written before 1940 were no longer in print and apparently not to be reprinted *as such,* for even if they were not being rewritten, reconceived, ultimately replaced, the important thing for this author's readers to know was that certain works had once existed, though they were no longer to be laid hold of. For instance her first fiction *Alexis*, published in 1929 when she was 26, was not reprinted in what Yourcenar would regard as its final form for 35 years. It was merely indicated, on all her subsequent books, as *épuisé*. The little novel affords proof of remarkable talents which required this kind of ripening into significance through a shadowy life of repudiation, a patient career in correctability. "The Treatise of Futile Combat," as it is subtitled in the French edition, concerns a young man's attempt to achieve self-awareness, and thereby self-acceptance, and thereby self-fulfillment. His discovery of sexual tastes which Alexis, an impoverished central European of noble stock, regards as unacceptably fixed on "beauty," decisively thwarts this 19th-century life, in which marriage and paternity fail to mend matters, and only art—musical composition, as it somewhat vaguely turns out—succeeds in releasing Alexis from his bad faith. The work assumes the form of a confession, a long letter to the wife he is "abandoning," and it concludes on a devastated note of triumph: "With the utmost humility I ask you now to forgive me, not for leaving you, but for having stayed so long."

Choosing for what she calls her "portrait of a voice" the tonality of the classical French moralists, the young author secured for herself, as ventriloquist, the possibility of a unity of tone exceptional in a beginner, and also the possibility of an aphoristic glamor which might compensate for a certain meagerness of incident. Not even *The Princess of Cleves* or *Adolphe* strews each page, each paragraph, with so many lustrous nuggets, so many neat lucidities. In the "definitive" preface of 1965 (which rather condescendingly dilutes what she had written for the second French edition of 1952, so that "for readers who may have forgotten Virgil" becomes "for those who may have forgotten the Latin of their schooldays") Yourcenar denies the influence of Gide's "great books" but acknowledges certain filiations with the author of *Corydon* and indeed devises formal parallels with the speaker of *The Immoralist*, whose confession antedates that of Alexis by some quarter of a century. Like Gide's Michel as he wrenches himself away from his wife Marceline in that celebrated breviary of estrangement (similarly unknown in its first edition to the public at large, but later to become a sort of classic), Alexis prompts his reader, even prompts his creator, to wonder about his wife Monique's possible response to such defection. "But for now," Yourcenar reports in her preface, "I have abandoned that project. Nothing is more secret than a woman's existence."

Uninterrupted, then, by any conflicting utterance—precisely in the manner of all those early Gidean "treatises"—Alexis tells his own story with the mild fluency of the 18th-century *maximistes*. Thereby he cuts down the blood-supply to the brain and instead maximizes, in another sense, a more general application of this cautionary tale. Given the stipulations of her chosen vocabulary and of the period taste to which she was admittedly appealing, Yourcenar could not use the word *homosexual*, or any of the rest of that technical vocabulary for "aberrations of the senses," as she observes they were called at the time: invert, pederast, pervert, uranist. Hence there is, for the reader, a certain mystification in all this "futile combat," without any very vivid apprehension of what it is that Alexis eventually surrenders to. Dostoievsky would not so leave us, as the French say, on our hunger.

Yet even granting a specifically *pallid* tonality, much transformed in later recitals into Hadrian's austere vivacity and the abrupt lyric cries of *Fires*, I should claim for this first tale in Yourcenar's canon a certain precision and an authentic power in her hero's admissions which derive from just the degree of ironic detachment so handsomely administered. In her preface she cites, helpfully and not a little vaingloriously, the influence of Rilke's *Notebooks of Malte Laurids Brigge* (1910), and indeed the recurrence of devices normally considered "poetic" is a pervasive character of this and of all Yourcenar's subsequent fictions. The alternation of narrative and aphorism is a much-honored procedure throughout, and if we recall that *aphorism* is etymologically a "wisdom broken," and that narrative is the healing impulse of language to put things together, we may observe how nicely this first brief recital fulfills the requirements of Yourcenar's ulterior imaginative genius, critical and lyric in close array.

Quite as instructive, in this kind of creative reorganization, is the fate of what Yourcenar calls one of her "forgotten texts," her first extended essay, the study of Pindar written in 1927, published in 1931 and withheld from subsequent readers until its posthumous appearance 60 years later in the Pléiade edition of her essays and memoirs. During the nineteen-fifties and sixties, Yourcenar had prepared—first for her own pleasure, then for publication, a series of translations of the Greek poets, from Homer to the Mimes of Herondas and beyond, to the lyrics of Byzantium, each selection provided with a brief but trenchant commentary, in her liveliest manner; these prose glosses, like the notes for *Hadrian*, are among her most striking works, and indeed she once suggested that these few pages on Pindar were a suitable substitute for that now unavailable early book. Here is a fragment of that later Pindar scholia, which gives some notion of how inclusive as well as how incisive her criticism can be:

Happy to the end, the poet is said to have died in his eighties on the steps of the theater at Argos, during a performance, his head resting on the shoulder of his young friend Theoxenos, for whom he had just composed an admirable erotic *Eulogium*. Granting the changes with regard to sentiment and propriety in the course of the centuries, this Theoxenos of Tenedos was for the old Pindar the equivalent of Ulrika von Levetzow for the old Goethe, and the poem for Theoxenos his *Marienbad Elegy*... The learned men of the Renaissance exulted in this brilliant and difficult *oeuvre*, which corresponded to their thirst for sublimity, and represented a sort of challenge to their erudition. Among the poets, Ronsard imitated him, but on a smaller scale and by quite external means; subsequent "Pindaric" odes, for all their obligatory "splendid disorder" escaped, in France, neither platitude nor absurdity. Seventeenth-century England was more fortunate, thanks to the Milton of *Lycidas* and the *Ode on the Morning of Christ's Nativity*, with their breadth of diction and their rhythmic virtuosity, the rare and somehow abrupt inclusion of a cogitation or of a personal emotion, at least in the former poem, and their religious fervor, at once magnificent and grave. Later, Dryden's *Ode to Saint Cecilia* was to imitate, somewhat academically perhaps, the form of the Pindaric ode and its rich deployment of sacred legends. With romanticism, a frequently mandatory admiration for "the great Ancients" occasionally gave way, with regard to Pindar, to a deeper understanding. In German-speaking lands, the young Goethe of *Prometheus*, of *Ganymede*, of *The Wanderer*, Hölderlin, and latterly Spitteler, splendidly attest to his more or less internalized influence. Hugo, with his startling critical flair, has defined the Theban poet in a single verse: "... serene Pindar filled with epic echoes," more aptly than any number of commentators, the five words summing up Pindar's two main aspects, majestic tranquillity and the perpetual murmur of epic transpiring through lyric song.

But before Yourcenar published her homage to a millennium of Greek poetry, including the seven or eight pages on Pindar, in 1970, she was still concerned about what she regarded as that unsatisfactory early essay: "I am currently working on revising, or rather rewriting," she reports to an archeologist friend, "a work I had the naiveté and audacity to undertake in my early twenties on Pindar's poetry, which both my French and my foreign publisher want to reissue. Since I clearly cannot let it be published as it stands, which is to say full of gaps only too obvious to me now, I am deeply involved in an enormous reconstruction job." Yet out of weariness or perhaps clearheadedness, that particular "reconstruction" never saw the light of day.

Despite Yourcenar's continuous disavowals of the little book, there are many clues in it to what would be her universe, her thought, even her style, as when she speaks—remember, Yourcenar is 22 when she is writing—of Pindar as "reaching the age when egoism is as much a virtue as a necessity" or again "every life contains a failure, and glory, in coming, only serves to call more attention to it." Finally, in evoking Pindar's old age and his amorous passions late in life, the young woman Yourcenar was when she wrote this book made some astonishingly premonitory remarks. Through Pindar, she sketched something of a self-portrait of the old woman she would become. "At all stages of his life, one could glimpse a lively sensuality in Pindar. This is a positive quality...That simple sensuality disciplined itself in art... With age, as always, his rather haughty reserve diminished: a weakening will could no longer hold instinct in check. It is toward the end, in the formless writing on the final pages, that intimate tastes and torments are revealed. Regret, that remembrance of desire... Let the reader not consider himself obliged to exhibit at this inappropriate juncture what few remaining principles he has. This taste for young beauty is a frequent one in those who are getting on in years." She who had her Alexis say, "As a child, I yearned for glory"—and who would admit much later on to having spoken of herself in this way—ends her first essay on Pindar with this sentence: "The only lesson we can learn from this life, so distant from our own, is that glory after all is nothing more than a temporary concession." Notice, though, how she revises away from the too-revealing confessional mode and in that later introduction to her translation of Pindaric fragments fastens her painful analysis of desire and regret to the old Goethe and the *Marienbad Elegy*.

Comparable revisions occur in the biography, of course. I have noted how several of Yourcenar's friends, lovers, and allies in the great campaign of cultural supremacy fell victim to the determined scission this author created in her life, much abetted by the drastic necessities of World War II: how the free-ranging, autonomous pre-1940 Marguerite seems an altogether different woman, and an altogether different writer, from the remote and hypochondriacal consort of Grace Frick, for the next forty years her translator, her domestic mainstay, and her unacknowledged lover. But perhaps, less sensationally, I can indicate the kind of transformation Yourcenar is always attempting—so that it becomes permissible, say, to print (and posthumously, at that) that early Pindar essay only when the later and shapelier and more stringent text is in place at the end of her career—by a more literary example which I believe has evaded Yourcenar's biographers.

On Tuesday, February 23, 1937, Virginia Woolf laments a lost opportunity to write in her journal, thus: "This extraordinary scribble means, I suppose, the translator coming. Mme or Mlle Youniac (?) Not her name." And then, after a page or so about what couldn't be written while indeed she was actually writing it, Woolf returns to the charge: "So I've no time or room to describe the translator, save that she wore some nice gold leaves on her black dress; is a woman I suppose with a past; amorous; intellectual; lives half the year in Athens; is in with Edmond Jaloux &c, red-lipped, strenuous; a working Frenchwoman; matter of fact; intellectual; we went through *The Waves*. What does 'See here he comes?' mean & so on." And then on the next day, writing to the composer Ethel Smyth (a difficult friend, whom Woolf was probably eager to put off at anyone else's expense), she concludes the dossier thus: "Yes, Ethel dear, I'd like to see you, but what's the use of seeing you against some intolerable necessary bore—this refers to a French translator who's wasted one of my rare solitary evenings." So much for the encounter, at least on Woolf's side, between these two women who were to become, each in her national fashion, Major Writers, insofar as majority status is conferred by academic consensus, critical esteem, and a continuous readership.

On Yourcenar's side, something more significant than a missed opportunity, an accidental oversight, is registered, indeed is enacted. For the encounter with Woolf and its treatment in Yourcenar's texts represents in little the characteristic procedure of this writer, its finesse and its excess, which I regard as the central symbolic effort of her life's work, and even of her life: the will to compose a figure of Olympian equilibrium which, as Dr Johnson said of Milton, would be "great by design."

In the essay which served as a preface to *Les Vagues*, first published as an article in *Les Nouvelles Litteraires* in 1937, Yourcenar sketches a portrait quite as telling as Woolf's informal one, though evidently given a high gloss for her French readers whom she assumes to be unfamiliar with the achievements of Leslie Stephen's daughter: "Only a few days ago, in the sitting-room dimly lit by firelight where Mrs Woolf had been so kind as to welcome me, I watched in the half-light as the profile of that young Fate's face emerged, hardly aged [Woolf was 55, Yourcenar 34] but delicately etched with signs of thought and lassitude, and I reminded myself that the reproach of intellectualism is often directed at the most sensitive natures, those most ardently alive, those obliged by their frailty or their excess of strength constantly to resort to the arduous disciplines of the mind."

Thirty-five years later, the high gloss has become something of a mirror in which Yourcenar (already incipiently identifying with Woolf's "sensitive nature," her "frailty or excess of strength" and most significantly with her "obligation to resort to the arduous disciplines of the mind"—though it is doubtful that Woolf would have characterized her own creative impulses in this highfalutin fashion) manages to articulate eternal contours for herself: "I translated *The Waves* into French, Virginia Woolf's next-to-last novel, and I am not sorry to have done so, since my recompense for ten months of work was a visit to Bloomsbury, and two short hours spent beside a woman at once sparkling and timid, who greeted me in a room taken over by twilight. We are always wrong about the writers of our time: either we overrate them or we run them down. I do not believe I am committing an error, however, when I put Virginia Woolf among the four or five great virtuosos of the English language and among the rare contemporary novelists whose work stands some chance of lasting more than ten years. And I even hope, despite so many signs to the contrary, that there will be a few minds aware enough in around the year 2500 to savor the subtleties of her art." Being overrated or run down—this was, as Yourcenar's latest biographer observes, a premonitory diagnosis: between the fetishists of her own productions, ever ready to launch into easy raptures, and those who regard her as in the worst sense an academic, even a *pompier* writer, Yourcenar has not yet been afforded a determinate status, nor do we possess, for all her rank as an "immortal," a satisfactory clue to how her work will be regarded "in the year 2500."

As for those subtleties of Woolf's art, Yourcenar seems to have been remarkably off-hand about them. In a letter written some forty years after her translation was published she comments: "I don't think the translation of *Les Vagues* caused me any particular problems, it was merely a question of letting oneself drift along with the current, not always too clearly aware of where that current was taking one; but Virginia Woolf herself seems to have desired that impression of vagueness (no play on words intended). In an attempt to be a conscientious translator, I went to see her at the time, to ask her certain questions about how she would prefer that I translate certain sentences containing allusions to themes or images from English poetry: literally, or by trying to achieve the same effects with similar themes familiar to French readers. But this problem was quite alien to her, as were problems of translation in general."

There is a discrepancy here, between Woolf's response to the encounter, which is described, however hastily, as a rather elementary process of textual scrutiny ("What does 'See, here he comes' mean, & so on"), and Yourcenar's lofty and perhaps after-the-fact discussion of French equivalents to "themes or images from English poetry." It is hard to believe that Mrs Woolf would be so obtuse about questions of equivalence in the translated language, if they had been presented to her. (As early as 1923, she writes in her journal: "I wonder if this next lap of my fiction will be influenced by Proust? I think his French language, tradition, &c, prevents that, yet his command of every resource is so extravagant that one can hardly fail to profit, & must not flinch, through cowardice.")

Yourcenar, however, was anything but a "conscientious translator," though she was frequently an inspired one, as we know from the testimony of her friend Constantin Dimaras, with whom, a year before her encounter with Woolf, she had collaborated on a translation of Cavafy's poems, a task perhaps facilitated by the fact that she did not know modern Greek, though as Dimaras tells us, "Marguerite was solely concerned with what she thought sounded good in French. . . I would give her word-for-word translations and she would 'arrange' things." In the case of her version of *What Maisie Knew*, completed in 1939 though not published in France until 1947, it may be of some interest to confront the texts, however briefly.

Here is James in 1897, on page 3 of the novel, breathing about the bush of Maisie's parents' divorce: "It was a society in which for the most part people were occupied only with chatter, but the disunited couple had at last grounds for expecting a time of high activity. They girded their loins, they felt as if the quarrel had only begun. They felt indeed more married than ever, inasmuch as what marriage had mainly suggested to them was the unbroken opportunity to quarrel."

And here is Yourcenar's version: "Dans ce monde là, les gens étaient presque uniquement occupés de commérages, mais ce couple désuni avait au moins devant lui de sérieuses occupations. Ils se ceignirent les reins, avec le sentiment que la lutte ne faisait que commencer. En vérité, ils se sentaient plus mariés que jamais, d'autant plus que le mariage n'avait jamais signifié pour eux qu'une perpétuelle occasion de disputes." The one slip in that first sentence, where "at last" is translated as "at least," is plausibly compensated for by the nice play on *occupied* which substitutes "sérieuses occupations" for "a time of high activity," nattily playing the phrase off "uniquement occupés" and giving a bit more point to a passage which in English seems to chew more than is bitten off.

More conclusive, though, than any inspection of Yourcenar's verbal surfaces is her continued interest—we are now in 1965, 26 years after the translation of *Maisie*—in James's thematics, the inveterate presentation of a child, especially of a girl, in a corrupt world of unloving adults. There are no children in Yourcenar's fictions, and all the more reason, then, to consider her own circumstances as a virtually motherless only daughter educated by her father in the manner of Montaigne and of Gargantua, of Mme de Sévigné and of Émile, when she discusses, with characteristic high-handedness, the procedures of Henry James: "[*The Turn of the Screw*] struck me yet again as a masterpiece and interests me all the more because, having translated *What Maisie Knew* into French quite some time ago, it prompted me to reflect on that other tale of childhood voyeurism, in which this time it is not with specters but with adults who are very much alive that the little girl forges strange bonds of complicitous knowledge. *The Turn of the Screw* goes much further than this nonetheless extraordinary novel because it is not, this time, only the problem of childhood innocence and perversity that preoccupies James, but that of our dealings with evil. James goes beyond the psychological, at once consciously and unconsciously, to enter into the theological and metaphysical as well as the occult. How right . . . to eliminate disdainfully Edmund Wilson's hypothesis reducing everything to hysterical fantasies on the part of the governess. A fine example of the flat and rudimentary aspect that spiritual problems take on in the minds of certain of our contemporaries. In reality [*sic*], sexual obsession fills *The Turn of the Screw* by virtue of the very fact that it is in the form of contacts with fornicators that James (typically a man of the nineteenth century) treats this problem of connivance with evil, and the first chapter, so offhandedly worldly, strikes me as proving *a contrario* that he knew how dangerous from all points of view was the terrain upon which he was advancing." It is hard to keep from feeling that Yourcenar's scornful dismissal of Wilson and of an emphatically psychoanalytical reading of James's tale is defensive, and that her own excitement about these texts is fueled by other concerns than "the problem of connivance with evil." Yet there is a certain grandeur, perverse perhaps but undeniable, in her approach to James—one consonant with her own metaphysical and religious traffic in *The Abyss*, which is both the *Salammbo* and the *Sentimental Education* of her career, accounting thereby for the curious dryness of this willed descent into chaos.

To return briefly to the matter of translation as an evidence of self-invention. My own dealings with Yourcenar, when I had occasion to translate her splendid volume of essays *The Dark Brain of Piranesi*, made me realize how troublesome, indeed how manipulative, as we have learned to say, such intercourse with a great writer can be. Yet it was evident throughout that all "our" efforts were to be in the service of the art, of a high and unyielding standard which would determine not only the nature of an author's prose but of her presence, as it were, in the English speaking world.

It is clear to me now that such demands were made continuously by Yourcenar, to the very end of a very long life, to good purpose: I believe that at least three of her novels (*Coup de Grace*, *Memoirs of Hadrian*, and *The Abyss* (for all its *acedie*), three volumes of her essays, the lyric prose of *Fires*, the French translations of Cavafy and of Greek poetry with its glosses, and the volume of *Oriental Tales*, are as likely to abide as any literature produced in the last 50 years. Moreover the arrangement, the design of these works and of all the lesser others which sustain them are as much the product of the maker's imaginative energy as the writing itself, though I also believe the author's determination to achieve the impregnable status of a monument will strike most of us as anything but sympathetic. With the help of her biographers, we may conjugate (surely the right word here) the largely concealed intimate drama of Yourcenar's life with the intensely intellectual drama of her literary progress, discerning how the nature of this astonishingly isolated woman—isolated by family circumstance, by sexual preference, and by actual exile from the comforting occasions of ordinary success—generated her writing and how such writing created her name, her body, and her life. I believe such an enterprise is worth our attention and our esteem.

Implicit in our modern cultural mythology is the assumption that the author is at the disposal of her works, servant of her inspiration, *umile ancella*, as Adrienne Lecouvreur puts it in the opera, of some external power, not hers at all. Like Nabokov, like Thomas Mann, Yourcenar opposes these assumptions; she has chosen, at the cost of how many grandiose inspirations of youth, of how many thwarted plans of maturity, of how many eloquent deliriums of her old age, to do nothing which is not a disposition of a conscious creative will. The two Pléiade volumes of Marguerite Yourcenar's works, the fictions and the essays, is a monument as purposefully determined as the Hanging Gardens of Babylon, laid out by Semiramis. Nowadays we are not so beguiled by monuments as we were once taught to be; they remain, nonetheless, among the wonders of the world.

Emerging from Censorship

BY J. M. COETZEE

I

Between the early 1960s and the mid-1980s, the Republic of South Africa operated one of the most comprehensive censorship systems in the world. Called in official parlance not censorship but publications control—censorship was a word it sought to censor from public discourse about itself—it controlled every form in which signs could be publicly disseminated, that is, not only books, magazines, newspapers, films, etc., but T-shirts, key-rings, dolls, toys, shop-signs—anything, in fact, that might carry a forbidden message or representation. Every new T-shirt, key-ring, etc., as well as every new book, film, etc., had to pass the scrutiny of the censorship bureaucracy before it could be released upon the public. In the old Soviet Union there were some 70,000 bureaucrats supervising the activities of some 7,000 writers. The ratio of censors to writers in South Africa was, if anything, higher than ten to one.

When a man reacts to the world around him as though the air is filled with coded messages deriding him or plotting his destruction, we call him paranoid. For decades the South African state behaved in a paranoid fashion. In itself, as a feature of what we can call the mentality of the state, the phenomenon is nothing new. Paranoia is the pathology par excellence of dictatorships. Among modern dictators Stalin was perhaps the most demonstrably and the most extremely paranoid. We can fairly say that of the millions who died at his behest a good proportion were victims of his paranoid delusions.

One of the features distinguishing modern dictatorships from earlier dictatorships is how widely and rapidly the modern dictator's paranoia, or the paranoia of a ruling clique, can be disseminated to infect the populace as a whole. In fact it has been a positive strategy of government among modern paranoid dictatorships to spread their paranoia. Stalin's Soviet Union is again the prime example: every citizen was encouraged to suspect every other citizen of being a spy or saboteur; the bonds of human sympathy and trust between people were broken down; and "Soviet society" became in fact just a name for tens of millions of individuals living on individual islands of mutual suspicion and terror of one another.

The Soviet Union was not unique. The Cuban novelist Reinaldo Arenas wrote of the atmosphere of "unceasing official menace" in his country that made a citizen "not only a repressed person, but also a self-repressed one, not only a censored person, but a self-censored one, not only one watched over, but one who watches over himself."[1] Exemplary punitive action in a context of "unceasing official menace" is an argument hard to resist: one effect to make certain kinds of writing and even speech a guilty activity, thereby reproducing the paranoia of the state in the psyche of the subject. Thus may the state look forward to the day when the censorship bureaucracy can afford to wither away, its function having been, in effect, privatized.

I may seem to fling the word paranoia around rather loosely. The paranoia of the tyrant—yes, perhaps. But if the writer stands a chance of being packed off to a real, objective reeducation camp, why should one call that paranoia rather than justifiable watchfulness?

My answer is, No. The watchfulness of the writer in the paranoid state has a pathological quality that truly tips it over into paranoia. The evidence I call upon here comes from writers themselves. Time and again they record the feeling of being touched and contaminated by the sickness of the state. In a move typical of "authentic" paranoids, they claim that their minds have been invaded; it is against this invasion that they express their outrage.

The Greek writer George Mangakis, for instance, records the experience of writing in prison under the eyes of his guards. Every few days the guards searched his cell, taking away his writings and returning those which the prison authorities—the censors—considered "permissible." Mangakis recalls accepting his papers back and suddenly "loathing" them. "The system is a diabolical device for annihilating your own soul. They want to make you see your thoughts through their eyes and control them yourself, from their point of view."[2] By forcing the writer to see what he has written through the censor's eyes, the censor forces him to internalize a contaminating reading; Mangakis's sudden, revulsive moment is the moment of contamination.

The ultimate proof that something has, so to speak, gone wrong with writers like Arenas or Mangakis is the excessiveness of the language of their response. To put the point in another way: as I use the term paranoia, it is not a figurative way of describing the situation of such a writer. Rather, the paranoia is on the inside, in the language, in the thinking; the terror and rage one hears in Mangakis' words is terror and rage at the most intimate of invasions, an invasion of the very style of the self, by a pathology for which there may be no cure. I suspect the same paranoia may be felt in my own language, as I write here: in the excessive insistency of its phrasing, in its vehemence, its demands for sensitivity to minutiae of style. The South African censorship began to wind down in the decade of the 1980s; today it is virtually dormant; yet I lived through its heyday, saw its consequences not only on the lives of fellow-writers but on the totality of public discourse, felt in my own person some of its more secret effects, and so must contemplate the possibility that I share (or feel I share) the position of an Arenas or a Mangakis because I too may have been infected with whatever infected them, real or delusional. That is to say, this essay may be a specimen of the same kind of paranoid discourse it seeks to describe.

I stress that the paranoia I am talking about is not the imprint of censorship on those writers alone who have become the objects of official persecution. All writing that in the normal course of events can fall under the censor's eye may become tainted in the manner I have described, whether or not the censor passes it. All writers under censorship are at least potentially driven to paranoia, not just those who have books banned.

Why should this be so? I can give only a speculative answer. It is an answer based not only on introspection, however: it is also based on a scrutiny (I should caution the reader, however: perhaps a paranoid scrutiny) of the accounts other writers (who may themselves have been infected with paranoia) have given of operating under regimes of censorship.

No one believes any longer that the self is the monadic unit described by classical rationalism. On the contrary, we picture the self as multiple and in many ways divided against itself. We picture it as a zoo, for instance, in which all kinds of strange beasts have residence, over which the anxious, overworked zookeeper of rationality has rather limited control. In this zoo there are few internal bars. At night the zookeeper sleeps and some of the beasts roam about (we call this dreaming).

Which, in this psychoanalytic fantasy, are the beasts in the zoo of the self? Some have names like figure-of-the-father and figure-of-the-mother; others are memories or fragments of memories in transmuted form, with strong elements of feeling attached to them; a whole subcolony are semi-tamed but still treacherous earlier versions of the self, each with an inner zoo of its own over which it has less than complete control.

Artists, says Freud, are people who move around in the inner menagerie with a degree of confidence and emerge from it when they wish more or less unscathed. Whether Freud's account of the creative process holds water is not my concern here. I poach from it one element: that artistic creation of a certain kind involves inhabiting and managing and exploiting quite primitive parts of the self. This is not a particularly dangerous activity but it is a delicate one, one that may take a writer years of preparation till he/she finally gets the codes and the keys and the balances right, and can move in and out more or less freely. It is also a very private matter, so private that it almost constitutes the definition of privacy: how I am with myself.

Managing the inner selves, making them work for one (making them productive) is a complex matter of pleasing and satisfying and challenging and extorting and wooing and feeding, and sometimes even of destroying. For writing not only comes out of the zoo but (I become hypermetaphorical now) goes back in again. That is to say, insofar as writing is transactional, the figures for whom and to whom it is done are also figures in the zoo: for instance, the figure-of-the-beloved in the zoo, who may or may not be an idealized representation of some beloved in the real world, though for Freud she is more likely to be a heavily disguised version of a parent.

Let us take the example of a kind of writing that is, in its essence, a transaction with some such figure of the beloved, that tries to please her (but that also tries continually though surreptitiously to revise and recreate her as the-one-who-will-be-pleased); and let us imagine what happens if into this transaction is introduced in a massive and undeniable way another figure-of-the-reader: the dark-suited, bald-headed censor, with his pursed lips and his red pen and his irritability and his censorious-ness (for no good reason I present the censor as a rather parodic version of the figure-of-the-father). Then the entire balance of the carefully constructed inner drama is destroyed, and destroyed in a way that is hard to repair. For, as is the way with these psychic operations, the more one tries to ignore (repress) the censor, the larger he swells.

Working under a censorship regime is like being intimate with someone who does not love you, with whom you don't want intimacy, but who is forced upon you. It is like writing for an intrusive reader, one who forces himself in upon the intimacy of the writing transaction, forces out the figure of the loved or courted reader, reads whatever you write in a disapproving and censorious fashion.

I cite an exemplary case from the Soviet Union, the case of one of Stalin's principal victims among writers, Osip Mandelstam. It tells several important and appalling lessons about the paranoid state.[3]

In 1933 Mandelstam, then 42 years old, composed a short but powerful poem about a tyrant who orders executions left, right and center, and relishes the deaths of his victims like a man munching raspberries. Though the tyrant is not named (he is identified only as a Georgian), the reference is clearly to Stalin.

Mandelstam did not write the poem down, but did recite it several times to friends. In 1934 his home was raided by security police looking for the poem. Though they did not find it—it existed solely inside the heads of the poet and his friends—they arrested Mandelstam. While Mandelstam was under arrest, the poet Boris Pasternak had a telephone call from the top man himself, Stalin. Who is this fellow Mandelstam? Stalin wanted to know. In particular, is he a master? (That was Stalin's word, the same in Russian as in English.)

Pasternak correctly inferred the second half of the question: Is Mandelstam a master or is he disposable? Pasternak replied, in effect, that Mandelstam was a master, that he was not disposable. So Mandelstam was sentenced to internal exile in the city of Voronezh. While he was living there, enormous pressure was brought on him to pay tribute to Stalin by composing a poem in his honour. Mandelstam gave in and composed an adulatory ode. What he felt about this ode we will never know, not only because he left no record but because—as his wife persuasively argues—he was mad when he wrote it, mad with fear, perhaps, but mad too with the madness of a person not only suffering the embrace of a body he detests, but taking the initiative, day after day, line after line, to embrace that body.

In fact the ode did not save Mandelstam. He was soon rearrested and sent to a labour camp, from which he never returned.

There is a great deal that can be said about the fate of this great and tragic poet. All I will comment on are two moments in his persecution: the moment when Stalin asks whether Mandelstam is a master, and the moment when Mandelstam is ordered to celebrate his persecutor.

"Is he a master?" We can be sure Stalin was not asking because he regarded great artists as above the state. What he meant was something like, Is he dangerous? Is he going to live, even if he dies? Is his sentence on me going to live longer than my sentence on him? Do I have to be careful?

Hence the command later on that Mandelstam write an ode (whether the command came from Stalin himself or from the toadies surrounding him need not concern us here). Making the great artists of his day kowtow to him was Stalin's way of breaking them, of making it impossible for them to hold their heads up — in effect, of showing them who was master, and of making them acknowledge him as master in a medium where no lie, no private reservation, is possible: one's own art.

To the case of Mandelstam let me add a case from South Africa that is comparable in its dynamic if not in its scale.[4]

In 1972 the poet Breyten Breytenbach published a poem in Afrikaans entitled "Letter to Butcher from Foreign Parts." As the poem made clear, the butcher to whom the letter was addressed was Balthazar John Vorster, then Prime Minister of the Republic of South Africa, the man who had done most to create a security-police empire with huge powers over life and death, a police force untouchable by the law, above the courts. Vorster did more than anyone to create an ethos of invulnerability among the police, an ethos whose terrible aftereffects still hang over South Africa. In the custody of Vorster's security police, scores of political detainees died unexplained deaths. It is important to remember that these people did not "disappear," as happened in Argentina and Chile. On the contrary, their bodies were produced for post-mortem examination; and, despite clear evidence that they had died under torture, patriotic or perhaps just frightened magistrates accepted the bland explanations produced by the police: that detainees had slipped on bars of soap and fatally concussed themselves while taking a shower, or had hurled themselves out of tenth-floor windows in fits of remorse, or had hanged themselves with their torn-up shirts.

In Breytenbach's long poem there are recorded the names of many of these victims, as if the poem says of itself, "It is I that will live in history, that will be remembered, not the court record." But the heart of the poem is a passage addressed to the butcher himself in which Breytenbach asks Vorster in the most intimate of ways what it is like for him to use fingers red with blood to fondle his wife's private parts. It is a shocking and obscene passage, all the more obscene for addressing the sex-life of a couple in late middle age, public figures in a highly puritanical society.

Some years later, Breytenbach—who had been living abroad when he wrote the poem, and had published it in the Netherlands, publication back home being out of the question—paid a visit to South Africa, using false papers and on a secret military assignment. He was soon picked up by the security police. He was not liquidated, he was not even tortured, but he was given a show trial. The formal charge was terrorism, but his writings, particularly the poem against Vorster, soon emerged as a subtext to the proceedings. The purpose of the trial, as it emerged, was to break him in much the same way as Mandelstam had been broken. In open court Breytenbach ultimately apologized to Vorster for what he called the "crass and insulting" poem he had written and thanked the security police for the humanity with which they had treated him. In return for eating crow he got nothing. The deal he had been promised—a lighter sentence—was reneged on.

There is a puzzling feature about both cases, Breytenbach's and Mandelstam's. Compared with the vast machinery of the state, including its well-developed machinery of censorship, the writer was clearly powerless. Yet the state, and particularly the head of state (the head of the state in which the paranoia buzzes), deemed these writers, these masterwriters, important enough in terms of their power—and power is the only quantity that power understands—to lavish much attention on. Why could the two poems in question, however insulting, not have been ignored like the pinpricks they were? Why do the activities of writers concern the state at all?

To answer this question, to understand the long history of troubled relations between writers and the state, we need to reflect on authorship as an historical phenomenon cradled in the early modern age, and on the ambitions opened up for the first time in history by a career in authorship.

Scribal culture, the culture of the West before the invention of printing, did not particularly foster the notion that by dint of writing a person could attain fame. This notion belongs to print culture. We begin to see evidence of it quite soon after the invention of printing, as printers begin to make a practice of attaching authors' names to the books they put out. What does this signing of the book mean? Of course it has legal and commercial implications: the author accepts a share of the legal responsibility for the book as he lays claim to a share of the profits.[5] But signing the book also has a symbolic meaning: the author uses the book as a vehicle for projecting his signature—and sometimes his portrait—into the world, in a multiplied form. It is this potentially endless multiplication of traces of himself that gives the author the sense of having the power to cross all spatial and temporal boundaries. In visions of fame and immortality authorship as we know it today is born: authorship and the mystique of the author.[6]

So much for the author; what of the state?

The people, as a concept in the political philosophy of the West, also goes back to the early modern state. The question may be McLuhanesque, but it is worth asking nevertheless: Which achieved its aims earlier—the state, fitting the concept of a people over the population under its control, or the early printer-publishers, creating a public (a reading public) for their products? Or, to put the question in a milder form: Does the reading public called into being by the invention of printing not constitute a model of the people as imagined in the philosophy of the early modern state?

Whatever the answer, it seems to be no accident that, as soon as printing arrived, state censorship took on a more systematic, widespread and rigorous form, as though in printers and their authors the state had identified not so much an enemy (though in fact that is what they were often labeled) as a rival. From the sixteenth century onward we begin to detect in the language of the state, when it turns to authors and their powers, a note of distinctly modern paranoia. Here, for instance, is England's Lord Keeper, Sir Nicholas Bacon, speaking in 1567:

> These books . . . [make] men's minds to be at variance one with another, and diversity of minds maketh seditions, seditions bring in tumults, tumults make insurrections and rebellions, insurrections make depopulations and bring in utter ruin and destruction of men's bodies, goods and lands.[7]

We tend today to think of blanket pre- and post-publication censorship as a feature of absolutist and totalitarian states: the Russia of Nicholas I, Stalin's Soviet Union. But censorship in early modern Europe was at least as relentless — draconian in its penalties and surprisingly sophisticated in its mechanisms too.[8] As early as the sixteenth century we find the state viewing authors and printer-publishers not only as an interest group with a strong (and self-justifying) sense of historical mission but as an elite with an ability to create a mass following, at least among literate people, in a way that is frustratingly similar to the ambitions of the state itself.

The history of authorship and the history of censorship are thus intimately bound together. With the advent of printing and the rapid multiplication of copies, the fortunes of the author rise; he grows in power but also becomes the object of the envy of the state. In the twentieth century, with the invention of radio and television, as the power of the author wanes, so does the state's interest in him wane. So it is no surprise that the great age of state censorship is the age of the preeminence of the print media.

II

"Is he a master?" Whether Mandelstam was a master-writer or not, what had Stalin, with the massive means of repression at his disposal, to fear from him? I return to this question in the context of the rivalry I have been discussing: between the power of the state to spread the word of its authority, and the power of the writer through publication to spread his.

The object of the state's envy, in this account, is not so much the rival content of the author's word, or even specifically the power he gets from the press to spread that word, as a certain disseminative power of which the power to publish and have read is only the most marked case. While the power of authors in general is slight without the multiplier effect of the press, the word of the master-author has a disseminative power that goes beyond purely mechanical means of dissemination. The master's word (as we know very well from Russian history) can spread by word of mouth, or from hand to hand in carbon-paper copies 'samizdat', literally self-publication; even when the word itself is not spread, it can be replaced by rumors of itself, rumors that spread like copies (the rumor that someone has written a poem about which the boss is furious, for instance).

Furthermore, a logic seems to spring into operation that works to the state's disadvantage: the more draconically the state comes down on writing, the more seriously it is seen to be taking writing; the more seriously it is seen to be taking writing, the more attention is paid to writing; the more attention is paid to writing, the more its disseminative power increases. The book that is suppressed today gets twice as much attention tomorrow, precisely because it has been suppressed; the writer who is gagged today is famous tomorrow for having been gagged.

No matter what the state does, writers always seem to get the last word; men and women of letters—the intellectual community, the academic community, even the journalistic community—whose sense of craft-solidarity can be surprisingly strong, are the writers, inter alia, of history. In an important sense it is they and not the state who make history.

This dynamic of reversal, powered by a strong belief among the intellectual community (at least in Judaeo-Christian cultures) in the vindication of the truth in the fullness of time, is clearly to be seen at work in our own age. In South Africa, for instance, writers, no matter how much persecuted, knew that in the long run the censors did not stand a chance—not only because apartheid was doomed to collapse because of its internal contradictions, not only because puritan moral standards were on the wane in a world-wide economy of consumption, but because as a community they would outlast their political foes and, more than that, would write their epitaph.

Writers in South Africa knew all this, and said so, sometimes loudly and publicly, though perhaps with too little explanation of the logic that weighted the outcome so heavily in their favor. Even more questionable was their readiness to embrace the status of victim, victims of the censor, when in fact they had uncensored access to the rest of the English-speaking world. (The South African government never went so far as to attempt to punish writers for publishing abroad, as happened in the Soviet Union, particularly in the 1960s.)

What I therefore ask, in a somewhat skeptical spirit, is whether writers under censorship are wholly disinterested in presenting themselves as embattled and outnumbered, confronting a gigantic foe. And since South Africa, where durable ties exist between (English-language) writers and foreign (principally British) publishers, may be a special case, let me spread my net wider to indicate that ready recourse to David-and-Goliath mythmaking, and in general to the rhetoric of battle, has not been a feature of literary life in South Africa alone.

A few years ago Seamus Heaney published an essay on the poets of Eastern Europe, particularly the Russian poets who suffered under Stalin, and on the impact upon the West of what he sees as their exemplary lives. Tsvetaeva, Akhmatova, the Mandelstams, Pasternak, Gumilev, Esenin,

Mayakovsky, says Heaney, have become "heroic names [in]... a modern martyrology, a record of courage and sacrifice which elicits... unstinted admiration." The refusal by these writers to compromise their art "expose[d] to the majority [of Soviet citizens] the abjectness of their [own] collapse, as they [fled] for security into whatever self-deceptions the party line require[d] of them."[9]

Heaney presents these great persecuted writers as heroes and martyrs despite themselves. They did not aspire to bring about the downfall of the state, he says, they merely tried to be true to themselves. Nevertheless, in being true they drew upon themselves the resentment of those many who had given in to the menaces of the state, and so were left in vulnerable and ultimately tragic isolation.

There can be no question about the power of the life-stories to which Heaney refers to evoke our pity and terror. What I draw attention to is the metaphorics of Heaney's account, a metaphorics of battle—of the radical oppositions of victory and defeat, suffering and triumph, courage and cowardice. Is not the very staging of the opposition between these writers and the Soviet state in terms of a metaphorics of battle in itself the declaration of a war which strangely betrays what Heaney admires in them: their unshakeable (but not wholly unshakeable—they were human, after all—their nearly unshakeable, and where it was shakeable wholly understandable) fidelity to their calling?

For Heaney's is of course a particularly intransigent kind of metaphoric, a metaphoric of black and white without shades of grey. It seems to describe an historical dynamic in which there are finally only two positions left open: for or against, good or bad, the self-censored cowardice of the herd or the uncensored heroism of the few. As a reading of life under Stalin, it seems, in its rhetorical violence, to issue a challenge to all grey readings, nuanced readings of those times. It constructs the writer-censor or writer-state relationship as one of rivalry that can only grow more and more naked till it issues in warfare.

Earlier in this essay I wrote of the paranoia of the state. But in the figure of the writer as the hero of resistance, the one who implacably attends to the voice of his daimon and goes on writing, is there not the potential for a certain megalomania? Paranoia on the one hand, megalomania on the other: not as unlikely a couple as may at first seem. Let me quote Mario Vargas Llosa:

> The congenital unsubmissiveness of literature is much broader than is believed by those who consider it a mere instrument for opposing governments and dominant social structures: it strikes equally at everything [that] stands for dogma and logical exclusivism in the interpretation of life, that is, both ideological orthodoxies and heterodoxies. In other words, it is a living, systematic, inevitable contradiction of all that exists.[10]

This extraordinary claim is made in the name of literature, but I take the liberty of reading it as a claim in the name of writers as a group. Let us be clear against whom Vargas Llosa speaks here. More than against the bureaucrat censor in the pay of the tyrant, he is speaking against the enemy of the tyrant, the revolutionary who hopes to employ the writer in the fight against the tyrant and thus draw the writer into his camp, enrolling the writer as a soldier in the grand army of the revolution. In their relations with the writer, says Vargas Llosa, tyrant and revolutionary are in fact more alike than they are different; or, to put it in another way, the dynamic of their opposition is a dynamic of illusionary differences. It is a dynamic in which the writer will not participate. His "unsubmissiveness" consists in being in "systematic... contradiction" at all times. In other words, true opposition consists in being in opposition to systems of opposition.

The maneuver practised by Vargas Llosa here of shifting his own opposition to a logical level one floor higher than the ground-level political battle cannot succeed in removing him from the play of oppositions. His claim that the writer occupies a position that simultaneously exists outside politics, rivals politics, and dominates politics, seems to me truly megalomaniac.

III

There is nothing that raises the hackles of writers like the threat of censorship, no topic that calls forth a more pugnacious instinctive response. In the first part of this essay I have tried to indicate why the threat of censorship is felt so intimately by writers, and in the second I have cast a skeptical look at the rhetoric in which their response is often cast.

The subject I have addressed has been a deliberately restricted one. When I have spoken of writers I have had in mind writers who originate their own work, and the censorship I have had in mind has been state censorship, pre- and/or post-publication, backed by the force of the law. I have thus not addressed the instance of writers in the employ of institutions that retain a contractual right to censor the work they pay for; nor have I had in mind the censorship of information through official press controls, though I acknowledge that the distinction between "writing" and information is not always easy to maintain.

I have particularly not addressed the question of whether there are circumstances in which legally enforced censorship may be justifiable, and in specific the question of whether language that is felt by broad groups of people to insult and demean them ought to be permitted public airing. This is part of a political debate about the relative weight of individual and group rights about which I will say nothing here except that, coming from a country in which political censorship was for decades carried out under the pretense of protecting ethnic and religious sensitivities, I may perhaps be excused a jaundiced view.

Notes

[1] Quoted in Carlos Ripoll, *The Heresy of Words in Cuba* (New York: Freedom House, 1985), p. 36.

[2] George Mangakis, "Letter to Europeans" (1972), in *They Shoot Writers, Don't They?*, ed. George Theiner (London: Faber, 1984), p. 33.

[3] The story of Mandelstam and Stalin is more fully recounted in my essay "Osip Mandelstam and the Stalin Ode," *Representations* no. 35 (Summer 1991), pp. 72-83.

[4] See my essay "Breyten Breytenbach and the Censor," *Raritan* 10/4 (1991), pp. 58-84.

[5] Lucien Febvre and Henri-Jean Martin, *The Coming of the Book*, trans. David Gerard (London: New Left Books, 1976), pp. 160, 84, 261; Elizabeth Eisenstein, *The Printing Press as an Agent of Change* (Cambridge: Cambridge U.P., 1979), vol. 1, p. 230; Alain Viala, *Naissance de l'ecrivain* (Paris: Editions de minuit, 1985), p. 85.

[6] As regards this mystique, we may note that even well-educated people misunderstood the etymology of the word author, believing that it went back not only to Latin *augeo*, to add something to something else—which it does—but also to Greek *autos*, self—which it does not. Thus there grew up around the word a field of connotations: the author was a man of authority, and his authority was backed by a certain parthenogenic power to create out of himself. See Viala, p. 276.

[7] Quoted in D. M. Loades, "The Theory and Practice of Censorship in Sixteenth-Century England," Transactions of the Royal Historical Society, fifth series, vol. 24 (London: Royal Historical Society, 1974), p. 142.

[8] The authorities in Tudor England, for instance, maneuvered writers into a position of

censoring themselves, and even invented the ploy of refusing to spell out the conventions of silence they expected writers to follow (in other words, imposing a silence about the conventions of silence). See Annabel Patterson, *Censorship and Interpretation* (Madison: U. of Wisconsin P., 1984), pp. 10-11.

[9] Seamus Heaney, *The Government of the Tongue* (London: Faber, 1988), p. 39.

[10] Mario Vargas Llosa, "The Writer in Latin America" (1978), in Theiner, ed., p. 166.

Gifts from Joyce[1]

The first gift James Joyce gave me arrived about forty years ago when I was ill with some now forgotten ailment and spent my three days of recovery reading *Ulysses* from cover to cover. The gift was twofold: it made me doubt my intelligence, and made me think English was not my native tongue. The book seemed like an artifact from an alien culture, about which I knew little; and it also seemed the product of another language, as impenetrable as a Sanskrit crossword puzzle. And yet the reading was a thrilling experience.

Of course it was ridiculous to think I had read the book in three days. I had grasped fragments, I had found that I liked Bloom and Molly enormously, thought Stephen a difficult and not-very-likable intellectual. I had ferreted out some of the book's scandalous passages, including the *Nausicaa* episode, in which Bloom and the young Gerty McDowell achieve simultaneous orgasms-at-a-distance, a section I thought I understood; but I'd missed totally the mockery of the sentimental cliches of the narrator that so ebulliently define Gerty's world.

I remember James Agee's reaction to this sort of confrontation with Joyce. He wrote in one of his letters that he'd been reading *A Portrait of the Artist* and added it "makes me ashamed ever to have thought I'd read it before, and exceedingly suspicious on the whole question of when or how or how soon to read what: unless there is certain to be re-reading; and suspicious even then; and suspicious for that matter of my illusion that I am reading it now. . . I am sick in myself and others of the illusion of reading which comes of somewhat intelligently skimming a great work, being somewhat excited by it, and thinking from that that you 'know' or 'understand' it."

I never thought I 'understood' all of *Ulysses* and still don't. But if I was overwhelmed by my early encounter, I was not daunted. I carried it with me whenever I moved anywhere, and I have the same copy still, yellowing and dogeared, the dust jacket gone, the pages marked, the text full of underlines; and while I understand it better now, it remains as strange a creation to me today as it was then. Much of *Ulysses* was a mystery I felt I would never fully solve, yet I loved its wit and wordplay, and valued it for the improbable ambition it presented to the youth I was. At some point it helped inspire me to begin thinking of an impossible enterprise: the creation of a book that would leap over my own conventional ambitions, a book that would be greater than what I knew I could do.

About twelve years after that first reading of *Ulysses*, I was on the phone with my father, who was then 77 years old, and he was remembering Van Woert Street, the long Irish block with an old Dutch name where he had been raised; also he was remembering his friends, the O'Connell brothers, a quartet of Irish-Catholic-Democrats who successfully entered Albany politics in 1921, took the city away from the Republican Protestants, and never gave it back; and he was also telling some of his World War One stories that I knew almost by heart. His memories coalesced in me with such significance that I wrote down what I called "Idea for an Albany fantasy," a page and a half of pencil notes that would reconstitute the city's past—which is as old as the country itself, in terms of European colonization. The fantasy would begin with such characters as the great Revolutionary War general, Philip Schuyler, the political wizard Aaron Burr; one of America's founding fathers, Alexander Hamilton, the British General John Burgoyne, all erstwhile denizens of 18th century Albany; then move along to Herman Melville and Henry James, our 19th century literary giants with an Albany connection, to Martin H. Glynn, a 20th century Irish newspaper editor from Albany who became Governor of New York State and who played a small role in the development of the Irish Free State; also those political O'Connell brothers and a vast crowd of priests, nuns, gamblers, gangsters, mothers, whores, and laboring men, including my father; and central to it all, by way of the pleasure principle, a stunningly beautiful and sensual girl I knew extremely well. All these Albanians would be contemporaries in my novel, all eternally living out their destinies, over and over again, as they discovered one another's present and past.

I added at the end of the notes: "Commit a decade to the creation of this book."

Alas, I did not create the monster, for it was beyond my ability not only to execute but even to imagine beyond the broad outline. I wrote instead a novel of average size, then another, and another. But, as it turns out, I have been creating some sort of oversize creature after all: for out of the novels I have written, and others I hope to write, has emerged a schema of interlocking stories that I call "the Albany cycle," and which seems to be not just a series of books, but an effort to invent and populate an entire world; and the writing of it will probably occupy the rest of my life. I recall the eminent critic Edmund Wilson writing about *Ulysses*, and the unknown future of its characters. We know Bloom has brought Stephen home after a day's and night's wandering, and that the sensual Molly immediately envisions an affair with Stephen, getting Italian lessons from him, giving him singing lessons in exchange; also we see Bloom asserting his absent manhood by demanding breakfast in bed from Molly, and one critic has suggested Bloom may even be ready to accept cuckoldry by Stephen in order to gain a son—letting Stephen father a child with Molly.

Of course we do not know what the Blooms or Stephen did, for *Ulysses* has no sequel. But so vivid are the people that we are able to imagine them in assorted future roles; and this is how it seems to be with me and my own characters—one novel begetting another, a secondary character demanding his or her own book, a story insisting on being continued. I believe this is partly a product of discovering my own excitement at meeting characters a second, or third time, in the short stories of Sherwood Anderson, Hemingway and J. D. Salinger, of seeing Stephen move from the *Portrait* to *Ulysses*, of being mesmerized by the work of William Faulkner, whose 30 interlocking volumes of novels and stories—the Yoknapatawpha saga—stand as perhaps the most ambitious undertaking in 20th century American literature.

Faulkner was a student of Balzac, another maestro of interconnectedness. The American novelist James Gould Cozzens, also a Balzacian, wrote about the phenomenon of related stories in a preface to a volume of 10 novels by Balzac. "The point on which we (Balzacians) agree," wrote Cozzens, "is that there comes an indefinable pleasure in meeting, in a Balzac novel, a character with whom we have had dealings before; an old acquaintance, who seems sometimes closer to us than a brother." Faulkner was a student of Joyce as well as Balzac, his most overt homage being visible in two of his greatest novels, *The Sound and the Fury*, and *Light in August*, in which he uses, to great effectiveness, the stream-of-consciousness technique and, with lesser success, the Joycean portmanteau wordplay. Faulkner's copy editor on *Light in August* conscientiously separated the words that Faulkner had willfully run together, and Faulkner restored the fusion and noted in the margin: "OK as set, goddamn it." And as the editing persisted he fumed anew and further noted: "OK as set, and written. Jesus Christ . . . (let the book) stand as it is."

Some critics in their reviews of these Faulkner novels noted the influence of Joyce, but Faulkner's retort was that he had never read *Ulysses*, had never even seen a copy until after his two novels were published.

"You know," he told an interviewer, "sometimes I think there must be a sort of pollen of ideas floating in the air, which fertilizes similar minds, here and there, which have not had direct contact." He admitted being told *about* Joyce and conceded he might have been influenced by what he had heard.

Writers frequently deny any influence from the writers who have gone before them, out of fear that their own work will seem derivative. But unless that fear is well grounded, and their work truly owes its existence to grand larceny, such a denial in the name of originality is the silliest sort of posturing. You might call it the immaculate conception theory of literature—the work created whole, its creator undiddled by any literary ancestor. But even Joyce owed, and acknowledged, a debt to Ibsen, Flaubert, Goethe, Dante, Shakespeare, among others, and, not least, Homer, whom he reinvented as himself, a Dubliner.

In his late years someone asked Faulkner what he thought of Joyce and he replied ungrudgingly: "James Joyce was one of the great men of my time. He was electrocuted by the divine fire. He [and] Thomas Mann were the great writers of my time. [Joyce] . . . might have been the greatest, but he was electrocuted. He had more talent than he could control."

T. S. Eliot, an admirer and booster of Joyce and *Ulysses*, wrote about this matter of literary inheritance: "No poet, no artist of any art, has his complete meaning alone. His significance, his appreciation is the appreciation of his relation to the dead poets and artists. You cannot value him alone; you must set him, for contrast and comparison, among the dead . . ."

I freely admit that I took heart and some direction from the ambition of the dead Joyce. I'm indebted also for his gift of courage in the face of the rejection, the opposition, and the censorship he encountered—in Ireland, France, the United States. I have never had to struggle against censorship, at least not yet. Joyce, Henry Miller, Norman Mailer and others cleared the way for all of my generation to say whatever we wanted to say in whatever way we wanted to say it. But I did have a few go-rounds with rejection of my early work, and then, surprising to me, *Ironweed*, my fourth novel, which I thought was my best book up to that time, had 13 rejections before being published with considerable success in the U.S., and, since then, in many languages around the world.

The arrogance with which Joyce confronted his detractors, censors and obstructors was admirable and inspirational, as was that cunning of which he has Stephen speak at the end of *Portrait*. But I was never much for cunning myself, never really knew how to get out of my own way, how to be anything less than the vulnerable witness, very like Bailey, the hero of my first novel, *The Ink Truck*, who when asked why, during a strike, he ran toward the company goons he knew would club him, responded, "That's all there is . . . Run to the glory of the club." Having been instructed by such gauntlet-runners as Joyce, and also Kafka, whose caveat was: "You are the problem, no scholar far and wide," I found myself clubbed and bloodied, taking the goon squad's worst, then found myself also getting up, having breakfast, and moving forward, making the goons irrelevant. This isn't much fun, but it certainly is Joycean.

* * *

I was in Dublin, in University College, 20 years ago, chasing after things Joycean, covering for an American magazine the doings of the 176 visiting scholars at the fourth annual James Joyce Symposium. I sat in on discussions of *Ulysses*, *Finnegans Wake*, and Joyce in general, and then went into the streets of Dublin tracking the man and his places — pubs and erstwhile homes, including the one in Bray where he set the Christmas dinner scene in *Portrait*, also The Gresham Hotel, which he used in *The Dead*, The Martello Tower, which was the opening setting of *Ulysses*, and Number Seven Eccles Street, the house where the Blooms lived and which I happened upon by happy accident when driving past it. All this attention to the real world had about it the feel of archeology, not literature; and yet there is a fine fascination about tracking the *world* in which Joyce actually lived, and discovering something palpable of the man who became the writer.

But the chief discovery for me was how the writer had *used* his world, how, when he left Dublin for exile in Paris and elsewhere, he took Dublin with him, venerating its memory by reconstituting it on the pages of his fiction. One of the Joyce symposiasts spoke of how Joyce "canonized the obsession with being Irish—the whole love of place, of knowing a particular street in Dublin and talking all night about it."

That is how it has been for me and Albany for many years. When I was in Puerto Rico I started to write stories about the expatriate life I'd chosen for myself. Puerto Rico was an exotic and romantic setting, a Spanish-language community full of hostility and reverence for the United States, with all sorts of volatile politics and left and right-wing beach bums to write about. I loved the place and yet I came to see that I really couldn't use it as a basis for my fiction because I wasn't Puerto Rican. I couldn't identify with, or even begin to read, the Puerto Rican mind, even though I'd married one. I didn't know the Spanish language as well as I wanted, and so could never possess the literature, or the complex world of Hispanic and Latin scholars and political theorists, who abounded in the Puerto Rican reality.

I had written short stories and had started a novel set in Puerto Rico, but I finally rejected all that and started a novel about Albany. I suddenly found myself ranging through sixty years in the history of an Albany family—the Phelans, whose lives have preoccupied me ever since. Making that transition from Puerto Rico to Albany had enormous consequences for me. To begin with I liked my own writing better, understood the people better. I found I understood the psychology of almost anybody in Albany—whether it was a baseball player or a politician or an artist or a drunk or a spinster or a clandestinely married woman—far better than I knew anybody in Puerto Rico. I called this novel *The Angels and the Sparrows*, and although it was never published, it did, in time, turn into the basis for my most recent novel, *Very Old Bones*. The *Bones* novel is much more complex than the early book, but the same people are present in both narratives. And so is the place.

The answer to why I liked the Albany novel better than my Puerto Rican stories is that I was doing what Joyce had done without knowing I was doing it; reconstituting a city that was long gone, and surprising myself every day with what was in my unconscious, what suddenly would make the leap into my imagination. I knew Albany far more intimately than I realized; and it would have taken me half a lifetime to know Puerto Rico in an equivalent way.

How can you possibly write about a place if you don't understand what the street names mean, or why the mayor is the mayor, or what political power means to your father, or how God is manifested in your neighborhood? I was little more than a tourist in Puerto Rico, and even when I began writing about Albany I discovered I didn't *really* understand the city's principal social force—the Irish Catholic Democratic bossism that held absolute power over the lives of almost everyone in the city. I hadn't paid sufficient attention to politics when I was working as an Albany newspaperman before going to Puerto Rico, hadn't observed my father and my uncles closely enough to know that they were truly political creatures.

I also disdained covering politics as a young newsman; and as a novelist I've always avoided political partisanship; for time very quickly changes political allegiances, and the novels premised on such allegiances blow away with the first winds of change. Yet if politics is missing from a novel about Albany then it would not be the Albany in which I grew up; for politics was a principal moral code of my city.

As a child and young man I heard very little condemnation of city politics on moral grounds, even from the church; especially from the church. For if you were Irish, which about forty per cent of the city's population was, by derivation—back in 1875 one in six Albany residents had been *born* in Ireland—then you probably also belonged to the Democratic Party; and if you were a Democrat, you stood a very good chance of also being a Roman Catholic. And if you were Roman Catholic you gave allegiance not only to the church on the corner, but also to the political boss, Daniel Peter O'Connell—namesake of a great Irish patriot—and Dan was, himself, a pillar of the church, inseparably linked to the Albany bishop and the local priests, who revered him and prayed for him, and whose prayers were answered regularly by his benevolence. Saint Daniel, one maverick Democrat called him.

But Saint Daniel was also running gambling parlors, profiting handsomely from the all-night saloons, the baseball pools, the illegal card games, and the whorehouses. He was in collusion with the grafters and bankers, getting rich with the paving contractors, not entirely for his own sake, for he lived frugally, but for the sake of perpetuating his political power.

Wherever you could make a holy vow or an illegal dollar, that's where the Irish were, that's where Dan and his politics were. I don't mean to imply that the church was in league with the whorehouses, but it was common knowledge that the madams all kicked in to Dan's coffers. And the bagmen who made the collections were often city detectives. The clergy, with bountiful self-interest, chose to look the other way when this knowledge surfaced, which it did regularly.

I remember vividly in the middle 1960s when a radical Franciscan priest, who was working with slum people to upgrade their neighborhood, took a list of addresses of South End whorehouses to one of the monsignors who was then a figure of authority in the Catholic Diocese. The monsignor looked at the list and told the young priest, "I don't believe this. Dan O'Connell wouldn't let these places exist in the city." But the South End, for forty years, had been notorious for its red light district. From the 1920s into the 1960s, Green Street, a very old thoroughfare, was the code name of Albany's bluest corridor of sin. It was as notorious and as widely known as Storyville in New Orleans, or the old Kips in Dublin that Joyce used for his Nighttown in *Ulysses.*

Within this peculiar prevailing morality, Albany families were interlocked in saintliness and chicanery; and chicanery was, sometimes, only another way of getting on in the world; and objective morality didn't interest the Albany Irish. They were more imaginative than that. They understood that they had been deprived, that in a previous era they had been social outcasts, unable to get jobs. Families were hungry, and hunger was immoral. Now the Irish were no longer hungry; they had jobs; they had power. Once Dan O'Connell became the political boss, he was as respected as the Bishop. Dan was the man who would save your soul by putting you to work. Of course he was also a rascal; and through the use of loyalty, ruthlessness, generosity and fear, he controlled Albany from 1921 until he died in 1977—a span of 56 years, unprecedented in the history of American machine politics.

Dan's last Mayor, Erastus Corning II, a wealthy patrician Protestant from an old Albany family, who had become Irish by osmosis, served as Mayor from 1941 to 1983—11 consecutive terms, another longevity record in American politics. Erastus continued controlling the city after Dan's death for another six years until he, too, died. This was how you removed a Democrat from power in Albany. You called the undertaker. Until this year.

Some months ago our then incumbent Mayor, an Irish Catholic Democrat by the name of Tom Whalen, announced that after ten years in City Hall he'd had enough. He was resigning, and it looked to some—and rightly so, it turned out—as if he might have a Federal judgeship somewhere in his future. This is unprecedented. Giving up city hall for the bench? The man must be daft. But no. He is of the new breed. Dan is dead, Erastus is dead. The machine is not dead but it is shrunken and arthritic. Albany is new, vigorous, even respectable. And can you believe it, our erstwhile metropolis of sin has been chosen as an All-American City. Dan O'Connell's bones must be dancing a scornful jig in their grave—dancing to that time-tested political theme of his bygone machine: *Honesty is no Substitute for Experience.*

* * *

I am proud of my Irish heritage and yet I don't consider myself an Irish writer, or even an Irish-American writer (just American, is my own perception). But I cannot escape the Irish connection, and neither do I try to avoid it. A writer like John O'Hara tried to bury his Irishness and came on as an Anglo-Saxon Protestant clubman; Scott Fitzgerald had a gift of Irish poetry in his soul, but he rarely identified it as such. A writer with whom I share the Irish-American political burden is Edwin O'Connor, whose novel, *The Last Hurrah*, was a marvelous piece of work that convulsed me with laughter through its very witty treatment of urban and ecclesiastical politics in Boston. Mr. O'Connor understood the social topography of Boston down to the last pew of the church, the last illegal vote. And yet I felt his politics were too hygienic, too bereft of the darker side of the comparable Irish political life in Albany.

A dozen years ago I came across a short book of conversations with Joyce, written by a friend of his, Arthur Power, who asked at one point, ". . . how do you feel about being Irish?" And Joyce responded, "I regret it for the temperament it has given me."

If anyone had asked me the same question I would have responded, "I am fond of it for the temperament it has given me." I am Irish all the way back on both sides of the family, and perhaps I have grown into the temperament, or resigned myself to it, but I would give no thought to exchanging it for something else. As one of my fallen-away Catholic characters says to a minister about what she now was instead of a Catholic, "Well, I'm certainly not a Methodist."

The element of darkness in the personality that seems to go with being Irish has become increasingly important to me in understanding anybody's life. I copied out a few paragraphs of what Joyce said to Arthur Power, something I already agreed with and had already put into practice in my novels, yet had never understood quite so clearly until I read Joyce's words.

He said: "When we are living a normal life we are living a conventional one, following a pattern which has been laid out by other people in another generation, an objective pattern imposed on us by the church and state. But a writer must maintain a continual struggle against the objective: that is his function. The eternal qualities are the imagination and the sexual instinct, and the formal life tries to suppress both. Out of this present conflict arise the phenomena of modern life. . . . Idealism is a pleasant bauble, but in these days of overwhelming reality it no longer interests us, or even amuses. We regard it as a sort of theatrical dropscene. Most lives are made up like the modern painter's themes, of jugs, and pots and plates, backstreets and blowsy living rooms inhabited by blowsy women, and of a thousand daily sordid incidents which seep into our minds no matter how we strive to keep them out. These are the furniture of our life."

When I wrote my novels on matters akin to what Edwin O'Connor had written, I felt I had to bring in that furniture that Joyce speaks of—the violence and the gambling and the sexuality, along with the shenanigans of the political thieves and the haughty clerics of the church. O'Connor's comic ward heelers in Boston, and O'Hara's country club social climbers, didn't have anything to do with what was going on down on Albany's Broadway among those raffish people I knew—the Irish, German, Jewish, Dutch, and Italians — tough, dirty-minded, foul-mouthed hustlers and gamblers and bigots and whoremongers, and, at the same time, wonderful, generous, funny, loyal, curiously honest and very complex people. I felt that this way of life had to be penetrated at *all* levels; and I felt it also required the surreal dimension that is part of any society in which religion plays such a powerful role.

Even before my family and I moved from San Juan to Albany in 1963, I had started doing long interviews with my parents and uncles and neighbors, and I began to see the political and religious ramifications in everything. I was learning what lay beneath the surface of the worlds that I thought I knew—city hall, the church, the newspapers, jazz music, night clubs, sports, family life in North Albany. I discovered the gangsterish life lived in Albany during Prohibition, the 1920s and early 1930s. I learned what it was like to make a living cutting ice on the river in the 19th century, what it meant to work in the Lumber District when Albany was known as the White Pine Center of the World.

And so gangsters populated my first Albany novel, *Legs*, and the writing took six years of my life, immersing me in not only Albany's history, but the history of the nation in those vicious years that were called the Jazz Age. That book propelled me into a novel called *Billy Phelan's Greatest Game*, which concerned the night world that my father and my favorite uncle had inhabited. In that book I wanted to dramatize the power of Irish-American politics in the city: how the bosses—Dan O'Connell and his associates—could impose their will on everybody in town. They controlled the flow of beer in the city both during and after Prohibition. Dan owned a brewery, and if you didn't take his beer, called Hedrick's, the police would suspend your privilege of staying open after the legal closing hour, or they'd close your saloon down as a firetrap. And so Hedrick's beer was sold on tap in 200 of the city's 259 saloons. The bosses could raise the taxes on your house or your grocery store if you disagreed with them. Merely by spreading the word they could force a small-time gambler like Billy Phelan to be "marked lousy"—a phrase I still have never heard used outside of Albany, which meant if the pols wanted to isolate you, they could; and you wouldn't even be able to buy a glass of beer in your own neighborhood saloon.

That was real power, and the individual was subordinate to it. Billy didn't understand the way his own world functioned, although he thought he did, and so my novel became a study of his imagination, his extraordinary moral code, his misreading of the ways of power. And in order to show all this, I had to reconstruct the city-that-was—the Albany of 1938—the *place* that was at the heart of the communal behavior that shaped my story.

In my most recent novel, *Very Old Bones*, politics is not a dominant issue, though I know it is everywhere unseen in the life of the family. What *is* visible is the peculiar behavior of certain people in the family who force their inherited morality, or their religious or sexual madness, on their wives, husbands, children, siblings, often with disastrous results. In *Very Old Bones* the story concerns the Phelans, an Irish and Irish-American family; but I have been struck by a broad reaction to the book by critics, friends, even strangers, who say that the novel tells the true story of *their* own families. It is hardly news that once a story is developed with the specifics of a single place, it can then transcend that place and take on meanings that were neither intended nor even suspected by the writer. But I do believe that the key word here is specifics, which is how any provincial fictional world becomes transcendent.

Without those specifics the place remains unrealized; and you do not have fiction as I value it. The writer can do all the navel-gazing, all the private psychological analysis, that the novel can bear, but until it's centered on a place, then it's a vagrant pursuit, a discursive soap opera, a Sunday afternoon in the park counting leaves on a generic tree. It is disembodied life, lacking the dynamics that create the movement that defines the imaginations of the people who make the story. And they're very different people in Mississippi, or Puerto Rico, or Dublin, or even Boston, from the people in Albany.

Joyce was insistent on the essentiality of place. In his talk with Arthur Power he spoke of Turgenev's *Sportsman's Notebook*, and he said, "You remember . . . how local it was—and yet out of that germ [Turgenev] became a great international writer. For myself, I always write about Dublin, because if I can get to the heart of Dublin I can get to the heart of all the cities of the world. In the particular is contained the universal."

My literary ancestors of place have been Irish in part, but many and various really, and I owe equivalent debts to Kafka and Hemingway and Nathanael West and John Cheever and Isaac Babel and Saul Bellow and so many more in whose work the sense of place is central. Even an abstractionist like Samuel Beckett is secure in his place—that cellar, that ash heap, that desolate room, that sterile plain—where his characters suffer the terminal torments of their cancerous souls.

There are cancerous souls everywhere, and pure souls, and lost souls; and Joyce put his in Dublin, and Hemingway put his in Paris, and Babel put his in Odessa, and Beckett put his in garbage cans. I put mine in a house on Colonie Street in Albany. Souls are where you find them, I say, and one place to find them is as good as another. But it's never the same place. And because it isn't, it's never the same souls.

The last gift from Joyce is probably the greatest, and also the most unusable—his language. Whether it's the exquisite ending to *The Dead*, or Molly's exultation as she yields to Bloom for the first time, or any given passage of *Finnegans Wake* that affects the mind like a Bach suite, it is always the recurrence of proof that literature can exist without plot but not without language.

Faulkner was once asked whether an author has the prerogative to create his own language, and he answered, "He has the right to do that provided he don't insist on anyone understanding it." He added that a writer assumes an obligation with his vocation to write in a way that people can understand. "He doesn't have to write it in the way that every. . . imbecile in the third grade can understand it, but he's got to use a language which is accepted and in which the words have specific meanings that everybody agrees on. I think that *Finnegans Wake* and *Ulysses* were justified, but then it's hard to say on what terms they were justified. That was a case of a genius who was electrocuted by the divine fire."

I wonder why Faulkner kept electrocuting Joyce? But maybe I don't wonder.

Hugh Kenner wrote of the coherent specificity of Joyce's language. In his essay on the occasion of Joyce's 100th birthday in 1982 Kenner wrote of the secret of *Ulysses* being "utter cohesion, thousands of details quietly supporting one another." And he mentions how Joyce thought it was "stupid" of George Moore to "make a character look up the time of a train that stopped in his suburb at the same time every day: rather like looking up the time of the 11 o'clock mass." Such inattention was unJoycean.

"Joyce," wrote Kenner, "worked with tireless attention to what had previously been inadvertent. He knows how much change a character is carrying, and in which pocket (Bloom set out on that famous morning with four shillings ninepence). He knows the brand of Bloom's hat, Plasto's. He knows that 'wrote' for 'write' is a plausible error in Martha Clifford's typed letter, because *i* and *o* are adjacent on the keyboard."

Joyce waged war, Kenner wrote, "against nescience, inadvertence, against the supposition that anything is anything else. Insofar as he could change the world of the mind, he changed it toward order."

But Joyce's order is of a particular kind, and is in many respects unusable by anyone else, a form of sudden death to imitators. Eliot said that the price of having a Dante or a Shakespeare [and he could have added

Joyce] is that literature can have only one, and those who come later must find something else to do.

Any person who aspires to serious writing knows this. I constantly purge my work of anything that seems to be even slightly Joycean, though that word now has such a broad context that I would have to stop writing and take up mathematics to be rid of its implications entirely. Joyce's gifts to the art of writing are so abundant, so pervasive, that some things have ceased to be his. The interior monologue that he didn't create but popularized is only Joycean if it is used to excess; otherwise it is just another tool in the writer's kitbag.

That said, I must also say that I used Joyce overtly in my last novel, *Very Old Bones*, an interlude of homage to *Finnegans Wake* that was the fictionalizing of a true event in my life. That event took place at a closed-down Catholic summer camp on Lake Luzerne in the Adirondack mountains, not far from Saratoga. I stayed there by myself for two weeks in 1971 when I was working on my novel *Legs*, trying to write enough text so my publisher would send money to avert foreclosure on my home and allow me to continue living at the genteel poverty level to which I had become accustomed. I was staying in a one-room cottage heated by kerosene.

It was October, when the temperatures fluctuate between the radiant heat of an Indian Summer day, and the sub-freezing mountain temperatures of the impending winter night. I had worked all day and, as usual, after cooking a very late supper, I settled in for some reading, which this night was *Finnegans Wake*. I was drinking *Old Crow* whiskey and smoking small Tiparillo cigars. I was up to about 30 cigars a day as a way of cutting down on cigarettes. Slowly I felt the chill in the room, and I put on my overcoat, checked the heater, found it cold, kept reading, smoking, drinking, put on my muffler, put on my hat and one glove, leaving the right hand free to turn the page, and in that condition, warmed by the whiskey and the language of the *Wake*, I defeated the weather utterly.

As usual, I read the *Wake's* pages without knowing very much about what I was reading, loving the jokes and the wordsmithery, thinking perhaps I had a grip on a meaning only to lose it, pushing onward into evermore mysterious and meaningless word games, continuing with the

belief that surely something would come clear, ever so slowly getting the
rhythm of the pages and feeling the onset of a response that was akin to
the subliminal suggestions music creates in me—free-floating then,
captivated by the growth of sensation first, then in the grip of a confound-
ing emotion; for I found myself moved, almost to weeping, by the beauty
of the meaning I could not put into words of my own, and from knowing
I was being as genuinely touched in the unconscious as Finn himself is
touched by his river of sleeping thought and memory, and I read through
to the final pages, experiencing the sublimity of Ana Livia's monologue,
as the River Liffey that she is, flows into the Irish Sea, and into Finn's
mind, and my own, and I decided when I closed the book that this was
probably the premier reading experience of my life, for never had I been
moved to tears and beyond by something that was fundamentally incomprehensible, a supreme lesson in the power of language alone to touch
what is deepest in our memory, our imagination. I decided in a much later
year to pass this experience on through the medium of my narrator in *Very
Old Bones*, Orson Purcell, who undergoes the same experience I did, but
in a summer hotel on the shore of Saratoga Lake. He lifts from that
glorious monologue of Ana Livia this fragment, and quotes it to make a
point in his story of his life among the women who were all the world to
him.

> '*Why I'm all these years within years in soffran, allbeleaved. To hide
> away the tear, the parted. It's thinking of all. The brave that gave their.
> The fair that wore. All them that's gunne. I'll begin again in a jiffey. The
> nik of a nad. How glad you'll be I waked you! My! How well you'll feel!
> For ever after*'

Orson finds abundant allusions to his own life and love in this and
other segments, as anyone must in Joyce's singular book. And then
Orson, this young man who has been so put-upon by life, quotes again in
conclusion:

> '*I done me best when I was let. Thinking always if I go all goes. A hundred
> cares, a tithe of troubles and is there one who understands me?*'

That last question was what Joyce had asked his wife Nora in Dublin
three and a half decades before he wrote that page of the *Wake*. And I think

it's safe to say, even *nine* decades after he asked it, that the answer is no, no one. But we are trying.

Brian Nolan wrote this about Joyce: "Perhaps [his] true fascination. . . lies in his secretiveness, his ambiguity (his polyguity, perhaps?) . . . His works are a garden in which some of us may play. All that we can claim to know is merely a small bit of that garden."

But even that small bit of Joyce's garden: what a splendid gift it has been to us all.

Note

[1] This essay was first delivered as a lecture on Bloomsday Eve, 6/15/93, at University College, Dublin; and later at the New York State Summer Writers Institute, 7/26/93.

On Milan Kundera

On Two Photographs

Back jacket of The *Unbearable Lightness of Being*: his body muffled in a padded black raincoat, he is self-consciously and uncomfortably cocked, leg and arm, against a scuffed urban wall: an image of the novelist as mock scheming Samson, all shoulders and pushing limbs. On his face, beneath the enormous, waspish eyebrows, a smirk-smile says: Like everything else regarding that absurd creature, social man, this rite of posing is ridiculous.

Above the title of the interview "The Art of Fiction LXXXI" in the *Paris Review* 92 (Summer 1984): his arm extending before him on a table or a desk, one hand clutches the massive root of the other, the fingers of which extend up and splay out like the rooster's comb of the bird-of-paradise flower-flora the novelist's body creates out of itself as it remembers "life in Paradise," a vegetal monotony that "bred happiness, not boredom" (*The Unbearable Lightness of Being*). Above this adjunctival tableau a face that, under its warm, caterpillar-on-leaf brows, beams back a lot of reflected light, plus an inner glow of agreeableness, of cooperation with the "media." A likeable mug. Broad nosed. Full lips widening to where they seem to catch in the deep grooves winging out from each side of the nose, the crowned head of an Egyptian king in the shape thus inscribed, or a plump nun in a habit, a nun who smiles over the hands, recollecting the myth of a peaceable kingdom.

The Kundera of the first photograph is identical with the old-fashioned, incessantly "obtrusive" narrator of his fiction—a born instructor with lemon juice in his veins, perpetuator of the famous Czech sternness. He it is who has also authored a series of passionately serious, stunningly lucid and summatory essays and interviews that, appearing in translation in American journals in recent years, and in conjunction with his novels, have brought back into our consciousness a sense of the historical momentousness of the novel.

This Kundera trusts nobody. Nothing escapes the withering glance of his irony except art, memory, and animals—the first two for their spiritual depth (such as it is), the third for a restful unconsciousness of depth.

And as for art, perhaps he trusts only the novel, with its inveterate skepticism, its "wisdom of uncertainty." Particularly the central European novel (Kafka, Broch, Musil, Hasek). Here he finds the great enemy of "totalitarian Truth," of the regimented abstraction that "excludes relativity, doubt, questioning." Here he finds "concrete existence," for instance "hated irony" and dialogue and jokes and "the centuried roots of jazz" and benign patches of irrelevance, such as the tongue of the bulldog in *The Farewell Party* "waving like a gay little flag."

The Kundera of the second photograph is the tender creator, in particular, of two heroines, Tamina in *The Book of Laughter and Forgetting* and Tereza in *The Unbearable Lightness of Being*. He would sooner pick his hand than pick a flower. Being is as safe with him as with anyone. His brilliant discursive flights are entertainment for her vacant mind. His irony is a boyish show of muscle; he would like to make even bitterness blossom into lyricism, to delight her ears. (Indeed, he can hardly think except to sing.) His sentences are tersely masculine just for her, teasingly rough caresses of the sandpaper tips of his long, peculiarly long, fingers.

On Not Being Serious

A novelist whose work has been banned for political reasons—as Kundera's has in Czechoslovakia—is naturally defensive about being read politically. He wants to believe that his work "transcends" politics; he wants to keep the children of his imagination out of danger.

Kundera's other reason for categorizing his fiction as "hypothesis" or "play" is his refusal of what Czeslaw Milosz, in *The Captive Mind*, calls "enslavement through consciousness." Logic may be limitingly self-born, out of phase with "concrete existence." A joke can set you free.

Yet Kundera also believes that thinking can free the mind, and the more he emerges as a formal authorial presence in his work, the more he appears as one who incessantly thinks. What is the purpose of all this thought? Ludvik, in Kundera's first novel, *The Joke*, thinks "that life in its day-to-day events speaks to us about itself, that it gradually reveals a secret, that it takes the form of a rebus whose message must be deciphered, that the stories we live in life comprise the mythology of our lives and in that mythology lies the key to truth and mystery." He adds: "Is it all an illusion? Possibly, even probably, but I can't seem to rid myself of the need to *decipher* my life continually."[1] Kundera displays the same need, satisfying it through his characters, those "playful" elaborations of himself. His books are, then, *serious* play. They press "concrete existence" for its secrets; they are intent (as Kundera says great novels are) on making discoveries. On the other hand, the author defends them as being only playfully serious, because seriousness, in his experience, strong-arms concrete being. Marketa, in *The Joke*, with her "fatal inability to grasp any joke whatsoever," is "the type of woman who takes everything seriously," and this "made her totally at one with the spirit of the age." Her "major gift from the fates was an aptitude for credulity." Seriousness, then, is a form of stupidity. That being so, who would want to claim that his or her work is serious?

Can Kundera have it both ways? He cannot decipher without being serious; he cannot be serious without being stupid. At times, as will be noted more fully, I think he is stupid, and precisely because he appears overeager to be serious (this usually means a cynical thinker, with cynicism acting as a reverse form of credulity). But that, for the moment, is not the issue. The issue is the contradiction between the intention to use thought to gain freedom and the insistence, at the same time, that the medium of that thought, the novel, is not "a territory where one. . . make[s] assertions; it is a territory of play and of hypothesis."

We can respect Kundera's fine scruples, his flight from either suffering or inflicting enslavement of consciousness, while concluding that, where an author obtrudes as a thinker so frequently and piquantly as

Kundera does, the distinction between play and assertion disappears. In a novel, an authorial assertion is precisely that; it may be relative to a concrete situation, but it is not automatically relativized by the novel "form," which bears it along as the barge bore the preening Cleopatra. Only a character's reflection may be lusciously changed by the medium of fiction, like an ice-cream bar when it is dipped into chocolate.

In any case, to assert is not to compel, whereas not to assert may be to abet the age's stupidities. Thought that isn't serious isn't worth thinking—indeed, cannot be thought. Kundera is worth reading, quite largely, because he thinks, and because his thought would befriend "concrete existence." (In fact, just as he is not gifted at laughter—his laughter is all pain—so he is no great friend to the flesh. In this, he is the opposite of Joyce. His special love is for the trembling or embittered "I." But more on this later.) Kundera's thinking is a continual agitation against received ideas, as exciting and alarming to break into as a hornet's nest, and as multiple, as incessantly active. This author may make himself audible in his work as an earnest that it is only fiction, but the result is the opposite: the fiction becomes serious because he, Milan Kundera, being in the midst of it, is savagely caring.

Reverse Kitsch

For Kundera, the novel is an aggressive complexity, a kitsch destroyer. (Kitsch: a sentimental group lie.) It is, precisely, rebelliously intelligent. A Boston Tea Party of a genre, a defiance against the taxation of ideological absolutisms, a serious mischief of both conceptual and formal complication, it is ethical to the degree that it remains an axiological gadfly, to the degree that its aesthetics disorient and buzz.

If this puts it precariously on the offensive, if it makes an affirmation of "being" hard to get to (but Kundera has never promised an *affirmation*), it also creates the hazard of reverse kitsch.

Reverse kitsch is the meaning of the smirk of the Kundera in the first photograph. If kitsch excludes shit, the kitsch-denier must shovel some into his work, as a lesson.

The Unbearable Lightness of Being begins, as if wanting to be unbearably, heavily frank, with an example. The first brief section concludes:

> Not long ago, I caught myself experiencing a most incredible sensation. Leafing through a book on Hitler, I was touched by some of his portraits; they reminded me of my childhood. I grew up during the war; several members of my family perished in Hitler's concentration camps; but what were their deaths compared with the memories of a lost period in my life, a period that would never return?
>
> This reconciliation with Hitler reveals the profound moral perversity of a world that rests essentially on the nonexistence of return, for in this world everything is pardoned in advance and therefore everything cynically permitted.

This analysis coarsely equates "*my* childhood" and the deaths of relatives ("*my* family"). Childhood and Hitler. To long for the first, it is implied, is to long for the second ("I was touched by some of his portraits"). But the meaning of the first is life (the *puer eternus*, once below a time, the unspilt seed); and the meaning of the second, death. The first relates to what is essential to the speaker, the "I" climbing up to exult in its first tree-crotch, whereas the second was, to the child, a temporal rustle of contingency.

What explains this leveling of legitimate, of just, distinctions? Does Kundera want to be antilyrical at any cost, brutal toward the "heart" for its failure to be entirely virtuous? The phrase "this reconciliation with Hitler" is dishonest. To begin with, an exaggeration. Second, a reification: a once-and-for-all status conferred on a passing emotion. There is a further confusion between pardon and cynicism. The first combines bewilderment and charity. The second is all weary condemnation.

Yes, it seems that Kundera wants us to look with him into his heart and see the monster there, the one produced by "the nonexistence of return." Diametrically opposed to the stupidity of Marxist or republican progressiveness, he keeps up an open fire on the unbearable lightness of existing only once (i.e., not only is there no recurrence or progression, but, bewilderingly experimental and fugitive, life never gains enough certainty and solidity to be heavy, to be real, to be just). "We can never know what to want, because, living only one life, we can neither compare it with our previous lives nor perfect it in our lives to come"—this thought is characteristically arresting, but listen to its undermessage: "this one life is not worth living." It makes short shrift of the imaginative extensions of experience in literature, of the lessons of history, of the pragmatic guidelines of organic societies, and of learning from one's own past mistakes.

Life: a tabula rasa. A grief of uncertainty. Perversely attached to its own imperfect past, so as to thicken itself with duration. And so everything is pardoned in advance, or at least in retrospect. Everything is cynically permitted. The thinking in all this is darkly, antisentimentally slick, not really thinking, but topsy-turvy kitsch.

Mystifications

Kundera feels "an irresistible desire to demystify myths" ("Conversation with Milan Kundera," *The Threepenny Review*, Winter 1986). That is, he has the aggressive and melancholy soul of a novelist. He has also a penchant for dramatic philosophy, a contradiction in terms whose folly he does not escape.

The opening pages of The *Unbearable Lightness of Being* form a mare's nest of "brilliant"—of stage-conscious—ideas. There is space to take up a few of them:

I. "In the world of eternal return the weight of unbearable responsibility lies heavy on every move we make." This idea assumes that we ourselves determine what will eternally recur (as opposed to being determined). And Nietzsche did indeed suggest that "your most solid center of gravity" should be the thought that, whatever you will, will its eternal return. But a solid center of gravity is a sustaining weight, not an unbearable one.

The ethical gravity of the ideal of eternal return is not "why Nietzsche called the idea the heaviest of burdens." Rather, Nietzsche understood that recurrence could only fake Being (Being as what stands). The relentless sewing machine of becoming could whir and whir as long as it liked, but would lack thread for its needle.

In the world of the eternal recurrence of the same, every move we made would be emptied, lightened, by the demon of duplication, with his taunt: "To repeat is not the same as Being in and for itself; it is to die a hundred thousand times."

Suppose that Gilles Deleuze is right when, in *Nietzsche and Philosophy,* he says that Nietzschean eternal return is the strict opposite of a circle that makes the same return, that what returns is active becoming itself, so active that it is being. Then the idea is indistinguishable from the great theme of the novel, namely the burden of "living only one life," a theme that only the Dionysian artist can make soar.

II. "If eternal return is the heaviest of burdens, then our lives can stand out against it in all their splendid lightness." How fortunate that eternal return is only a "myth," how splendid to live only one life. The pictorial appeal of contrast ("can stand out against") lures Kundera into this patent insincerity.

III. "Parmenides. . . saw the world divided into pairs of opposites: light/darkness, fineness/coarseness, warmth/cold, being/ nonbeing." Again: Parmenides judged "lightness . . . positive, weight negative." But in point of fact miracle-minded Parmenides corrected those taken in by "the deceptive order of my words," those who "divided form contrariwise and established characters apart from one another." Name two opposites: "There is nothing that does not belong to either. Being is indivisible" ("ungenerated, imperishable, whole, unique, immovable, and complete").

No philosopher of Being more divinely antidivisional than Parmenides. What a pity to see his pure white egg of a theory (too good, of course, for this world) broken on the edge of Kundera's sizzling habit of logical dualism.

IV. "What then shall we choose? Weight or lightness?" If eternal return exists, we cannot choose lightness; if we live only once, we cannot, so Kundera insists, choose weight. What, then, is there to choose?

But the impulse behind Kundera's question is not merely to make us tense with the drama of a choice; the obscure impulse is to recognize that, if we trust the tale and not the teller, weight (or the unavoidable "myth" of weight) is crucial. For I suggest that Kundera's novel discovers not the unbearable lightness, but the scarcely bearable burden, of living (living once only).

Consider Tomas: this donkey of a character bears several rocks in his panier: his passion for surgery, his passion for women (for the " 'I' [that] hides itself," for "what is unimaginable about a person"), and his passion for truth, which underlies the other two passions and which leads to his seditious, ruinous article on Oedipus' willful blindness to the truth. Or consider Tereza: this sweet little donkey is terribly burdened by the need for a master (master of her soul and master of her body). Her "I" is sunk like a trapped diver, and only Tomas (such is her destiny) could possibly free her, releasing her lungs to the unbearable lightness of metaphysical air (her unique being awaits his detection of her unique flesh). In short, she is rather horribly referenced to one man, a man whose passion for discovery exceeds her, leaving her deserted, inert.

Sabina, Tomas's mistress, is burdened by the need to betray others. Franz, whose mistress she becomes, bears every leftist's burden, the myth of the march of history, the need to keep faith with everyone.

The unbearable lightness of being is a myth—a metaphysical fancy. Implicit in the oxymoron "unbearable lightness" is the paradox of a lightness too heavy to be borne. This is a negative inversion of Parmenidean indivisibility: opposites meet, because neither offers any support to being.

Kunderean Thought

All told, Kundera's thinking is, as intimated, an ambivalent mixture of motives, plus a proposition. Cynical antilyricism accounts for its glumness; a dramatic sense of important fresh discovery for its flair; a sensual love of shaping a sharp-edged idea for its piercing concision; hope in its potentially freeing results, for its quite remarkable salience and watchfulness; the need to escape from traps (e.g., central Europe) for an occasional blithe myth.

At its worst, it might be labeled Contra-Sweet ("Physical love is unthinkable without violence"; "if we have one life to live, we might as well not have lived at all"). At its best, as in his essays, it is an elegance of forceful, plain persuasion. In between it belongs to that bastard category, the provocative ("The individual composes his life according to the laws of beauty even in times of greatest distress"; "If a love is to be unforgettable, fortuities must immediately start fluttering down to it like birds to Francis of Assisi's shoulder")—thoughts that flutter down to us, impose their delicate, alien lightness of weight, and then fly off. Hypothetical? For the most part, his style of thinking eschews conditionality and qualifiers—phrases like "for the most part" and writerly, pressed-flower words like "eschews." It means to bite, to have instant, hard effect.

Attack and Dodge

Cognitive totalization? Leave that to the enemy, who loves it as a path back to a lost paradise.

Kundera's two masterpieces, *The Book of Laughter and Forgetting* and *The Unbearable Lightness of Being*, are like territories that defy mapping, that refuse to be small cohesive nations that can be wiped out by the squat tanks of a lineal, ideological paradisaicism.

In the sense developed by Gilles Deleuze and Felix Guattari in *On the Line*, the novels are continually self-decentering rhizomes—irisstands with a stemmed flow-head here, another there, and so on, all springing from the same promiscuous self-multiplying root (a root with a passion for the lateral). The contrast between Kundera's habit of reductive binary differentiations (body and soul, east and west, and so on) and the open circles, the broken chains, the deterritorializations and reterritorializations of his masterpieces (in terms echoed from *On the Line*) is peculiar.

In fact, however, the first serves as the means to the second. Kundera's way of creating a fictional map (and not a tracing: "a map is opposed to the trace. . . because its whole orientation is toward establishing contact with the real experimentally" [Deleuze and Guattari]) is to externalize his subject matter (lives, events) by placing it under the burning glass (under several in turn) of "universal ideas." Two twice-occurring chapter headings in *The Unbearable Lightness of Being*—"Lightness and Weight," "Soul and Body"—read like entries indexed in a philosophical dictionary. Other titles, in both books, announce not fictional "concreteness" but themes, ideas ("Words Misunderstood," "The Grand March," "Karenin's Smile," "The Angels," "Litost," "The Border"). Afraid of creating a climate like Dostoevsky's "a universe where everything turns into feeling. . . . where feelings are promoted to the rank of value and of truth" (in words from the Introduction to *Jacques and his Master*); determined to be a Cartesian nut that no one, that nothing, can crack, Kundera invents fictions whose multiplicities are defined and united by means of "outside" lines, the flight of his own authorially elaborated ideas, themselves multiple. His texts are thus opposed in every way to the classical or romantic book, which, as Deleuze and Guattari observe, is "constituted by the interiority of a substance or a subject." If Kundera himself is present, it is not as a universe of feeling, but as an activity of thought.

In what Schoenberg called "developing variation," as Theodore W. Adorno observed, "intellectualization becomes a technical principle." The result is that "all develops more concentratedly and more rapidly than is deemed acceptable by the sluggish habits of culinary [consumption]; polyphony functions with real parts." Like Schoenberg's art, Kundera's is one of "identity in nonidentity," in which, "amid radical change, melodic economy prevails."

Unlike Schoenberg's art, however, Kundera's is not, in Frederic Jameson's terms, "symptomatic of an objective tendency in the socioeconomic structure," of "an inhuman systematization of the world itself." It is not organized down to the least phrase, straitjacketing. What the various ideas compose, at any rate, is less a system than a grid, through which the characters are viewed (our nose pressed to the screen) but not captured.

Like Beethoven melody, a typical Kundera paragraph forms a short-lived synthesis of the functional (the development of an idea) and the expressive (the "poetry" of unique experience). But that it is disposed with a view to the whole structure of a chapter, as well as to social structure, does not keep it from seeming, tough luck, alone, indeed bereft.

Kundera's serial compositions (avoiding what he calls the "key signature" of unity of action, that "king's court in miniature") are the likely fictional home of those displaced from power, those who no longer belong, those experiencing cultural and personal vertigo.

The gain reciprocal with this forlornness is a certain deceptive dodging of the external reign of necessity. Kundera's ideational orientations relieve him of the burden of singleness of action, with its passive, unbroken, and "unbearable" submissions (when the action is novel length) to inexorable orders, not least temporality. A rhizomic structure does not, and cannot, end: its proliferation through segmentation or reterritorialization (that enchantment, that serial eternity) simply leaves off . . . Kundera's architectonics are important to him—as contrapuntal "music," as a victory over the political marketing and miring of ideas, over death—and they are subtle enough; but, and this is their secret aim, they never create the expectation of a certain formal satisfaction that they subsequently disappoint, as disappoint they inevitably would.

Are the two novels in question aesthetic triumphs, at least where "architectonic clarity" (in Kundera's phrase) is concerned? I think not. They are radiant only because certain of their characters come to mean more than the ideas that illuminate them, and not because of any architectonic light. (Their architectonics break up the path of the light they contain.)

In particular, they end poorly. *The Book of Laughter and Forgetting* leaves off with Jan, a dully repulsive character, not least so because he is conceived of as primarily sexual, hence biologically subject to repetition, bored. (Oh, Tamina, where are you, now that we have come to love you?) As for *The Unbearable Lightness of Being*, it drags to a nominal close with poor Karenin's mute, doggy death, generating a nostalgia for the animal paradise of unreflective circular repetition—a fictional luxury, surely, in the shadow of the Hegelian harrow that advances on everything in the book, requiring from those in its path a sleepless cunning. (Besides, isn't repetition boring? Isn't Karenin Jan in canine form?)

From their scattered bushes, Kundera's novels cry: "Life is not paradisal, and least of all when someone means to make it so. In the presence of a utopian idea, mock and jump clear." Smelling the paradise of socialist brotherhood turns Kundera into a hornet with a rage to relativize space, to decenter it and break it up, to create a "vertiginous complexity," to send the official picnickers packing. A negative role, perhaps, limited by its oppositional stance, its antiabsolutism that imposes a commitment to not making a commitment, its fondness for the idea that "in this world of iron laws there should remain a little human disorder" ("Symposium," *Laughable Loves*).

So Kundera's novels, piece by piece, sting and depart. Fleeing "revolutionary eschatology," they leave themselves no future, even as they twist this way and then that to avoid their own, or the very thought of, death. (News of the deaths of Tomas and Tereza, who are crushed by the truck they were riding in after it goes off the road, reaches us in one chapter; in the next, they are back among the living, ignorant of the accident still ahead of them, revived by the mercy of the narrative's own rhizomic flights from time.)

Novels so Czech after all, so discouragingly familiar with the forces that flatten and scatter, yet persisting, persisting.

Kundera's Art: (1) Essentialization

What makes Kundera's two masterpieces superior to his earlier work, in my view, is their essentializing (piercing, condensing) use of the "essayistic." Analysis, here, is strength (such is its posture, its air of aggressive alertness). It incessantly and searchingly sifts the narrative material, both lightening it and, as if finding nuggets, locating its weight. It is selective, summary, generalizing, and caring. (This last is a word that, though experiencing danger as it enters the force field of Kundera's irony, is necessary, and in the full Heideggerian sense of a shepherding of Being. After the initial shock—for Heideggerian Being is at once more an *extasis* and more formal than anything suggested by Kundera—one sees the logic of the latter's homage, in his essay "The Novel and Europe" [*The New York Review of Books*, July 19, 1984], to Heidegger's "beautiful and almost magical phrase 'the forgetting of being,'" where the shared sense is that this nihilistic lobotomization must be stopped.)

In Kundera's mature art, nothing waits for its caring interpretation (or the pained statement "I don't know"). Everything is instantly interrogated for its proximity to the "border" between being and emptiness.

In a novelist of less burning care, of less elegance of intellect, of less essentializing power, of more limited cultural experience, the method might be a famine. With Kundera, it is meat and drink for grown-up, human hunger, a breathtaking elimination of what he calls "novelistic word-spinning," "the automatism of novelistic technique."[1]

This development, so long overdue, so unforeseen, is part of his complex achievement.

Kundera's Art: (2) Co-feeling

The philosophical symposium would be Kundera's ideal literary form, were it not for his penchant—more, his creative passion—for co-feeling. If he aspires to write, like Broch, a "gnoseological" novel, the novel as above all "an act of cognition (of 'gnosis')," he wants at the same time to create works of imaginative sympathy. For "understanding means merging, identifying. That is the secret of poetry. We burn in the. . . thought we espouse, we burn in the landscape that moves us" (*The Book of Laughter and Forgetting*).

What is the good of co-feeling with others? How value it?

In *Jacques and His Master*, the master wonders "whether or not we're good inventions," and Jacques observes: "We should love the master who made us what we are. We'd be much happier if we loved him." But how love him? Jacques and his master, because imperfect inventions, love and depend on one another.

Kundera loves his native country because it is an imperfect invention (too many masters). He loves it because it is weak. Tereza realizes "that she belonged among the weak, in the camp of the weak, in the country of the weak, and that she had to be faithful to them precisely because they were weak and gasped for breath in the middle of sentences. She felt attracted by their weakness as by vertigo." (Vertigo: "the intoxication of the weak," "the desire to fall.")

Tereza is weak, Tamina is weak: they must be loved, these allegorical figures of the soul as a small nation trying to avoid being overwhelmed— by the body, by alien erasures of culture, by time's identity-smearing thumb.

Kundera's genius for co-feeling is greatest in these two heroines of fragility. Yes, they must be loved, not for their weakness exactly, but for their vertigo. The characters for whom and to whom their respective novels were written (to expand on Kundera's statement that *The Book of Laughter and Forgetting* is "a novel about Tamina, and whenever Tamina is absent, it is a novel for Tamina"), they are also the only characters who know too well the terror of being in a position to fall.

"It takes so little"—this the closing idea of *The Book of Laughter and Forgetting*—"so infinitely little, for a person to cross the border beyond which everything loses meaning: love, convictions, faith, history." When Tamina enters the island of the children, the children torment her, not because they are bad, so the narrator says, but because she does not belong to their world. "If anyone is full of bitterness and hate, it is Tamina, not the children. Their desire to cause pain is positive, exuberant." This Nietzschean valorization of the bad—as what is not "positive, exuberant"—is perverse. It makes a fetish of strength. For a moment, Kundera crosses the border beyond which weakness appears defensible, lovable. He loves the children, the idea of their organic potency. He abandons Tamina.

Tamina escapes the island, if only to drown in the attempt. The risk of being an "I" (the attempted, solo master of death) is the liability of growing weak, indeed the constant desire to go under, to give up. The Cartesian fortress is a tower built on air, an effort to create strength on a foundation of weakness (of nothing).

Co-feeling can be from strength to strength, or from weakness to weakness. Kundera's runs to the weakness of those who, remembering time and fighting death, have tried to found Being in the vigilant and loving powers of the "I."

Contra the "Reign of Mucus"

Temperamentally, Kundera is a metaphysical (Cartesian) puritan whose works betray a loathing of sex and the body—the reduction of the former to comedy and nausea (has any male writer made male genitalia seem more alien to the women in his fiction?), of the latter to heavy or killable flesh. (If he is also a hedonist, as he has said, it is only secondarily, and sorrily, and cynically.)

Tamina escapes the children's island because her "I" wants to revive, to pull away from the children's hot medium of flesh.

Kundera's antipathy to youth-and-body culture, both east and west, glances at the stupidity of flesh from the privacy of a memory-quieted room. He predates—and, equally, postdates—the "process" philosophers

(from the German romantics on) and their profound task of
reconciling God and earth, soul and body. In his existential world, there
is only the embattled, increasingly embittered "I am" (i.e., "I remember,
I am attached to this and that: this is my spirituality, the
unsleeping knowledge of death"). Kundera takes his place in the Socratic,
rationalist tradition of irony, with its relentless suspicion of
spontaneous life.

Hence, though he may aim for "phenomenological poetry" such as he
honors in Broch (by citing a coldly ironical portrait of a woman in the
throes of sex!), his fiction lacks descriptive appetite and trust, descriptive
density and love.

But with Tereza and Tamina his skepticism toward the body at least
softens into the poetry of compassion. He understands Tamina's body
through its loss of her husband's love, and through the children's
impersonal curiosity. He understands Tereza's body (as she comes to do)
through the metaphor of the death camps, where it disappears toward
anonymity and excrement.

His books mourn the flesh and its lost ticket to paradise. But, for all
that, they are not elegiac; they are alive with what remains, the jealously
independent "I."

Kundera is not one of those, like Nietzsche, who beats the minutes to
flush the "unhistorical." He is a cultural, that is, a vulnerable man,
difficultly checking ("everything cynically permitted") a desire to fall.

An Unspoken Utopia

The value in defense of which Kundera writes is the self as "the sum of
everything we remember"—as what resists death more savagely than can
the blindly acquiescing flesh. And the particular potency of his position
(as it unfolds in his novels) is his understanding that death is therefore as
much a political as a biological or an ontological issue. Certain cultures
are cultures of death. (Kitsch involves *organized forgetting*.") Kundera
loves Europe, loves what Husserl called its "passion of knowing,"
because it attempts to house, and always to quicken, the "I remember"
("forgetting is a form of death ever present in life").

What does Kundera want above all? If he were to let himself go, to blurt out in a few unstoppable phrases what the country after his heart would consist of (besides fond familiar things, such as Janacek's music, Broch's and Kafka's novels, etc.), it might be something like "a nation of supple and athletic minds, well trained, intuitive, used to depend on themselves." The words in fact come from Whitman, who uttered them as what America might, with great cost, become—like Kundera, only more openly, with new ground to stand on, Whitman was a spokesman for Europe's latest and most advanced and most probably improbable dream.

Whither?

"The process of the novel's development has not yet come to an end. It is currently entering a new phase. For our era is characterized by an extraordinary complexity and a deepening in our perception of the world; there is an unusual growth in demands on human discernment, on mature objectivity and the critical faculty. These are features that will shape the further development of the novel as well." (Mikhail Bakhtin, "Epic and Novel," *The Dialogic Imagination*)

So it has done in Kundera, as in Broch. But what has become of the inspiriting affinity of the novel (the only genre to appear, as Bakhtin notes, after "writing and the book" and in the full historical light of day) with "development as a process"? The Kunderean "I," which is or wants to be more of the past than of the future, cannot encourage this folly (it finds historical "progress" too hateful). Hence what Bakhtin calls the "surplus of un-fleshed-out humanness" that even the novel, that fluid and swallowing form, always leaves disincarnate, as unrealized human possibility, cannot look, in him, to the future for its appeasement and place.

The burden of the unrealized is thrust on the author in his courageous assumption within his work of "the author's point of view," however he may dismiss this courage elsewhere as "play" or "entertainment." But human possibility is not happy, not hopeful there, and the experience of reading Kundera can indeed seem not only necessary for furthering "human discernment, . . . mature objectivity and the critical faculty" but also, in his own shameless hyperbole (one that tells all), "unbearable."

Note

[1] In his preface to the American translation of *The Joke*, Kundera says: "Ever since *Madame Bovary*, the art of the novel has been considered equal to the art of poetry, and the novelist (any novelist worthy of the name) endows every word of his prose with the uniqueness of the word in a poem." But although *The Joke* is translated by the same highly talented individual who translated *The Book of Laughter and Forgetting* and *The Unbearable Lightness of Being* (Michael Heim), it is prosy, whereas they are not. *The Farewell Party* (translated by Peter Kussi) is prosy too, if relieved by numerous arresting passages. Only the two recent novels have a piercingly fine touch throughout, *The Unbearable Lightness of Being* especially, in the form of a moving condensation.

Proust and the Ideological Reader

BY ROBERT ALTER

Of the heroic generation of modernists who fashioned a new order of fiction in the first quarter of this century, there are three writers who remain commanding figures above all others, their work still a compelling challenge to the reader and a fascinating labyrinth for the critical expositor. Two of the three were exiles: Joyce, a self-banished Dubliner wandering from Trieste to Zurich to Paris; Kafka, a German-speaking Jew in Czech Prague, pondering an ancestral tradition from which he knew he was irrevocably estranged and dreaming, toward the end of his life, of a Zion he realized he would never reach. The third of these writers, Marcel Proust, was a homosexual, a condition he himself equated, in the famous prefatory chapter of *Sodome et Gomorrhe*, with the state of exile. Marginality, vulnerability, the uneasy consciousness of dual identities were, as critics have often observed, at the heart of the modernist enterprise, spurring both its experiments with literary form and its exploration of uncharted, ambiguous realms of moral and psychological life. After six decades of critical investigation, Joyce's Irishness and his awareness of himself as a lapsed Catholic have come to be pretty well understood. Kafka's Jewishness remains more elusive, perhaps inevitably for a writer who was so acutely concerned with Jewish matters and who so scrupulously avoided explicit allusion to them in his fiction, though the Jewish dimension of Kafka has inspired some illuminating commentary, from Walter Benjamin's two remarkable essays in the 1930's to Marthe Robert's recent book, *Seule, comme Franz Kafka*. Proust, one might think, treats homosexuality exhaustively enough in both the *discours* and the *récit* of his vast novel to make the character of his own inward exile perfectly clear, but in fact the ramifications of homosexuality in Proust have often been peculiarly misunderstood, as J. E. Rivers argues persuasively in his new study.[1] Regrettably, this revisionist critic also perpetrates a new sort of misunderstanding, which, as I shall try to show, derives from his ultimately ideological conception of homosexuality and the concomitant assumptions he makes about the relation between the realist novel and the reality it purports to represent.

To set the discussion square at the outset, let me say that neither the title nor the subtitle of the Rivers volume corresponds very accurately to the contents of the book. If one could infer something like an Ovidian *Ars Amatoria* from Proust, that is not really Mr. Rivers's subject, which is rather Proust's sexual identity, the historical context of homosexuality in fin-de-siècle Europe, and homosexuality as a theme in *A la recherche du temps perdu*. The subtitle invokes sexuality rather than homosexuality as a matter of principle because Mr. Rivers sees homosexuality and hetero-sexuality as symmetrical bifurcations of the human animal's intrinsically bisexual nature, but in fact his book, apart from one section of a dozen pages, is concerned specifically with homosexuality in Proust. The subtitle also includes a fine phrase, "the aesthetics of sexuality," but only Mr. Rivers's admirable concluding chapter engages that issue, while the rest of the book is devoted to an exposition of the general nature of homosexuality, theories of homosexuality and *causes célèbres* involving homosexuals in Proust's time, Proust's own homosexual entanglements, and the discussions and representations of homosexuality in *A la recherche*.

Before I consider what seems to me problematic in Mr. Rivers's conception of this subject, I should like to indicate some of the sensible and genuinely helpful aspects of his study. Critics like Justin O'Brien have assumed that Proust's homosexuality imposes an intrinsic limitation on his imaginative scope: according to this view, all the heterosexual relationships Proust represents in such intricate detail must be masked homosexual relationships, every alluring woman in Proust must be construed as a male in brilliantly deceptive drag. Mr. Rivers counters such arguments chiefly by pointing out that sexual identity is not an exclusively one-directional phenomenon: even men who conduct actual liaisons only with other men have some psychological potential for heterosexual experience, while the proportion of males, according to Kinsey's figures, who admit to having had sexual feelings for both sexes may be more than 40%. In the specific case of Proust, Mr. Rivers, following the lead of George Painter and others, interestingly shows that the novelist's erotic life may not have been so entirely homosexual as is generally assumed. Proust was seriously attracted to a number of different women; perhaps these were no more than elaborate flirtations, but there may well have been a deeper erotic element—even to the point of having an affair—in at least some of these involvements. This ambiguity of sexual identity, Proust's and perhaps everyone's, is well to keep in mind, though more weight still could be put on the polymorphous elasticity of the creative imagination, its uncanny ability to stretch beyond the literal biographical experience of the writer. If Tolstoy could imagine such splendidly convincing women, if Jane Austen could create male characters that seem so plausible in speech, gesture, and psychological nuance, it is hard to see why a novelist whose chief erotic attachments are homosexual should be denied the ability to penetrate into the nature of heterosexual relationships and to create credible women as well as men. Mr. Rivers is thus quite right to resist the various attempts that have been made to represent Proust's homosexuality as a set of blinders, or, alternately, as an uncontrollable obsession which skews the picture of reality in what is otherwise the work of a writer of genius.

The early sections of *Proust and the Art of Love* are devoted to this sort of valuable correction of readings based on hostile preconceptions of the homosexual imagination. The middle portion of the book usefully elucidates the background of European discussions of homosexuality during the period of gestation of Proust's novel, with particular attention to a series of sensational jury trials, fraught with political implications, from the trial of Oscar Wilde in England in 1895 to the Eulenberg affair in Germany, 1906-1909, all of which appear to have impinged on Proust's awareness and affected the course of his novel. Finally, in his extremely interesting concluding chapter, Mr. Rivers proposes that for Proust homosexuality—or inversion, as the writer himself likes to call it—is not merely a phenomenon to be studied in its own right, but also a kind of overriding metaphor as well as a source for the artist's difficult and peculiar vision of reality. "I am he," Mr. Rivers paraphrases the implicit position of Proust's narrator, "who sees and feels things the opposite of the way they are usually seen and felt. I am he who lives his life backwards in order to make it meaningful, he who organizes his experience by approaching it *à l'envers*. I am he who has understood more and practiced more inversion than any one else in my book. In short, I am a Sodomite, and my struggle with the agony and the inspiration of that destiny is a fundamental basis of my art." By this point of the argument, the invert in Proust makes contact with the alienated Jew in Kafka, the ex-patriate Irishman in Joyce. Seeing things thus from the margins, from the other end of conventional perspectives, *à l'envers*, leads the writer to a daring imagination of moral and aesthetic possibilities—Ulysses in Nighttown, Gregor Samsa as dung beetle, Charlus in Sodom—which, as Mr. Rivers aptly observes, goes quite beyond issues of double sexual identity. "Androgyny . . . is a trapdoor through which we enter realms of even greater ontological complexity: man-bird, man-fish, man-horse, manflower, and so on through the whole range of cosmic possibility."

If *Proust and the Art of Love* at its best clears away intellectual debris and illuminates the power of Proust's work, it also exhibits an opposite tendency, which is to sanitize Proust and by so doing in effect to emasculate him. The underlying difficulty here is that Mr. Rivers has a very firm and, to my mind, simple notion about a *correct* view of homosexuality, and by the unwavering light of that conviction he measures not only all previous critical assertions about Proust but also everything Proust himself wrote concerning homosexuality. Mr. Rivers repeatedly invokes the authority of empirical studies in order to give his generalizations a 'scientific' grounding, but his citation of sources is tendentious, and there is scarcely any discussion of the serious methodological criticisms that have been leveled against the validity of the studies he uses. In the end, then, his view of homosexuality is scientific more or less in the sense that Marxism-Leninism is regarded as scientific in certain parts of the world: it is an explanatory system whose validity cannot be questioned because it dictates what is perceived to be the only just politics, and that is why I have said it is ultimately ideological.

Mr. Rivers's treatment of psychoanalysis is a revealing indication of this ideological tendentiousness. Since psychoanalysis challenges his axiom that homosexuality is absolutely normal, he cannot accord it serious consideration, cannot allow it to appear in his argument except as a crude caricature. Here is a characteristic passage:

> As is well known, psychoanalysis holds that the creation of art is a symptom of neurosis. The artist creates in obedience to repressed, subconscious urges and in an attempt to compensate for various personality defects or traumata of early life. In the Freudian view the artist has very little conscious control over his choice of symbols and themes: they are dictated to him by his subconscious fears, desires, and aspirations.

The passage goes on, predictably, to toilet training, primal scenes, and Oedipal complexes, catchwords trotted out with the same degree of accuracy exhibited in the sentences just quoted. It is astonishing that a serious writer commenting on Freud should not even know that the actual psychoanalytic term is "unconscious," not the popularized spatial metaphor, "subconscious," which has rather different implications, and it is certainly hard to imagine how in the Freudian system the unconscious can have "aspirations," or how emotional problems can be called "personality defects." As for Oedipality, Mr. Rivers is so far from understanding what it might mean in psychoanalytic theory that he can say Proust's closeness to his mother "does not mean, however, that he had an Oedipus complex," as though it were something like measles contracted by certain unfortunate children and not others. His general insistence that psychoanalysis reduces art to little more than a helpless symptom of neurosis may accord with some of Freud's flagrantly reductive followers, but surely misrepresents the theory in general and Freud himself, who both privately and in his writings expressed the profoundest respect for the shaping and intuitive powers of the artistic imagination. The bibliography appended to *Proust and the Art of Love* includes close to eighty items under the rubric, "Works About Sexuality and Homosexuality," but, astoundingly, there is not a single text in the lot by Freud, and the more recent works are either by apologists for homosexuality or the findings of empirical researchers that confirm Mr. Rivers's views.

Let me quickly summarize those views, not in order to debate them, something which I do not claim to be within my competence, but in order to see what the consequences are when such notions are used to measure 'objectively' Proust's imaginative representation of homosexuality. Homosexuality and heterosexuality are thought to be equally normal, equally possible manifestations of the human sexual potential. Indeed, the etiology of heterosexuality is supposed to need as much explaining as the etiology of homosexuality. Since every man and woman is potentially either or both, there can be no such thing as a homosexual or a heterosexual. Rather, we may speak only of a person with homosexual tastes, preferences, inclinations, orientation. (Mr. Rivers himself follows this language rule with unvarying consistency, an ideological stylistic tic which has certain critical effects I will comment on momentarily.) Any idea that all homosexuals, or even many homosexuals, share certain character traits, such as femininity or passivity or aesthetic sensitivity, is categorically false. In fact, popular thought gravely confuses inversion, in which the typical traits of one gender are salient in a member of the opposite gender, with homosexuality, when actually there is no correlation whatever between the two, inversion being as likely to appear among heterosexuals as among homosexuals. In sum, humanity may be very roughly divided into those who usually prefer sexual congress with members of their own sex and those who usually prefer sexual congress with members of the opposite sex, but no other characteristics, psychological, moral, aesthetic, or somatic, can be attributed to either of these groups.

Whatever validity these views may have, it should be apparent that if they are pressed too hard on *A la recherche du temps perdu,* Proust's splendid architecture begins to collapse. To begin with, there is an unsettling dissonance between the 'correct' terms Mr. Rivers imposes on homosexual characters in *A la recherche* and Proust's own perception of them. Thus, in summarizing a crucial episode in *La Prisonniere,* Mr. Rivers informs his readers that "Charlus is, in fact, homosexually inclined." This is rather like saying that Satan in *Paradise Lost* tends, in fact, to yield to impulses of envy, and the terminological absurdity is symptomatic of something seriously awry in the critic's conception of the subject. Proust, of course, firmly believed that people could be homosexuals, not merely 'inclined' to homosexuality, and he even spoke of homosexuals as a race. In the signal instance of the Baron de Charlus, he imagined homosexuality as the very matrix of the character's identity. When the narrator at the beginning of *Sodome et Gomorrhe* peers out at Charlus from his vantage-point in the stairwell and sees the lubricious smile of the Baron as the aristocrat meets Jupien for the first time, the hidden observer is suddenly struck by the revelation that this seemingly virile figure resembles nothing so much as a woman. Here, of course, Proust sins twice against correct doctrine, assuming that someone can be quintessentially a homosexual and confusing homosexuality with inversion. Mr. Rivers on his part follows with meticulous care what actually goes on in *A la recherche* —he even allows himself at one point to refer to "the discovery of Charlus's true nature in *Sodome I* "—but he repeatedly puts a hedge around Proust's powerfully imagined figures by calling them people of homosexual tastes or preferences when the novelist himself saw them as offspring of the race of Sodom, bearing their heavy destiny as homosexuals quite beyond any consideration of mere inclination.

What is at stake in this shift of terms is how human sexuality, not just homosexuality, is conceived. Mr. Rivers frequently and admiringly quotes C. A. Tripp, author of *The Homosexual Matrix*, who returns the favor by providing a blurb for the jacket of *Proust and the Art of Love*. In one of the passages cited, Tripp revealingly says that homosexuals are "a behavioral category of individuals who are about as diffusely allied with each other as the world's smokers or coffee drinkers, and who are defined more by social opinion than by any fundamental consistency among themselves." To say that one is a homosexual or a heterosexual, or for that matter, a sadist, a masochist, a fetishist, as a matter of taste, preference, or inclination, is precisely to equate sexuality with coffeedrinking, smoking, chess-playing. Sexuality in these terms becomes a purely volitional matter, or, alternately, a casual and transitory habit, a kind of variable hobby. All connections between sexuality and the unconscious are in this fashion brushed aside. There is, of course, a vast body of clinical evidence that would suggest this is a superficial view of human sexuality; but more to our present purpose, this view is hopelessly out of phase with so many of the masterworks of literary tradition, from the Bible and Euripides and Virgil to Shakespeare to Joyce and Proust, in which man's sexual urge is seen as imperious, overpowering, rooted in a chthonic realm of fantasies and fears and dreams not subject to the control of reason. At the very least, the Freudian unconscious is a hypothesis with considerable explanatory power for the understanding of literature, and a critic who rejects it categorically is under some obligation to propose a workable alternative.

Since Mr. Rivers holds Proust's genius in the highest regard, and since Proust's understanding of homosexuality is in many ways thoroughly at odds with his own, he has to resort to certain exegetical acrobatics, the sum effect of which is to discount the power of some of Proust's central insights by defining them as something other than insights. Occasionally, he adopts toward this end the strategy of the *Nouvelle Critique*, which severs the referential nexus between fiction and reality and defines the former as an intricate system of self-referentiality. Thus, Proust's notion that there is a freemasonry of homosexuals is explained away as one of many systems of "encoded signs and signals" in *A la recherche* that have purely internal functions in the complex structure of the novel. "And so we can say that the narrator's delineation of a worldwide homosexual brotherhood with its own secret language is artistically 'true,' since it corresponds to a pervasive aesthetic and epistemological pattern in *A la recherche*." Lest we be inclined to brush away the gossamer frame of quotation marks around 'true,' he hastens to add: "But by any criterion other than the novel's own web of self-referential metaphor it is false."

More typically, Mr. Rivers disposes of all those uncomfortable ideas, images, allusions, and characters in Proust by asserting that the great writer's work was marred by "constant eruptions of Proust's internalized homophobia." The author of *A la recherche*, in other words, presented many misleading and distorted notions about homosexuality, presumably also falsifying to himself his own experience as a homosexual, because he was brainwashed by a hostile and repressive heterosexual culture. An alternate version of this tack is that Proust culled from the homophobic sexologists of the day certain received ideas about homosexuals which he introduced into his work in order to make it more acceptable to readers. One hardly needs to comment on the terrible discredit both these strategies of explanation do to Proust's intellectual integrity and to the strength and authenticity of his independent perceptions. But since Mr. Rivers has the scientific truth about homosexuality firmly in hand, he has a perfect implement for separating the grain from the chaff in *A la recherche*:

> The parts of the novel which "groan and wail" over the tragedy of being a homosexual "man-woman" and of suffering from homosexual disease have little to do with reality as it was then or as it is now. They are endorsements of stereotypes. The parts of the novel which depict girls and women in rebellion against traditional female roles, on the other hand, shatter stereotypes and challenge some of the most fundamental assumptions of Western culture.

One man's stereotype, it is apparent, may be another man's truth, and *vice versa*. This is ideological reading with a vengeance, for the implicit criterion of truth in the novel is political, i.e., what is most liberating, and that in turn is defined by the degree of correspondence to a scheme of reality which is an article of unquestioned faith for the liberated critic. Whatever agrees with the scheme can be described as a discovery of the writer's genius; whatever contradicts the scheme can be written off as a lamentable "internalization" by the writer of distorted stereotypes.

The recurrent notion in Proust of the homosexual as a freakish, mysterious, paradoxical "man-woman" is a case in point. Mr. Rivers shows with abundant documentation that a key definition of the homosexual in the sexology of the late 19th and early 20th century was "the soul of a woman enclosed in the body of a man." Since the idea seems to him utterly without basis, he must conclude that Proust never really observed on his own such hermaphroditic monstrosity but introduced it into his work because he had been "persuaded" by the writings of Karl Heinrich Ulrichs, Richard Krafft-Ebing, Magnus Hirschfeld, and other dubious theoreticians of a benighted era. Even Proust's own effeminacy, noted by many who knew him, can be explained as having been "inculcated by the medical and social opinion of his age." Mr. Rivers elsewhere complains about Freud's determinism, but his own approach attributes the most far-reaching determinist power to social and ideological institutions while leaving little margin for the autonomy of individual experience. One may grant that the "man-woman" is a simplistic stereotype, that statistically many homosexuals are perfectly virile and do not identify psychologically with the opposite sex. A realist novel, however, is not a statistical study by the Kinsey Institute. It is not obliged to portray a statistically representative reality but, on the contrary, may often choose to explore the meaning, the freight of possibilities, of the typical through a depiction of the extreme. One need not assume that Paris in the Belle Epoque was swarming with Barons de Charlus, but I find it hard to believe that Proust invented Charlus and the whole vision of homosexuality that surrounds him merely out of what he had read in Karl Heinrich Ulrichs, rather than from his own keen observation, his own homosexual liaisons, and from the most unflinching introspection.

Fatality, compulsion, blight, conspiratorial secret, vice, primal sin—these are the terms through which Proust often chooses to conceive homosexuality, these are what give his representation of homosexuality such power as an absorbing, danger-fraught moral drama, and these are what in Mr. Rivers's sanitizing view should be set aside as mere prejudices of the age. Proust's sense of homosexuality, to be sure, was richly ambivalent, and if the Cities of the Plain suggested an infernal image of degradation and fiery destruction, he could also imagine Sodom as a kind of distant utopia, conflating, as Mr. Rivers shrewdly observes, the myth of Sodom with the myths of Eden and Zion.

But why the symbolic insistence on Sodom? "Sodomite" of course had been a standard epithet for homosexual in European languages since the late Middle Ages, and the symbolic use of the Cities of the Plain had some currency in the 19th century, Vigny assigning Sodom to men, Gomorrah to women in a poem from which Proust quotes for the epigraph to *Sodome I*. Mr. Rivers proposes that Proust invokes the Sodom story chiefly to transform it from dystopia to utopia, effecting "a transvaluation of one of the primary sources of the Western prejudice against homosexuality." But this is too onesided in regard to both Proust and the Bible. In fact, though the townsmen of Sodom are eager to rape the two male strangers who have come into Lot's house (Genesis 19), the emphasis of the story is clearly not on homosexuality but on the wholesale violation of the host-guest bond, sacred throughout the ancient Near East, and, by extension, on a society (like the society of the Cyclops in Homer) that has barbarically cast off all moral restraint. In the biblical view, of course, homosexuality is an abomination, but there are still graver abominations.

Lest this seem like special pleading, let me point out that there is an exact heterosexual companion-piece to the story of Sodom in the Hebrew Bible—the grisly tale of the concubine in Gibeah told in Judges 19. The author of the story in Judges makes line-by-line allusion to the story in Genesis, thus invoking it as the archetype of depravity, laying out a narrative situation virtually identical in its outlines to the earlier one, even putting the same dialogue, phrase after phrase, in the mouths of his characters as that used in Genesis 19. The difference here is that the guest who has been given shelter and is the object of unbridled lust is a woman, and there is no blinding angelic light in this story to ward off the assailants. The concubine is brutally gang-raped all night long and left to die on the doorstep of the house from which she was thrust. What follows—for the Bible characteristically moves from moral conflict to political consequences—is that the concubine's master hacks her body into twelve pieces, sending them out to the tribes of Israel to rally them against the Benjaminites whose members have perpetrated this horror, and a devastating civil war ensues.

I am not, of course, proposing that when Proust symbolically invoked the story of Sodom he had explicitly in mind its heterosexual double in Judges 19. What the existence, however, of the second story does suggest is where the central moral dynamic of the Sodom story lies, a dynamic to which Proust himself was surely not insensitive. Sexual desire, both these biblical writers keenly understood, is an awesomely potent force. In order for any society to maintain civilized coherence, desire must be circumscribed, channeled, delayed, and, as we now would add, sublimated. Sodom and Gibeah embody terrifying visions of places where the immediate, total satisfaction of violent desire is given precedence over all moral considerations, over all traditionally respected bonds and obligations. The result, as the second story, building on the first, makes particularly clear, is the unleashing of mere anarchy on the earth. This glimpse into chaos in the Sodom story is, I think, something Proust understood with the deepest penetration of his extraordinary artistic intuition. He knew what it might mean to make one's eroticism the first of all motives and values, and he understood that the consequences of such a focusing on the erotic might be all the more disastrous if one's sexuality were 'adversary' in nature, forced underground by the dominant culture. What he called inversion could lead to the achievement of perspectives on daring new ontological possibilities, but the trapdoor also opened on an infernal landscape of male whorehouses where whipped figures swung in chains for the exquisite pleasuring of the flesh, where nobleman was humiliated by plebeian, where imperious desire tore the bonds of civilized order to shreds. This was not all of Proust's vision, but it was an essential part of it, and we ought not to permit any latter-day ideological thirst for supposed justice to deprive a great writer of what he saw.

Note

[1] *Proust and the Art of Love: The Aesthetics of Sexuality in the Life, Times and Art of Marcel Proust* (New York: Columbia University Press, 1981).

IV
The Art Scene

Snippets and Seeds:
Picasso and Co.[1]

BY RUDOLF ARNHEIM

Paul Klee's use of letters in his paintings, on which Michel Foucault meditates, is the final Declaration of Independence by modern painting. All other shapes, even the purely geometrical ones, can be seen, directly or indirectly, as representations of the outer world. Klee's letters, however, identify the surface on which they appear as indisputably that of a picture. They thereby move the representation definitively from the world of nature to that of the canvas. The picture still refers, but it refuses to depict.

* * *

In Nicholas Cusano's *De Ludo Globi*, which a friend has just translated, the perfect spheres of medieval cosmology are reduced to ungainly spheroids stumblingly trying to follow the eternal circles. What more impressive image of the shocking disturbance brought about at the beginning of the Renaissance by the encounter with the new reality, which replaced the abstraction of perfect *idola* with the incalculable irrationality acknowledged by the new explorers. One senses, however, also the tipsy pleasure of the individual liberated from the geometrical constraints of a conceptual universe, and the tolerant smile responding to one's own ambling course, unsteady but happily ours.

* * *

There is fundamentalism in art when it dips back to the elements of the medium. The Byzantine icons took refuge from the subtle naturalism of Hellenistic refinement by limiting themselves to basic shapes, simple colors and symmetrical composition—the fundamentals of visual form. Moving the opposite way, Renaissance art returned with Giotto to nature, the foundation of artistic subject matter. At the beginning of our own century, Malevich's square proclaims the fundamentals of plain geometry in protest against the dismemberment of shape and the color nuances of Impressionism. Nor is the religious type of fanaticism absent from fundamentalism in the arts: Piet Mondrian broke with his closest ally, Theo van Doesburg, who violated the parsimony of the horizontal and the vertical by introducing diagonals into his paintings.

* * *

The painter Chuck Close has said he chose to work from photographs because that gave him an objective criterion of whether he was doing right or wrong. Actually, the literal copying of photographs should reveal the very opposite of faithfulness to nature. Looked at closely as a model for the painter, the photograph dissolves into irrational shapes that alienate the picture from the objects it represents. The discovery of this new, visually incomprehensible world suits today's fascination with accident. But accident makes for sterility when it leads to masochistic surrender instead of urging the sense of form to find meaning in the amorphous hints at many different meanings.

* * *

In the early drawing of children things are related by mere addition. A head, a neck, or an arm is independently complete uninfluenced by what happens next to it. Similarly at early levels of "primitive" thinking, processes such as dying or coming to life are not understood as modifications of the body but as mere additions or withdrawals. Diseases invade and possess the body like incubi. The soul is an independent entity applied to the body or taken away from it. Functional modification is a concept of a higher order. In the arts also, the modification of shapes comes late.

* * *

So wholly are we caught in the naturalistic tradition that we interpret any deviation from "reality" as a monstrous deformation. I suspect that actually very few of Picasso's variations of the human figure are to be understood as aggressive or polemical. Instead they are endless explorations he carries out by changing size relations, shape, or spatial orientation, or by establishing new, paradoxical connections between parts of the body. The atomization of figures and objects in Cubism is no more destructive than the physicists' discovery that solids are made up of particles. And just as physics must return to the normally perceived macroscopic shapes if it is to avoid a one-sided view of nature, Picasso returns from his eager dissections to the classical solidity of nudes and apples.

* * *

It almost looks as though Picasso worked out a particular style for the representation of each of his women—a style that went beyond portrait resemblance and applied to the painting or drawing as a whole. It is as though a cool smoothness of shape and color went with one of them, a lusty trumpeting of bright primaries and vigorous action of shapes with another, a classical calm with a third.

* * *

Unity requires that all parts fit the context of the whole. But in several varieties of twentieth century art, single units are made strongly independent so that their self-sufficiency resists being submerged with ease in the structure of the total composition. This is true not only for the subject matter, when, for example, a part of a leg or arm is given such closure that the effort to see it as fitted to the whole figure creates high tension. It holds also for the purely visual relations between the shapes. Cubism carries this principle to its extreme: not only gives each element a completeness of its own, which has no counterpart in the represented objects; it even equips every such element with its own space, which penetrates the spaces of its neighbors as though it were unaware of them. And yet the composition as a whole hangs so perfectly together.

* * *

In comparing the various forms of Cubism, it is helpful to distinguish paintings whose shapes could be reconstructed in a coherently carpentered wooden model from others in which the elements penetrate one another "blindly." To obtain the latter effect, Picasso omits the corner edges that would come about if the units met at spelled-out angles in traditional unitary space.

* * *

Surprisingly often Picasso adopts the traditional device of creating the roundness of volume by using red for the highlights and green for the shadows. We are familiar with this use of the complementaries from Rubens, Delacroix, or Cezanne. It returns as one of the pictorial constants that modernity does not wish to do without.

* * *

In his large cartoon for a tapestry, *Women at Their Toilette,* of 1938, Picasso offers a two-step representation. In oil and pasted paper on canvas he portrays a tapestry, which in turn portrays women with a mirror and flowers in a room. The figures and objects are made up of textured materials, which prevent us from reading the picture as a direct representation of the subject matter. We must take the intermediate step of seeing a picture that shows us how familiar objects can be constructed from fabrics and wallpaper and other manmade ornaments. Quite properly Picasso regards tapestry not as a medium of direct representation but as "twice removed," as Plato might have said.

* * *

To Picasso, the horse is a woman, guided, mounted, victimized, and often beautiful. Its partner is the bull.

* * *

Again and again throughout the work, Picasso is tempted to emancipate the contour from the planes and volumes it defines. This goes beyond the conspicuous black lines resembling the lead strips of stained glass. At times, for example in the *Embrace* of 1925, the contours become objects of their own. They produce calligraphic ornaments that transform the picture space into surface grids, reminding one of wrought iron. Even so, they remain loyal to the areas they enclose until, quite late, they free themselves more radically from the planes and volumes that created them. In some of the late works there is a struggle between two incomplete pictures, one made up of colorful objects, the other of linear strokes and curves—works of a disturbing complexity that begin to look like De Kooning. Picasso begins to look "modern," which is resented by some who followed him willingly through his most capricious variations on the safe tradition.

* * *

Picasso's sculptured guitars bridge the mutual exclusiveness of inside and outside. They are open, to show the hollow interior as an essential aspect of the instrument's nature. He never does the same with the human body. Children or "primitives" sometimes depict the innards of animals and human figures, and the body of Paul Klee's *Ventriloquist* is a container for the creatures to whom the performer gives voice. But the inner organs of the human body become a part of a painter's or sculptor's statement about the nature of man only when the person is disemboweled and has joined the world of matter in death.

* * *

Unlike painting, sculpture cannot rely on the verticals and horizontals of a surrounding frame for a skeleton on which to hang the composition. In the manner of the vertebrates, sculpture has to supply its frame-work through its own inner anatomy. In a wooden construction of 1914, Picasso uses the backbone of the mandolin as the central vertical and the clarinet as the horizontal base, on which the diagonals and curves can safely sway.

* * *

A realistically drawn *Still Life with Biscuits* of 1914 reminds us that Cubism is prefigured in the discordant interplay of objects, to be found already in the still lifes of the seventeenth century. The same is true for the Rubens-like intertwining of figures in Picasso's scenes of rape, fighting or acrobatics. Cubism applies the mutual invasion of separate objects to the make-up of a single object, a human body or a guitar, thereby reinterpreting its integrity as a balanced antagonism of opposites. The more harmoniously unified and gracefully symmetrical the model, the stronger the urge to reveal the precariousness of its inner equilibrium.

* * *

What we see as transparency is originally only the superposition of pictorial objects which respect each other's integrity by ignoring the presence of their neighbors. The animals on the walls of Lascaux cross one another's contours quite unconcernedly. But when some twenty thousand years later the generation of Picasso returns to this early recklessness, transparency in painting has been acknowledged and practiced for centuries. Therefore it is no longer possible for two objects to occupy the same place without a loss of material solidity. They turn each other into wraiths—a welcome side effect.

* * *

The straight front face and the straight profile are too complete within themselves to be usable as phases of a stroboscopic flip. The pink front face of *Woman with Sculpture* of 1925 is placed uncompromisingly on her black profile. We are enjoined to see the two as one without resorting to the time dimension, which would permit us to make them, in a traditionally acceptable manner, two momentary aspects of the same face.

* * *

In traditional painting, the underlying eidola of circle, triangle, and square supply form without making themselves conspicuous. They must never be spelled out explicitly, lest nature trespass on geometry. Picasso, however, constructs the face of his *Girl with a Hoop* of 1919 frankly out of square, triangle, oval, and lozenge, thereby disclosing the creative tension between man's two realms of existence, nature and rational shape.

* * *

After its delivery to the Prado, Picasso's *Guernica* is now displayed in a huge showcase, much like the glass box that holds Rembrandt's *Night Watch* in the Rijksmuseum in Amsterdam, and for the same reason. Both paintings had been attacked with a knife. *Guernica* hangs as the only exhibit in a tall historical hall of the Cason del Buen Retiro and thereby arrests visitors as it was never permitted to do on the second floor, busy with transients, of New York's Museum of Modern Art. By having more space around it, the painting expands into a monument, and its figures move more freely. It is also better lit. But although incomparably more powerful at its new location, the painting chills one by its solitary confinement. It misses the company of other works, which in the usual museum room relieves somewhat the meaninglessness of art displayed without the original context for which it was intended. Also the painting suffers from its spatial isolation from the visitors: it does not share the floor and walls and light of the room in which they approach it. Remote in its glass box, it is something between a slide projection and an epiphany, that is, something less and something more than the painting. And as I was privileged to lecture on *Guernica* right in front of the work, it all seemed like a pious legend about a worshipper of images who is rewarded for his effort by the miraculous apparition of the radiant original itself.

Note
[1] Rudolf Arnheim, born in 1904, has contributed journal entries to *Salmagundi* since 1972.

The End of Art
According to Arthur Danto[1]

Over the past six years or so, a new voice has been heard in the often
peevish world of art criticism, a reasonable and reasoning voice, clear,
elegant, sometimes impish, half-J. L. Austin and half-Addison and Steele,
a voice seemingly disinterested and free of both formalist and
deconstructionist cant. This voice belongs to Arthur Danto, Johnsonian
Professor of Philosophy at Columbia University and author of numerous
philosophical works, among them *Narration and Knowledge* and
Nietzsche as Philosopher, both in the analytic mode. In 1981 he
published *The Transfiguration of the Commonplace*, a philosophy of art
which grew out of a long reckoning with the apparently overwhelming
shock Danto experienced upon seeing Andy Warhol's *Brillo Boxes* in
1964 at the Stable Gallery. This work, which he considers paradigmatic
of art in the twentieth-century, led him to analyze the interesting philosophical problem of what he calls indiscernibles, i.e. why, if we take two
ordinary objects otherwise seemingly indistinguishable from one
another (say Duchamp's famous *Fountain* and just an ordinary urinal, or
Warhol's *Brillo Boxes*, and ordinary Brillo boxes), we can identify one as
a work of art and the other as, well, just a thing. The process of exploring
that question led him into complex discussions of content, aesthetics,
representation and style—matters both traditional and at the heart of
much post-modern and post-formalist theory—and finally to a consideration of rhetoric in art that holds style to be a representation of the artist's

self—a surprisingly old-fashioned and wholesomely humanist notion hardly consonant with the post-modern critique of artistic individuality or originality. At any number of points along the way, however, Danto repeatedly emphasized the idea that in works like Duchamp's *Fountain* and Warhol's *Brillo Boxes*, art has "evolved in such a way that the philosophical question of its status has almost become the very essence of art itself, so that the philosophy of art, instead of standing outside the subject and addressing it from an alien and external perspective, became instead the articulation of the internal energies of the subject." This quite fascinating idea obsesses him again in *The Philosophical Disenfranchisement of Art*, a work that not only delves further into the philosophical history of art but draws upon Danto's experience since 1984 as art critic for *The Nation*.

Danto develops *The Philosophical Disenfranchisement of Art* around two principal and corollary ideas. To summarize them briefly, the first is that since western philosophy beginning with Plato has waged a successful campaign to deprive art of standing and power in the real world, art has finally, in the twentieth-century, achieved its revenge by becoming philosophy, that is, by concerning itself totally with issues of its own ontology, and in the process re-enfranchised (or re-privileged) itself, not as a ground for effective action, but as a superior form of consciousness. The second idea is that since art has in fact solved the problem of satisfactorily defining itself to itself, and has in effect become philosophy, it has nothing left185 to do as an historical phenomenon, and has reached its end, that is, fulfilled its destiny, and, much like Marx's ideal state, more or less withered away into inconsequence. This means—in case you didn't know it—that we are in a post-historical phase, in which artists continue to make works of art, but without necessity, without purpose, and without the intellectual dynamisms that made art until the end of modernism (i.e. Brillo boxes) historically compelling. Should we need evidence for this last conclusion, we need only, Danto claims, look about us at the art of the eighties, which is, according to him, dismal, pointless, and proof of the triumph of market forces in an art world rendered empty by historical exhaustion.

The title (and central) essay, "The Philosophical Disenfranchisement of Art," takes as its starting point Auden's well-known line, "For poetry makes nothing happen." Oddly enough, Danto reads this line without irony (a really fatal lapse when it comes to Auden) as a point of departure for his argument that Platonic metaphysics, with its hierarchy of first and second order appearances, has defined a place for art in philosophy "from which it is then a matter of cosmic guarantee that nothing can be made by it to happen." Taking this thought even further, he argues that "since Plato's theory of art *is* his philosophy, and since philosophy down the ages has consisted in placing codicils to the platonic testament, philosophy itself may just be the disenfranchisement of art—so the problem of separating art from philosophy may be matched by the problem of asking what philosophy would be without art." He surveys more recent (post-Renaissance) theories of art, and sees Kant's idea of *disinterest* in art, of art's "purposiveness without any specific purpose," for example, as simply another chapter in the "systematic neuter[ing]" of art, a process that has continued all the way into contemporary aesthetics. This philosophical consensus has been so uniform, he says, that it makes us wonder "whether, rather than art being something the philosopher finally deals with in the name of and for the sake of systematic completeness—a finishing touch to an edifice—art is the reason philosophy was invented, and the philosophical systems are finally penitentiary architectures it is difficult not to see as labyrinths for keeping monsters in and so protecting us against some deep metaphysical danger."

In this rather Piranesian view the metaphysical idealization of art as beauty is finally as politically ruthless a move as that which "turned women into ladies." Thus, by this account, modern art's program of "uglification," of deliberately de-aestheticizing works of art (Duchamp's *Fountain* again, and *Mona Lisa* with a moustache) and its rejection of ideas of The Beautiful, has been tantamount to a rejection of its disenfranchised status. Duchamp, as Danto sees him, was a philosophical, as distinct from an artistic genius, because, for him, getting rid of prettiness wasn't enough; some deeper transformation away from aesthetic objecthood was required to free art from the demeaning trivialization of Platonic metaphysics. By not just raising but in effect embodying or one might even say *acting* the question, "namely why—referring to itself—should this be an artwork when something else exactly *like* this, namely *that*—referring now to the class of unredeemed urinals—are just pieces of industrial plumbing?" Duchamp's urinal actually achieved the unprecedented historical feat of not only turning a work of art into philosophy, but of freeing art from an inferior stage of consciousness to its ultimate and destined awareness of itself as itself, a conclusion Danto bases on Hegel's idea of history as the dialectical unfolding of consciousness to itself through the progressive identification of subject with object ("since consciousness of consciousness is consciousness"). Art then becomes one stage in history and philosophy another, higher one, "and it is the historical mission of art to make philosophy possible, after which art will have no historical mission in the great cosmo-historical sweep." Thus, Hegel's philosophy of history gets a resounding confirmation in Duchamp's work, which, in questioning the philosophical nature of art from within the artwork, implies "that art already is philosophy in a vivid form, and has now discharged its spiritual mission by revealing the philosophical essence at its heart. The task may now be handed over to philosophy proper, which is equipped to cope with its own nature directly and definitively. So what art will have achieved as its fulfillment and fruition is the philosophy of art."

Apparently oblivious to the problems suggested by the vagueness of the idea that something has a "philosophical essence" (does it mean a built-in capacity for internal criticism? can things also then have an aesthetic or artistic "essence"? and if so, what would that mean?) Danto nonetheless anticipates objections by pointing out that his Hegelian view of Duchamp can still be seen as simply part of the Platonic agenda, still a way of substituting philosophy for art, and still a way of condescending to art by seeing it as a quest for self-clarification as philosophy. Even so, he believes that his hypothesis is not only true but borne out by the history of modernism, a history he sees in rather orthodox Greenbergian terms as an in-house critique (although he seems to ignore the motive of *renewal* crucial in Greenberg's theory of modernism). As he puts it, "When art internalizes its own history, when it becomes self-conscious of its history as it has come to be in our time, so that its consciousness of its history forms part of its nature, it is unavoidable that it should turn into philosophy at last. And when it does so, well, in an important sense, art comes to an end." From the history of philosophy's attempt to "emasculate or to supersede art:" Danto sees the whole force of modernism to be an attempt to win back art's priority (or should we say *manhood*?) by actually claiming status for itself as philosophy, relieving itself in the meanwhile of its nambypamby aesthetics and status as the gimp of the humanities.

Of course the paradox here, as Danto acknowledges, is that if art makes nothing happen, neither does philosophy: "Philosophy makes its appearance just when it is too late for anything *but* understanding." Art re-enfranchises itself as philosophy only to discover that it has no more effectiveness in the "real world" than it had before. And this brings Danto to the notion that "there is an incentive in philosophically curing art of philosophy: by just that procedure we cure philosophy of a paralysis it began its long history by infecting its great enemy with." So what then, he asks, are the powers of art independent of philosophy? Well, Danto is so much the philosopher, and so unable to desist even momentarily from his habitual privileging of philosophy, that no sooner does he attempt to separate art from philosophy than he finds the question of whether art "makes anything happen" no longer philosophically interesting! It becomes a question for history or psychology "or some social science or other." Art, it turns out, may not be especially more ineffective than anything else in making things happen; it just doesn't necessarily bring them about. It is really, he says, simply "a matter of fact" whether it does so or not. Citing the anagrammatic poem which happens to encode the formula of the atomic bomb, the folksong in "The Lady Vanishes" that reveals a special secret, and "The Murder of Gonzago" in *Hamlet*, he suggests that "art makes something happen only adventitiously, when it is put to an extra-artistic use: and that leaves the familiar thought that intrinsically it makes nothing happen as art." But this has to be wrong, he says, if he has been right in *The Transfiguration of the Commonplace* to argue that "the structure of artworks is of a piece with the structure of rhetoric, and that it is the office of rhetoric to modify the minds and then the actions of men and women by co-opting their feelings." Poetry (or art) may therefore "make something happen if it is successful in promoting action of a sort that may make something happen." And this is not just an added feature of art, but intrinsic to it, "if indeed the structure of the work of art and the structure of rhetoric are of a piece." So if we look at art as rhetoric, then "there is reason after all to be afraid of art."

This cheerful conclusion, which might go far to explain the possible effect of *The Clouds* on the eventual trial and execution of Socrates, not to mention the questions one could raise about the meaning of the last line of Rilke's "Archaic Torso of Apollo" ("You must change your life"), simultaneously leaves philosophy and Danto's whole enterprise with a pie in its face. For if the structure of art is "of a piece" with the structure of rhetoric, and if, as Danto argues, art has latterly become philosophy, then the structure of philosophy and the structure of rhetoric must be the same, and philosophy (as indeed the deconstructionists have been telling us for some time now) can no longer justify its claim to truth but instead has to be seen along with literature (or as literature) in terms of rhetorical strategies and effects. Danto acknowledges this problem but seems undaunted and unembarrassed by it. He's not sure, he says, that rhetoric and philosophy do share the same structure, "since it is the aim of philosophy to prove rather than merely persuade," but he doesn't then ask, for instance, "What was Duchamp trying to prove?" as a way of testing his hypothesis about indiscernibles (I myself think of Duchamp as more of a rhetorician than a philosopher, in that I severely doubt whether his works lead us to a new sense of *necessary* conditions in art. He seems rather to be concerned with ways of seeing, irony, play, the arbitrariness of aesthetic categories, the falseness of fixed positions). Danto's task, he says, somewhat vaguely and evasively, is to "disassemble portions of the philosophy of art from art," and rescue it from the deconstructionists, who are, he charmingly acknowledges, out to disenfranchise *him*.

His way of doing this, in "The End of Art," another version of which can be read in *The State of the Art*, a recent collection of Danto's Nation reviews that should be read in tandem with the present volume and *The Transfiguration of the Commonplace*, is to seek an explanation for "the dismal state of the artworld" in the theory of modern art and then use it to justify his theory of art's re-enfranchisement of itself as philosophy and simultaneous liquidation of whatever parts of it aren't philosophy as a meaningful practice. Having fulfilled its ontology in Hegelian teleology, and having achieved in Duchamp's Ready-Mades and Warhol's *Brillo Boxes* a perfect consciousness of itself, art simply has nothing more to do and can either close shop or go romp in the trivial resorts of human sensibility. Art today is bad not because it has lost its historical direction, but because it has no historical direction to lose (how otherwise explain pluralism and the proliferation of one awful style after another?), "and we have to ask whether this destructured condition *is* its future: a kind of cultural entropy. So whatever comes next will not matter because the concept of art is internally exhausted." No matter how much fuss our museums, galleries, critics and collectors make about the next step in an on-going dialectical future, and no matter how many of the ninety thousand or so artists in New York City alone are living in cramped, miserable and inhumanly expensive quarters hoping to bite off a slice of art history for themselves, Danto asks whether "a point has been reached where there can be change without development, where the engines of artistic production can only combine and recombine known forms, though external pressures may favor this or that combination? Suppose it is no longer a historical possibility that art should continue to astonish us, that in this sense the Age of Art is internally worn out, and that in Hegel's stunning and melancholy phrase, a form of life has grown old?" His questions are rhetorical; he really does believe that art is finished. And if that indeed is what has happened, he later concludes, in "Art, Evolution, and the Consciousness of History," post-historical art will not require a further history, and the best kind of artist will be the one "with the keen sense of play that survival in the artworld now demands."

As a debating position, Danto's theory of the end of art seems to me professionally constructed, and only another professionally trained analytic philosopher could probably sort out its logical flaws. Yet, interesting as it might be to hear a truly rigorous philosophical analysis of Danto's position, it nevertheless seems to me that the best response to it—and I include the ideas not simply in *The Philosophical Disenfranchisement of Art*, but in his other two volumes on art as well—should be primarily non-philosophical and "institutional" in nature, that is, based on the actual experiences and ideas of artists, critics, curators and art historians, people who work within the art world itself. For there is, for me, a very non-philosophical obstacle to taking Danto's notions about the end of art seriously. Unlike Danto, who never privileges art, never centers it as the source of ego satisfaction in his life, who has nothing at stake as far as art is concerned except what he can make of it as a philosopher, and therefore no internal position for which he must take responsibility, people in the art world, whatever their motives, biases and affiliations, do, which means that art's value, which may admittedly be intolerably vague, different and contradictory for each one of them, and possibly convertible into the venal terms of money or fame or power, is nevertheless one that "enfranchises" them to pursue more or less meaningful activities in the world. A young artist seeing Jackson Pollock's *Autumn Rhythm* for the first time may be so moved that he stops painting like Philip Guston and spends the next fifteen years trying, through his art, to understand what Pollock was doing. A critic may be so moved by an artist's work that he risks his reputation defending it. A museum curator may spend hundreds of boring hours with self-infatuated millionaires in order to acquire a major collection in the belief that it truly enriches the country's cultural heritage.

All of these, in my view, are instances of art's making things happen, and those things are something more than a response to rhetoric. What Danto has done, however, is to situate himself within this fluid, fickle, unendingly competitive art world—a world that has been since the middle of the nineteenth-century, in both Europe and America, fiercely social and conventional, and ruled more often than not by forces as arbitrary as taste and fashion—as a critical journalist who then attempts to certify his perceptions about the current art "scene" as philosophy, i.e. as necessary and true propositions about the world. Any critic wants to be right, and not just factually so, but logically so as well. But Danto's trust in the persuasive force of philosophy as a way of analyzing the contemporary art situation seems both naive and unwarranted. Lots of people have predicted the end of art: from beginning to end, the history of modernism has been plagued by both gloomy and joyful apocalyptic forecasts, most of them philistine and *retardataire*, others offered, as Danto's is, in the name of some inexorable historical or aesthetic logic. Danto's contribution to this chorus is disheartening, not just because the very idea of predicting a programmatic future in art is nonsensical in fact, if not in theory, but because we need critics who care desperately about whether and how good art gets made, and Danto doesn't care enough or believe enough in art's capacity for self-renewal to analyze with sufficient philosophical rigor or aesthetic passion what it would take for art to be good (I mean of course *historically* good) again in whatever senses he would like it to be.

The art world is a universe richly unstable and notoriously inhospitable even to those willing to educate themselves in public, who recognize that even their most passionately held convictions can be at best provisional and relative. What bothers me the most is not that Danto's analysis and accompanying prophecies may turn out to be true, but his tone of detachment, as if he were describing a natural catastrophe like a flood or an earthquake, in which human accountability plays little or no role. This tone is all the more irritating because it comes clothed in his stylistic *niceness*, his extreme amiability. There he is, critic and philosopher, softly deploying his wonderfully trained intelligence with unoffending cordiality, a mere bystander to an era not just ordinarily bad but terminally so, as it were, and purveyor of philosophy's Hellenic sweetness and light, simply soaking up things as they are, as opposed, it may be inferred, to the gloomy Hebraic fulminations of those pitiful souls (wherever and whoever they are) who care desperately about the future of art and have only their irrelevant and contingent aesthetic convictions to live and die by. As a critic he sees that things are terrible; as a philosopher, he analyzes them as historically and logically inevitable, and thus marks out for a rather minor and possibly banal piece of guesswork a sort of Thucydidean logic of cause and effect. Yet another, rather major peculiarity in Danto's way of thinking about art is that despite the multiplicity of great achievement in the twentieth century, the rich and far from exhausted problems presented by the work of Cezanne, Picasso, Matisse, the Futurists, the Constructivists, the Surrealists, the Abstract Expressionists and many other movements and individuals, he collapses the whole burden of twentieth century art history into those issues raised by Duchamp and Warhol, the only two artists he seems ever to have looked at. In excluding or at the very least simply ignoring works from Manet to Pollock whose creation of a new aesthetic demanded the rejection of "Beauty" as it was understood by nineteenth-century post-neo-classical academicians and genteel patrons, he simply clears the window of painting—which on the one hand was committed to a complex, intellectually difficult, critical investigation of itself, and on the other to sensuous visual experience (i.e. aesthetic experience) demanding comparison with the best of the old masters.

Danto, however, rejects aesthetic experience and pleasure as philosophically uninteresting; he completely swallows the all-too-prevalent idea that "formalism" means the exclusion of "content" and is thus "empty." This is too bad, because if he didn't, he might have saved himself a lot of trouble: his beloved "indiscernibles," Duchamp's *Fountain* and Warhol's *Brillo Boxes*, are in fact not as indiscernible as he thinks, if the testimony of the eye is to be admitted. *The Fountain*, for instance, while a "real" urinal, was turned upside down when first shown in New York in 1917; it had a signature, "R. Mutt" and, however much it scandalized people, nobody peed in it, at least not to my knowledge; had it been placed in a real men's room, nobody would have. *The Brillo Boxes* were in fact made of wood, not paper; they *imitated* the originals, and *resembled* them, but were not *indistinguishable* from them. This is visual, "aesthetic" information, but Danto comes to his visual experience conceptually, not sensuously.

Indeed, if the pieces in *The State of the Art* are any indication, Danto's eye is not to be trusted. He comes across in his *Nation* columns as a companionable, frequently witty, delightfully open-minded haunter of museums and galleries. There is something of the late eighteenth-century *amateur* and nineteenth-century *flaneur* in his enjoyment of leisurely reflection and the activity of discrimination. And he does make judgments—perhaps not often enough, but with creditable regularity. Yet his descriptions of objects, and the actual judgments themselves, often fall flat; they don't live up as convincingly felt criticism to the great pleasure he seems to take in the critic's role. Too often they have a kind of dead visual accuracy, a precious but juiceless well-writtenness that lacks the tactile, plastic, almost erotically engaged sense of materials and relationships essential to good art-writing. I have been following Danto's *Nation* pieces from the beginning, and have found them amusing, interesting and sometimes passionate in their enthusiasms. They have too a wondrous clarity (the analytic legacy here) and freedom from the typical snarliness and infighting of much current art-writing. But Danto hasn't made me see a single work of art in a fresh or unexpected way. His deliberately-chosen marginality, his cultivated-amateur's voice, his own tone of relative disinterestedness finally create inertia. What he says just doesn't matter. He isn't highhanded enough, or demanding enough; his approvals and dismissals strike me as often facile and unearned—what anyone would say. As an actual looker-at-objects, he, like Harold Rosenberg, does better with contexts than texts, with exhibition rhetoric, art-world social analysis, and biographical commentary than with actual works, about which he is often inconclusive and banal.

Because Danto does not see current aesthetic and cultural issues as interesting unless they take the form of conceptually exact philosophical questions, he cannot help but respond passively to the "dismal state" of the art world of the eighties—a state he has no stake in setting right, since according to him this is a post-historical age. Certainly, aesthetic issues per se have no autonomy for him; and as for cultural criticism, of the kind done by Walter Benjamin or Adorno, or Clement Greenberg or Harold Rosenberg, or the October critics, for instance, or T. J. Clark, no doubt that for him belongs to "some social science or other." To him the current deplorable art scene is simply a result of modernism's historical devolution and not, as I think it ought to be seen, a continuation of what Flaubert, in a letter to Turgenev, identified as "the rising tide of shit" that has been engulfing bourgeois civilization since the middle of the nineteenth-century, a new wave of kitsch in a society that has developed an insatiable appetite for junk and legitimized it as general, as distinct from popular, culture. Danto the antiaesthetic anti-formalist, who appears to have no interest whatsoever in Kant's view that art is non-cognitive (but not anti-cognitive), and that it can absorb concepts even as it remains operative as a perceptual phenomenon, and who assimilates Kant, when he does take him into account, into the disenfranchising tradition, is the most rigid, narrow and unimaginative historicist I have ever read, even though, as a writer, he sounds flexible, broad, and infinitely taken with art's capacity for play. He has certainly embraced, in his Hegelianism, the same or nearly the same structural model of argument as a good deal of German art history and hardcore (i.e. Greenbergian) formalism, with their talk of dialectical movement and historical stages, but he has done so without apparent awareness of that fact, and without the commitment to the aesthetic values and notions of style which were originally part of the impetus for such theories. If there is one truly legitimate task that the best post-modernist artists and critics have set themselves, it is to work their way out of (rather than simply dismissing) the deadly historicism of formalist aesthetics, with its dreary next-stage forecasts, and its reduction of art to nothing but convention. Yet their strategy has been to raise other issues Danto can't understand because he can't see the fertile and originating irony in, to return to his heroes, Duchamp and Warhol, an irony that critiques or begins to deconstruct all kinds of fascinating questions about the role of taste, context, rhetoric, situation, authorship, "aura" (to borrow Walter Benjamin's terms), uniqueness and originality in art-issues which spell out not the end of art but the terms upon which legitimate, i.e. historical, renewal of art may possibly occur. Certainly the question of "indiscernibles," of what it means for something to be a work of art, is entertained in the Duchampian universe, but it isn't the only question, or a question that necessarily dominates all other questions. Danto, however, in fetishizing the urinal, sees only the apocalyptic reduction of art to philosophy, not art's Kantian capacity to absorb and embody any number of questions, including philosophical ones.

Danto, like a lot of people, myself included, hated the 1985 Whitney Biennial, but he hated it in the name of what values? I keep asking myself, if Danto is right and art is over, then why is he an art critic? What's the point of churning out those charming *Nation* columns? He never indicates just why he gives a damn about art one way or the other. Philosophy isn't his problem; it's the need for philosophical answers to radically uncertain situations that throws him off course. Philosophy is a kind of habitual secondary process for him that obscures the bafflements and confusions that inevitably accompany the primary responses of any really good and honest critic. It keeps him from the terrible feeling of being at a loss, the anxiety of not knowing what to make out of the general awfulness of much contemporary art. This chronic translation of the journalistic into the philosophical comes out as a strange lack of instinctive tolerance for the struggle good artists go through during bad aesthetic times and it makes me unwilling to take him very seriously. Incapable of the kind of aesthetic agnosticism, or even the holding action of any number of dedicated and insufficiently known good artists (and they really are out there, whether Danto knows it or not), who don't know whether what they are doing is history or not, but are trying to come to terms with the art of the century, he has none of the good critic's negative capability, the talent of living with the in-betweenness of awkward ages and bad patches, and neither the patience, faith nor curiosity to seek out and fight like hell for those few artists who are risking everything to put themselves on the line historically. That such a line exists, that the art of the past, whether rationalized as history or mythologized as chronicle, always puts pressure on the present, that modernism may undergo any number of revisions, including that in which the idea of "art history" itself is savagely deconstructed, means only that art will, phoenix-like, renew itself out of its own ashes, which it has been doing stunningly, if not regularly, since the Renaissance. Art is both indeterminate and overdetermined, deeply hooked into desire and need, and unlikely to be brought to a state of inanity because at a certain point in its history some artists made works which looked like things which aren't art. It's true, as Robert Hughes has said, that much art today "aspires to the condition of muzak," but in seeing this condition as historical necessity, Danto becomes its accomplice, lacking the courage to switch channels on the synthesized strings even as he deplores their cheap, meretricious sound.

To go back to the beginning, art in the West may indeed have been disenfranchised (if Danto is right) as real action, but it seems in most cases to have been better off for this so-called deprivation, and lots of intelligent people have said that its efficacy as symbolic action is far superior to any merely practical consequence it might have. What, after all, is so almighty wonderful about "making things happen"? Who wants to live in Plato's boring old Republic, anyway? Some recent accounts of post-modern art speak joyfully about art's finally merging once again with a mainstream culture, finally sharing communal values, finally getting to political concerns the way "traditional" culture did. But a good deal of great art, visual and literary, has more often than not refused to endorse the cultural status quo. At the very least it has undermined it by using irony to distance itself from power and authority, and at the very best its ironies have been tragic, uncompromising and transcendent, not local and offered in appeasement of a dominant ideology, as much so-called post-modern image appropriation and media-based art has been. I suspect that much of this hoopla about the return to communal values disguises a very real relief at the return of recognizable images. Most people never "got" Cubism and abstraction, and some of the pleasure in the new idea of antiformalist "content" is at heart an old-time philistine joy in the recognizable, dressed up in colors borrowed from pop culture, watered-down deconstruction and conveniently anthologized Marxist theory. Danto participates in a very similar kind of philistinism far more than he realizes. His theoretical position couldn't be farther from David Salle's, for instance, or Cindy Sherman's, or Jeff Koons's, but as much as he says he dislikes the art that's around, he just loves having recognizable images to look at. In *The Transfiguration of the Commonplace* he accepts the "action painting" theory of Abstract Expressionism with such unquestioning alacrity, and seems so visually unengaged in its actual achievements, that it makes me suspect that he has never been comfortable with abstraction as a question of convention and style. But the dead give-away comes in "Approaching the End of Art," the final essay in *The State of the Art*, where he gaily recites the compensations of the post-historical age. Art can now return to "the serving of largely human ends. There is after all something finally satisfying in making likenesses, and it is not surprising that there should have been a great upsurge in realism. There is something finally satisfying in just moving paint around."

It would come as a great surprise, I think, to the great modernists and those who love them to hear that their work had not been made in the service of "human ends," and that those ends are apparently synonymous in Danto's mind with representation. And the great realists in art history would, I think, be equally surprised to learn that their frequently philosophical investigations of reality in the end amount to just "moving paint around." Art has no doubt had a difficult relationship with philosophy, but it has developed internal conventions, traditions, problems and codes of struggle and meaning which have incorporated the idea of criticality from a very early stage without posturing as philosophy and without foregoing the immediate and the sensuous. It has thus enfranchised itself by not only actively resisting its incorporation into philosophy, but by incorporating only so much philosophy as it needs, having other tasks, and serving other ends which Danto finds too philosophically uninteresting to question, much less embrace.

Note

[1] Review of Arthur C. Danto, *The Philosophical Disenfranchisement of Art* (New York: Columbia University Press, 1986).

Anselm Kiefer and the Shapes of Time

BY CHARLES MOLESWORTH

One of the overriding sensations generated by the Anselm Kiefer exhibit[1] is that of being caught in a curious time warp. On the one hand Kiefer paints with many of the attributes, such as egoistic theatricality, heroic scale, and a rough-house attitude towards materials, that are clearly and heavily indebted to Abstract Expressionism. But just as convincingly he goes about his art with an attitude that could only be sustained by someone for whom that fabled American school of the 1950's never existed. Kiefer seems to escape from the context of Abstract Expressionism by extending it, as if none of its problems, self-questionings, and revisionary histories were at stake. Kiefer has accomplished one thing crucial to all artists, and it helps to strengthen his supporters and quiet his critics: namely, he paints as if what he does, in all its grandiosity, was the way painting *ought* to be done. The sensation of the time warp, however, creates a further sense that Kiefer is supported by history and at the same time contemptuous of its rigidities. The highest claim one might make for him is that he creates his own historical context, that he warps time in probably the only way it can be warped—disdainfully.

But it is not time pure and simple with which Kiefer wrestles or succeeds, it is more specifically with art historical time, that special construct that is open to the winds of change, celebrity, media exposure, and a dozen other forces even more difficult to harness. From time to time, art historical schemes return back to the histories of society and politics from which they spring, somewhat as a prodigal child returns. But is it out of duty or instinct that such returns occur? And is the homecoming the occasion of rejoicing or retribution? But Kiefer's work occurs, or at least is famously exposed, at a time when art history is back among the historical constructs offered on the larger canvases of society and politics. It is this painter's tribute, and his special burden, that his work raises with new force the questions of how and why art should deal with "real life" subjects, such as historical ideologies, personal will, and emotional qualities, as opposed to the formalist concern with purely "painterly" issues. In fact, Kiefer's art engages several issues, but they can be grouped under at least three headings: social and emotional content, visual pleasure, and technical abilities. A full response to his work, of course, would try to integrate these issues into some coherent view.

Kiefer has executed several large canvases that feature cultural, historical, and mythical heroes of Germany, often posed against grand, even grandiose, backgrounds, and labeled with a script lettering that suggests, in part, the sort of hand one sees in the work of admiring school children copying out the lesson of the day. One person's patriotism is another's chauvinism; one person's burgeoning nationalism is seen by someone else as incipient fascism. Kiefer, of course, fully realizes that German nationalism, since Nazism and the horrors of World War II, is not just another nationalism. So what is the viewer, especially the non-German viewer, to make of Kiefer's work in this vein? Having raised so explicitly the issues of historical and political values and responsibilities, what can he expect the viewer's response to be? In one painting the names and portraits of Rilke, the mystical poet, and von Clausewitz, the hard-nosed theoretician of war, among several others, are present; in a different painting, effigies (in the form of flaming torches ensconced in an empty hall) representing Joseph Beuys, the radical artist, and Richard Wagner, the great composer and notorious anti-Semite, appear together with famous German cultural figures. In a post-structuralist, postmodern world, we might read such juxtapositions as ironic, but forgivingly ironic, as if the target or butt of the joke were not any particular person or group, but rather history itself. If any nation or group can produce such disparate figures, Kiefer might be understood to suggest, and still call itself one people, one entity, then the boundaries of self-delusion are infinite, and infinitely comic.

But is it all a joke? Perhaps the visual pleasures of the work help us answer this question, though again Kiefer is and is not a painter who offers such pleasures readily. Indebted in part to the same impulses that produced Arte Povera, with its use of crude, "everyday" materials, the canvases are startling in a way that combines seductive textures and details with a brusque un-painterly impatience or directness. So the questions return in another context. Do the dark palette and the roughened textures, the burnt-out look of the canvases and their harsh elementarity, complete with paint-encrusted hay, stretches of paint thickened with sand and clay, often on a backing of lead plating, suggest destruction and historical desolation? Or do they rather suggest some nearly silent but proud reaffirmation of a national soul, a "volkish" spirit, that survives in spite of its own self-destructiveness, in spite of unending brutality from both inner and outer forces, in spite of modernity itself?

Kiefer's mentor was the late Joseph Beuys, and Beuys drew considerable influence from the modernist attack, elaborated by Duchamp and others, on retinal pleasure. This would account for the more or less directly "semantic" side of Kiefer. But he never allows such interest in conceptual or intellectual issues to overwhelm his concern with pigment, texture, and plastic values. Yet even here the issues are complicated. By using several impractical techniques, such as painting on clumps of hay and fastening blobs of poured lead onto the canvases, Kiefer creates a curatorial nightmare. Much recent concern has been aired about the state of many of the works of the Abstract Expressionists —Rothko's canvases, for example, have already begun to fade less than a dozen years after his death. For a painter like Rothko, whose commitment to the qualities of color approached something like a religious level, such fading represents a virtual destruction of the spiritual. If Kiefer wants a monumental art, as his sense of scale and content would clearly imply, his use of ephemeral and brittle materials suggests at the same time an attack on the very notion of durability and a triumph over time.

By using lead sheeting for the background of several paintings, Kiefer indulges in a modernist exploration of material. The properties of lead are such that it can seldom be rolled absolutely smooth, so it creates an effect similar to that of color field abstraction, where slight variation in tone and surface creates visual interest. Sometimes Kiefer scores the lead with acid, but even here there is almost a chaste result, as the corroded surface is not all that gouged or discolored. The blobs of poured lead, generally used in paintings with scorched or roughened backgrounds, are attached to the canvas by small staples; apparently the lead is not poured directly on to the painting, but added later in collage fashion. Such uses of lead might very well connote some interest in industrial techniques, a way of signaling some modern impulse at work in Kiefer's mind. But because of the softness and its interesting texture, the lead also connotes malleability and elementariness, and thus suggests a medieval or alchemical context. It is as if Kiefer were harking back to Mime, the dwarf Vulcan-like figure from the Niebelung who mans the foundry that produces Siegfried's sword. Kiefer has been quoted as saying that "symbols create a kind of simultaneous continuity and we recollect our origins." Such concern with origins extends beyond the semantic content to the materials themselves.

The use of hay in the paintings is combined with polymer paint, emulsion, and shellac; traditional media such as oil pigments are not prominently featured and something like tempera is noticeable by its absence. On at least one occasion the hay connects in a challengingly literal way with Kiefer's use of landscape. In a painting entitled "March Heath, March Sand," he covers large areas in a photographic image of a landscape with irregular strips of sand glued onto the surface. The literalness here is almost comic, as if he were trying to plow up the image. As it turns out, the title refers to a patriotic tune used for inspirational effect by Hitler, and, further back, the area depicted is a locale in Brandenburg that figures importantly as a battleground in Prussian history. The thematics of plowing and regeneration would seem to suggest the possibility of a new start, but they could just as well suggest, with typical equivocality, the penchant to plow under unpleasant episodes and the resultant irruption of unresolved destructive impulses. If the latter suggestion is dominant, then the picture could also be taken as a sort of literalized pun, representing the "real" area beneath all the associations of memory and misused history.

Such literalizing of metaphors and puns occurs in the work of some Pop artists. Kiefer is perhaps as far removed from a Pop sensibility as one could be, at least at first glance. But then we remember his use of words, often for the sake of "identification," as part and parcel of the visual images, and we might recall the work of Jim Dine, or even the Magritte of "ceci n'est pas un pipe." And Kiefer's sculpture, "Palette with Wings," is a metal construction over nine feet tall, composed of a palette board (a favorite motif) flanked by a pair of wings (with an eleven foot span), and a lead snake entwined around the piece's supporting single pole. The snake is both a symbol of trouble in Eden, and a caduceus, suggesting medical health. The artist's tool can soar, Kiefer seems to tell us, but only if we admit that such soaring is either subject to corruption, or is itself a putative cure for our fallenness. But the tone of this particular equivocal conjunction has about it something like a Pop playfulness. Even the notion of sculpting a pair of lead wings echoes an aesthetic disposition that stretches from Duchamp's marble sugar cubes to Johns's "Painting with Two Balls," with its witty mockery of macho attitudes. And is the raggedness of the wings' feathers a gesture towards mimetic naturalism, or an ironic send-up of it?

There is some indication that Kiefer is moving away from a narrow German focus, as recent works deal with the French Revolution and the myth of Isis and Osiris. But the latter indulges in a liberalization, as the myth of the scattered limbs of the Egyptian deity are represented by shards of porcelain scattered about a huge canvas and tied back to a central point by strands of copper wire. There is also the vantage point of the viewer situated just outside and a little above the horizon line. The revolution painting is titled "The Ladies of the French Revolution," and consists of five panels covered with lead sheets; mounted on the panels in a random order are wildflowers framed under glass, each named for a woman involved in the historic events. But as with the ironic juxtaposition of German cultural heroes, here we have both Charlotte Corday and Marie Antoinette joined in the same work, denying any consistent political partisanship. What links these more recent works with the German paintings is a play with materials, a sense of historic irony, and a sense that Kiefer is developing technical skills of execution (the French

Revolution work being especially impressive) under the guise of expanding his subject matter.

Kiefer is an interesting artist because such questions about his use of materials continue to be asked alongside the queries about his social content and historical themes. One of the main legacies of formalism in painting and in art history was the notion that these two areas of art—matters of style and the manipulation of materials on the one hand, metaphoric or thematic or ideational content on the other— were linked in some abstract sense, though what really mattered was the first area. Only if the first area were accorded something like absolute primacy of aesthetic significance, would the second area be allowed a place; otherwise, opinionated, gullible, and temperamental as most of us are, our opinions, fancies, and ideas would lead us away from the purely aesthetic. While Kiefer lets us have opinions and fancies, he still lets us know, unlike the conceptual artists, for example, that visual pleasure is not only a noble but a necessary aim in easel painting.

Another way to approach Kiefer's relation to art history is to trace through his work traditional or mythic motifs that he has himself bent to a personal expression. For example, he often uses landscape frontality in his work; the viewer is presented with a large expanse, generally empty. Even in those paintings that have a building, room, or other structure in them, the feeling is one of an empty expanse. The viewpoint is often just above such expansive emptiness, so that Kiefer may be suggesting that we are not exactly immersed in or trapped by our historical horizons, but we are far from being free of them in any way. He also often paints trees or ferns or flowers, even occasionally incorporating actual plants into the work. These can be seen as emblems of frailty, but also as signs of eternally self-regulating forms; in either case, they seem to serve as something of a rebuke to the orders of culture and human intention that are otherwise so dominant in the paintings. Such appeals, through traditional motifs, to the themes of domination and frailty of responsibility and detachment would indicate a standard humanistic attitude, though one deeply felt and sincerely expressed, that tells us we are, as Shakespeare would say, "poor forked things," simultaneously the victims and the observers of our fate.

Now many of our historical schemes, and by extension our art historical schemes, are impoverished when it comes to setting up polarized dichotomies. Despite many warnings and good intentions, such polarities turn out to have no really useful mediating term or category that will keep the scheme from becoming mechanistic or reductive. So Kiefer may turn out to represent a continuation of formalism by other means, or else he may be hailed as a precursor of a return to painting made significant through social and historical content. It is hard to see him as representing both possibilities (even harder to see him as representing neither), because the two "parties," that of formalism and that of socially conscious art, have no room for overlap. The most cynical reading of Kiefer would be that he realizes all this but has chosen to set it against itself by subtly manipulating just enough of the stylistic markers from each camp so as to appear equally at home in both. For what does seem unavoidable is the conclusion that Kiefer is nothing if not self-conscious about style even to the point of being stylish.

One of the ways that art historical schemes are drawn up is to attend to questions of skill, or rather, to try to use levels of skill, and even attitudes to skill itself, as historical markers. In some fairly radical versions of such history there is even a hoped-for equation between skill and political content. This is true in other than art historical schemes, by the way. One slogan, for example, heard during the 1960's in America was that "good writing is counter-revolutionary." The equation here seems to involve a notion that pleasure can have a specific class function and a specific class identity; certain forms of frippery or a concern with variations rather than with themes, for example, might be assumed to be "bourgeois." Contrariwise, rough externals or a thematics of disrespect, even resentment, are assumed to be proletarian, or at a minimum, anti-bourgeois. Such equations are rejected by many critics as too simplistic, reductive, or tendentious. But establishing the truth of such claims is tricky, much trickier than the all-too-ready willingness of many to discard them completely would seem to warrant. A considerable part of the excitement generated by Kiefer, and also some of the dismay, is tied to this recurrent predilection to make an easy assumption about the relatedness of technical and stylistic questions on the one hand, and ideological and political values and concerns, on the other.

Kiefer's work contains a number of equivocal aspects and these make such relatedness hard to spell out. In the face of such ambiguity, many people want some resolution. One immediate temptation might be to argue that Kiefer, by returning political and social issues to painting, is ipso facto a radical artist. Another temptation might be to add that his style is deliberately rough, that it abjures not only the polished surfaces of commercial art but also the by-now tame standard forms of avant-garde outrageousness; hence his project must constitute a truly challenging new direction. These readings of Kiefer would echo the sense of a time warp mentioned earlier, for they would implicitly suggest that he becomes truly avant-garde by outstripping the avant-garde at its own game, that is by ignoring precedent. The irony in Kiefer's case comes from that fact that the precedents he ignores are those of the avant-garde itself. As a friend of mine remarked after seeing the Kiefer show, "After post-modernism comes modernism." In a way what we might be seeing is the turning back on itself of an art historical consciousness, and that turning back results in a challenge—even a deconstructive challenge—to art history itself. If the Pop and then even more so Minimalist movements were examples of art conceived by people who knew art history but chose to mock its "truths," then Kiefer is an artist who works with and against the structures of such history.

One way to understand a history that turns back on itself is to see it as a form of myth, a recursiveness that would be traceable back to a scheme from a philosopher like Vico, with his love of cycles and completions. Kiefer is certainly a mythic artist, at least in terms of much of his ostensible content. And the mythic disposition always has a tendency to mock chronological history, to see it as an inferior temporal order— "those dying generations," as Yeats said. What is there by way of motif may be there by virtue of a guiding vision, though that doesn't mean that Kiefer has a consistent or programmatic attitude towards the competing claims of myth and history. But at the very least it would help clarify the mixture of tones, allowing the grave historical irony and the painterly play with materials and semantics to coexist. It would also help us see why it is possible, perhaps necessary, to regard Kiefer as both an historical and a formalist painter.

This may be the clue to his political meaning as well. Most of the major political revolutionary movements have both a forward and a backward looking aspect. This may come from a desire to capture and even shape time by freezing it into a recurrent pattern. Sartre has written of how the Girondin party in the French Revolution, for example, adopted Roman values, and even wore Roman togas in their Republican assault on the order of the monarchy. But it is not enough to say that Kiefer must look back in order to move ahead, or that we can trust his forward lookingness to "decontaminate" or ironically correct the possible ethnocentrism or racialism in his subject matter. It is not enough to make such arguments, but it may be all we are able at this time to make of Kiefer's work. History, as the poet said, has many cunning corridors, and much may well depend on who is willing to follow Kiefer down his particular route. Marx's famous remark in The Eighteenth Brumaire, that men make their own history but not always as they would wish, has been glossed many times. Marx used the plural advisedly, for the history any of us makes must in turn be further made or unmade by those that follow. But this applies to Kiefer with something like special force, not only because he seems to have an ability—or at least the desire—to make his own history as he goes.

Note

[1] At the Museum of Modern Art in New York City until January 3, 1989. The show traveled from Chicago to Philadelphia to Los Angeles before closing in New York.

The Aesthetic Alibi

BY MARTIN JAY

In a recent essay decrying the General Services Administration's dismantling of his site-specific public sculpture, *Tilted Arc*, in 1989, Richard Serra made his case in terms of what he called "moral rights" against property rights.[1] Although the government had paid for the work, he argued, it had no right to destroy it, for the result was to override "the right to freedom of speech, the right of expression, the right to protection of one's creative work."[2] Instead of "maintaining the integrity of its artworks,"[3] the government was exercising a kind of censorship, which threatened to introduce political considerations into the realm of art.

More than a reaction to the special case of "public art" like *Tilted Arc*, Serra's alarm was fueled by an increasing number of challenges to the unhindered expression of transgressive ideas and symbolic actions in the past few years. Such a development in the United States seems especially ironic at a moment when elsewhere in the world, most notably the former Soviet bloc, restrictions are being relaxed. At times the threat has been directed at "high art," as in the case of Serra's sculpture, at others against "low" or "popular art" as exemplified by the reaction to performances by the rap group *2 Live Crew*. Sometimes the charge has been obscenity, as with the photographs of Robert Mapplethorpe, or the corruption of minors, in the case of Jock Sturge's photos of nude children, or something akin to blasphemy in the case of Andres Serrano's infamous *Piss Christ*.

Politically, the menace has usually been identified as coming from the right, with figures like Jesse Helms, Patrick Buchanan and Donald Wildmon the major culprits; but with the hysterical (and often hypocritical) inflation of "political correctness" into an equally ominous threat, it has also now become linked at times to the left.[4] No less variable have been the threatened punishments, which range from the destruction of already existing works and the imprisonment of offenders against standards of decency to the loss of funding from the National Endowment for the Arts or the General Services Administration. But whatever the justification, source or penalty, a pattern has emerged in which freedom of expression seems very much under siege. With the Ayatollah's death threat against Salmon Rushdie as the *reductio ad absurdum* of this trend, artists and their supporters have recognized how high the stakes can get in this struggle. As a result, the ghost of Senator McCarthy has been sighted with greater frequency than at any time since he seemed to be mercifully buried in the 1960's.

Sorting out all the complex issues raised by these events would be an impossible task in the modest compass of this column. Even venturing yet another attempt to discuss the limits of free speech seems foolishly ambitious, especially for someone with no expertise in the intricacies of the law. What I would prefer to do instead is focus on one aspect of the debate, which concerns the question of what is normally called "artistic freedom." For in response to efforts at restricting free speech, the assumed special right of the artist has frequently been claimed. Serra may talk loosely of "moral rights" and worry about free expression in general, but it is clear that, say, a "non-signature" architect with no artistic pretensions who protested against an alteration to a house he designed would get nowhere. Even Madonna in *Truth or Dare* could brazen her way out of a threat to close her concert down for public lewdness in Toronto only by righteously wrapping herself in the flag of *artistic* free expression.

Broadly speaking, artistic freedom can be defined as a special case of freedom of speech, which raises it to a more purified level. That is, the restrictions on free speech in a liberal society are generally relaxed still further when that speech (or any symbolic action) is deemed to have aesthetic value. It may be prohibited to shout "fire!" from the audience of a theater, because of the panic it will engender, but there is no problem with the same cry on stage, just as long as it remains understood as part of the play. For as speech act theorists have been telling us for some time, the "perlocutionary" impact of the same words, their ability to make something happen, varies with the context. What would be libelous or offensive in everyday life is granted a special dispensation, if it is understood to take place within the protective shield of an aesthetic frame. One of the distinguishing marks of liberal, secularized Western societies is precisely our claim to recognize such a protective shield. When it is pierced, and works of literature or art are burned for their repugnant ideas, transgressive language or distasteful imagery, we grow indignant at the failure to observe what seems to us almost a natural boundary. Although we may disagree over what justifiably can claim protection under the doctrine of aesthetic freedom, virtually all of us honor the distinction between art and its other, and are willing to tolerate in the former sphere what would be troubling in the latter. We even invent new categories like "performance art" to permit behavior that without its protection would in all likelihood threaten the perpetrator with immediate incarceration in a mental institution, if not a jail.

The ideal of "artistic freedom," it can safely be said, is one of the most sacrosanct in our culture, and we relish any opportunity to reaffirm its value. Not for us, we tell ourselves proudly, are there exhibitions of "degenerate art" designed to humiliate artists who fail to conform to the state's authoritarian tastes. Not for us are there laws forcing heterodox writers to circulate their work in samizdat editions or seek exile abroad. Even post-modernists, who pride themselves on challenging the liberal pieties of the Enlightenment tradition, can find ammunition for the defense of aesthetic freedom in the claim of Jean-Francois Lyotard that a radical incommensurability—a "differend" in his vocabulary—exists between art and other "regimes of phrases."[5] The right to free aesthetic expression is in fact so much a part of our self-understanding that it often seems to have its own intrinsic justification beyond that provided to free speech in general by the first amendment.

What, however, makes all of this appeal to artistic freedom so paradoxical, what in fact should force us to reconsider its self-evident truth, is that the challenge to its integrity has come not only from the troglodytes who fail to understand the rules of the aesthetic game, but also from another source, and one far more difficult to dismiss out of hand.

That is, it comes from within the discourse of the aesthetic itself, or more precisely from those artists and intellectuals who have called into question the very idea of a distinct and inviolable realm of experience called "art." For if they are right and we are no longer permitted to assume that such a realm exists, a realm radically apart from other spheres of life, then it becomes highly problematic to grant what used to be thought of as contained within its boundaries any special dispensation.

The critique of the integrity of the aesthetic has come, broadly speaking, from three directions, which we may designate historical and sociological criticism, avant-garde practice, and post-structuralist theory. The first of these has established the chronological origins of the idea of what the literary critic M. H. Abrams calls "art-as-such," [6] which rather than being an eternal cultural given, came into being only in the 18th century in England and Germany. Encompassing the so-called "fine arts," enjoining an attitude of contemplative appreciation akin to religious worship, defining works as autotelic, disinterested and autonomous, this new appreciation of a generic category called "art" generated a discourse called "aesthetics" developed with great power by writers like Shaftesbury, Burke and Addison in England and Baumgarten and Kant in Germany. Its practical value was perhaps first put to the test during the French Revolution, when the art treasures of the discredited monarchy were saved from the iconoclastic fury of the mob and protected in the Louvre, itself thus wondrously transformed from a king's palace into a museum preserving the artistic patrimony of the nation.

The subsumption of discrete artistic crafts under the generic category of art, and the discursive isolation of aesthetics from ethics, metaphysics, epistemology and other philosophical fields, was accompanied by the institutional creation of networks of evaluation, preservation and commodification, which invested the idea that art was a realm apart with social rather than merely cultural force. In an age when traditional hierarchical standards were under pressure, the concept of aesthetic taste and the market judgments of value that went along with it provided new ways to distinguish high from low, worthiness from worthlessness. Bourgeois pretensions to distinction through aesthetic connoisseurship went hand in hand with the substitution of the marketplace for aristocratic patronage systems.

Along with these changes went the construction of the creative genius as a figure of unconstrained power, who produced art by breaking rather than following rules. Although often heroized as a victim of bourgeois philistinism, the genius was ironically in large measure a function of the aesthetic system engendered by the same changes that led to the market demand for his creations. Like art itself, the genius was often construed as unbound by non-aesthetic considerations, cognitive, ethical or whatever. His pursuit of aesthetic perfection could, to be sure, lead to a chilling indifference to more conventionally humane concerns, an attitude brilliantly captured in Oscar Wilde's observation that "When Benvenuto Cellini crucified a living man to study the play of muscles in his death agony, a pope was right to grant him absolution. What is the death of a vague individual if it enables an immortal work to blossom and to create, in Keats's words, an eternal source of ecstasy?"[7] But by and large, such attitudes were tolerated as the cost of untrammeled artistic freedom.

There is a great deal more that could be said about the historical construction of the category of Art and the aesthetic discourse surrounding it, a topic of considerable current scholarly interests.[8] But suffice it to note for now that once we have come to appreciate "art's" contingent, historical roots, it has inevitably grown more difficult to defend free aesthetic expression as if it were a self-evident truth. Indeed, in the hands of sociologists like Pierre Bourdieu, an awareness of the historical construction of aesthetic value can lead to a denial that art in any way transcends its institutional roots in the system of social distinction that it helps maintain.[9] In this reading, culture becomes "cultural capital" and artistic freedom is little more than the right to assert hierarchical superiority in a more "tasteful" way than mere money or breeding would allow.

From a very different perspective, that of the so-called avant-garde movements of the late 19th and early 20th centuries, a complementary assault on the integrity of the aesthetic was launched. Dadaist manifestations, Duchamp's ready-mades, Surrealist automatic writing and found objects, all of these challenged the ideology of the creative genius and the permanent, transcendent value of the works he created. Although at times descending into a nihilist "anti-art for anti-art's sake," the avant-garde by and large held onto a belief in the redemptive potential of art. Here the value of art as a realm of autotelic and autonomous disinterestedness was not challenged *per se*; what was at issue instead was the continued separation of that realm from everyday life. As Peter Burger has argued, the avant-garde often sought to infuse everyday life with the emancipatory energies of art.[10] That is, it sought not the abolition of the separate sphere of the aesthetic as much as the realization of its "promise of happiness" in the realm of quotidian existence. Unlike the modernists, who Burger claims remained within the institution of art and disrupted only conventional notions of the artwork, the avant-garde actively sought to heal the wound that split art from life.

The emancipatory outcome they sought has not, to be sure, been realized, surviving only in the parodic form that we can identify with the post-modernist version of reintegrating art and life. Nor has their own "work" successfully escaped being re-aestheticized by the powerful institutions of collection and preservation that still determine what is art and what isn't. What Walter Benjamin made famous as the aura around works of art has not dissolved as easily as he and others in the heyday of the avant-garde had hoped. But in challenging the integrity of the institution of art and debunking the claim that artists are creative geniuses above the law, they have also helped undermine the premises of the discourse on which the idea of aesthetic freedom is based.

Still a third stimulus to this debunking has been more recently provided by the theories called post-structuralist. Jacques Derrida's *Truth in Painting* is perhaps the best-known locus of an argument that has been elaborated by others in the same camp, such as Philippe Lacoue-Larbarthe, Jean-Luc Nancy and Paul de Man.[11] For Derrida, the absolute distinction between the work, or *ergon,* and its surrounding frame, or *parergon*, is impossible to maintain. Intrinsic and extrinsic, text and context, cited works in quotation marks and "direct" words spoken without them,[12] all of these are intertwined in ways that undercut the ideal purity of the aesthetic realm. Aesthetic discourses, such as Kant's Third Critique, are likewise invaded by the parergonal cognitive and ethical considerations they try to keep at bay. Thus, although deconstruction is often taken to mean the imperialism of the aesthetic, because of its refusal to segregate literal from metaphorical meanings and rhetoric from philosophy, it might be understood just as well to imply a belief in the opposite: the pollution of the pure realm of art by "extraneous" considerations from outside. Not surprisingly, something called the "aesthetic ideology" has been its target as often as it has in the work of Marxist cultural critics like David Lloyd or Terry Eagleton.[13]

As a result of these and comparable critiques, the integrity of the institution of art no longer seems as inviolable as it did from the era of, say, Matthew Arnold to that of Clement Greenberg. This is not to suggest, however, that it has simply collapsed or is even on its last legs. For the social and economic exigencies that called it into being are still very potent. The ironic complicity between commodification and the ideology of unique genius can scarcely be doubted in an age of fifty million dollar Van Goghs. But what has become dubious nonetheless is the practice of evoking artistic freedom by those who must surely know that the ground on which they base their case has turned into quicksand.

Interestingly, this is not the first time such inconsistencies have appeared. Take, for example, a celebrated episode in the history of Surrealism, the furor surrounding Louis Aragon's poem "Front Rouge."[14] Containing the memorably lyrical lines, "Shoot Leon Blum, Shoot Boncour Froissard Deat, Shoot the trained bears of social democracy," the poem caused Aragon to be indicted on charges of incitement to murder and provocation of desertion in the army in January, 1932. Breton and the Surrealists rallied to his defense, organizing a giant petition on his behalf, which some 60,000 people signed. Many who did were won over by the Surrealists' invoking of the general principle that a poem should not be confused with a political tract. Falling back on what can be called the "Aesthetic alibi" for what he acknowledged was only a mediocre "poem of circumstance," Breton wrote, "I say that this poem, by its situation in Aragon's work on the one hand and in the history of poetry on the other, corresponds to a certain number of formal determinations which do not permit the isolation of any one group of words ('Comrades, kill the cops') in order to exploit its literal meaning, whereas for some other group ('The stars descend familiarly on earth') the question of this literal meaning does not come up . . . The meaning and significance of the poem are *different* from the sum of all that analysis of the specific elements it involves permit to be discovered in it . . ."[15]

Here we have the peculiar spectacle of one of the leading avant-garde critics of art for art's sake, one of the most dogged believers in transgressing the barrier between art and life, resorting to traditional notions of the inviolable integrity of the organic work, the formalist distinction between form and content, and the radical distinction between literal and metaphorical uses of language. Not surprisingly, Breton was roundly attacked as a hypocrite by writers like Andre Gide and Romain Rolland, who claimed that symbolic action inevitably had moral and political consequences, which could not be so easily evaded. To claim a special immunity on the part of the poet, they furthermore argued, was to raise him above the common man, whose prosaic challenges to authority were unprotected by the alleged disinterestedness of the aesthetic realm.

Aragon, for his part, ultimately repudiated Breton's defense, partly because the Surrealist pamphlet contained subtle criticisms of the Communist Party, to which he soon gave his uncontested loyalty. The "Aragon Affair," as it became known, ended with Aragon, against whom all charges were dropped, leaving behind his Surrealist affiliation entirely and Breton sputtering with rage at the betrayal. What he seems to have been a bit less outraged by was the betrayal of his own principles by the appeal to aesthetic purity he had made on behalf of the ungrateful Aragon. The interpenetration of art and everyday life, he seemed to be saying, was only a one-way affair; it was justifiable when art sought to influence the everyday or made raids on it of its own choosing for inspiration, but should everyday concerns invade the sacrosanct realm of the aesthetic, then its freedom was being violated.

Today, the same logic seems to prevail among those who most piously defend artistic freedom against the incursion of the state, the church, or social groups offended by what they see or read. It is tempting as a result to repeat the charges of Gide and Rolland and simply dismiss the appeal to a special dispensation for artistic expression as self-serving and hypocritical. Salman Rushdie, we might be inclined to conclude, was right to disappoint his defenders and accept some responsibility for the offense his book caused Moslem believers. Madonna, by the same token, should have been woman enough to shoulder the blame (or accept the credit) for the fact that her material challenged the sensibilities of the good citizens of Toronto.

And yet this is a temptation that must be resisted. For what would be left, the nagging worry remains, to protect us from the censorious efforts of the Helms, Wildmons and Khomeinis of the world, if the fiction of aesthetic integrity were utterly abandoned? How might we fend off the wholesale invasion of the aesthetic realm by those who want to subordinate it to non-aesthetic considerations—moral, political, economic, etc. This concern, I agree, is not an idle one, as threats to free expression (artistic or otherwise) should never be taken lightly. The recent disclosures about the explicit political pressure on decisions at the National Endowment of the Arts show how easily such threats can be translated into action.

There are, it seems to me, three ways to preserve what the doctrine of artistic freedom in its naive form can no longer be expected to protect. The first draws on a solution recently suggested by feminists concerned about the problematic practical consequences of deconstructing the centered subject, female or otherwise. Rather than accepting the dissolution of subjects entirely into discursive systems, with the accompanying danger of robbing women of their potential for self-realizing agency and the solidarity of their group identity, theorists like Gayatri Chakravorty Spivak and Rosi Braidotti have introduced the idea of "strategic essentialism."[16] Acknowledging that collective subjects like "woman" are ultimately artificial constructs rather than natural givens, they have claimed that it is nonetheless permissible to adopt an essentialist discourse when it is strategically useful in combating discrimination against people who are the victims of negative essentializing.

Although the parallels are not perfect, perhaps a similar strategic essentialism might seem warranted in the case of artistic freedom. That is, even though it may be impossible to ontologize the aesthetic as a separate realm apart from mundane values and interests, it may be useful in certain circumstances to claim that it is such a realm as a bulwark against the pressures to subordinate what we normally include in "the aesthetic" to what is extrinsic to it. Such an approach, however, may well invite the rebuke that fictions can work only so far as they remain persuasive to the people who hold them. If those who defend the integrity of "art" know it to be more than a concocted category, what is to keep this knowledge out of the hands of those who attack that integrity? How long can a strategy effectively operate that is built on a distinction between those who are privy to the truth (which they only pretend to forget) and those who are not?

A second, possibly more fruitful defense arises from the observation made above that despite all the efforts to historicize, deconstruct or render obsolete through realization in the lifeworld the differentiated realm of art, it nonetheless survives as an ideology because the social and economic reasons for its existence persist. That is, just because we can denaturalize a category like the aesthetic and expose it as historically relative does not mean it necessarily goes away. Nor does showing its boundaries to be porous mean that they are entirely effaced. Art may no longer be legitimated in traditional terms, but if it successfully functions as "cultural capital," then it is likely to be around for a long time to come.

If this is the case, then why not still draw on some of the residual power of the category, without foregrounding its deeper socioeconomic function, to protect transgressive symbolic action? Although such a solution, like that of strategic essentialism, may seem a bit duplicitous, it does seem to keep the less theoretically astute thought police at bay. Or at least so one might conclude from the trial of the Cincinnati museum exhibition of the Mapplethorpe photographs, when the jury accepted "expert testimony" (by eminent "cultural capitalists") as to their artistic merit.

A final, somewhat more candid alternative would be to accept the collapse (or at least moribund status) of the category of the aesthetic and fall back on a more general defense of free speech of all kinds. Such a *soidisant* would spare us the embarrassment of saying that an elite of *soidisant* artists can claim more protection than the average citizen. It also would avoid the no less elitist implications of the first two defenses, based as they are on the difference between those disabused of the aesthetic ideology and those still in its thrall. Such a defense, to be sure, would do little to help in cases such as Serra's *Tilted Arc*, where something more fundamental has to be assumed to justify the continuing rights of the "creator" after he or she has sold the work created, but in other instances, it might be sufficient to resist censorship.

Here a potential problem arises, however, at a time when challenges to the absolute exercise of free speech, whether through the invocation of community as opposed to universal standards or the controversial critique of "fighting words," threatens to narrow the definition of the permissible. The 1973 Supreme Court decision in the case of *Miller v. California* opened the possibility of local juries deciding what was obscene or offensive. More recent opinions, I am told, suggest that a broader category like the universally construed "public sphere" may get us beyond the potentially stifling judgments of narrowly defined "communities," which never, *pace* the Helms and the Wildmons of the world, have any one shared set of standards. But there is still no reason to assume that the offensive and transgressive symbolic action hitherto defended on aesthetic grounds will automatically survive, because there remains the inevitable struggle to define who has the power in such a public sphere to decide what is permissible and what isn't. And as the recent Supreme Court decision curtailing free speech in publicly funded abortion clinics suggests, this power may well be wielded by the current court with a narrow definition of what is permissible.

It may therefore be necessary to draw on all of the defenses outlined above—and still others yet to be invented—to resist the implications of the unraveling of the aesthetic alibi. "The freedom of the artist," like the ideology of *l'art pour l'art* on which it rests, may be a myth in its classical form but without some less vulnerable version of the same notion, we are in danger of losing more than a faded ideal. For insofar as the category of "art" provides a shelter not only for cathartic and consoling experiences of beauty, but also for experiments in cultural transgression and innovation, it serves a vital future-oriented function that transcends its status as mere capital in the cultural economy of our day. It is perhaps for this reason that we stubbornly hold on to its privileged status, even as we have paradoxically come to recognize that it is built on foundations of extremely porous clay.

Notes

[1] Richard Serra, "Art and Censorship," *Critical Inquiry,* XVG, 3 (Spring, 1991). See also, Barbara Hoffman, "Law for Art's Sake in the Public Realm," in the same issue.

[2] Ibid., p, 575.

[3] Ibid., p. 576. This phrase refers to a bill submitted by Senator Edward Kennedy protecting the artist's "moral rights" supported by Serra. It was passed in October, 1990 as the "Visual Artists Rights Act." For details and implications, see Hoffman,p. 568f.

[4] That this is not entirely a fantasy is demonstrated by the controversy over David Nelson's portrait of the late Chicago mayor Harold Washington in women's underwear in May, 1988. It was seized by officials of the city government from the student exhibition, where it was being shown, and returned only after it was slashed.

[5] Jean-Francois Lyotard, *The Differend: Phrases in Dispute,* trans. Georges Van Den Abbeele (Minneapolis, 1988).

[6] M. H. Abrams, "Art-as-Such: The Sociology of Modern Aesthetics," in *Doing Things With Texts: Essays in Criticism and Critical Theory,* ed. Michael Fischer (New York, 1989).

[7] Wilde as quoted in Ernest Raynaud, *Souvenirs sur le symbolisme* (Paris, 1895), p. 397.

[8] In addition to the Abrams essay cited above, see Terry Eagleton, *The Ideology of the Aesthetic* (Cambridge, Mass., 1990); Luc Ferry, *Homo Aestheticus: L' Invention du gout a l'age democratique* (Paris, 1990); Howard Caygill, *Art of Judgment* (Cambridge, Mass., 1989).

[9] Pierre Bourdieu, *Distinction: A Social Critique of the Judgment of Taste,* trans. Richard Nice (Cambridge, Mass., 1984).

[10] Peter Burger, *Theory of the Avant-Garde,* trans. Michael Shaw (Minneapolis, 1984).

[11] Jacques Derrida, *The Truth in Painting,* trans. Geoff Bennington and Ian McLeod (Chicago, 1987); Lacoue Labarthe and Jean-Luc Nancy, *The Literary Absolute: The Theory of Literature in German Romanticism,* trans. Philip Barnard and Cheryl Lester (Albany, N.Y., 1988); Paul de Man, *The Rhetoric of Romanticism* (New York, 1984) and *The Resistance to Theory* (Minneapolis, 1986).

[12] This issue was at the center of the celebrated debate between Derrida and the speech act philosopher John Searle in *Glyph* in the late 1970's.

[13] Elsewhere, I have sought to grapple with the implications of this critique. See my "'The Aesthetic Ideology' as Ideology; Or What Does it Mean to Aestheticize Politics?," *Cultural Critique* (Forthcoming).

[14] For accounts, see Maurice Nadeau, *The History of Surrealism,* trans. Richard Howard with intro. by Roger Shattuck (London, 1987), chapter XIV; and Helen Lewis, *The Politics of Surrealism* (New York, 1988), chapter VI.

[15] Breton, "The Poverty of Poetry: The Aragon Affair and Public Opinion," in *Selected Writings,* ed., Franklin Rosemont (London,1989), p. 77.

[16] Gayatri Chakravorty Spivak, "Criticism, Feminism and the Institution," in *Intellectuals: Aesthetics, Politics, Academics,* ed. Bruce Robbins (Minneapolis, 1990); Rosi Braidotti, "The Politics of Ontological Difference," in Teresa Brennan, ed., *Between Feminism and Psychoanalysis* (London, 1989).

Painterly

BY JED PERL

A complaint frequently heard from the artists here in New York is that the most important shows of paintings by old and modern masters do not visit our museums. To out-of-towners—who think back on the 1989-90 season, when New York had a Velasquez show at the Metropolitan and "Pioneering Cubism" at the Modern—this can sound a little crazy, a mix of big-city irrationality and big-city greed. But for New York artists, who depend on the classics to keep their sense of proportion in the midst of all the big-city hype, the thought that a great show is passing them by can be the occasion for a big-city-size anxiety attack. How can artists ever forgive the hometown museums for denying them (that's how they'd describe it) Chardin (mounted in Boston more than a decade ago) or Watteau, "Matisse in Nice" and "Late Braque" (all mounted in Washington, DC in the 1980s)? The truth is that New York artists don't forgive the hometown museums. But the artists do take action. They get into cars and trains and planes and buses and go where the art is. Sometimes, there are so many New York artists at the shows in Washington or Boston that these out-of-town events become New York events. And when the artists come back to New York, they assimilate what they've seen and learned into the hometown mentality. Watteau didn't happen in New York, but New York artists feel it happened to them.

"Titian, Prince of Painters," mounted at the National Gallery, was the show that had the most artists trooping down to Washington this past fall. It is close to an impossible task to mount an American retrospective of an artist who was born five hundred years ago and did much of his most important work for public buildings half a world away. Under the circumstances, the show that the National Gallery put together in collaboration with the Palazzo Ducale in Venice, where a different (and larger) version was seen this past summer, was the best that could be hoped for. This compilation of paintings by one of the greatest painters who ever lived contained some of his greatest achievements. There were paintings that are sensuous, mysterious, marvelously clear: *Venus with an Organist and Dog* (from the Prado), *The Annunciation* (from Chiesa di San Salvador in Venice), *The Entombment* (from the Prado), and *Tarquin and Lucretia* (from the Fitzwilliam in Cambridge) give us about as much as we can expect from a single work of art. What was missing at the Titian show was something that not even the finest curator could have given it: the end-to-end coherence that's possible when a museum presents a retrospective of an artist whose essential work is all in an easel-painting scale. The Titian show doesn't hold in the mind as a totality: it was not a perfect experience. But on its own terms, it was a totally satisfying experience. Once you'd tuned in to the exhibition's astronomical high points, the rest of the show somehow came up to meet them. Titian's masterpieces became the open sesame to a whole universe of experience. That this universe had its good moments and its less good moments, its plateaus and valleys and confusing terrain, was part of its grandeur.

When contemporary artists travel to see the work of an old master, it's because they believe that the artist has something important to teach them. In the case of an enormous, complex career like Titian's, there are any number of lessons to be learned—what one takes away from the work will depend on what one brings to it in the first place. But every contemporary view of Titian will probably hinge on some idea of Titian as a—as the—natural painter.

By natural painting, I mean to suggest the freedom of the brushwork, the directness of the color. We feel that Titian is in some easy relation with the essential elements of the painter's art—pigments, oils, canvas. Yet there is a paradox hidden away here: what we think of as natural painting is the product of an extremely refined culture. Only with Titian, in sixteenth century Venice, does painterly painting become an established mode in European art. That loose brushstroke of Titian's is something that had to be championed, that people *learned* to value.

In the century following his death in 1576 Titian's art influenced painters as diverse as Rubens, Velasquez, Rembrandt, and Poussin (in his first maturity). Titian's painterliness came to be associated with feeling, passion, impulsiveness. This hot, emotional kind of painting was, in turn, opposed to a cooler, drier kind of painting—to a kind of painting that was thought to suggest reason, detachment. Even during Titian's lifetime, in Paulo Pino's *Dialogo della Pittura* of 1548, this opposition was being framed geographically, as a difference between Venetian and Florentine art, between *colore* and *disegno*. The opposition between a painting organized in terms of color and a painting organized in terms of linear design has become, for us, a habit of mind, a way of understanding the variety of art. From the seventeenth to the twentieth centuries, painting has been mapped in terms of changing but related oppositions between the Classical and the Baroque, the Neoclassical and the Rococo, Constructivism and Expressionism. In the twentieth century, *disegno*—an art that is in some way conceptual—has sometimes been seen as disappearing into the ideas of Marcel Duchamp, whose mental elegance is viewed by his admirers as suggesting a twentieth-century version of Leonardo, the Florentine idea-man who invented the High Renaissance style but painted very few paintings. Duchamp's personal rejection of painting has dominated thinking about art for half-a-century. Just now center-stage in the art world belongs to work that takes its inspiration or materials (or both) from the worlds of advertising and photography.

As for painterly painting, it has become a victim of its own prestige. We tend to see Titian's coloristic brushwork through the prism of the modern movement—through the work of painters from Delacroix to Kandinsky, for whom the colorful brushstroke was a force for revolutionary change. Manet and the Impressionists used the painterly brushstroke to shatter the conventional image of reality. Thus painterliness was mixed up with the heroism of modern art; and as that heroic idea of modern art began to look like a cliché of the textbooks, painterliness began to look old hat. The brushstroke that announced, in Fauvism and German Expressionism and Abstract Expressionism, a reconsideration of experience, is now viewed by the art world thought police as a reactionary gesture—an imitation of a revolutionary spirit to which we no longer subscribe. Delacroix's incendiary romanticism (with its recollections of Rubens, who recollected Titian), can look like a form of narcissism, a denial of the realities of life. Life, we are told by the thought police, does not allow room for individual expression.

Yet painterliness, even if it is sometimes imagined to be a terminal patient, is in pretty good health. In New York it is always present, as it were under the surface, as the active agent in painting culture. Paris taught New York to appreciate the power of the brush, and if it has sometimes been said that the brushstroke disappeared from view in the 1960s, this is to a large degree a PR-machine perception. It is not for nothing that Hans Hofmann was the greatest art teacher that this city has ever known. He believed in the brush as a carrier of meaning and metaphor, and, of course, of emotion. One feels the eloquence of the painterly brush, Paris's legacy to New York, in the work of an Abstract Expressionist like Joan Mitchell, who is painting more interestingly now than she has in quite a long time. It's a hedonist's taste for the magic of the brush—and that's a very New York taste—that enables Joan Snyder, a painter sometimes given to overly literary ideas or overly expressionistic gestures, to win through to paintings of elegance and concision. Gretna Campbell, who died in 1987, produced in her last years landscapes in which an unpicturesque variety of hedges and trees and fields is united, through the nervous energy of the brushwork, into stirring gray-purple-green dramas. Louisa Matthiasdottir, the finest still-life painter at work today, uses a clear, forceful brushstroke to give her geometric tabletop arrangements of kitchen implements and fruits and vegetables a classical brilliance and precision. Nell Blaine, with jumpy, zippy strokes of high-keyed color, is painting the most beautiful bouquets of her long career. Leland Bell's iconic figure compositions—three figures around a table, a man and a woman in a bedroom— have achieved a marvelous combination of fullness and pared-down-ness. And John Heliker's interiors have a poetic blue-green atmosphere that is mysteriously eloquent. All of these artists are past fifty. A new generation has grown up since then: among those whose work has interested me in the past few years are Rita Baragona, Temma Bell, Richard La Presti, Stanley Lewis, and Ned Small.

These artists would not be unhappy to be called tradition-conscious. Indeed, they're the artists who are sometimes said to be inhibited by their reverence for the art of the museums. To me, their exhibits are essential events: they paint what they must paint, and in doing so they demonstrate the relevance of the painterly impulse. But they are not the only artists who are responding to "Titian, Prince of Painters." I have a sense that the appeal of this show has to do with a sea change in the art world: people want a way out of the hi-tech mentality that's dominated them for decades. The brushstroke has, just now, a glamour, an appeal. It reappears in unexpected places, in unpredictable forms. We see painterliness treated ironically, as a jokey (perhaps fondly jokey) suggestion of a romantic individualism that the artist doesn't quite believe in. This could be the motivation behind Gerhard Richter's retreads of Abstract Expressionist style. Or painterliness is used for nostalgic effect: as a shorthand invocation of an earlier, supposedly more interesting period in the history of art. Perhaps this is part of the motivation behind Carroll Dunham's recent work, those ambitious abstract paintings that look more than a little like the paintings of the Dutch Cobra group of the 1950s. The granddaddy of all nostalgic or ironic painterly work of today can be found in a little drawing that Duchamp did in 1953. Called *Moonlight on the Bay at Basswood*, it's a scene of trees silhouetted against the sky and reflected in a lake, done in "ink, pencil, crayon, talcum powder, and chocolate on blue blotting paper." This bit of American atmosphere is little more than a few smears of pigment: it's painterliness reduced to an ironically sentimental gesture.

The painterly ironic is at its most engaging in the work of Sigmar Polke. This contemporary German artist has an impressive yet somehow disembodied gift for paint-handling. I have not yet seen the retrospective of his work which opened at the San Francisco Museum last fall and is now touring the country; but I have seen, here and there, much of the work that is in that show. Polke's images are all second hand stuff: his stenciled figures and objects invoke Western industrialized culture, his abstract compositions invoke the work of the New York School of the 1940s and

1950s. I understand that this self-consciously retro pose is at the essence of what Polke is about: he's suggesting that today all feelings are in quotation marks, that everything has been experienced before. If that were all there was to his work, I wouldn't care to think about it at all. But Polke has an instinctive feeling for paints and surfaces that lends some of his compositions a genuine animation. In some of his large recent paintings (which are done in oddly mixed media: powdered meteoric material and silver nitrate suffused through artificial resins) nothing much goes on, there's nothing but mystical vapor. Still, Polke's easy command of the materials holds me. This is Dadaist painterliness. Even some of the works with stenciled figures, such as *Jeux d'enfants*, with its Rococo angels and swishes of purple and green paint, have an authority. Polke's painterly gifts can't make up for the deadness that's at the heart of his work. But it is the painterliness that gives his canvases their eerie decadence. It's curious to see such beautifully heartless works.

In the 1980s, painterly painting was a fashionable idea: the free brushstroke was a seductively ambiguous gesture, simultaneously romantic and ironic. Titian's very late style, with its harum-scarum brushwork, was very much on artists' minds. Paul Georges, an artist who likes both classical structures and off-the-wall ideas, had a show at the Anne Plumb Gallery in 1988, in which he presented his own versions of the Diana and Actaeon story, from Ovid's *Metamorphosis*. This story—of Diana's destruction of Actaeon, who has seen the chaste goddess naked—was the inspiration for some of Titian's greatest mythological paintings. The rhapsodic craziness of Titian's late style seems to have spurred Georges on, to have given him a way to connect the two sides of his personality as a painter. Georges's big, expansive Diana and Actaeon paintings—with their verdant vistas and jolts of red—are a witty and compelling reconsideration of painterly passion.

One late Titian in particular, *The Flaying of Marsyas* (which is in the Archepiscopal Palace in Kromeriz, Czechoslovakia), has been widely discussed since it came to London for "The Genius of Venice 1500-1600" show in 1983. (The *Marsyas* was in Washington—its second visit to the capital in five years—for the Titian show.) This painting has astonished people with its shifting levels of illusion, its chaotic exploding strokes and counterstrokes of paint. When I first saw the *Marsyas* a few years ago, I was very excited by it; but since then I've come to feel that people put it up a little too high, that what they really love about it is not its struggling-for-coherence quality but its painting-for-the-hell-of-it quality. (Georges's achievement in some of his recent work has been to join these two impulses in an uneasy but exciting union.)

Marsyas depicts the pipe-playing goat-man after he's lost his competition with Apollo to determine who's the greatest musician. Marsyas, hanging upside down from a tree at the center of the painting, is receiving his punishment: he's being flayed alive. One figure tears at his flesh with a knife; another plays a violin; a dog leaps at Marsyas's blood; Midas (the judge) sits deep in thought. When the painting was first shown in London, the late painter and critic Lawrence Gowing wrote in the *London Review of Books* that "London has been half under the spell of this masterpiece, in which the tragic sense that overtook Titian's poesie in his seventies reached its cruel and solemn extreme. At most hours on most days there is a knot of visitors riveted and fairly perplexed in front of it." The painting does have a weird, dissonant poetry, which comes from the shifts from passages of almost sharp-focus realism to passages of brushy vagueness. But I think there's something overly dissonant about the image. I think that the *Marsyas* has become a cult painting because it can be seen as Titian's endorsement of anarchic painterly gestures.

When I consider the current taste for the instability of the *Marsyas*, I find that the taste is related to the taste for those gorgeous amorphous surfaces of Polke's. The paintings of the Englishman Howard Hodgkin have a related appeal. Hodgkin, who's nearly sixty, broke through into stardom in New York this past winter, with his show at Knoedler. His paintings, which are often rather small, are filled with a few large, summary brushstrokes that invoke, in a sort of posterish telegraphic manner, the places and things that the titles announce: *Rain, Fire in Venice, In Tangier*. Hodgkin is presented as a traditionalist: as an artist who reforms the intimist poetry of Vuillard and Bonnard into a virtually abstract form of utterance. But I can't get involved with Hodgkin's paintings: they're so damn airy and imprecise. While Hodgkin may be a traditionalist and Polke may be a Dadaist, I feel a connection between their work. Both artists see painterliness as an attitude, as a way of giving a knowing nod to the values of the past. They present painterliness in quotation marks: it's a "hot" style to be opposed to the "cool" styles.

During the fall, the Pace Gallery mounted, in its downtown space on Greene Street, a show called "Painting Alone," which included work by seven youngish artists. Much of the work in the show recalled the more recent abstract Polkes—it was Polke without Polke's brute talent. It was an indifferent show, and yet the theme had a certain of-the-momentness that made the catalogue an interesting read. Here curators Rainer Crone and David Moos opposed painting to photography and observed that painting "is the one independent medium most detached from the surrounding world in its quest for self-formulation. With its vast array of materials and their impossible articulations, painting is borne open and thrust into the realm of the infinite and endless." This sounds appealing— it's an argument for painting-as-painting. Yet in a footnote to this sentence, the curators begin to backtrack. "This possibility of the infinite," they explain, "may resonate like an all too Romantic reflection about man's capabilities in our present world, that is dominated and regulated by the economic structures and pressures." They then go on to argue against our being constrained by these economic structures and pressures. Nonetheless, the discussion in this catalogue suggests a danger that's inherent in much of the recent painterliness: it is ideologically fueled. Painterliness is presented as a defense or argument against something else: the hi-tech. Polke, Hodgkin—and Julian Schnabel, when he's being painterly—are, in their various ways, ideologues of painterliness.

As artists come, more and more, to believe that the age of abstraction has ended—as they look for increased contacts with the world "out there"—the art of Titian takes on a new interest. This master of appearances was also, at least in his very late work, a master of abstract brushwork—or so the theory goes. He was there before us; and the abstractness of his late style can be seen as providing a bridge that we can cross back to representation. But the idea that Titian's painterliness expresses a duality—that for him paint is simultaneously a representation of the world and an exploration of the abstract value of materials—this does not quite jibe with the seamless unity of the very great Titians. I find the *Marsyas* to be an extreme case in Titian, a confusing and not entirely satisfactory painting that rather muddles our understanding of the artist. For me the essential Titian is a little earlier—the 1560s rather than the 1570s—and remarkable for the unselfconsciousness of his effects.

With Titian, painterliness is not an end but a means. What holds us when we're in front of the paintings—and holds in the mind—is not a surface covered with lively colors and brushwork, but a three-dimensional world that is charged with the sense of life. The nature of Titian's painterliness is discussed with beautiful clarity in Erwin Panofsky's book, *Problems in Titian: Mostly Iconographic:* "While Titian never sacrificed plastic, spatial and luminary values at the altar of color, he did conceive of all these values as functions of color, and not the other way around." Titian's glory is in his ability to show us the colors and forms that he observes in the world: warm pink flesh against cool gray sheets; the Madonna's grave response to the appearance of the iconic Angel; a dagger pointed at a breast; a precious gold clock placed before a window that frames a deep, lustrous landscape. If Panofsky is right to say that Titian "was not an intellectual," he also insists that this "does not mean he was unintelligent." On first glance, Panofsky's book, which emphasizes the iconographic side of Titian, may seem to take an odd approach: it deemphasizes the formalist in Titian. But I think Panofsky—who can write magnificently about formal matters when he chooses to—is making an important point. What Panofsky shows is that Titian's sense of the world is grounded in culture and history, in literature and thought. Titian is a clear-headed sensualist. Titian is a painter of bountiful lyrical gifts; but without his powers of analysis those lyrical gifts would not—could not—have their expressive power.

Maybe the real test of a good—and then, of course, of a great—painterly painting is that after you've looked at it for a while the brush work takes its discreet place in a larger drama of form. I think that *The Flaying of Marsyas* is a less great Titian than *Tarquin and Lucretia* because the brushwork stays so much at the fore. Yet one can learn from this late, strange problematic painting. The most interesting Expressionist to come out of England in many years, Leon Kossoff, has done a series of free copies of *Marsyas* . Obviously Kossoff was moved by the insistent symmetry of the work, its tight frontality that holds in check a shivering movement of brushwork. For Kossoff the *Marsyas* has been a lesson in the selflessness of the painterly brush. In the years that he's been studying that Titian, Kossoff has become a better painter: his portraits and London streetscapes have achieved a hardness and a clarity—they're remarkable paintings. Kossoff's forms are built up from his barrage of brushwork— a barrage that is covered over with an odd splatter of drips and skeins of paint. It's a strange paint surface, yet it works: there's method to the madness. Painterliness becomes a way of knowing the world.

That's what the painterly was for Titian—a way of making sense of the world and its experiences. In Titian's work painterliness is married to what we sometimes think of as opposites: narrative and spatial clarity, moral and psychological imagination. But these are only further dimensions of Titian's naturalness as a painter. It is natural for so many levels of experience to come together in a work of art.

Some Things I Saw

BY MARY GORDON

The Case of Berthe Morisot
(Losing my temper in the National Gallery
and types of feminist shame)

It is the first one-woman show of hers in America. The National Gallery, a place I had been happy. Official, 19th century America got together and built these marble halls, these splashing pools so you can hear the sound of water while you're looking at the pictures, the pictures of the great collectors, making their money God knows how. I have never seen many of Morisot's paintings, and the ones I saw I found rather disappointing, a secret I don't tell anyone, but they seem pale to me with nothing of Cassatt's draughtmanship or bold coloration—although it may be unfair to compare them simply because they were contemporaries and friends. And of course, female. Renoir said female painters were like a five legged calf, a version of Dr. Johnson's dancing dog, I wonder if he knew it. But Morisot was important because there is no doubt that she is a serious and highly accomplished painter, and, unless one is comparing her to the greatest geniuses—Manet and Monet and Degas (I am not saying Cassatt, although I mean it)—as good as the best of her age. I'd rather look at Morisots than most Renoirs and Sisleys and Pisarros; the faults I find in her I find in them, and I find her subject matter more interesting.

But before I am allowed to look at the work of Morisot, I am forced to look at her image. Forced sounds like a highly ungrateful language for the privilege of being allowed to look at a very beautiful painting: Manet's

Le Repos. The curves of the sofa and the female figure (Morisot), the creaminess of the white dress—it is a beautiful picture of a beautiful woman. But it is a portrait *of* Berthe Morisot not *by* Berthe Morisot. I feel angry for her, insulted, as if a virtuoso had been invited to her first recital and stole the attention by perfectly playing a solo before she got on stage. I enjoy the Morisots, particularly the pictures of her daughter, and I am compelled by a self-portrait she does in late middle age: the face is serious, heavy, matronly, the eyes are deep-set, the hair is severely pulled back. But I keep thinking about *Le Repos.* Nothing Morisot has painted is as beautiful as this portrait of her. I have to keep thinking about her as a female body, as the object of an erotically charged vision greater than her own. I didn't want to think of her as a painter, dislodged from her biography, from her physical beauty—separated from the admiring and powerful male gaze.

I keep thinking of the other painter who was also a famous object of male artistic vision: Georgia O'Keeffe. I had an odd reaction to seeing Steigletz's photographs of her, a reaction unshaped by anyone I knew. I resented Steigletz for presenting her to me as so much the object of his desire. I resented her for *posing.* I didn't understand why she did it. It must have taken up a lot of time. And to *pose,* and to make oneself immobile, fixed, seemed to me an act of obedience, a loss of autonomy I couldn't forgive. In those photographs, the immediacy of the camera's eye means that the subject of the photograph, particularly when she is photographed incessantly, has something of an aspect of pornography. I was ashamed of those feelings. But I didn't want O'Keeffe lolling around on sheets for Steigletz, her hair loose, her breasts unflattteringly droopy. I wanted her up, girt, on her feet, her hair pulled back, her eye not resting on the camera's, but on something in the world she could make the object of her own vision: the heart of a flower, red stones in the desert, a window frame of a Lake George house. Of course Steigletz's photographs of O'Keeffe helped to make her famous; they made her 1924 show a *cause celebre* : no one could separate the paintings from the body of the painter. Did she use that, consciously? Was it a strategy, an opening up of a private erotic contract to the art-buying world? I see those photographs and I'm angry. K. suggests that this may be because of a severe puritanism about female exhibitionism; I suspect she's right. She says that in *Chanson De Roland*, which she's now teaching, there's passage after passage about military male posing. And no one judges *that* harshly. H. thinks O'Keeffe is a lousy painter: too full of self love. I find her great. H. likes the photographs better than the paintings. For me it is no contest, so I can forget about them, dislodge the object of male vision from the painter when I see her work. But I cannot dislodge the memory of her face: so arresting it appeared in *Vogue* as often as a model's. Is it possible to separate the image of the beautiful woman's face and body from her work? The question is more difficult for a visual artist. We know, for example, that Virginia Woolf was a beautiful woman, but because the visual aspects of her art are privately apprehended and symbolically rendered by black signs on a white page, we can forget that a physical woman held a pen in her fleshy hand to make these impressions. The writer is always more ghostly than the painter; there is a possible modesty in the hiddenness, the abstraction, of our re-creation of the world.

I tried to think if all this could ever be an issue for a male artist whose appearance is so much connected to his work that we would look at it differently if he looked different. I tried to think of a male artist who existed with equal importance as the object of artistic vision and the creator of art. I could not think of one possible example, nor could I easily imagine it for the future. The primacy of the female body as the locus of erotic charge seems immutable as long as the male heterosexual's is the dominant vision.

The truth is that for me, and I feel ashamed of it, Berthe Morisot's biography—as well as her physical beauty—is inseparable from her art. Perhaps this wouldn't be true if I loved the art more purely, as I do Cassatt's and O'Keeffe's. And the fact is that what is important for me is not Morisot's beauty or her happy erotic and marital life, but her maternity. Morisot introduces into the artistic language the daughter as object of mother's adoring gaze. Julie Manet is painted in all her stages of babyhood and young womanhood. Was that sensuous mouth an anxiety to the mother, even as the painter rejoiced in it? Mothers desire their daughter's flesh, we desire it to be near our own with an ardor we are afraid to speak of—largely for the daughter's sake. We have been told over and over again that mothers are jealous of their daughters' youth, and this is perhaps the truth in many cases. But we also rejoice in our daughters' growing and beauty, and there is an extraordinary poignance to me in Morisot's depicting herself as a sober matron at the same time that she paints her daughter at the dreamy brink of her sexual ascent. I love the drawing of Julie looking over Morisot's shoulder as she sketches, interested in her mother's work, but also luxuriating in her usually forbidden nearness to the body of the working mother. The combination of art and life makes me much more emotionally engaged with Morisot's paintings than I am with what I know to be a greater work, Manet's *Le Repos*. Trained in the modern tradition, this makes me feel uneasy, immature. I am supposed to know better. But it shakes up, as well, the notion of modernist purity because, like it or not, what I know about Morisot's life has deepened my experience of her work.

A final admission, nothing of her work moves me as deeply as her final letter to her daughter. Morisot died young, at fifty four. Julie was only seventeen.

> My little Julie, I love you as I die, I shall love you even when I am dead; I beg you not to cry, this parting was inevitable. I hoped to live until you were married. Work and be good, as you have always been; you have not caused me one sorrow in your little life. You have beauty, money, make good use of them. I think it would be best for you to live with your cousins . . . but I do not wish to force you to do anything . . . Do not cry; I love you more than I can tell you.

So that, in the end, both the physical beauty, and the depth and tenderness of the connection between mother and daughter, were cut down by death. Inevitable, yes, but still unbearable, and worse because we have such palpable evidence of intensely lived physical and affective life.

Abel Gance's *Napoleon*

In the minds of middle-class young men life is associated with a career, and in early youth that career is Napoleon's. They do not, of course, necessarily dream of becoming Emperor, because it is possible to remain

like Napoleon while remaining far, far below him. Similarly, the most
intense life is summarized in the most rudimentary of sounds, that of a
sea-wave, which from the moment it is born until it expires is in a state
of continual change. I too like Napoleon and like the wave could at any
rate look forward to a recurring state of birth and dissolution.

—Italo Svevo
The Confessions of Zeno

That was exactly the problem. I was neither middle class nor male.
Nor European. Napoleon was to me a figure of boredom or a joke. Then
there is the shame—to be bored or amused by a figure so important to so
many great minds and lives (Stendhal, Tolstoy), reamed over by so many
passionate girls of the nineteenth century. And to me—what? Someone
famous for tucking his hand inside his jacket pocket, a sausage in fake
Roman curls, a conqueror, the prototype for Hitler, rampaging through
Europe cutting countries up like lunch. Jane Austen is meant to be small
minded because she didn't include him.

Shame drives me to see this film, shame and its relations, snobbery
and cultural avarice: I can't miss this thing that is not to be missed. And
I may have been lying for years about having seen it—the way I lie about
having read *The Charterhouse of Parma*, which I have never been able to
finish. I go with M. to Radio City, a locus of pure happiness. I came here
with my father. It's a place I can *know* we visited; I know I didn't make
it up. I can pin down the memory. I remember standing in freezing lines
with him for the Christmas show, sitting in silence with him for the Easter
show, where the Rockettes, dressed as nuns, formed themselves into a
Cross. And our last movie together: Grace Kelly and Alec Guiness in *The
Swan*. My father adored the idea of this movie. Two Catholic stars. And
this was no Bing Crosby playing Father O'Malley. This was about
Europe: the real thing. Somehow it had to do with what he had in mind
for me. Thinking me royal, did he imagine some deposed prince of the
blood would recognize what he did—my royalty—and take me to reign
in absentia with him, in Spain perhaps, in an obscure castle? Waited on
by devoted servants proud to work for nothing? A private chapel, with our
own saintly, live-in priest?

On the night that I was brought into the hospital in grave danger of losing the baby I was five months pregnant with, *The Swan* was showing on television. I took it as a sign. The television in my room was broken and I made a fuss demanding to be moved. I watched the movie and it wasn't very good. Ten days later, I lost the baby, and with it my belief that my father was looking down on me, watching out for me, communicating with me in amiable humane ways conducive to my comfort. I lost the habit at that time of years of primitive faith. I have not been happier for the loss.

In 1958, I saw *Gigi* in Radio City with my mother. After my father's death. It's the only time she took me into the city. She must have wanted to see that movie badly. It was our only linkage as a family: our love of Hollywood romance.

At that time, she didn't need a cane for walking, only her built-up shoes. Still I remember walking up the great staircase with her anxiously. It was difficult but she was able to do it. I remember being as happy there with her as I had been with him, and feeling a bit bad about it, I had let *her* into *our* place, where I knew *he* wouldn't have wanted her to be.

Everyone is happy in Radio City. It's the size, the thrill that something so monumental should be devoted to the most familiar and accessible of pleasures—movies—The Art Deco Style—opulence with a built in touch of self parody so no one feels left out. This time I notice a statue, a classical huntress formed of cast iron, made not with the usual chaste, noble self-effacing breasts but with big modern boobs, their large nipples pointing straight out. The girlie magazine elevated to the status of the eternal. "Well, he knew what he liked," M. says, and the statue is a comfort. For all its grandeur, there's no serious pretentiousness about Radio City, which is why it's the perfect place for me to see *Napoleon*, the "classic" I have so pretentiously come to see.

There's a real orchestra in the pit, conducted by Francis Ford Coppola's father, Carmine. I like that familial touch. It's sentimental, but I think of all silent film as partaking of the sentimental, the overdone. The music is over-rich, over-heroic but I am charmed by it, as I am charmed by the absurd music of the huge Radio City Wurlitzer that had ushered us in.

The first scene is a snowball fight at Brienne, the school Napoleon attended as a boy. Almost immediately we see the face of Rudenko, who plays the child Napoleon. At once I stop simulating interest; the extraordinary face of the child peering above the snow bank arrests me entirely. I am no longer here able to say, in the world outside the theatre, that I have been here. This is the world I inhabit now, the world of the intense visions of childhood, the world of dream.

The face of Rudenko. Delicate, androgynous, proud, horrified at being stared at. It is almost an affront to look at this child. He should be left alone, but he was born to be looked at. Who could protect him? What relation could he have to a mother, a father? You would have to stand back from such a child if you were a parent, and let him go, into the world, into his sorrow.

He is leading his fellow students in a snowball fight. At first, he looks out of place, as if he should be home practicing the piano. But then he stoops to an almost absurd posture: he is on one knee in the snow, his back to the boy troops. And we see that he is born to do this, to give orders and then to separate himself from his followers. In real life, children were made ill by the constant repetition of the snowball scene during the filming. Rudenko, the son of poor Russian Jews, had a difficult life. He never wanted to talk about having played Napoleon.

The lighting of *Napoleon* is the lighting of the unconscious, of the unclear world of dreams. Some of the scenes are shot through a blue lens, some through a sepia colored lens, as though Gance were making us experience our fantasy of what pastness is, of what it means to be walking in Hades, among the dead. Of being voyeurs of the lives of the dead. The half-light: as if we were travelling in a tunnel between two things: waking and sleeping, consciousness and unconsciousness, as if we were at a doorway, having already died, waiting for what is to come after, looking behind at history, looking forward into shadows.

The crowd scenes have the menace of a nightmare. It has always been a fear of mine to be killed, namelessly, by a nameless crowd. The citizen who is hung outside Napoleon's window could be anybody, guilty or not, someone who just happened to be at the wrong place at the wrong time. Even Napoleon cannot stop his death from happening. He considers trying; he reaches for the gun on his desk, but decides against it. My childhood glimpses of the French Revolution were all from the point of view of the murdered aristocrats: the *Tale of Two Cities*, the *Scarlet Pimpernel*. Probably because, even in the '50's, the church, source of my historical information, thought the Revolution was a drastic and disastrous mistake.

Why am I so afraid of mobs? I've never really experienced one. But I think of the idea of Mardi Gras, of Carnival, as monstrous. Horrifying. At the end of it of course you could be dead. Statistics say that there are a disproportionate number of births nine months after Mardi Gras or Carnival in places where they are celebrated. Anonymous death, anonymous coupling.

The distressing, yet pretty, scene of the *Bal des Victimes*. The subtitle reads: "To be admitted to the Victims Ball, it was necessary to have been imprisoned, or to prove the death of a father, a brother, or a husband." It is 1792. The terror still reigns. But the fashionable have an unprecedented number of parties. Beautifully dressed ladies vie for attention, and have rose petals showered upon them as they make their entrances. In the midst of this staccato gaiety, Napoleon stands fixed, puritanical. He looks unhealthy—(pigeon breasted, stoop shouldered, with the hint of a pot belly despite his thinness)—the obvious fate of the finicky boy who walked through the school pillow fight, fastidiously shod, with the turned out toes of the careful child, who never allows his consciousness to lapse at the ball. Disorder reigns. As a joke, a man wears a balloon at the top of his collar where his head should be and pops it: the practical joker of the near victim of the guillotine. Women are passed from hand to hand; a virile man takes off his jacket and is barechested. Josephine appears. Napoleon courts her by beating her suitor in a game of chess. In the midst of increasingly manic activity, two men fight over a woman by the means of the stillest of games. Josephine uses her past hardship as an instrument of flirtation: "It was here, M. Bonaparte, that I was summoned to the scaffold." The actress playing Josephine is not exceptionally beautiful, but she has style; she's what in the twenties would be called a "fascinator". (It is interesting how styles of sexuality in mouths mark a period. For the twenties, lips were bowed. Aggressive teeth with a decided overbite signified the sexually experienced woman—the less obvious, more intelligent choice.) Puritanically, Napoleon walks around the ball casting baleful looks, making censorious comments. "With imbeciles and lay abouts like you, France is heading for the abyss." But his puritanism is the preserver of dignity. It is dignity in degradation. His puritanism is a form of stillness, infinitely desirable in the mayhem. Over and over, Napoleon is the center of our attention, the source of our comfort because of his stillness. The evocative power of the film, perhaps all early film, comes from the quality of the movement the camera gives us: jerky, and the light: unclear. The shift from frenetic unsmooth movement to iconic stillness. The stillness becomes the state ardently longed for, a spiritual condition, the peace of contemplation, the end point of the search for what is above us, not subject to us, to change and therefore loss. Napoleon's stillness seems eternal; it is the visual source of our belief in his heroism.

The visual source of all that is not heroic, all that is human and vulnerable, is Napoleon's hair. For a large part of the movie, I can't understand it. Where is the famous Napoleonic curly cap? Hair is important for Gance. The most dreadful bully at the school has wild, evil hair. Danton's is a thick mop, Robespierre's is a hyper-rational Enlightenment flip. Napoleon's hair is a deliberate decision on Gance's part. He rejected one wig for Dieudonné (who plays Napoleon) on the grounds that it made him look like an old woman. Napoleon's lank, unheroic hair is there purposely to fracture the icon, to force us to look at Napoleon as if for the first time. I later come to realize that the hair is as it is, long and lank, to remind us of Jesus. Sentimental, gentle Jesus. Meek and mild. In the Hollywood posters for *Napoleon* (the film was never distributed in America) his hair is short and curly.

Why does this film of Napoleon, about whom I know very little, about whom I have hardly thought at all, seem to be the travel folder of the territory of my dreams, the photo album of my unconscious? J. suggests that it's because we see dreams and the past—which we can't control— as existing in murky light. Emblem of our confusion. Can it be that our first visions after birth were half seen, or seen as half-illuminated, and the charge—depressive or elated—that we feel at twilight or at dawn, reminds us of that first sight? Or do we know, somehow, that the last things we'll see will be in the same way unclear, elusive, almost out of sight?

Who's Not Singing in *The Singing Detective*?

The dreaming boy alone in the lush tree. The crooner by himself before the microphone. The walking detective (hard boiled dick) solitary, gun in hand, his heels clicking along the rainy pavement. Is he by himself because he wants to be? Is the role of the isolate, in proximate relation to things longer than they are wide, the role he chose first for himself or is it the austere and wise second choice of the man who knows too much?

Dennis Potter's *The Singing Detective* is all about the stuff male dreams are made of: obviously, deliberately, self-consciously this is the case of the work. The brilliant technique is there to interweave dream and wakefulness, real (nineteenth century) reality and primitive fantasy, the numbing, nullifying pressures of present life and the simple voluptuousness of the old songs and the older stories. I watched, at first, transfixed by the verbal and visual facility but as the hours drew on I found myself more and more alienated from what I was seeing, more uneasy, until finally I had to force myself to watch. The techniques of the singing detective are new, but the message is certainly not. Dennis Potter is merely saying something we have heard for a very long time: at the center of the boy's dream is the treacherous, transgressing cunt.

The point of *The Singing Detective* is that it functions simultaneously on many levels. There is the level of the present: Philip Marlow, a washed up writer of third-rate detective fictions, lies in his bed in a hospital ward. He is the victim of arthritic psoriasis, which renders him loathsome to look at (his skin has turned to horrifying scales) and makes most movements of his limbs and head excruciatingly painful. Around him, the flotsam and jetsam of English society suffer, decay and die. (Men make far less attractive patients than women. Perhaps it's all those catheters, all those grizzled faces, degenerate looking because unshaved.) They reveal themselves to be, like the rest of Marlow's humankind, small-minded, mischief-making, lewd, self-deceiving, foolish, devoted to others' harm. The occasional ray of decency pierces the pervading fog: an Indian man, who has the good sense to understand that Marlow's racial slurs are ONLY A JOKE, offers Marlow a sweet and then dies. But sweetness and light come to the ward in the presence of a pretty nurse, who is not only cheerful and understanding, but covers every inch (*every inch*) of Marlow's damaged body with cold cream. This is an important part of his therapy, and Marlow tries to be good, but what would you do, male viewer, if a pretty girl were greasing your penis with cold cream? You might try, like the noble Marlow, thinking of the most boring possible things (the Arts Council, the Guardian Woman's page, your own work even) but against your will you would succumb. Against your will. The only other time we see Marlow as a sexual performer he is calling his partner (a whore) filthy names at the climactic moment. But at Nurse Mill's hands, there is no need for nasty language. Marlow's orgasm is entirely unvolitional. It occurs through the ministrations of a woman who asks nothing of him, not even money. She doesn't require so much as a touch. Contact is limited to his penis and her greasy plastic gloves. How could he possibly fail her? Wiping the semen with the Kleenex, she only half blames. She is the perfect woman. "You're the girl in all the songs," Marlow says, and he's right, not just because she's pretty and nice but because she offers sexual satisfaction while eliminating entirely the risk of sexual failure. Marlow loathes himself; of course he would expect that women would loathe him. How could sex with anything like mutuality be anything but terrifying for him? What reason would he have to *feel good about it*, that mandate that we have been given from the sixties on? Why would he trust women, when his early experience of them shows them to be betrayers and tormentors? How could he be other than he is?

Of course the *self* that Marlow is is enormously complicated: that is the point of *The Singing Detective* and particularly its technique. He is his present and his past, his psychoanalysis and his characters, his mordant, nasty, witty language and the soothing words of the songs, "Banality with a beat," he calls them. In the experience of the past which the suffering Marlow remembers, popular songs are an important backdrop. In fact, they solidify the tone of childhood wishes: simplicity and harmony, delicious temporary yearning with no sense that finally it cannot be fulfilled. In Marlow's memory of his childhood, his mother is hysterical, and frustrated, but she *moves*. She is imprisoned in her husband's family house with her appalling father-in-law who projects missiles of phlegm onto the fire in the middle of dinner, and her mother-in -law, who keeps reminding her that it is not her house. It is not surprising that she takes a lover. We are not surprised at this turn of events, but we are mournful. For who is she betraying? The kind, stoical, anxious to please father, his eyes always close to tears, his ears vulnerable below his too short haircut. And the father sings. The loving joyous words of the song come from his mouth, as he leads a sing-song in the pub. Impotent in life, he is potent in his singing. He owns the important language: the language of the songs. In *being the singer*, he is able to be self-expressive, to express the deepest desires of the community and therefore to be its point of cohesion. And what is mummy doing all the while? Accompanying him on the piano. She is the silent handmaiden. Only when she is deprived of language and it becomes the property of the father in a way that excludes her are there moments of family happiness. It is interesting to note who sings in *The Singing Detective*. The only solo female voice which is accompanied by a specific female face is that of Dietrich singing Lili Marlene. This is the voice of the foreigner, the one who could not be mother. "A tart," Phil's maternal grandfather calls her, tart being synonymous for him with non-English. The foreign spy, who is killed by the enemy, is a special locus of desire for Philip as he takes on the skin of his third self, the character of the Singing Detective he has created in his novel. The spy who sings Lili Marlene is given the face of Philip's real life mother. In Philip's detective-novel life, she is shot dead. She is the only female solo singer in the film. The important female characters— Philip's tormenting teacher and his complicated wife—are not allowed into the dream world of the songs.

There are important reasons for this, and they are connected with the ultimate failure of *The Singing Detective* to achieve cohesion or a satisfying end. When *The Singing Detective* works, it works because it embodies and indeed canonizes extremely pervasive and seductive elements of adolescent male fantasy. The Philip Marlow-Sam Spade character makes sacred, honorable, and noble the male fear of intimacy with the female. The detective is always the moral center of the fiction. He is poor and unsuccessful because his standards are incorruptible. For the same reason he is alone: he is purer than the rocks on which he sits.

Occasionally, he is tempted, either by a need for love or for sex, to join himself with a female, but it is always to his peril. The beautiful face is always the face of the betrayer and the murderer. Only his secretary understands him, and she is willing to love him in agonizing silence, making him coffee, bailing him out, helping him with his hangover, and being told that she's a great girl and he's sorry he's too ruined to be the man she really deserves. The fiction embodied by the '30's and '40's songs embodies as well a world of female un-dangerousness. One yearns and is yearned for; one loves and is loved, but the high point of erotic imagination is the kiss, not the fuck. Obviously we (contemporary men and women) are supposed to know better than all this, we are supposed to want the loving partnership of equals. But in fact, the loving partnership of equals has very little mythological furniture to make habitable its bare rooms. The stories and the songs that all of us grew up on are based on relationships of unequal and skewed power. There is simply nothing that has been imbedded in popular culture long enough to render luscious the model of two adults struggling in the modern world. Tracy and Hepburn, Russell and Grant, exist in the realm of comedy, whose touch by its very nature is light, too light to make the deep impress of melodrama on the molten wax of yearning. Too light and too far from death. We see Ingrid Bergman leaving Humphrey Bogart at the Airport and there is music in the background; there is no equivalent to "As Time Goes By" running through our brains as we see Russell and Grant in the newsroom or Tracy and Hepburn on the golf course or in court. There is no theme song for mutuality, just as there is no embodied romance for the female isolate. Humphrey Bogart can walk off alone or with Claude Rains, but Hepburn and Russell have to have a man. It is impossible to say that we can't believe in the female isolate because of our conviction of female bodily weakness. Even Amelia Earhardt went up in flames. Shane rides off into the sunset alone; the female on the frontier must be accompanied.

The romances of popular culture make no place for the solitary female. She can't look death in the face; she has to be saved from it. A stronger presence (male) has to intervene between her and death. She is the conduit of death but she can do nothing to keep it back. If she can never be alone, how can we ever know who she is? And if she is only death or betrayal, how can there be a truthful end that includes her in any of the traditional, delicious genres?

At the end of *The Singing Detective*, Marlow walks out of the hospital with his wife. Why isn't this woman singing? There is a perfect opportunity for her to do it. Near the end, in the process of Marlow's cure, the Ink Spots are singing "You Always Hurt The One You Love." The voice we hear next is Ella Fitzgerald's. But do we see Marlow's wife's face? No, the voice is disembodied.

In life real change does not amputate the child's life, or the dreamer's, it moves it along. In the context of the film's shaping myth, the force bringing about change would not be the psychiatrist or the sexy soubrette wife, but the pretty nurse, who cures by her unselfish love. In the last encounter with her, Marlow tells the nurse she is the nicest and most beautiful person he's met in a long time. He mentions how wonderfully her head sits on her neck. Then he quits, dropped; he becomes a grownup. We are meant to believe that the boy in the tree will stay there, he will come back, but he will not be powerful enough to defeat the good (adult) man and the good woman, walking down the hospital corridor into the modern world. In the context of everything that went before, this is unbelievable, the stuff of post-therapeutic thought against the heady concoction of non-linguistic, culturally enshrined desire.

Potter's techniques—this ability to harness television's fragmentariness and quick shifts—are new, but the story is a very old one. You can't put old wine in new bottles, and the final product lacks bouquet; the sediment settles at the bottom: the stuff of undigested dream.

Andy Warhol

I am trying to understand why he disturbs me, no, hurts me, yes that's it, causes me to be in pain. Did he mean to? Or mean nothing? The mockery in the face, always, under the fright wig (was he really frightened?): what a fool you are. Or perhaps, even less inflected than that: how uncool you are. That is the central mystery. What was he saying: where was the accusation—foolishness, which would imply some enduring value— which would be about constantly shifting trends? Was he saying something? No, that's not it, you know he was saying something,

you just don't like what he had to say. The central question was this:
What did he care about? Or was he all about not caring for one thing more
than another? Perhaps the most frightening posture of all, because if
he's right, and there's no point caring for one thing more than
another(except if it's pretty or cool) there is no point to your life or the life
of people you admire and look to for what?—guidance, meaning,
standards—and certainly no point to their deaths. What is his relation
to death?

    S. and I take Anna and Emily to see the Warhol show, thinking they'll
be amused by the Brillo boxes and the Campbell soup cans. A laugh for
the children. But it doesn't mean anything to them. They're bored. If only
I could be bored. Or amused. I look first at the fashionable, well drawn
shoes. The enjoyable re-productions of ads for corn plaster. The tabloids.
The disasters. The sexy boys who liked to kill. The empty electric chairs
where they ended up. The gawkers at the accidents, the wrecked cars, the
mangled bodies. Infinitely far away. Hundreds of Marilyns, their mouths
messy, violated. Or post-violation. The fashionable women. Edith Scull
with her still, rich hair. Elvis. James Dean. Sullen mouths available to
everyone. Not giving in. Julia Warhol. So he had a mother. I see anger
in his messing up her face. It is a violent reaction toward a mother. He
is in every way the opposite of Vuillard, whom I look to for solace.
Vuillard's muted palate, his interior lives not sentimentalized (there is
danger in the lurking women—mother, sisters, about to spring, in the
cavernous space in front of which the huge doctor bends looking as if he
could not possibly minister, that all his bulk, his scientific knowledge can
only smother, take away the little air the poor invalid so desperately
needs), but nevertheless endowed with tenderness, and of course art—he
can draw well, paint well. Good drawing, good painting matter to him.
I own a pencil drawing of his mother. She is serene, eternal: like Felicie
in Flaubert's *Un Coeur Simple.* That 19th century French stoicism of the
domestic. A place of rest. R. says I like it because I hope my son will think
of me that way when I'm old.

    Warhol lived with his mother for most of his life. They lived in the
same house until quite near her death. Closer than my mother and me.
She was an alcoholic, an embarrassment, crazy, perhaps, a rack rat, a

torment. But he kept her around. Until she became senile. Then he put
her in a nursing home and didn't get in touch with her. Didn't go to her
funeral. Lied to people when they asked how she was after she was dead.
"Fine," he told them. What did lying mean to him? What did it mean to
him to lie?

I start talking to everyone about him. N. tells me he went to church
all the time. This makes me angry at first, then scared. Warhol and me.
Post war, immigrant Catholics. If he is one then what am I? I am
everything not—him: female, susceptible, engaged. Yet he went to
church more than I do. It makes me furious, because of course it fits right
in with a tradition that was highly romantic for people like my father: the
decadent tradition, Huysmans, sinning, but devout. Devout. What can
that possibly mean in a life like Warhol's? A life of watching while people
fuck, shoot up, jerk off, kill themselves. Watching. Wishing they'd do
it for the camera. I am a camera. The I. The "eye." The unsusceptible
I/eye. Is this evil? To refuse to be engaged. To encourage the destruction
of others so that you can observe the spectacle. When he found out that
Edie Sedgewick had tried to kill herself, he said "I wish she'd done it in
front of the camera." If the Church is about anything, it's about
engagement. Yet for a certain stripe of priest, there's a real kick in having
the unrepentant sinner, the flagrant sinner, kneeling in front of you every
week. A proof of the sweep of the cloak of Holy Mother Church. Much
more interesting than the 99 who are not lost. They got the idea from Jesus,
after all. The Good Shepherd. I know mine and mine know me. But I keep
wanting to know what could it have meant to him, kneeling there? Did
he relish the perverseness of the posture? Was he covering his bets, just
in case the most orthodox things his mother believed in were true? What
does it mean to say of Warhol: What did it mean? What did meaning
mean? Was being in Church a goof for him? A laugh? Did he pray? What
was the face on the other side of prayer for him? There could not have
been a face. If there was a face, what does this mean for the way I live
my life?

I am of his time, not Vuillard's. This was his genius: he understood
what people really liked to look at. The sickly boy (faggot-in training)
wheezing while his mother buys him movie magazines to cut the pictures

of stars from. Rita Hayworth. Sonja Henie. Lush. Cute. All that was not his mother. In the pictures of him at art school, this picture of him from high school, you can see the unattractive boy trying to be well groomed. The young sissy trying to be careful. How did he get from there to where he was? Where was he? A genius. Knowing what people were really like, what they were interested in. He tells us that the nineteenth century is over. Nature, contemplation. Over. Now people love what they can consume. And what can be, had been reproduced. The day of the unique image, the unique object is over. When Walter Benjamin says it, it doesn't scare me, because for B. there is some relief in value, some hopefulness. For Warhol there is consumption. Which is death.

I start talking about him obsessively. I bore everyone talking about the end of the 19th century. Which I've just discovered (March 1989). I fall into depression, a depression that makes me want to stop writing. Literally contemplate taking my novel back from the publisher. I am ashamed of everything I have done. It is not of my time. It's a lie, a pathetic one, because I didn't realize I was lying, I thought I was telling the truth, but it's not the truth about the way we live, even about the way we pretend to live. In the 19th century, businessmen had to pretend to care about poetry, nature, music. To pass as *hautes bourgeoises*, they had to pretend to like these things. So maybe a few of their children did, by accident. But the arts were supported, and at least people had to pretend to believe. Was that better? Is the truth better? The truth about what people really like to look at, like to see?

The difference between Warhol and Cornell. Cornell took all the camp images that people love to look at and said: they are part of a wonderful dream, a dream of emptiness, eternal. And because they are boxed, separated, they have the uniqueness, the un-reproduceability of a dream. In a picture of Cornell I have his thumbnail is frighteningly long. Like a bird's claw. What does it mean about your life if you let your thumbnail grow that long? Cornell had a retarded brother. Some people think his work is about doing something that would make his brother happy, that his brother could understand. At the end of his life, Cornell had a friendship with a waitress who was murdered. When I read about it for the first time, I wondered if he could have murdered her. You wouldn't wonder that about Warhol. He might have watched somebody killing, but not have killed himself. Cornell would have hidden the body. Perhaps in a beautiful box he had made. A box of dreams to accompany her to the emptiness after death. Warhol would have photographed the body, then abandoned it for something newer, perhaps more freshly dead.

The white face under the white hair, Warhol's, says to everything I could possibly say: bullshit. But he wouldn't say that, it wouldn't be pretty or cool to say that, what he says is worse, much worse. What he says is it doesn't matter. It could be anything. Anything could be anything. One thing or another. Everything passes in front of you. You let the camera run. You take it in. But no, not in, because you are impermeable. The desirable state: To be susceptible to nothing, vulnerable to nothing. Fascinated with people sucking death into themselves while you watch. Terrified of death? But why? What is life, that it should be so valuable? Perhaps only the something as opposed to the nothing. The *only thing* that matters then. The only desirable. That the camera should always have something new to fix on. Should not stop.

V
Criticism

The Death of the Author

BY WILLIAM H. GASS

Popular wisdom warns us that we frequently substitute the wish for the deed, and when, in 1968, Roland Barthes announced the death of the author, he was actually calling for it.[1] Nor did Roland Barthes himself sign up for suicide, but wrote his way into the College of France where he performed *volte faces* for an admiring audience.[2]

Many of the observations which Barthes makes in his celebrated essay are suggestive, called for, and even correct; but none of them quite drives home the stake. The reasons for this are complex. The idea of the death of the author does not match the idea of the death of god as perfectly as the current members of this faith may suppose, because we know—as they know—that there *are no* gods. The death of the author is not an ordinary demise, nor is it simply the departure of belief, like an exotic visitor from the East, from the minds of the masses. The two expressions are metaphors which are the reverse of one another. The death of god represents, not only the realization that gods have never existed, but the contention that such a belief is no longer even irrationally possible: that neither reason nor the taste and temper of the times can condone it. The belief lingers on, of course, but it does so like astrology or a faith in a flat earth—in worse case than a neurotic symptom, no longer even *à la mode*. The death of the author signifies a decline in authority, in theological power, as if Zeus were stripped of his thunderbolts and swans, perhaps residing on Olympus still, but now living in a camper and cooking with propane. He *is*, but he is no longer a god.

Barthes is careful to point out the theological overtones of his announcement.[3] Deities are in the business of design; they order oftener than generals; the robes the painters put them in are juridical. God handed down the tablets of the law to Moses, and Jane Austen or Harriet Beecher Stowe hand down texts to us. While it is by no means necessary to put the author's powers and responsibilities in religious terms, Beckett's school-boy copy books are tablets, too, and attract lawyers and legalese as though they were papers sticky with honey. When John Crowe Ransom, in clearly secular language, praises Milton's *Lycidas* as "a poem nearly anonymous," he means to applaud the degree to which Milton has freed the poem from its poet, and consequently from the danger of certain legal difficulties.

> Anonymity, of some real if not literal sort, is a condition of poetry. A good poem, even if it is signed with a full and well-known name, intends as a work of art to lose the identity of the author; that is, it means to represent him not actualized, like an eye-witness testifying in court and held strictly by zealous counsel to the point at issue, but freed from his juridical or prose self and taking an ideal or fictitious personality; otherwise his evidence amounts the less to poetry.[4]

In this case the arrogance, the overbearing presence, of the author is at one with his disappearance. Joyce has Stephen Dedalus state the aim precisely:

> The personality of the artist, at first a cry or a cadence or a mood and then a fluid and lambent narrative, finally refines itself out of existence, impersonalizes itself, so to speak. The esthetic image in the dramatic form is life purified in and reprojected from the human imagination. The mystery of esthetic, like that of material creation, is accomplished. The artist, like the God of creation, remains within or behind or beyond or above his handiwork, invisible, refined out of existence, indifferent, paring his fingernails.[5]

The dramatist's curtained disappearance is not complete enough for Barthes. He knows that "*Madame Bovary—c'est moi!*" remains true despite Flaubert's celebrated detachment. He knows how the deity of tradition took delight in concealing himself. Hunt as hard as you cared to, he could easily elude you if he wished. Still, such difficulties did not dampen the desire of the faithful to find him, or weaken in any way their belief that he was there. Circumstances have kept Shakespeare's life hidden from us, yet he has been hunted like a criminal. In volume after volume, his unknown character is cleverly constructed like a ship in a bottle. So Barthes wants to slay a spirit. He would bruise a bodiless being. It is the demise of that confident, coldly overbearing, creator—that so palpably erased and disdainful imperial person of the artist—that he longs for.

It is apparent in the quotation from Joyce that when the work of writing has been done, the essential artistic task is over. The freedom from himself which the artist has given to his composition is the indifferent freedom of the Rilkean *Dinge*, an object which exists like a tree, a hat, or a stream, and like the stream scarcely needs canoes or campers to complete it; yet it is a thing whose modulated surfaces betray the consciousness it contains, and which we read, as we read words, to find the hand, the arm, the head, the voice, the self which is shaping them, which is arranging those surfaces—this second skin—into a leer, a grimace, or a happy grin that tells us of the climate of life inside. In the old theological mode, we either thought to find god through his revelations in sacred scripture, or by studying his other world; we applied ourselves, that is, to natural or to revealed religion. Nowadays, when the artist deliberately disappears, he may wish it to be thought that his work "just came about" naturally; grew the way crystals collect to create a flake of snow, perhaps, or more slowly, as deltas silt, or suddenly the way islands rise up calamitously out of the sea; or, more ideally, in the manner a mollusk exudes a chamber about itself, or quietly from within, brooding as the old gods did upon a basin of dark cloud and wind, the way, with a cluck now and then like an errant clock, the chicken intuitively shapes a shell. To hide, in this case, is to represent skill as instinct, intellect as reflex, choice as necessity, labor as slumberous ease. Valéry writes:

> Perhaps what we call *perfection* in art (which all do not strive for and some disdain) is only a sense of desiring or finding in a human work the sureness of execution, the inner necessity, the indissoluble bond between form and material that are revealed to us by the humblest of shells.[6]

For Joyce, of course, this writing from which its designer—the deity—disappears, seems authorless because there is no book to weigh in one's hands, no print, no page, no poet's voice: it is *performed*; the theater buries the text inside the bodies of its actors where their organs are. But we are also aware of the similarly scenic art of Henry James, of his effaced narrators and substitute selves, of various Ishmaels and many Marlowes, or of those poems which appear on parchmented pages as though scratched there by creatures long extinct.

> Calm covers the peaks.
> Among the treetops
> a breath hangs like a leaf.
> In the deep woods
> birdsong sleeps.
> At the foot of hills
> slopes find their peace.
> Be patient. Wait.
> Soon, you too, will cease.[7]

Richardson slips onto the title page of *Clarissa Harlowe* disguised as S. Richardson, the simple printer who has collected and edited the letters which comprise her unhappy history; Defoe suggests that Moll Flanders is the pseudonym of a well-known lady who tells her somewhat unwholesome story in his book; *Gulliver's Travels* is introduced by one Richard Sympson, an "ancient and intimate friend" of the author, and the man into whose economizing hands these papers have fallen (he tells us he's cut out dull stretches of seafaring stuff); while *The History of Henry Esmond* is brought before us by that late Virginia gentleman's daughter, Rachel Esmond Warrington, now, alas, a widow. These novels have authors, to be sure, but they are artificial ones, replacement pens or "dildoes." Still, no one will imagine that Defoe or Swift or Thackeray felt that by placing these fictions in front of themselves they were risking their lives. No one is done in by a dildoe.

Actually, a volume of letters, however modestly brought before the public, inordinately multiplies "authors," whose names appear, we suppose, at the end of every communication. These artful dodges (and it would be awful if they fooled anyone) strengthen the concepts of source and voice and purpose, control and occasion, which are central to the notion of a commanding creator, precisely because they call them into playful question. Thackeray pretends not to be responsible for *The History of Henry Esmond*, neither for writing it nor for bringing it to public notice, but Thackeray intends to accept all praise and monies due. A few writers like us to believe that they are simply telling a story they have heard elsewhere; that they are therefore just "passing on," somewhat as any gossip might, some juicy bits, and cannot be held accountable for the sad and sordid facts involved; but many authors accept their responsibilities calmly enough and make no effort to conceal themselves or minimize the extent of their powers. Trollope, for instance, is a comfortable theist who appears in page after page in order to sustain and continue and comfort his creation. He is invariably concerned and polite. "We must beg to be allowed to draw a curtain over the sorrows of the archdeacon as he sat, sombre and sad at heart, in the study of his parsonage at Plumstead Episcopi." Furthermore, he will try to talk the reader out of what might be, perhaps, a too hasty judgment of character and motive. "He was avaricious, my readers will say. No—it was for no love of lucre that he wished to be bishop of Barchester."

The appearance of the author by our fireside; his chatty confidential tone; his certainty that he knows what we think and how we feel; his slightly admonitory manner; the frequent comparisons he draws between our condition and that of his characters; the comfortable clichés he draws around us like a shawl: these devices more readily make his world and his people real; whereas deists like Flaubert, like Henry James, like Joyce, who are satisfied to kick their creations out of the house when they've come of age; who wind their works up and then let them run as they may, and who cannot be recalled to rejoin or revise or reconsider anything by any plea or spell of magic or sacrifice or prayer; who leave it up to us to calculate and judge: their world is far less friendly, far less homey, far less "real." When Trollope comments: "Our archdeacon was worldly—who among us is not so?" he deftly implicates us in his activities.[8] We are all together in this, he suggests; I am speaking of the world each of us lives and loves and suffers in—no other, he implies; whereas the brilliant opening of *The Fifth Queen* is so immediately vivid and pictorial we must be somewhere outside it, viewing it as we might a painting or movie screen. Trollope's relaxed and slippered style is just as skillful in its way as Ford's, but Ford's world is unmediated and set adrift; we shall never find a path through its cold and passionate landscapes on which our feet can be set; we shall only be able to observe these historical figures connive and betray and ruin, and the light fall unsteadily on walls wet with the cold sweat of another age.

Pantheism is not out of the question as a possibility either. *The Notebooks of Malte Laurids Brigge* invent "another self" whose very name is a rhythmic echo of Rainer Maria Rilke; yet this other self, its almost unendurably beautiful and squalid encounters, these records of lonely reading and empty rooms and lovely yet lost objects, this static parade of exquisite perceptions that constitute the frozen frieze-like flow of the book, are so infused with the poet's presence, the poet's particular sensibilities, that Malte, his surrogate, cannot avoid surrendering his self to his author's *style*, even when the outcome of his life appears to be different than his creator's. We might permit Malte to possess the thought that *Denn Verse sind nicht, wie die Leute meinen, Gefühle (die hat man früh genug),—es sind Erfahrungen*, but the movement of the mind (from cities, people, and things, to animals, birds, and blooms), the music of the words (*Um eines Verses willen muss man viele Städte sehen, Menschen und Dinge, man muss die Tiere kenned man muss fühlen, wie die Vögel fliegen, und die Gebärde wissen, mit welcher die kleinen Blumen sich auftun am Morgen* [9]), the romantic innocence of the idea, are unmistakably Rilkean. As we read along, Trollope's manner discreetly retires from sight and Mrs. Proudie or Mr. Slope are shortly there before us as plainly as two dogs in the yard. Malte feels, to be sure, yet what Malte feels can only have been informed and inhabited and carried to him by his ceaselessly zealous holy spirit.

When authorship is denied, it is often in order to extol certain sources or origins instead. It is easier for poets to pretend that they are merely an eartrumpet for the muse; that they have been so smitten with inspiration they scarcely recognize their own rhymes; because the creative pain of the poet can sometimes be measured in moments, especially if she scribbles; but the novelist cannot persuasively invent a spirit whose relief requires several years of sluiced transcendence, as if somewhere a spigot had been left on. Our author, in this unlikely case, is simply a conduit, or a place where the collective unconscious has risen up to refresh us like a bubbler in the park.

The *Geist* has been known to gather up unwary authors somewhat as Zeus used to do with fleeing maidens and plump them with proper thoughts and attitudes. If writers were not the instruments of history, as often princes and politicians were, they were at least a showcase, a display of the spirit, like a museum's costumed effigies, if not one of its principal actors. Historical forces of this sort are as crudely imaginary as deities have always been, although probably not nearly as harmful since they cannot capture the imagination of millions the way divinities do. But of course the *Geist* can go behind a curtain and come back out as the *Volk* or the *Reich* instead of the *Zeit*. Taine's version of this recipe would certainly have been familiar to Barthes, whose notion combines the concept of the author as a conduit with that of the author as focal point: that hot spot where many causal rays have been concentrated.

Taine wished to understand his subjects (whether Spenser, Lyly, or Milton), in the first place by recreating the so-called outer image of the man; by setting him out in the kind of clear hindsight which is the common sense and direction of history; and then to penetrate that picture to the moral condition which lay behind those features and animated them. Finally, he sought in race, epoch, and environment, the conditions which came together to create the local climate of his case. He fashions, in other words, a chain of authors: the public figure, the inner man, the milieu. It is the right pull upon that chain which brings the gush.

There is clearly considerable satisfaction to be had in the removal of the poet from his or her position in the center of public adulation. Taine maliciously observes that:

A modern poet, a man like De Musset, Victor Hugo, Lamartine, or Heine, graduated from college and travelled, wearing a dresscoat and gloves, favored by ladies, bowing fifty times and uttering a dozen witticisms in an evening, reading daily newspapers, generally occupying an apartment on the second story, not over-cheerful on account of his nerves, and especially because, in this dense democracy in which we stifle each other, the discredit of official rank exaggerates his pretensions by raising his importance, and, owing to the delicacy of his personal sensations, leading him to regard himself as a Deity.[10]

Indeed, it is no longer the painter or the poet whom the public looks for, talking or scribbling away in some café's most prominent corner, but (after Cocteau, who taught everyone the trade), a Sartre or a Barthes whom we hope to catch a glimpse of—a Lacan or Foucault, or some other impresario of ideas.

Parlor games, in which a poem is composed one line at a time by inebriated guests, cancel out authorship by allowing too many cooks to stir the broth. Occasionally, for sport and in despair, fiction writers will alternate the writing of a novel's chapters, and equally rarely, talents like Ford's and Conrad's will collaborate with a modest sort of success. In most cases, the schoolboy botches which result are so far from creating "a sense of a world" that no one would think to wonder about that world's authorship anyway.

The *renga*, a chain poem which made its first appearance in Japan in the 8th century, is a more serious collaboration; it is more serious simply because the participants generally are. When contemporary poets turn to it, their feelings are not dissimilar to Barthes's:

> In contrast with the conception of a literary work as the imitation of antique models, the modern age has exalted the values of originality and novelty: the excellence of a text does not depend on its resemblance to those of the past, but on its unique character. Beginning with romanticism, tradition no longer signifies continuity by repetition and by variations within repetition; continuity takes the form of a leap, and tradition becomes a synonym for history: a succession of changes and breaks. The romantic fallacy: the literary work as an odd number, the reflection of the exceptional ego. I believe that, today, this idea has reached its end.[11]

When, however, the *renga* turns out to be a chain forged in four different languages, we can justifiably suspect that oddness, and difference, will be its most striking distinction, and that the four authors will neither hide themselves behind one another nor disappear into the collective anonymity of the text, but will sign their names to the poem, and write of the feelings they had while composing it in reports which remind one of the ecstatic early accounts of group sex.[12]

It is not that "authorless" work in any of the senses I have so far suggested can never be excellent, or that novels with a great degree of authorial visibility must always be romantic, bourgeois, and decadent, because fine work of both kinds exists; rather, it should be recognized that the elevation or removal of the author is a social and political gesture, and not an esthetic one. We can characterize art as anonymous or not, but this characterization will tell us nothing, in advance of our direct experience of the building, the canvas, the score, or the text, about its artistic *quality*. Furthermore, this "anonymity," as we've seen, may mean many things, but one thing which it cannot mean is that *no one did it*.

Unless one imagines a computer which has been fed every rule of language, the principles of every literary genre, the stylistic tics of all the masters and their schools, *etc.* Then poem and story might emerge from this machine, to the astonishment, boredom, or ruin of readers, like race or market results; and it could say, if asked, as Polyphemus was, that no man did it.

So art can seem authorless to me because I don't *know* who did it; or because I can't *tell* who did it; because I don't *know* who did it; or because it simply doesn't *matter* who did it; or because it just *happened* and nobody did it. That is: there is the piece of sea wrack I pick up from the beach; there is "ding dong bell, pussy's down the well"; there is your average TV serial segment; there is that tune I know from somewhere, but can't remember, and can't guess; there is that enigmatic couplet carved on an ancient rock whose author has vanished forever into the hard lilt of its cruel vowels.

It might at first seem that the effacement of the author was an act of modesty, and the familiar fatherly storyteller's style of Trollope, and other writers like him, was authoritarian and manipulative, in as much as they gave nothing away to the reader, and took on the point of view of a tower; but the opposite is clearly the case. Trollope knows everything necessary to tell the tale, to be sure, and presents himself comfortably in that cloth; but Flaubert is not telling a tale, he is constructing a world; he is putting it together atom by atom, word by word. Trollope is merely inserting his characters into the well-known world of his readers, readers who take their daily life enough for granted that long ago they stopped looking at it; they scarcely any longer even live it, but use all their inner tubes to float on top; so that when Trollope looks and lives, his readers are surprised at what they see and feel. Flaubert, however, cannot count on the comfortable collusion of his readers to solidify his world through their inattention and neglect; it is not the reader's funny bone he wishes to tickle, but the text he wishes to shape so securely a reader will not be necessary. Flaubert wants to expose his "readers" to their world of overpapered problems and bloated hopes by unupholstering their souls, lowering their ceilings to the true level of their aspirations; he wants to demonstrate to them that they are only devouring the world and making shit of their lives; he can hardly count on their help; their "help" would subvert his enterprise. Flaubert cannot ask for, cannot count on, readers in the old sense then, for each is only too likely to be another *hypocrite lecteur*, however much each also is *mon semblable, mon frère*. Thus the author becomes a god, instead of someone's garrulous uncle, because the author now disdains those lower relations, and has left home in disgust. *Madame Bovary* is not a chair for a fat burger's Sunday snooze; it *is* the fat burger himself, breaded and greasy, and mostly buns. His home is a White Castle.

When the author detaches himself from the text, he detaches the reader at the same time, then, and it is this unpleasant consequence which Barthes is responding to. Trollope is telling his story to someone, and even when, as in the case of the epistolary novel, the messages are not addressed to the reader directly, they are addressed to someone; they remain communications; and the three-term relation of writer-letter-recipient is maintained. But if no one is written or posted the word, then no one is addressed by the word. The letter is no longer a letter. A does not equal A. What would the sign, BUY BILGE'S BEER, mean or be, if it were carefully posted at one of the poles?

The author becomes a god at the moment he no longer believes in them, and just because the gods are dead; yet not because, as Taine implies, he suddenly sees a vacancy (although socially that might very well describe his motives), but because a world without god must be a world without true believers too. Yet this writerless, readerless world must be made by someone, a deity of the undivine kind, a god in lower case.

The moment god goes, the text becomes sacred (unalterable, revered, studied, paraphrased, guarded, handed on). Consider the deist's contention. If god is on permanent vacation elsewhere, then this world is all there is; it is the entire text; only from it can truths be learned; and if this world is to run on successfully, it must run on by itself, on its own four wheels; while, finally, if god has given us a message when he made this world, he did not wait around for our understanding or reply, both of which become, if not irrelevant to us, certainly irrelevant to him (since he is out of hearing), as well as to the world itself (which is blind and dumb and deaf and thoroughly uncaring). It is not clear that it is a text in the traditional sense. Suppose that idling down an alley as is my wont, I pick up a scrap of paper which has blown from some pile of trash. Examining it I read:

WILL'S WHEEL ALINEMENT SERVICE
sugar
nappies
strong clock for Aunt Helen
33 BAD CLIMATE ROAD

Like the sign that said BUY BILGE'S BEER, these words have wandered away, even from one another. A reminder without mind, purpose or point, like works of modern art, they merely appear. Made of words, they are not now a message. What is there here to take to heart, to puzzle over, to believe?

The basic folly of Bouvard and Pécuchet (those two aforetime Beckettean clowns) is that, in a world like WILL'S WHEEL ALINEMENT SERVICE, they do, nevertheless, believe things; they believe them right into the ground; they sincere systems to death; they accept explanations like a crematorium its corpses. In *Finnegans Wake* a hen scratches a meaningless message out of a midden. Both world and work are simply *here.* No one asked for either. As far as the world goes, one can do X or Y, live or die, it doesn't matter. John Barth's Todd Andrews has enormous difficulties making up his mind which or whether.[13] The world we're in is one of authorless accident, comical suffering and confusion; it is the world of WILL'S WHEEL ALINEMENT SERVICE, while the *Wake* is entirely internal, its "nothing" signifying sound and fury. The *Wake* is a replacement for the world. Unlike the world, it is made of meanings. Like the world, it does not mean.

If the author goes, taking the reader with him into some justifiable oblivion, he does not omit to leave his signature behind, just the same. Indeed, he not only signs every sheet, he signs every word. Erased, Flaubert's care cries out, "me me me." Removed, Henry James's late manner *maître d's* everything. The *Wake* calaminates, just before it doesn't conclude: mememormee! Till thousands-thee. Here is a further example of pure signature prose:

> . . . I felt acutely unhappy about my dutiful little student as during one hundred and fifty minutes my gaze kept reverting to her, so childishly slight in close-fitting gray, and kept observing that carefully waved dark hair, that small, small-flowered hat with a little hyaline veil as worn that season and under it her small face broken into a cubist pattern by scars due to a skin disease, pathetically masked by a sunlamp tan that hardened her features, whose charm was further impaired by her having painted everything that could be painted, so that the pale gums of her teeth between cherry-red chapped lips and the diluted blue ink of her eyes under darkened lids were the only visible openings into her beauty.

The "I" of this brief instructional tale[14] is not that of the great Vladimir, Napoleon of Prose, but the style certainly is his. We are meant to be dazzled, humbled, tossed into awe as though it were a ditch alongside the road.

The "I" is not Nabokov—no—yet this "I" teaches literature (French not Russian) at a girl's college (not a woman's college, not Cornell) in an Ithaca, N.Y., climate (no mistaking that upper New York snow and ice, icicles carefully described), so that we are led roundabout to wonder. Again, this sort of teasing is deliberate.

Whether the scholar sees the genial Trollope seated comfortably in the text, or the irascible Flaubert skulking angrily behind his, critics continue to "tyranically center," as Barthes puts it, "the image of literature on . . . the author, his person, his life, his tastes, his passions . . ." but they have reached their quarry by different routes: content in the first case, style in the second. Of course, Trollope's tone tells a tale as well as Nabokov's does, but Nabokov's arrogance is formal, relational, and his control is not that of a fatherly Czar but that of the secret police. The performative "I declare," "I sing," "I write," does not, in fact, cut the text off at the point of the pen, as Barthes seems to think. Nabokov's passage *is* a performance . . . and a good one. In this sense, Trollope's touch could only dull the master's quill.

The problem is not, I think, whether the author is present in the work in one way or another, or whether the text will ever interest us in her, her circle, her temper and times; but whether the text can take care of itself, can stand on its own, or whether it needs whatever outside help it can get; whether it leads us out and away from itself or regularly returns us to its touch the way we return to a lovely stretch of skin. Certainly some readers are anxious to be distracted, and arrive in a work like an anxious traveler at a depot. There are four winds, and four cardinal points of the compass, and four trains out of the text:

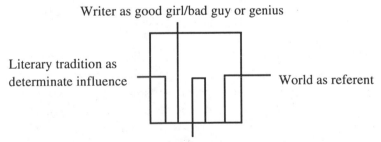

Writer as good girl/bad guy or genius

Literary tradition as determinate influence

World as referent

Reader as interpreting subject or rhetorical object

When Nabokov halts his "I" on its walk in order to render an icicle in full formation, there is no question that the world, with its notions about the proper procedures for freezing and thawing, is partially directing his pen. Is it, then, the artful author of this passage?

. . . I had stopped to watch a family of brilliant icicles drip-dripping from the eaves of a frame house. So clear-cut were their pointed shadows on the white boards behind them that I was sure the shadows of the falling drops should be visible too. But they were not. The roof jutted out too far, perhaps, or the angle of vision was faulty, or, again, I did not chance to be watching the right icicle when the right drop fell. There was a rhythm, an alternation in the dripping that I found as teasing as a coin trick.

And are the laws of light and shadow determining this?

And as I looked up at the eaves of the adjacent garage with its full display of transparent stalactites backed by their blue silhouettes, I was rewarded at last, upon choosing one, by the sight of what might be described as the dot of an exclamation mark leaving its ordinary position to glide down very fast—a jot faster than the thaw-drop it raced.

And is the world of melting snow and forming ice our readerly destination? Do we want to stand in the snow, too, with this "I" which is soon then to be ourselves? But this "I" cannot be ourselves, for its observations are both beyond us, and the world.

This twinned twinkle was delightful but not completely satisfying; or rather it only sharpened my appetite for other tidbits of light and shade, and I walked on in a state of raw awareness that seemed to transform the whole of my being into one big eyeball rolling in the world's socket.[15]

Physical phenomena clearly have a finger if not a hand in the composition of these passages, but the choice of event, selection of details, arrangement of elements, turns of phrase and pace of words, all the higher functions of relevance and association, imagery and implication: these are controlled by Nabokov and increasingly by the character of the little device he is creating; that is, a short story about two sisters, Cynthia and Sybil Vane (Sybil will be a suicide, Cynthia a victim of heart disease), and Cynthia's belief in haunting shades and interfering spirits. As the text grows, its demands grow; but the text can make these demands only in terms of certain principles of composition which the author accepts: coherence, for instance, fulfillment of expectations, and so on.

Actually, Barthes, while appearing to free the text from externals, is going to tie it rather firmly to two of them: the literary tradition and social usage, on the one hand, and the reader's caprices on the other. He sees the writer as a kind of whirling drain sucking texts into itself and concentrating their fall upon her page. The text, Barthes argues, is

> a multidimensional space in which a variety of writings, none of them original, blend and clash. The text is a tissue of quotations drawn from innumerable centres of culture. Similar to Bouvard and Pécuchet, those eternal copyists, at once sublime and comic and whose profound ridiculousness indicates precisely the truth of writing, the writer can only imitate a gesture that is always anterior, never original. His only power is to mix writings, to counter the ones with the others, in such a way as never to rest on any one of them.[16]

Let us shape a situation to fit Barthes' conditions. The lanky young man who bags our groceries has just dropped the flour on top of the broccoli. He hoists the sack into the cart, and says, with a vacant smile pointed vaguely in our direction: "Have a nice day." Our young man is scarcely the author of this unmeant hope we have just now been commanded to realize. The English language provides its grammar and vocabulary; our present sales and marketing customs furnish the expression itself; the manager of the store supplies the impulse and determines its timing (so that the bagger does not utter his platitude and *then* bruise the broccoli). The carry-out boy (whose jacket says, "I'm Fred," but this is a bit misleading since he's borrowed the coat from a friend, having forgotten, in his habitual a.m. haste, to wear his own) is a willing automaton. Still, we can see his lips move inside that smile like a little wrinkle in a wrinkle, and we hear the words issue from him. Suppose they were written on his jacket?—that jacket whose name is Fred. In that case, there wouldn't even be a cartoon balloon around the words, with a string depending from it toward his mouth. The expression would resemble our odd scrap on which WILL'S WHEEL ALINEMENT SERVICE was found— 'alignment' spelled, we would have to observe, in a typically lowerclass way, obedient to the social code. As Barthes argues, writing removes the writer from her words.

Our author thinks, *Orlando –Orlando was*, and then writes "He" (to stand for Orlando, for there could be no doubt about his sex, though the fashion of the time did something to disguise it); writes that Orlando was in the act of slicing, in words which are transcribed by her secretary's

typing machine (losing the effect of that lovely swirling hand, so especially graceful at crossing tees), and subsequently mailed to an editor who
will peevishly mark it up (wondering if our author shouldn't write
'blackamoor' instead of simply 'moor' and a whole lot else in the same
vein), only to pass the ms. on to a printer who, in due course, will produce
new and original errors in the galleys. When the galleys are finally
corrected, everyone within reach of the words will have had a hand in
them. During this process it even might look for a time as if Orlando were
going to be replaced by Rudolph at a copy editor's suggestion, but, to the
relief of literature, at the last moment a *stet* is put beside his name,
allowing Orlando to remain. So now he can be seen (for there can be no
doubt about her sex) at the top of the book's first page, slicing at the head
of a moor which is swinging from the rafters.

Office memos, guidelines, brochures, official handouts, architectural
programs, presidential speeches, screen plays, are oftener in worse case
because they are customarily constructed on assembly lines, by gangs and
other committees, by itinerant troupes of clerical assistants. The Surgeon
General warns us that smoking is hazardous to our health. Does he
indeed?

Every step I have described has taken us away from the vocal source
(if there was one, for perhaps she never said aloud or to herself, "Orlando," since it is a name people are often embarrassed to utter), and
removed its original maker from significant existence the way Will's
scrap of paper, which we fetched from the wind and took to the pole, was
removed; yet this is hardly surprising because no one *authors his speech*;
we simply speak it. It is necessary to say we author what we write
precisely because what we write is disconnected from any mouth we
might actually observe rounding itself for the Os required to produce Or
lan dO; so that the question imperatively arises: who, indeed, has made
these marks? Whose is the responsible pen?

*Suddenly a burst of applause which shook the house greeted the prima
donna's entrance*, Balzac writes,[17] after carefully collecting the correct
clichés, for applause always bursts; when it does so it always shakes the
house; it invariably greets an entrance, which, of course, is what actors
and actresses *make*. No wonder Barthes uses "Sarrasine" as an example

of the dead hand of the author, for it would be hard to compose a more dismally anonymous sentence, except that Balzac has had practice, and this one is succeeded and preceeded by hundreds of others its equal. *The Marquis went out at five*, Paul Valéry's *bête noir* (it was certainly not his *béte bleu*) is, by comparison, inimitable. Balzac creates strangeness out of phrases which his readers will be *completely used to*. As they sail along through the story, they will not have to think or realize or recreate or come to grips with anything. Nothing can trouble this salve-like surface. "Sarrasine" is a story whose merit is to seem not to be there, and one can imagine Balzac removing originality from it like unwanted hair.[18]

Virginia Woolf no doubt changed many things while she wrote, adding images, crossing out details, removing words, exchanging paragraphs, perhaps pages, reconceiving the entire enterprise, falling into foul moods, later climbing out of them, altering herself when she mooned over Vita Sackville-West and remembered Knoll, somewhat as her hero progresses from one sex to another. Was Joyce the selfsame man who began *Finnegans Wake* when, fifteen years later, he woke from it? Certainly Malcolm Lowry's bout with *Under the Volcano* (begun when he was a much younger and certainly less well-formed writer than Joyce was when he began the *Wake*) involved more than one personality and bears witness to different levels of skill and conception. *Malte Laurids Brigge* is many things, and one of them was to be a course of therapy for a deeply troubled Rilke so that he would not become "his other self." It is unlikely that one inflexible self wrote *Orlando*, nor did it spring into being all at once as it does when we open its covers now.[19] We know how all the other Orlandos influenced her; how she researched the Great Frost before she composed that amazing description of it; how faithfully she frequented the British Museum, and how much she loved memoirs, biography, and other historical texts.

A poet's life, like Chatterton's, may be no longer than a mayfly's, and yet many poems might be appended to his name, because poems can occasionally be blurted, but works of prose, as I've pointed out, involve time in an essential way, and can have a single author only in the traditional metaphysical sense that they possess (as even the saddest of ordinary mortals does) an enduring, central, stubbornly unchanging self, that "me" that is the permanent object of the "I", perhaps within the child as a state of lucent potentiality, and translucent to the point of invisibility when past its prime, but an unshakable unity nevertheless.

It is commonly felt that a unified work of literature should seem to have a single author (unless, like the style of much of "Sarrasine," the work is so undistinctive, bland, and featureless—so collective, so corporate—as to suggest a corporate, collective style), so that what any actual author must do, divided as she often is into whore and housewife and shrew and mum and cook and clothes horse and eardrum off which the brags of men bounce—sissboom, boomsiss—girlscout, nannie, and nursemaid, left breast and right, choirgirl and choregirl and cheerleader and hash slinger and Model C and Gentle Annie and Madame La Mort and La Belle Dame Sans Merci and eye in whose loving gaze great men grow up from little lads and finks and fat louts into troubadors and totem designers and business thieves and all that. . . and all that. . . is to infer, is to construct, contrive, the ideal author of her text, and then try to accommodate, corset, constrict, her multifarious nature to that less variable but often more reliable and likeable though artificial being. From the poem the reader projects the poet, too—not a person—but the poet of the poem.

Hume has warned us that if we wish to infer a creator solely from the evidence of a creation, we cannot attribute to it any other character, qualities, or power, than would be strictly necessary to produce the thing, the song, or world in question. Nor can we forget (when we are busy imagining the author of *Waverly* or *Lady Chatterley's Lover* or *The World as Will and Representation* or *The Life of Reason*) the silly, incompetent, or wicked things the work accomplishes as well; the insane mix of planning and chance, absurdity and design, incompetence and skill, which is the rule in most cases; just because we wish to bring "good ole glory" to a name, for the name will no longer designate the necessary author or the less necessary personality behind the art, but still another kind of slippery fiction.

The intention of the author is only occasionally relevant, but if we believe at all in the Unconscious, or in the impossibility of literally nothing escaping the author's clear awareness and control, then the artificial author (the author which the text creates, not the author who creates the text) will be importantly different from the one of flesh and blood, envy and animosity, who holds the pen, and whose picture enlivens the gray pages of history. Strictly speaking, Scott is both more and less than *the* author of *Waverly.*[20]

In certain cases, further complications arise. When an author devotes a great portion of a writing life to one work, as Dante did, or Spenser did, or Proust, then the likelihood that the work itself will begin to overwhelm and almost entirely occupy the arena of ordinary life grows great, because the writer will surely have imagined marriages more interesting than her own, deaths more dismaying than that of Uncle Charley, or invented characters with more quality than her children, who simply sniffle, skin knees, and fail in school; she will not carry on her fictional affairs like boring conversations; she will have fallen in love with a rake of her own devising. Proust's book became a second cork-lined room around him; Flaubert's letters reflect the fact that his writing desk is both board and bed; the nighttime life of the *Wake* compensates for a failing sight. That is, works not only imply an artificial author, they profoundly alter, sometimes, the nature of the historical one. God, himself, I suspect, has been made worse by the world.

That characters get out of control, that the uncompleted text takes over its completion, was a commonplace long before E. M. Forster complained of it, or Flann O'Brien made it a compositional directive.[21] And Vladimir Nabokov's little story about the Vane sisters doubles the dialectical interference of text with intention, intention with text. Cynthia's death provokes in the narrator the expectation of her ghostly appearance. His sleep is soon troubled by a dream about her, but this is hardly the apparition he hopes for and fears. Though the narrator puzzles himself about it, the dream yields him nothing. He and the story conclude:

> I could isolate, consciously, little. Everything seemed blurred, yellow-clouded, yielding nothing tangible. Her inept acrostics, maudlin evasions, theopathies—every recollection formed ripples of mysterious meaning. Everything seemed yellowly blurred, illusive, lost.[22]

Nabokov, however, has not concluded *his* fun, for the first letters of the words which make up that final paragraph provide a message:

IciclEsbycyntHiameterfrommesybil; that is: Icicles by Cynthia, meter from me, Sybil.

If the author had not waited until the 20th century to pass on, but had gone off more quickly, rather like fish, Galileo wouldn't have had to publish his work anonymously and in another country far from his own place of residence; neither would all those amiable works of erotica have had to hide their heads, but they could have ridden out happily headless, written simply by a raunchy world; Charlotte Bronte wouldn't have had to give birth to Currer Bell or die as C. B. Nicholls while trying to carry her baby; neither should we have seen originate a distinct species of posthumous writing, a genre practiced so perfectly by Kafka, and one to which some work of Descartes, and the *Dialogues* of Hume, belong. The pseudonyminal pranks of Saki, Kierkegaard, and Brian Ó Nualláin (a.k.a. Brian O'Nolan, Myles na gCopaleen, John James Doe, George Knowall, Brother Barnabas, the Great Count O'Blather, and Flann O'Brien) would not have been necessary.

If Roland Barthes had been interested in radically simplifying the final solution to the Author Question (and I've tried to indicate and describe, here, some of the members of this rather heteronomous race), by removing these authors who come to claim every fresh text like red ants to a wound, he could have adopted the "single author" theory, either as it is alluded to by Borges, or proposed by Gertrude Stein or implied by Hegel. Then, with this plurality of persons—both real, inhuman, artificial, and imaginary—reduced to manageable proportions, a single stroke across the top of the word would have been enough. An author can't author anything.

Stein distinguishes (to consider her version for only a moment)[23] between what she calls human nature, on the one hand [a physical existence which established for the writer a notable identity in time and a visitable locale in space; the person whose likeness is taken up to put on postage stamps, who cashes the checks, and whose character can be counterfeited if one gets hold of the appropriate documents and facts; the "I am I because my little dog knows me" borderpatrol identity], and the human mind, on the other [a universal level of creativity and thought which moves evenly between Kant-like entities; that elevation we refer to when we speak of the way a work may transcend its Oxford, Mississippi milieu, for instance, its Colombian quaintness, the author's alcoholism or mushy obsession with mom, to achieve a readily understandable meaning and an immediately shareable emotion; the "I am not I any longer when I see" *en soi*].

Every author has an identity, but masterpieces are written by the human mind, not by human nature, which only lends them their common smell and color, their day to day dust. The implication is that readers differ in the same way. A masterpiece can be read as if it were by James Michener (it is the principal way Proust suffers from his society— swallowing fans), but the works of the human mind are really addressed to other human minds. That ineffable persona which a poem implies will be "the human mind" if the poem achieves greatness; however, the fatuous little *New Yorker* story will fasten the reader to a rock in Westchester and leave him to be eaten up by trademarks and localisms and proper names. It will flatter his determinate and causal—his chemical— self. The anonymity which the superb poem or fiction presumably possesses, according to some theories, may consequently be a kind of spiritual consanguinity.

Because we borrow, beg, buy, steal, or copy texts; because texts enter our eyes but remain in the blood; because we are, as authors, plagiarists and paraphrasers and brain pickers and mocking birds; because of these and other like habits we are, in effect, translating texts from one time to another and one context to another and one language to another. If, instead of repeating, "have a nice day," we suggest to strangers that they "lead a good life," we have simply rearranged a slightly different little cluster of clichés. But all that any author works with, in the beginning, is given her by one corrupted magi after another: the language, the life she leads, the literary tradition, schools she attends, the books she reads, the studies she has undertaken; so she cannot lay claim to some syntax or vocabulary, climate of ideas or custom of entertaining, as hers, and hers alone, and therefore as special as she is. Neither is that inadequacy she is supposed to feel at the close of her office hours the feeling of a freak. Of course, all of this wisdom and experience, this shit and sublimity, is shared, and of course a great deal of what we all do and think and feel and write is no more uniquely had or imagined than the balloon of the bagger; the stream of life is rarely more than a pisser's trickle; and literally millions of sentences are penned or typed or spoken every day which have only a source—a spigot or a signboard—and not an author[24]; they have never been near a self which is so certain of its spirit and so insistent on its presence that it puts itself in its syllables like Mr. Gorgeous in his shimmering gown.[25] When all that was was fair, Joyce writes, describing Paradise, and in that simple rearrangement of the given and the inevitable and the previous, he triumphs, making something new, in Pound's sense,[26] and *breaking through the circle of society*, transposing a him- and a herself into the mode known as *authoring*.

The Goethe poem, which I quoted earlier with deceitful intent, is scarcely his any more (nor would he claim it).[27] None of the formalities match. The idea may still be there like an ancient tree in a neglected park. But that's what we do: for good or ill we incessantly transmute. What I am emptying my bladder of, behind that tree in that neglected park, was once a nice hot cup of green tea.

Balzac never betrays the bourgeois, never breaks through the circle of society, because he employs forms which they understand and use themselves [for instance, the step-ladder like structure of life in school (1st grade, 2nd grade, 3rd grade, and so on), the step-ladder like structure of life in the family (birth, bawl, crawl, walk, speak, etc.), the step-ladder like structure of life in the church (birth, baptism, confirmation . . .), in business, in society, and so forth, each of which points the way and evaluates all progress, not from cradle to grave, but from birth to bequest]; Balzac relishes their stereotypes and pat phrases and vulgar elegancies;[28] his taste is that of the turtle which has found itself in a robust soup; he, too, would flatter the reader, the public, the world which receives him until it receives him well and warmly; and Roland Barthes, for all his fripparies like lace on a sleeve, for all his textual pleasures, which imply a more courtly era, is no better, accepting a pseudo-radical role as if it were the last one left in the basket. Balzac's revelations, however critical and "daring" and suggestive, pet the bourgeois to the purr point because they are revelations which remain in their world and language like dummies in a window. Though more perceptive than most, more sensitive, even more moral and upright (let us grant), and undoubtedly a genius, Balzac is more moral the way more money is more money; his is the ultimate hosanna of utility; however hard his eye, his look will land light.

"Sarrasine" is corrupt in both its art and its attitudes, and this is the one thing Roland Barthes' extensive commentary neglects to point out.[29] Rodin's statue of a nude and arrogant Balzac is a bother, but not Balzac, whose arrogance is the arrogance of the best men of business, and who deserves to be wearing at least a hat. That is why we need authors: they refuse. Readers, on the other hand . . . readers . . .readers simply comprise the public.

Notes

[1] Roland Barthes. "The Death of the Author," *Image, Music, Text*, transl. Stephen Heath (New York: Hill & Wang, 1977), pp. 142-148.

[2] Jonathan Culler, *Roland Barthes* (New York: Oxford U. Press, 1983), p. 119.

[3] Barthes, *op. cit.*, p. 149

[4] John Crowe Ransom, "A Poem Nearly Anonymous," *The World's Body* (New York: Charles Scribner's Sons, 1938), p. 2.

[5] Stephen says this during a one-sided conversation with Lynch in the middle of the final chapter of *A Portrait*. Lynch shortly follows this with the joke that God must have hidden himself after perpetrating Ireland.

[6] Paul Valéry, "Man and the Seashell," *The Collected Works in English, Aesthetics*, Vol. XIII, trans. Ralph Mannheim (New York: Pantheon, Bollingen Series XLV), p. 27.

[7] Adapted from Goethe.

[8] These quotations are, of course, from the opening chapter of *Barchester Towers*.

[9] "For poems are not, as people think, simply emotions (one has emotions early enough)— they are experiences. For the sake of a single poem, you must see many cities, many people and Things, you must understand animals, must feel how birds fly, and know the gesture which small flowers make when they open in the morning." From Bk. 1, Sec. 14; "I think I ought to begin to do some work. . ." Stephen Mitchell's translation.

[10] *History of English Literature*, Hippolyte Adophe Taine, vol. 1, trans. by Henry Van Laun (New York: the Colonial Press, 1900), p. 2.

[11] Octavio Paz, "Introduction," *Renga: A Chain of Poems*, Octavio Paz, Jacques Roubaud, Edoardo Sanguineti, and Charles Tomlinson (New York: George Braziller, 1971).

[12] *Ibid.* Paz speaks first of a "feeling of abandonment," then a "sensation of oppression," followed by a "feeling of shame," a "feeling of voyeurism," a "feeling of returning." It is all very operatic. They are only writing a poem, after all, these poets; but they must pretend they are having a religious experience. The fiction is that the poem is all important, when only the fact that they are writing it together really is.

[13] In *The Floating Opera* (New York: Appleton Century Crofts, Inc., 1956), Barth is not to be seen. Andrews is writing his own story, but he immediately points out how limited his powers are: he is stuck with the truth. I look like what I think Gregory Peck, the movie actor, will look like when he's fifty-four . . . (The comparison to Mr. Peck isn't intended as self-praise, only as description. Were I God, creating the face of either Todd Andrews

or Gregory Peck, I'd change it just a trifle here and there.) When a fictional character speaks to the reader the way Trollope spoke to him, and as Todd Andrews not infrequently does, he intends the reader to become a fiction. How else will they hold a conversation?

[14] Vladimir Nabokov, "The Vane Sisters," *Tyrants Destroyed and other Stories* (New York: McGraw-Hill, 1975), pp. 222-3. The balance of "between . . . lips" and "beneath . . . lids" is particularly artful, as is the repeated use of "small," and the music of passages like "the diluted blue ink of her eyes . . ."

[15] Barthes, *op. cit.*, pp. 143, 119, 120.

[16] Barthes, *op. cit.*, p. 146. These views are the consequence of Barthes' work on S/Z, and his disclosure of all the "codes" which come together in "Sarrasine," the example he has taken from Balzac and quotes again in this essay.

[17] (216)*ACT.: "Theater": 6: entrance of the star, in Roland Barthes, S/Z, trans. by Richard Miller (New York: Hill & Wang, 1974), p. 111.

[18] Every attempt at something striking, such as the features of a beautiful woman where *each pore has a special brilliance*, is catastrophic. *Ibid.*, p 34.

[19] I make some similar points about "Sarrasine," Roland Barthes, and style in my essay "The Habitations of the Word," *The Kenyon Review*, 1985.

[20] For example, consult the little parable, "Borges and I," in *Labyrinths*, edited by Yates & Irby (New York: New Directions, 1964), pp. 246-7. Borges writes: I live, let myself go on living, so that Borges may contrive his literature, and this literature justifies me.

[21] In *Aspects of a Novel* (New York: Harcourt Brace, 1927), p. 102. *At Swim-Two-Birds* (London, 1939). O'Brien is a text weaver, his novel is "a book-web," and he even uses a pseudonym, yet few novels belong more completely to their maker.

[22] Nabokov, *op. cit.*, p. 238.

[23] Gertrude Stein, *The Geographical History of America*, intro. by W. H. Gass (New York: Vintage, 1973). This book develops, perhaps at unnecessary length, ideas contained in her somewhat earlier essay, "What Are Masterpieces, and Why Are There so Few of Them?"

[24] (439) *This was woman herself, with her sudden fears, her irrational whims, her instinctive worries, her impetuous boldness, her fussings, and her delicious sensibility* SEM. Femininity. The source of the sentence cannot be discerned. Who is speaking? Is it Sarrasine? the narrator? the author? Balzac-the-author? Balzac-the-man? romanticism? bourgeoisie? universal wisdom? The intersecting of all these origins creates the writing. S/Z, *op. cit.*, pp 172-3. In "Death of the Author" (*op. cit.*, p142) this condition is suggested for *all* writing.

[25] On putting the self in syllables, see "The Soul Inside the Sentence", *Salmagundi*, No. 56, Spring, 1982, pp. 65-86.

[26] *Make It New* (New Haven: New Directions, 1935)

[27] Über allen Gibfein
    ist Ruh,
    in allen Wipfeln
    spurest du
    kaum einen Hauch.
    Die Vöglein schweigen im Walde.
    Warte nur: balde
    ruhest au auch.

[28] See Richard Howard's benevolent description of this phenomenon in his introduction to S/Z, *op. cit.*, pp. x, xi. I find now that when I go to get a book off the shelf, I pick something I've read before, as if I didn't dare try anything new.

[29] Although the typically faithless quote from George Bataille, which is included in S/Z as an appendix, suggests that "Sarrasine" is more than ok.

The Conduct of Criticism:
How We Do What We Do

BY IRVING HOWE

Literary criticism resembles the Jews: easy to recognize but hard to define. Without some flicker of imagination, literary criticism must sink to pedantry or chatter, yet it falls short of being imaginative literature. Largely a mode of discursive writing, it is something a little more than just discursive. Dependent upon and secondary to imaginative texts, it nevertheless strains, though seldom with attractive results, to arrive at a full expressive independence. Criticism keeps asking itself—no one else especially cares—what it is and should be. And it thrives most when not sure of the answer.

No one has yet established fixed boundaries for literary criticism, or more accurately, no one has yet established boundaries which most critics will accept. Volunteers police the area, eager to establish rules, but violators still roam about freely. How then can we speak of criticism as a discipline, if we can't even say where it begins and where it ends? Yet this very imprecision can become a major source of the interest criticism can exert as a meditation upon the work of the mind in its imaginative bearings—a meditation that may draw upon almost anything, history, metaphysics, science, politics, psychology, even the puzzle called life, just so long as the critic steers us tactfully back to the poem or fiction itself. For literature is really too important an enterprise to be confined within the literary: it will steadily break past the boundaries that zealous guardians of method and rule strive to erect.

I want here to propose a view of criticism—unsystematic, untheoretic—or at least, of how critics do what they actually do. This is not the only possible or legitimate view, of course, nor perhaps even the best one; but at least until about a decade ago, a view that many critics would have taken for granted. I nourish the expectation that in another decade or so that will be happening once more.

I

In our time the main circumstance for the writing of literary criticism has been the constant pressure exerted by extra-literary concerns and interests. It is not just a paradox to say that because the most serious critics have been committed to the idea that literature should command an autonomous status, they could not often keep their extra- literary persuasions and biases—the very core of their identities—from entering their critical work, sometimes as invigoration, sometimes as contamination. At least since Matthew Arnold found that reflecting upon the place of poetry in the modern world led him to worry about "a girl named Wragg," the most influential critics have assumed the role of cultural commentator and literary criticism has become an occasion for the testing, usually through oblique ways, of cultural inclinations and moral values.

There follows inescapably a clash between the desire for coherence within a formal discipline, which means first of all a scrupulous loyalty to the text under consideration, and the need to ground our responses to literature in the most urgent experiential concerns. This tension has been a source of the best, but also the worst, in criticism, and except for certain specialists, those critics who succeed in escaping such tensions seldom merit serious consideration. Even the seemingly neutral study of prosody and fictional structure cannot, if undertaken with any imaginative flare, remain self-sufficient for very long. Soon breaking past technical notation, primary as that notation may often be, such critical or partly critical tasks proceed, well or badly, into the perils of cultural discourse.

Edmund Wilson once wrote that he wished to explore "the history of man's ideas and imaginings in the setting of the conditions which shaped them." While this does not yet specify the critic's actual procedures, which are notoriously elusive and diverse, it does indicate something about the critic's ends: to examine structures of social life, ranges of individual feelings, styles of language as these emerge through the mediated disclosures of literature. But before even approaching these ends—we all hurry to affirm—there must come the descriptive analysis of the work itself: genre, form, tone, style, etc. Such analyses are not likely to go very far without becoming entangled with problems of judgement; and no sooner does this happen than there ensues a critical effort, sometimes a very hard struggle, to locate some "larger significance" in or of what the poet or novelist has made. Works of literature, as the Israeli theorist Benjamin Harshav says,

> convey meanings and meaning complexes as well as rhetorical and aesthetic import; they. . . call for interpretations and elucidations. However, the experience and interpretation of literary texts are not a matter of language alone: language in literature can be understood only as imbedded in fictional constructs . . . are mediated through language alone. This is one basic inherent circularity of works of literary art. It is not necessarily a vicious circle, but can be understood as an interdependence between the two domains: language and fictional constructs.

The interdependence of which Harshav speaks necessarily implies a distinction, if only for analytical purposes, between language and fictional construct. Serious critics shuttle between and often are torn by— they may even suppose it a professional obligation to allow themselves to be torn by—the opposing demands or pressures of language and fictional construct.

As a refraction, however conceived, of human experience—and if not that, then what? or why does it matter?—literature frequently contains a substratum or potential of moral criticism, sometimes an explicit statement. *Ought* shadows *is*: imaginative renderings bear normative implications, and no rendering of human behavior, no matter how abstruse or oblique, can be quite value-free. Critics besotted by ideology suppose, these days, that this justifies reducing the literary work to a political or philosophical "position," but usually these are bad critics. The substratum or potential of moral criticism in a literary work is rarely systematic, sometimes marked by internal contradiction, often elusive. It can form a running line of commentary, as in George Eliot's novels, or can be realized through flickers of comic negation, as in Samuel Beckett's plays. But it is there, most of the time, and a central job of the critic is to find it, gently, lightly. This critical substratum or potential may be progressive, rational and optimistic; but it need not be, it can readily be their opposite. But any imaginative text moving beyond the most rudimentary of depictions will be marked (I quote John Dewey) by "a sense of possibilities that are unrealized . . . When they are put in contrast with actual conditions [they may form] the most penetrating 'criticism' of the latter that can be made."

These remarks may help explain why literary criticism in our time has served as a vehicle through which cultivated persons could reflect upon the human situation as disclosed in imaginative works. The double seeing—the work itself and "through" the work—is tricky and a frequent cause for critical missteps. I recognize that I may here be gravely minimizing the pleasures to be had, in their own right, from certain literary genres or from what might be called the sheer "doing," the sheer performance of the literary work: for example, the lyric of personal feeling, the fiction of mimicry, the story of absorbing incident. And also that I risk underestimating the value of literary criticism as technical scrutiny, though I hope soon partly to remedy this. But in an age of fragmented and fractious beliefs, it seems all but inevitable that critics should also serve as guardians of taste, priests of value, protectors of the word—or their violators and betrayers. At its best, however, criticism has been one of the last humane disciplines in which it remains possible to take a comprehensive and, at times, shared view of our condition while still making very large claims for the solitary reader who must finally depend on personal sensibility and knowledge. The "classic kind of critic," as Delmore Schwartz has described T. S. Eliot, is "expert precisely because he depends upon the quality of his own experience, while at the same time being aware that the more experience of literature he has, the more expert he becomes" in the sifting of his own experience.

It's a risky business, with an appallingly high rate of failure. While pedestrian scholarship can have a certain secondary value, filling in some cracks of knowledge, pedestrian criticism rarely has any. To cling fanatically or programmatically to the text is to risk the dryness of literalism. To range everywhere is to risk not knowing or seeing anything. To chase after general ideas is to subvert literature in behalf of something that might be considered without invoking literature at all. Still another major peril for the critic—I sometimes find that in thinking about criticism I see nothing but perils—is to slacken the tension between the act of reading and placing the work in its proper context. Theoretical sectarianism, which can be both formalist and anti-formalist, is an ever-present danger—the danger of narrowness, dryness and righteousness. What makes a good critic is not the possession of an invulnerable method, but a breadth of feeling and a canniness of sensibility that enable him to chart a course among looming perils. Odysseus had no theory for steering past Scylla and Charybdis, he had to rely upon powers of craft.

Perhaps, in the last analysis, disinterestedness is beyond our reach. Perhaps it is a sign of vanity even to hope for it. But a reaching toward disinterestedness is one mark of the serious critic even as he is quite aware of bias, crotchets, predispositions. The fashionable notion that all critical writings release interest, strikes me as an intellectual vulgarity debasing both Marxism and the sociology of knowledge. It also happens to be a libel on many critics who do sincerely strive for a sense of justness, even generosity, in dealing with writers whose opinions they cannot share and whose tastes they question.

Precisely because it is all but inevitable that modern critics should expand—sometimes shrink—into cultural and moral commentary, we ought to give a place of honor to at least some critics who concentrate on the formal aspects of literature. Critics like me, always in danger of straying from the matter at hand, need critics like them to keep us, if not honest, then at least on track. I read the Russian formalists with such admiration, not for their method—do they even have one?—but for their attentiveness to the words on the page. If I were to offer any criticism of their work, it would be something like that of Bakhtin, namely, that the "contaminating" influences of experience which they would like to banish from critical discourse have a way of infiltrating even the most stringent of their scrutinies—see, for example, Boris Eichenbaum's brilliant study of Gogol's "The Overcoat," in which everything is focussed on verbal usage yet the wretched overcoat as object and symbol persists in obtruding.

II

Little wonder that some critics want methods and theorists sometimes decree them. But in the actuality, the conduct of criticism, method seldom plays the role its advocates claim. In the actuality, the conduct of criticism, method has a way of fading and crumbling, it is something far more frequently asserted than employed. In actuality—in what critics do—far more depends on temperament and talent. Much depends on gifts of intuition, gifts that cannot be decreed but can be nurtured, so as to enable what F. R. Leavis calls the critic's "first concern... [which is] to enter into possession of the given poem . . . in its concrete fullness." The best criticism is often brief, aphoristic, lapidary. Much depends on "fit," or what an earlier age called decorum. Do my inclinations and capacities of response match up with the work of a given writer? Zola may "fit" for me, but not Gide; I may "see" Frost, but not Hart Crane. The critic's limitations define (sometimes are) the critic's powers, and as we come to know his / her work we appreciate the limitations quite as much as the powers. *To see, to see*: that is the prime task, the overwhelming difficulty. As Yogi Berra once said, "You can observe a lot, by just looking." Which I take to be a gloss on T. S. Eliot's remark that "the only method is to be very intelligent."

III

But what does the critic actually do? How does the critic conduct him/ herself? It would seem an easy question to answer, but it is terribly difficult, since we are about as good at describing what we do as most people are at giving street directions. Let's begin modestly, simply.

Presented with a poem or a fiction, we know that our first task is "just" to describe it. Perhaps we begin by trying to place it in a line of tradition from which, of course, it will necessarily deviate, and in order so to place it—T. S. Eliot tells me—I must possess "the historical sense . . . a feeling that the whole of the literature of Europe from Homer and within it the literature of [my] country has a simultaneous existence." A sufficiently imposing prospect, but there are further difficulties Eliot failed to mention, one of them being that there is more than a single literary tradition or more than a single view of tradition(s) and that I, for instance, count as major figures in my tradition writers like Isaac Babel and Sholem Aleichem whom Eliot, in his Tory-ish insistence, either did not know or did not care to know. It is hard these days, what with shattered canons and shifting curricula, simply to insist upon an overriding tradition, though I believe that if taken with a sufficient quantity of the "historical sense" Eliot demands (though in practice often narrows), the idea of a central literary tradition is still an imperative for critical discourse. In any case, it seems that I need to know a very great deal "just" to describe a poem.

To describe is also, very soon, to stumble toward a preliminary and tentative approximation of value, if only in order to enable the act of description. Notoriously imprecise as the language of criticism is in general, the only word for our terms of valuation is scandalous—so scandalous that one almost assents to Northrop Frye's improbable refusal of valuation as a central task of criticism. For which practicing critic has not felt depressed before those weary adjectives, "great" and "distinguished," or has not seen through Harold Bloom's weak surrogate of "strong"? Still, there is no choice (short of inventing a new language). Our language tilts us toward judgement, and of course serious valuation is far more than a matter of finding the right adjective. It may emerge through complex acts of recognition and slow penetrative appreciations. "Explication in the neutral sense," writes William Wimsatt, can be "so integrated with special and local value intimations that it rises from neutrality gradually and convincingly to the point of local judgement."

One can only hope so: it is the optimal condition. But from my reading of critics and my own limited experience I conclude that we do not often achieve this optimal condition. All too often there looms a gap between "explication" and "local judgement," across which, on the wobbly skates of personal sensibility, the critic tries to glide. Finally, what matters is the reader's sense of how trustworthy, how seasoned, even how disinterested the critic is. Since the critic can hardly "prove" his "value intimations" to be right or unassailable, our readiness to accede to them, if only provisionally or only as the ground for later dissociations, depends on our criticism of the critic, our judgement of his/her reliability, capacities, tastes.

Beginning as reading, criticism, writes Eliot, "is an instinctive activity of the civilized mind." It begins as an immersion, a submission, exactly of the sort that you, who may be fortunate enough never to have written a word of criticism, engage in whenever you come upon a new work of literature. It is an act of immersion and submission beautifully evoked in Wallace Stevens' poem, "The House Was Quiet and the World Was Calm":

> The house was quiet and the world was calm.
> The reader became the book; and summer night
>
> Was like the conscious being of the book.
> The house was quiet and the world was calm.

The reader became the book: is this not the condition to which the wary critic, eager to rise out of the rut of professional maneuver, aspires? Perhaps even aspires with an innocence of pleasure? Of course, this response may be no more than a tactical simulation: first love can happen only once, and even in America, only three or four times. But ideally that is the state of receptivity toward which the critic aspires, and without which everything that may follow, all the methods and maneuver, count for very little.

Let us say that our critic has "placed" a war poem in a proximate tradition. It resembles one of Isaac Rosenberg's trench poems, a comparison that may be a neutral point of approach: the revelation of the new requires familiarity with the old. Now comes difficulty. Does she like this war poem because it confirms her own predispositions? Can she be sure that she is engaged with the poem and not the poem's external motive? And how, in any case, can she separate the one from the other? Or may not this poet actually be writing out of other, less attractive premises which a close study of the language might disclose? Here is where the critic's integrity is severely tested, and the test consists in a readiness to turn upon the text.

Now come the formal steps, seeking out patterns of imagery, wondering if any relation can be established between meter and meaning (our critic once read Yvor Winters), etc. And of course the steps I've put down as a sequence will in practice occur as a jumble of simultaneous responses, far more entangled and complicated than I can here detail.

Finally, the critic wants to locate a crux of individuality, what we call the writer's voice or signature. Perhaps that is in part what George Poulet meant when speaking of the writer's "point of departure." As glossed by Paul de Man, the point of departure "serves as a unifying principle within a single corpus while also serving to differentiate between writers . . ." Perhaps in using the loose but suggestive term, a "writer's vision," we have in mind what the writer moves toward, seeks to cohere, once having left Poulet's "point of departure." It is what makes Hardy Hardy and not someone else. Your pedestrian critic will catch Hardy's fatalism (anyone could), but a good critic will move past that commonplace, toward Hardy's feelings about locale, his elegaic sentiments about his own past life, his mixed responses about a religious experience felt most acutely at the moment of refusal, and then further still, into local passages, plays of language, quirks of literary conduct.

I turn now to a simple example from my own experience, useful perhaps because it is elementary. Some 30 years ago I reviewed Bernard Malamud's first book of stories. A significant new writer: no earlier body of judgement to fall back upon: no choice, then, but to fumble toward original response.

At first I noticed, as anyone might, Malamud's familiar setting, "the Jewish immigrant neighborhoods of the depression years." This brought a temptation to drop him into the worn slot of immigrant Jewish fiction, that is, into a ready-made mini-tradition. But it wasn't good enough, since "he treats {this milieu] as no writer before him." So I got to the harder task of evoking whatever was distinctive in Malamud's work: "it is as if the speed of the movie reel were crazily impaired, as if the characters leapt clear of the earth, as if a Chagall painting snapped into motion . . ." Thirty years ago I was rather pleased with that sentence, but now I look at it askance. Those repeated "as if's" are a sign that I was substituting evocative similies for precise description, rarely a good procedure (though at times unavoidable) in criticism. A few sentences later I did somewhat better: "Everything—action, dialogue, comment—is sped up, driven to a climax in which gesture compresses and releases an essential meaning, and the characters . . . rise to a fabulous sort of 'Yiddish' articulateness." But then I got into trouble, writing that Malamud's stories are "not realism at all" yet in another sense do invoke realism since "they aim . . . to indicate that this is the way things really are." An unfortunate remark. I didn't consider that all literary modes aim to "indicate that this is the way things really are" and that such an aim is not a sufficient ground for evoking realism.

Clearly, there were unacknowledged esthetic suppositions, probably internal contradictions, in this little review, so that it might be argued that I should have straightened myself out to a decent consistency. Perhaps so. But would that really have helped me do a better job in evoking whatever was fresh in Malamud's stories? I doubt it. For it does not follow that because a critic has theoretical suppositions imbedded in his work—as who does not?—he should set about to use theory in the act of criticism or opt for a premature and predictable system.

The relation between literary theory and critical practice was discussed a few decades ago in an exchange between the literary historian René Wellek and the literary critic F. R. Leavis. Where, asked Wellek of Leavis, where is your theory? How do you explain or justify whatever it is that you do? Most of us might have been intimidated by this probe, but Leavis was not. A critic, he replied, "might just be the better for a philosophical training [in esthetic theory] but if he were, the advantage . . . would manifest itself partly in a surer realization that literary criticism is not philosophy."

The critic's aim, continued Leavis, "is, first, to realize as sensitively and completely as possible this or that which claims his attention . . . The business of the literary critic is to attain a peculiarly strict relevance in developing his response [to a literary work] into commentary; he must be on guard against abstracting improperly from what is in front of him . . ."

The charged words here are "peculiar completeness of response" and "abstracting improperly." To, perhaps, sharpen our sense of what the critic does, let me try to illustrate Leavis' meaning with two instances.

Reading the poems of Robert Frost we may wonder why we occasionally hear a jarring note, a Philistine jeer. It's not the main thing we hear, for if it were, Frost's poems would not merit much attention; but simply to miss this note would mean to fail in a "peculiar completeness of response." That would require from the critic a balancing of Frost's evident wish to convey the voice of a sage together with the voice of a simple feller, to combine the mind presumably superior to that of mere urban literati with a mind uncomfortable with all urban types. Achieving here a "peculiar completeness of response" would require some knowledge of the Emersonian tradition, which means partly a tradition disparaging tradition. It might then be possible to attack Frost, in Wintersian style, as an enemy of rationality, but to do that would, I think, be to "abstract improperly," for it would be to ignore a great deal, and certainly the best, in Frost's work. But it would not be "abstracting improperly" to notice that Frost's posturing can result in a strain of intellectual and emotional vulgarity, creating in the reader a touch of irritability.

My second example concerns the talented novelist V. S. Naipaul. His recent novels have kept returning to the corruptions and delusions of Third World countries. A blend of indigenous brutality, decadent leftist rhetoric and nationalist frustration is portrayed by Naipaul in a manner that seems (to me) honestly corrosive. Also unnervingly keen and comic. Yet one remains uneasy. The "peculiar completeness of response" that is the critic's obligation requires that we fret about a punitive impulse, perhaps even vindictiveness, in Naipaul's work. One senses, at times, an illicit, unacknowledged emotion, beyond the needs of the fictions themselves. Is it "abstracting improperly" to ask whether some ideological alloy disturbs his fictions?

In the case of Frost, the critic is beset with problems regarding the "character" of the poet as the voice that comes through in the poems; in the case of Naipaul, the critic must confront questions of intellectual tact regarding the relation of ideology to literature, as well as the still more difficult matter of moral tone. The Frost problem is secondary, confined to his inferior poems; the Naipaul problem is primary, characteristic of his distinguished work. If there is a theory that can dispose of these difficulties in the conduct of criticism, I shall be glad to receive it. My own experience, for what it's worth, suggests that I have to rely here on my slender resources of knowledge and sensibility, for what they are worth. With Frost, whose poetry I love, I must restrain an occasional irritability, because I sense he is intent upon baiting people like me and I say to him: "No, I will not provoke." With Naipaul, whose novels I admire, I must bring to bear an awareness of the political problems attached to the idea of the Third World. All these strains of awareness are at work in critical judgement; they can only be individual, local, provisional; they are always susceptible to the frailties of error.

IV

The view of criticism I've been edging into implies certain notions and attitudes. Let me notice a few, in no special order:

I. Whatever the differences between New and New York critics two or three decades ago, both believed in a sharp demarcation between discursive and "creative" prose. Criticism can only be adulterated, made puny and pretentious, by injections of "creative" writing, usually third-rate prose poetry. But criticism is a branch of writing to be undertaken with force, economy, vividness. The critics I have admired wrote in a wide range of styles—Lionel Trilling sought elegance, George Orwell blunt strength, Harold Rosenberg epigrammatic thrust, Yvor Winters gravity of voice, Robert Penn Warren a fine translucence. But all saw themselves as writers, and almost all would have agreed with Allen Tate that "critical style ought to be plain as the nose on one's face; that it ought not to compete in the detail of sensibility with the work which it is privileged to report on . . . I have tried to remember . . . that I was writing, in the end, opinion, and neither esthetics nor poetry in prose."

Alas, poor Tate: we knew him well, and how sadly is he out of fashion. Today bad prose blots the literary scene, not the kind that comes "naturally" to all of us, but a bad prose that has to be learned: a kind of code.

II. Criticism usually constitutes a short-breathed enterprise, fitting comfortably into a longish essay. Often, that essay can be compressed into a few sentences, crystallizing judgement and insight. When Henry James writes that Hawthorne's "tread is a light and modest one, but keeps the key in his pocket," the vivid trope projects a sense of a writer who releases his values stealthily. When T. S. Eliot writes that Hamlet suffers from "the intense feeling, ecstatic or terrible, without an object or exceeding its object, which every person of sensibility" has known, even readers unpersuaded by Eliot can feel that they have been granted a brilliant perception in economical form. When W. H. Auden writes that in "an ideal production, Faust and Mephistopheles should be played by identical twins," this one sentence suggests an entire moral view of the connection between tempted and tempter. When V. S. Pritchett writes, "Chekhov is at one with all who travel alone," he tells us more than any number of close studies. When Bakhtin writes that "for the prose artist the world is full of the words of other people," he brings to immediate life the meaning of his notions about the "dialogical" novel. In such remarks, thought and expression fuse; illumination flares.

III. Is this not partly a matter of taste? I approach the word nervously, aware that it can suggest a dilettantish impressionism or a snobbism masquerading as cultivation. Well, of course it can, quite as any category of value can be tipped into its contrary. But the taste for which one turns to critics is rarely any sort of innate gift confined to an aristocracy of privilege; it is the distillation of a lifetime of disciplined reading and intellectual work. John Dewey has called taste not an "arbitrary liking" but "the chief matter wherever values enter . . . Instead of there being no disputing about tastes, they are one thing worth disputing about. Taste . . . is the outcome of experience brought cumulatively to bear on the intelligent appreciation of the real worth of likings . . ."

Or to transpose into my own shorthand: Taste is a judgement which can occur as an instantaneous apprehension, though behind it there is likely to be a prolonged experience. Taste functions as an approximate index of cultural and moral values, with proper allowance for individual predilections and a pluralism of sensibility. Our response to a critic dealing with a new novel or book of poems will depend less on his declared theory than on our experience of his taste—which is really to say, our apprehension of his entire being as critical reader.

IV. Some years ago the poet-scholar J. V. Cunningham published an attack on a New Critic who had read "Ripeness is all" as signifying that "man may ripen into fullness of being." In this reading, said Cunningham, "we discover in Shakespeare's phrase the secret morality of our time. It is a meaning I can enter into quite as deeply as anyone, but it is not what Shakespeare meant." For

> Shakespeare meant something much more traditional . . . The context is the desire for death. The conclusion is that as we were passive at the hour of our birth so must we be passive to the hour of our death . . . We must endure our going hence, be it when it may, since the hour of our death is in the care of Providence: the readiness is all.

How this view of things is so deeply entrenched in Shakespeare's culture as to render impossible the sympathetic reading of the New Critic, is a burden of Cunningham's little book. For we cannot say everything about a literary text that our desire or ingenuity prompts; both history and language impose limits; and knowledge must serve as a brake upon the critic's speculations or perhaps better, as the disciplining ally for the expression of taste.

V. So perilous an undertaking is criticism that the better critics become at it, the more they grow dubious about it. Just about every good critic I've ever known expressed a certain skepticism about criticism, Tate in print, Trilling in conversation.

A lifetime of writing criticism prepares one for little more than more of the same. It also arouses a certain impatience with the calling, so that many critics turn to other things, to politics, history and prophecy, to verse and fiction. Winters and Leavis became gurus of sects. Anyone who heard R. P. Blackmur intone his lectures could easily imagine him as a New England preacher wrestling with damnation. Philip Rahv was in part a Leninist functionary. Right now, Geoffrey Hartman has turned from fine critic of romantic poetry to apprentice in Judaica. Harold Bloom romances the sublime, and if he could find it anywhere else he might not be so assertive about its place in American literature. One of the few major critics of our time apparently content with being only a critic was F. R. Leavis, and that because he held to the sweet illusion that criticism might serve as an agency of social salvation.

How well one understands these temptations and yearnings! They lead, probably, to disaster? Yes; but only dullards wholly escape them.

V

Let me finally say a few untheoretical words about the avalanche of literary theory that has recently poured out of the academy. Habitually uneasy about what I do as a critic, suspecting that no really first-rate mind would be content to do it all the time, I confess myself a little unnerved by the bustle of self-assurance, the dialectical prowess, the Gallicized jargon of the moment. Having grown up a qualified partisan of literary modernism, I feel uneasy at seeming to resist the new and the radical. I squirm a little when charged, as I suppose I shall be, with being an empiricist, since I suppose that is what I've always been—and it's not been a bed of roses either. But an empiricist in my own way, quite different from the ways of others, with (for better or worse) my own distinctive experiences and interlocking strengths and weaknesses.

There are scholars, like Meyer Abrams, who respond to the recent theorizing with refutation. There are critics, like Alfred Kazin, who loftily ignore the whole thing and attend to their own work. The English critic John Bayley cries out: "So far have things gone that a simple exclamation from a perceptive critic about an author he knows and loves . . . seems today like the past retrieved." And Denis Donoghue refuses, or so he says, to grow agitated:

> I do not see much point in haggling . . . over theories of literature. Theory begins to matter only when it determines practise; prescribes it, predicts it, sets limits upon it. So: take the theories lightly until they darken into practise; then intervene.

Good advice, but who has a character good enough to follow it? For while in the past I could at least read the work of critical antagonists, and very often learn from them, now my problem is that I can hardly find a common basis of discourse with some of the theorists. A glaze of oppression thickens before my eyes when I try to read them. No doubt, my fault.

By now several times burned and more than once shy, I find myself nervously alert to the dangers of fixed doctrine. "The worst evil of fanatic falsification," wrote R. P. Blackmur, occurs "when a body of criticism is governed by an *idée fixe* . . . when a notion of genuine but small scope is taken literally as of universal application."

In my own lifetime, literary theories have come and gone. Come and gone with disconcerting rapidity, as at first with majestic certainty. Each school—the Marxists, the New Critics, the neo-Aristotelians, and now the post-structuralists—was utterly persuaded it had demolished its predecessors. And perhaps it had. So I take some comfort from reading Tzvetan Todorov, a born-again humanist, in a recorded conversation with the French critic Paul Bénichou:

> The first general reproach you [that is, Bénichou] address to the contemporary critical debate is that you observe in it a belief in a sort of verbal fiction called 'method.' Critics 'think they are talking about method,' tend to 'christen every discovery a new "method"' whereas in fact the issue is entirely different. If I decide to carry out a sociological approach, I have no particular method at my disposal; I choose rather to concentrate on only a part of the object (literature) and sometimes to adopt a set of hypotheses concerning this part.

Exactly! No approach rules out totally any method, and no method rules out a critical practice, by which I mean the actual moves a critic makes while engaged with a text.

As I read the theorists hoping for a bit of help, a lift, a clue in the actual practice of criticism, they can be more interesting than their theories. With Paul de Man theory matters less than temperament: a deep and, as it now turns out, guilty sadness at the imperfections of being. With the Russian formalist Boris Eichenbaum, a triumph of perception regarding the "life" banished as against the principle that proclaims an imperative to banish. With Bakhtin I find myself moved by a gallantry that prompts him to acknowledge the powers of the formalists. None of this provides me, or anyone else, with a method. I must still stumble along as best I can; but it does stimulate. It slows the hardening of arteries. And meanwhile, as a prescriptive lucidity, there is William Empson's mild remark: "Perhaps the real test of an esthetic theory, or at any rate while so little is known about the matter, is how far it frees the individual to use his own taste and judgement."

Hard to justify, full of pitfalls, "each venture . . . a raid on the inarticulate with shabby equipment always deteriorating . . ." Yet there is something fine, occasionally exalted about finding oneself in the company of Dr. Johnson and Hazlitt, Arnold and Eliot, Wilson and Winters, Empson and Eichenbaum, unequal of course to their talents but still sharing in the pleasures of scrutiny.

The Political Turn in Criticism

BY DENIS DONOGHUE

In the January-February 1953 issue of *Partisan Review*, John Crowe Ransom reviewing R. P. Blackmur's *Language as Gesture* took issue with him upon one consideration, that in appraising the social and political issues which inhabit Yeats's major poems Blackmur remarked only their function within the work, not the ideas as such, even though they might be "ideas from which, at the very moment, out in the world of action, the issues of life and death are hung." Blackmur, according to Ransom, was repudiating "the ideas as ideas, and reckoning their usefulness for the poem."[1]

Ransom had especially in view "The Later Poetry of W. B. Yeats" (1936) in which Blackmur spoke of Yeats's "Byzantium" as "the poetry of an intense and condensed declaration; not emotion put into doctrine from outside, but doctrine presented as emotion." Blackmur spoke, too, of the companion-poem "Sailing to Byzantium" as exhibiting "the doctrine in action, the doctrine actualized in a personal emotion resembling that of specific prayer." Then he concluded the essay with a large consideration:

> When we call man a rational animal we mean that reason is his great myth. Reason is plastic and takes to any form provided. The rational imagination in poetry, as elsewhere, can absorb magic as a provisional method of evocative and heuristic thinking, but it cannot be based upon it. In poetry, and largely elsewhere, imagination is based upon the reality of words and the emotion of their joining. Yeats's magic, then, like every other feature of his experience, is rational as it reaches words; otherwise

it is his privation, and ours, because it was the rational defect of our society that drove him to it.[2]

I have adverted to this little episode between Ransom and Blackmur because it anticipates many of the issues I shall try to describe in my own terms, and partly because we might clarify the issues by requiring each of the disputants to be somewhat more forthcoming. We might ask Ransom what status he assigned to ideas as such, and how they acquired such privilege, and whether or not he thought the ideas so considered remained intact in that character during and after their involvement in the poem. Are they already a virtual poetry, or merely as Blackmur seemed to imply, raw material for a possible poem? We might ask Blackmur whether he was really content to regard the production of ideas as a matter of ad libbing, of informal play before the commitment of the words is made. Was he content to give the poet every latitude till the play transpired in decisive words, and to judge the degree of decisiveness by an unexplained correlation of emotion and rhythm, the emotion animating a rhythm till that moment merely virtual? When Blackmur says that Yeats's magic is rational as it reaches words, he seems to mean that the poetical character is wayward till it finds a proper syntax for its emotions, and that, so much found, nothing that has preceded the finding matters, every caprice is forgivable as merely auxiliary to the order arrived at. But we might have to ask Blackmur how he could be sure that the syntax found is the order of the rational imagination and not of some sinister force that has assumed the mask of reason and has had no difficulty in appearing plausible. Blackmur's answer would probably invoke the evidence of form; as in writing of Allen Tate he said that for Tate events do not become experience till the imagination creates them in objective form, and further and more comprehensively that "the act of experience, in the arts, transpires only in form." What has not transpired in its particular form cannot be said to have been experienced. For the moment, however, we need only advert to the gist of the episode. For Blackmur, ideas in a poem have merely opportunistic or otherwise instrumental value. For Ransom, the question was: must they not also have constitutive value, and be judged by correspondingly strict criteria?

II

It is a commonplace that recent critical theory has taken a distinctly political turn. After twenty years in which theory was in a dependent relation to epistemology, linguistics, anthropology, and psychoanalysis, it now proceeds in a parasitic relation to politics, either of the Right or, more loudly, of the Left. The wind is now blowing from Germany, not from France: the main sources of authority are Marx and the neo-Marxist Frankfurt critics, especially Benjamin, Adorno, and Horkheimer, with selective acknowledgement to Lukacs. Debates between Habermas, Gadamer, and Ricoeur are best understood in that setting. For the time being, the Frankfurt way of being serious has displaced the Parisian way of being rueful.

III

I shall cite two examples of the political turn, the first from close to home. In Ireland, readers of Yeats, Joyce, and Synge are interrogating these writers in a far harsher spirit than any I recall. It is regularly suggested that Yeats, in particular, bears some responsibility for the violence and death-dealing in Northern Ireland since 1968. Seamus Deane, for instance, has argued in his *Celtic Revivals* (1985) that Yeats turned a misreading of Irish history into an extraordinarily potent mythology which in some sense is being acted out by young people who have never perhaps read a word of his poetry. Yeats, that is, construed the Protestant Ascendancy as an aristocracy, so that he could endow it with the power and grace he ascribed to Italian Renaissance princes, while in fact the Ascendancy was "a predominantly bourgeois social formation." To fulfill the logic of his enterprise, Yeats also conjured into existence the Irish peasant, so that the kinship of peasant and aristocrat, predicated on the working of land, would provide a paradigm of an Ireland heroic in its difference; most tellingly, in its difference from an England given over to science, positivism, empiricism, and industrialization. It follows, according to Deane, that Yeats derived a politics from an aesthetic: he sought "to obliterate or reduce the problems of class, economic development, bureaucratic organization and the like, concentrating instead upon the essences of self, community, nationhood, racial theory, Zeitgeist."[3] To some extent, therefore, Yeats is responsible for the situation in the North, where ostensibly political actions are propelled in fact by ancestral images and powerfully deployed symbols.

In this spirit, Deane refers to Yeats's "Ancestral Houses." The poem, he says,

> owes its force to the vitality with which it offers a version of Ascendancy history as true in itself. The truth of this historical reconstruction of the Ascendancy is not cancelled by our simply saying No, it was not like that. For its ultimate validity is not historical, but mythical. In this case, the mythical element is given prominence by the meditation on the fate of an originary energy when it becomes so effective that it transforms nature into civilization and is then transformed itself by civilization into decadence. This poem, then, appears to have a story to tell and, along with that, an interpretation of the story's meaning. It operates on the narrative and on the conceptual planes and at the intersection of these it emerges, for many readers, as a poem about the tragic nature of human existence itself.[4]

Deane repudiates what he calls this humanist reading of the poem, on the grounds that it claims that a work of literature "can arrive at a moment in which it takes leave of history or myth...and becomes meaningful only as an aspect of the 'human condition'." It endorses, he maintains, the humanist conviction that literature, in its highest forms, is free of ideology.

I shall comment a little on Deane's position before citing my other example of the political turn. It strikes me that his invidious distinction between history and myth is itself ideological because he has not established it, he has merely assumed it. Whether we approve or not, myth is as real as history; language offers hospitality to both, with little show of favor to one more than the other. Neither of them is given by nature or arises spontaneously. Nor has Deane established that a consideration of Ireland in terms of class, economic development, and the like is ideologically innocent by comparison with discriminations in terms of caste and race which are ideologically guilty. Deane is reading "Ancestral Houses" as if it were an editorial in a newspaper.

Besides, there are indeed human experiences of which the appropriate account is not historical but mythological. I am persuaded by Northrop

Frye to distinguish between mythology and ideology in this respect. An ideology, he says, "expresses secondary and derivative human concerns": ideologies are derived from mythology, "which expresses the primary desires of existence, along with the anxieties attached to their frustration."[5] The ground of the distinction is biological, it is based upon one's bodily form and its relation to the earth; upon a metabiology rather than a metaphysic, to invoke a distinction by Kenneth Burke. Mythology, in Frye's sense, doesn't float free of history, it may be verified upon historically acceptable evidence at any moment. But it calls, too, for a description which recognizes the primordial character of the experiences it expresses. "Ancestral Houses" posits a certain primordial mode of experience, which Yeats regards as analogous to an organic sequence— birth, growth, maturity, decay, death—which, he is hardly obliged to prove, may be verified by recourse to historical evidence. I can't see that Yeats's rhetorical position in this poem is more vulnerable than Deane's or mine.

IV

My second witness is Fredric Jameson, a critic for whom a political passion provides every incentive, literature, film, and architecture providing the occasions of acting upon it. In his essay on *Ulysses*, his study of Wyndham Lewis, and *The Political Unconscious*, Jameson has developed a theory of Modernism according to which many of the received works of modern literature constitute only a scandal. Briefly, he argues that Anglo-American modernism has been dominated by an impressionistic aesthetic:

> The most influential formal impulses of canonical modernism have been strategies of inwardness, which set out to reappropriate an alienated universe by transforming it into personal styles and private languages: such wills to style have seemed in retrospect to reconfirm the very privatization and fragmentation of social life against which they meant to protest.[6]

The modernist strategy issues from Symbolism, which Jameson regards as featuring "the illicit transformation of existing things into so many visible or tangible meanings."[7] Illicit, because the transformation surreptitiously brings into a single act of perception the experienced and the intelligible. Any work of literature, therefore, that is founded upon Symbolism is to be rejected, since it offers to turn a predicament into a privilege, it provides an otherwise alienated reader with an unquestionable recourse to his own privacy and subjectivity, and encourages him to feel that his truth is to be found and enjoyed there. In *Ulysses*, whatever Bloom encounters is mediated through his subjectivity, and the whole is "unified by the stylistic tone in which all contradictions are ironically resolved as well as by the overall unity of Bloom's personality." So "the Joycean phantasmagoria, even in the Nighttown chapter, serves to reconfirm the unity of the psyche, and to reinvent that depth-psychological perspective from which these private fantasies spring."[8] Joyce has played into the hands of the enemy; he has given his reader the consolation prize of a restored subjectivity.

Jameson's reading of *Ulysses*, to go no further than that book, is disabled by his insistence that literature will serve a political cause: what the cause is, it makes no theoretical difference to specify. Jameson's immediate authority for his rejection of Symbolism, I would guess, is the passage in *The Origin of German Tragic Drama* where Benjamin juxtaposes the allegorical and the symbolic ways of seeing, much to the moral advantage of allegory:

> Whereas in the symbol, destruction is idealized and the transfigured face of nature is fleetingly revealed in the light of redemption, in allegory the observer is confronted with the *facies hippocratica* of history as a petrified, primordial landscape. Everything about history that, from the very beginning, has been untimely, sorrowful, unsuccessful, is expressed in a face—or rather, in a death's head. And although such a thing lacks all "symbolic" freedom of expression, all classical proportion, all humanity—nevertheless, this is the form in which man's subjection to nature is most obvious and it significantly gives rise not only to the enigmatic question of the nature of human existence as such, but also of the biographical historicity of the individual.[9]

(I might note that "hippocratica" denotes the livid, shrunken image of the body, immediately before death; it is so named because Hippocrates was the first to describe it.) It follows from Benjamin's invidious meditation on allegory and symbol that the moral superiority of the allegorical vision consists in its refusal of comfort, redemption, and unity: according to Benjamin, the occasional felicities of man in nature are specious, anthropomorphic delusions, to be set aside by a relentless sense of history as death. Allegory testifies to a refusal to be appeased, it resents every token of unity, the seeming conjunction of existence and meaning. Jameson contrasts *Ulysses* with *The Childermass*, much to the advantage of the latter; because Lewis refuses to be comforted, seeks the dispersal rather than the unification of subjectivity, takes precaution against homogeneity of tone, "composes by phrase, by larger word-units drawn from various sources which are never completely subdued and mastered by the overall form of the sentence itself."[10]

Jameson's comparison of Joyce and Lewis serves a political purpose. It doesn't matter that Lewis's own political attitudes were flagrantly Right. What matters is that he devised a style which refuses to conspire with personality, subjectivity, homogeneity. The resentment which is the most evident feature of his common style can be dealt with later: for the moment, Jameson can produce him as the *facies hippocratica* of a modern literature otherwise rotten with inwardness and its consolations.

V

My objection to such procedures as those I have recited from Deane and Jameson would be just as severe if they served another political cause: in any case, they compromise the literature they read by subjecting it to a test of good behavior. They defeat the literature in advance. But the question now arises: what form would a serious engagement with literature take, if not a political form which turned it into propaganda?

In approaching an answer, I disclaim any originality for it by alluding to its constituents, these being the work of other hands. I merely bring the pieces together to suggest a programme all the better for its slightness.

I begin with a passage from "Yeats and the Language of Symbolism", where Frye distinguishes between the natural man and poetic man:

> Once a poet finds his mask, and it becomes the outward form of his creative life, it loses all real connection with his natural life . . . The poet,

by presenting us with a vision of nobility and heroism, detaches that vision from our ordinary lives. He thus works in a direction exactly opposite to that of the political leader who insists on trying to attach it, and so perverts its nature, as fascism perverted the Nietzschean gospel of heroic virtue into the most monstrous negation of it that the world has ever seen... The artist, of course, is always, like Narcissus, apt to become enamored with the reflecting illusion of his own mask. Yeats himself did not possess every kind of high intelligence, and some affectations resulting from a pedantic streak in his make-up led him into a certain amount of social and political dithering. But for all that we should not be too quick to plaster a fascist label on Yeats's myth merely because a conspiracy of thugs happened to debase that myth instead of some other one... Poetic symbolism is language and not truth, a means of expression and not a body of doctrine, not something to look at but something to look and speak through, a dramatic mask. "The poet", said Sir Philip Sidney, "never affirmeth"; when he does affirm, he not only ceases to be a poet, but is as likely to be wrong as anyone else.[11]

I assume that when a poet affirms, in Frye's sense or Sidney's, he voids the distinction which Hegel makes, in the *Encyclopedia of Philosophical Sciences*, between Imagination and Reason: "Imagination . . . is reason, but only a nominal reason, because the matter or theme it embodies is to imagination *qua* imagination a matter of indifference; while reason *qua* reason also insists upon the truth of its content." (Section 457).

This implies—and it leads me to the second constituent, a passage from Frank Kermode's *The Sense of an Ending*—that a poet does well to remain among his fictions, and to regard them as "heuristic and dispensable."[12] A myth, in Kermode's sense but not in Frye's, is a fiction which has congealed because the poet has forgotten that it is a fiction and proposes to put it into practice as if it were true. *King Lear* is a fiction, anti-Semitism is a myth. Kermode aptly quotes Sartre's observation that "the final aim of art is to reclaim the world by revealing it as it is, but as if it had its source in human liberty." The "as if" is the grace note that prevents a poet's fictions from becoming myths.

The third constituent is clearly compatible with Frye and Kermode; it is a composite factor, a motive common to Ernst Bloch's *The Spirit of Utopia* and Herbert Marcuse's *The Aesthetic Dimension*. Bloch defends modern art and literature by saying that they represent the future of mankind by expressing mankind's desires, especially the desire for freedom. Bloch's work is a philosophy of hope, of futurity, of Utopia, a stirring of possibility. Marcuse is more specific. "By virtue of its aesthetic form," he maintains, "art is largely autonomous vis-à-vis the given social relations." Literature can be called revolutionary "only with reference to itself, as content having become form." Indeed, the political potential of art lies only in its own aesthetic dimension: its relation to *praxis* is inexorably indirect, mediated, and frustrating. Marcuse goes further to say something which must be a scandal to such readers as Deane and Jameson, that when the subjectivity of individuals is dissolved into class consciousness, a major prerequisite of revolution is minimized, namely, the fact that the need for radical change must be rooted in the subjectivity of individuals themselves. Marxist theory was mistaken, according to Marcuse, in interpreting subjectivity as a bourgeois notion:

> But even in bourgeois society, insistence on the truth and right of inwardness is not really a bourgeois value. With the affirmation of the inwardness of subjectivity, the individual steps out of the network of exchange relationships and exchange values, withdraws from the reality of bourgeois society, and enters another dimension of existence. Liberating subjectivity constitutes itself in the inner history of the individuals—their own history, which is not identical with their social existence.

The scandal is not yet complete. Marcuse goes on to defend "art for art's sake" "inasmuch as the aesthetic form reveals tabooed and repressed dimensions of reality: aspects of liberation." The domain of art is the freedom of inwardness and subjectivity. This freedom is not, Marcuse says, illusory, it is just as real as the public reality it contradicts. "Art breaks open a dimension inaccessible to other experience, a dimension in which human beings, nature, and things no longer stand under the law of the established reality principle." But this does not mean that the world according to art is a fantasy or an illusion; it is that of another 'reality principle', of estrangement "and only as estrangement does art fulfill a cognitive function: it communicates truths not communicable in any other language; it contradicts."

When Marcuse encourages us to believe that "a work of art is authentic or true not by virtue of its content [i.e. the "correct" representation of social conditions], nor by its 'pure' form, but by the content having become form,"[13] one is impelled to say to a politically-minded reader—Deane, Jameson,—that his reading is at best incomplete. Incomplete, unless it eventuates in an aesthetic judgment, a judgment of the particular work of art as "content having become form."

The only remaining constituent I see as necessary is a certain capacity in the reader: imagination. It is a sufficient justification of art that it enables us to imagine experiences which we have not had, and to participate in those experiences within the accepted limits of form. It offers us the possibility of complete knowledge of the work in question, by comparison with the partial knowledge which is the most we can practice in our ordinary lives.

Is there a clear objection to this programme, apart from the obvious objection issuing from propagandists who lay violent hands upon the work of art on behalf of a political aim? The only one I have found is in Paul de Man's Introduction to Hans Robert Jauss's *Toward an Aesthetics of Reception*. As in his "Hegel on the Sublime", de Man repudiates "any valorization of aesthetic categories at the expense of intellectual rigor or political action, or any claim for the autonomy of aesthetic experience as a self-enclosed, self-reflexive totality."[14] I am content with that; especially in a work of literature, where the saving commonness of language, the heterogeneity of every work, makes the dream of totality and self-enclosure absurd. In the Introduction to Jauss, de Man argues against any "concatenation of the aesthetic with meaning-producing powers of language." The aesthetic, he says, is by definition a seductive notion "that appeals to the pleasure principle, a eudaemonic judgment that can displace and conceal values of truth and falsehood likely to be more resilient to desire than values of pleasure and pain." It is strange to find de Man saying this, since according to his normal view, all such values are merely different functions of language, they have no independent character. But in any case de Man brushes the aesthetic category aside; aesthetic reactions are interesting only as symptoms. "Whenever the aesthetic is invoked as an appeal to clarity and control, whenever, in other words, a symptom is made into a remedy for the disorder that it signals, a great deal of caution is in order."

But de Man's idea of the aesthetic is specious. "It is impossible to conceive of an aesthetic judgment that would not be dependent on imitation as a constitutive category," he claims. Why? Because the easiest notion of form is that of a visible object; and the easiest notion of cognition is the apprehension of such an object? De Man refers to "Hegel's massively misunderstood treatment of the aesthetic as a provisional (*vorlaufig*, a word that also occurs in Benjamin) form of cognition" and says that it is "entirely in the spirit of his continuators Kierkegaard and Nietzsche."[15] But it is not misunderstood if we relate it to the other activities I have invoked as constituents of an aesthetic stance: provisional cognition, nominal reason, the production of "consciously false" fictions, imagery of a future consonant with desire, and the antithetical cognitive function which Marcuse called estrangement or contradiction.

VI

I shall make a few remarks about "Ancestral Houses", since Deane has given it a distinctly ideological reading. Not that I think it a superior poem; by Yeats's standards, it is somewhat flaccid, and in that character best taken as the dispirited beginning of a series of meditations, in the last and best of which Yeats shakes himself out of a weary mood by thinking of "eyes that rage has brightened." It will be clear that Deane and I differ in our readings of the poem. Where he is scandalized by Yeats's movement from bad history to no-history-at-all, I read the poem as expressing one of Yeats's recurrent moods, his worry that the next phase of history may not be the antithetical one he prophesied and longed for; it may continue to be the primary culture he partly despises, partly fears, the Christian culture of meekness, the common man, democracy. Great men, out of phase, may be brought low by the common herd.

We have a poem in five stanzas, eight iambic pentameter lines each, end-rhyming strictly in the sequence abababcc. Each stanza coincides with a long, complex sentence, although a repeated phrase at the beginning of the second—"Mere dreams, mere dreams!"—postpones its sentence for a moment. It is possible to follow Harold Bloom in taking the poem as sardonic on the whole, as if Yeats were scorning the aristocrats for not holding on to their possessions. But that interpretation ignores the degree to which Yeats recognizes the satisfactions—the sweetness, the gentleness—which also mark the defeat of once-great men.

The first stanza invokes the familiar Romantic contrast between organic and mechanic form. The distinction is most readily found in Coleridge, but its imagery comes from Shelley and Blake; from Shelley, to whom water was the great symbol of existence, according to Yeats's "The Philosophy of Shelley's Poetry"; and from Blake, who says in *The Marriage of Heaven and Hell* that "the cistern contains: the fountain overflows." In "The Philosophy of Shelley's Poetry", again, Yeats refers to Blake, "who was always praising energy, and all exalted overflowing of oneself." It is decent of Yeats to ascribe to the rich man the powers to be admired: at least he doesn't suggest that anyone might have them merely by taking thought. The stanza is a reply to Yeats's "Adam's Curse"; it makes no bones about the exhilarating conjunction of power, inherited property, and genius, as if it might stave off the inevitable decay of beauty and other proud forms of achievement.

The second stanza begins with the most rueful concession—"Mere dreams . . ."—but it sets it aside at once by invoking Homer, Yeats's type of another conjunction, that of genius and the natural or unchristened heart, the poet of life itself with nothing but its own conviction in its favor. This stanza contains the first crisis; the fountain of life becomes "the abounding jet", but it is then given up, as if Homer were now defeated. The proper symbol, Yeats admits, is the "marvelous empty seashell." In *The Island of Statues* Colin addresses the shepherd boy:

Who art thou?—speak,
As the sea's furrows on a sea-tost shell,
Sad histories are lettered on thy cheek.

The sea-shell has been flung "out of the obscure dark of the rich streams", so it can speak with authority of everything it has been through, but now it can only recite its sad history, shadowing "the inherited glory of the rich." This stanza goes back not only to the worn shell of "Adam's Curse" but to every instance of greatness brought down.

In the third stanza, Yeats celebrates the Renaissance princes and the artists and architects they employed, and here a major disjunction is recognized, between the artists, "bitter and violent men", and the sweetness and gentleness of their creations. In "Ego Dominus Tuus" and *Per Amica Silentia Lunae* Yeats is fascinated by artists whose works are entirely different from themselves, by William Morris and by Landor, the latter a man of notable violence who "topped us all in calm nobility when the pen was in his hand." Or in the version of Landor which Yeats gives in *A Vision*: "The most violent of men, he uses his intellect to disengage a visionary image of perfect sanity...seen always in the most serene and classic art imaginable."[16]

This third stanza contains another crisis: a violent artist may produce works of surpassing gentleness, and satisfy that in us which longs to be appeased, but his master's power, in a generation or two, may lapse, his descendants decline into mice; it is a theme of several poems, including the next meditation of the sequence, and *Purgatory*.

The fourth and fifth stanzas brood upon the same fear, that these works of grace and beauty may domesticate our greatness as thoroughly as our violence and bitterness. The beauty Yeats celebrates is that of women, the gardens where they walk, their patron Juno:

> O what if gardens where the peacock strays
> With delicate feet upon old terraces,
> Or else all Juno from an urn displays
> Before the indifferent garden deities;

(I assume a "that" after "all"; meaning all the beauty and high spiritedness that the figure of Juno displays, attended by the peacocks sacred to her.) The sentence has to wait through three rather slack clauses before finding its verb, "take", in the last line; it is an extravagance of suspended revery, repeated with somewhat less risk to the grammar in the final stanza which anticipates a similar revery in "To Dorothy Wellesley". These beautiful women were always a danger to Yeats's syntax.

It is a well-recognized mark of Yeats's rhetorical power that it can turn into terms of praise many words normally held for rebuke: violent, bitter, haughty, and in many societies "rich". Much of this effect is achieved in "Ancestral Houses" by setting up a concatenation of values which go together only when compelled to do so; the attachment of "life", the

Blakeian imagery of flowing fountains, and the greatness commonly ascribed, in Pound as in Yeats, to Renaissance patrons of the arts who happened otherwise to be monsters. Yeats's word "greatness" forces us to acknowledge this concatenation as a single force, even though we would ordinarily want to distinguish its constituents along an unYeatsian system of values. Andrew Marvell's "Horatian Ode on Cromwell's Return from Ireland" makes it similarly difficult to dissent from the values he celebrates: active virtue—another equivocation—is ascribed to Cromwell, only aesthetic decorum to the defeated Charles.

Deane's reading of "Ancestral Houses" errs in two respects: it maintains that the poem takes leave of history or myth, and that it becomes meaningful only as an aspect of the "human condition." In fact, the poem doesn't even take leave of history; it refers vaguely but clearly enough to eighteenth century accomplishment—"a haughtier age" points in that direction, though there is no need to assume that Yeats meant Ascendancy Ireland, even though in "Blood and the Moon" the haughty man praised is Burke. The theme is the alleged decline of culture between the Augustan age and our own: the anomaly which gives the poem whatever life it has is the fact that the images which please our passivity are those, now long domesticated, which we have inherited from great and violent men.

More thoroughly than most other poets, Yeats knew that a vocabulary, a diction, incorporates a totalizing ambition. When we bring together a few cognate words, they think their kinship so compelling that they preen themselves and set out to take over the world. So much so, that by apt choice and repetition of such words it is easy to convey a conviction that this way of construing the world is ordained by natural law. Yeats recited his high words so imperiously that his poems nearly prescribe a way of being in the world; like a cavalry officer, assured of rank, dignity, and power. The experience of reading any of these central poems is one of imagining a world other than one's own, and assenting to it at least provisionally, and holding back from it, swaying while the reading lasts between assent and refusal. If Jameson retorts that such an experience merely gulls the reader into thinking that he is acting out his freedom in the presence of the poem, I would defend the reader's freedom precisely by not claiming that it is absolute. It is a conditional felicity, and I would reduce every extravagant claim made on its behalf and then speak up for the value as so reduced.

As for the "human condition": it is a reasonable merit to ask of a poem that it spill over from its local circumstances and speak of the universal fate of being human. We value Donne's poems, and Shakespeare's, and Hardy's because, whatever the local circumstances which provoked them, they transcend that origin and speak beyond their occasion. Besides, to read "Ancestral Houses" uninvidiously, which on the present occasion means unideologically, it is only necessary to imagine what it would be like to be different, to feel differently, to have the experience of living by another system of values, according to which it would not be sufficient to deem Yeats's word "greatness" to amount to nothing more than monstrous behaviors. Once we receive it as an imagined experience, we are free to discard every piece of merely local evidence in its favor: it is not necessary to remain infatuated with the greatness of a Renaissance prince. Deane's reading of the poem, like Jameson's reading of *Ulysses*, would ensure that these works are never read but censored in advance.

VII

I revert to the dispute between Ransom and Blackmur, and remark that Ransom thought it serious enough to conclude it by saying that "there are substantive as well as formal values" in a poem, just as in a novel where their existence is generally admitted. Ransom did not mention that in writing about T. S. Eliot's criticism, Blackmur had been more specific in defining the several relations between thought, experience, belief, feeling, and emotion; so that in Eliot's context rather than in Yeats's, Blackmur's notion of "doctrine presented as emotion" becomes clear. It is hardly surprising that Blackmur ascribed to Eliot a programme much the same as his own. What Eliot did was simple, according to Blackmur: "he excluded thought *as such* from poetry and said that poetry dealt with the experience or feeling of thought which might or might not—probably *not*—have been the poet's thought; and similarly he said that poetry dealt with belief as the experience or feeling of belief which probably had to be, from the nature of belief, the poet's own belief."[17] A page or two later

Blackmur gave working definitions of feeling and emotion. Feeling "is the fundamental term: concrete, sensory, nuclear, somehow in experience, whether actual or imagined, always particular." Emotion is "feelings organized by a force whether within or without the psyche: emotion is feelings, organized, generalized, abstracted, built into a form, theoretic or not." Ad libbing between the words, we can say that doctrine presented as emotion may be translated now to read: an apparently systematic body of ideas, presented so far as they are feelings, which in superior poems is far enough. The feelings in the case are sufficiently organized, the writing of the poem is the mode of organizing them within the constraints of language. Otherwise put in Blackmur's terms: emotion is the theoretic form of feelings which, lacking that form, are disordered and personal beyond communicative redemption. Blackmur says of the theoretic form, the emotion, that it is good only in that instance; which I take to mean that the defect of an idea is that it claims to be good in any and every instance. This is Deane's error, and Jameson's; that having arrived at an idea—a political stance, a position which can only be reasserted since its history as an idea is already complete—they insist on its being good in every instance.

So the question to ask about "Ancestral Houses" is not: do I find its political attitude congenial? but rather: am I willing to read it, and to let it at least provisionally read me? If I am willing to read it in that spirit, I suspend for the time being not my disbelief but my economy, the nearly automatic dispositions of attitude I for the most part practice. It is vain to read a poem unless we are on every occasion willing to ask ourselves: what would it be like to be different?

The best reader is not the one who murmurs to himself, "I have seen what I have seen, see what I see!", but the one who says to the poem: "Help me to feel what you have felt."

Notes

[1] John Crowe Ransom, "More than Gesture" *Partisan Review*, January-February 1953: reprinted in his *Poems and Essays* (New York: Vintage Books, 1955), p. 104.
[2] R. P. Blackmur, *Form and Value in Modern Poetry* (Garden City, New York: Doubleday Anchor Books, 1957), p 58.
[3] Seamus Deane, *Celtic Revivals* (London: Faber and Faber, 1985), p. 33

[4] Seamus Deane, "Heroic Styles: The Tradition of an Idea" (Derry: A Field Day Pamphlet, No. 4, 1984), p.6.

[5] Northrop Frye, "In the Earth, or in the Air?" *Times Literary Supplement*, January 17, 1986, p. 52.

[6] Fredric Jameson, *Fables of Aggression* (Berkeley: University of California Press, 1979), p.2.

[7] Fredric Jameson, "*Ulysses* in History" in W.J. McCormack and Alistair Stead (eds), *James Joyce and Modern Literature* (London: Routledge and Kegan Paul, 1982), p. 129.

[8] Jameson, *Fables of Aggression*, p. 57.

[9] Walter Benjamin, *The Origin of German Tragic Drama*, tr. John Osborne (London: NLB, 1977), p. 166.

[10] Fredric Jameson, 'Wyndham Lewis as Futurist" *The Hudson Review*, July 1973, p. 318.

[11] Northrop Frye, *Fables of Identity* (New York: Harcourt, Brace and World, 1963), p. 238.

[12] Frank Kermode, *The Sense of an Ending* (New York: Oxford University Press, 1967), p. 145.

[13] Herbert Marcuse, *The Aesthetic Dimension* (London: Macmillan, 1979), pp. ix, xii, 4, 19, 72, 10, 8.

[14] Paul de Man, "Hegel on the Sublime'' in Mark Krupnick (ed.), *Displacements: Derrida and After* (Bloomington: Indiana University Press, 1983), p. 141.

[15] Paul de Man, *The Resistance to Theory* (Minneapolis: University of Minnesota Press, 1986), pp. 64, 66.

[16] W. B. Yeats, *A Vision* (London: Macmillan, 1962), pp. 144-5.

[17] R. P. Blackmur, *The Lion and the Honeycomb* (London: Methuen, 1956), pp. 169, 172.

VI
Intellectuals

The Responsibility of Intellectuals: A Discussion[1]

WITH GEORGE STEINER, CONOR CRUISE O'BRIEN
LESZEK KOLAKOWSKI, ROBERT BOYERS

BOYERS: The American sociologist, Philip Rieff, has written very instructively about the shifting character structure or ideal of the intellectual. Twenty years ago, in *The Triumph of the Therapeutic*, he wrote that "many intellectuals have gone over to the enemy without realizing that those they still considered the cultural elite have actually become spokesmen for what Freud called 'the instinctual mass.' " What sort of character ideal do you think is implicit in Rieff's sense of the intellectual? Do you agree that something more or less sacred has been traduced as the intellectual has become a recognizable contemporary social type?

STEINER: I think any human being probably will try to live his life, if he can at all, in harmony with his inner convictions. Most of us cannot quite do it; we try. But the intellectual has a very special task. He belongs, we belong, to the most spoiled caste in mandarin history. Very often today the intellectual is rewarded for his passions, for his obsessions beyond what most of us certainly might have hoped. And that means that he must really try and live what he professes. For example, to be sitting in opulent safety in some rewarded university chair and make oneself a spokesman for terrorism in a far part of the earth is contemptible. It's sheer cant. For my part, I teach, or try to teach, and live by, the masters, the great texts, the philosophic traditions, the things handed on to us. And to do this while deriving every privilege—and what's much more important, every discipline of ecstasy, of inner joy—from one's position, and then to mouth egalitarian or radical or populist slogans, to attempt to run with the wolves of Philistinism as did so many in '68 and '69 is, I think, suicidal. So, I would interpret Rieff's remark as saying, "have the pride of being what you are." That's how I would understand it, and would certainly concur with it.

BOYERS: Leszek, would you care to speak to this point as well?

KOLAKOWSKI: Intellectuals are often subject to a special psychological phenomenon, reflecting the fact that they are torn asunder between incompatible desires or attitudes. On the one hand, they are proud of their superiority and independence. On the other hand, this very feeling of independence they are so proud of produces in them a kind of uncertainty about where they belong. There is, of course, in every human being, a need to belong somewhere. And this is one of the reasons why it is relatively easy for intellectuals to identify themselves in a cerebral way with the cause of the people while keeping their feelings of superiority intact. In other words, they want to belong to an elite which doesn't have ordinary needs, but they suffer at the same time because of this very feeling of aloofness and isolation. The best way of escaping from this dilemma is precisely the cerebral identification with the cause of the underdogs. Marxism is the best way of expressing this conflict, of reconciling at least partly these contradictory feelings. Another tendency common to intellectuals is their constant and desperate search for their own legitimacy. After all, nobody asks what the plumbers are for or what the physicians are for, but the question what are intellectuals for is quite natural and understandable. And it is intellectuals who put this question incessantly. They hope eventually to find a kind of social legitimacy which they feel they lack. The other problem is that the intellectual wants to be heard, and the only institutional guarantee that an intellectual can be heard is for him to become part of a totalitarian establishment. This explains why so many intellectuals long to be court thinkers or court philosophers in a totalitarian system which provides certain comforts, and which guarantees at least a hearing to loyal intellectual servants, no matter what the ultimate result may be.

Many of those who are with us here are certainly acquainted with the memoirs of Nadezhda Mandelstam, which provide extremely instructive reading for all intellectuals. From these memoirs we can see how the Russian intelligentsia was itself partly guilty of its own destruction. Various schools in literature vied with each other for recognition by the despotic Communist government in order to eliminate their rivals. And this rivalry eventually gave the despots an extremely convenient tool with which to tame, or domesticate, and eventually destroy Russian culture. Behind this phenomenon we perhaps can discern the contradictory feelings and desires we've noted, both to be in the elite and to be on the side of the underdogs, to be independent and to be acclaimed a herald of reason and a prophet to the people. Incompatible demands, but characteristic, perhaps, of this class.

In the anti-Americanism of many European intellectuals you can see precisely a dimension of this attitude. Think of the Frankfurt School thinkers' hatred of America. These people came from German universities and found themselves in the United States, in a world where intellectuals or professors are not considered demi-gods, but just workers like anybody else. In addition, they found a culture where anybody can buy for very little money a record with the best music, whereas, previously, concerts had been a privilege of the elite. They hated, really, democracy in America—not the various democratic institutions themselves, but the democratic spirit and its effect on daily life. The situation was unacceptable to them. And so you see how this feeling of an outraged elite expressed itself paradoxically in semi-Marxist, semi-Revolutionary ideology which contained a great many confusions and contradictions.

BOYERS: Conor, in a useful, but irritating book called *Political Pilgrims*, a sociologist named Paul Hollander studies the attraction of Western intellectuals to various tyrannical regimes in Cuba, China, the Soviet Union, and elsewhere. Hollander's intellectual visitors to places like Cuba and North Vietnam saw, he claims, what they wanted to see, and typically perceived, above all, a radiant sense of community, a rejection of alienation, social isolation, and so on. Are intellectuals more peculiarly susceptible to the sort of illusion described by Hollander than other citizens? And, if they are, mightn't the case be made that the illusion has not been limited in the way Hollander proposes?

O'BRIEN: I'd like to make several points in response to this. One is that all the examples given by Hollander are of Left wing regimes about which intellectuals certainly have had illusions, but I think it would be misleading to suppose the insight applies only to the Left wing. Think of Ezra Pound, W. B. Yeats and T. S. Eliot who, in different degrees, but in similar ways, were attracted to Fascist or Rightist regimes. Ezra Pound was, as we know, right to the end with Mussolini. I think that intellectuals are probably more likely to con themselves and one another about extreme regimes than other people are. We are, all of us participating in a meeting like this, more used to inhabiting constructions of the mind than other people are. We are therefore more prone to the temptation of believing in the realization on earth of our constructs than others are. Utopia is, after all, a fiction. We are inclined to create fictions and then to believe that they have actually happened, whereas more down to earth people are probably more aware. You know, if there had been trade unionists that had gone along with the Webbs to the Soviet Union in the 1930's, they probably would have thought, "it's not so great; it's rather bloody awful." That truth ordinary, sensible persons would have seen. But the Webbs didn't see; they got worked up in their heads about a cause.

But I'd like also to make a couple of related points, drawing a little on Christopher Lasch's very useful typology which he elaborated at the beginning of our proceedings. He distinguished between the intellectual as the voice of reason and the intellectual as the voice of conscience, referring also to a third category which doesn't so easily lend itself to summary and which I'll avoid for now. I do want to talk about the important contrast between the voice of reason and the voice of conscience. Christopher Lasch didn't find it necessary to say about this what may be too obvious to need saying. But I like making points that are so obvious that people sometimes forget they are there. Sometimes I think that's my main function in life. The obvious point is this: that if an intellectual says that he is the voice of reason or that he is the voice of conscience, he isn't necessarily either one, and in fact can't be either. I am not, please, at all suggesting that Christopher Lasch meant that an intellectual could actually be these things. He is far too sensible to mean anything of the kind. But—to make another obvious point in relation to what is obvious—an intellectual may well aspire to being one of these things or both of these things, and that's fine. When an intellectual sets out to be the voice of reason (and why should he not aspire? I aspire, slightly), he is at the same time a fallible human being, and that's a limitation on his being a voice of reason. When an intellectual sets out to be a voice of conscience, he must know that he is at the same time a sinner, and that's a limitation on his being a voice of conscience. Now there may be children of the Enlightenment in this room (I am a kind of step-child of the Enlightenment myself), who say, "sin, what's that?" I don't quite know what sin is, but I do know a little about what greed is, what ambition is, what rapacity is, what cruelty is, and I have never been convinced that intellectuals are more immune to these infections than other people. So, limitations of sin and fallibilty are there, and we can't ignore them when we set about defining what we do and what we're good for.

It's also necessary to remember that even good evidence may not satisfy those who listen to the intellectual as voice of reason. I come forward, George comes forward, Leszek comes forward, each a voice of reason. We present our arguments, we set out our evidence, and you can say, "I don't believe that evidence; it's contradicted by this, by that, and furthermore, in your reasoning from such evidence there is a fallacy." And then we, voices of reason, have to answer you. The cards at least are face up on the table when the intellectual is acting, or endeavoring, quixotically, to act as the voice of reason. On the other hand, if one of us comes forward saying, "I am the voice of conscience," you will have a much harder time testing what we are saying. I say I am moved by profound compassion for the third world. Very possibly I am and very possibly I am not. You have no way whatever of knowing which it is or what I would do if you were to entrust me with power. Pol Pot was spilling with compassion for the Third World before he came into power in Cambodia and enacted the most bloody regime we have seen since the death of Adolf Hitler. Pol Pot was a Western Intellectual, and he was widely accepted, but there was no means of testing his integrity.

Either way, it seems to me that if an intellectual addresses you, whether as the voice of reason or the voice of conscience, you must challenge him. There was a phrase which David Ben-Gurion had, which he used about the United States, about their political intentions. He said, "Respect, but suspect." I would suggest that would be a good principle to apply to the intellectual generally: Respect but suspect.

KOLAKOWSKI: May I make a short comment here? What you've said, of course, is true; both so-called Left and so-called Right regimes were very attractive to many intellectuals. Nevertheless, the attraction of the so-called Left despotic regimes was incomparably greater, and there were reasons, probably, for that. People like Ezra Pound or Heidegger, who became at a certain moment spokesmen for fascist ideology, were rather exceptional, whereas praisers of Stalinism, even at the peak of its horror, were very common. I remember that just after the death of Heidegger, there appeared posthumously a long interview with him in *Der Spiegel* and, curiously enough, he did not, in fact, repudiate his earlier convictions. He tried to explain away his commitment of the thirties by alluding to political circumstance. When asked about his attacks on academic freedom he said, "No, it was perfectly alright what I said then because it was a matter of purely negative freedom." As if there were any other freedom but negative! And so, in fact, he seemed to have basically retained his intellectual approval of tyranny. Even so, perhaps he was not ready to admit that he still thought he was right in supporting Hitler.

But is there a very big difference between commitment to Rightist or Leftist despotic regimes? They do differ, of course, in many ways. One German historian whose name escapes me at the moment said that the war between the Soviet Union and Germany can be seen as a dispute between Left Hegelians and Right Hegelians. A horrifying homage paid to philosophy.

STEINER: I think I would like to protest a little against this note of cynicism. I think that for a very long time, certainly since the Bolshevik

Revolution, there has been a characteristic movement of hope among intellectuals. Intellectuals have needed, for no base motives, but rather for very essential reasons, windows on hope. The windows opened, in turn, have been many. They were the Bolshevik Revolution for many, at other points they were the Prague Spring, the Dubcek regime, for others Cuba, for others the Chile of Allende. Postfacto, each time, it is very easy to say what a bloody fool one was; it was foreseeably going to end in catastrophe and tyranny and corruption. It is very easy to say "Really! How could one have been taken in again!" As it happens, personally being of an entirely stoical and pessimistic and perhaps anti-democratic conviction, I did not harbor any false hopes. But I am not proud of that; I am ashamed. What really interests me is now, what is to be the quality of thinking, the epistemology of thought if there are no more windows, if we are now (and I would argue that, almost for the first time certainly since 1789, we are indeed) in the midst of a situation where you are taken for a damn fool if you invest in such hope? Let's get down to concrete cases. Suppose your student comes to you, as mine have, as they must have to you, and says, "They're burying people alive in San Salvador. I can't bear it any more. I am a human being; I've got to do something," as did students whose notes we found in Cambridge (in England), saying, "Have gone to Prague," whose fathers had perhaps gone to Spain leaving similar messages behind. Now what do you do when someone comes to you and says "I know that if I go on the Left, it will end up, if we win, in Stalinist thuggery of the worst kind; it will end up in murder, in slave camps. And if I go on the Right it will end up in one more fascist colonel or generalissimo or whatever. It's no use, is it?" Does one now say it is our obligation to grow up by accepting a Freudian reality principle? By accepting that there is no choice in such situations because whichever side wins it will all end up in some kind of horror? Does one say, as we are trained to do by our profession, "Look, we need nuance, we need detail, we need relative comparisons. There are horrors and horrors"? "Bliss was it that dawn to be alive," said Wordsworth of the French Revolution.

O'BRIEN: And recanted shortly after.

STEINER: And recanted, and then ended writing sonnets on behalf of capital punishment. They also happened to be lousy poetry. So the question is a very real one. I don't know how one operates without certain errors. The errata of conscience, the mistakes one makes, are very often the ennobling ones, and I will now put my fate in Leszek's hands on something which we have both thought about a great, great deal. I was only a student in Paris on one of the big Sartre evenings, a long time ago. It was the time of the David Rousset libel action in regard to Soviet labor camps.

Sartre, about whom I know every doubt is allowed (I still think he is one of the master presences of our century), said, "I want to make a distinction. Suppose it's all true, about the Gulag." Of course he knew by that time; one knew since Borkenau; one knew even before Borkenau if one wanted to know. One didn't need . . .

KOLAKOWSKI: Weisberg.

STEINER: Yes, Weisberg. And even earlier. Sartre said, "Alright. Suppose it's all true. There are two possible reactions for a human being. One is to say 'Ha! I told you so. What a fool you were to expect otherwise. How much easier it is for you and me now that we know.' The other reaction is to say, 'Damn it to hell! One more great human hope gone to bits.'" And he said, "Ontologically, they are not the same reaction." Now I know there is everything to be said against him, but I remember this. I still want to bear that remark in mind and worry about it and think about it and try to analyse the difference between the two reactions. And in doing so, here, I find myself suddenly in a most surprising position between two great lions of the Right. So, about the Hollander remark, with which we began these reflections, I would like briefly to ask: what do we do if there are no more mistakes of hope to be made?

O'BRIEN: Can I ask you a question? You said let's be more concrete. We have known each other for quite some time. We have crossed swords, we have always respected one another; we have a relationship going back a while. Now, during the Viet Nam War, as you remember, I was in a mild version of the protest movement. I used to sit down in various places. I occasionally got booted by an Irish cop or whatever. No great martyrdom, no big deal, I agree, but I was in the business of protesting against that war. And George, you at that time were not against the war. We have now transposed our positions. I think that's true; do you agree?

STEINER: Yes.

O'BRIEN: I have moved perceptibly to the Right; George has moved towards something that appears to be the Left. (Laughter from the audience.) It may not appear to other people to be the Left, but it appears so to me! What do you think, George, about your attitude towards that war at that time?

STEINER: I still believe that, corrupt as it was, the regime in South Viet Nam was preferable to the tyranny and extermination that would come from the North. I have never thought of Viet Nam as a window of hope. But if we were now to bring the conversation around to American intervention elsewhere in the world, if we were to put the problem of Central America on the table, Conor, between us . . .

O'BRIEN: I don't think we'd differ.

STEINER: I don't think we'd differ either. So that, of course, one must look at each case. But I was hoping also that you, Leszek, would help on the other point. The point is that there are differences of disappointment, or there are different ways of saying one should always have known, or one was a fool to hope.

KOLAKOWSKI: Yes. I do not deny at all that many people have been drawn to this or that historical experience, which proved so disastrous and disappointing, for good reasons. However, there are distinctions to be made here, for example, between intellectuals who joined the Bolshevik Revolution enthusiastically, in good faith, with great hopes, against the forces of evil, against something which they rightly might have thought was wrong, and people who are so trained in self-deception that they cannot see anything wrong in lying to others. There is a difference between good faith and bad faith, between the commitment arising from naivete and errors and the commitment of people who, after decades of experience where everything could have been seen clearly, when there were many documents which they simply refused to see, to read, or to believe, and continued (or even frequently began) their commitment to what was then an obvious, indubitable despotism of the worst kind. I mean there is a difference, say, between Mayakovsky and Aragon, because Aragon was a damn liar, and Mayakovsky was a man who committed himself to what he genuinely believed was a good cause, the cause of the oppressed, of the people, and perished of disappointment for this reason. And Sartre's 'ontological' distinction is good enough to serve as an excuse for the worst kind of commitment. He himself never, to my knowledge, analysed or recanted his own blunders.

STEINER: My dislike of Monsieur Aragon joins yours gratefully. But, again, if I have to define an intellectual: he is one who is constantly uncomfortable with his own ideas and assents. The point is, the same man in Crevecoeur in '40 and '41 wrote great poems of resistance, poems like "Je resterai roi de mes douleurs" or many others which were life-giving at the time. They were the voice of resistance. The same man who wrote those poems we condemn today; and that's an absolutely central part of our problem. I would still like to try and get your help, Leszek. How does thought work when the future tense has no Messianic quality? I took the liberty of asking you at dinner again about one of your books, not yet translated into English, a very fine book on the heretical churches of the seventeenth century, *Chretiens sans eglise*. This work deals specifically with this problem of chiliasm, with heresies of hope. What do we do when the negation principle asserts itself?

KOLAKOWSKI: Don't you think that there is a variety of hope which is within the limits of our resources? Because, after all, we live, and we have always lived, in a world which is full of horrors, and it is not unreasonable (it may even be constructive) to hope that something surprising will happen, that the world will perhaps be made better. Without this hope, perhaps we could not survive. There is, however, an apocalyptic hope of the kind preached by Ernst Bloch, implying that we have the technical tools to implement perfection. This hope, if practically pursued, necessarily ends with the simulation of perfection in the form of despotism. And I don't think there is another possibility. Therefore we cannot, we must not, blame hope as such. But I think we are right in blaming apocalyptic hope, that hope which suggests, either implicitly or explicitly, that we can master a special technique which will bring us a world of perfection.

O'BRIEN: Yes, I think this is very interesting. First of all, I think that to lay wreaths on the tomb of chiliasm or millenialism—call it what you like—is premature. That stuff is going to be around an awfully long time. It already has been around a long time. Were it dead, I would not mourn it; I would not. I would like to see human hopes a bit more humble, a bit more limited, a bit more rational. But I don't think they're going to be limited by anything I think about how rational they ought to be. This millenial thing is very deep. It's very deep, for example, as we know, in the history of this nation, and it's one of the binding features of America. It's at the core. It's knocking around in the back of Ronald Reagan's rhetoric. He doesn't quite know what's knocking about in the back of his head, but that's it. When he links God and Nation, he's in the direct tradition of the New England pulpits, raising up new children of Abraham, new Chosen People. That stuff is busting out all over, and some of us intellectuals are going to be carrying the fiery cross for it. And no doubt it is necessary that this be so. But I would like to keep my bottom in my chair and not rise up and not carry any fiery cross and not plug the Millenarian tradition or chiliasm or whatever, but be very interested in them and aware of their power.

STEINER: But it is, I think, a very new situation when there is no place which enlists the imagination. From the point of view of teaching, or education, a process which we are all in, for better or worse, it is highly problematic and perplexing that dreams have no—what Shakespeare called—'local habitation, and no name.' That is, in fact, when one thinks back about the many illusions one may have had about, say, Dubcek's Prague, one may feel a bit silly.

O'BRIEN: Yourself, George?

STEINER: Very well, I was there at the time, and it was rather marvelous. But in a situation where the best to be offered is a kind of very ironical self-deconstructive meliorism—and perhaps that is the best to be offered—I think certain philosophic problems—problems of how to teach, and problems of how to dream forward (yes, that is Ernst Bloch's phrase, "to dream forward") do arise, and they seem to me to spring out of the quotation from Hollander's book. One of the profound problems of intellectuals is their divorce even from the possibility of action. Not in Conor's case, but with most of us, there has been a divorce from action. And so these illusory voyages, the Voyage en Icarie. Plato did go to Syracuse several times.

O'BRIEN: And a right mess he made of it!

STEINER: That's right!

KOLAKOWSKI: I think the comparison between the illusions connected with the Prague Spring and the other cases you quoted is perhaps a little bit unjust. It was a process which did not degenerate into something opposite but was simply crushed. We cannot say with any certainty what might have developed if the new situation had been allowed to develop in the direction in which it started. It might have degenerated. But so far we are left with the so-called idea of socialism with a human face. To which we can add the soviet expression, "is it possible to have a crocodile with a human face?" Perhaps. Show me.

BOYERS: I would like to move our discussion in a slightly different though clearly related direction. In Milan Kundera's recent novel, *The Unbearable Lightness of Being*, one of the principle characters says, "My enemy is kitsch, not communism." Is this a sentiment attractive to many

Western intellectuals, so far as you can tell? And what validity do you ascribe to this idea that the enemy, in the West, as in the Soviet East, is kitsch?

O'BRIEN: I don't buy it at all as a categorization. First of all, it is far too limited: How can the enemy be some one thing in the world? It might be communism; it might be kitsch. I feel that the enemy is mainly in oneself, as religious people say, in one's own sinfulness.

STEINER: We have other enemies, Conor.

O'BRIEN: So you have. No, but I meant that to say "my enemy is one thing in the world"—kitsch or communism—is, frankly, childish.

KOLAKOWSKI: But I understand this in another way, that the implication, not explicitly stated, of such a saying is that communism is an example of kitsch, kitsch being an inept imitation of something good. Communism is an imitation of something good, but an imitation so ludicrous as to become its opposite. So it's possible to say I despise kitsch, therefore I despise communism. But, even so, I am not particularly enthusiastic about such a saying, because this implies that I despise Communism for aesthetic reasons. It is ugly, to be sure, but I wouldn't want to be associated with that attitude.

STEINER: I wonder of what capitalism is an imitation?

KOLAKOWSKI: What is it an imitation of? Well, that's quite a question. Please answer it.

O'BRIEN: It might be original—as in original sin.

STEINER: In which case we might do well to come back for a moment to the point about the Frankfurt School thinkers in America. Of course what they feared here most was not, in any simple sense, democratic institutions: it was kitsch. It was mass vulgarisation. They were very afraid of what lay ahead in what they took, rightly or wrongly, to be a mass media culture. They may have been wrong, but I think the question raised by Kundera was certainly important to Horkheimer and Adorno.

BOYERS: In *The Captive Mind*, which is now thirty years old, Czeslaw Milosz writes of *Ketman*, a term which stands for the condition of intellectual life in Eastern Europe under Soviet domination. "Life in constant tension," Milosz writes, "develops talents which are latent in man. He does not even suspect to what heights of cleverness and psychological perspicacity he can rise when he is cornered and must either be skillful or perish. The survival of those best adapted to mental acrobatics creates a human type that has been rare until now. The necessities which drive men to Ketman sharpen the intellect." Does this passage from *The Captive Mind* seem to you still persuasive? Does it in fact describe the difference between intellectuals who have lived in a place like Poland and most intellectuals who live in this country?

O'BRIEN: I think everybody in this room would first like to hear Leszek Kolakowski on this question.

KOLAKOWSKI: I should admit that it was many years ago that I read Milosz's book and I don't have it fresh in my memory. So it is somewhat difficult for me to comment on the book in detail. But I can speak briefly about the passage you just quoted, a passage in which Milosz stresses certain virtues, or rather beneficial results, of a regime which compels people to sharpen their minds in order to outwit or get around the various barriers which a despotic regime imposes. There is a truth in this, I would say, but a limited one. I don't think the insight is generally valid if the despotism goes beyond certain limits. I don't think that it is true of the Soviet Union where practically the entire inherited culture was ruthlessly crushed by physical extermination and the use of unspeakable terror. It is true that in Poland, in spite of various monstrosities, terror has never reached the Stalinist extreme. There it has always been somewhat easier to exercise the kind of ingenuity which of course might have led to something good. Of course it was not Milosz's intention to praise the

Polish Communist regime for the unintended good results which it might have brought about.

O'BRIEN: Does Milosz intend us to see the results as good? That's not clear to me. What he is saying is literally true: tough conditions sharpen the mind. We all know this is so . . .

KOLAKOWSKI: But not extermination camps.

O'BRIEN: Well, no. Tough conditions that you can survive, and survive with a bit of a margin, may produce a sharpening of the intellect. But is the human being equipped with an intellect sharpened to that degree and in that way a better type of human being than a human being whose intellect has not been sharpened in that way?

BOYERS: In *The Captive Mind,* Milosz describes a whole variety of intellectual figures to whom he assigns character types. In the course of the work he demonstrates again and again the deterioration of mind and spirit which is more or less inevitable for those forced to live over many years under such conditions.

O'BRIEN: The sharpening of the intellect goes hand in hand with the deterioration of character?

BOYERS: Exactly. Implicit in that particular kind of sharpening and the stresses associated with it is the progressive deterioration of character.

O'BRIEN: Yes, well that's what I rather suspected he did mean. Forgive me; it's been a long time since I read Milosz.

STEINER: In some way I think this is the central issue we have to face, and the one which probably divides us most deeply. Borges, remember, when urged to leave Argentina, at the time when they were closing in on him and he was in constant physical danger, said, "Don't be a fool, censorship and oppression are the mother of metaphor." Joyce, when questioned on the question of censorship and Catholic oppression—and Conor, correct me, if I've got the context wrong—said, "Squeeze us; we are olives." Asked to leave South Africa, Nadine Gordimer, whom I put very near the top of novelists now writing in the English language, has over and over again refused to leave. It is quite clear that it is not only for reasons of integrity that she wishes to stay, but that the very nature of her gifts depend on this situation. It is her very material. I lack Russian—I have to read it in translation—so I may be getting it all wrong. But I would say that Russian poetry from Akhmatova and Tsvetyeva, from Mandelstam to Brodsky has been an uninterrupted stream of great works possibly to be compared with that of classical Greek literature. What is coming from Eastern Germany, which I do see first hand, is so much superior to what is being produced in West Germany that it is almost embarrassing. What history will one day say about the literary stature of a Pasternak or a Solzhenitsyn or a Grossman (many put his big new novel, the latest of the giant samizdats, beside Pasternak and Tolstoy), I am not qualified to judge. I am a reader in translation. But again, coming out of some of the worst oppression we know, that of the Latin American police states, is a literature of astounding energy. Roughly—I stick my neck out the whole way—the KGB and I totally agree that the next essay on Hegel is the most vital and dangerous thing around. We concur on the danger of a great Russian phrase that is as old as Pushkin, if not older: the writer and thinker are the alternative state. The facts for me are manifest. We are an animal which when cornered becomes eloquent. Conor has written about it wonderfully in the context of the Irish situation. We know when a book, a poem makes all the difference. It was at the dawn of the Congress in '37 when Pasternak was told, "If you speak, we arrest you; if you don't speak we arrest you." For two days he said nothing. On the third day he rose, and he said a number. He only said a number, and then the audience got up and began reciting his translation, which in Russia is as classic as Pushkin, of Shakespeare's "When to the sessions of sweet silent thought/ I summon up remembrance of things past," in chorus. There is no danger there for great literature. None whatever! It is so safe as to overwhelm one, because it is breathing. It is an absolute bloody necessity: you die without it. God, look at our literature in free Britain. Mountains of trivia and pretentiousness! Now, if you say that the poems of Pasternak and Mandelstam are not worth the price, you may be completely right. If you say to me that what I'm really getting at is a peculiar character of a great oral/poetic civilization which Eastern Europe and parts of Latin America share, that may be true. But can you tell me what poem would matter in the United States?

KOLAKOWSKI: You know better than I do about this. I know nothing of poetry. But it is not a matter of choice for us. Nobody asks us what we would prefer: a tyranny in which great poets may possibly emerge, or a mild, hedonistic democratic society in which there is no great literature because there are no tragic conflicts to produce it.

STEINER: Borges could have left Argentina any time. Nadine Gordimer could leave South Africa tomorrow.

KOLAKOWSKI: Some can leave, yes. But I don't know of any example of a writer or intellectual who, for the sake of great literature, might have chosen to go and live under tyranny.

O'BRIEN: Nadine Gordimer, whom I respect greatly, is a very good writer indeed. But I can't accept your equating her situation with others living under tyranny—in Eastern Europe, for example. If she were here I'm sure she would not accept it either. Nor was, in my opinion, the position of Joyce in the Catholic Ireland of his day comparable. Joyce was nearly bored blind by the Irish of his day, and I don't blame him. His sight was not, in any case, very good. He chose what he called silence, exile and cunning. There was a lot of cunning, there was a lot of exile, and not very much silence. But okay, he made his choice. But the cases George has cited are not, in my opinion, all closely similar. I think it was a very remarkable statement that we have just heard from George, nevertheless, and I'm sure it's all happening a great deal in our heads. And there certainly is an enormous puzzle regarding literature of even greater significance written under tyranny. This pressure cooker situation that you have had for so long, particularly in Russia, doesn't date from the Bolshevik Revolution. It existed long before. Turgenev wrote, "we are on the eve of the great Revolution; there will be wonderful changes," and so on—as many intellectuals of the period did. And I think it was Bloch who said "We are the sons of Russia's dreadful day, the day that came after that eve."

BOYERS: I thought we might speak a bit about the intellectual career of Jacobo Timmerman. Timmerman's first book on his awful experiences in Argentina was much heralded, though it was attacked in this country by writers for magazines like *Commentary*, who argued that a frontal assault on an anti-communist government in Argentina was, in effect, a way of giving aid and comfort to our enemies abroad. Were you disturbed by this approach to Timmerman, which was a very mild instance of the effort in this country, certainly, to discredit Timmerman's book? And, by the way, what did Timmerman's subsequent work on Israel and Lebanon say of his political acumen and his intellectual stature?

KOLAKOWSKI: I haven't read the articles you mention in *Commentary* or any other magazine, but assuming, of course, that you have given us a fair summary of the argument, I can only say that I find it outrageous.

O'BRIEN: Well, I read Timmerman's two books, but I only saw references to the articles you mention. First, I would distinguish between the two books. In Timmerman's Argentina book, which impressed me, it seemed we were given testimony of an experience which he had undergone. The experience has been impugned. People say that the testimony was made up, that he had not actually had these experiences. It seemed to me that he probably had. I believed him, and I thought it was a very moving testimony from someone who had been right on the floor under a despotism and had survived. I thought the book impressive in other ways. Then, when I read his book on Israel in Lebanon I was much less impressed. He was going along with the popular judgments of the moment. He was not situating anything. He even went so far, in the epilogue of the book, written after the Sabra and Shatilah episode, as to say that Israel's society was so corrupted by its Right Wing movements that there could not possibly be any proper investigation into the massacre. This society could only produce a white-wash. I reviewed that book when it was published and said I didn't believe there would be only a white-wash. And I was right. The commission appointed to investigate was really quite exceptional, as we realize when we consider that there are very few countries which could tolerate an investigation into something like that. My own country is the Republic of Ireland, which is a decent little democracy, but I think we would have white-washed more. And I know that our neighbor, Britain, or this country, for that matter, would have white-washed more because they have done so in the past. So I think Timmerman was wrong. But he has every right to be wrong, and to my mind, his wrongness on this does not invalidate his early book which he wrote as a witness; and it shouldn't destroy our respect for him. I think he is entitled to respect, and to being wrong.

STEINER: Perhaps we can extend this a little by remembering that the most influential teacher in the history of modern France was a philosopher who preferred to stay a school teacher, namely Alain. We were brought up under his terrifying dictum (remember, this is taught to very young people): "Every truth is the refusal of your body." He was Spinozan, totally committed to contempt for the human body. Torture is the one thing that we are, I think, as perfectly privileged people—I refer to those comfortably gathered in this kind of room— peculiarly ill-equipped to imagine or to handle. Conor's memory has just given us a very beautiful example. He said that Timmerman was on the floor of the Galtieri regime. The most terrible scene in that book is when he is on the floor being tortured, and your memory, Conor, brought that horror back. I do think we don't know how to handle torture. It's extraterritorial, isn't it, to our categorical imperatives of hope, of rationality? For me it is of a theological order; it is hell; it is the attempt to institute, as Baudelaire said, *l'enfer preparatoire*: to introduce, as De Maistre predicted, the building of hell into a nontheological situation. In Timmerman, I believe the account, which calls up again the extreme complexity of our inability to handle certain things, the questions raised again and again in theories of evil. Those who have undergone torture are really probably in another world of knowledge from even the most vivid imaginers among us. And in front of a human being like that I feel . . . if there were a word which makes embarrassment transcendent, it would describe my feeling before such a person.

But let me give you an example of where the intellectual really comes up against the fact of evil, where evil is incarnate. Faced with the accusations on his conduct in Algeria, General Massu showed a film which, as far as we can tell, was authentic. He had had himself subjected to the same tortures they were using on the Algerian insurgents, in the bathtub, with the electric shocks, and so on, and came out saying, "They exaggerate the pain." Now if there is absolute evil, it lies in that answer. And I don't think we're at all well-equipped to handle it. And whether one agrees with everything contained in Timmerman's first book or not, I think the best response one can make to it is to simply shut up. And that is what the authors of the articles you mention did not know how to do.

BOYERS: Some years ago Isaiah Berlin wrote an influential book about the distinction between what he called the hedgehog and the fox. Is Berlin's distinction useful in telling us something about different classes of intellectuals or in distinguishing between intellectuals and, say, academics? Is it in any way a useful, living distinction?

STEINER: That dichotomy, intellectual/academic, has been debated often enough, but maybe it would be useful to try to get it into focus again. There is this mysterious business of being interested in something utterly, with a supremely uncompromising interest which is stronger than love, or hatred, or any loyalty. The object of that interest can be inherently bizarre. A man may give his life to chamber pots of the T'ang bronze period. He wants to catalogue them all, to get the damn thing right. One of the few very, very great novels we have on this sort of life of autistic ecstasy is Dumas's *Black Tulip*. When you are interested in something beyond life or death or anything, I think that's when you are an intellectual. It's a pathological condition; it can lead to murderous social injustice or indifference or stupidity. It can lead to self-destruction. The real treason of the cleric is even for a moment to try to negotiate it or justify it. To do so is to betray one's calling. It wouldn't occur to me ever to negotiate or justify my passions, ever. Nor would it occur to me that they are to be shared by others. They are infinitely self-rewarding, agelessly autistic. But that's what it's about. You don't choose your cancer, the leprosy of obsession which directs you towards a supreme effort. Princeton has just celebrated with proper modesty the publication of a complete catalogue of the mosaics of San Marco in Venice. The author had written his German thesis on certain problems in certain mosaics in San Marco in 1927, but had instantly withdrawn it because of errors, imperfections. Now in 1985 the two volumes, three thousand pages, are ready. The specialist's life is complete. Every stone of every mosaic in that one church has been indexed, studied: the work is done. *Opus perfectum est.* And you do not negotiate such a passion, you do not justify or validate it. You don't give a damn if anybody ever opens the book. You have been chosen. *Une vocation*: a summons. And I don't think one can belong to our clerisy if one hasn't had some measure of that summons. So I would like to reject the difference between intellectual and academic and modulate to something much more simple. In our present culture we have increasing numbers of intense specialists as against the diminishing numbers of generalists. This is a large and complicated subject, involving the displacement by technicity or *techné* of *sophia* or wisdom. In the process, the fox smelling his way around with joy, not closing his bristles into a single ball of monomaniacal specialization, comes to seem terribly vulnerable. But what this tells us of the distinction you mention, that between the intellectual and the academic, I'm not prepared to speculate about.

BOYERS: A perhaps related question: Recently Sidney Hook wrote a piece on Bertrand Russell in which he said that Russell could restate stale and familiar positions on the perennial problems of philosophy in a way that made them seem fresh and challenging. Do you regard Russell's willingness to traffic with the familiar and to write countless books and articles for a general audience as having contributed in a positive way to his stature as an intellectual?

O'BRIEN: I think there's a contradiction in the formulation. I don't think you can state the stale and familiar in a form which is fresh and challenging. If what you have said is fresh and challenging, your material will not by its nature be stale and familiar; it will be or seem something new. So Sidney Hook seems to me to have written a rather bogus formulation.

BOYERS: Well, you may be right, Conor; at least the formulation could probably be more precise. But the idea that Russell often wrote about matters that seemed too familiar to be made interesting still seems to me to be worth talking about. And you haven't responded to Hook's statement that Russell—unlike many professional scholars—was able and willing to write for a general audience.

O'BRIEN: I have known other sinners who have done just that.

BOYERS: And, presumably, without much in the way of grave misgiving.

O'BRIEN: Very little.

KOLAKOWSKI: Once at a conference I attended, a German colleague of mine read a paper to a rather large audience which, it was obvious, was not made up of philosophers or of people at all familiar with German philosophy. The paper my colleague delivered was utterly incomprehensible to most people there. Afterwards I asked him, "Why did you offer such a paper to this audience? You should have guessed that nobody would understand." And he answered me, "You know, in Germany, if a philosopher writes in a way which is intelligible to the general public, he makes of himself a laughing stock. He is just ridiculous." Never before had I heard this attitude stated so boldly, though of course I knew it was an attitude implicitly shared among philosophers in Germany more than elsewhere. But one would never think of Bertrand Russell in this company. He did write, of course, a number of very technical things, but I always admired him for his ability to communicate sometimes difficult questions in a language which was accessible to a general educated public. I don't think there is a problem in his case at all, though I think the issue raised here may be worth looking at.

O'BRIEN: The issue, here, has much to do with language and nationalism. Fichte, in his *Addresses to the German Nation*, produced a most ingenious and interesting thesis which concerns the inferiority on linguistic grounds of non-Germans because the original Germans who remained in Germany managed to keep their original language. This Fichte established "clearly", to the satisfaction of most reasonable Germans. On the other hand, there were other Teutons such as the Franks (he doesn't mention the French, as the French were in actual occupation of Berlin, though it is about them that he is talking) who took unto themselves a language full of foreign words with Romance roots. And the consequence of this for them was that they died intellectually. They could no longer understand what they themselves were saying. They became non-people linguistically. Whereas the Germans, by reason of having stuck to their original language, retained a seriousness about the use of language which the French could never have. The result was that the Germans could understand French more than the French, whereas the French, even if they worked all their life at it, could never understand German, at least in what was most German about it. And all around this argument is the idea of German profundity and French Enlightenment superficiality. It seems to me that a lot of the complexity of philosophical language from that time on, basically in Germany, has to do with making that original nationalistic point: The Germans are clear; others, therefore, are frivolous and silly. We are extraordinarily complicated, and are therefore saying something profound that the foreigners, who don't in any case exist and are mentally dead, can't possibly understand. I know there's more to the thing than this, and I've certainly left a flank there for George. But I'm willing to see him have a go.

STEINER: If you were to ask Russell in the Elysian fields about the point at which he shifted into more popular writing, that wonderfully impish aristocrat would, in a Mozart/Salieri situation, read to you a letter he wrote to Ottoline Morell at Garsington when Wittgenstein had done the critique of his early papers. There he writes that he is destroyed, that he knows he is not in Wittgenstein's class. So I would stress, as a very important point, that there are certain motives for becoming a master of haute vulgarization. One realizes that one cannot do the supremely difficult, creative thing. The Russell case is particularly intriguing. About the obscurity of German philosophical writing we will not convince each other, of course. Hegel's *Phenomenology* is one of the masterpieces of prose by any standard. Nietzsche is incomparable in his clarity, in his force; he is a supreme lyric writer. Other recent German philosophers of importance, like Ernst Tugendhat, write pellucidly. Kant's *Critiques* are models. Many, many pages in Hume are less penetrable than anything in Kant's *Critiques*. I think we all have a bit of a problem with the fact that from Herder to Kant and Schelling, from Hegel, Schopenhauer and Nietzsche down to Wittgenstein and Heidegger German philosophy and metaphysics have dominated. I don't know who would be at this table as a thinking being without what Kant and Hegel brought about in the history of the mind and consciousness.

O'BRIEN: I'm not sure I want to be included in this company.

STEINER: I have tried to pay you a great compliment, Conor. Accept it, for once.

O'BRIEN: You know, George, I fear you most when you are offering me enormous compliments.

KOLAKOWSKI: I would subscribe to everything George has said, with perhaps the exception of the statement that Hegel was a master of prose. But my German might not be good enough to appreciate his literary merit. Anyway, I would certainly always prefer Lessing.

STEINER: I love Lessing, too, but wouldn't you like to write the *Phenomenology*?

KOLAKOWSKI: No, I would not like to write it.

O'BRIEN: I think, George, it's already been done.

STEINER: As Borges would point out, that's where the problem of rewriting begins!

BOYERS: This seems a good time—now that we've gotten into "rewriting" Hegel's *Phenomenology*—to turn to our audience.

AUDIENCE: The American intellectual, especially the liberal, has always been troubled by the prospect of entering the world of "real" politics. But he's always had to deal with the nagging thought that he was somehow obligated not to evade it, even when he's done nothing but evade it.

O'BRIEN: Well, is there a world of real politics? And do you have to get into it? I was in it for eight years—four years in Parliamentary opposition and four years in office (I'll not say "power"). Then the electorate threw me out on my head, and I was very sore in my head, for about six months, and then I was very glad, I felt liberated from the political process, from having to say things which I didn't necessarily believe. I didn't say all that many of them; I was no more mendacious than was absolutely required by the nature of the political process, but there was some mendacity and it sickened me. In light of this experience, I'd have to say that one of the great advantages of this country is that most intellectuals I've met feel they can live quite contented lives without being involved in the political process. This is a condition not vouchsafed to intellectuals elsewhere, who may be regimented or required to be in politics. So, I am not, frankly, quite sure how sincere American intellectuals are when they demand to be involved in the political process. It seems to me that they are, on the whole, despite certain attitudes of more or less ritual discontent, unusually happy and indeed pampered people. And long may they and all of us remain so.

AUDIENCE: I suppose we are, most of us, pampered if not always happy people. And this does, as you seem to suggest, lead on to the question of bad faith. Does a comfortable and successful intellectual have the right not only to sympathize with terrorist movements but to espouse things which represent no threat to him and have nothing to do with his way of life? This is the point that George Steiner made earlier in the evening, and it is a point that obviously troubles each of us. Can we afford to say, I wonder, that it is "normal" to be troubled and necessary sometimes to avow or espouse things in which we have no direct personal stake? Is bad faith even an appropriate term for this utterly familiar condition?

STEINER: I think every one of us has to answer these questions for himself. But however we regard the political challenge represented by the status quo or by some outrage against the status quo, we are driven back to the nominal theme of this session, to the responsibility (the word I prefer is answerability) of the intellectual. We feel we must try as best we can to live our convictions. We want to be taken seriously. Is this always possible? Suppose that an ardent Zionist, who has read a recent essay of mine which argues that Judaism may well perish as a great moral presence because of the activities of the new Israel, says to me, "you are a stupid son of a bitch, you don't know what Israel can mean;" then I shut up. If an American parlor Zionist comfortably ensconced in a major American university, yells at me, I respond differently. I think the person who lives the risks of his convictions may be a very dangerous person, he may be a terribly mistaken person, but I think he won't sizzle at the last judgment.

O'BRIEN: Would that apply to so sincere a person as Adolf Hitler?

STEINER: I have, as you know, gotten in a bit of trouble on that very matter. And there's no reliable way of answering adequately, even in respect of a Hitler. I don't know the answer even when the question is posed in Milton's *Paradise Lost*. But, surely, Conor, we have always agreed that "the trimmer who bloweth neither hot nor cold" is a quotation worth pondering.

O'BRIEN: I have no very strong objection to the trimmer who bloweth neither hot nor cold. I think he is Everyman.

STEINER: Certainly you used to, and not so many years ago, speak rather differently of the trimmer.

O'BRIEN: Yes, I used to do this, you used to do that. Now we've both of us changed a bit, and that's okay. But now it seems to me that if you despise the trimmer you are despising Everyman, and you may be also taking it upon yourself to despise what is quite real in yourself.

STEINER: Maybe, maybe.

AUDIENCE: I'm interested in the implications of the trimmer position, as it is spoken for by Mr. O'Brien. I have heard him at this conference and elsewhere refer to the condition of rational hope, but what this can mean in the face of stagnating conditions, enduring problems of poverty, repression and inequality I can't quite understand.

O'BRIEN: Yes, well, I don't see the trimmer position generally as so very difficult to understand as you make out. The word trimmer isn't, or oughtn't to be, the issue. My point is, if you place your hope in the millenium, that may be very stimulating to you personally, and it may give a great charge or purpose or effectiveness to your life, as it did in the case of Oliver Cromwell, and other, later figures. It is a very, very powerful thing, this hope, and I don't underestimate it at all, but it is not a rational sentiment. There ain't going to be any millenium; it's not going to happen. But you elect in any case to go for the irrational drives, for prophecy; you may decide to go for broke in general, to try to set the world aright one way or another. I can't make myself go for broke in that way, and I don't want to. I realize that this is quite possibly a spiritual limitation in myself. But I prefer to see what the chances are of making things marginally better for those I care most about—not for all humanity, since I know I'm not going to redeem all humanity. I care, in circles going out, about my family, my city, my country, people with whom I identify—like yourselves—in other countries, not an indefinite and inexhaustible number of countries, but concentric communities. I care about those and I would like at least that my own intellectual activity should not make things worse or more dangerous for those people, and preferably that it would make things, by a tiny margin, a little bit better, a little bit clearer, a little bit more rational, even a little bit more compassionate. That's what I would like to do, and I don't set myself any larger goal than that. I'm not even sure that I'm going to achieve that. I associate myself in this with Burke who deplored and condemned those who preferred a longterm advantage to humanity, as they conceived it, to the actual lives and interests, and these are the words he used, "of those whom we daily see and converse with."

AUDIENCE: I'm still not satisfied that the concrete responsibility of the intellectual has been addressed. Isn't it possible to say that the function of the intellectual is to serve those who most need the attention and help of enlightened persons?

KOLAKOWSKI: I'm always suspicious of the word "responsibility" when it is used in this way. Usually when people talk of the responsibility of intellectuals they mean not that I should be a responsible person, but that I should be responsible for one particular thing, that I should take a specific position. "Verantwortung" was a very popular word in Nazi ideology, we should remember. It meant that if you were not a Nazi you were not just wrong but irresponsible. This, of course, is nonsense and it is no less nonsensical when the concept is used by communists or by supporters of other causes. I can be responsible for good things or bad things as I go about my business, but I cannot be required to be responsible *tout court.* That's meaningless. So the point is, what are causes which are worth being responsible for? And this is a moral and political issue quite different from the other. If you ask what right intellectuals have to be what they are, what right they have *not* to serve the cause of this or that group which needs them, I think you are asking an unfair question. Why should there be a particular way of being an intellectual? Why should someone feel guilty for doing this thing or that, so long as it is not morally reprehensible? What's wrong with merely being an historian or a poet? Why should I ask myself what right I have to be an archeologist? We know that people are driven by various motivations and that there are different ways of doing good.

As to the identification with the oppressed: those who urge this usually have particular reasons of their own for urging it. This doesn't mean that one shouldn't identify with the oppressed if the instinct is genuine. But usually it is an ideological and purely cerebral identification which satisfies the intellectual without demanding anything of him.

STEINER: May I take up the question in another way? Almost every profession has certain absolute constraints, what used to be called in an older dispensation "sins against the Holy Ghost," that is to say, the unpardonable, the irremediable. I think our profession does, and I think these codes are not talked about enough. Some of these may seem too small or petty to notice. I think, for instance, a real intellectual is one who, even on the page of the article or pamphlet, or I would almost say newspaper, which he is about to put in the wastebasket, would correct a misprint; that is an almost sacramental obligation. More serious, I would say a real teacher is one who knows that as the process of teaching has in it a terrifying ease of charismatic power, any sexual abuse of a student is unpardonable.

But to get at the larger issue of responsibility, we may have to consider the origins of the modern concepts of the intellectual and the intelligentsia in the Dreyfus Affair. The central understanding that developed there is that you leave any city, any *polis*, rather than sacrifice to it what bit of truth possesses you, what you believe to be the truth. No city, no nation, no loyalty, is worth the sacrifice of a truth. Others learned something no less important: that we have the obligation of pressing the unpleasant questions, the questions which are in bad taste, the embarrassing questions, the taboo questions. Being so privileged as we are it is almost our imperative job not to ask the nice questions, not to ask the comfortable questions. At the moment, of course, looking about us even in the most liberal of societies, there is an astonishing list of taboo questions, the raising of which ruins one's professional hopes, or one's friendships, or whatever. Well, if that is what matters most then the intellectual is in the wrong business.

In discussions of this sort the name of Julian Benda is invariably invoked. He is a strange and talismanic figure, fearfully disagreeable. He had fought very hard for the Dreyfus affair as a young man. And the night when at last the captain was to be freed a great dinner celebration was thrown. Proust was there, Leon Blum was there, Jaures was there, along with others who had fought. And the champagne flowed. Benda just sat there grim and cold, and when asked why he said, "None of you understands: the man has been pardoned, but the pardon is not in the proper form of the juridical code; I am not going to feast." Now that is an intellectual. Benda's is in some ways an appalling attitude, though there was nothing precious in the man, nothing mystical. He simply felt that form in the matter of law was important, possibly beyond mercy or compassion.

KOLAKOWSKI: Yes, George, I agree with you about these things. There is a specific responsibility of the intellectual. It is not political. It is a responsibility to use words precisely and without trying to mislead. Intellectuals are not wiser or saner in their political choices than others, but if they espouse what I believe are bad causes, I do not say they are irresponsible. I say they have made a bad choice, that they have attached themselves to a bad or unworthy cause.

O'BRIEN: I think this is a very important point. You can say about the anti-semite or the anti-democratic terrorist that they are responsible in a sense. First of all they are responsible to their constituency, those who believe the same things they do. Secondly, they are responsible to the community at large in that the community at large has the right to reject them and tell them to go elsewhere and eliminate them from such processes as they may be involved in. And this rejection or elimination I, for one, would push pretty far. Beyond these two concepts, but attached to the concept of responsibility to one's community at large, there is the right of a demo-cratic society to defend itself against people whose concept of responsi-bility makes them enemies of democracy. It may not be the responsibility of the intellectual to believe any of these things, but this is about as far as I want to go in speaking of responsibility.

STEINER: Can we say, then, that the primary duty of the intellectual as intellectual is simply to tell the truth? And, more particularly, where that telling may damage him?

O'BRIEN: His duty, I should say, is to pursue truth, and if the consequences of this pursuit are inconvenient, that shouldn't limit his pursuit. On this we can surely agree.

Note

[1] This is an edited transcript of a panel discussion held at Skidmore College on April 11, 1985.

Intellectuals in the Post-Colonial World

BY EDWARD W. SAID

I

It isn't just the strident calls to arms of The Committee for the Free World (formerly the Committee on the Present Danger) that are evidence for a renewed sense of 'Western' or 'free-world' or 'Judeo-Christian' embattlement. There is the equally impressive, but always maliciously portrayed and essentialised evidence pointed to in the non-Western world of ferocious denunciations of America the devil, of imperialism, of a continued policy of perceived hypocrisy and racism. Whether it is admitted or not, however, these claims and counterclaims derive to a substantial degree from the common colonialist past, insufficiently analysed and theorized, which is being re-experienced belatedly in a variety of combative forms, many of them reducing contemporary history rather rigidly to instant retrospective views of a long and extremely affecting relationship: that between a group of Western metropolitan powers, and a whole range of variously weaker peripheral cultures, areas, states, and peoples.

For whereas it is largely true that direct colonial rule ended in the middle years of this century—and it is good to be reminded that between them a small handful of European powers controlled 85% of the earth's surface in 1914, and that in the period between 1878 to 1914 outlying territories and peoples were included within direct European domination at an astounding annual rate of 240,000 square miles—the meaning of colonial rule was by no means transformed into a settled question. This is perfectly obvious in the Western or metropolitan societies whose connections with Africa, Asia, and Latin America were so long, productive and at the end, so embattled and traumatic. And although I wouldn't say that there is a majority of people in England who feel remorse for and totally regret the Indian experience, there are many people for whom on the one hand the good old days inevitably had to end, even though, on the other, the value of those days, the reason for their end, and attitudes towards native nationalism are all highly volatile issues. But what may perhaps be surprising to many, is that debate in various countries of the Third World about colonialist practice and the imperialist ideology that sustained it is extremely lively and diverse. There are, for example, large groups of people who believe that the bitterness and humiliations of the experience that virtually enslaved them nevertheless delivered the benefits of a national self-consciousness, liberal ideas, and technological goods, benefits over time that seem to have turned colonialism into a much less unpleasant thing. Other people have used the post-colonial occasion for a retrospective reflection on colonialism, the better to understand the difficulties of the present in newly independent states. There, the problems of democracy, development and destiny are real ones, attested to by the persecutions of intellectuals who have carried on their thought and practise publicly and courageously. One thinks of Faiz Ahmed Faiz in Pakistan, or Ngugi wa Thongo in Kenya, major artists both whose sufferings did not impede the intransigeance of their thought, nor inhibit the severity of their punishment.

But neither Ngugi nor Faiz, nor many others like them, were anything but unstinting in their hatred of colonialism. The irony of course is that they were listened to only partially, both in the West and by the ruling authorities in their own societies. They were considered by many Western intellectuals to be wailers and whiners who denounced the evils of colonialism, and as agents of outside powers by the regimes at home who imprisoned or exiled them. The tragedy of this experience, and indeed of all post-colonial questions, lies in the constitutive limitations imposed on any attempt to deal with relationships that are polarized, radically uneven, remembered differently. The spheres, the sites of intensity, the agendas, the constituencies in the metropolitan and ex-colonized worlds overlap only partially. The small area that is common does not, at this point, provide for more than what I'd like to call *a politics of blame*. In what follows I want first to consider the actualities of the intellectual terrain common as well as discrepant in the post-colonial cultural discourse, especially concentrating on what in it gives rise to and encourages a rhetoric as well as a politics of blame. Then I shall consider the ways in which a reconsidered, or revised notion of what might be called a post-colonial intellectual project is likely to expand the area of overlapping community between metropolitan and formerly colonized societies. Here I shall be trying to formulate an alternative to a politics of blame, that is, a more interesting *politics of secular interpretation*, which I hope will strike you as an altogether more rewarding activity than denunciations or simple regret.

II

One way of getting hold of the commonest post-colonial debate is to analyse not its content, but its form, not what is said so much as how it is said, by whom, where, and for whom. But even trying to do this sort of analysis requires a kind of *askesis* not easily come by, given that the arsenal of enunciative strategies is so well-developed, so tempting, ready at hand. Take as a recent instance Salman Rushdie's critique of the Raj revival—his diagnosis of the spate of recent films and articles about India that include *Jewel in the Crown* and Lean's *Passage to India*. Although Rushdie's analysis argued that the nostalgia pressed into service by affectionate recollections of British rule in India coincided with the Falklands war and that "the rise of Raj revisionism, exemplified by the huge success of these fictions, is the artistic counterpart to the rise of conservative ideologies in modern Britain," numerous commentators simply responded to what some of them considered to be Rushdie's wailing and whining in public. Moreover, to the extent that Rushdie was trying to make a larger argument that would presumably appeal to intellectuals for whom Orwell's division of the intellectual's place in society into inside and outside the whale no longer applied—modern reality in Rushdie's terms was actually "whaleless, this world without quiet corners [in which] there can be no easy escapes from history, from hullabaloo, from terrible, unquiet fuss"—to the extent that *that* was Rushdie's main point, it was not the point considered worth taking up and debating. Instead the main issue for contention was whether things in the Third World hadn't in fact declined after direct colonialism had ended, and whether it might not be better on the whole to listen to the rare— luckily, I might add, extremely rare—Third World intellectuals who manfully ascribed most of their present barbarities, tyrannies, and degradations to their own innately native histories, histories that were pretty bad before colonialism and that have reverted to that state after colonialism. Hence Naipaul over Rushdie.

Thus you could conclude from the emotions stirred up by Rushdie's case that many people in the West had come to feel that enough was enough. After Vietnam and Iran—and note here that the names of those countries are usually employed equally to evoke domestic traumas (the student insurrections of the sixties in the case of Vietnam, the hostage episode in the Iranian instance) as much as international outrages, the "loss" of Vietnam and Iran to radical nationalism—after Iran and Vietnam lines had to be defended. Western democracy had taken too much of a beating, and even if most of the physical damage had been done abroad there was a sense, as Jimmy Carter once rather grotesquely put it, that there had been mutual damage. This feeling in turn led to a re-thinking of the whole process of decolonization. Was it not true, ran this new evaluation, that "we" had given "them" progress and modernization? Hadn't we provided them with order and a kind of stability that they haven't been able since to provide for themselves? Wasn't there some atrocious misplaced trust in their capacity for independence, which has quite logically led to the Bokassas and the Amins, whose intellectual correlates are people like Rushdie? Shouldn't we have held on to the colonies, kept the subject or inferior races in check, remained true to our civilizational responsibility?

I realize that what I have just reproduced is not the thing itself, but a caricature. Nevertheless it does bear an uncomfortable, if skewed, resemblance to what has been said by enough people who have imagined themselves to be speaking for the West. There seemed little enough skepticism that no monolithic "West" in fact exists, anymore than one could speak convincingly of the entire ex-colonial world in one sweeping generalization after another. The leap to essences and generalizations was accompanied by a whole set of appeals to an imagined history of one-way Western endowments and free hand-outs followed by a reprehensible sequence of ungrateful bitings of that grandly giving "Western" hand. Why don't they appreciate us, after what we did for them? The thing to be noticed here of course is how easily everything could be compressed into that simple formula of unappreciated magnanimity. Gone are the ravages to the colonial people who for centuries endured summary justice, unending economic oppression, the total distortion of their societies and their intimate lives, and a recourseless submission given to them as a function of unchanging European superiority. Gone most of all are the traces, an infinite number of them, that comprised the immensely detailed and violent history of colonial intervention—minute by minute, hour by hour—in the lives of individuals and collectivities, on both sides of the colonial divide.

The first thing to be noticed about the form of this kind of discourse is how totalizing it is, how all-enveloping its attitudes and gestures, how much it shuts out even as it includes, compresses, and asserts a great deal. Its paradigm, I think, will remain the narrative form of Conrad's *Heart of Darkness*. Marlow on the one hand acknowledges the tragic predicament of all speech—that "it is impossible to convey the life-sensation of any given epoch of one's existence—that which makes its truth, its meaning—its subtle and penetrating essence. . . . We live, as we dream—alone."—and yet conveys the overwhelming power of Kurtz's African experience through his own overmastering narrative. And this narrative in turn is connected directly with the redemptive force, as well as waste and horror, of Europe's mission in the dark world. Whatever is lost or elided or even simply made up in Marlow's narrative is compensated for in the sheer historical momentum its temporal movement forward describes, digressions and all. For within the narrative whose source and authority he is, Marlow can move backwards and forwards in smaller spirals, very much the way lesser episodes in the course of his journey up river occur and are finally compelled by the principal trajectory.

What makes Conrad different from all the other colonial writers who were his contemporaries is that, for reasons having nothing to do with colonialism, he was a great deal more self-conscious about what he did than they were. Like most of his other tales, therefore, *Heart of Darkness* is not just a recital of Marlow's adventures: it is also a dramatisation of Marlow telling his story to a group of listeners, at a particular time and in a specific place. Although the almost oppressive force of Marlow's narrative leaves us with a quite accurate sense that there is no way out of the sovereign historical force of imperialism, and that it has the power of a system representing everything within its dominion, Conrad at least shows us that what Marlow does is contingent, it is acted out for a set of like-minded hearers, and it is limited to that situation. Neither Conrad nor Marlow offers us anything outside the world-conquering attitudes embodied by Kurtz, and Marlow, and Conrad. By that I mean that *Heart of Darkness* works so effectively precisely because its politics and aesthetics, so to speak, are imperialist; and that, by the time that Conrad wrote, seemed an attitude that was inevitable and for which there could be no alternative. For if we cannot truly understand someone else's experience and if, as a result, we must depend simply upon the assertive authority of the sort of power Kurtz wields in the jungle or that Marlow possesses as narrator, there is no use looking for non-imperialist alternatives in a system that has simply eliminated, and made unthinkable, all other alternatives to it. The circularity of the whole thing is unassailable. Except, as I said a moment ago, that Conrad is self-conscious about setting and situating the narrative in a narrative moment, thus allowing us to realize after all that far from swallowing up its own history, imperialism has in fact been placed and located by history, one that lies outside the tightly inclusive ring on the deck of the yawl *Nelly*. As yet, however, no one seemed to inhabit that region, and so Conrad left it empty.

It bears repeating that Conrad himself never, and probably never could have, presented anything other than an imperialist world-view. But because he also had an extraordinarily persistent residual sense of his own exilic marginality, he instinctively protected his vision with the aesthetic restraint of someone who stood forever at the very juncture of *this* world with another, always unspecified but different, one. Conrad's realization is that if like narrative, imperialism has monopolized the entire system of representation which allowed it, in the case of *Heart of Darkness*, to speak for the blacks as well as for Kurtz and the other adventurers (who include Marlow and his audience), your self-consciousness as an outsider can provoke in you an active comprehension of how the machine works, given that you are usually out of synch with and at a distance from it.

The form of Conrad's narrative has had two lives in the post-colonial world. Its assertive sovereign inclusiveness has been reproduced by those who speak today for the West, what the West did, and what the rest of the world is, was, and may be. The inflections of this discourse are to exclude what has been represented as "lost" by showing that the colonial world was, religiously and ontologically speaking, lost to begin with, irredeemable, irrecusably corrupt. Moreover, it focusses not on what was shared in the colonial experience—I shall return to this a little later—but on what must never be shared, namely power and rectitude. Rhetorically, its terms are, to borrow from Julien Benda's attack on modern intellectuals, the organization of political passions which, he was prescient enough to know, lead inevitably to mass slaughter; and if it is not literal mass slaughter then it is certainly rhetorical slaughter. What it resolutely fails to acknowledge is that the colonial encounter continues, as much in the drawing of lines and the defending of barriers, as in the enormously complex and interesting interchange between former colonial partners. The effect of this discourse is to draw like-minded people—the aggressive Westerners and those people outside the West for whom the Ayatollahs speak—away from the ongoing interchange into a regrettably tight little circle. Inside the circle stand the blameless, the just, the omnicompetent, those who know the truth about themselves as well as the others: outside the circle stand a miscellaneous bunch of querulous whining complainers who have spilt the milk and continue to cry over it.

It is no accident that an important ideological shift that occurred during the past decade or so has accompanied this contraction of horizons. The simplest way of describing the shift is to point to a dramatic change in emphasis and quite literally in directions among thinkers noted not for their conservative philosophies but for their insurrectionary attitudes.

The examples of Lyotard and Foucault, whose estimable work came to be surrounded by the far lesser figures of the *nouvelle philosophie,* describe a striking lack of faith in what Lyotard was to call the great legitimising narratives of emancipation and enlightenment. Foucault also turned his attention away from the oppositional forces in modern society he had studied for their insurgent resistance to exclusion and confinement—delinquents, poets, outcasts, and the like—and had decided that since power was everywhere it was probably better to concentrate on the local microphysics of power that surround the individual. In both Lyotard and Foucault we find precisely the same trope employed to explain their disappointment in the politics of liberation: narrative, which posits an enabling *arché* and a vindicating *telos*, is no longer an adequate figure for plotting the human trajectory in society. There is nothing to look forward to: we are stuck within our circle. The line is now enclosed by a circle. After years of support for the anti-colonial struggles in places like Algeria, Cuba, Vietnam, Palestine, Iran, that came to represent for the Western Left their deepest engagement in the politics and philosophy of decolonization, a moment of exhaustion and disappointment was reached. This is when one began to hear and read accounts of how futile it was to support revolutions, how barbaric the new regimes that came to power, how—this is an extreme case—much to the benefit of Moscow decolonization had been.

Enter now terrorism and barbarism. Enter also the "I told you so" formerly superannuated colonial experts like John Kelley whose well-publicized message was: these colonial peoples deserve only colonialism or, since we were foolish to pull out of Aden and India and everywhere else, invasion. Enter also the Borchgraves, Sterlings, and Laqueurs, the theoreticians of the relationship between liberation movements, terrorism and the KGB. There was a resurgence of sympathy for what Jeanne Kirkpatrick called authoritarian (as opposed to totalitarian) regimes who were Western allies, and with the onset of Reaganism a new phase of history had clearly begun.

However else all of this might have been historically understandable, drawing the circle around the West certainly was and is not an attractive or edifying role for the post-colonial intellectual. Constitutively it shuts out the possibility of knowledge and of discovery of what it means, to return to Rushdie now for another quotation, to be outside the whale:

> Outside the whale is the unceasing storm, the continual quarrel, the dialectic of history. Outside the whale there is a genuine need for political fiction, for books that draw new and better maps of reality, and make new languages with which we can understand the world. Outside the whale we see that we are all irradiated by history, we are radioactive with history and politics; we see that it can be as false to create a politics-free fictional universe as to create one in which nobody needs to work or eat or hate or love or sleep. Outside the whale it becomes necessary, and even exhilarating, to grapple with the special problems created by the incorporation of political material, because politics is by turns farce and tragedy, and sometimes (e.g., Zia's Pakistan) both at once. Outside the whale the writer is obliged to accept that he (or she) is part of the crowd, part of the ocean, part of the storm, so that objectivity becomes a great dream, like perfection, an unattainable goal for which one must struggle in spite of the impossibility of success. Outside the whale is the world of Samuel Beckett's famous formula: *I can't go on, I'll go on.*

The terms of Rushdie's description, while they borrow from Orwell, seem to me to resonate even more interestingly with Conrad. For here, in its explicit references to the outside, is the second consequence, the second life of Conrad's narrative form, which indicates the existence of a perspective from outside the representations provided by Marlow and his listeners. It is, above all, a profoundly secular perspective, and it is neither beholden to notions about historical destiny and the essentialism that destiny always seems to entail, nor about historical indifference and resignation. To the extent that being on the inside results in shutting out, editing and subordinating the full experience of colonialism to the dominance of one Eurocentric and totalizing view, this one adumbrates the presence of a field without special historical privileges in it for one party over all the others.

I don't want to over-interpret what Rushdie means, nor do I want to put ideas in his prose that he may not have intended. Insofar as he is engaged in a controversy with the British media he is of course claiming the privilege of someone who does not recognize the truth of his experience in popular representations of India. Now I myself would go further and say that it is one of the virtues of such conjunctures of the political with the cultural and aesthetic as also to provoke partial realizations of a common ground obscured by the controversy itself. Perhaps this common ground is especially hard to see for the combatants directly involved who seem to do more fighting back than reflecting. I can perfectly well understand the anger that fuels Rushdie's argument because like him, I feel outnumbered and outorganized by a prevailing consensus that has come to regard the Third World as an atrocious nuisance. Whereas we write and speak as members of a tiny tokenized minority of marginal voices, our journalistic and academic critics belong to a considerably wealthy system of interlocking informational and academic resources. This has newspapers, TV stations, journals of opinion and institutes at its disposal. Most of them have now taken up a strident chorus of rightward-tending damnation in which what is non-white, non-Western, and non-Judeo-Christian is herded together under the rubric of terrorism and/or evil. To attack this is to defend the Western democracies.

The irony, as I said a moment ago, is that people like us are in fact at even greater risk in the formerly colonized world, where in many places critical ideas are considered a menace. So you find yourself isolated and criticised here, and isolated and criticised there, even though your constituency is a fairly large one. The most attractive and immoral move, however, has been Naipaul's, who has allowed himself quite consciously to be turned into a witness for the Western prosecution. There are others like him who specialize in the thesis of what one of them has called self-inflicted wounds, which is to say that we "non-Whites" are the cause of all our problems, not the overly maligned imperialists. Two things need to be said about the small band whose standard bearer Naipaul has become, all of whom share the same characteristics. One is that in presenting themselves as members of courageous minorities in the Third World, they are in fact not interested at all in the Third World—which they never address—but in the metropolitan intellectuals whose twists and turns have gone on despite the Third World, and whose approval they seem quite desperate to have. Naipaul writes for Irving Howe and Joan Didion, not for Eqbal Ahmad or Dennis Brutus or C. L. R. James who, after noting his early promise, went on to excoriate Naipaul for the scandal of his "Islamic journey," *Among the Believers*. Second, and more important, what is seen as crucially informative and telling about their work—their accounts of the Indian darkness or the Arab predicament— is precisely what is weakest about it: with reference to the actualities it is ignorant, illiterate, and cliché-ridden. Naipaul's accounts of the Islamic, Latin American, African, Indian and Caribbean worlds *totally* ignore a massive infusion of critical scholarship about those regions in favor of the tritest, the cheapest and the easiest of colonial mythologies about wogs and darkies, myths that even Lord Cromer and Forster's Turtons and Burtons would have been embarrassed to trade in outside their private clubs. Roughly the same goes for recently favored witnesses on the Arabs, scholars whose manipulation of Orientalist formulae about the degenerations of Islamic culture and the hopeless impotence of Arab political life were seen as learned, eloquent confirmations of what "we" have always known.

All of this dramatises the problems of constituency and of where the post-colonial discourse, and in particular the politics of blame, in fact takes place. There is no question, I believe, that the overwhelming and influential preponderance of opinion is circulated in the circle that I have been characterizing, a circle where—and this is very important—colonialism is seen exclusively as an experience that has ended, and about which any claims about or reparations for its damages and consequences into the present are dismissed as both irrelevant and preposterously arrogant. Whereas it does seem to me extraordinarily important to remember that the continuing debate that has been stimulated by critics and, in a sense, reminders of colonialism such as Salman Rushdie, Eqbal Ahmad, and others—intellectuals whose work has attracted attention in the West, in that very same circle whose closure has been a central project for the ideologists of an affirmative Western, Judeo-Christian tradition— this debate testifies to an experience of colonialism that continues into the present and which, I strongly believe, it is the role of the post-colonial intellectual to clarify and expand.

Let me return to Conrad once more. Outside the group of Marlow's listeners lies an undefined and unclear world. Conrad sometimes seems to want to fold that world into the imperial metropolitan discourse represented by Marlow, while, as I said, by virtue of his own dislocated subjectivity he resists the effort and, I have always believed, succeeds in so doing. For Conrad's self-consciously circular narrative forms encourage us to sense if not the actuality, then the potential of a reality that has remained inaccessible to imperialism and which in the post-colonial world has erupted into presence.

Even if we confine ourselves to cultural and ideological artefacts, the evidence for this is both impressive and rich. For not only has there been a whole literature and a theory of resistance and response, there has been in the greatly disparate post-colonial regions, a tremendously energetic attempt to engage with the metropolitan world in a common effort at re-inscribing, re-interpreting and expanding the sites of intensity and the terrain contested with Europe. Some of it—for example, the convulsively irate writing produced by disciples of Fanon like Shariati and Jalal Ali Ahmed—interprets colonialism by asserting the native culture opposition. In other instances, novelists like Ngugi and Tayib Salih reinscribe in their fiction such great topoi of colonial cultures as the quest and the voyage into the unknown, reclaiming them for their own, post-colonial purposes.

Between colonialism and its genealogical offspring there is thus a holding and crossing-over. Many of the post-colonial writers bear their past within them—as scars of humiliating wounds, as instigation for different practices, as potentially revised visions of the past tending towards a future, as urgently re-interpretable and re-deployable experiences in which the formerly silent native speaks and acts on territory taken back from the colonialist. And, for the first time, these writers can read the great colonial masterpieces that had not only misrepresented them, but had assumed their inability to read and respond directly to what had been written about them, just as European ethnography depended in very real measure upon the natives' incapacity to intervene in scientific discourse about them. Let us try now to review the new situations more fully.

III

I think we should begin by accepting the notion that although there is an irreducible subjective core to human experience, this experience is also historical and secular, it is accessible to certain kinds of analysis, and—

centrally important for me—it is not exhausted by totalizing theories marked and limited by doctrinal lines or by analytical constructs. I mean simply that if you believe with Gramsci that an intellectual vocation is socially possible as well as desireable, it is an inadmissible contradiction at the same time to build analyses of historical experience around exclusions, exclusions that stipulate, for instance, only women can understand feminine experience, only Jews can understand Jewish suffering, only formerly colonial subjects can understand colonial experience. Nor does what I am talking about have to do with saying glibly that there are two sides to every question. For the difficulty with theories of exclusiveness or with barriers and sides is that once admitted these polarities absolve and forgive a great deal more ignorance and demagogy than they enable knowledge. Even the most cursory look at the fortunes of theories of race, of the modern state, of modern nationalism itself, verify the sad truth of this. If you know in advance that the black or Jewish or German experience is fundamentally comprehensible only to Jews or Blacks or Germans you first of all posit as essential something which, I believe, is both historical and the result of interpretation—namely the existence of Jewishness, Blackness, or Germanness, or for that matter of Orientalism and Occidentalism. Secondly, you are pretty likely to construct defenses of the experience rather than promote knowledge of it. And, as a result, you will demote the different experience of others to a lesser status.

If at the outset we acknowledge the massively knotted and complex history of special but nevertheless overlapping and interconnected experiences—of women, of Westerners, of Blacks, of states, etc.—there is no particular intellectual reason for granting each and all of them an ideal and essential status. And yet, we would wish to preserve the *quidditas* of each so long as we also preserve some sense of the human community to which they all belong. An excellent example of what I mean is Terence Ranger's and Eric Hobsbawm's collection of essays on *The Invention of Tradition*, which includes essays on invented traditions that are highly specialized and local, yet all of them bearing traces of similar socio-political and ideological impulses. The comparative or, better, the contrapuntal perspective then proposes itself and with it, Ernst's Bloch's notion of non-synchronous experiences. That is we must be able to think through and interpret together discrepant experiences, each with its particular agendas and pace of development, its own formations, its internal coherence and its system of external relationships.

Let us contrast two roughly contemporary texts, the *Déscription de l'Egypte* in all its massive, impressive coherence and, a comparatively slender volume, Abd el Rahman al Jabarti's *Journal*. Both date from the 1820's. The *Déscription* was the 24 volume account of the French expedition to Egypt produced by Napoleon's team of scientists, which he had with him. Abd el Rahman al Jabarti was an Egyptian notable and *'alim*, or religious leader, who witnessed and lived through the French expedition. Take for example, the following passage from Fourier's introduction to the *Déscription*:

> Placed between Africa and Asia, and communicating easily with Europe, Egypt occupies the center of the ancient continent. This country presents only great memories; it is the homeland of the arts and conserves innumerable monuments; its principal temples and the palaces inhabited by its kings still exist, even though its least ancient edifices had already been built by the time of the Trojan War. Homer, Lycurgus, Solon, Pythagoras, and Plato all went to Egypt to study the sciences, religion, and the laws. Alexander founded an opulent city there, which for a long time enjoyed commercial supremacy and which witnessed Pompey, Caesar, Mark Antony, and Augustus deciding between them the fate of Rome and that of the entire world. It is therefore proper for this country to attract the attention of illustrious princes who rule the destiny of nations.
>
> No considerable power was ever amassed by any nation, whether in the West or in Asia, that did not also turn that nation toward Egypt, which was regarded in some measure as its natural lot.

He speaks as the rationalizing mouthpiece of Napoleon's invasion of Egypt in 1798. The resonances of the great names he summons, the placing, the grounding, the normalizing of foreign conquest within the cultural orbit of European existence—all this transmutes conquest from an event into a process that is much longer, slower, and more acceptable to the European sensibility enfolded within its own cultural superstructure, than such an event could have been for any Egyptian enduring the conquest.

At almost the same time Jabarti records in his *Journal* a series of anguished, but not unperceptive reflections on the conquest; what he says, he says as an embattled religious notable recording the conquest of his country and the destruction of his society. "This year is the beginning of a period marked by great battles; serious results were suddenly produced in a frightening manner; miseries multiplied without end, the course of things was troubled, the common meaning of life was corrupted and destruction overtook it and the devastation was general. [Then, as a good Muslim, he turns back to reflect on himself and his people.] 'God,' says the Koran (xi,9) does not unjustly ruin cities whose inhabitants are just."

Whereas the French expedition was marked by the presence of a whole team of scientists whose job it was to survey Egypt as it was never surveyed before—the result of course was the 24 volume *Déscription*—Jabarti has eyes for, and only appreciates, the facts of power. They bear upon his existence as a conquered Egyptian, an existence for him compressed into that of a subjugated particle, barely able to do much more than record the French army's comings and goings, its imperious decrees, its overwhelmingly harsh measures, its awesome and seemingly unchecked ability to do what it wanted according to imperatives none of the natives could affect. The discrepancy between the politics producing the *Déscription* and Jabarti's prompt response is therefore total, a fact that highlights the terrain they contest so unequally between them.

It is not difficult to follow out the results of Jabarti's attitude, as in fact generations of historians have done. One can almost immediately see how his experience produced a deep-seated anti-Westernism that becomes a persistent theme of Egyptian, Arab and Islamic history; one can also find in Jabarti the seeds of Islamic reformism which, as promulgated later by Abdu and Afghani, will argue either that Islam had better become modern in order to compete with the West or return to its Meccan roots the better to combat the West; and, to cut the list short, Jabarti can also be seen as initiating the immense wave of national self-consciousness that culminates in Nasserite theory and practise.

On the other hand we have not always found it necessary to read the development of nineteenth century French culture and history in terms of Napoleon's Egyptian expedition. The same has been true of British colonialism in India, a reign of such immense range and wealth as to have become for members of the imperial culture, a fact of nature. Yet what later scholars and critics say about all the European texts made literally possible because the *Déscription* consolidated the conquest of the Orient, is also a function, attenuated and late, of that earlier contest. To write today about Nerval and Flaubert whose work depended so massively upon the Orient then is very allusively to repeat the French imperial victory, consolidate its traces, and extend them into 150 years of European experience, although in saying such a thing we once again highlight the discrepancy between what is symbolised in the opposition of Jabarti to Fourier. It is not a matter of exclusion, as Foucault and Lacan would have us see such things, but of a silent and incorporated disparity that persists in a variety of forms. "They," the colonials, must always take us, the European conquerors, into account; for us, however, they are an episode we experienced, before we went on to other things.

The asymmetry is striking. On the one hand we assume that the whole of history in colonial territories was a function of the imperial intervention; on the other, there is an equally obstinate assumption that colonial undertakings were a phenomenon marginal and perhaps even eccentric to the central activities of the great metropolitan cultures. Thus, to focus principally on attitudes in Europe and the U.S., there has been a tendency in anthropology, history, and cultural studies to treat the whole of world history as viewable by a Western meta-subject, whose historicizing and disciplinary rigor either took away or, in the post-colonial period, restored, history to people and cultures "without" history. Interestingly, therefore, there have been no full-scale critical studies of the relationship between modern Western imperialism and its culture, the occlusion of that deeply symbiotic relationship being a result of it. More particularly, the extraordinary dependence—formal and ideological—of the great French and English realistic novel on the facts of empire has also never been studied from a theoretical standpoint. All these elisions and denials are, I believe, reproduced in the strident journalistic debates about decolonization, in which imperialism is repeatedly on record as saying in effect, you are what you are because of us; when we left, you reverted to your deplorable state. Know that or you will know nothing. For certainly there is little to be known about imperialism that might help either you or us in the present.

Were the disputed value of knowledge about colonialism just a controversy about methodology or about academic perspectives in the writing of cultural history, we would be justified in regarding it as perhaps worth notice, but not really serious. In fact, however, we are talking about a small corner of what, in the world of power and nations, is a compellingly important and interesting configuration. I do not want to spend more than a moment talking about what is perfectly obvious. There is no question, for example, that in the past decade an extraordinarily intense reversion to tribal and religious sentiments has accompanied and deepened many of the discrepancies between polities that have existed since— if they were not actually created by—the period of high European colonialism. Moreover, the various struggles for dominance between states, nationalism, ethnic groups, regions and cultural entities has without question been amplified as well as conducted to a very large degree by the manipulation of opinion and discourse, the production and consumption of ideological media representation, the simplification and reduction into easy currency of vast complexities, the easier to deploy and exploit in the interest of state policy. In all of this intellectuals have played an immensely important role, nowhere in my opinion more crucial and yet compromised than in the overlapping region of experience and culture left as a legacy of colonialism where the politics of secular interpretation are carried on for very high stakes. Naturally, the preponderance of power has been on the side of the self-constituted Western societies, but the reactive responses to this imbalance on the part of many formerly colonized states has been remarkable too. Recent work on India and Pakistan by Eqbal Ahmad and Tarik Ali has highlighted these complicities between the post-colonial security state and the intellectual elite; similar studies have been produced by Arab, African and Latin American oppositional intellectuals.

The entire legacy therefore of what can metaphorically be called the struggle between Conrad and Fanon, with only a few exceptions to it, has been disastrous. Let us concede that, given the discrepancy between European colonial power and colonized societies, there was a kind of historical necessity by which colonial pressure created anti-colonial resistance. What concerns me is the way in which, several generations later, the conflict continues in an impoverished and for that reason more dangerous form, thanks to the underlying complaisant alignment between intellectuals and the present institutions of power. The result, as I noted earlier, has been an intellectual politics of blame and a drastic reduction in the range of material proposed for attention and controversy by intellectuals.

There isn't time here to plot the various strategies that might be employed to widen, expand, deepen the area of post-colonial intellectual activity in order to treat the rich residual actualities of the colonial encounter more usefully. I shall be very brief and schematic, and I shall confine myself to two or three points and illustrative examples. I hope I'll be forgiven for re-stating the problem anecdotally. Two years ago I had a chance encounter with an Arab Christian clergyman, who came to the United States, he told me, on an exceedingly urgent and unpleasant mission. As I myself happened to be a member by birth of the relatively small, but significant, minority he served—Arab Christian Protestants— I was most interested in what he had to say. Since the 1860s there has been a Protestant community of a few sects scattered throughout the Levant, largely the result of the imperial competition for converts and constituents in the Ottoman Empire, principally in Syria, Lebanon, and Palestine. In time of course these congregations—Presbyterian, Episcopalian, Baptist, as well as a few others—acquired their own identities and traditions, their own institutions, all of which, without exception, played an honorable nationalist role during the period of the Arab Renaissance. Roughly one hundred and ten years later, the very same European and American synods and church authorities who had authorized and indeed sustained the early missionary efforts had reconsidered the matter. It had become clear to them that Eastern Christianity was really constituted by the Orthodox Church from which, it should be noted, the overwhelming majority of converts to Protestantism came: the nineteenth century missionaries were totally unsuccessful in converting either Muslims or Jews. Now, in the 1980s, the Western principals of the Arab Protestant communities were encouraging their acolytes to return to the Greek orthodox fold. There was talk of withdrawing financial support, of disbanding the churches and schools, of, in a sense, cancelling the whole thing. The missionary authorities had made a mistake 100 years ago in severing Eastern Christians from the main church. *Now* they should go back.

To my clergyman friend this was a cataclysmic eventuality, and were it not for the genuinely aggrieved sensibility involved one could have considered the whole matter a joke, a cruel joke, but a joke nonetheless. What struck me most strongly, however, was the way in which my friend put his argument: this was what he was here to say to his ecclesiastical principals. He could understand the new doctrinal point being put forward now, that modern ecumenism had better go in the direction of dissolving small sects and preserving the dominant community, rather than in encouraging these sects to remain independent from the main church. That you could discuss. But what seemed horrendously imperialist and belonged entirely to the realm of secular interpretation, he said, was the total disregard with which over a century of Arab Protestant experience was simply scratched off as if it had never happened. What they do not seem to realize, my gravely affected friend told me, is that while we were their converts and students once, we have been their partners for well over a century. We have trusted them and our own experience. We have developed our own integrity, and lived our own Arab Protestant identity within our sphere, but also modern history which we consider to be an independent one. How can they say that the mistake they made a century ago could be rectified today by a stroke of the pen in New York or London, leaving us absolutely nowhere?

You will note that this touching story concerns an experience of colonialism made up essentially of sympathy and of congruence, not of antagonism, resentment, or resistance. The appeal by one of the post-colonial parties was to the value of a mutual experience. True there has been a principal and a subordinate, but there had been dialogue and communication. What you can see in the story is, I think, the power to give, or to withhold, attention, a power utterly essential to interpretation and to politics. The implicit argument made by the Western missionary authorities was that the Arabs had gotten something out of what had been given them, but we, the givers, were now pulling out. Their point seemed to be that in such a relationship of historical dependence and subordination, all the giving went one way, the value was mainly on one side, the ties were significant only as they benefitted the recipient. And so mutuality was constitutively impossible.

I take this to be a parable about the area of attention, made greater or lesser in size, made more or less equal in value if not in quality, furnished for interpretation by the post-colonial situation as that has followed from the colonial encounter. The intellectual imperative here appears to be clear, at least to me, so I needn't embellish it.

The second schematic point I want to make can also be made by example. One of the canonical topics of modern intellectual history has been the development of dominant discourses and disciplinary traditions in the main fields of scientific, social or cultural inquiry. Without any exceptions that I know of, the paradigms for this topic have been drawn from what is considered exclusively Western sources. Foucault's work is one instance of what I mean as, in another domain, is Raymond Williams's. I mention these two formidable scholars because in the main I am in almost total sympathy with their genealogical discoveries to which I am inestimably indebted. Yet for both of them the colonial experience is quite irrelevant and that theoretical oversight has become the norm in all cultural and scientific disciplines except in occasional studies of the history of anthropology—like Johannes Fabian's book *Time and the Other* and Talal Asad's *Anthropology and the Colonial Encounter*—or the development of sociology, such as Brian Turner's book *Marx and the End of Orientalism*. Part of the impulse behind what I tried to do in *Orientalism* was to show the dependence of what appeared to be detached and apolitical cultural disciplines upon a quite sordid history of imperialist ideology and colonialist settlement.

But I will confess that I was also consciously trying to express anger at the consolidated wall of denials that had been built around policy studies passing themselves off as uncontroversial scholarly enterprises. Whatever effect my book achieved would not have happened had there not also been some readiness on the part of a younger generation of scholars, here and in the formerly colonized world, to take a fresh look at their own collective history. Despite the acrimony and recriminations that have followed such efforts, many important revisionary works have appeared. Most of them are valuable because they get beyond the reified polarities of the East vs. West kind, and in an untotalizing way they attempt some grasp of the heterogeneous and non-synchronous developments that have eluded the so-called "world-historians," like Wallerstein, as well as the colonial Orientalists. As examples it is worth mentioning Peter Gran's study on the Islamic roots of modern capitalism in Egypt, or Judith Tucker's research on Egyptian family and village structure under the influence of imperialism, or Hanna Batatu's magisterial work on the formation of modern state institutions in the Arab world, or S. H. Alatas's great study of *The Myth of the Lazy Native*. But there are dozens more such works, all of which characterize interesting intellectual research that is self-consciously post-colonial. Not surprisingly, a great deal of this is cast in terms borrowed from and conducted within the debates between experts of modernization, dependency, and Marxist theories of post-colonial development.

Yet few works have dealt with what I said earlier was a more complex field, the genealogy of contemporary culture and ideology. One of the most notable and recent has been the as yet unpublished work of a Columbia doctoral student from India, herself a trained professional scholar and teacher of English literature, whose brilliant historical and cultural research has, I think, uncovered the political origins of modern English studies, and located them in the system of colonial education imposed on natives in nineteenth century India. A great deal about Gauri Viswanathan's work has unusual interest, but the central point she seems to be making is that what has conventionally been thought of as a discipline created entirely by and for British youth was first created by colonial administrators for the ideological pacification and re-formation of a potentially rebellious Indian population, and then imported into the metropolitan center for a very different but related use there. The evidence, I think, is incontrovertible and refreshingly clear of nativism, one especially besetting hobble of most post-colonial work. Most important, though, this kind of study maps out a much more varied and intertwined archeology for knowledge whose actualities lie considerably below the surface hitherto assumed to be the true texture, and textuality, of what we study as literature, history, culture, and philosophy. The implications are vast indeed and, once again, provide the benefit of pulling us away from routinized polemics on the superiority of Western over non-Western models.

My very last point is simply made. There is no way of dodging the fact that the present ideological conjuncture is deeply inhospitable to the alternative norms for intellectual work that I have been discussing. There is also no escape from the pressing and urgent calls many of us respond to from embattled causes and turbulent fields of battle. Nevertheless, a resistant, perhaps ultimately subjective, component of oppositional energy resides in the intellectual vocation itself, and it is on this that one has to rely, particularly when collective energies seem mostly harnessed to movements for domination and coercion. And we should not be too optimistic about standing up to them.

Intellectuals in the Post-Colonial World: Response and Discussion[1]

WITH EDWARD W. SAID, JOHN LUKACS AND CONOR CRUISE O'BRIEN

O'BRIEN: I think we're much indebted to Edward Said for a large retrospective on those matters which have produced present situations. I would like to try to supplement and complement—and I must say I feel it is very necessary to complement what Edward has said—by talking a little more directly about our announced subject, "The Intellectual in the Post"—I stress "Post-"—Colonial World. What we've heard most about here is the pre-colonial world. I don't dispute the relevance of that to the other. But I'd like to concentrate in my own remarks on 20th century developments, on the role and position of intellectuals both in the decolonization process and in the post-colonial world. Edward has had very little to say about how intellectuals now live, how they express themselves, what freedom they have, what they are. I would like to have a look at that too. But I want to begin with the expectations of intellectuals in the initial period of decolonization. And I come from that country which was first in the process of decolonization, an Ireland whose example in 1921 was to be followed by many in India, Egypt and other places.

What did people expect? Intellectuals, throughout that whole area of the former colonial world, expected to be the inheritors of their newly liberated countries because they had been the challengers of the colonial governments. The people who first challenged British or French power were intellectuals: teachers, writers, publicists. I call them intellectuals because they were people who used concepts, who used words, and who used these to challenge the imperial power, principally Britain and France, knowing that they had an echo for their words and concepts in London and in Paris, and knowing that because they had that echo they were respected in their country. They were the spokesmen for their people. It was an intoxicating role, and a splendid one, as long as it lasted.

Very often these people knew less about the actual conditions in their own countries than they knew about the currency of ideas learned from books which were current in Western Europe at the time. They thought that when the British or the French or the Belgians were gone, their legacy would be what had always been denied them before, an enlightened world. Democracy, for example, had not been shared. The British and the French, who were democrats in their own countries, were not democrats in their colonial administration. And those who were struggling against them assumed the natural development of democratic tendencies in their decolonized countries, along with the continuation of things like freedom of expression, and the rule of law.

So the colonial powers withdrew. And how did they withdraw? Partly by handing over power to intellectuals. Some of these intellectuals were what Christopher Lasch has called "Voice of Reason" intellectuals, persons essentially associated with the status quo, or relatively conservative intellectuals like Leopold Senghor in Senegal. But there were also "Voice of Conscience" intellectuals, persons who claimed to be speaking for the poor and the underdeveloped and the oppressed, though desiring in many cases simply to win power for themselves and their cronies in the name of all that. Typically both types of intellectuals became involved in the first phase of decolonization. Then there was the second wave, wherein the elite that had won the elections could only survive if it satisfied the military. At least throughout most of the decolonized world, this was the phase of the military coups, when the soldiers came in and said to the intellectuals, "Chatterboxes, shut up." And they either shut up or else they went onto the radios and the press of the decolonized world, and said what the soldiers wanted, or what the dictators wanted.

We do not always like to remember this aspect of the decolonization process, but if we are going to talk about the postcolonial world, we can't forget it. The source of all the evil we've heard about was not just in London or Paris. The evil in so many situations has its source in the heart of human beings, whenever they have an advantage, whenever they wish to use that advantage against those whom they may be able to dominate. Now, we here are a group of overwhelmingly Western-based intellectuals. We're not going to be able to change all that out there. But I do think one of the responsibilities that we have is not to romanticize what is happening, not to avert our eyes from dictatorships, from one-party states, not to pretend that it's not happening. I lived for three years in Ghana, West Africa. I lived for a while also in the Congo; I spent some time in Nigeria. Like many of us when we travel, I was in touch there mainly with intellectuals, with the people who teach or write for publication. All of those I met were far less unhappy about colonial residues and the bad thoughts of people in London or Paris or New York than with the situation they were currently living under. And they had reason to fear that situation. At one point, coming from Ghana, in Nkrumah's time, I used to visit the university in Nigeria, a university built up essentially on international consolidations. It had never been seriously honored in the colonial period. In the immediate post-colonial period there was probably more respect for it as a university than there had been. But on the verge of the Nigerian civil war, the entire university was cracking apart on tribal lines. That is to say, the Yoruba in the university were saying, "the Ibo are horrible, let's get them out, let's throw them back to where they came from." And I felt terror in that place, at the time, talking with the families of the people who were in danger of death. Now I refuse to say, with the Jeanne Kirkpatricks of the world, "the whole world is reverting to barbarism, we alone preserve civilization." That is false; there are seeds of renewal in the post-colonial world, as everywhere. But if we tell the people there that there's nothing wrong, if we fail even to hint that there are dictatorships, that there are tyrannies, if we fail to assert that those are wrong, we are then letting down the people who live under those undemocratic regimes, the very people whom it is our duty to support, and who are, in the main, silenced. They do not have access to a free press;

there is no freedom of expression. This is certainly true for most of Africa, and I believe it's true for most of the middle east. If we pass over these conditions in silence, we are in breach of our responsibilities.

LUKACS: I want to return to what Edward Said said in passing about the writer V. S. Naipaul. And I want to take exception to those remarks. Naipaul is a very interesting thinker, and contrary to what Mr. Said has said, he does not write for or pander to Western intellectuals. Naipaul writes a fine English prose, but it is not his style alone that makes him such an unusual writer. Unlike most other intellectuals, particularly those from ex-colonial countries, Naipaul is not a strident collector of injustices. In fact, he castigates some of the post-colonial countries themselves. He does not write principally about the trains not running on time, or the streets being dirty, or the garbage not being collected, though obviously he is not above noticing such things. His principal concern is not with injustice, or justice, but with truth. He is not bothered as much by the prevalence of injustice as by the prevalence of untruth. He is deeply concerned with the rhetoric of those who address public issues. And he wishes that not only more Easterners but also more Westerners were concerned with the ethics of rhetoric. Because this is the fatal sickness of intellectuals in the West, too. They are obsessed with injustice but are little concerned with the prevalence of untruth, not only in Uganda but on American television and in some "enlightened" journals of opinion. There hangs over our world a filthy, polluting cloud of untruth. And in this respect, a person like Naipaul should really merit all of our respect, because he is concerned by the easy acceptance of lies in our society, by the propagation of catchwords and formulas.

WILLIAM PFAFF: I have a question about Mr. O'Brien's remarks regarding the role of the intellectual in the pre-colonial period. It seems to me that there's a point of difficulty, which Mr. Said did not address and which is central to the point of the post-colonial intellectual. This is the problem of conversion. The third world intellectual, the Asian intellectual, was a victim of cultural conversion. It's not enough to say that imperialism conquered these countries. If one looks into the literature of the Indian intelligentsia of the 19th century, of the Chinese new thought of the turn of the century, of the Arab awakening, one sees that they were not saying the West was more powerful, or had technological tricks that they must learn. They were saying that Western values were superior to their own values, at least as regards the way people are treated, questions of justice, of administration, of government. So that there was a cultural conversion on the part of the intelligentsia, which naturally led to a self-loathing as well. These people became, in a real sense, a Westernized intelligentsia. We see, even today, that the vocabulary of the third world still shows a tendency to pose problems in the language of the West—of Marxism, socialism, democracy. So the fact is that the Western agenda, so to speak, is the agenda of the post-colonial world, whether it likes it or not.

A second reaction to the West, which we see today in Iran, is the attempt to move completely away from the West and go back to the old civilization so as to reanimate it. Perhaps I'm wrong, but I don't see this solution as a viable one; you cannot live in the modern world in those terms. Perhaps you can cut yourself off from the modern world. Obviously the desirable solution would be an intelligent synthesis of what is good in the West and what is valid in the old civilization. But nobody seems to have achieved this in a really balanced way. Anyway, it seems to me wrong to discuss the problem in terms of the aggression of the West, or the defense of the third world, just as—here I agree with Mr. Said—it's wrong to talk about it in the triumphalist language of the West, i.e., "we are right and see that they're all barbarians, reverting to savagery." We have here a question of the collision of civilizations, and it's not a simple matter. It is an especially grave problem for societies which have had their own formidable cultures, like China and Islam, cultures which have been undermined in crucial ways by the impact of the West. They're left today with much in ruins and not much reconstructed. This seems to me the main dilemma of post-colonial life.

SAID: I think that Mr. Pfaff puts it very well, defining possibilities in a way I find persuasive. But I draw quite different insights from all of this. I think, first of all, the schematic attempt to talk about the post-colonial dilemma as if it were a single thing, the same thing happening in India that happened in Algeria and elsewhere, is not really appropriate. There are similarities of a certain kind, but those are really not the interesting aspects. That's the first point I want to make. The second point is that I'm not sure if in fact the break between the colonial and post-colonial period is that great. Look at the relations between Algeria and France. I suppose the ties could be closer between these countries, but the ties between them are nonetheless impressive, and worth considering.

The third point I want to make is that I don't think what we see in the post-colonial or post-independence world is necessary—necessary as understood through the eyes of Western-style intellectuals. Take Iran, for instance, an example which is horrible, politically and on every other ground. But if you get around the politics of blame issue, what is going on in Iran is really interesting and constantly in flux. There are different, independent cultures involved in Iran. We need to examine the distinction between what is native and what is foreign there. The over-riding dogma promulgated by the historiography of the colonial world has been, in fact, that the main thing that counts in these societies is the impact of the West. And that—certainly in my part of the third world—is what every historian has written about. But the new generation of historians is looking at that impact as simply another episode among many in a much longer history than that provided by "The impact of the West."

At some point, part of the post-colonial intellectual's agenda should be to leave aside the immediate politics in which we're all engaged. We need to understand the nature of Islam, for example, as something not necessarily defined by the powers that be that are interested in it only as it bears upon Western security. Isn't there another tradition here, that has been hidden and invisible to the scrutiny of scholars shaped by the dominant Western traditions? Take for example the whole notion of Oriental despotism. There's been a lot of research lately on this, but the actual model is deeply flawed. The most interesting aspect of the post-colonial intellectual's job is not in the arena of combat. What is most valuable and interesting and necessary is the intellectual's task of reexamining the issues completely. Looking at the issue of "religion" as a category of "traditional society" doesn't make adequate sense because the model adopted is essentially Western. By Western here I mean a particular, disciplinary history. We can't simply take our models and apply them to other cultures as if they were perfectly capable of doing them justice. These are the kinds of things I'm interested in.

O'BRIEN: Just in supplement to what Edward has said I'd like to offer, not an answer to William Pfaff's question, but an exhibit. Several years ago, in Kyoto Japan, I attended a conference under the auspices of the United Nations University, which had the rather grand title of "Endogenous Elements in National Culture." It was an Asian conference; I was, I believe, the only European there. But it presented a very interesting peculiarity. There were representatives from all over Asia: India, Pakistan, Burma, etc. The interesting peculiarity was that although it was about endogenous elements in national culture, every one of the representatives there, with the exception of one nation, spoke English exclusively, including the Chinese. English was the language of the conference, used throughout by all except the Japanese. And, except for the Japanese, the themes of the contributors were about the impact of the West, generally negatively conceived, but still the West, the West, the West. The only people who talked about the endogenous elements endogenously were the Japanese. They discussed what were to outsiders extremely abstruse aspects of Japanese diversification in a particular five-year period of the late 17th century. And that's all they talked about—they never referred to the West at all. They ignored it totally. I was reminded of Auden's famous line about the Sphinx turning a vast behind on shrill America. That is what they were doing, but nobody else was; everybody else was obsessed with the West. As I say, draw your own conclusions.

AUDIENCE (CHARLES MOLESWORTH): I found Edward's anecdote about the missionaries to be quite striking. It seems to me to catch a moment in the Post-Colonial experience that merits reflection. And it calls to mind a very rough analogy with the relationship between Marlow and Kurtz's intended. Marlow claims that women cannot bear a lie, but in fact he tells her a lie in the course of completing his tale. And it seems to me, in a sense, that that's what your American Episcopalians are doing:

they're opting out of a situation by telling the colonized what the colonizer thinks the colonized need to hear. But does the colonizer really know what is going on? Does Marlow? Does Conrad?

SAID: It's hard to jump from one situation to another. The thing that impressed me about the whole Marlow episode and Conrad's staging of the story is that Marlow, in fact, makes it clear that he does know what he's doing, and he can more or less do anything. And even when he says that he can't really tell us what's happened, because language isn't good enough, or words to that effect, he does it anyway. What Conrad is representing is a total grasp of the whole situation. And we're led to believe that Marlow is impressed by the horrendous experience that both he and Kurtz have gone through. I don't know if he felt sorry for the Africans that he saw, but at least he felt something. That's why I think Conrad is more interesting as an imperialist kind of consciousness. He does seem to be aware of some alternatives, though not all of them.

O'BRIEN: I must mildly differ with you there, Edward, in that it doesn't appear to me that Conrad's *Heart of Darkness* is in any sense an imperialist statement. It's certainly not imperialist in the sense of offering any defense of the Leopoldine system. It is, on the contrary, along with Roger Casement's exposé, very powerfully, and in all of its implications, an anti-imperialist work.

LUKACS: I would say that it's not exactly anti-imperialist. It's really directed toward the futility of imperialism.

O'BRIEN: Certainly it's opposed to the Leopoldine system. Conrad may have favored, in other locales, the milder British and French systems.

SAID: Certainly it's true that Conrad—or Marlow—lets us think that it's futile, that there are these terrible abuses and so on and so forth. And yet I wonder whether that is all that could be said about Conrad's view of imperialism. I think the way in which the work is constructed, with a kind of emptiness and, as Marlow says, the total demoralization of the geography, the backwardness of the natives and the Blacks—it does seem to me too simple to say of all this, "well, it's meant as an attack upon imperialism." I think that in many ways it's an account that pretty much follows the standards of a *Mission Civilisatrice* . . .

O'BRIEN: Oh, God! *Mission—Mission Civilisatrice?*

SAID: Yes

O'BRIEN: *Heart of Darkness?*

SAID: Yes

O'BRIEN: Oh, God.

LUKACS: A very important clue in all this, if you remember, occurs when Marlow starts his trip, and gets his job in Belgium (he and Baudelaire were the two people who most despised the Belgians); and he says, "I have to go out of this horrible country."

SAID: And yet he says that the wonderful thing about this civilization, our British or Western civilization, is that it's unlike Rome, in that it is really all about serving an idea. That's the way the story starts, really...

O'BRIEN: Oh, come on, but that's turned into a horrible irony.

SAID: Well, it's turned into a horrible irony, but it's also turned into the basis of a profoundly imperialist work.

O'BRIEN: I'll be sticking straws in my hair in a moment.

AUDIENCE: We may not be able to agree exactly on Conrad's intentions, but certainly Marlow is a fan of British imperialism, at the opening of *Heart of Darkness*, looking at the flag, feeling the warmth of the colors and so forth.

O'BRIEN: If you saw Leopoldine imperialism you'd like British imperialism too.

SAID: Isn't that really the point?

O'BRIEN: Yes, that is the point. But we're speaking here of quite different things.

SAID: Different, yes; but we're speaking of imperialism. I'm aware that there are different kinds of imperialism, but you have the thing I'm talking about wherever you read that there is a kind of inevitability to the white man in the dark world. Of course there are different kinds of white men. As Conor was saying, there are the Leopolds, and there are the Kurtzes, and so on. Conrad says that all Europe went into the making of Kurtz, of course. But I think that Conrad distinguishes very carefully among the various kinds. What I am saying—it seems to me so completely obvious—is that *Heart of Darkness* is not only a work about imperialism, it is a work of imperialism itself. It is a kind of modified imperialism, with a certain consciousness that Conrad had of a natural course of things where the superior people went out and conquered the rest of the world. Some did it for what they considered to be the good of the natives, and Conrad deals with them in *Nostromo*, which is a great work. But it's inevitable that even great works of that moment should support, in some sense, imperialism. There are criticisms of the abuses of particular adventurers. But the enterprise itself is presented by Conrad (like Marx before him) as, (a)-inevitable, given the relevant historical forces, and (b)-inevitable as understood by a certain kind of personal mythology held by the adventurer, whom he profoundly admired. Casement, for example, is also in Kurtz. And this type of man, who goes into the other world, so to speak, is someone that Conrad had great admiration for.

O'BRIEN: How can you say that Casement is Kurtz? Casement did nothing similar to what Kurtz did. And Casement exposed, publically, the Kurtzian system, as Conrad did. How you identify Casement with Kurtz absolutely baffles me.

SAID: You were also baffled earlier when I said imperialism, but you finally came around to my use of the word, I believe.

O'BRIEN: No, no, no, Edward. What I did was to make distinctions between one imperialism and another, quite as you do: every sensible person must do no less.

SAID: You accept, I believe, that Conrad could write about British imperialism as inevitable and still dislike other forms of imperialism?

O'BRIEN: I think that Conrad, in *Heart of Darkness*, is producing a *reductio ad absurdum* of all imperialism by taking the worst case. The worst case, incomparably, is Leopoldine. There has been nothing like it, there never was anything like it before. To smear all this over and say British, French, at bottom it's all the same, it's all imperialism is rubbish. In taking the worst case, Conrad was saying that the whole thing was a mess; it's not going to do anybody any good, so why not just get out. In my opinion it's all profoundly anti-imperialist, but anti-imperialist with nuances.

AUDIENCE (JEAN BETHKE ELSHTAIN): I'm interested in the way we see others as foreign, or read the foreign as synonymous with the enemy. Mr. Said probably knows a small book by Glenn Gray called *The Warriors,* in which he argues that one major function of a nation state at war is to construct as powerful and abstract as possible an image of the enemy, in order to distinguish as sharply as possible the act of killing from the act of murder. So we think in terms of "the enemy," as though it were concrete and definitive. We take one small part of what those foreign people might be and turn it into "the enemy." Now, with that in mind, I'm thinking of an experience I had in a class last week. We were talking about Gray's book, and I asked my students which group they most naturally see as the abstract enemy in the way Gray describes. We talked about various candidates. The students were finally unanimous that the Nicaraguans didn't fit; neither did the Chinese, nor the Russians. But the Arabs did. That is, in terms of the images that we are saturated with through the media, and the fact that we sort of owe them (we think here of oil prices, Iran, blowing up Marines in Lebanon), it's hard not to see "the Arabs" in an abstract and thoroughly undiscriminating way.

SAID: Some of this has to do with religion. There is a tension with the Arab-Islamic world that's at least partly based on religion, which is held to be deeply competitive with, and later than, Judaism and Christianity. I think, for example, the fairly recent use of the term Judeo-Christian includes an implicit reference to Islam as "other." And this in part comes out of a certain fear.

Certainly what's going on in South Lebanon today is an example of events Westerners see in a way almost completely dictated by fear. For here we have an attempt by Westerners to ascribe events to some fundamentally intransigeant Islamic component which is supposed to feature suicide and terror over a rational sort of acceptance of permanent occupation. I think Israel plays a very important role here. The relationship between Israel and the West, and the United States in particular, has had the effect of more or less condemning the surrounding world, which is now pretty large, to one undifferentiated mass. They're all thought of as Arabs and Communists and Islamic terrorists, all these fantastic categories, one blending into another.

One can't ignore, either, a particular kind of ignorance about the Middle East which is quite remarkable when you think of the great burgeoning of area studies in this country after world war two. You see Soviets, Chinese and Indians on television discussions; the area of scholarship that has remained a kind of poor cousin and has never made any contribution to the larger culture of the West is the study of Islam. If you ask a Western intellectual to name a writer of that world, he can't. Very little is available for that reason. And very little specific sympathy with Islamic thought is likely to develop.

AUDIENCE: To the author of *To Katanga and Back* I want to say that it is necessary to recall how much that went wrong in places like the Congo was the result of the underhanded maneuverings not only of the Belgians but of external powers of various kinds, often abetted by the United

Nations itself. This Mr. O'Brien knows probably better than anyone else. In other words, it seems to me that before one points the finger at emergent peoples who are made to take a bad spill, we also have to take into account the tripwire which is almost invariably set in their path.

Second, I don't think it is entirely correct to say that third-world intellectuals have routinely corrupted their own revolutions. In many instances the intellectuals have been trampled underfoot by leaders who were supported by the West because they were perceived as our allies and as "good guys," resolute anti-Communists. These people were able to take hold of the levers of power and to use this power against the up-and-coming generation of intellectuals who, had they been given an opportunity, might have come out looking somewhat more impressive as intellectuals.

O'BRIEN: Yes, that does certainly supplement what I've said here. I don't think we are in fundamental disagreement. It is true, as I wrote in the book to which you refer, that in the post-independence Congo, which is now Zaire, there was a great deal of Western intervention. It's also true that many of the principle figures were, in the main, agents of Western powers, or at least were building up their own positions with the help of Western aid. But where I differ from Edward in relation to his presentation, just as you differ from me in relation to my presentation, is on the question of balance. Some of the troubles of post-colonial Africa certainly came from Western intervention and manipulation. But not all, by no means all of them. The Congo experience is one thing. Ghana, for example, is another. When I lived in Ghana in the sixties I saw that most of Ghana's troubles were being manufactured by a new elite. When decolonization was well under way, in many places, it was clear that intellectuals would formulate the demands and launch the critiques. This was the case from 1947 on, from the time of Indian independence and all through the years when other countries would press their claims. And it had been true under colonialism too. In the Gold Coast, which became Ghana, the old intellectual elites, known in colonialist mythology as the educated Africans, were preparing to take over; they were expecting to take over. But then the scenario speeded up, and they couldn't follow. So a new elite of less educated people, people who were not University graduates mainly, and had done maybe one year in high school, realized that if they stepped up their rhetoric and shouted "get out," the highly educated would leave, because they were ready to get out anyway. And they did, most of them. So you had the second-rate intellectuals pushing out the old elite. This phenomenon was quite frequent in Africa, though there were other patterns also. One doesn't, in recognizing this, speak with general contempt about the intellectuals who remained. Some of the new leaders were quite capable. Tshombe never pretended to be an intellectual. He was just an ordinary guy. Lumumba was a very ill-prepared intellectual, but he had a very good mind, however much circumstances caused him to grope for his way. But Jomo Kenyatta, were he here today, would be making a real impact on this gathering. So would Leopold Senghor of Senegal. Some of the heirs were in fact intellectuals of exceptionally high quality.

But the thing I did want to stress here, the fact we should not lose sight of, is that in most colonial countries there is little or no freedom of expression, that intellectuals who want to write will have to work for state-controlled newspapers or state-controlled broadcasting systems, that those who want to teach and engage in research will be in universities which are under a very heavy shadow of state control. And this is not invented by the ex-colonial power; it is the work of the new elites who are partly shaped by the old colonial experience.

AUDIENCE: I want to return to something suggested in Edward Said's opening remarks. We can't pretend that telling the truth amounts to the same thing in one context as it amounts to in another. It's important to talk about oppressive state control in Africa or in Central America, but it's just as important to recognize what that talk means in some places. To stress in the United States the infringements on freedom of the press imposed by the Sandinistas in Nicaragua is in effect to support the Reagan policy in Central America. You may deny that is what you intend to do, but there it is.

O'BRIEN: Obviously I don't want anything I said here to be construed as justifying American foreign policy in Nicaragua, which I think is fundamentally wrong-headed; I think it's also addressed to American domestic concerns and not to any genuine international interests of the United States. I want to be quite clear about that. But I don't think that we who want to criticize American policy in Central America or elsewhere are doing ourselves any good if we try to sweep under the rug the tyrannical and negative aspects of many post-colonial regimes. (Whether Nicaragua is post-colonial or pre-colonial would be very hard to say right now.) In the main I've been talking of regimes I know best, African regimes primarily. And frankly, most of them are bloody awful. And I don't think we should pretend that they are anything else, not if we are to preserve what I might call our intellectual commitment to honesty.

SAID: But who would disagree with a denunciation of tyranny? The wrinkle comes when you ask, "where does one do that?" I mean, to denounce tyranny is not necessarily to advance the cause of freedom.

O'BRIEN: I'm satisfied simply to tell the truth. I can't be sure about which of my statements will or will not advance the cause of freedom.

SAID: But "telling the truth" will seem to some people very easy if the truth they tell is designed to appeal to an obviously receptive constituency which wants to hear one kind of truth but no others. The value of testimonials to freedom and democracy will vary in accordance with the circumstances in which they are made. And that is exactly the point I would make about V. S. Naipaul. Naipaul's constituency is not the world of truth seekers everywhere. He writes to the Western liberal who wants very much to be reassured that, after all, after "we" left Pakistan, after "we" left Malaysia and after "we" left Iran, things got worse. To flatter a prejudice is not "simply" to tell the truth.

LUKACS: Naipaul hasn't spared anyone in his writings. He has had harsh things to say about people in Argentina and in Trinidad, about Africa and Pakistan. He's not at all selective in the manner of most intellectuals I know.

ROBERT BOYERS: It does seem to me that you're right, Edward, that Naipaul does write for an audience of Western intellectuals.

O'BRIEN: And what other audience would he write for?

BOYERS: But I can not agree with Edward that Naipaul's Western audience is typically charmed by what he has to say or receptive to his message, such as it is. Naipaul's most pressing insights go directly against the grain of the standard liberal bias held in common by most Western intellectuals today.

SAID: Wait a minute. When V. S. Pritchett reviewed *Journey Among the Believers* in *The New Yorker*, he said that Naipaul had done something that no one else had done; he had revealed to us the fundamental laziness of the Islamic mind. Now Pritchett is a very good writer, but he is also in this respect a representative spokesman for a Western view of the Islamic mind. You don't think that before he read Naipaul he believed in the incredible energy of the Islamic mind. No? So what are you trying to say about Naipaul? I'm simply saying that, on the basis of his being an Indian Trinidadian, he has had ascribed to him the credentials of a man who can serve as witness for the third world; and he is a very convenient witness. He is a third worlder denouncing his own people, not because they are victims of imperialism, but because they seem to have an innate flaw, which is that they are not whites.

O'BRIEN: That's not true. He's talking about human beings living in very confused and desperate situations. There is no trace of a racialist bias in Naipaul, and I don't see why when you disapprove of his views it's necessary to bring in the question of race or of innate characteristics.

SAID: Why, I wonder, doesn't Naipaul talk about the confused and desperate situation in which people live in the white countries? The only whites he dislikes intensely are those who believe that blacks can redeem themselves.

BOYERS: Naipaul need not balance what he says about Africa with comparable complaints on the state of affairs in London. The question you're raising has to do with whether or not he deliberately falsifies his material on the third world so as to pander to the biases of a Western audience. That audience, I would contend, is not disposed to believe that conditions in the third world are as awful or as hopeless as they seem in Naipaul. And they are surely resistant to the idea that people in Africa or in India or Pakistan are victims of their respective cultures. An important dimension of Naipaul's argument is that as long as Indians and Africans continue to think in ways mandated by their own cultural institutions, they will be unable to deal effectively with their problems. This is hardly the sort of thing Western liberals, with their obligatory respect for alien cultures, are prepared to like. How often do we hear serious writers tell us that one culture is not as good as another, that some cultures positively obstruct or even forbid the kinds of intellectual growth we are supposed to admire? Some readers may like to read that the Islamic mind is lazy, but most Western liberals want to believe that one culture is as valid as another and that problems are the consequence of "imperialism." Naipaul can hardly be said to pander to these people.

SAID: The Naipaul phenomenon is the phenomenon of a certain context, of a certain moment and above all, of a certain ignorance. I mean, Naipaul didn't just happen. He attracted great attention at a particular time. He had this great impact because he contributed to an already growing disenchantment with the third world, and with the decolonization process generally.

BOYERS: I don't think that anyone will deny that, by the time Naipaul became very influential, in the mid-1970's, the promise attributed to most third world revolutions had gone sour. It was no longer possible even for devout enthusiasts to sustain the hope in those revolutions that they had formerly entertained.

SAID: But the question is, how well, how honestly, does Naipaul address problems in the countries he says he's talking about? How much of the effect he produces is a matter of his knowing how to anticipate dissatisfaction with what happened in Iran or in some other place? Don't just listen to what I say about Naipaul: read what C. L. R. James and Salman Rushdie say.

O'BRIEN: Would the Iranian revolution have satisfied you, if you had been living there?

SAID: Of course not. I've attacked it frequently, and loudly, although I am still a solid supporter of the revolution against the Shah. But my view of the revolution there is not in question. The moment Naipaul defines and crystallizes for the Western audience is the moment of *our* disappointment with the prospects of other peoples. And that disappointment, based as it is on our tendency to grow bored with something we can't control, is at the root of the acclaim Naipaul has won.

O'BRIEN: Obviously we're not going to agree on much of this, and there's really a good deal we haven't touched on. We haven't debated, for example, the question of how much Naipaul really does know about the Islamic world. What Edward regards as a prejudice may be the leading edge of a perfectly valid insight. But for now I think we'll have to leave our differences where they are.

Note

[1] This is an edited transcript of a panel discussion held at Skidmore College on April 10, 1985.

Intellectuals and History[1]

BY CORNELIUS CASTORIADIS
(TRANSLATED BY DAVID AMES CURTIS)

First of all, the term "history." I do not understand by it merely history-already-made but also history-in-the-making and history-to-be-made. In this sense, history is essentially creation—creation *and* destruction. Creation signifies something entirely different from the objective indeterminacy or the subjective unforeseeability of events and of the course of history. It is ridiculous to say, for example, that the advent of tragedy was unforeseeable, and it is stupid to see in *St. Matthew's Passion* an effect of the indeterminacy of history.

History is the domain in which human beings create ontological forms—history and society themselves being the first of these forms. Creation does not necessarily—nor even generally—signify "good" creation or the creation of "positive values." Auschwitz and the Gulag are creations just as much as the Parthenon and the *Principia Mathematica*. But among the creations in our history, Greco-Western history, there is one that we judge positively and take credit for: putting things into question, criticizing them, requiring a *logon didonai*—accounting for something and giving a reason for it—which is the presupposition for both philosophy and politics.

Now, *this* is a fundamental human posture—and, at the outset, it is in no way universally given. It implies that there is no extrahuman authority responsible, in the last instance, for what occurs in history, that there are no true causes or author of history. In other words, it means that history is not made by God or by *phusis* or by "laws" of any kind. It is because they did not believe in such determinations (besides the ultimate limit of *Ananke*) that the Greeks were able to create democracy and philosophy.

We ourselves resume, reaffirm, and will to prolong this creation. We are and will to be in a tradition of radical criticism, which also implies both responsibility (we cannot put the blame on an omnipotent God, etc.) and self-limitation (we cannot invoke any extrahistorical norm for our conduct, which nevertheless must be provided with norms). As a result, we situate ourselves as critical actors in relation to what is, what could and should be, and even what has been. We can contribute to the character of ''what is'' so that it may be otherwise. We cannot change what has been, but we can change how we gaze upon it—and this gazing is an essential ingredient of our present attitudes (even if it is most often done unconsciously). In particular, we do not grant, in a first approximation, any philosophical privilege to historical reality, past or present. Past and present are nothing other than masses of brute facts (or empirical subject matter) except insofar as they have been critically reevaluated by us. Since we are downstream from this past and since it therefore has been able to enter into the presuppositions of what we think and what we are, we may say, as a second approximation, that this past acquires a sort of transcendental importance, for our knowledge and criticism of it form a part of our self-reflective activity. And this is so not only because it clearly shows the relativity of the present, through our knowledge of other epochs, but also because it allows us to glimpse the relativity of actual history, through reflection upon other histories that were actually possible, even if they have not been realized.

Secondly, the term "intellectual." I have never liked it or accepted it, for reasons that are at once aesthetic: the miserable and defensive arrogance implied therein, and logical: Who is not an intellectual? Without entering into basic questions of biophysiology, let us observe that if one intends by the term "intellectual" someone who works almost exclusively with his head and nearly not at all with his hands, one leaves out people whom one would clearly want to include (sculptors and other categories of artists), and one includes people who certainly were not intended thereby (computer specialists, bankers and brokers, etc.).

It is unclear why a talented Egyptologist or mathematician who wanted to know nothing outside their respective disciplines would particularly interest us here. From this remark one might conclude that, for purposes of the present discussion, we ought to include all those who, irrespective of their profession, try to go beyond their sphere of specialization and actively interest themselves in what is going on in society. But this is, and ought to be, the very definition of the democratic citizen, irrespective of his occupation. (And let us note that this is the exact opposite of Plato's definition of justice: minding one's own business and not getting mixed up in everyone else's—which is not at all surprising, since one of Plato's aims is to show that democratic societies are unjust.)

I will not try to respond to this question here. My remarks are aimed at those who, by their use of speech and through their explicit formulation of general ideas, have been able or are now able to attempt to have an influence on how their society evolves and on the course of history. The list is immense, and the questions raised by their words and deeds are endless. Therefore, I will also confine myself to a brief discussion of three points.

The first concerns two different kinds of relationship between the thinker and the political community, as exemplified in the radical opposition between Socrates, the philosopher in the city, and Plato, the philosopher who wants to be above the city. The second relates to a tendency that began to take hold of philosophers during a certain phase of history—namely, the tendency to rationalize the real, that is, to legitimate it. The era that is just now coming to a close has witnessed some particularly grievous instances of this tendency, with the fellow-travelers of Stalinism of course, but also, in an "empirically" different but philosophically equivalent fashion, with Heidegger and Nazism. I will conclude on a third point: the question raised by the relationship between, on the one hand, the criticism and the vision of the philosopher-citizen and, on the other, the fact that, from the standpoint of a project of autonomy and democracy, the great majority of men and women living in society are the source of creation, the principal bearers of the instituting imaginary, and that they should become the active subjects of an explicit politics.

Socrates and Plato

In Greece, the philosopher was, during a long initial period, just as much a citizen as a philosopher. It is for this reason too that he was sometimes called upon to "give laws," either to his city or to another one. Solon offers the most celebrated example of this role played by the philosopher-citizen. But still in 443 B.C., when the Athenians established in Italy a pan-Hellenic colony called Thurioi, it was Protagoras whom they asked to establish a set of laws.

The last in this line—the last great one, at any rate—is Socrates. Socrates is a philosopher, but he is also a citizen. He discusses matters with all his fellow citizens in the agora. He has a family and children. He takes part in three military expeditions. He takes up the supreme magistracy, and he is the epistates of the prytaneis (President of the Republic for a day) at perhaps the most tragic moment in the history of the Athenian democracy: the day of the trial of the victorious generals of the battle of Arginusae, when, as president of the people's assembly, he braves the furious crowd and refuses to initiate illegal proceedings against these generals. Similarly, a few years later he will refuse to obey the order of the Thirty Tyrants to arrest a citizen illegally.

His trial and conviction are a tragedy in the proper sense of the term. It would be inane to search for the innocent and the guilty here. Certainly the *demos* of 399 B.C. is no longer that of the sixth or the fifth centuries, and certainly too, the city could have continued to accept Socrates as it had accepted him for decades. But we must also understand that Socrates' practices transgress the limit of what, strictly speaking, a democracy can tolerate.

Democracy is the regime founded explicitly upon *doxa*, opinion, the confrontation of opinions, the formation of a common opinion. The refutation of another's opinions is more than permitted and legitimate there; it is the very breath of public life. But Socrates does not limit himself to showing that this or that *doxa* is erroneous nor does he offer a *doxa* of his own in its stead. He shows that all *doxae* are erroneous, and still more, that those who defend these *doxae* do not know what they are talking about. Now, no life in society, and no political regime—democracy least of all—can continue to exist based upon the hypothesis that all its participants live in a world of incoherent mirages—which is precisely what Socrates is constantly demonstrating.

The city certainly should have accepted even this; it had done so for a long time, with Socrates as well as with others. But Socrates himself knew perfectly well that sooner or later he would have to account for his practices. He did not need anyone to prepare his apology, he said, because he had spent his life reflecting upon the apology he would offer, were he ever accused. And Socrates not only accepts the judgment of the tribunal made up of his fellow citizens; his speech in the *Crito,* which is so often taken as a moralizing and edifying harangue, is a magnificent development of the fundamental Greek idea that the individual is formed by the city: *polis andra didaskei,* it is the city that educates the man, as Simonides wrote. Socrates knows that he was brought up by Athens and that he could not have been so brought up anywhere else.

It is hard to think of a disciple who has, in practice, betrayed the spirit of his master more than Plato. Plato withdraws from the city, and it is at its gates that he establishes a school for his chosen disciples. One knows of no military campaign in which he would have participated. One knows not of a family he would have reared. He furnishes to the city that raised him and made him what he is none of those things that every citizen owes it: neither military service nor children nor acceptance of public responsibilities. He calumniates Athens to the most extreme degree, and, thanks to his immense genius as a stage director, a rhetorician, a sophist, and a demagogue, he will succeed in imposing, for centuries to come, an image of the politicians of Athens—Themistocles and Pericles—as demagogues, of its thinkers as "sophists" (in the sense imposed by him), its poets as corruptors of the city, and its people as a vile herd given over to their passions and illusions. He knowingly falsifies history—and in this domain he is the first inventor of Stalinist methods. If one knew the history of Athens only through Plato (from the third book of the Laws) one would know nothing of the battle of Salamis, the victory of Themistocles and of that despicable *demos* of oarsmen.[2]

What he wants to do is to establish a city removed from time and history, governed not by its own people but by "philosophers." But he is also—contrary to all of previous Greek experience, where the philoso-

phers have shown an exemplary *phronesis*, a wisdom in their actions—
the first to display that basic ineptitude which has, since then, so often
characterized philosophers and intellectuals when faced with political
reality. He wants to be the counselor to the prince, in fact a tyrant— this
has never stopped since—and he fails miserably because he, the subtle
psychologist and admirable portraitist, cannot tell apples from oranges
and takes Dionysius the Younger, tyrant of Syracuse, for a potential
philosopher-king—as, twenty-three centuries later, Heidegger will take
Hitler and Nazism for the incarnations of the spirit [*esprit*] of the German
people and of historical resistance against the reign of technique. It is
Plato who inaugurates the era of philosophers who wriggle out of the city,
but who, as possessors of the truth, want to dictate to it laws while
completely ignoring people's instituting creativity and, at the same time
being politically impotent, have as their supreme ambition to become
counselors to the prince.

The Adoration of the *Fait Accompli*

Nevertheless, Plato is not at the source of this other deplorable aspect of
the activity of intellectuals when confronted with history: the
rationalization of the real, that is to say, the legitimation of the
powers-that-be. And for good reason. In Greece, at least, adoration of the *fait
accompli* is unknown and impossible as an attitude of the mind [*esprit*]. We
must move ahead to the Stoics to begin to find its first seeds. Though it
is impossible for us to discuss its origins here and now, it is evident that,
after an enormous detour, this attitude harks back to the archaic and
traditional phases of human history, when the institutions given at each
time were considered sacred, and accomplishes the amazing feat of
putting philosophy, born as an integral part of putting the established
order in question, into the service of the conservation of this very order.

However, it is impossible not to see that Christianity, from its very
inception, was the explicit creator of the spiritual, affective, and existential postures that will, for eighteen centuries and more, provide a basis for
the sanctification of the powers-that-be. The dictum, "Render unto
Caesar the things which be Caesar's," can only be interpreted along with
the statement that "There is no power but of God: the powers that be are

ordained of God.'' The true Christian kingdom is not of this world and, moreover, the history of this world, by becoming the history of Salvation, is immediately sanctified in its existence and in its "direction," that is to say, in its essential "sense."[3] Exploiting for its own ends the Greek philosophical *instrumentarium,* Christianity will furnish, for fifteen centuries, the conditions required for acceptance of the "real," such as it is— up to Descartes' "Better to change oneself than the order of the world" and, obviously, to the literal apotheosis of reality in the Hegelian system ("All that is real is rational"). Despite appearances, it is this same universe—an essentially theological, apolitical, acritical universe—to which belong both Nietzsche, when he proclaims the "innocence of becoming," and Heidegger, when he presents history as *Ereignis* and *Geschick,* advent of Being and donation / destination of and through the latter.

Let us be done with this ecclesiastical, academic, and literary "respectuosity." Let us finally speak of syphilis in this family, of which half the members are clearly suffering in general paralysis. We should take by the ear the theologian, the Hegelian, the Nietzschean, the Heideggerian, bring them to Kolyma in Siberia, to Auschwitz, into a Russian psychiatric hospital, into the torture chambers of the Argentine police, and require that they explain, on the spot and without subterfuges, the meaning of the expressions "There is no power but of God," "All that is real is rational," "the innocence of becoming," or "releasement toward things."[4]

But we encounter the most extraordinary *mélange* when the intellectual, in a supreme *tour de force,* succeeds in tying the critique of reality to the adoration of force and power. This *tour de force* becomes elementary once a "revolutionary power" arises somewhere or other. Then begins the golden age of fellow-travelers, who were able to afford the combination of an apparently intransigent opposition to a part of reality— reality "at home"—with the glorification of another part of this same reality—over there, elsewhere, in Russia, in China, in Cuba, in Algeria, in Vietnam, or, if worst came to worst, in Albania. Rare are those among the great names in the Western intelligentsia who have not, at some moment between 1920 and 1970, made this "sacrifice of conscience," sometimes (the least often) in the most infantile kind of credulity, other times (most often) with the most paltry sort of trickery. Sartre, stating in a menacing tone: "You cannot discuss what Stalin is doing, since he alone has the information that explains his motives," will remain, no doubt, the most instructive specimen of the intellectual's tendency to make him/ herself look ridiculous.

Faced with this debauchery of pious perversity and of fraudulent use of reason, we must forcefully state the following, deeply buried evident truth: *reality possesses no privilege,* neither philosophical nor normative; the past has no more value than the present, and the latter exists not as model but as material. The past history of the world is in no way sanctified—and it might be rather that it is damned, for it has shunted aside other, effectively possible histories. These latter have as much importance for the mind [*esprit*]—and perhaps more value for our practical attitudes—than "real" history. Our daily paper does not contain, as Hegel believed, "our morning realist prayer" but rather our daily surrealist farce. More than ever, perhaps, this is so today. If something should appear in the present year, it should create in us, initially and until there is proof to the contrary, the strong presumption that it incarnates stupidity, ugliness, maleficence and vulgarity.

The Citizen

Certainly, to restore, to restitute, to reinstitute an authentic task for the intellectual in history is, first of all and above all, to restore, restitute, and reinstitute his critical function. Because history is always both creation and destruction at once, and because creation (like destruction) concerns the sublime as much as the monstrous, elucidation and criticism are, more than anybody else's, in the custody of those who, by occupation and by position, can place themselves at a distance from the everyday and from the real. That is to say, in the custody of the intellectual.

At a distance, too, and as far as it is possible, from oneself. This takes the form not only of "objectivity" but also of an ongoing effort to go beyond one's specialty, to remain concerned by all that matters to men and women.

Such attitudes would certainly tend to separate the subject from the great mass of his contemporaries. But there is separation and there is separation. We will not leave behind us the perversion of the intellectual's role that has characterized it since Plato's time, and again for the past seventy years, unless the intellectual genuinely becomes a *citizen* again. A citizen is not (not necessarily) a "party activist"—but someone who actively claims his/her participation in public life and in the common affairs of the city on the same footing as everyone else.

Here, quite evidently, appears an antinomy which has no theoretical solution; only *phronesis*, effective wisdom, can permit one to surmount it. The intellectual should want to be a citizen like the others; he also wants to be spokesperson, *de jure*, for universality and objectivity. He can abide in this space only by recognizing the *limits* of that which his supposed objectivity and universality permit of him; he should recognize, and not just through lip service, that what he is trying to get people to listen to is still a *doxa*, an opinion, not an *episteme*, a science. Above all, he must recognize that history is the domain in which there unfolds the creativity of all people, both men and women, the learned and the illiterate, a humanity in which he is only one atom.

Nor should this become a pretext for swallowing uncritically the decisions of the majority, for bowing down before force because it is the force of numbers. To be a democrat and to be able, if this be one's judgment, to say to the people "You are mistaken," this too is what should be required of him or her. Socrates was able to do it during the Arginusae trial. After the fact the case seems clear-cut, and Socrates was able to rely upon a rule in formal law. Things are often much hazier. Here again, only wisdom, *phronesis*, and *taste*, can permit one to separate the recognition of people's creativity from blind adoration of "the power of facts." And be not surprised to find the word *taste* at the end of these remarks. One only had to read five lines of Stalin to understand that the revolution could not be *that*.

Notes

[1] Speech given to the "Intellectuals and History" round-table discussion at the International Conference of Intellectuals and Artists in Valencia (June 16, 1987), commemorating the fiftieth anniversary of the 1937 Congress of Antifascist Writers in Valencia. Published as "Les Intellectuels et l'histoire" in *Lettre Internationale* 15 (December 1987), pp. 1-16.
[2] Pierre Vidal-Naquet has reminded me of this point during friendly conversations.
[3] Translator's Note: In French, the word "sens" means both "direction" and "meaning" or "sense."

⁴Translator's Note: I have followed the actual English translation of the German phrase, "Die Gelassenheit zu den Dingen." (Martin Heidegger, "Memorial Address," in *Discourse on Thinking,* trans. John M. Anderson and E. Hans Freund [New York: Harper and Row, 1966, p. 54. The original German title of this book is *Gelassenheit.*) The French translation reads: "L'ame egale en presence des choses," which could be translated as "the soul unruffled in the presence of things."

Author's Note: Cf. *ibid.,* p. 52, where Heidegger says, "No single man, no group of men, . . . no merely human organization is up to the task of taking in hand the governance of our atomic age." [Translator: Translation slightly altered to accommodate both French and English Translations.] And: "We are to do nothing but wait" ("Conversation on a Country Path," *ibid.,* p. 62). Translator: This "Conversation" between a scientist," a "scholar," and a "teacher" was noted down in writing by Heidegger circa 1945, i.e. at the end of the Nazi regime in Germany. The statement quoted here is made by the "teacher" who expounds upon the meaning of "releasement."

The Descent of de Man

BY MARTIN JAY

"In a profession full of fakes he was real..."

—Barbara Johnson[1]

"I look forward to seeing what I will produce and know as little about it as anybody else. "

—Paul de Man[2]

During the fall semester of 1987, the news of an unfolding scandal passed like a shudder through the body of American humanist scholarship. Through word of mouth and the haphazard circulation of a few xeroxed pages, the rumor quickly spread that something deeply disturbing had been unearthed about the background of one of the most distinguished and influential figures in our intellectual life, a figure who still cast a long shadow four years after his death in December, 1983. The subject was Paul de Man, the Sterling Professor of Humanities at Yale and for many years the dominant presence in the so-called Yale School of literary criticism, which had initiated a generation into the intricacies of deconstruction. The revelation concerned his initial writings, composed when de Man was still in his early twenties in his native Belgium. Thanks to the research of a young Belgian scholar from Leuven, Ortwin de Graef, a cache of some hundred or so articles were discovered that had appeared in the newspaper *Le Soir* in 1941 and 1942. Much to the dismay of their discoverer, who is an admirer of de Man, they gave clear evidence of his fascist and anti-semitic sympathies. On December 1, 1987, *The*

New York Times forced the underground rumor to surface with a sensational, unsigned essay entitled "Yale Scholar's Articles Found in ProNazi Paper." Within a very short time, other journals like *The Nation* rushed to comment on the scandal. Any thought that the disturbing story could somehow be kept only local knowledge quickly was dissipated.

As this is being written, the full import of the materials is still uncertain and even more so are their implications for the ideas de Man so effectively promulgated . "Effectively" is the right word here, for there can be few scholars who so spontaneously and fervently engendered the praise of his colleagues and students. As Frank Lentricchia noted back in 1980, "Reading the prefaces and acknowledgments of Harold Bloom, Geoffrey Hartman, and J. Hillis Miller (the other Yale School critics), one is struck by the tone of respect, even reverence, with which the name of Paul de Man is mentioned."[3] What Lentricchia called de Man's "rhetoric of authority" was even more strikingly evident in the tributes that followed his premature death at the age of 64. In the memorial statements gathered in a special issue of the *Yale French Studies* as "The Lesson of Paul de Man"and in the deeply felt encomium written by Jacques Derrida to his late friend,[4] the remarkable power of de Man's intellect, personality and pedagogical talent was clearly acknowledged.

Although de Man was a master of irony—Derrida once called him *"l'ironie meme"*[5]—it is difficult to believe he would have taken much joy from the ironic undercutting of his reputation at precisely the moment when his admirers were paying him such heartfelt homage. They themselves must doubtless feel a mixture of shock, chagrin, sadness, and anger as the result of what may well seem a kind of posthumous betrayal. When so much is invested in the personal stature of a master thinker, when his own warnings against such a deeply transferential relationship go unheeded, the consequences can indeed be devastating. Whatever those of us who were never under his considerable spell may think about his intellectual legacy, it is impossible not to empathize with the traumatized victims of these disclosures.

With hindsight, however, it is possible to wonder if certain questions might have been asked before about the roots of de Man's thought that were not. No secret, after all, had been made of his relationship to another de Man, his uncle Hendrik, whose political attitudes and actions were part of the public record. Yet, when it was treated by his supporters, its sinister implications were unexplored. Thus, for example, Stanley Corngold's essay on de Man in the 1983 collection, *The Yale Critics: Deconstruction in America*, entitled with an irony only now apparent "Error in Paul de Man," a footnote explained that he was "a nephew of the Belgian Socialist Hendrik de Man, at one time titular leader of the Belgian labor party."[6] Corngold then added a sentence from the elder de Man's biographer Peter Dodge that "in 1941 (Hendrik) de Man retired from public life and left Belgium to lead a solitary existence in an Alpine hut on Mont Blanc, where he devoted himself to reflection and writing. . . . In the end he concluded that the Socialist movement unavoidably participated in the decadence of the capitalist world order, and the best the responsible individual could do was to cultivate his garden."[7] What is remarkable about this description of the uncle is that it maintains a discreet silence about what de Man did before his "retirement" into horticulture. According to Zeev Sternhell, the distinguished historian of fascism, "It was in his capacity as leader of Belgian socialism that in June 1940 [Hendrik de Man] announced the dissolution of his party as a gesture of welcome to the new world the Nazi victory had brought. In his view, the collapse of the parliamentary parties had cleared the way for the construction of a true and authoritarian socialism which, in its essential aspects, would be based on the Nazi model."[8] In fact, well before the Nazi invasion, the elder de Man's penchant for anti-democratic corporatism and technocratic state planning meant he was already on the road from radical left to radical right travelled by others from Mussolini to Doriot. After the war, he was convicted in absentia of treason by a Belgian military tribunal.

Corngold, who acknowledges his "indebtedness—and that of many others—to Paul de Man as a teacher,"[9] can be forgiven his understandable reluctance to highlight the unsavory dimensions of the uncle's career at a time when the nephew, still then alive, seemed in no way besmirched by them. Now, of course, the context is very different, as a quick glance at one of the unearthed essays makes clear. On March 4, 1941, the twenty-two year old Paul de Man addressed the vexed subject of "The Jews in Contemporary Literature" in *Le Soir*. Beneath his signature in a box was a quotation attributed to Benjamin Franklin claiming that "A leopard can't change its spots. The Jews are asiatics; they are a menace to the country that admits them, and they must be excluded by the Constitution." Whether or not de Man approved this filler, whose source was not cited, his article was fully in tune with its sentiments. Arguing against the allegation of "vulgar anti-semitism" that the Jews were responsible for modernist literature, a myth also spread by the self-aggrandizing Jews themselves, he contended that the truth was very different. The modernists of the first rank, de Man protested, were never Jews. Moreover, modernist art has developed from intra-aesthetic impulses, which have nothing to do with anything external, such as the racial origins of its creators. Thus, he concluded, "one can see that a solution to the Jewish problem that aimed at the creation of a Jewish colony isolated from Europe would not unleash deplorable consequences for the literary life of the West. It would lose, on the whole, some personalities of mediocre value and would continue, as in the past, to develop according to its great laws of evolution." Thus a *Judenfrei* modernism would survive the "isolation" of the mediocrities whose fate seemed to have troubled the young de Man far less than that of the literature they were wrongly accused of fostering.

What such deeply distasteful outbursts suggest is that the relationship between the two de Man's needs to be examined more seriously than has hitherto been the case. Can, for example, the nephew's attitude toward history, which will be discussed below, be understood without acknowledging the uncle's pessimistic embrace of the idea of "post-histoire" after the war as an antidote to totalizing notions of progress?[10] Can Paul de Man's acceptance of a Nietzschean vision of repetition and displacement be grasped without taking seriously Hendrik de Man's gloomy prognosis of impending catastrophe as the "return"[11] of senselessness?

What such questions do not imply, however, is that we must now believe in the discovery of a hitherto repressed or forgotten "true" source of de Man's work or, even less plausibly, deconstruction in general. For although one can certainly point to the importance for deconstruction of thinkers like Heidegger and Blanchot, whose own attitudes during the Nazi period may well have been consonant with those in de Man's essay,[12] it is no less plausible to make a case for the contrary assertion. That is, certain of its roots can be seen as nourished by Jewish soil. As Susan Handelman has argued in *The Slayers of Moses*, Derrida was covertly indebted to a tradition of heterodox rabbinic hermeneutics based on an absent God whose textual traces never reveal an ontological plenitude.[13] The influence of the great Jewish phenomenologist Emmanuel Levinas on Derrida has also been widely acknowledged. And other Yale School critics like Geoffrey Hartman and Harold Bloom have never been reluctant to emphasize their Jewish preoccupations.

Moreover, de Man himself wrote sympathetically of the figure of the wandering Jew in his late essay on Walter Benjamin. Arguing against the interpretation of Benjamin's account of translation as a messianic project of homecoming to an *Ursprache*, he contended that instead it valorized "a wandering, an *errance*, a kind of permanent exile if you wish, but it is not really an exile for there is no homeland, nothing from which one has been exiled."[14] Rather than trying to save modernism by sending the Jews into exile, as the 1941 *Le Soir* piece suggested, de Man came to equate all that was attractive in literature, modernist or otherwise, with the very condition of perpetual wandering, a linguistic correlate of the diaspora shorn of its messianic hopes.

These very inadequate and underdeveloped reminders of the possible links between deconstruction and Jewish traditions and experiences are useful as a counterweight to the premature assumption that de Man's youthful writings have somehow exposed the real roots of the movement. There may, however, be more subtle links between de Man's version of deconstruction and his earlier political sympathies than any straightforward anti/philo-semitic dichotomy would suggest. In a provocative and controversial 1986 essay in *Representations* entitled "Writing and Deference: The Politics of Literary Adulation,"[15] Jeffrey Mehlman spun out an elusive argument about the putative links between the American reception of deconstruction, which de Man had done so much to orchestrate, and the forgetting of Franco-German intellectual collaboration during the Second World War. Making what he admitted were "a few particularly vigorous intertextual leaps" to substantiate his claim, Mehlman concluded that one should "imagine Derrida's opus as the textual instantiation of the amnesty or radical forgetting"[16] that characterized postwar French politics.

As might be expected, such a charge could only arouse enormous resistance among partisans of deconstruction, many of whom saw Mehlman as a disgruntled apostate from a cause he once championed. But now in the aftermath of the de Man disclosures, Mehlman's intuition seems worthy of at least serious discussion, rather than mere contemptuous dismissal.

Indeed, if anything, what this sorry episode demands is a more sober and less polemicized reappraisal of the sources, internal tensions, and implications of deconstruction than has hitherto been demanded. It is likely, alas, to generate, at least initially, precisely the opposite. The selfstyled "liberal humanist" opponents of deconstruction with their Arnoldian reverence for cultural hierarchies are doubtless gleefully indulging in *Schadenfreude* at the debacle. Spared the difficult task of evaluating complex arguments they were rarely able to meet with commensurate ones of their own, they now can take comfort in the claim that their suspicions of inherent nihilism or worse have been borne out by the facts. Others further to the left, who have worried about the political ambiguities of deconstruction because of its debt to Nietzschean "irrationalism," will also perhaps allegorize the de Man scandal into a microcosm of the "essential" elitist, anti-democratic message of the movement, which among other things would mean forgetting de Man's elaborate defense of allegory as precisely that which resists such easy passage from one level to another.

Equally probable is an attempt on the part of certain of de Man's loyalists to exercise a kind of damage control, distancing the lessons he taught them as far as possible from his "youthful errors." To focus on a thinker's overt politics, they may claim, is to indulge in precisely the kind of ad hominem reductionism and psychologistic trivialization that deconstruction with its emphasis on texts rather than authors has so insistently warned against. In the light, however, of their own effusive tributes to the person of de Man as teacher, colleague, and intellectual palladin, such a defense quickly crumbles. And moreover, it is precisely the intertextual pollution of de Man's later criticism by his early political writings that is at issue. The disastrous example of another notorious attempt to build a wall between a writer's "serious work" and his political "errors"—that of Heidegger —should be avoided at all costs.[17] Indeed, if deconstruction has taught us anything, it is the impossibility of creating watertight boundaries between different discourses or genres. And it has drummed into us as well an awareness that the most seemingly marginal texts are those that may reveal most about a corpus of writings .

Without therefore succumbing to the temptation to polemicize mindlessly against a body of thought that cannot be reduced to any one forgotten point of origin, it is nonetheless imperative to ask hard questions about the implications of these deeply troubling writings. Although considerations of space preclude anything but the most cursory inventory of those questions, let me suggest a few obvious openers. It has, for example, often been claimed, perhaps most insistently by Rodolph Gasche, that the American transformation of deconstruction from a genuine philosophy into a variant of literary criticism—a shift of emphasis between the work of Derrida and that of the Yale School—"must be understood as originating in New Criticism; it is a continuation of this American-bred literary scholarship."[18] Is it now perhaps as plausible to see the origins in a *European* tradition of aesthetic modernism that privileged the realm of the literary as irreducible to anything external to it? Although the later de Man was anxious to challenge idealist notions of literary organicism and aesthetic totalization, he nonetheless strongly defended the poetic as "the most advanced and refined mode of deconstruction"[19] because of its self-exposing powers. There was no need, he insisted, to add a deconstructive reading to a text from the outside; literary texts already deconstructed themselves.

While admitting the inevitable intertwining of the figural, rhetorical and tropological dimensions of language, on the one hand, with the referential, communicative and grammatical, on the other, de Man nonetheless devoted his considerable critical energies to stressing the power of the former. Understanding the rhetorical function of tropes, he argued, served to undermine a straightforward semantic or semiological concept of language. It also made clear the inadequacy of conceiving language as an expressive medium fully adequate to the task of communicating ideas or describing objects in the world. All language was therefore tendentially revealed in literature, which was most explicit about its problematizing of reference and representation.

Although on one level this expansion of the realm of the literary might be construed as breaching the *cordon sanitaire* his early texts built between modernist literature and its alleged extra-literary origins in the Jews, on another it paid it subtle tribute. For if literature was the highest manifestation of the truth that no linguistic practice can speak the "truth" about an external world, then it was impervious to the determining force of anything "outside" it. Whereas in "The Jews and Contemporary Literature," de Man's strategy was to make literature a privileged enclave, in his later work he tended to inflate it into the most rigorous and revealing variant of language in all of its forms. In both cases, however, the literary retained its special place, unbeholden to anything external to it. A related issue concerns de Man's controversial attitude towards history. According to critics like Lentricchia, his later writings "reveal a critical intention to place literary discourse in a realm where it can have no responsibility to historical life."[20] One way in which this intention was accomplished may have been de Man's celebrated insistence that the modernist moment in literary history was somehow always already anticipated by earlier literary practice. In so doing, as Stephen Melville has noted, "de Man has implicitly done away entirely with any real temporal structure to either history or literature."[21] In the past, such an attitude was often attributed to de Man's embrace of Heidegger's distinction between the realm of mere ontic representation (where what normally counts as historical change takes place) and a deeper realm of ontological reality, which to be sure de Man never interpreted in as positive a way as Heidegger.

Now, however, it is hard to avoid wondering if de Man's complicated critique of historical thinking—or more precisely, of fictionally narrativized historical accounts resonant with genetic or teleological meaning—might be understood as anxiety over his own unmastered personal past. Might his sympathy for a kind of Nietzschean "active forgetting" bespeak a certain desire to efface the memory of his youthful mistakes by denying their meaningful connection with his later career? Or was he struggling in subtle and covert ways to exorcise it, as some of his defenders may be tempted to suggest? Only a careful reconstruction of de Man's intellectual trajectory, as Gayatri Spivak has argued, will provide a possible answer. Only a willingness to risk narrativizing his development, even as we remain wary of overly pat "stories" of his life's meaning, will suffice.

The outcome of such an endeavor cannot be foreseen until more evidence is available. But what is certain is that some attempt of this kind must be made. For no aspect of the de Man scandal is so galling as his own failure to confront in an explicit and unequivocal manner the unpalatable implications of his tainted writings. Although it may be possible to read certain of his works, such as his tortured essay on Rousseau's *Confessions* in *Allegories of Reading,*[22] as a coded explanation for his silence, it ultimately served him ill. Now when it is too late for de Man himself to explain or apologize for his youthful texts, the revelation of their existence has created an irreparable damage to his reputation. Those who want to salvage the still powerful implications of his work must be willing to assimilate a lesson that de Man by his example neglected to teach: the historical past must be worked through, not repressed, if its hold over us is to be shaken.

Finally, de Man's well-known aversion to politics has to be reconsidered in the light of the disclosure. Even so close a colleague as Geoffrey Hartman once commented on de Man's disdain for the political that for him, *"Language* rather than politics is fate." For de Man, he wrote in 1980, "politics is part of a counterfeit Great Tradition that arrogates to itself the impositional strength of performative language. Yet de Man's position has become too absolute."[23] One dimension of that absoluteness was his insistence in *Allegories of Reading* and elsewhere that the performative power of language was due as much, if not more, to its figural as to its literal power, its rhetoric as to its argument. Might such a contention, we may wonder, be a reflection of his unease with the perlocutionary effects of his early writings, taken at their literal word? Or was his general silence about politics a reaction to the recognition that even rhetorically their effects were deeply noxious? Was his spirited defense of the undecidability of all readings a covert apologia for the apparently explicit implications of those texts? Or was he denying himself the right to speak about politics out of a well-earned shame about his earlier follies?

In de Man's own defense, it might be noted that in his last writings, collected in *The Resistance to Theory,* he had begun to inch toward a recognition of this problem, acknowledging the importance of the critique of ideology. Planned articles on Marx's *German Ideology* and Adorno's *Kierkegaard: Konstruktion des Aesthetischen* were unfortunately never completed. What he did produce suggests, however, that de Man still held on to the belief that the primary tool in unmasking ideologies was what he called "the linguistics of literariness."[24] Whether it would be sufficient as a way to unmask the ideological past that we now know may have been lurking in his own work is highly unlikely.

De Man's celebrated reflections on the relationship between blindness and insight help us to see why.[25] A thinker's blindspots, he always insisted, were in complicated ways constitutive of the insights he reached, not an impediment to them. Whereas the scientific method sought to purge errors and rectify mistakes, critical practice acknowledged its permanent inability to "see" with unobstructed clarity. Like the foreign substance that stimulated the oyster to secrete a pearl, blindness was actually productive of insight. Error was inevitable because of the impossibility of ever bracketing the rhetorical dimension of language in the hope of perceiving an unmediated truth. The main source of ideology, therefore, was precisely such a quest to purge knowledge of error.

Although this argument is not without its power, it cannot be applied to the ideological dimension of de Man's own work. For the essays in *Le Soir* can in no sense be understood as an insightproducing blind-spot in de Man. They were, it is safe to presume, willfully suppressed instead, all too actively forgotten rather than part of the tropic unconscious of the author. Thus no amount of attention to the linguistics of literariness would help us expose their ideological residues in de Man's later work. Here a little bit of straightforward error-correction would be a lot healthier than insight-generating blindness.

De Man's admirers often spoke of his Olympian bearing, his ironic detachment and his uncanny ability to generate reverence and awe. Now that he has been forced to descend from Mount Olympus and his spell has been broken, we can finally approach his legacy without the piety it once occasioned. We can now finally *read* de Man, to use his favorite verb, with the cold and unforgiving eye that he himself turned with such penetration on the texts of others.

Notes

[1] Barbara Johnson, "In Memoriam," *Yale French Studies*, 69 (New Haven, 1985), p. 10.

[2] Paul de Man in "An Interview with Paul de Man," by Stefano Rosso, in Paul de Man, *The Resistance to Theory*, foreword by Wlad Godzich (Minneapolis, 1986), p. 121.

[3] Frank Lentricchia, *After the New Criticism* (Chicago, 1980), p. 293.

[4] Jacques Derrida, *Memoires for Paul de Man* (New York, 1986).

[5] Jacques Derrida, "In Memoriam," *Yale French Studies*, 69, p. 14.

[6] Stanley Corngold "Error in Paul de Man," in Jonathan Arac, Wlad Godzich, Wallace Martin, eds., *The Yale Critics: Deconstruction in America* (Minneapolis, 1983), p. 106.

[7] Ibid.

[8] Zeev Sternhell, "Fascist Ideology," in Walter Laqueur, ed., *Fascism: A Readers Guide* (Berkeley, 1976), p. 352.

[9] Corngold, p. 106.

[10] Hendrik de Man, "The Age of Doom," in Peter Dodge, ed. and trans., *A Documentary Study of Hendrik de Man. Socialist Critic of Marxism* (Princeton, 1979), p. 345. De Man borrowed the term "post-histoire" from the French mathematician A.A. Cournot and called it "adequate to describe what happens when an institution or a cultural achievement ceases to be historically active and productive of new qualities, and becomes purely receptive or eclectically imitative. Thus understood, Cournot's notion of the posthistorical world would, in a more general way than intended by him, fit the cultural phase that, following a 'fulfillment of sense,' has become 'devoid of sense.' "

[11] Ibid. p. 346.

[12] Heidegger's sympathies are well-known. For an account of similar attitudes on the part of Blanchot, see Jeffrey Mehlman, *Legacies of Anti-Semitism in France* (Minneapolis, 1983). Mehlman reads Blanchot's "Comment la literature est-elle possible?" as at once "a discreet inauguration of French literary modernity and coded farewell to plans for a French fascism in the 1930s" (p. 13). De Man's attraction to Blanchot may well have been motivated by a recognition of the same impulse in his own work.

[13] Susan A. Handelman, *The Slayers of Moses: The Emergence of Rabbinic Interpretation in Modern Literary Theory* (Albany, 1982).

[14] Paul de Man, "Conclusion: Walter Benjamin's 'The Task of the Translator'," in *The Resistance to Theory* p. 92. It might, of course, be argued from, say, a Zionist point of view, that the consigning of the Jews to a permanent exile is a denial of the messianic dimension of Judaism, but from de Man's perspective, the latter could only be a myth.

[15] Jeffrey Mehlman, "Writing and Deference: The Politics of Literary Adulation," *Representations*, 15 (Summer, 1986); see also the exchange between Mehlman and Ann Smock on the article in *Representations*, (Spring, 1987).

[16] Mehlman,"Writing and Deference,"p. 12.

[17] The most recent account is Victor Farias, *Heidegger et le nazisme* (Paris,1987); see also Hugo Ott,"Martin Heidegger als Rektor der Universitat Freiburg," *Zeitschrift fur die*

Geschichte des Oberrheins, 132 (1984).

[18] Rodolph Gashche, *The Tain of the Mirror: Derrida and the Philosophy of Reflection* (Cambridge, Mass., 1986), p. 3. American New Criticism was, to be sure, itself largely a reflection on European modernism.

[19] Paul de Man, *Allegories of Reading: Figural Language in Rousseau, Nietzsche, Rilke and Proust* (New Haven, 1979), p. 17.

[20] Lentricchia, p. 310.

[21] Stephen W. Melville, *Philosophy Beside Itself: On Deconstruction and Modernism,* foreword by Donald Marshall (Minneapolis, 1986), p. 133.

[22] The essay is significantly entitled "Excuses (*Confessions*)" and argues that "to confess is to overcome guilt and shame in the name of truth: it is an epistemological use of language in which ethical values of good and evil are superseded by values of truth and falsehood . . ." (p. 279).

[23] Geoffrey H. Hartman, *Criticism in the Wilderness: The Study of Literature Today* (New Haven, 1980), p. 108.

[24] Paul de Man, "The Resistance to Theory," in *The Resistance to Theory,* p. 11.

[25] Paul de Man, *Blindness and Insight: Essays in the Rhetoric of Contemporary Criticism* (New York, 1971).

Foucault's Politics in Biographical Perspective[1]

BY JAMES MILLER

For the past five years, I have been working on a book, now finished, about Michel Foucault. My book is not a biography, though in outline it follows the chronology of Foucault's life; nor is it a comprehensive survey of his works, although it does offer an interpretation of a great many texts. It is, rather, a narrative account of one man's lifelong struggle to honor Nietzsche's gnomic injunction, "to become what one is." Through a blend of anecdote and exegesis, I have approached Foucault's writing as if it expressed a powerful desire to realize a certain form of life; and his life as if it embodied a sustained and at least partially successful effort to turn this desire into a reality. In order to obtain evidence for the second half of my hypothesis, I have conducted interviews in the spirit of an investigative journalist, gathering information about various aspects of Foucault's life, particularly in the United States, that have been hitherto undocumented and, therefore, largely unexamined. In the spirit of an intellectual historian, I have sketched the broader cultural and social context within which this life unfolded. And in the spirit of a literary critic, I have highlighted a handful of recurrent phantasies and imaginative obsessions that gave to Foucault's life a characteristic color and mood, informing both his composed texts and his everyday behavior. My aim has been to conjure up "neither the pure grammatical subject nor the deep psychological subject," as Foucault himself once put it, "but rather the one who says 'I' in the works, the letters, the drafts, the sketches, the personal secrets." What follows is a brutally condensed summary of a much longer argument about Foucault's changing political convictions, drawn from my book; which will give some idea of where my approach has led.

All of Foucault's work hinges on an idea of experience. Near the end of his life, Foucault briefly defined his basic idea in this way: "experience," he explained, was a form of being "that can and must be thought," a form "historically constituted" through "games of truth." The appearance of the word "game" in this formulation underlines the claim, fleshed out in Foucault's various historiographic studies, that truth is part of a human activity, a form of life; its rules are not something fixed, given once for all; new games of truth—scientific and political, poetic and psychological—come into existence, while others, falling into disuse, are forgotten. "The history of thought," as Foucault once explained his lifework, was an "analysis of how an unproblematic field of experience, or a set of practices" that had long been accepted "without question," came to seem questionable, inciting "discussion and debate," provoking the formulation of fresh concepts, which articulated experience in fresh ways—and, in turn, provoked new questions, in a process of unending critique.[2]

Foucault's own thought grows out of an empirical conviction that *any* field of experience is *always*, in some way, problematic. In practice—so his various historiographic critiques of reason suggest—we can probe any boundary, question any limit, challenge the rules in any game of truth we may find ourselves playing. And that is not all: More often than most people dream, we can *change* the rules of the game. We have that kind of power; it is merely a question of using the power, even if few of us ever will, inhibited as we are by the conventions of ordinary language, common sense and conscientiousness, reinforced by the threat of punishment and a more diffuse, hence insidious set of fears: of being branded as queer, crazy, abnormal. The goal—the trick—is to *unleash* the power in our selves; and thus to tap the energy essential for realizing Nietzsche's injunction, "to become what one is."

Extending a tradition of critique inaugurated by Kant and rendered properly historical by Ernst Cassirer, Gaston Bachelard and Georges Canguilhem, Foucault sometimes studied games of truth in what he called their "positivity." In *The Birth of the Clinic* and in *The Order of Things*, he showed, for example, how in the nineteenth century clinical anatomy, economics, zoology, botany and linguistics each crystallized as internally coherent "discourses," organizing new patterns of perception, constituting new disciplines of understanding, informing the structure of institutions and, ultimately, regulating conduct. At the end of his life, in *The Use of Pleasure* and *The Care of the Self*, Foucault also investigated how classical thinkers from Socrates to Seneca had elaborated their own *personal* regimens of "truth," in an effort to bring order and beauty to their lives.

As a connoisseur of modern art and eroticism, on the other hand, Foucault, following in the footsteps of Nietzsche, was passionately interested in approaching experience in what he sometimes called its "negativity." In *Madness and Civilization*, he took away from his encounter with the infernal vision of Goya, the cruel sexual phantasies of Sade and the insane glossolalia of Artaud "something that can and must be thought," something that startles and illuminates—something at different times in his life he called "unreason," "the thought from outside," or, more simply still, "freedom." Emboldened by the examples of Baudelaire, Rimbaud, Andre Breton and Georges Bataille, Foucault sought out "limit experiences" for himself, trying to glimpse Dionysus beneath Apollo, hazarding the risk of "a sacrifice, an actual sacrifice of life," as he put it in 1969, "a voluntary obliteration that does not have to be represented in books because it takes place in the very existence of the writer." At this breaking point, "experience" becomes a zone full of turbulence, unformed energy, chaos—"*l'espace d'une exteriorite sauvage*," as he called it in *The Order of Discourse*, "the space of an untamed exteriority." Like few thinkers before him, Foucault was at home in this no-man's land: indeed, the inner logic of his philosophical odyssey, and also his public political statements and actions, is unintelligible apart from his lifelong, and highly problematic, preoccupation with limiting the limits of reason, and finding ways—in dreaming, at moments of madness, through drug use, in erotic rapture, in great transports of rage, and also through intense suffering—of exploring the most shattering kinds of experience, breaching the boundaries normally drawn between the unconscious and conscious, order and disorder, pleasure and pain, life and death; and in this way, starkly revealing how distinctions central to the play of true and false are pliable, uncertain, contingent.[3]

In a 1978 interview with the Italian journalist Duccio Trombadori, Foucault enumerated three crucial implications of his lifelong preoccupation with understanding the meaning of his various experiences, and in unlocking the power at play in the various games of truth that ordered the different domains of possible experience. The first implication, he said, was that there was "no continuous and systematic theoretical 'background,'" or rule of method, that governed his work, despite periodic books, interviews and essays suggesting otherwise. The second implication, said Foucault, was that "there is not a book I have written that does not grow, at least in part, out of a direct, personal experience"—with madness, with death, with sexuality, with forms of behavior commonly branded as criminal. In effect, all of his books amount to a kind of involuntary and unnoticed memoir. The third implication, as Foucault explained it, is more complex. Of course, he said, "starting from experience, it is necessary to open the way for a transformation, a metamorphosis, that is not simply individual but has a character accessible to others;" for this reason, he always labored to connect his own "experience," in a "certain fashion, to a collective practice, to a manner of thinking." At different times, he played the language games of structuralism, of Maoism, of the most superficially impersonal sort of classical philology. Yet even at this public and exoteric level, he stressed, much that others might find puzzling or esoteric about "the relationship between 'limit-experience' and 'the history of truth'" could be clarified only by picking up "the threads of certain episodes in my life." "*What I say does not have objective value,*" he concluded with disarming candor: but viewed through the lens of his own investigation of the limits of experience, what he had said, and written, could nevertheless "perhaps help to clarify the problems that I have brought to light, and their consequences."[4]

The early episodes of Foucault's political life, and some of the problems they brought to light, may be summed up briefly. When he was in his early twenties, Foucault was recruited into the French Communist Party by his teacher at the *Ecole normal superieure*, Louis Althusser. He stayed in the Party for roughly four years between 1950 and 1954, not only toeing the Stalinist line but learning something firsthand about the pliability of the truth—and also about the ability of a trained mind to believe, and find reasons for believing, almost anything. But he never really felt at home in the Party, he would later say; not least, so he claimed, "because I was homosexual. It was an institution that reinforced all the values of the traditional bourgeois life." The same values, as he discovered, prevailed in social democratic Sweden, and also in Communist Poland, the two countries where he lived between 1955 and 1958. Returning to France in 1960 (after a year in Germany), Foucault withdrew into a kind of inner exile, disdaining all 57 varieties of French Marxism, from the Sartrean brand to the structuralist brand. Superficially, he lived the life of a conventional professor. At the same time, he became the close companion of a young militant named Daniel Defert, who quickly became his political alter-ego. And between 1960 and 1968, while Foucault himself was keeping a low public profile, he was expressing in no uncertain terms his fascination with moments of madness and rapture and erotic ecstasy, particularly in the essays that he wrote about Artaud and Bataille, Klossowski and Blanchot; in the constantly astonishing pages of these essays, as in the dizzying climax to *Madness and Civilization*, bold claims are made for the Marquis de Sade and his literary heirs; they are said to be stoking "volcanoes of madness;" their works promise to "destroy the oldest laws and pacts;" the evident insanity of their dreams amounts to a "total contestation" of Western culture. These are not the words of a man resigned to his fate.[5]

Foucault's first important political epiphany occurred in March, 1968 in Tunisia, where he was then living, while teaching at the University of Tunis. In March of 1968, the University blew up. "I witnessed student riots, very strong, very intense," Foucault later recalled. Up till then he had stood apart from the mounting agitation, put off by the students' adhesion to various Marxist formulas, many borrowed from the work of Althusser, then at the height of his prestige among francophone radicals. But the more he saw, the more he became convinced that the Tunisian student movement embodied "an utterly remarkable act of existence." Marxism in this setting seemed to function as a kind of myth, in George Sorel's sense—a body of images capable of inspiring "a kind of moral energy," exciting "a violence, an intensity, an utterly remarkable passion," enabling students to accept "formidable risks." Exhilarated by their courage and defiance, Foucault helped the rebellious students to escape arrest. "It was a formative experience for me," Foucault recalled in 1978. It was, in fact, his first inkling that politics, like art and eroticism, could occasion a kind of "limit experience."[6]

More riots occurred in Paris in May 1968, confirming the new political possibilities revealed for Foucault in Tunis. During the Night of the Barricades, when French students renewed the liturgies of Revolution in a kind of delirious ritual of Dionysian abandon, Daniel Defert, who was on the Left Bank at the time, called up Foucault in Tunis, and held up the telephone receiver to the radio, so they could listen together to the pitched battle with police. A few months later, Foucault moved back to France for good—and plunged, along with Defert, into a new world of radical politics. This phase of his life would last for about five years. During these years, as he later recalled, he was fascinated by forms of political action that required "a personal, physical commitment...From that moment on, what I was trying to do was to constitute for myself a certain manner of recapturing both what had preoccupied me in my work on madness, . . . and also what I had just seen in Tunisia: one rediscovered, then, *experience*."[7]

Foucault's activism took a variety of forms. He marched, signed petitions, issued provocative interviews, and also participated actively in various demonstrations, getting arrested on more than one occasion. Brave, physically courageous, he put his body on the line. In most of these activities he was allied with the *Gauche Proletarienne*, or "GP" (or, more loosely still, the "Maoists"), which became the first decisive political association of his life. Founded at the end of 1968 by a young militant named Benny Levy (who in these years operated under the alias Pierre Victor), the GP united veterans from May 1968, some of them avowed anarchists, others ultra-Marxists. Relatively small though it was, the GP's prestige was great: embodying the most stringent standards of ardor and commitment, the group managed to combine the delight in disorder evinced by Bakunin with the genius for strategy displayed by Lenin. In a way that no other group could rival, the GP promised to carry forward the movement started in May 1968, prolonging the moment by mastering its chaotic energies. Its forte was show-stopping direct action: for example, stealing paté from a luxury food shop to give to immigrants; distributing free subway tokens to needy commuters; handing out blank teaching certificates to anonymous passersby. The government was not amused. An underground organization was set up. And in 1970, shortly after the GP had been outlawed, Daniel Defert became a clandestine member. The prison information group Defert and Foucault started the next year was aimed, in part, at challenging conventional ways of thinking about good and evil, innocence and guilt, honor and punishment. At the same time, their prison group played a more practical role in helping to stir up discontent inside French jails, where the conditions were often deplorable—and a number of Maoist militants were serving terms. The efforts of Defert and Foucault, in conjunction with the agitation of Maoists, played some role—how much is hard to say—in helping to spark a series of prison revolts that rocked France in 1971 and 1972.[8]

In the middle of 1971, Foucault summed up his political convictions in an interview conducted by insurgent French lycee students and published in *Actuel*, at the time the most outré magazine of the French counter-culture. The title of the piece was "Beyond Good and Evil." At the outset of this conversation, Foucault criticized "humanism," which he defined as "everything in Western civilization that restricts the desire for power." His political goal, he said, was "a 'desubjectification' of the will to power." To reach this goal required "a simultaneous agitation of consciousness and institutions." The institutional objective was simple, but sweeping: "'The unity of society' [*L'ensemble de la societe*] is precisely that which should not be considered except as something to be destroyed." At the same time, those in revolt could engage the enemy at close quarters. If one crux of the political problem was "subjectification," each individual might approach his or her soul as a field of combat in which to overthrow "the subject as pseudosovereign." This could be done through a variety of concrete practices: "the suppression of taboos and of the limitations and divisions imposed upon the sexes; the exploration of communal existence; the loosening of inhibitions with regard to drugs; the breaking of all the prohibitions that form and guide the development of the normal individual . . . I am referring to all those *experiences* that have been rejected by our civilization," said Foucault, "or which it accepts only within literature."[9]

At about the same time in 1971, a debate began to simmer in the *Gauche Proletarienne* about the meaning of justice and the limits of violence within a movement that was avowedly beyond good and evil. On February 5, 1972, Foucault sat down with Pierre Victor to discuss these matters in an interview taped for *Les temps modernes*. "Now my hypothesis," Foucault explained, "is not so much that the court is the natural expression of popular justice, but rather that its historical function is to ensnare it, to master and to repress it." Popular justice, Foucault suggested, was better served by expressions of uninhibited outrage. The September Massacres, during the French Revolution, were exemplary. So too was the revival, during the Revolution, of "the old German custom" of parading "the head of an enemy on a stake, for public viewing when he had been killed." Of course, the people could not always be left to its own devices; "a revolutionary state apparatus" had some utility—but only if it was used "to educate the masses and the will of the masses in such a way that it is the masses themselves who come to say, 'In fact we cannot kill this man,' or, 'In fact we must kill him.'"[10]

Murder was not an academic issue for the *Gauche Proletarienne*. The group maintained a paramilitary wing and a commando unit; like the Red Brigades in Italy and the Baader-Meinhoff gang in Germany, it had cultivated an ability to kidnap, to torture and to kill. On February 25, 1972, after a Maoist worker named Pierre Overney had been shot to death by a Renault plant guard, a GP commando unit retaliated by kidnapping a company official. A furious row erupted on the French left; criticism was heaped on the Maoists for their action; stung by the criticism, the GP commando unit quickly released the kidnapped Renault official, unharmed. Among the Maoists themselves, the debate over violence and terrorism deepened. "A libidinal Marxist, a joyous immoralism" (as Benny Levy later characterized it) had led the French ultra-left into an apocalyptic game of political poker: it was time to call the bet, or fold.[11]

Perhaps unleashing the will-to-power by committing acts of "popular justice," no matter how cruel, no matter how murderous, was a useful way to conjure up Dionysus beneath Apollo. It was this kind of logic that had evidently led Foucault to endorse the September Massacres. But it was an ominously similar kind of logic that had led a number of fascist and Nazi philosophers, many also intoxicated by fantasies of Dionysian revolt, to welcome the prospect of war, seeing in its violence and devastation an opportunity to will "the unprecedented," hurling the human being through a "breach" in which "suddenly the unbound powers of being come forth and are accomplished as history"—thus Martin Heidegger in 1935.[12]

The complex and highly ambiguous connections between the Nietzschean wager, a kind of Faustian pact with the death-instinct, and the hecatombs of the fascist adventure were lost neither on Foucault, nor on such political allies as Gilles Deleuze and Andre Glucksmann. The drift of the ultra-left toward terrorism, like the drift of a Nietzschean politics toward an affirmation of power "without statute and limit, without structure and order," made urgent, paradoxically, precisely a reaffirmation, somehow, of statute and limit, structure and order: "Power without limitation," as Foucault remarked in 1983, "is directly related to madness." (For the author of *Madness and Civilization*, of course, this statement cuts two ways.) But how could an affirmation of statute and limit be made effective? What kind of structure—and what kind of order—could be affirmed?[13]

For a Nietzschean, such questions admitted of no easy answer. As Nietzsche himself had insisted, a thin line separated the "superhuman" from the "inhuman," above all in those commanding souls who, by shattering the laws and entering into the no-man's land of total revolt, proved strong enough to practice a "great" politics. For anyone committed to exploring the "unbound powers" of the human being, the effort to identify and uproot the inhuman—and to identify, and tear out, the "fascism in us all"—had therefore to be ruthless and unrelenting.

"How," wondered Foucault in 1977, "does one keep from being fascist, even (especially) when one believes oneself to be a revolutionary militant? How do we rid our speech, our acts, our hearts and our pleasures of fascism? How do we ferret out the fascism that is ingrained in our behavior?"

In the last decade of his life, Foucault worked with renewed energy to ferret out the lusts for power and death that, so he argued, had been encoded in the beliefs, institutions and practices of modern society—and, hence, inscribed in "our speech, our acts, our hearts and our pleasures." His own struggle against fascist impulses he joined publicly in the pivotal but enigmatic last chapter of *The Will to Know*, on "The Right of Power and Death over Life." One "rallying point for the counterattack" against the Faustian pact with the death-instinct, he declared there, must be a transcendence of "sex-desire," combined with a fresh exploration of "bodies and pleasures."

The most important political episodes of Foucault's last decade of life occurred in North America, not France. In San Francisco in 1975, he discovered that exploring the body and its pleasures could be a shared public venture—that is, a *political* project. Gay liberation, as it was practiced in America, was, after the *Gauche Proletarienne*, the second decisive political experiment of Foucault's life.

In France after 1975, Foucault moderated the tone of his political commitments, evincing a new modesty and restraint in the causes he supported, speaking out on behalf of various Soviet and Eastern European dissidents, mobilizing support for Vietnamese boat people, defending the Solidarity trade union in Poland, and so on. In practice, he became an Amnesty International-style human rights activist; in theory—particularly in his College de France lectures in 1979—he implicitly defended the value of a libertarian kind of liberalism, if only as an incitement to a critique of all forms of government. He no longer viewed every legal code, as he once had, simply in terms of the method of subjugation that it instituted. Asserting certain rights against the power of government now seemed to him a useful and worthy enterprise. He had his students read Hayek and von Mises; and he publicly endorsed the work of Francois Furet on the French Revolution. Paradoxically enough, Foucault in these years became one of several prominent figures who helped inspire a renaissance in French liberal thought.

Still, Foucault could not and did not commit himself wholeheartedly to any conventional understanding of liberalism. Dangerous and potentially lethal forms of disorder and revolt still sometimes held out the promise of a total spiritual and institutional transfiguration of human existence—such, at least in Foucault's view, was the great promise, tragically betrayed, of the revolution in Iran in 1978. Given his continuing fascination with the creative possibilities opened up by such political limit-experiences, Foucault could not rest content, as liberal theorists are often wont to do, with the assertion of various rights. Indeed, he could not regard rights as anything other than a partisan invention, won through struggle and maintained only through the readiness of vigilant individuals to challenge abuses of power. As Foucault freely admitted, his conception of rights was therefore essentially strategic. His forerunners, as he implied in his lectures at the College de France between 1976 and 1979, were not Locke and Mill, but rather critics of absolutism who mythologized the past, men such as Sir Edward Coke and John Lilburne; and also romantic liberal historians like Augustin Thierry, who appreciated the value of political conflict. Like such forerunners, Foucault could never imagine himself in the shoes of the liberal jurist or Kantian moral philosopher, struggling to formulate dispassionate and impartial laws of universal applicability. And that was not all: for even in societies where human rights and a certain measure of personal freedom were protected by law, the work of the philosopher, as Foucault understood it, had scarcely begun. "If what we want to do is create a new way of life"—and this was certainly one of his lifelong goals—"then the question of individual rights is not pertinent."

The possibility of creating an entirely new way of life was at the heart of the gay "politics of the self" that preoccupied Foucault at the end of his life. This is not the place to discuss in detail the arcana of his own "erotics of truth" which, for most of his life, he transmitted only under a "stamp of secrecy," although his Manichean gnosticism informs the allegorical figures of *Madness and Civilization*, the glad tidings of man's death in *The Order of Things*, and also the overt argument of *The Will to Know*. Suffice it to say that, through the alchemy of sado-masochistic eroticism, acting out with consenting partners the most harrowing scripts of domination and submission, Foucault thought it possible to confront, and grapple with, the most deeply-ingrained of normally unthinkable impulses and temptations, exorcising murderous and suicidal lusts—and, at the limit, perhaps even momentarily breaking out of what he regarded as the "prison" of the soul. Surrendering "to the slow motions of pleasure-pain," as Foucault once evoked the experience, buffeted by wave after wave of unfamiliar sensations, the habitual dispositions of the body could be broken down, its historically-constituted instincts and drives reduced to a teeming mass of "formless pseudopods"—as if every zone of the body, like an amoeba through its pseudopodia, was now able to change constantly its shape, returning one's *bios* to an innocent and formless flux. "There is a creation of anarchy within the body," explained Foucault: "This is something 'unnameable,' 'useless,' outside of all programs of desire," beyond genital sex—and, at this breaking point, perhaps beyond as well the "fascism that causes us to love power, to desire the very thing that dominates and exploits us." For Foucault, the personal *was* political—and the political *was* personal—in ways that may be impossible to fathom fully. Besides being a master of a certain type of positive historiographic inquiry, he was, I believe, a kind of mystic—philosophically; sexually; politically.

Foucault himself at the end of his life repeatedly suggested that any philosophy worth taking seriously embodied a singular fusion of idea and existence. One of these occasions bears directly on the character of his own political life. In March of 1983, he met Jurgen Habermas over dinner. They swapped notes on their philosophical biographies. Habermas explained how Heidegger's involvement with the Nazis was for him a pressing and important problem. "One thing he said has set me to musing," Foucault later recalled: "He mentioned one of his professors who was a great Kantian...and he explained how astonished and disappointed he had been when, while looking through card catalogues one day, he found some texts from around 1934 by this illustrious Kantian that were thoroughly Nazi in organization." But what did it all mean? Presumably the Kantian Nazi had subscribed to a rational moral code;

still, he had been a dutiful Nazi; what did that tell us about the limits of reason in a realm like politics? Why should the thought of Nietzsche be rejected on political grounds, but not that of Kant? "I do not conclude from this that one may say just anything without the order of theory," said Foucault, "but, on the contrary, that a demanding, prudent, 'experimental' attitude is necessary; at every moment, step by step, one must confront what one is thinking and saying with what one is doing, *with what one is*." The key to appraising the values held dear by *any* philosopher was therefore "not to be sought in his ideas, as if it could be deduced from them, but rather in his philosophy-as-life, in his philosophical life, his ethos."

By the time of his dialogue with Habermas, Foucault himself had come to exemplify, by design, a highly unusual kind of "philosophical life." In his last seminar at Berkeley in the fall of 1983, and more powerfully still in his final lectures at the College de France in February and March of 1984, Foucault implicitly illuminated the paradoxes and peculiarities of his own philosophical quest by analyzing the strikingly similar quest of Diogenes and the ancient Cynics. Like the pagan Cynics, Foucault expressed and explored his philosophical convictions in his way of life as well as in his composed texts, in the process illustrating an "extremely radical conception," in which one's *bios*, or life as such, is "the immediate, explosive and savage presence of truth." Resorting at various times to "critical preaching" and "provocative dialogue," and pursuing, in Foucault's words, "the *bios philosophicos*" as "the animality of being human, renewed as a challenge, practiced as an exercise, and thrown in the face of others as a scandal," the Cynical philosopher forced his audience out of the safe harbor of Socratic inquiry and onto potentially stormy seas. Viewing a life led in such terms as an inward s well as outward adventure to be faced in the spirit of Odysseus, the Cynic supposed that a man might find his way home, but only by setting sail and leaving solid land behind, fearlessly grappling with unfamiliar dangers, like Odysseus at grips with the Sirens; or Saint Anthony wrestling with his demons; or Baudelaire struggling with "the essential, permanent, obsessive relation that our age entertains with death."

In the course of his own philosophical odyssey, Foucault too, fought bravely—against conventional ways of thinking and behaving; against intolerable forms of political power; against intolerable aspects of himself. With a curiosity and courage that I find admirable, Foucault persevered in his great Nietzschean quest, fearlessly trying to get free from himself ("se deprendre de soi-meme"), in the process becoming what he became: one of the most challenging thinkers of this century.

I will conclude with a comment made by one of Foucault's American friends, the novelist Edmund White. The comment is surely exaggerated but also, perhaps, pertinent. In one of our conversations, White summed him up this way: "Michel Foucault was a man deeply attracted to power in its most totalitarian forms, politically and sexually. Throughout his life, he struggled against this attraction. That is what I most admired about him."

Notes

The assertions and anecdotes in this paper have been culled from a study of Foucault's lifework, based on interviews as well as an interpretation of texts, published by Summit Books in the fall of 1992. When citations appear in a paragraph in this paper, I give the French source below (with a page reference to the standard English translation in parentheses).
[1] A lecture delivered at an international conference on "Le siècle de Michel Foucault" held at Tokyo University, Japan, November 2-4, 1991.
[2] *L'usage des plaisirs* (1984), pp. 12-13 (English translation, [hereafter "et"]: pp. 6-7). "Discourse and Truth: the Problematization of *Parhessia*," ed. Joseph Pearson (unauthorized 1985 transcription of Foucault's fall 1983 seminar at Berkeley), p. 48.
[3] "Qu'est-ce qu'un auteur?," *Bulletin de la Societies francaise de Philosophie*; July-September, 1969, p. 78 (et: p. 117). *L'ordre du discours* (1971), p. 37 (et: p. 224).
[4] *Colloqui con Foucault* (Salerno, 1981). I am translating from the original (and so far unpublished) French transcript.
[5] Quoted in Otto Friedrich, "France's Philosopher of Power," *Time*, November 16, 1982, p. 148. "Un si cruel savoir," *Critique*, July, 1962, pp. 610-11. *Historie de la folie a l'age classique* (2nd edn, 1971), p. 552 (et: p. 282).
[6] *Colloqui con Foucault*, loc. cit.
[7] Ibid.
[8] Daniel Defert reported becoming a clandestine member of the GP in a letter to the author, 1/8/91.
[9] "Par dela le bien et le mal," *Actuel*, November, 1971, pp. 43-47 (et: "Revolutionary Action: 'Until Now,'" in *Language, Counter-Memory, Practice*, pp. 218-33).
[10] "Sur la justice populaire," *Les temps modernes*, No. 310, bis, 1972, pp. 335, 340, 346 (et: "On Popular Justice" in *Power / Knowledge*, pp. 1, 6, 13). The Bastille's commanding officer—whose head was paraded on a stake on July 14, 1789—was de Launay, whose name is mistakenly transcribed in this text as "Delaunay."
[11] Benny Levy (a.k.a. Pierre Victor), quoted in Herve Hamon and Patrick Rotman, *Generation*, Volume II (Paris, 1988).
[12] Martin Heidegger, *An Introduction to Metaphysics*, trans. Ralph Manheim (Garden City, N.Y., 1961), p. 137.
[13] Ibid, p. 111. "Discourse and Truth," loc cit., p. 14.

The Revenge of the Subject /
The Return of Experience

BY LYNN HUNT

I came to my reading of James Miller's book amply forewarned. He presented a paper based on his research at a conference to which I had also been invited, and I watched in amazement during his session as many members of the audience reacted with fury and indignation to what he said. I confess that I found the reactions to his paper even more interesting than the paper itself, not because of the content of the discussion that ensued, but because of the extraordinary tumult generated by his remarks. The usual placid surface of a scholarly presentation turned into roiling waters as people stood and almost screamed their disapproval. They accused Miller of every imaginable intellectual offense and clearly felt that they had to defend the memory of Foucault against a threatening assault by an unsympathetic outsider. I imagine that some of the readers of this book will have similar reactions as they turn the pages.

I have to confess, however, that I did not have that reaction, either to the talk or to the book. I did not feel enraged, betrayed, manipulated by sensationalism, or used by an opportunist out to make money (all comments I have heard in public discussions of earlier drafts of the book). How can it be, then, that a book written in the most "traditional" (not modernist, not postmodernist) manner throws some readers into a fury? How can an author whose own moral position remains unclear— for I believe that Miller is forthright about his own ambiguous reaction to what he has found—provoke so many readers into moralizing attitudes either about the subject (Foucault's life) or the author himself (Miller)?

If Miller has manipulated us, it is in a most unusual way. He has generated a reaction—a visceral feeling, whether it be fury, rejection, amazement, disgust or just uncertainty—that in some sense proves his central contention: that experience matters. It sounds simple, but it actually involves very big stakes. At issue is not just the correct interpretation of Foucault's work but by implication the interpretive strategies of postmodernist criticism. Miller uses the most traditional tools of history and literary criticism (biography and thematic analysis) to paint a new picture of one of the leading masters of postmodernism. In the process, he raises disturbing questions about the relevance of an author's life and more profoundly still, about the possibility of liberating the self in the modern world.

As Miller himself admits, he has written a very un-Foucaultian book about Foucault. He has put the man (not generic) at the center, the very man who argued that "man" (generic) will soon be "effaced, like a face drawn in the sand at the edge of the sea." Foucault may have wanted to efface himself or decenter all of mankind, but Miller just won't let it happen. He has searched out every trace of Foucault's own face drawn in sand in order to explain its lasting imprint. He has taken everything that Foucault ever wrote or said, and much that was written and said about him, and tried to get at the psychological and philosophical strands that unified the thought as well as the life.

In this endeavor to reassemble a life and give it philosophical and ethical coherence, Miller has proved himself a very adept student of his much admired model, Jean Starobinski, who wrote what was probably the single best intellectual biography of our time, *Jean-Jacques Rousseau: Transparency and Obstruction* (French edition, 1971). Starobinski took the seeming contradictions of Rousseau's life and thought—his abandonment of his children, his railing against his erstwhile allies in the Enlightenment, to take only two examples—and managed to relate them all to a few central principles informing Rousseau's vision of the relation of individuals to each other. If this was a problematic undertaking in the case of Rousseau, because it necessarily sacrificed some of the author's quirks and gyrations on the altar of aesthetic unity, it is even more so in the case of Foucault, who after all never wrote anything remotely resembling *The Confessions.*

In his effort to provide similar unity and coherence to Foucault's life and work, Miller runs counter to the apparent spirit of Foucault's own work, since Foucault almost never emphasized the unity or consistency of either his thought or his life. On the contrary, Foucault constantly underlined the importance of disruption, displacement, and discontinuity in the development of Western discourses and practices. Foucault wanted surfaces; Miller gives him depth, and in defiance of all the deconstructionist denunciations of "the metaphysics of presence," Miller relentlessly pursues the underlying, unifying presence of a self.

Ironically, even perversely, then, Miller turns the tables on all of Foucault's own techniques of analysis. In the first pages, he talks in terms altogether different from Foucault's own references to the "games of truth": Miller asserts simply, and in tones reminiscent of a judicial proceeding, "Above all, I have tried to tell the truth." (It seems, throughout, moreover, that Miller considers himself as much on trial as Foucault.) For Miller, truth seems to mean being frank about the evidence for Foucault's preoccupation with death, whether in the form of his writing or his interest in sado-masochistic eroticism. It means linking Foucault's presumed philosophical quest for a "limit-experience" to his experiments with his own body and ultimately tying both of them to AIDS, which appears here as a kind of tragic truth that Foucault found, as if on purpose, at the end of his life. Hence Nietzsche, phenomenology, poststructuralism, Maoist politics, mind-altering drugs, sado-masochistic sex rituals, and AIDS all appear to be linked in one, inexorable project that demanded death as its only possible outcome.

Miller does not look for Foucault where Foucault taught us to look for any self: as a being produced by broad disciplinary practices and the discourses of modern institutions. The man who uncovered the workings of asylums, prisons, and hospitals, and who insisted that discourse shaped experience, is here portrayed as an intellectual and psychological loner who played the games of structuralism, poststructuralism, Maoism, and academic advancement in order to discover himself. Some readers will find that too much of Miller's intellectual analysis rests on a few, often obscure, personal interviews. By the very nature of the enterprise, personal experience looms much larger in those interviews than in Foucault's published work. This evidence gets its power, however, from Miller's skillful interweaving of material from interviews with the analysis of the published work. Both resonate in new ways.

Most striking in this portrayal of the intensely individualized self is Miller's depiction of Foucault as a determined self-fashioner. Foucault seems to fit the Loyola-Sade-Fourier psychosexual mode (remember Miller's suggestive title, "The Passion of Michel Foucault") uncovered by Roland Barthes in his wonderful analysis of that unlikely threesome. The philosopher-historian who devoted his life to analyzing our production as human beings by forces outside of ourselves—discourses, practices, and total institutions—is presented as an individual self very much in charge of remaking his identity according to his developing inner precepts, according to his own particular version of visionary and sometimes cruel self-discipline.

Nothing is more central to that emergent inner self than sex. Sex is not put forward by Miller as a discourse, the terms in which Foucault so strikingly analyzed it in his published work, but rather as a limit-experience, indeed, as an experience akin to, next to, and eventually in the circumstances of the 1980s, almost inevitably leading to death. If Foucault thought that "sex is worth dying for," Miller argues while quoting Foucault himself, it was because he saw himself engaged in a very personal "relentless search for a certain truth of pleasure," an "erotics of truth." Miller claims that Foucault found this truth in the S/M subculture of San Francisco.

Foucault never said this directly, however, so Miller juxtaposes Foucault's published remarks about sex—"the erotics of truth" were "transmitted by magisterial initiation," in secrecy, and only "to those who would make use of it...to intensify it, and to make it more acute and fulfilling"—with information he gathered from Foucault's friends and intimates. They describe Foucault's fascination with the limit-experiences available in the leather bars and bathhouses of the San Francisco warehouse district around Folsom Street. Foucault's ideas of power and discipline consequently become concrete in ways that are probably unimaginable—and perhaps unbelievable—to many people, as Miller uses the literature about the urban S/M subculture to fill in the blanks purposefully left by Foucault himself.

It is the leap from Foucault's own abstractions about sex to Miller's concrete particularities about male homosexual S/M sex and back again that will in particular shock, infuriate, or irritate many readers. Where Foucault's discourse of sex focussed on institutions, language, and virtually agentless practices of discipline, Miller's recounting of Foucault's own sexual practices concentrates on particular places, individuals, and choices. Some might question the success of the leap from one to the other, but the procedure that Miller follows seems to me to be credible; he has used everything at hand to supplement his account of what Foucault himself said, he compares his sources whenever possible, and he writes about potentially sensational subjects with a judicious, even sympathetic tone.

What interests me, however, is not the particular truth of Miller's rendition of Foucault's sex life but rather the way that Miller uses this concrete information about the webbing of the author's life to reinterpret the main directions of Foucault's intellectual endeavor. The stories of S/M subculture, like the accounts of Foucault taking drugs, being hit by a car, or making youthful suicide attempts, all feed into Miller's general line of argument that Foucault's work was always, from the very first writings, concerned above all else with self-becoming through experience, in particular experiences that were linked in some way or another to death. This emphasis on experience is the central thread on which Miller hangs his effort to provide a unified explanation of Foucault's life and work.

Although some readers might legitimately complain that Miller occasionally makes Foucault seem like the latter-day Husserlian he explicitly claimed not to be, Miller's emphasis on experience, and especially sado-masochistic experience, does illuminate much about Foucault's work, even on the most detailed level. It certainly highlights in a new way, for example, the gruesome opening pages of *Discipline and Punish*, in which Foucault almost lovingly recounts the tortures inflicted on the would-be royal assassin Damiens (a passage deleted from the standard anthology of Foucault's works). It also helps to explain Foucault's evident fascination with Sade, who appears in many of his works as a kind of icon, but who is never analyzed in any extended fashion. But the importance of sado-masochistic experience to Miller's analysis goes far beyond the details of tone or representative figures.

Miller claims that lived experience—what Foucault called "the space of an untamed exteriority"—provided the single, almost unvarying touchstone of Foucault's lifelong quest as a philosopher. Foucault's fascination with death appears in the first pages of Miller's book, but sado-masochism only emerges as a dominant theme in the last part of the book, the part that concerns Foucault's life after 1975. Miller asserts that Foucault reached a decisive turning point with his California experiences in 1975 and afterward. Foucault's life therefore seems to have had its own major displacement or breaking point. Before 1975, before California, as Miller recounts it, Foucault had known exactly what he wanted to say. After 1975, during his years of frequent visits to Berkeley and San Francisco, he fell into a period of intellectual and personal crisis, described as depression by some of his friends in Paris.

In the post-1975 period, moreover, Foucault simultaneously pursued very different projects on the personal and philosophical planes. Personally, according to Miller, he pursued his interest in S/M subculture and the limit-experiences provided by drugs, bondage, discipline, and even intense physical suffering. Philosophically, in contrast, his work (published as volumes two and three of *The History of Sexuality*) turned philological, and his prose, previously alternating between the shocking, the flashy, and the abstract, became increasingly austere and careful. Could there have been a greater contrast, a greater dissonance between the public austerity and the private revels? Can this be termed unity of experience, either across a lifetime or between the personal and the philosophical?

Miller does not see the contrast as dissonance or even disruption. Uniting both planes of experience, the philosophical and the personal, he argues, was a concern with "the problem of individual conduct." Foucault, in short, had become a strange kind of ascetic, in whose life the bondage and the discipline of S/M sex filled in for the spiritual exercises of Loyola or the self-chosen torture of St. Anthony. Foucault himself claimed to have moved away from his earlier preoccupation with power, toward an interest in the self or the subject and the experience of subjectivity. But this does not mean that the essential purpose of his quest had changed. The search for "a possible transcendence" (whether of the system or of the self) supposedly united Foucault's early interest in Nietzsche and Raymond Roussel to the concerns of the last years with both personal erotic abandon and Stoic models of sexual conduct. Discipline had become intensely personal, something exercised not by anonymous structures like the Panopticon of the ideal prison but by individual self mastery.

Can these parts of a life really have fit together so well? If they did, then why was Foucault in intellectual crisis after 1975? Why are the works written after 1975 so different in tone from those before? Why aren't they filled with the exhilaration of personal discovery? Can their stolid, unruffled, pedantic soberness really be explained as an effort at transcendence through an aesthetic self-fashioning? Does the personal experience of bondage and discipline really provide a model for an ethics of self-mastery? What was the meaning of Foucault's quest to "get free of himself," as Foucault himself called it: self-mastery or self-annihilation?

When I find myself asking such questions, I have to admit that Miller has already succeeded in much of his endeavor. He has put Foucault's intentions as an author of his work and his life front and center on the agenda. He has made the personal life of the usually discreet and reticent philosopher seem crucial to any analysis of his works. He has shown that despite Foucault's own protestations at various points in his career, the philosopher had never entirely emancipated himself from the grip of the transcendental subject and its experiences. The man who predicted the death of man lives on as an interesting, singular, individual even after his own death.

Yet Foucault manages to have a last, doubting word about this provocative attempt to unify his life and work. In an informal discussion near the end of his life—recounted by Miller—Foucault worried about the kind of self the modern world (and he himself) might be seeking to create: "Have we found a positive foundation, instead of self-sacrifice, for the hermeneutics of the self? I cannot say this, no. We have tried...And we can't find it." Thus Foucault to the end expressed doubts about any possibility of real liberation, of "getting free of the self," of getting beyond the denial and negativism in self mastery. Despite his enigmatic suggestions in *The History of Sexuality: An Introduction* that we might escape the identification of ourselves with our sexuality through a return to "bodies and pleasure," he apparently remained a sceptic to the end.

Foucault, according to Miller, "had waged a kind of guerrilla war . . . against the imperative to tell the truth." Unlike Rousseau, Foucault hated any form of confession, and throughout his life he seemed to desire a kind of effacement or self-disappearance. Miller tries to tell the truth for him, insisting that Foucault confessed himself involuntarily in his books. He won't let this man disappear behind the smoky mirrors of his rhetoric or the often labyrinthine structure of his arguments. I found this attempt to track Foucault down and make him speak fascinating and ultimately convincing in most regards. But there are some limits to the old-fashioned approach to history and criticism, especially when the author is constrained by his own feelings of bad conscience.

If Miller hadn't felt a little guilty to be writing about male homosexual S/M culture from the outsider's point of view and perhaps even more guilty to have started on his inquiry on the basis of malicious gossip about Foucault's readiness to deliberately spread AIDS (I presume Miller's feelings of guilt on the basis of his comments in the postscript), then he might have pushed a little further into the conundrums of gay and S/M sexualities, conundrums that are central to Foucault's entire intellectual endeavor because they concern the possibility of "being different." Even if Miller had not felt guilty, however, it may have been impossible to fully penetrate those questions by way of the kind of biographical and thematic analysis that Miller employs.

As Foucault taught us more insistently than any other cultural critic, sexuality is a social construction. If that is so, then can "deviant" sexualities ever be anything other than refractions of what is defined as normal? Intimately linked to each other, both the normal and the deviant are defined by the general processes of delineation of sexual practices and discourses that take place on a social and discursive level rather than on a personal one. How then could a deviant sexuality ever offer liberation from the stranglehold of disciplinary discourses and practices? It would simply be another reflection, another mirroring, however parodic or convoluted, of the definition of the normal. Foucault taught us to see, in other words, that bodies bound in chains and dangling from meathooks in the backrooms of San Francisco bars reflected back the self tortures and self annihilation inflicted by the smothering French provincial Catholicism of Foucault's youth. Foucault's own decidedly nontraditional approach to the production of sexuality and deviance—through the analysis of discourses and practices rather than personal agency—necessarily put these questions about difference, resistance, and liberation on our agenda. It is not clear that the traditional approach, with its emphasis on self, choice, and a possible transcendence, can answer them any better.

Paroxysms and Politics

BY RICHARD RORTY

James Miller runs together two questions which I think should be kept distinct. The first, meta-ethical, question is: "Is there any immutable, ahistorical, backup for our present beliefs about right and wrong?" The second, substantive, question is: "Do our present beliefs about right and wrong need major revision?" This distinction is obscured in the writings of both Nietzsche and Foucault. But it is one thing to say that philosophy cannot underwrite our politics, and another to say that we should have a different politics.

At the beginning of *The Passion of Michel Foucault*, Miller summarizes Nietzsche's challenge by saying that "there is no Aristotelian mean, no Platonic idea of the good, no moral compass implicit in our ability to reason, and no regulative ideal of consensus that could smooth away the rough edges of competing forms of life and enable us to reconcile their incommensurable claims." He summarizes his own motives for writing about Foucault by saying:

> Nietzsche's philosophy has therefore always been for me a puzzle and a provocation, if only because, in terms of its inner logic, which I have yet to see refuted, I can find no easy way to rule out the sort of cruel and murderous practices embraced by some of his followers. What might it mean, after Auschwitz, to live a life thoughtfully 'beyond good and evil' is, in short, worth finding out. And what better way than to study the life of the most revolutionary—and deeply serious—of post-war Nietzscheans?

Toward the end of his book, Miller says "Unless I am mistaken, Foucault issued a brave and basic challenge to nearly everything that passes for 'right' in Western culture—including nearly everything that passes for 'right' among a great many of America's left-wing academics."

Plato and Kant wanted to rule out cruel and murderous practices by an appeal to what Miller nicely calls "a moral compass built into our ability to reason." Nietzsche gave us some good reasons to think that we have no such built-in equipment, and Foucault and Miller that the mode of life of a person who finds happiness and fulfillment in supervising a death camp, or in consensual sado-masochism, usually cannot be "ruled out" on the basis of anything internal to that person. If he or she is to be changed rather than killed, he or she must be re-educated, or disciplined and punished, rather than reasoned with.

On the other hand, neither Nietzsche nor Foucault gave us any good reasons for thinking that the part of Kant which overlaps with Christianity as opposed to the part which overlaps with Plato—roughly, the idea of an egalitarian commonwealth in which we shall all respect each other's dignity—is wrong. Nor does either give a good reason to disbelieve the common core of Kant, Mill and Habermas—the conviction that this commonwealth should be one in which the "rough edges of competing forms of life" are, in so far as possible, smoothed away by a consensus about the desirability of living and letting live.

Miller suggests that, once we give up on the notion of "reason" common to Plato and Kant, our notion of 'right' has been challenged. But it is one thing to challenge a moral consensus and another thing to deprive it of philosophical support. One explanation for the marked behavioral differences between the French and American intellectuals is that the French ones read a lot of philosophy in high school, and are expected to take it pretty seriously. By contrast, if an American intellectual is told that a moral consensus rests upon a questionable philosophical assumption, he is likely to suggest keeping the consensus and skipping the philosophy. American intellectuals think that the only way to issue "a brave and basic challenge" to our present consensus would be to lay out a new utopia—one bravely and basically different from Kant's, Mill's and Habermas'—for our consideration. Notoriously, Foucault refused to sketch such a utopia.

The same sort of Franco-American difference prevails when modifications are made in the reigning consensus. Acquiring the conviction that it is OK to find one's happiness in consensual sado-masochism, or that the present consensus among the males engenders and protects violence against women, often leads a French intellectual to entertain large questions about the relation between the history of civilization and what Foucault called "the body and its pleasures," or to call for the dissolution of "the humanist subject, a subject which is inevitably gendered male."

When an American acquires such convictions he or she is likely to express it in fairly banal terms. In the case of consensual sado-masochism, the reaction is something like: "Hey, as long as nobody gets really *damaged*, why not?" Americans whose first information about what happens in gay bathhouses comes from Miller's book, and are intrigued to learn, for example, that "Once penetration has been achieved, internal massage coupled with in and out motions generates paroxysms of intense euphoria" (Geoff Mains, quoted in Miller's book), will be inclined to wonder if perhaps we might not be able to get the same paroxysms in the comfort and convenience of our own homes. Maybe the FDA-approved paroxysms pill? An Underwriters' Approved bedside widget for stimulating the relevant paroxysm-center in the brain?

This sort of reaction is why Americans often strike French intellectuals as just what Nietzsche had in mind when he described "the last men" as having "their little pleasures for the day and their little pleasures for the night". On the other hand, French intellectuals often strike Americans as hoping for paroxysms where nobody should want them—in politics. Such a paroxysm is suggested when Foucault says

> humanism, at least at the level of politics, might be defined as every attitude that considers the aim of politics to be the production of happiness. Now, I do not think that the notion of happiness is truly thinkable. Happiness does not exist—and the happiness of men exists still less.

If happiness is not the aim of politics, what is?, we Americans (even we left-wing academic Americans) ask ourselves. Didn't we and the French fight the Nazis precisely because the Nazis thought that German Greatness was the aim of politics, and thereby made a lot of people unnecessarily miserable? Why do we think of gay bathhouses and Auschwitz as very different, if not because one contributes to the happiness of men and the other destroys it? Why are we feminists if not because we have come to realize that women are being made unhappy merely in order to give men the kind of happiness made possible by an arrogant sense of mastery?

A lot of left-wing American academics still think that you can get some new sort of politics out of Foucault, one aimed at something more exciting than happiness. But Miller's book makes it clear that Foucault found nothing better to suggest. Miller shows us Foucault drifting into politics and drifting out again, getting a kick out of dropping bricks on policemen's heads at Vincennes in the wake of 1968 and commending von Hayek and von Mises to his students in 1979. Foucault is often thought of as a philosopher who synthesized theory and practice by organizing the *Groupe d'information sur les prisons* (GIP), but the appearance of synthesis breaks down when Foucault says that "the ultimate goal of its [GIP's] interventions was not to extend the visiting rights of prisoners to thirty minutes or to procure flush toilets for the cells, but to question the social and moral distinctions between the innocent and the guilty." Prisoners need flush toilets for their cells a lot more than anybody needs to question the distinction between the innocent consensual sado-masochists and the guilty non-consensual torturers, or the distinction between the guilty male rapist and his innocent female victim (or, for that matter, the distinction between dutiful policemen and those ecstatic left-wing academics at Vincennes, trying to crush the policemen's heads).

Instead of sketching an alternative utopia, Foucault keeps hinting that if we could only break out of the meshes of power which have formed our subjectivity, we would appreciate how contemptible the last men are, and would realize that their and our "humanist" desire for shared happiness is not only an artifact of acculturation, but one which we should repudiate. But he never, as far as I can see, makes clear whether he thinks that (a) there is something deep inside us which is repressed by *any* socializing, subjectivity-forming, process, and nevertheless needs to be freed, or (b) that prior to the modern state we were socialized into a different, better, sort of subjectivity than we have now, or (c) that the sorts of "limit-experiences" he found in LSD trips and in gay bathhouses are a token of the existence of human possibilities which no society has yet explored, but which might somehow become the basis for a new, non-humanist, politics.

The first of these alternatives (with its "humanist," Rousseuvian-Kantian, overtones) is one which Foucault often explicitly repudiated, even though it still seems to lurk beneath the surface of much that he says. The second alternative is suggested by such passages as the following:

> . . . the political, ethical, social, philosophical problem of our day is not to try to liberate the individual from the state, and from the state's institutions, but to liberate us both from the state and from the type of individualization which is linked to the state. We have to promote new forms of subjectivity through refusal of this kind of individuality which has been imposed on us for several centuries.

But what other kind of individuality did we have before those centuries? The one we had when our subjectivity was shaped by the pre-literate village? By the Athenian polis? By the medieval church? If Foucault thought that his historical research had revealed that in earlier times, before the state really got the hang of exercising bio-power, we (who? everybody? a few lucky intellectuals?) had a very different, and really terrific, sort of subjectivity, he certainly failed to make clear just when and where this was so.

Miller's book has convinced me that the third alternative is the most plausible. His book shows us how Foucault's lifelong infatuation with death (an infatuation shared with Sade, Poe and Baudelaire, but not, it is worth noting, with Nietzsche) came together with his experience in California to produce, at least in the last ten years of his life, a belief that there is a kind of death-in-life which has nothing to do with happiness, and which was, for him, "thinkable" in a way that happiness was not.

If we do have to fall back on this third alternative, however, we can see all the more clearly why we should not hope to get a new *politics* out of Foucault. Politics is supposed to include, and help, all those people who *do* find happiness thinkable, who save limit-experience for occasional weekends, and who do not share Foucault's interest in death. Contempt for these people is not a good beginning for political deliberation. Or, at least, not for political deliberation within democratic societies—societies in which compromise is the name of the game, in which different sorts of people try to rub along together by smoothing out the rough edges of their incommensurable claims.

It seems to me that the power and originality of Foucault's work conspired to reinforce a conviction which leads us to be suspicious of Foucault's criticism of the forms of subjectivity characteristic of the last several centuries. He confirmed, willy-nilly, our sense that individuality has been getting bigger and better recently. For Foucault himself was an admirable example of the sort of figure whom he honored in his deservedly famous reprise of Kant's "What is Enlightenment?". There he offers Baudelaire as an example of Kant's *sapere aude!*, and says that the Baudelairean, "just when the whole world is falling asleep . . . begins to work, and he transfigures that world. His transfiguration does not entail an annulling of reality, but a difficult interplay between the truth of what is real and the exercise of freedom."

Surely this difficult interplay is one of the things we have been getting better at? Strikingly individual thinkers—Americans like Whitman and Chomsky as well as Frenchmen like Baudelaire and Foucault, Germans like Weber and Habermas as well as Germans like Nietzsche and Heidegger—have become better and better at spotting the freedom-limiting dangers lurking behind the latest attempts at happiness. The increasing ability of the state to exert "bio-power" has been matched by the increasing ability of the post-Kantian intellectual to spot what the state is up to, and to warn us about it. Despite all the ink that has been spilled in the so-called "Habermas-Foucault debate", Habermas and Foucault are really in the same line of business: they both try to continue the pursuit of happiness by warning us of present dangers to freedom which have resulted from our success in overcoming past dangers.

For my American money, however, Habermas shows (especially in the sensitive and instructive chapters on Foucault in *The Philosophical Discourse of Modernity*) a much better understanding of, and appreciation for, Foucault than Foucault ever bothered to have of most of his dialectical opponents. The biographical information Miller provides helps us understand why Foucault had so little interest in talking things over with his opponents (why, as Paul Rabinow puts it, Foucault's "basic metaphor is one of battles and not conversation"). But I do not think that this information does as much for us as Miller may believe. It may explain why Foucault wanted to bring paroxysms and politics together, but it does little to convince us that this attempt is worth making, or that Foucault formulated a "brave and basic challenge" to our sense of right and wrong. Knowing more about Blake's life helps us understand why he wrote that it was better to strangle a baby in its cradle than to nurse an unsatisfied desire, but little to convince us that he was right on this point. (Apart from anything else, it is hard to forget the possibility that the baby at hand might grow up to be the Blake or the Foucault of the next age.)

The sort of integration of Foucault's biography and his texts which Miller attempts had to be attempted, but in the end it may be as hopeless as an attempt to link Wittgenstein's sad homosexual yearnings with his eventual repudiation of Frege's formalism, or Heidegger's distaste for democracy with his passion for the pastoral. When it comes to the great post-Kantian self-inventors, we are unlikely to find very tight connections between the life and the work. Maybe Foucault's claim that "every great philosophy so far has been . . . the personal confession of its author and a kind of involuntary and unnoticed memoir" is true of a few of the great system-builders of the past. But I think he was wiser when, in a splendid image, he cautioned us against "deep" interpretation of his thought:

> It has struck me that I might have seemed a bit like a whale that leaps to the surface of the water disturbing it momentarily with a tiny jet of spray and lets it be believed, or pretends to believe, that down in the depths where nobody sees him anymore, where he is no longer witnessed nor controlled by anyone, he follows a more profound, coherent and reasoned trajectory.

Foucault did a lot to break the spell of the idea that if we just read an author (or the prose of the world, or the historical record) long and carefully enough we shall always find a hidden coherence. We should imitate his appreciation for the role of chance and genealogy, and not try too hard to find whalepaths leading from the hard-working, danger-spotting historian of the present to the romantic who thought that nothing could be more beautiful than "to die for the love of boys."

Despite my doubts about Miller's attempt to spot a reasoned trajectory behind a sequence of brilliantly original, very diverse, quite unpredictable, eruptions, I am tremendously grateful for his immense labor of research, and for the very sophisticated and intelligent book he has written. We have been getting some really first-rate lives of the great philosophers recently. Miller on Foucault ranks with Nehamas on Nietzsche, Westbrook on Dewey, and Monk on Wittgenstein.

Art and Ideas

BY ROGER SHATTUCK

The pages printed below were read in April 1994 to a fairly large, mixed, and (I thought) inscrutable audience at the New School in New York City. Five of us formed a panel to discuss James Miller's *The Passion of Michel Foucault* on the occasion of its appearance in a paperback edition.[1] To my amazement the Board of Trustees of the New School had been invited to attend the event. Few of the Trustees—mostly New York business and professional figures—knew anything about Foucault. Two were carrying Miller's book under their arm and seemed all the more perplexed for having read a few pages. I doubt that their perplexity was much dispelled by the end of the evening. After David Halperin read a page from one of Foucault's books, two members of the audience asked what the passage was about. The discussion following our statements revealed that few members of the audience understood the extent of Foucault's influence on certain segments of intellectual life, particularly in universities, and the significance of that influence.

Across the United States departments of sociology, philosophy, and literature are still offering courses in Foucault. One recent advertisement for such a course carried a slogan that makes me wonder what goes on in some classrooms: "Take this course. Get a life." Miller's book has been attacked from all sides because it breaks the code of silence about Foucault's personal life and its close relation to his philosophy and politics. For the same reason I welcome Miller's book—with certain reservations.

Second Thoughts on a Wooden Horse

"Let us be content with provoking second thoughts and not worry about convincing anyone."

—Georges Braque, *Cahiers*

After quite a few youthful years of geographic and intellectual wandering, I finally began steady work as a teacher of modern French literature. That field brought me into contact very early with the work of Michel Foucault in the original French. Before the end of the sixties I had read both *Histoire de la Folie* (1961) and *Les Mots et Les Choses* (1966). The strenuously paradoxical *pensée* of Pascal that opens the first and the discussion of Borges' taxonomies and Valasquez'_Las Meniñas_ that opens the second seemed to be intellectual Siren songs directed at me personally. The social construction of madness during the Great Confinement of the insane following the decline of leprosy struck me as incontrovertible; I did not know then that Foucault's chronology and interpretation were highly speculative. He also talked intelligently about *Rameau's Nephew*. And in *The Order of Things* he had startling things to say about Don Quijote and about Port Royal grammarians. Twice I succumbed— and twice I drew back. For, barely ten years earlier, I had gone through the same infatuation— over Sartre. *Being and Nothingness* had inoculated me. I recovered from Foucault in time to see around his brilliance and to discover his disabling weaknesses and his immense debt to Nietzsche. Many of you have done so for yourselves, I trust.

Foucault writes in cantata style. It is not necessary to understand the words and sentences in order to be swept up by the intellectual song. Dr. Johnson wrote that men are very prone to believe what they do not understand. Foucault has the knack of evasive language. I shall cite three examples. His historical argument in book after book rests on his notion of *episteme*, a Greek borrowing meaning the network of mental and cultural conditions dominant in a period. The *episteme* supposedly produces the thought of the period. Carefully scrutinized, *episteme* reveals itself as a recostumed version of the Hegelian *Zeitgeist*—the fully discredited idea of History personified as an agent.

Foucault also increasingly exploits the ambiguity in French—lost in English—of the word *représenter*. It can mean to represent by imitation or by signs, and it can mean to act out or practice. "The duty to represent one's most furious desires" (*The Order of Things*) also means "The duty to act out one's most furious desires." *Discourse*, a term popularized by Foucault among others, comes to mean not linguistic communication produced by human beings or authors but the spontaneous generation of meaning in language without attribution to an author and without distinctions of literary genre. Presumably the *episteme* itself produces all our discourse and responds to it. Writers and readers are an illusion obstructing the free proliferation of meaning. (See "What is an Author?") Do we wish to honor this legerdemain?

Finally I began to be troubled not only by Foucault's flashy vocabulary but also by other problems like his contradictions. He borrows one of his principal mottoes from Pindar via Nietzsche, "To become the thing one is." (see Miller, 68-69). Yet in the course of time this forceful claim to personal integrity has been turned 180 degrees into a very different message. "One writes to become something other than who one is," Foucault states in a 1983 interview on Raymond Roussel. In *The Uses of Pleasure* (1985) he advocates the kind of curiosity "that permits one to get free of oneself." Consistency may be the hobgoblin of little minds, but on such a fundamental shift one expects some explanation from a professional philosopher. My own work on the case of the Wild Boy of Aveyron revealed to me how tendentious Foucault's history of psychiatry is for the early years at the opening of the 19th century. For he treats the institution of the asylum as a cruel technology of power and dismisses the strong philanthropic and humanitarian motives that drove Pinel and Tuke to develop a "moral treatment" of the insane that recognizes their humanity. Foucault's attempt to establish a new periodization bringing the classical era to a close only in 1800 serves to eliminate the Enlightenment and to reinforce another maneuver I shall discuss at the end.

So in the seventies I read no more Foucault. There were far more important writers to deal with—Proust, for example. And I believed that Foucault had yielded to the temptation of becoming a guru, a *maître à penser*, a practitioner of intellectual mystification. Before long a friend sent me from Paris the devastating criticisms of Foucault's history and philosophy by Gladys Swain and Marcel Gauchet (*Penser la maladie mentale*, Gallimard, 1980). For this discussion it is an essential book.

In the eighties graduate students began showing up in my courses at the University of Virginia who made use of *discourse*, *desire*, and—a bit more rarely—*episteme*. They had not always read Foucault, but all had studied with a professor somewhere who had succumbed to the new gospel. I read a few more of his writings without finding reason to change my previous estimate.

In early 1992 an advance typescript of Jim Miller's book sent out by the publishers lured me back to Foucault. I knew Jim slightly as a fellow contributor to *Salmagundi* and as a friend of friends. To my amazement during a busy season I found time to read all 700 pages. Each time I picked up Miller's typescript, it made me feel more vividly the wonderment of the child in the story of the Emperor's New Clothes. Could this adulation of a Svengali truly be taking place among people of discriminating intelligence? I woke up to the fact that the past century has produced no powerful rebuttal of Nietzsche. Partly in consequence, no one has called Foucault to task on a scale equal to his influence.[2] But Miller goes a long way. Let me mention a few of the episodes and arguments documented in Miller's book, many of which were little known before its publication.

I. Over the years Foucault aimed his heaviest weapons at humanism in all forms. And he defined what he meant. "Humanism is everything in Western civilization that restricts *the desire for power*" (199).

II. In his 1971 debate with Chomsky, Foucault invoked as the ideal social model Maoist China and denied the need for law, justice, and responsibility. That same year Foucault was welcoming from Nietzsche the acceleration of "instinctive violence" and "something of the murderous" (218). Our cruelest phantasms "should be freed from the restrictions we impose on them . . . and allowed to conduct their dance" (223-24).

III. As a prominent intellectual Foucault was consulted in 1978 about the reform of French Penal Law. He argued for abolishing the age of consent for all sex acts, heterosexual and homosexual. "It could be that the child, with his own sexuality, may have desired that adult" (257). All sexual behavior, including rape, should be freed from constraints—

except the physically violent element.

IV. Increasingly Foucault advocated the association of sex with cruelty (rather than with love) and with impersonality and strangers (rather than with intimacy) (259-69).

V. Foucault's celebration of "transgression" as a way of life and of psychological quest turned before long toward sadomasochistic eroticism and "la joie suppliciante"—that is, the joy of torture (86-89). When homosexual promiscuity in San Francisco bathhouses and the reality of AIDS were added to this equation, Foucault pronounced the logical and nihilistic result: "Sex is worth dying for" (34). He did not specify whose death. Fully informed by his medical colleagues about the seriousness and the highly controllable nature of the AIDS epidemic threatening him and his friends, this prominent philosopher took the position of advocating promiscuity among male homosexuals. "'If sex with a boy gives me pleasure'—why renounce such pleasure? *We* have the power, he said again: *we* shouldn't give it up" (353).

We readers should be grateful for the steadiness with which Miller demonstrates how Foucault spurns any middle ground of moral constraints and political institutions that human beings may have constructed between total power and total anarchy. Foucault cannot decide which extreme to favor.

But I am deeply puzzled, sometimes appalled, by Miller's responses to what he is so conscientiously recording. On the page after reporting Foucault's recommendations about age of consent and rape, Miller writes, "Though Foucault's specific proposals are highly questionable. . . his courage is beyond dispute." Courage? Foucault was a privileged and protected insider at the summit of French and American educational establishments. Under our "bourgeois" system of justice he did not face one shred of danger. This was no Robin Hood taking risks to help the downtrodden, no brave explorer dying on the way to the South Pole. Foucault was defending and normalizing his own homosexual, sadomasochistic tastes and pleasures. Proust, who dealt extensively with these subjects, would not have sympathized. Nor would Wilde, who wrote a sentence beyond Foucault's grasp as a thinker: "Kindliness requires imagination and intellect."

In his Postscript, Miller speaks of his sympathy toward the foolhardiness of "any sexually adventurous gay man in 1983," of a "certain dignity" in Foucault's regarding AIDS as a "limit-experience," and of Miller's "conviction that what Nietzsche and Foucault have written about the genealogy of moral judgment is, in some broad sense, 'true'"(383). The wish to stimulate the mind through the senses belongs to every era, including the most primitive and the most sophisticated. Religious sects have sought mystical experience through many forms of asceticism and also of licentiousness. It is as if the lesson of temperance can rarely be learned without the experience of excess. But certain intellectual and artistic minds have come to cultivate excess for its own sake, not as a path toward restraint or humanity. Excess itself is knowledge. The most dazzling formulation of the program came from a sixteen-year-old.

> The poet makes himself into a *seer* by a long, immense, and deliberate *debauchery of all his senses*. All forms of love, suffering, madness. He must search by himself. He runs through all the poisons in order to hold onto the most essential... He becomes the great leper, the great criminal, the great outcast—and the supreme Knower.

Rimbaud's manifesto of *dérèglement* has often been used as a blanket justification for the most dissolute and self-indulgent behavior. Foucault convinced himself and his admirers that his own crapulous behavior merited some kind of perverse moral justification. But what he referred to as "the limit-experience" of sadomasochistic experimentation led—so far as we can tell—to no illumination beyond itself. It led to self-destruction; Foucault died of AIDS. In professing to find "dignity" in Foucault's life of passion, Miller makes me wonder how far he has swallowed a romantic doctrine that welcomes sheer experience for experience's sake. Or perhaps Miller is preaching a new shamanism. In either case we are drifting very far from the shore.

To my mind, Miller's own book belies every aspect of Miller's evaluation. Could I, then, would I, write a blurb for this book, which reveals the truth and then seems not to grasp it? I'll read you my blurb in its original version, slightly longer than the one that appears on the jacket of the hardback edition.

Miller has written truer than he knows. Foucault, the most mesmerizing of the recent French conquistadors, flirted seriously with terrorism, hoped to invent an ungovernable New Man, and tried to convert homosexual sex into an impersonal sadomasochistic experiment. Miller strips the intimidating and evasive terminology away from this intellectual horror story. Miller's scrupulousness should help bring us to our senses.

I see no reason to retract any part of that statement.

Another way of understanding Foucault's place on the scene today, as partly revealed by Miller, is to employ an ancient analogy. Publishers and admirers offer us Foucault's accumulated writings as a new departure in intellectual history, philosophy, and anthropology. I see his works as forming a remarkably successful wooden horse, like the Trojan Horse Odysseus devised to introduce Greek soldiers into Troy in order to conquer the city. On the outside Foucault's writings make ambitious claims about periodization, epistemes, discourse, and institutions of repression. Anyone who reads attentively will see before long that these claims veil a doctrine of total liberation from all social and moral constraints in order to act out our most violent instincts—above all, sexual.

In *The History of Madness* he refers to "a massive cultural fact that appeared precisely at the end of the 18th century and that constitutes one of the greatest conversions of the occidental imagination. . . madness of desire, the insane delight of love and death in the limitless presumption of appetite"(210). The corresponding passage in *The Order of Things* refers to the same "reversal" of values and the great author who produced it. "After him violence, life and death, desire, and sexuality will extend, below the level of representation, an immense expanse of darkness, which we are now attempting to recover . . . in our discourse, in our freedom, in our thought" (211).

The message recurs at the very end of *Madness*: "Through him the West has regained the possibility of surpassing reason through violence." *The Order of Things* closes with the claim that the knowledge we have gained from this author and the "mutation" he has brought down on us is the only knowledge that "has allowed the figure of man to appear" (386). Who is the great thinker who will become the savior of humanity? It is the Marquis de Sade. He rides in the belly of this great wooden horse. A few times he is named; more often the reader must identify him. Sometimes Sade is misleadingly flanked by the mainline figures of Goya, Nietzsche, and Van Gogh. But they have been rung in to provide camouflage. The rehabilitation and imitation of Sade represents Foucault's attempt to introduce a major revision of cultural and personal values unencumbered by moral considerations.

Foucault never quotes Sade. He never pauses to examine the nature of Sade's sustained episodes of orgasmic pleasure directly stimulated by sodomy, cruelty, torture, and murder, or to examine the philosophy used to justify them as superior to so-called virtue. Writing on what appears to be a high level of scholarly "discourse," Foucault simply invokes Sade as the heroic, model figure of the modern era. Readers who do not know Sade's work are left dangling with hortatory phrases like "the living body of desire" and "the secret nothingness of unreason." They may well be moved to seek out that vicious author as teacher and prophet. Readers familiar with Sade's work may perceive the true direction of Foucault's project: to seduce and to pervert, following the doctrine that elevates power above truth. But you would not grasp this project from an uncritical reading of Foucault's abstract, obscurantist prose.

There is a disturbing dishonesty at work here. How has it contrived to reach so high in the social and humanistic disciplines? Intellectual fashion, I believe, has become more powerful than ever. The Divine Marquis, brought secretly into the city in the wooden horse of Foucault's writings, lives again among us, not as hyena but as hero. For Miller and his readers it is time for second thoughts. We should listen carefully for the answer to our challenge: Who goes there?

Notes

[1] The panel consisted of James Miller, presiding, David Halperin, Janice Sawicki, Steven Seidman, and Roger Shattuck.

[2] Beginning in the seventies Foucault was welcomed in prominent American newspapers and reviews by Richard Poirier, Leo Bersani, and Alexander Nehamas among others, and more cautiously by Jean Starobinski, Steven Marcus, and George Steiner. Sterner criticism came a little later, from Lawrence Stone, Paul Robinson, Gordon Wright, and Erik Midelfort.

VII
Politics

The Fragility of Liberalism

BY CHRISTOPHER LASCH

The collapse of communism as a serious competitor to liberal capitalism has generated a state of euphoria among liberals of the right and center, qualified only by the reflection that the "end of history," in Francis Fukuyama's celebrated phrase, will be a "very sad time" for those who value "daring, courage, imagination, and political idealism." The "unabashed victory of economic and political liberalism," as Fukuyama sees it, means the universal rule of law, the globalization of the "classless society" that has already been achieved in the United States, the "receding of the class issue," a steady expansion of the supply of consumer goods, a "universal homogeneous state," and a "post-historical consciousness" in which "ideological struggle . . . will be replaced by economic calculation, the endless solving of technical problems, environmental concerns, and the satisfaction of sophisticated consumer demands."

Fukuyama's article recalls earlier predictions of the end of ideology by liberals; but it is curiously reminiscent, as well, of Marcuse's one-dimensional man and the Frankfurt School's horrifying vision of a totally administered society without contradictions and therefore completely resistant to change. Since Fukuyama, like Marcuse and his friends, takes his inspiration from Hegel, it is not surprising that their different versions of the end of history have so much in common. For that matter, the convergence of technical optimism with cultural despair, the worship of progress with nostalgia, has been a persistent current in modern thought ever since the Enlightenment. The triumph of reason looks like the promised land of harmony and freedom until we remind ourselves that men have learned to value freedom only in the course of competition and conflict. At that point, Max Weber's "iron cage" of rationality looks like a more accurate description of the future. Fukuyama, after dwelling at length on the beauties of liberalism and the feebleness of the forces now opposed to it, unexpectedly leaves us with the prospect of "centuries of boredom." The new order, he says, calls up the "most ambivalent feelings"—on the one hand, the satisfaction of knowing that liberalism no longer faces an ideological challenge of any importance; on the other hand, a "powerful nostalgia for a time when history existed."

But the liberal order is far from secure in fact. In the hour of its seeming triumph, its fragility is exposed more clearly than ever before, nowhere more clearly than in the United States. Having defeated its totalitarian adversaries, liberalism is crumbling from within. The absence of an external threat makes it more difficult than before to ignore this decay. The Gulf War provided a momentary distraction, but it ended all too quickly; and although we can look forward to further distractions of this kind, it will be impossible, in the long run, to avoid the day of reckoning. Already the signs of impending breakdown are unmistakable. Drugs, crime, and gang wars are making our cities uninhabitable. Our school system is in a state of collapse. Our parties are unable to enlist the masses of potential voters into the political process. The global circulation of commodities, information, and populations, far from making everyone affluent (as theorists of modernization used to predict so confidently), has widened the gap between rich and poor nations and generated a huge migration to the West and to the United States in particular, where the newcomers swell the vast army of the homeless, unemployed, illiterate, drug-ridden, derelict, and effectively disenfranchised. Their presence strains existing resources to the breaking point. Medical and educational facilities, law-enforcement agencies, and the available supply of goods—not to mention the supply of racial good will, never abundant to begin with—all appear inadequate to the enormous task of assimilating what is essentially a surplus population.

But even the children of privilege are no longer assimilated into the culture of liberalism. One survey after another shows that college students no longer command even a rudimentary knowledge of Western history, literature, or philosophy. A kind of deculturation has clearly been going on for some time, a process of unlearning without historical precedent (which explains why we don't have a better word to describe it). What E. D. Hirsch calls illiteracy is probably a more serious danger than the most obviously ideological attacks on liberal culture. The right repudiates "secular humanism," while the left denounces any attempt to uphold a core of common values as cultural imperialism and demands equal time for minorities. The "modernization" of the world, as it was conceived when liberals were running the show, implied the creation not only of a global market but of a global culture in which liberal values—individual freedom, open inquiry, religious tolerance, human dignity—would be universally respected. We have a global culture all right, but it is the culture of Hollywood, rock and roll, and Madison Avenue—not a liberal culture but a culture of hedonism, cruelty, contempt, and cynicism.

So much for the symptoms of liberal decline—which should elicit just as much ambivalence, incidentally, as its supposed ascendancy and the resulting "end of history." I turn now to the causes of this decline. It is pointless to speculate about what is to be done—whether we should seek to rescue liberalism, to replace it with something else, or resign ourselves to the decline not just of liberalism but of our national experiment as a whole—until we get a better understanding of exactly what is happening to our political traditions and why. If liberalism retains the capacity for growth and development along new lines, it would be foolish to desert our dominant tradition. If, on the other hand, it has reached the outer limits of its growth, we should probably turn to submerged traditions in American life, which have been overshadowed but never altogether extinguished by the reigning political creed.

To speak of any kind of limits at all is another way of speaking about the plight of liberalism, a political tradition predicated on unlimited economic expansion. In its most persuasive form, liberalism rests on a chastened belief in progress, one that does not presuppose any naive illusions about the perfectibility of human nature but assumes merely that a steady growth of consumer demand—a revolution of rising expectations—will sustain economic expansion indefinitely. Liberalism has identified itself with policies designed to assure full employment and thus to expand the capacity to consume. The promise of universal abundance has contained egalitarian implications without which it would have carried very little moral authority. Those implications, to be sure, were open to conflicting interpretations. Some people argued that it was enough to increase the general pool of goods and services, in the expectation that everyone's standard of living would rise as a result. Others demanded more radical measures designed not merely to increase the total wealth but to distribute it more equitably. But no one who believed in progress conceived of a limit on productive capacity as a whole. No one envisioned a return to a more frugal existence; such views fell outside the progressive consensus.

The belated discovery that the earth's ecology will no longer sustain an indefinite expansion of productive forces deals the final blow to the belief in progress. A more equitable distribution of wealth, it is now clear, requires at the same time a reduction in the standard of living enjoyed by the rich nations and the privileged classes. The attempt to extend Western standards of living to the rest of the world, on the other hand, would lead very quickly to the exhaustion of nonrenewable resources, the irreversible pollution of the earth's atmosphere, drastic changes in its climate, and the destruction of the ecological system, in short, on which human life depends. "Let us imagine," Rudolf Bahro writes, "what it would mean if the raw material and energy consumption of our society were extended to the 4.5 billion people living today, or to the 10-15 billion there will probably be tomorrow. It is readily apparent that the planet can only support such volumes of production . . . for a short time to come." Let us imagine further an India in which every family owned a pair of cars and every house came with air-conditioning, stereo sets, VCRs, and a kitchen fully equipped with the latest appliances.

The growing importance of environmental issues provides the most dramatic but by no means the only indication that we have entered a new age of limits—limits not only to economic development but more generally to human control over nature and society. It is a commonplace observation that technological innovations have unforeseeable consequences that often render them self-defeating, compounding the very problems they were meant to solve. The widespread use of antibiotics leads to the proliferation of bacteria resistant to antibiotics. Medical technologies that prolong life create still another class of dependent, superfluous persons whose numbers overwhelm the facilities for taking care of them. Automobiles, supposedly a fast, cheap, and efficient means of transportation, merely disguise the cost of getting from one place to another. By taking account of the time required to maintain and pay for these machines, to drive and park them, and to earn the money to buy gas, insurance, and repairs, Ivan Illich once calculated that the average driver achieved an average speed of only 4.7 miles an hour—not much faster than he could walk. David Ehrenfeld, after citing many other examples of self-defeating technologies in his *Arrogance of Humanism*, argues that it is no longer possible to avoid the conclusion that our inability to make long-range predictions with any accuracy, to control the innumerable complexities that enter into such calculation, or to allow for unanticipated effects caused by our own procedures of diagnosis and measurement impose severe limits on our capacity for control. In a recent article, not yet published, Ehrenfeld continues his analysis of our "misplaced faith in control" by showing how over-management, in the private as well as the public sector, makes society increasingly unmanageable. The sheer volume of paperwork absorbs energies that might be used more constructively. Obsessive record-keeping makes it more and more difficult to distinguish useful from useless information or to locate appropriate information when it is needed. Obsessive supervision undermines the judgment and competence and self-confidence of those under supervision and creates a need for still more supervision. The cost of maintaining elaborate structures of management drains resources away from more productive investments. The administered society, it appears, is inherently unstable. There are limits beyond which it cannot operate without collapsing under its own weight—limits we are rapidly approaching.

In its classic version, liberalism reduced the functions of government to a bare minimum. Diplomacy, war, police, and education pretty much exhausted the responsibilities of the state, as it was conceived by liberals in the 18th and 19th centuries. This drastic simplification of government was an important source of liberalism's appeal, together with its promotion of religious tolerance and free speech. Yet the liberal state has now evolved into a leviathan, and even the misnamed private sector is dominated by huge bureaucracies exercising quasi-governmental powers and closely linked to the bureaucracy, notwithstanding their impatience with regulation. What explains this curious line of historical development, as a result of which liberalism has come to be associated with a special order that would have seemed completely repellant to the founders of liberalism? Is it simply that liberals have betrayed their own heritage, as right-wing critics argue when they try to recall liberalism to its free-market origins? Or is there something in the very nature of liberalism—some inner contradiction, as we used to say—that gives rise to the need for elaborate structures of management, supervision, and control?

Through all the permutations and transformations of liberal ideology, two of its central features have persisted over the years—its commitment to progress and its belief that a liberal state could dispense with civic virtue. The commitment to progress alone generated many of the difficulties that now threaten to bury the liberal state, since progress meant large-scale production and the centralization of economic and political power. The belief in progress also contributed to the illusion that a society blessed with material abundance could dispense with the active participation of ordinary citizens in government—which brings us to the second point, the heart of the matter. In the aftermath of the American revolution, liberals began to argue, in opposition to the older view that "public virtue is the only foundation of republics," in the words of John Adams, that a proper system of constitutional checks and balances would "make it advantageous even for bad men to act for the public good," as James Wilson put it. According to John Taylor, "an avaricious society can form a government able to defend itself against the avarice of its members" by enlisting "the interest of vice . . . on the side of virtue." Virtue lies in the principles of government, Taylor argues, not in the "evanescent qualities of individuals." The institutions and "principles of a society may be virtuous, though the individuals composing it are vicious."

The trouble with this agreeable paradox of a virtuous society based on vicious individuals is that liberals didn't really mean it. They took for granted a good deal more in the way of private virtue than they were willing to acknowledge. Even today, liberals who adhere to this minimal view of citizenship smuggle a certain amount of citizenship between the cracks of their free-market ideology. Milton Friedman himself admits that a liberal society requires a "minimum degree of literacy and knowledge," along with a "widespread acceptance of some common set of values." It is not clear that our society can meet even these minimal conditions, as things stand today; but it has always been clear, in any case, that a liberal society needs more virtue than Friedman allows for. A system that relies so heavily on the concept of rights presupposes individuals who respect the rights of others, if only because they expect others to respect their own rights in return. The market itself, the central institution of a liberal society, presupposes, at the very least, sharp-eyed, calculating, and clear-headed individuals—paragons of rational choice. It presupposes not just self-interest but enlightened self-interest. It was for this reason that 19th-century liberals attached so much importance to the family. The obligation to support a wife and children, in their view, would discipline possessive individualism and transform the potential gambler, speculator, dandy, or confidence man into a conscientious provider. Having abandoned the old republican ideal of citizenship along with the republican indictment of luxury, liberals lacked any grounds on which to appeal to individuals to subordinate private interest to the public good. But at least they could appeal to the higher selfishness of marriage and parenthood. They could ask, if not for the suspension of self-interest, for its elevation and refinement. Rising expectations would lead men and women to invest their ambitions in their offspring. The one appeal that could not be greeted with cynicism or indifference was the appeal summarized in the slogan of our own times: "our children: the future"— a slogan that makes its appearance only when its effectiveness can no longer be taken for granted. Without this appeal to the immediate future, the belief in progress could never have served as a unifying social myth, one that kept alive a lingering sense of social obligation and gave self-improvement, carefully distinguished from self-indulgence, the force of a moral imperative.

Thomas Hopkins Gallaudet, a prominent educator and humanitarian (a pioneer in education for the deaf, among other things) expressed a view widely shared by liberals when he wrote, in 1837, that the "good order and welfare of society" had to rest on "that indescribable parental attachment to offspring which secures to the child every particular, constant, and fond attention which its peculiar condition demands." Neither "legislative enactments" nor prisons nor a large police force could guarantee social order. Even the school, on which liberals characteristically put so much of the burden of social control and improvement, could not succeed unless it saw itself as "co-operating with the [family and] . . . greatly aiding its operations." Now that the family's educational role has been so greatly diminished, with the result that the schools expend most of their efforts in teaching things that should have been learned at home, we can appreciate the wisdom of these 19th-century platitudes about the dependence of the school on the family. Educators in the 20th century have tried to assure us that well-managed schools can replace the family, in effect. John Dewey's version of this new consensus was more modest than most. Since modern industry had "practically eliminated household and neighborhood occupations," he argued, the school would have to "supply that factor of training formerly taken care of in the home"—training, that is, in the "physical realities of life." Abraham Flexner and Frank Bachman went much farther. "Social, political and industrial changes," they wrote in 1918, "have forced upon the school responsibilities formerly laid upon the home. Once the school had mainly to teach the elements of knowledge, now it is charged with the physical, mental, and social training of the child as well." In our own day, it is charged, in addition to all that, with the still more sweeping task of instilling a sense of racial and ethnic pride in disfranchised minorities, at the expense of the basic education that is really needed. Yet it is more and more widely acknowledged, even by educators, that the schools can't teach anything at all unless the importance of learning is upheld in the home. Without a substructure of strong families to build on, the school system will continue to deteriorate.

The history of education provides an especially striking illustration of a general principle, namely that the replacement of informal types of association by formal systems of socialization and control weakens social trust, undermines the willingness both to assume responsibility for oneself and to hold others accountable for their actions, destroys respect for authority, and thus turns out to be self-defeating. The informal associations that have been allowed to wither away (except when they have been deliberately and systematically destroyed by ill-conceived adventures in social engineering) include not only the family but the neighborhood, which serves, much more effectively than the school, as an intermediary between the family and the larger world. Jane Jacobs speaks of the "normal, casual manpower for child rearing" that is wasted when city planners and other well-meaning reformers seek to get children off the streets into parks, playgrounds, and schools where they can be professionally supervised. The whole thrust of liberal policy, ever since the first crusades against child labor, has been to transfer the care of children from informal settings to institutions designed specifically for that purpose. Today this trend continues in the movement for day care, often justified on the grounds not merely that working mothers need it but that day care centers can take advantage of the latest innovations in pedagogy and child psychology. This policy of segregating children in age-graded institutions under professional supervision has been a massive failure, for reasons suggested by Jacobs in *The Death and Life of Great American Cities*—an attack on city planning that applies to social engineering in general, right across the board. "The myth that playgrounds and grass and hired guards or supervisors are innately wholesome for children and that city streets, filled with ordinary people, are innately evil for children, boils down to a deep contempt for ordinary people." In their contempt, planners lose sight of the way in which city streets, if they are working the way they should, teach children a lesson that cannot be taught by educators or professional caretakers—that "people must take a modicum of public responsibility for each other even if they have no ties to each other." When the corner grocer or the locksmith scolds a child for running into the street, the child learns something that can't be learned simply by telling him about it. What the child learns is that adults unrelated to each other except by the accident of propinquity uphold certain standards and assume responsibility for the neighborhood. With good reason, Jacobs calls this the "first fundamental of successful city life"—one that "people hired to look after children cannot teach because the essence of this responsibility is that you do it without being hired."

Neighborhoods encourage "casual public trust," according to Jacobs. In its absence, the city has to rely on formal agencies of law-enforcement. In Los Angeles, a city that has turned its back on the street, we see this pattern in its most highly developed form—the "militarization of city life," as Mike Davis calls it in his *City of Quartz*. A vastly expanded police force, equipped with the technology and increasingly with the mentality of a police state, still finds itself unable to assure safety and order and has to be supplemented by an army of private policemen. According to Davis, the private sector specializes in labor-intensive law-enforcement, the public sector in aerial surveillance, paramilitary operations, wiretapping, and the maintenance of its elaborate criminal files. "Fortress L.A.," as Davis calls it, is becoming a city of "enclosed communities," heavily guarded compounds prepared to repel intruders at the slightest hint of trouble.

Los Angeles, the triumph of counter-urbanization, embodies the triumph of liberalism, together with its collapse. It is literally the end of the road, simultaneously the last refuge of the liberal dream and the nightmare that was always implicit in the dream. Liberalism promised progress, abundance, and above all privacy. The freedom to live as you please, think and worship as you please—this privatization of the good life was liberalism's greatest appeal. Having set definite limits to the powers of the state, at the same time relieving individuals of most of their civic obligations, liberals assumed that they had cleared away the outstanding obstacles to the pursuit of happiness. What they allowed themselves to forget was that public order is not just a function of the state, which can safely be entrusted with the responsibility for education and law-enforcement while citizens go about their private affairs. A society in working order has to be largely self-policing and to a considerable extent self-schooling as well. City streets, as Jacobs reminds us, keep the peace and instruct the young in the principles of civic life. Neighborhoods recreate many features of the village life that is celebrated in American folklore, even as Americans reject the promiscuous sociability of the village in favor of "life-style enclaves," as Robert Bellah calls them, in which they associate exclusively with those who share their own tastes and outlook. Neighborhoods provide the informal substructure of social order, in the absence of which the everyday maintenance of life has to be turned over to professional bureaucrats. In Los Angeles, a city deliberately designed to maximize privacy, we see how this hyperextension of the organizational sector is the necessary consequence of the retreat from the neighborhood. But Los Angeles is exceptional only in its single-minded dedication to a deeply anti-social version of the American dream and in the scale of the social problems that result. The same pattern can be seen in every other American city, where the police, the educational bureaucracy, and the health and welfare bureaucracies fight a losing battle against crime, disease, and ignorance.

I want to explore one more illustration of the principle that the atrophy of informal controls leads irresistibly to the expansion of bureaucratic controls. I refer to the growing demand for the censorship of pornography, obscenity, and other forms of unacceptable speech, not to mention the outcry against flag-burning. Here is another instance where liberalism seems to be reaching its limits—in this case, the limits of more or less unconditional guarantees of free speech. It is suggestive that the strongest case for censorship today does not come from professional patriots and right-wing advocates of ideological conformity—that is, from the kind of people who never grasped the importance of free speech in the first place. It comes instead from the kind of people who formerly upheld the First Amendment against its critics—from people on the left, especially from feminists who take the position that pornography exploits women and ought to be subject to some kind of public regulation. It is not necessary to accept their contention that pornography represents an invasion of women's civil rights (a contention that stretches the concept of civil rights out of all resemblance to its original meaning) in order to see the justice of their opposition to pornography. But pornography is not just a women's issue, and the best argument against it is not simply that it demeans women, corrupts children, or injures some other class of victims, but that it "offers us an unacceptable mirror of ourselves as a people," in the words of Elizabeth Fox-Genovese. Like obscene speech, it corrupts our public culture. The pervasiveness of obscene images and speech, not just in the media but in everyday conversation, reminds us that morality is a public matter, not just a matter of private taste (except when someone can claim to be injured) and that what makes it public is the need for common standards, not just the possibility that pornography or obscenity will impinge on the rights of women or demean them in some other way. As Fox-Genovese observes, "A society unwilling or unable to trust to its own instinct in laying down a standard of decency does not deserve to survive and probably will not survive."

Every culture has to narrow the range of choices in some way, however arbitrary such limitations may seem. To be sure, it also has to see to it that its controls do not reach too far into people's private lives. Still, if it allows every impulse a public expression—if it boldly declares that "it is forbidden to forbid," in the revolutionary slogan of 1968—then it not only invites anarchy but abolishes the distinctions on which even the category of truth finally depends. When every expression is equally permissible, nothing is true. The heart of any culture, as Philip Rieff rightly insists, lies in its "interdictions." Culture is a set of moral demands, of "deeply graven interdicts, etched in superior and trustworthy characters." This is why Rieff can describe the United States today as a "cultureless society." It is a society in which nothing is sacred and nothing, therefore, can be effectively forbidden. An anthropologist might say that a cultureless society is a contradiction in terms, but Rieff objects to the way in which liberal social scientists have reduced the concept of a culture to a "way of life." In his view, culture is a way of life backed up by the will to condemn and punish those who defy its commandments. A "way of life" is not enough. A people's way of life has to be embedded in "sacred order"—that is, in a conception of the universe, ultimately a religious conception, that tells us "what is not to be done."

If Rieff and Fox-Genovese are correct in their belief that culture rests on a willingness to uphold public standards and to enforce them, then the "remissive" culture of liberalism cannot be expected to survive indefinitely. In the past, liberals could afford a broad definition of free speech only because they could take for granted the existence of informal sanctions against its misuse. The First Amendment was not designed to protect obscene or pornographic speech, which eighteenth-century conventions relegated to strictly private circulation. Here as elsewhere, liberalism presupposed a morality inherited from the pre-enlightened past. The persistence of that morality, supported by the family, the church, and a code of common decency so widely accepted that it hardly needed to be articulated, concealed contradictions in liberalism that are beginning to surface now that a certain reticence and propriety can no longer be taken for granted. The danger is that a belated recognition of the importance of common standards will lead to a demand for organized repression that will endanger hard-won rights of free speech. We see this not only in the movements for censorship of pornography or (at the opposite end of the political spectrum) in the officially sanctioned pressure for an amendment against flag-burning but in the ill-advised measures adopted by universities against "verbal harassment" and more generally in the attempt to enforce a stifling standard of politically correct speech.

The search for organized controls where informal controls no longer seem to operate promises to extinguish the very privacy liberals have always set such store by. It also loads the organizational sector, as we have seen, with burdens it cannot support. The crisis of public funding is only one indication, although it is also the clearest indication, of the intrinsic weakness of organizations that can no longer count on informal, everyday mechanisms of social trust and control. The taxpayers' revolt, although itself informed by an ideology of privatism resistant to any kind of civic appeals, also grows out of a well-founded suspicion that tax money merely sustains bureaucratic self-aggrandizement. The state is obviously overburdened, and nobody has much confidence in its ability to solve the problems that need to be solved. Of course a disenchantment with the welfare state does not in itself imply a commitment to some other kind of solutions. It may well signify nothing more than indifference, cynicism, or resignation. Although almost everybody now believes that something has gone radically wrong with our country no one has any clear ideas about how to fix it. The increasingly harsh, intemperate quality of public debate no doubt reflects this shortage of ideas and the frustration to which it gives rise.

As formal organizations break down, people will have to improvise ways of meeting their immediate needs: patrolling their own neighborhoods, withdrawing their children from public schools in order to educate them at home. The default of the state will thus contribute in its own right to the restoration of informal mechanisms of self-help. But it is hard to see how the foundations of civic life can be restored unless this work becomes an overriding goal of public policy. We have heard a good deal of talk about the repair of our material infrastructure, but our cultural infrastructure, as we might call it, needs attention too, and more than just the rhetorical attention of politicians who praise "family values" while pursuing economic policies that undermine them. It is either naive or cynical to lead the public to think that dismantling the welfare state is enough to insure a revival of informal cooperation—"a thousand points of light." People who have lost the habit of self-help, who live in cities and suburbs where shopping malls have replaced neighborhoods, and who prefer the company of close friends (or simply the company of television) to the informal sociability of the street, the coffee shop, and the tavern are not likely to reinvent communities just because the state has proved such an unsatisfactory substitute. They still need help from the state, in the form of policies designed to strengthen the family, say, and to enable families to exert more control over professionals when they have to depend on them or at least to give them more freedom in the choice of professionals. A voucher system for schools is the type of reform that answers this need, and the same principle might be applied to other professional services as well.

Such reforms will not, in themselves, be enough to restore the structures of informal self-government in an over-organized society. But even these modest beginnings require far more energy and vision than our leaders have shown in recent years. The belief that liberal societies have achieved a state of almost perfect equilibrium—that "liberal outcomes are stable once reached," in the words of one of Fukuyama's admirers, Stephen Sestanovich—adds one more reason to the list of reasons that appear to justify a policy of drift. The "end of history" contributes to the disinclination to undertake fundamental changes. The stability of liberal states is an illusion, however, and the sooner we recognize it as such, the sooner we can hope to summon up the "daring, courage, imagination, and idealism"—qualities prematurely consigned by Fukuyama to the dustbin of history—that will enable us to address the unsolved problems that will otherwise overwhelm us.

Hannah Arendt:
Democracy and the Political

BY SHELDON S. WOLIN

The question of democracy is not one that has received much attention from those who have written about Hannah Arendt. This omission seems understandable because Arendt herself never systematically addressed the topic in any of her writings. Yet it is not difficult to show that many of the major categories that compose and distinguish her political outlook were either critical of or incompatible with democratic ideas. This I believe to be the case with the distinction on which her political ideals were grounded, the distinction between "the political" and "the social." Her critical attitude toward democracy rested on a correct intuition that the impulse of democracy has been to override that distinction. For historically, democracy has been the means by which the many have sought access to political power in the hope that it could be used to redress their economic and social lot. The "natural" state of society contains important distinctions of wealth, birth, and education that are typically extended into political power. Thus social power is translated into political power which is then used to increase social power. Democracy is the attempt of the many to reverse the natural cycle of power, to translate social weakness into political power in order to alleviate the consequences of what is not so much their condition as their lot-tery.

Democracy would also obliterate these Arendtian distinctions because it wants to extend the broad egalitarianism of ordinary lives into public life. It is at odds with the emphasis on authority, ambition, glory, and superiority that figured so importantly in Hannah Arendt's conception of authentic political action. It was not accidental that she excluded the sentiments of fellow-feeling—compassion, pity, and love—from the political realm, or, more important, that she was silent about "friendship" (so central to her ancient Greeks) and "fellowship" (so basic to Hebraic and Christian conceptions of community). These democratic sentiments and virtues do not accord with the agonistic conception of action she extolled. Democratic action is, perforce, collective; its mode is cooperation; and its presupposition is not a small audience of heroes but shared experience.

In what follows I propose to explore the origins of the antidemocratic strain in Arendt's thought, tracing it from its beginnings in her classic study of totalitarianism to its apogee in her next major work, *The Human Condition*. Then I want to show that in her later writings a change is evident. It appeared first in the last chapter of *On Revolution* (1963) and more strikingly in the collection of essays, *Crises of the Republic* (1969). While on the way to what can fairly be described as a leftward position, she modified some of her most characteristic categories. Within limits, and in her own way, she was, in the course of reflecting upon the political events of the 1960s, radicalized.

Hannah Arendt's first major work, *The Origins of Totalitarianism* (1951), was completely silent about democracy. Although *prima facie* there seems to be no necessary reason why an analysis of totalitarianism should discuss democracy, the historical and political context of the subject-matter and the book suggest otherwise. The book was written in the immediate aftermath of World War II. During the war years in the United Kingdom, the British Commonwealth, the United States, and in a significant part of Nazi-occupied Europe, the single, most universal theme that set the interpretation of the war in the minds of ordinary people everywhere was of a struggle between "democracy" and "dictatorship." The books, newspapers, magazines, radio and movies of the time conveyed a pretty unanimous viewpoint that the nature of totalitarianism was to be grasped almost entirely in terms of the political antitheses between democracy and totalitarianism: between democratic freedom of speech and education and totalitarian thought-control and mass manipulation;

between democracy's system of free political parties and government by consent and the totalitarian one-party state with its use of terror and intimidation.

While it would be an exaggeration to argue that the *Origins of Totalitarianism* reversed the accepted perspective, it is no overstatement to say that the work adopted a viewpoint that interpreted totalitarianism by means of categories that were drawn from intellectual traditions that were deeply anti-democratic. One tradition was associated with Nietzsche, the other with Tocqueville. A fundamental category of both traditions was the "mass." For Nietzsche democracy was primarily the political expression of the atomistic, unheroic, security-loving culture which had emerged after the defeat of the agonistic, aristocratic political culture of antiquity by the slave morality of Christianity. "The democratic movement," Nietzsche wrote, "is not only the form of the decay of political organization, but a form of the decay, namely, the diminution, of man, making him mediocre and lowering his value."[1]

Tocqueville, whose general influence on Arendt, particularly in her understanding of the founding of the American republic and of the nature of the French Revolution, has not been fully appreciated, not only anticipated Nietzsche's nostalgia for a politics on an heroic scale[2] but was the first nineteenth-century theorist to revive the ancient notion that certain forms of tyranny might have a popular basis.[3] Tocqueville envisioned "an immense protective power," operating benignly rather than brutally, that "hinders, restrains, enervates, stifles, and stultifies" by "a network of pretty complicated rules" that "covers the whole of social life." Democratic "equality," Tocqueville held, "has prepared men for all this," encouraging them to pursue "petty and banal pleasures," to "exist in and for himself," isolated and politically passive.[4]

The echoes of these writers can be heard in the main themes of Arendt's analysis of totalitarianism: ". . . totalitarian movements," she wrote, "depended less on the structurelessness of a mass society than on the specific conditions of an atomized and individualized mass."[5] "Mass man" was characterized by "isolation and lack of normal social relationships" caused in part by "the breakdown of the class system."[6] Totalitarian movements, she continued, were built on "sheer numbers" of "indifferent people. . . who never before had appeared on the political scene."[7] Totalitarian leaders, such as Hitler and Stalin, "had the confidence of the masses" and enjoyed "indisputable popularity."[8] The triumph of totalitarian movements, she concluded, shattered the "illusion" that the existence of "democracy" had been made possible because the majority had taken an active part and had positively supported democratic government. In reality the majority had been indifferent. This proved that "a democracy could function according to rules which are actively recognized by only a minority." Insofar as democracy rested on the masses at all, it had rested "on the silent approbation and tolerance of the indifferent and inarticulate sections of the people." The moral was that while democratic freedoms might be defined in terms of formal, legal equality, they were viable "only where the citizens belong to or are represented by groups or form a social and political hierarchy," that is, where there was political and social inequality.[9]

The Origins concluded with a warning, that unless human beings resolved to undertake a fresh political start (a "planned beginning of history") that would include the creation of "a new polity," the future was bleak. "There are plenty of indications that the mob. . . will take over and destroy where we were unable to produce."[10]

She undertook that project herself in *The Human Condition* (1958), and offered her conception of a new beginning that would furnish the ground for withstanding the masses. There was little in the *Origins* that would have prepared a reader for the archaic vision of "a new polity" that was inspired by the version of pre-Socratic Hellenism associated with Nietzsche and Heidegger. *The Human Condition* did not present a sketch of a political constitution as Plato had done, but it did offer, in the Platonic sense, an "idea" that embodied an ideal. And like Plato's, her ideal owed virtually nothing to the facts of history and only slightly more to the history of political ideas. "The political" was the ideal. The intention behind it was to combat a different version of the masses than the one which had figured in her analysis of totalitarianism. Although "mass society" remained the danger, the analysis was focused on the phenomenon of "work" and on the transformation of society and politics effected by the modern emphasis upon productivity and economic growth. These and other notions were assembled under the idea of "the social"; and behind that idea was her main opponent, Karl Marx, who symbolized the destruction of the Western tradition of politics.

Arendt's conception of "the political" had several aspects. It signified not a state or a society but a determinate public space, a forum, an agora, set aside, jealously defended so that those men who wished to test themselves by the highest standards of excellence might compete, by speech and action, in the presence of their peers. It was to be a politics of lofty ambition, glory, and honor, unsullied by private interest or the material concerns in the larger society "outside": a politics of actors rather than citizens, agonistic rather than participatory, encouraging qualities that would enable men to stand out rather than to take part in, share (participation = *pars* (part) + *capio* (seize)). It was a combination of Periclean democracy, idealized so as to expunge the democratic elements of law courts and assemblies, and an Homeric assembly from which the merest suggestion that a Thersites might arise to "quarrel with kings" (*Iliad* 2.211-78) had been removed.

It is difficult to exaggerate either the severity with which she drew boundaries around the political in order to separate it from the banality and low concerns of ordinary life, or the historical distortions which had to be introduced in order to claim for her construct the authority of the Greeks. Among the distortions she ignored the acute class conflicts that were a familiar feature of the Greek city-states and had generated continuous pressure for the broadening of citizenship and for the enlargement of political access so that excluded social elements might enjoy the benefits of political membership. As a result she gave us a politics without the divisive conflicts that have presented the main challenge to politicians, just as she had given us what was said to be a Greek-inspired conception of action but without analyzing the vital place accorded violence and war in Greek conceptions of the *polis* and of noble action.

In the same bowdlerizing vein, she made no mention of the periodic efforts, as early as the Solonic land reforms, to expand the meaning of equality (*insonomia*) so as to include a socio-economic content and not just an equality of formal legal rights.[11] So insistent was she that political equality had to be confined among the few that she tried to maintain that the "real" meaning of equality as understood by the Greeks had not to do with fair treatment or even with equal rights but with a condition in which the individual was free because he was neither a ruler (or superior) nor a subject (or inferior).[12] In support of this interpretation she claimed that "the whole concept of rule and being ruled. . . was felt to be prepolitical and to belong to the private rather than the public sphere."[13] The claim is, however, flatly contradicted by Aristotle's familiar definition that "citizens, in the common sense of the term, are all who share in the civic life of ruling and being ruled." [14]

The fragility of her ideal was underlined by the condition which it required. A politics devoted to the production of memorable actions had to be not only exclusive but subsidized. The ancient Athenians had compromised their democracy by excluding slaves, resident aliens, workers, and women, that is, practically the entire work force of the *polis*. Arendt accepted this notion and dressed it out by adopting Aristotle's justification that these human activities were "functions" which embodied the metaphysical principle of "necessity," that is, they were necessary to sustaining human life and, by extension, the collective life of the *polis*. But because these forms of "labor" were bound endlessly to produce and reproduce the means of life, and because the fate of the products and services was to be consumed and thus to pass away without trace, and because the laborer depended on employers or masters, the activities were unfree, without choice or lasting significance. Parenthetically, one might note that this contrast between "freedom" and "necessity" was comparable to the one developed by Marx, but, unlike Marx, Arendt wanted to preserve necessity rather than develop a complex strategy, as Marx did, for exploiting it, overcoming it, and consorting with it. For Arendt freedom resided essentially in the political realm where men could exercise choice. In her eyes, Marx's exaltation of labor, his claim that it should constitute the principle around which society should be reorganized, represented an inversion of the true hierarchy of values. It meant enshrining an activity that was essentially mindless, routinized and repetitious in place of political action with its drive for the unpredictable and memorable deed. "The art of politics teaches men how to bring forth what is great and radiant. . . Greatness. . . can only lie in the performance itself and neither in its motivation nor its achievement."[15] Labor, on the other hand, entails a form of sociability that involves "the actual loss of all awareness of individuality and identity." The "*animal laborans*" is marked by "an incapacity for distinction and hence for action and speech."[16]

The distinctive nature of the political or public realm was developed by the contrasts which Arendt drew between it and the concept of "the social." The latter signified all of the activities and relationships which, by nature, were "private." They included work and labor, love, sex, family, and household. These, she contended, were matters that could not withstand the glare of publicity that attends all political actions without being distorted or perverted. Private things, such as labor, "material concerns, " and "bodily functions," should remain "hidden." [17]

The crisis of modernity is that the political realm has been invaded by the social realm, especially by private economic interests and private values of consumption and pleasure. The most dangerous invader is the mass whose power has increased with the growth of conformity. The value of equality has been realized in the fact of sameness. Politics has given way to administration as bureaucracies regulate daily life and render it more uniform. The triumph of necessity, and of the labor principle that embodies it, is realized in the form of a society dedicated to the ignoble ideal of mere life. She described that society in a passage that is pure Nietzsche:

> Society is the form in which the fact of mutual dependence for the sake of life and nothing else assumes public significance and where the activities connected with sheer survival are permitted to appear in public.[18]

In retrospect *The Human Condition* seems a work that is highly suggestive at the margins of its chosen problems and irrelevant, even misleading, at its center. There are marvelously perceptive comments about the nature of action and of work, but the main construct, "the political," could not carry the burden assigned to it. This was because two of the most fundamental political problems were either ignored or treated superficially: power and justice. Power, she declared, "exists only in its actualization." It "springs up between men when they act together and vanishes the moment they disperse . . . Power is to an astonishing degree independent of material factors . . ."[19]

This formulation was fully consistent with her discussion of work, labor, technology, and private property which never succeeded in grasping the basic lesson taught not only by Marx but by the classical economists as well, that an economy is not merely work, property, productivity, and consumption: it is a structure of power, a system of ongoing relationships in which power and dependence tend to become cumulative, and inequalities are reproduced in forms that are ever grosser and ever more sophisticated. It is a system of power whose logic contains no inherent principle of justice, and it is doubtful that, in the absence of the devoted labors of philosophers over the past two decades, it would have ever acquired one. But justice was not discussed by Arendt at all; it simply did not figure for her as it had for Plato and Aristotle, as the main objective of political action.

Arendt's silence about justice was related to another extraordinary omission: the state. That one could claim to have a politics without discussing the state is perhaps the result of her Greek starting-point. As is well-known, the concept of the state does not make an appearance until the early 16th century. Its absence, both in theory and practice, allowed her attention to be focused on the political actor and action itself to be treated in dramaturgical terms, with not much attention given to institutional constraints, to the difficulties of "action-at-a-distance," and to the dependence of actors upon their own instrumentalities. When the modern state appears and acquires its centralized apparatus of power, the actor anticipates the fate of the contemporary author in a structuralist critique: the text no longer needs him. The presence of the state has even more important consequences for ordinary citizens. It represents not only the greatest concentration of coercive power in history, and it not only demands obedience, but it asks for loyalty, even affection, from its subjects. The conditions which the modern state requires—enormous revenues, a managed economy and labor force, a huge military establishment, ever-more lethal instruments of violence, a vast bureaucracy, and a compliant citizenry that will produce legitimation upon demand—make it increasingly plain that the "democratic state" has become a contradiction in terms.

On Revolution (1963) saw Arendt exchanging the paradigm of Athens for the early American republic, the agonal actor of Homer for the revolutionary of 1776, and Pericles for John Adams. Many of the categories developed in The Human Condition were retained, particularly the dichotomy between the "political" and the "social" with its anti-democratic and even anti-political implications. Now, however, the opposition between the political and the social was developed by means of a contrast between the two great 18th century revolutions, the American, which was guided by an authentic political impulse, and the French, which catalyzed the "many" who, since antiquity, had remained outside history, that is, the history of memorable actions. The French Revolution marked the moment when those who had been hidden away in the lower depths of society had suddenly erupted. ". . . this multitude, appearing for the first time in broad daylight, was actually the multitude of the poor and the downtrodden, whom every century before had hidden in darkness and shame."[20] It was as though, she continued, "the slaves and resident aliens [of antiquity], who formed the majority of the population without ever belonging to the people, had risen and demanded an equality of rights."[21] Themselves preoccupied with their "needs," they generated a type of physical "necessity" from their own "misery" and unleashed it upon public space. Thus out of a primal necessity revolution emerged, not as the inspired action of a desperate people unable to secure redress for their grievances, but as an "irresistible process," a necessity so overpowering as to defy human control, and hence signifying—as necessity always does—the denial of freedom.[22]

In the American Revolution, she maintained, "the exact opposite took place."[23] The Americans conducted a genuinely political revolution, one that "concerned not the order of society but the form of government." Among the reasons for the difference, as Tocqueville had argued before her, was nature's bounty rather than colonial virtue. Although there was "poverty," there was little of the "misery" and "want" that would later goad the sansculottes to revolt. At the same time there was just the right amount of deprivation to discourage improper political aspirations. The majority of colonists, she noted approvingly, being occupied with "continuous toil," "would [be] automatically exclude(d) . . . from active participation in government."[24] Acknowledging that while misery may not have been the lot of the white majority, it may have been the experience of the black slaves, she insisted that the main point was that "the social question" was absent from revolutionary America "and with it, the most powerful and perhaps the most devastating passion motivating revolutionaries, the passion of compassion."[25] The demands of the miserable that the political order remedy their distress could fall on sympathetic ears in Europe because moderns had come to feel compassion, not because there was any widespread belief that social and economic opportunities ought to be open to all. "The game of status seeking," she wrote in a passage that is simply historically untrue, ". . . was entirely absent from the society of the eighteenth and nineteenth centuries...."[26] And with a fine Nietzschean aside she chided contemporary social scientists for believing that "the lower classes have, as it were, a right to burst with resentment, greed, and envy. . ."[27]

Although Arendt was full of praise for the Framers of the American Constitution for having succeeded in giving lasting institutional form to revolution, something which most modern revolutionists have failed to do, her account of the Constitution displayed again her antipathy toward material questions, in this case, the economic motives of the Founding Fathers, even though many of the founders were not hesitant to argue them openly in public space, as it were. By ignoring these matters her account of the Constitution left uninterpreted the drive for centralization, the determination to curb the power of the colonial legislatures, and the Hamiltonian vision of a national economy presided over by a strong state. Her failure to recognize that the Founders were more concerned to halt the democratic social movement that had captured some of the state legislatures and initiated economic legislation favoring small farmers and that their own plans included a capitalist's version of the social question returns to undercut the proposals for a new conception of the political—or rather, a new embodiment—advanced toward the end of *On Revolution.*

She criticized the Framers for having introduced a system of representative government which meant that "the people are not admitted to the public realm." She charged the Constitution with having caused the withering of the "revolutionary spirit" because it had failed "to incorporate the townships and the town-hall meetings, the original springs of all political activity in the country" into the new political order.[28] Her charge, however, merely accused the Framers of what they openly avowed. The new national government, as its architects made clear, had to break the monopoly which State and local institutions had on the affections of the people.[29] Incorporating local institutions was not something the Founders failed to do; it ran counter to their political vision. They made the Constitution into a triumph of state-sponsored capitalism, an elite version of the "social question" which included the defense of property rights, the encouragement of a national economy through currency reforms, tariffs, taxation, commercial policies, state subsidies, a military power able to extend American commerce, and an enlightened bureaucracy to nurture infant industries. The vision of the Founders was national rather than local, expansive rather than stationary. Consequently, for Arendt to praise the Founders for having kept the rabble and their social concerns from invading public space, and then to tax that same elite for being insensitive to the value of local participatory institutions was to strain at a gnat and swallow the camel.

Arendt's criticism of the Framers was an expression of her unease at the spectacle presented by modern representative government and its system of political parties: they had made politics the monopoly of a professional elite and closed it off to natural elites who are inspired, not by careers, but by genuine love of politics. Her solution was to resurrect an obscure proposal advanced by Jefferson in a private letter written nearly a quarter century after the ratification of the Constitution. Jefferson had envisaged a system of "elementary republics" located in the wards, counties, and states and forming a "gradation of authorities," each with a share of power, that would serve to check and balance each other.[30] Although Jefferson's proposal suffered from some of the same shortcomings as ancient Greek democracy in making no provision for the political admission of women, slaves, and aliens, there were genuinely democratic features to it. "Every man in the State" was to be "an acting member of the Common government, transacting in person" according to "his competence." Each would thus feel himself to be "a participator in the government of affairs, not merely at an election one day in the year, but every day. . ."[31]

Arendt then proceeded to integrate Jefferson's proposal with a tradition of participation which extended back to the likes of the Committees of Correspondence during the American Revolution and forward to the revolutionary councils and committees that had sprung up spontaneously with the outbreak of revolutions. She found them in the French Revolution, the Paris Commune of 1871, the Russian revolutions of 1905 and 1917, and the Hungarian Revolution of 1956. And doubtless she would have included the Solidarity movement in contemporary Poland.

Most of these examples fulfill her exacting criteria of heroic politics and spontaneous appearance. Whether they were purely political and unmarred by social and economic objectives may be more contestable. But granting their importance, it may still be the case that the fact of their existence casts doubt on her entire thesis concerning the corrupting effects of the social question, of material misery upon the capacity of ordinary citizens to act in a genuinely political way. If modern societies were mass societies, how is it possible for ordinary citizens to escape the deadening effects of routinized labor and the corruptions of consumer society and to display an appetite for politics and political action? How is it possible, first, to congratulate the elites for keeping the masses at bay and, then, to welcome these committees and councils as "the political elite of the people"? Arendt did not attempt to answer the question, but it is not difficult to find a plausible explanation, although it involves getting behind the "darkness" which Arendt repeatedly found to be surrounding the lives of laboring people. Thanks to social historians and cultural anthropologists we learn that the poor are not without rich cultures of their own. Once this is appreciated their capacity to act ceases to be inexplicable and the suspicion arises that the concept of the "mass" may be of limited utility. It may even be primarily an intellectual conceit, a displacement of the intellectual's resentment at what capitalist culture does to the status of intellectuals: It restricts "high culture" to the few and then subsidizes the intellectual to protect the few from the cultural banality of capitalism.

Arendt's indifference, to put it blandly, to the culture of ordinary and poor citizens produced a severely impoverished notion of the historical meaning of the political. Here I have in mind what has been one of the most important, perhaps the most important, sources of the popular understanding of a wide range of political notions, such as equality, justice, community, authority, and power. The historical contribution of Western religions to the political education of ordinary and poor people is almost impossible to exaggerate. Religion supplied a first hand experience in what it meant to be a member of a community, to sacrifice and share, to be an object of power, to make not just promises but commitments of long duration, to refuse to conform for conscience's sake, and, not least, to found new communities.

At the end of *On Revolution* there was an element of pathos to Arendt's project. Beyond extolling the value of these new forms of elitism, nothing is said about how they might be maintained because institutionalizing them would destroy the spontaneity which was an essential element of their political authenticity. Their appearance, therefore, is accepted as one would accept the inexplicable workings of Divine Grace. These elites are "chosen by no one," they constitute themselves. "Politically they are the best and it is the task of good government and the sign of a well-ordered republic to assure them of their rightful place in the public realm." "To be sure," she added, the recognition of these elites "would spell the end of general suffrage" for recognition would mean that the elite had won "the right to be heard in the conduct of the business of the republic," and that they cared "for more than their private happiness." As for those who would be excluded, they had not only chosen their fate by remaining passive, but they had, unconsciously, affirmed "one of the most important negative liberties we have enjoyed since the end of the ancient world, freedom from politics."[32]

This last remark illustrates Arendt's profound equivocality about politics, an equivocality that led her to welcome spontaneous political action but to distrust action when the stakes became so large as to threaten to incorporate the concerns that are located closer to or within "private" life. She wanted a pure form of politics, one that was consistent with the claim that "power is to an astonishing degree independent of material factors."[33] Political institutions, she declared flatly, should be made independent of economic forces.[34] It was her vision of pure politics that led her during the late 1960s to oppose the Viet Nam War, to defend civil disobedience, to criticize the involvement of universities in the war business, and, within limits, to welcome some aspects of the student protest movements. In all of these commitments one can see a common element: a support of actions that were primarily political, or at least could be seen that way, and without economic motives or broad social aims.

In closing let me offer some remarks intended as a contribution to an alternative, democratic conception of the political. What would such a conception look like? How can it escape being merely another arbitrary construction? One answer is that, historically, the idea of the political and the idea of democracy have shared so many common meanings as to seem almost synonymous. This cannot be said of the relationship between the idea of the political and, say, the idea of a political order that would be controlled by or responsive primarily to the wealthy. Marx expressed this point in one of his early writings:

> . . . it is evident that all forms of the state have democracy for their truth, and for that reason are false to the extent that they are not democracy.[35]

Marx's point can be rendered like this: It is the nature of the state that, insofar as it claims to be political, it will govern for the good of the entire community and not serve primarily the interests of a particular class or group: this is the democratic "truth." But insofar as the state in question takes a particular form, say, one mainly controlled by the wealthy or by corporations, it will by virtue of its actual nature rule in the interests of a part of the society, that is, be false to the democratic principle of the good of the whole community. It follows that only a democratic state has the possibility of acting as a genuine political state. It might be added that most political theorists, from antiquity to the present, have accepted the premise of this point and resisted the conclusion. They have accepted the

principle that the political defines a distinct kind of association that aims
at the good of all, depends on the contributions, sacrifices, and loyalties
of all, but they have then bent their ingenuity to devising structures that
would allow the few (whether kings, aristocrats, representatives, or
bureaucratic officials) to use collective power for the good of all while
exacting from the population at large the various contributions needed for
that task.

These are, however, mainly formal considerations, and while they
help to identify correctly the principle that the political means the
common wellbeing is the end and the definition of what is authentic
political action, it does not specify what the political has to include so that
the common well-being is furthered. Nor does it tell us what the nature
of the common well-being is: is it something that is "made" or "created"
? And, if so, out of what? Or is it disclosed? Is it a pure good, or equivocal,
even ironic? What are the conditions that are needed for the political to
come into being so that the common well-being becomes possible and
how do these conditions entail democracy?

We can begin not by ignoring the state but by avoiding the error of
assuming that the state is identical or coterminous with the political. The
state is a modern phenomenon and its *raison d'etre* was to develop, or
better, to capitalize the power of society—the power resident in the
human activities, relationships, and transactions that sustain life and its
changing needs. The state became a coercive agency, declaring and
enforcing law, punishing miscreants of all descriptions, systematizing
taxation, encouraging commerce and manufacture in the direction of
national economies, conducting diplomacy, waging war, and seeking
empire. Its characteristic form of action is the decision which it "makes"
with relentless regularity; its typical expression is the announcement of
a "policy," and its mode of governance ranges from inducements to force.

The appearance of the state signifies that surplus power is available,
that collective life has succeeded in producing more power than the daily
needs of the members require. The existence of surplus power is a sign
that the political has come into being in the common life that makes the
state possible. Common life resides in the cooperation and reciprocity
that human beings develop in order to survive, meet their needs, and begin

to explore their capacities and the remarkable world into which they have been cast. The political emerges as the shared concerns of human beings to take care of themselves and the part of their world that they claim as their lot. The political emerges, in the literal sense, as a "culture," that is, a cultivating, a tending, a taking care of beings and things. The common life and the political culture emerge to the accompaniment of power. Shared concerns do not eliminate the need for power; they depend upon it. This was partly glimpsed in a remark by the late Roland Barthes:

> One must naturally understand *political* in its deeper meaning, as describing the whole of human relations in their real social structure, in their power of making the world.[36]

There is, of course, an irony here in that the skills of social cooperation, which human beings acquire through experience and apprenticeship, and which enable them to settle their existence, eventually are made to work against them. Their skill produces more power than they need. Surplus power enables them to project: to control more of the future and so to develop plans and expectations, i.e., projects. The dynamics of collectivity then take hold. The search for surplus power then gets institutionalized, which is the organizational language for talking about the routinized manufacture of surplus power. Surplus then becomes the province of administration; it is managed and administered in the form of programs, including programs for the deployment of power converted into weapons and man-power. In all of this the political, which had emerged as shared concerns and involvements, has disappeared.

The loss of the political is a clue to its nature: it is a mode of experience rather than a comprehensive institution such as the state. The thing about experience is that we can lose it and the thing about political experience is that we are always losing it and having to recover it. The nature of the political is that it requires renewal. It is renewed not by unique deeds whose excellence sets some beings apart from others, but by rediscovering the common being of human beings. The political is based on this possibility of commonality: our common capacity to share, to share memories and a common fate. Our common being is the natural foundation of democracy. As beings whose nature displays common elements, we have an equal claim to participate in the cooperative undertakings on which the common life depends. We are not equal in power or ability, and that is precisely why equality is crucial. The development of power upon which the common life depends requires different qualities and it produces different beings, differences which are interpreted as inequalities. At the same time, and stated somewhat differently, our human being is not exhausted by its common being. It is, as Hannah Arendt so often and eloquently reminded us, a being that is capable of expressing the most remarkable and glorious diversity. That diversity has important implications on how power is exercised democratically.

Each of us is a contributor to the generation of power without which human life cannot endure. The problem of the political is not to clear a space from which society is to be kept out but it is rather to ground power in commonality while reverencing diversity—not simply respecting difference. Diversity cannot be reverenced by bureaucratic modes of decision-making. Diversity is the nightmare of bureaucracy. The bureaucrat's response to it is either to invent another classification or, in the corporate world, to manufacture 57 varieties. The mode of action that is consonant with equality and diversity is deliberation. Deliberation means to think carefully. We must think carefully because what is at stake is the exercise of human power. To exercise power democratically, that is, with the fullest possible participation by equals, far from being an exercise of crude mass power, is the most sensitive way of handling power. Democratic deliberation implicates our common being in decisions which are bound, in a complex society, to threaten harm to our diverse beings. It requires not that we come to terms with power— representatives and bureaucrats can do that for us—but that we face it.

Notes

[1] Cited in Tracy B. Strong, *Friedrich Nietzsche and the Politics of Transfiguration* (Berkeley and Los Angeles, 1975), p. 201.

[2] See, for example, *Democracy in America,* tr. George Lawrence (Garden City, New York, 1969), p. 15

[3] A. Andrewes, *The Greek Tyrants* (London, 1956).

[4] *Democracy in America*, p. 692

[5] *The Origins of Totalitarianism* (New York, 1951), p. 312

[6] Ibid., pp. 310, 308

[7] Ibid., p. 305

[8] Ibid., (New York, 1951), p. 301.

[9] Ibid., p. 306

[10] Ibid., pp. 438, 439

[11] See G. Vlastos, "Isonomia," *Classical Philology,* Vol. XLI (1946), 65-83; J.W. Jones, *The Law and Legal Theory of the Greeks* (Oxford, 1956), pp. 16-23, 84-90; M.M. Austin and P. Vidal-Naquet, *Economic and Social History of Ancient Greece: An Introduction* (Berkeley, Los Angeles, 1977), pp. 24-26

[12] *The Human Condition* (Chicago, 1958), pp. 32-33

[13] Ibid., p. 32

[14] *Politics* III.xiii. 1283 b 45.

[15] *The Human Condition,* p. 206

[16] Ibid., pp. 213, 215

[17] Ibid., p. 77

[18] Ibid., p. 46.

[19] Ibid., p. 200.

[20] *On Revolution,* p. 41.

[21] Ibid., p. 33.

[22] Ibid., pp. 33, 41-44

[23] Ibid., p. 44.

[24] Ibid., p. 63.

[25] Ibid., pp. 66, 90

[26] Ibid., pp. 66-67

[27] Ibid., p.67

[28] Ibid., pp. 241-242.

[29] See Hamilton's remarks in *Federalist 27 ad finem*

[30] *On Revolution,* p. 258

[31] Cited, *On Revolution,* p. 257.

[32] *On Revolution,* p. 284. See also *Crises of the Republic,* pp. 231-233

[33] *The Human Condition,* p. 200

[34] *Crises of the Republic,* pp. 212-13.

[35] *Critique of Hegel's 'Philosophy of Right',* tr. Joseph O'Malley (Cambridge, 1970), p. 31.

[36] *Mythologies,* tr. Annette Lavers (New York, 1972), p. 143.

Letter From Paris:
Racism

BY TZVETAN TODOROV
(TRANSLATED BY MARY MAXWELL)

Political life in France has entered, little by little, into a new phase. The shift began in 1983 when the government of the left, then in power for two years, conducted a dramatic revision of its politics that led to its rupture with the Communist party, and the latter's return to the opposition (thereafter, its virtual disappearance). The Socialists, left alone at the head of state, renounced at that point all prospects for societal upheaval and adopted a social and economic policy that was, more or less, that of previous governments. The new policy, dubbed "obligatory," appeared no longer as distinctly that of the left or the right, but as the only one possible if France were to remain an integral part of the European community and the world market, and continue her "development."

The second great stride, clearly, was achieved in 1989 with the collapse of Communist regimes in Eastern Europe. The process had begun before, and is still not completed; but, since this year, the shift has become irreversible. As a result, the great East-West axis that structured the political representation of the world, the opposition of totalitarianism and democracy, has lost much of its relevance. In a word, the ideological war came to an end, both within and without, the democratic ideal and the civic consensus allowing everyone to come to an agreement, if not on every point, at least on the framework in which one might wish to see discussed each new question.

On this idyllic picture nevertheless appeared a shadow that canbe named in abridged form by one word: racism. It may cover over, however, several distinct realities. One is the recrudescence of overtly racist acts: raids of persecution that sometimes end in murder; the refusal of service to persons physically different from oneself; antisemitic attacks. At the same time, the party of the extreme right, whose program nearly amounts to "Arabs and Africans, get out!", has advanced steadily since 1983, so as to attain, in certain regions, fifteen, twenty, and even twenty-five per cent of the vote.

Finally a discourse descended from the old racist tradition placed itself in the public forum, all the while distinguishing itself from that tradition on several essential points, with the result that those who practice it can declare, "I am not a racist." The discourse of the old racist stressed differences in the physical characteristics of beings; the one who replaced him today openly speaks only of cultural traits. "I am not a racist," recently announced Brigitte Bardot, taking part in a crusade against the sacrifice of sheep practiced by certain Muslims in France. "I don't see the color of skin, but the soul of people." The old racist affirmed the superiority of certain races over others; these days one is content to stress the insurmountable difference that separates them. In sum, not long ago one aspired to the submission of other races (their extermination, in the extreme case of Hitler); one wishes now their separation from us, their return to their country of origin (if they don't want to conform to our customs, continues Bardot, let them leave). The ideological conflict responsible for supplying us with a good Enemy therefore finds itself replaced by a conflict that one may call ethnic, since it refers to differences at once national, cultural and racial; the fear of the Reds is supplanted by fear of the Blacks and the Browns. I believe we've lost in the exchange.

Facing the Rise of Racism

This phenomenon surprised as many traditional political classes as it did the analysts, and reactions in the face of it have remained a little chaotic. The issue in which *Le Debat* celebrates its tenth anniversary (60, 1990) offers a sample that is probably representative of these reactions among French intellectuals.

A first attitude (evoked rather than assumed in *Le Debat*) belongs to a number of leftist militants; they take the rise of the extreme right and of racism with absolute seriousness and decide to combat it with repression. Antiracist legislation has been reinforced, a new law has been passed that criminalizes falsification of the history of the Second World War (as in the denial of the gas chambers), and the National Front today has the greatest difficulty finding halls and grounds in which to hold their reunions. Some call for their prohibition pure and simple.

One can ask oneself whether such reactions don't risk aggravating the illness they're designed to relieve. To begin with, the adherents of the National Front don't transgress the rules of the democratic game, they don't call for armed struggle or promise the installation of a dictatorship; they make use of the same political instruments as the other parties: the ballot box and the television. Next, as was remarked at the time of the vote on the new laws, to combat a fever, it's not enough to break the thermometer: if a party receives fifteen per cent of the vote, it will not disappear following its prohibition: in a democracy one can't prohibit people from thinking in their own way. To criminalize the tendentious interpretation of history is grotesque, and can only produce effects contrary to those anticipated. Truth does not need a law in order to be protected; if law becomes necessary, it's because the legislator has doubts about its being a truth. In short, to fight against racism by repression, without trying to understand what provokes it, seems the same kind of short-sighted practice that the left of yesteryear loved to criticize among its adversaries.

A second attitude, on the contrary, consists of minimizing the importance of the phenomenon and of seeing in it a somewhat perverse manifestation of a process nevertheless identical, that of the expansion of democratic individualism, the victory of the "hedonistic-communicational age." According to this altogether optimistic hypothesis that Gilles Lipovetsky, for example, develops, the rise of fundamentalism or of national passions demonstrates what collective membership has yielded to the autonomy of the individual and his choices. "In the society of superchoice, why would there not exist the existential gamut of religious intransigence, including the possibility of strict traditionalism?" Religious or racial extremism would then be only one product among others in the "supermarket of lifestyles"; that one could choose it would prove our accrued liberty, not our dependence. Such a vision is rather reassuring for the long term; in the immediate, however, it does not permit us to make crucial distinctions between tolerance and intolerance.

A third reaction widespread among French intellectuals led them to throw doubt upon the legitimacy of antiracism. As a first step, racists and antiracists were opposed as two extremes equally undesirable and equally responsible for the malaise in contemporary society, "two demagogic movements of opposite meaning" (Marcel Gauchet). It was further contended that, no more than the human rights from which it proceeds, antiracism can't serve as the basis for a politics (political action has need of the framework of the state, therefore of the nation). But if it is true that human rights, and therefore antiracism, does not suffice to found a politics, to content oneself with stating that impossibility is, in its turn, a bit insufficient. It's because we don't want to abide by it that we no longer approve one hundred per cent of the General Bugeaud, conquering Algeria in the nineteenth century, who declared: "I will always prefer French interests to an absurd philanthropy for foreigners"; or Marshall Goering who justified himself in this way at Nuremburg: "Where questions of the nation's interest are, there morals come to a stop." The national state is the framework in which one can impose rights, certainly; but morality (and morality consists in large part of a defense of human rights) must be able to contain and check reasons of state. It is perfectly possible, contrary to what this factitious opposition suggests, to be a responsible politician (or only a citizen) and not need to reduce oneself to a demand for "the right to difference."

And finally one last reaction returns to make banal the arguments of the extreme right and attempts to discover in them a grain of truth; it is illustrated in *Le Debat* by the intervention of Paul Yonnet. The politicians of this cast are to begin with credited with the best intentions: "Le Pen denies being a racist and throws the invective back at his adversaries"; it is time to put back in its place "the red flag of the holocausts." What is stressed, in order to convince us, is the unbridgeable gap that is supposed to separate racism, though little recommended, and xenophobia, omnipresent and, why not, good (it's "the body's rejection of a graft," what's more natural?). Antiracism itself is assimilated to an endeavor to establish "the moral order." Several familiar themes are, at the same time, adopted. On the one hand, scorn for other civilizations (heavy irony in the intention of the government to "teach the hidden beauties of foreign cultures"); it's a good thing that "it will be a long while before the French accept the Maghreb as their future." On the other hand, we have the defense and promotion of a national identity: there may be today the danger of a "cultural deportation of the French identity," in particular, of the "pillar of French identity" that is red wine, and which needs to be defended against the socialist government (a deputy of the extreme right, the old cinéaste Claude Autant-Lara, has already distinguished himself by his attack against the destabilizing, cosmopolitan drink that is Coca-Cola, and by his concomitant promotion of our national wine).

Collective Passions

There are undoubtedly reasons (Marcel Gauchet suggests some of them in his analysis) that explain why exactly of the Western European countries it is in France that the rise of the extreme right is the strongest. All the same, other countries know a similar phenomenon: the increasing hostility toward "visible" immigrants, exploited with more or less entitlement by the parties of the extreme right. For my part, I'm going to look for my explanation a little further away. It must be understood that the hopes one may nourish for a definitive end to hostilities and for the elimination of the image of the Enemy, in the name of a quiet pursuit of pleasure, must rest on a rather simplistic analysis. A passion seizes us today, even when one least expects it, a passion specifically *collective*, that each of us is more or less familiar with: this consists of identifying with one group and of pledging the others to exclusion. A fundamental division rises up between Us and Them, a division which is at the same time a division between good and evil.

A democracy where the consensus reigns and where there are no more great ideological conflicts (left-right, East-West) isn't able to satisfy this passion: people are deprived of an object. Clearly it's not that there's nothing more to do to improve each of our societies, notably France: democracy here is far from ideal and the condition of ordinary citizens leaves much to be desired. Such flaws, nevertheless, don't light up the collective passion for they don't let us divide the world into Us and Them or play the game of exclusion and identification. It's necessary therefore that passion find a new object. There are certainly predictable and timely substitutes, as in the passion for sports like soccer which can electrify stadium crowds and make us applaud one team and boo the other. But this displacement—that can inspire a murderous instinct of its own—touches only one part of the population and has no long-lasting effect.

So in Europe today there rises up another serious candidate for this role: the ethnic conflict which is continually referred to by the terms North-South. It has all the qualities needed to replace its predecessors effectively and to maintain itself for some time. I enumerate them: the familiarity—it may be superficial—with each other's way of life, thanks to the circulation of peoples and even more of images; mutual economic dependences (notably due to petroleum); the growing disparity in standard of living here and there; the presence of representatives of each group in the bosom of the other; workers immigrating to the North, tourists and experts to the South; the ease of identifying these representatives (White, Brown or Black). The conflict as yet rarely breaks out with unmistakable clarity, but we already know it well in its larval stage when the representatives of the other community become scapegoats: whites risk serving as hostages in the South (as has happened in Libya, Iran or Iraq); people of color are victims of a different hostility in the North. This is the new form of racism, even if those who practice it are not always aware of it. It is also that which makes us see in Europe no longer, as during the East-West conflict, a space of liberty and integration, but a means of distinguishing ourselves from others and of separating ourselves from them: we prefer to remain "among ourselves."

Are there remedies to this situation? George Orwell, who raised the question of collective passions in "Notes on Nationalism," asked himself whether it wasn't necessary to adopt a policy of voluntary vaccination, adjusting ourselves to the benign passions in order to protect ourselves from the malignant forms. One would inculcate patriotism to escape nationalism, choose monarchy in order to avoid dictatorship, and adopt conventional religion in order to fight superstition and fanaticism. (Similarly, Bruno Bettelheim suggested that, rather than deceive ourselves as to the nonexistence of the violence in ourselves, we should find innocent outlets for it; but he was content to suggest, for example, chopping wood with a hatchet). I fear such solutions are never chosen voluntarily (one would, at the very least, have trouble attracting a crowd to a project that aimed exclusively to introduce them to evil); it is only in retrospect that we discover the beneficial effects of imperfect solutions. Orwell proposed that each of us, including humble citizens remote from the spheres of government, learn to battle in his own way against the grip of unwanted passions; and he went on to remind us that this effort, whether we like it or not, was by its nature a way for us to participate in the moral life.

Eastern Europe: Annus Mirabilis

BY STANISLAW BARANCZAK

Then all at once the quarrel sank:
Everyone felt the same,
And every life became
A brilliant breaking of the bank,
A quite unlosable game . . .

—Philip Larkin

Had Mark Twain been among the living last December, he would probably have said about the totalitarian oppression in Eastern Europe what he had once remarked about the New England weather: If you don't like it, wait a minute. Feeling uneasy at the sight of the Berlin Wall? Take a week's rest: next time you pick up the paper, look at its front page and you'll find a photo of the Wall being torn down. Hating to see a brilliant Czech writer put in jail for the umpteenth time in his life? Just go to bed Wednesday night and sleep on it: he'll become president of his country before you manage to pronounce *ctvrtek* (Thursday in Czech). A Romanian dictator giving you the creeps? Turn on the news, quick: you may have missed the ten-second shot of a rebellion in his capital. Make another wish. Any miracle is possible.

One precondition, though: the year on your wall calendar must be 1989.

It was indeed an Annus Mirabilis, a year of instant gratification for all the impossible dreamers and incorrigible believers in the final triumph of right over might (in some cases actually happening, to cap it with a rhyme, overnight). It was also a year of instant and merciless punishment for all the political theorists and futurologists, authors of sweeping generalizations and fail-safe predictions. Irrational hopes have proven infinitely more realistic than the supposedly sober cerebral work of rationalistic analysts. (I'm reminded, in particular, of a Western political scientist who, at the outset of Solidarity in Poland, wrote a book about its alleged "romanticism" as opposed to the "realism" of the Communist party apparatus: what does he have to say now, with his realistic foot in his scientific mouth?) What had seemed totally out of the question for decades, could prove entirely feasible a minute later. And the wildly increasing speed of it all! In the history of mankind there had been, I guess, no comparable period of such a dizzying acceleration of crucial changes. Timothy Garton Ash has captured this perfectly in his famous summary of different lengths of time needed for the reform to pass in different countries: "Ten years for Poland, ten months for Hungary, ten weeks for East Germany, ten days for Czechoslovakia." We might add: "Ten hours for Rumania," and we wouldn't be very far from the truth.

Throughout that autumn, exhilarating events literally tripped over each other, making the trivial act of reading the morning newspaper an everyday wonder. If someone happens, like this writer, to serve as a columnist writing twice a year on Eastern Europe, he may well have missed the 1989 "Autumn of Nations" for the simple reason that it occurred before the deadline for his next installment. In my case, this situation has had a particularly ironic twist. My last column's protagonist happened to be no one else but Vaclav Havel, who, at the moment of my writing, was just being put behind bars for another of his alleged political offenses. Before I managed to collect my thoughts for this essay, not only had Communism in Czechoslovakia folded down like a sloppily assembled May Day grandstand, but my hero had moved from his prison cell to Prague's presidential palace. Instead of another letter from jail or another one-act play—two concise genres of which he is a certified master—he had to write his first New Year presidential address, which, incidentally, turned out to be not a shabby piece of prose either. (There are certain obvious advantages in having a president who has a good command of his native language—a truth we are painfully reminded of in this country whenever President Bush or Vice President Quayle opens his mouth.) Things like that don't happen very often to a columnist, even in this rollercoaster century and even if he writes his column just twice a year.

I'm often asked these days by my American friends how I, an Eastern European after all, feel in the wake of all these astounding developments. There is no single adjective that would adequately describe my feelings. I feel great, exhilarated, liberated, vindicated, of course: who wouldn't? What else is there to feel after the final (knock on wood) collapse of the colossal structure of the absurd, lie, and oppression that weighed down and left its ineffaceable imprint on each of the years of your life, including years spent in emigration? But I also feel sad—sometimes very sad. This happens especially when the euphoria gives way to the sober thought: all right, but why did all this monstrous absurdity last so long? Why didn't it collapse earlier? Were those excruciatingly long decades (from our four in Czechoslovakia to seven in the Soviet Union) of unimaginable suffering and hopelessness, those millions of people executed, frozen to death, tortured, imprisoned, orphaned, exiled, those innumerable lives poisoned with fear and deceit, that immense human potential wasted—was all this experience necessary for mankind to finally learn the obvious truth that the idea concocted by a bearded gentleman in the 19th century and put into effect by another bearded gentleman in 1917 simply doesn't work and harms everything from the nation's economy to your physical and mental health?

And what about the devastation that's left behind? Devastation, in fact, is the only lasting heritage that Communism bestowed on those who were lucky enough to survive it, and its scope is indeed hard to grasp if you know Eastern Europe only from your TV screen. We watch the original national flags of Lithuania or the Ukraine paraded through the streets of Vilnius and Lvov (which may soon be called Vilna and Lviv again), but behind these flags there is the polluted Baltic Sea and the deserted villages around the Chernobyl reactor. We see people thrusting up their spread fingers in a victory sign for the CNN cameras filming them in a Warsaw street, but these people are standing in long lines which, no matter how much foreign aid is pumped into the perforated tank of their country's economy, will continue to be a constant element of Polish reality for years to come. We catch a glimpse of thousands of Bulgarians carrying banners in a Sofia square, but this particular demonstration's objective is, of all things, to protest against the legislation that gives the Turkish minority in Bulgaria the rather basic right to speak in their own language in public. We see crowds dancing beneath the now-opened Brandenburg Gate, but how many of those exuberant faces belong to former secret policemen taught to torture during interrogations, border guards taught to shoot trespassers without warning, party hacks taught to keep the masses under the poverty level while choking themselves with opulence, informers taught to squeal on their neighbors, journalists taught to misinform and deceive, censors taught to suppress the slightest trace of independent thought, sports officials taught to feed children with drugs and hormones so that they would win more golden Olympic medals for their Socialist homeland?

Devastation of landscape, devastation of economy, devastation of the fabric of society, devastation of the human body, devastation of the human soul—you name it, Eastern Europe has them all. This is the garbage that for all these decades was swept under the rug of propaganda and the heavy furniture of the military and police apparatus of control. Now all this reveals itself to our eyes at once: industrial fumes and poisoned rivers, factories falling apart and collective farms unable to produce food, chauvinistic hatred substituting for social cohesion, twisted mentalities making individuals unfit to function in the new conditions of democratic openness and economic competition, millions of lies and wrongs that have to be rectified. This is the terrible burden with which Eastern Europe will now have to cope.

And yet, it is precisely among this all-devouring devastation that the miracle of East European "refolution" (to borrow an apt term from Garton Ash again) has taken root and borne the fruit that we can see today. It is nowhere else but among these disillusioned, despondent, and deadly tired men and women that all the Sakharovs, Havels, and Walesas of that part of the world rose and lived to see their ideas realized, if not yet unequivocally victorious. It is in these countries of Eastern Europe that the dirty trick played by twentieth-century history on millions of human lives brought the worst to humans *and* brought out the best in them.

If the decades of Communism in Eastern Europe have not been a total waste, it is mainly—perhaps only—for this reason. If there has been some meaningfulness in that much too long, much too costly, and much too painful experience—regardless of whether we call it a providential plan or logic of history or the masses' irresponsible spirit of resistance or just the clearsightedness and conscientiousness of a handful of individual minds that started it all—it lies perhaps in the fact that after this unforgettable Annus Mirabilis we will understand better what the human being is all about. Some day, maybe tomorrow, maybe years from now, a historian of ideas will make up a balance sheet showing, more precisely than is possible today, what concepts of humanity have been refuted and what have been affirmed by the dissolution of the Communist empire in the fall of 1989. One thing is sure: in the loss column there will be an ample pack of ideas and ideologies of the most various and incompatible sorts but unified by their shared contempt or neglect of the natural plurality, diversity, and unpredictability of the human world. Needless to say, the first place in that loss column will be occupied by the Communists themselves, with their conviction that the advantages of the future paradise on earth they offered would be appreciated and patiently awaited by anybody whom they could force to break his back while digging excavations for the system's foundations.

But there will be others in the same loss column as well. There will be the conservative opinion- and policy-makers in the West, unable to discover the authentic anti-totalitarian movements behind the facade of the totalitarian "evil empire" (after all, it's so much easier to have a conveniently uniform enemy than to extend some genuine help to those who fight it from within), while also unable to see the horrific human rights abuses behind the front of a country's supposed independence from the Soviet bloc (the case of Rumania under Ceausescu). And there will be the left-wing opinion-makers, too, always interested not so much in how the oppressed people in Eastern Europe lived and what their true aspirations were as in checking whether these aspirations did not stray beyond the pale of "a Socialism with a human face." (I can't help recalling here the response of the dissident Vladimir Bukovsky, who, freshly kicked out of his country after years of prison abuse and force-feeding, was asked by a Western journalist what he thought of the idea of a Socialism with a human face in the Soviet Union: "Socialism? No thanks. Just to see a human face would be nice enough.") There will be those who believed that Communism was the end of history (as we see rather clearly today, it wasn't). And there will be those who, more recently, believed that Communism's collapse would be the end of history (again, as we see quite clearly today, in some places it is precisely this collapse that opens new cans of nationalistic and chauvinistic worms or lays bare the hidden social conflicts: history will continue as long as human evil exists). There will be those who maintained that, because of the Soviet tanks, Communism would never transform itself into democracy by means of a peaceful evolution (once the lid of the Brezhnev doctrine had been lifted from Eastern Europe, the examples of Poland, Hungary, Czechoslovakia, East Germany, and, let's hope, the Baltic republics would prove otherwise). And there will be those who claimed that where no Soviet tanks were involved a bloodbath could always be avoided (Rumania's example showed us that sometimes it couldn't). There will be those who believed that Communism's collapse might be caused only by the conditions of a profound economic crisis and therefore it would never happen in East Germany or Czechoslovakia. And there will be those who prophesied that such a collapse would take place only in a country with a strong tradition of anti-Soviet sentiment, and therefore it would never happen in Bulgaria; or only in a country with a strong tradition of armed resistance against the oppressor, which precluded Czechoslovakia; or only in a country with a strong tradition of intellectual dissent, which eliminated Rumania; or only in a country with a strong tradition of disregard for any authority, which excluded East Germany... There will be those who were convinced that a collapse would never happen unless it happened first in the Soviet Union; and those who were sure that it might start only as a rebellion of some of the Eastern bloc countries against the Soviet Union. This list could be extended *ad infinitum*.

But the pride of place in our loss column will undoubtedly be awarded to one single thinker—ironically, a former Soviet dissident and (at least before his emigration) one of the staunchest, most merciless critics of

Communist ideology and mentality. I have in mind Alexander Zinoviev and his theory of Homo Sovieticus, a definite, unchangeable "new type of man" produced by the Communist system, one characterized by his absolute loss of desire and need of freedom, and one whose destiny is to carry the germ of his spiritual enslavement to the remotest corners of the earth to finally conquer it all. True, someone who would try to refute this ambiguous, both catastrophic and triumphalistic vision by maintaining that human nature has remained unaffected by Communism's devastating pressure would be equally wrong. As I have said, the swarms of social and moral ills inflicted on Eastern Europeans by all the years of their living under totalitarian rule will most certainly haunt them for years to come. Yet the recent series of belated miracles occurring one after another from the Elbe to the Black Sea can find an explanation only in the fact that, apparently, there is some indestructible core of humanity in most human souls—something that no pressure, no matter how long lasting, cruel, perfidious, and limitless in the means it has at its disposal, is able to take away from us or suppress in us once and for all.

This core compresses in itself the most human part of our nature: our individual uniqueness, our unquenchable thirst for freedom, our need to live in dignity, our craving for truth. Like stubborn moss, all these values may be trampled upon but they will grow on and never die. Homo Sovieticus may well have been a genuine historic phenomenon of the twentieth century, but even his name indicates that, forcibly Sovietized as he was, he has still remained human. And as long as we are human, no system, ideology, political leadership, or apparatus of oppression can succeed in turning us into an army of obedient robots. If there are any lessons for humanity in what happened on this planet in the miraculous year 1989, this one is the first to memorize.

Beyond Individualism: The New Puritanism, Feminism and Women

BY ELIZABETH FOX-GENOVESE

A new puritanism may well be stirring among us, but the visible evidence leaves room for doubt. For whatever else this puritanism may entail, it has done little to banish the display of flesh and sexuality from the public consciousness. Looking at the pages of the spring's fashion magazines, at television and films, or at young people out for a good time, the substance of puritanism seems more than a little elusive. Once again, skirts are getting shorter, midriffs are being bared, and, if we are to credit the established fashion press, clothing for spring and summer will explicitly resemble diaphanous, sexy underwear. There is little here that Cotton or Increase Mather would recognize, much less claim as anything they intended. There are days I even wonder how many people still know what the word adultery means. The tendency that Christopher Lasch precociously identified as the culture of narcissism, has, in the years since he published his book, flowered in ways that even he might not have foreseen.[1]

Our age is becoming one in which the qualifiers of sex are rapidly disappearing. Premarital and extramarital sex are still recognized categories, but even they are less and less frequently evoked, yielding ground to the encompassing category of sex, which recognizes fewer and fewer social markers. This is a world in which the use of the term "unwed mother" has become politically suspect on the grounds that any reference to weddings implies an inappropriate value judgment. Mothers are not married or unmarried, they are single or partnered, or better yet simply mothers. In a world in which Murphy Brown has made it into the pages of textbooks as an example of the impermanence of marriage, the image of Hester Prynne bearing her scarlet A and struggling to raise her daughter Pearl has devolved from quaint to irrelevant.[2] What place is there for Hester in a world in which married women are encouraged to revel in the delightful freedom of taking a younger man or perhaps a woman as a lover on the grounds that such lovers permit them to enjoy the new delights of sex freed of the encumbrances, economic dependence, or emotional obligations of marriage?[3]

No, puritanism seems a very strange quality to ascribe to a society in which it would be easier to find people who would admit to being shocked by the notion that twenty year-old women are virgins than that fifteen and even thirteen year-old girls are having sex and babies. The apparently unending sexual revolution of the past thirty years has flooded American society with graphic images of sexuality, uprooting sexual taboos the way the swollen Mississippi uproots trees. From record jackets to sex magazines to pornography, the visual images of sexuality defiantly proclaim a fierce determination to exorcise the lingering ghosts of puritanism and Victorianism—usually lumped under the sneering label of hypocritical bourgeois morality. Puritanical restrictions upon behavior and representation provoke the contemptuous anger that restrictions upon the unlimited freedom of individual self-expression are automatically taken to merit.

At the core of this defiantly exhibitionist anti-puritanism lies the determination to sever any persisting links between sex and morality, or, to put it differently, to validate the sexual desires of individuals as inherently good. The problem with puritanism from this perspective is that it made people feel bad about themselves by forcing them to repress the instincts and inclinations the realization of which would presumably have made them happy. In this sense, Lasch was doubtless right to link the commitment to instant and complete gratification to a narcissistic personality type that from another angle might best be described as an unending adolescence. Puritanism becomes one with Freudianism, notwithstanding their radically different views in other respects, by confronting individuals with the necessity to relinquish or repress some of their desires in return for membership in society or civilization.[4]

In the event, the attempt to sever sex from morality has apparently triumphed, at least in the measure that it has become increasingly difficult to condemn any specific form of sexual behavior or display on strictly moral grounds.[5] Some, notably those who take religion seriously, persist in the conviction that sex only acquires meaning within a moral context, but they are increasingly an isolated minority at least with respect to our public discourses.[6] For those discourses have been recast in such a way that individual freedom invariably takes precedence over social order, with the result that freedom is invariably presented as the ultimate moral good. Attempts to counter this assumption with arguments about the good of families, the good of society, or even the larger good of individuals are impatiently dismissed as benighted, if not malicious, attempts to curtail the freedom, which is to say the pleasure and self esteem, of individuals. On what grounds has any one of us the right to tell any other that he or she is a bad person because of whom he or she prefers to sleep with, at what age, and under what conditions? Even so-called nature, if we are to credit the more extreme militants, has no such right, so why should human prejudice?

In retrospect, any number of Americans have tended to identify puritanism more closely with the rigid imposition of authority than with morality per se. Presumably, the ease with which puritanism was discredited throughout the late nineteenth and, especially, the twentieth centuries had much to do with changing attitudes toward both authority and morality. The emergence of adolescence as a recognizable stage in human lives, the successive appearance of bicycles and automobiles, the expansion of leisure activities, the advent of radio and film, the increase in the divorce rate all played a role. But the discrediting of both authority and morality acquired an unprecedented and self-revolutionizing momentum during the 1960s when blows upon things as they had been assumed to be fell with accelerating frequency from all quarters. From thence forward, the association of moral precepts with illegitimate authority appeared irreversible.

Prior to the 1960s, even as the residual vestiges of puritanism were coming under mounting attack, there appears to have lingered an assumption that puritanism represented bad, externally imposed morality in contrast to good, internally assumed morality. That was the period in which many assumed that individuals might internalize and respect moral imperatives, even if they increasingly mistrusted authorities and institutions that presumed to tell them what to do. The attractiveness of this compromise position successfully masked the extent to which the mistrust of authority might be expected to end in the mistrust of morality as well. It also produced a widespread disposition to delight in H. L. Mencken's celebrated quip that puritanism represented the haunting fear that someone, somewhere might be happy. Mencken and those who appreciated his wit presumably assumed that human beings were capable of a self-regulated liberty without falling into license—that adults did not have to be told what to do in order to do right and that to do right might include a wider spectrum of behavior than anything the Puritans would have countenanced. In other words, they did not necessarily assume that an attack on Puritan authority need result in an attack on morality per se.

Presumably, Mencken and his contemporaries glossed over the association between authority and morality because of their implicit willingness to distinguish between internal and external authority. They were, nonetheless, shortsighted. Since the 1960s, if not earlier, the war against illegitimate authority has been carried into the interstices of human minds. External authorities remain as much of a target as ever, but they are increasingly taking second place to the internalized authorities that make people feel bad about themselves. Once it became clear that prying neighbors—the old biddy down the street—had lost the power to dictate behavior, it also became clear that their defeat would not automatically result in the defeat of persisting guilt and self-doubt. What good did it do to vanquish the neighbors if you did not immediately feel good about yourself? The concern with feeling good about oneself led directly to the assumption that any connections between sex and morality were inherently suspect. No less portentously, it also pointed toward a growing tendency to discredit the claims of individuals upon one another. Thus, in the case of the freedom and self-realization that a married woman is taken to gain from one or more extramarital affairs, it is considered inappropriate to evoke her possible failure in loyalty to her husband. After all, have not men imposed marriage upon women for their selfish advantage? Have not men regularly abused women within marriage and betrayed their marriage vows without? Which of us would presume to tell a weaker party to live up to standards that were designed and enforced for the advantage of the stronger party?

This seesaw evolution in the relation between the elements of authority and morality in puritanism predictably ended in their reunification as the target of a full scale sexual revolution in which any link between sex and morality was discredited as inherently and debilitatingly authoritarian. But contrary to what some might have expected, the virtual defeat of morality did not automatically settle the problem of authority, which showed a disconcerting tendency to reemerge in new forms, notably in the relations between women and men. In effect, puritanism returned, not as a carrier of morality but as an effort to impose authority. The danger, to which I shall return, lies in the steadfast refusal to resuscitate moral norms as a justification for the legitimate imposition of authority.

For those of us who are not willing to condemn the original puritanism out of hand, the apparent character of the new puritanism seems more than a little ironic—and perhaps ominous as well. For the new puritanism more closely resembles the image created by the critics of puritanism than it resembles the original puritanism. Today's puritanism, in other words, has a good deal more to do with that of Nathaniel Hawthorne and Arthur Miller than with the puritanism of the Mathers or even John Winthrop. The case of Miller is especially telling. Despite Miller's denials, most readers saw the use of puritanism in *The Crucible* as the prototype for the McCarthy hearings of the 1950s. The Salem witch trials of the 1690s emerge as a parable for the arbitrary and intrusive inquisition of the Un-American Activities hearings. In the measure that Miller was attacking puritanism—and one may plausibly argue that he was not much concerned with puritanism at all except as a familiar cultural symbol—he was attacking it for its inherently anti-democratic, virtually police state tendencies. Sexual morality was not his primary concern; the abuse of political authority was.

The new puritanism is similarly more concerned with authority— or rather power—than with morality. Significantly, those who most staunchly promote a new puritanism would not think of themselves as puritans at all. For, in the opinion of Catharine MacKinnon, who, together with Andrea Dworkin, has emerged as the leading exponent of the new puritanism, the issue is not sex but power, specifically the power of men over women. To begin to redress this imbalance of power, Dworkin and MacKinnon have been waging an unrelenting war against pornography, which they regard as a direct cause of men's abuse of women and, hence, a violation of women's civil liberties. According to MacKinnon, "Men's power over women means that the way men see women defines who women can be."[7] From this perspective, questions of morality—of decency and obscenity—are irrelevant, for obscenity laws define morals "from the male point of view," in the interests of continued male dominance.[8] The goal, accordingly, must be to eradicate the male pornographic imagination from its privileged position in our society and laws.

MacKinnon and Dworkin's initiative has found solid support among one tendency in feminism, which regards most expressions of male sexuality as inherently an abuse of power—claiming, at the extreme, that an erection is an act of aggression. Thus the opposition to pornography in particular and male sexuality in general has led a significant group of feminists to describe ours as a "rape culture."[9] According to the editors of *Transforming a Rape Culture*, the transformation of that culture requires "a revolution of values" and a systematic opposition to the "vile conditions of life in a country where rape and fear of rape are a means of social control."[10] Women must learn to assert themselves, for they live "in a culture whose belief system is based on massive distortions about women's sexual availability. Like any oppressed people, women must lose no chance to correct these misimpressions."[11] Hence, opposition to sexism should be viewed as analogous to the abolitionist and Civil Rights movements. The transformation of our rape culture requires "rethinking and reshaping attitudes internalized from childhood" so that a "critical mass of people believe that violence against women is neither natural nor legitimate."[12]

These claims and the many others like them confirm the transformation of authority into power in the feminist and perhaps the popular imagination. Morality per se has no place in this lexicon, except in passing as it relates to power. Thus the eradication, or better the reversal, of prevailing power relations must uncritically be accepted as a moral good. But those who equate the moral good with the transformation of the power relations between the sexes or, by extension, between any group of victims of oppression and their oppressors remain ominously silent about the possible moral abuses to which the implementation of their goals might give rise. As a rule, they dismiss questions of traditional sexual or personal morality as so many weapons in the male arsenal that has (violently) kept women in their place. And this dismissal permits them to restrict moral considerations to the redressal of power imbalances or, further, the triumph of those who have suffered power over those who have wielded it.

A moment's reflection should confirm that, under these conditions, it is hardly surprising that feminism itself has recently thrown up a counter-tendency manifest in the ideas of those whom *Esquire* magazine has recently dubbed the "do me" feminists.[13] Katie Roiphe, Naomi Wolf, and others have declared war upon the image of victimization that, in their view, the new puritanism promotes. Not least, they reproach what, for lack of a better term, we might call puritan feminism for turning men into objectifying predators who are only interested in sex. Perhaps more important, they insist that women, too, enjoy sex, including violent sex, and should drop the outdated pretenses that cast them as the passive victims of male lust. Lust is good—for women as well as men.

Katie Roiphe launched the attack, in her polemical *The Morning After: Sex, Fear, and Feminism on Campus*.[14] In a scathing attack on young women who wallow in their own vulnerability and victimization, she mocks the sex and harassment codes that, in her view, exonerate young women of responsibility for their own actions by permitting them to hold young men accountable for every encounter that they regret after the fact. She especially mocks the "take back the night" events in which young women are encouraged to tell openly of their own experiences of sexual abuse. Roiphe is merciless, self-assured, and, above all, young. From her perspective, the excesses of take back the night rituals frequently appear to have more in common with the formulaic confessions of the Chinese cultural revolution than with the conventions of adult sexual relations in a society that prides itself on its freedom. Her perspective contains too much truth for comfort. But Roiphe is preaching a taste for sexual adventure that many young women do not share.

Naomi Wolf, for her part, preaches the delights of a predatory female individualism in economics as well as in sex.[15] A *bona fide* member of the upscale, professional feminist elite, Wolf celebrates the joys of making money with the same relish she brings to the joys of making sex. Clearly she believes that life is too much fun for women such as herself to throw it all away out of a misplaced fear that you might take a few knocks and bruises along the way. The inescapable message of her wanton intermingling of sexual and economic freedom is that girls, too, are entitled to have fun and, above all, to shed the outmoded constraints of a protection for their purported vulnerability that only keeps them out of the most exciting games. In her world, sex emerges as a kind of power, money as a kind of eroticism. If it feels good, do it. But if you want to do others, you must be prepared occasionally to be done yourself. As they say about the lottery, you have to be in it to win it.

For the Wolfs and Roiphes of this world, the new puritanism threatens to return women to the backwaters of a domestic sphere from which they have been (with considerable success) struggling to escape. It embodies precisely what Mencken thought all puritanism embodies, namely the fear that someone might be having fun. Wolf and Roiphe's self-congratulatory attacks, nonetheless, contain some salutary points, although not necessarily the ones they think. Born to considerable privilege, both take much in the way of material comfort, education, opportunity, and physical safety for granted. Their impatience is primarily directed toward young women like themselves who are allowing fear and self-pity to blind them to the wealth of opportunities that are there for the seizing. And they are especially impatient with the possibility that this misguided puritanism might foreclose yet more opportunities—might prematurely exclude women from the seductive world of erotic individualism that is opening to them.

Wolf and Roiphe are not noticeably troubled by the larger issues at stake in the battle they have so lightheartedly joined. For openers, they assume that women should embrace the opportunity to enjoy the sexual freedom and economic independence that have traditionally been reserved for men. They thus assume that women must naturally aspire to equality with men. But the equality to which they wish women to aspire has to do with the freedom, verging on license, that men, especially privileged men, enjoyed precisely because women did not. To take the specific case of college students, young men were frequently allowed to do pretty much as they chose because everyone took for granted that internalized conventions would prevent their doing it to the "nice" young women of their own class. Once those conventions had been brushed aside by the sexual revolution, it was easy to assume that young women would do pretty much the same and, above all, would lose their valid reasons for not doing so.

There ensued the confusions with which all of us have become too familiar: drunken fraternity parties in which young women were raped, or gang-raped, by young men who thought that everything was permitted; co-educational dormitories in which young people might return to their rooms to find their roommate in bed with a lover; singles bars in which anyone might end up going home with a stranger; blind dates in which young men assumed that young women might be expected to "do it" on a first date. This was a world in which the rules were not simply blurred, but non-existent. Disconcertingly, however, many young women's attitudes did not change as rapidly as the rules collapsed. So, as Roiphe suggests, they would start an evening in quest of excitement and end it by regretting the results. And, Roiphe concludes, if they seek revenge through the intervention of external authorities, they dodge responsibility for their own actions and, worse, they threaten to deprive others of the opportunity for any adventure at all.

Roiphe, like Wolf and other "do me" feminists, assumes that the unlimited opening of sexual possibilities for individuals is a positive good and that any curtailment of those opportunities must automatically be condemned as a misplaced puritanism. For rules interfere with women's quest for power and sexual pleasure. In this respect, the "do me" feminists implicitly concur with the new puritan feminists that sex is not the real issue. Recently, I was approached, after a lecture, by a young woman, who wanted to assure me that she and many others like her warmly embraced my views. And to give me a sense of the irresponsible feminists she opposed, she told me with genuine puzzlement that her own mother— would you believe?—did not think that a young woman who was naked in a young man's room with the door closed had a clear right just to say "no." Did I not believe, she pressed her point, that women always had a right to say no?

As it happens, I do believe that women always have the right to say no. I also know that there are situations in which one kind of no is more effective than others and that the most effective kind occurs before you take your clothes off. The issues of responsibility in sexual encounters are endlessly complex, but to define all subsequently regretted encounters as rape, independent of the woman's role in shaping the encounter in the first place, must end by diluting and trivializing the crime of rape itself. For the determination to define—and punish—any ambiguous sexual encounter as rape rejoins the new puritan view that all heterosexual relations should be understood as exclusively (unequal) relations of power. In that view, women must always be cast as victims and must always enjoy the license of victims to combat their oppression by any means, fair or foul, they can mobilize.

The most alarming aspect of our current situation lies in the assumption that the means to be mobilized are those of external authorities—not the despised traditional authorities of fathers, neighbors, or even the young woman's concern for her reputation, but the authorities of university administrations or the state itself. This mindset has given us the proliferation of speech codes, sex codes, discriminatory harassment codes, and all the rest. Make no mistake, these new codes do not represent the return of the older parietal rules under different guise. Those, some of you may recall, were the rules that prohibited men from women's dormitory rooms, or prohibited their presence there after specific hours, that required women to return to their dormitories by a specific time, that, in some instances, prohibited married or pregnant women from registering as undergraduates at all. Parietal rules, as their detractors insist, did embody assumptions about female sexuality, its differences from male sexuality and the protections it required. They fell equally upon all undergraduates and, in this sense, simply defined the situations in which sexual encounters would occur. They also acknowledged the college or university's assumption of a certain *in loco parentis* responsibility. Above all, they embodied the conviction that a civilized community required some norms of appropriate sexual behavior.

Today the justification for any norms of sexual behavior has gone by the boards. No college or university and few parents any longer claim the right or accept the responsibility to tell any single individual how to behave. And the behavior of the single individual is precisely the point. For current mores hold that if any individual genuinely derives pleasure from sadomasochism or anything else, no other individual has the right to judge, much less to interfere. Thus the Wolfs and Roiphes may comfortably take the ground of individual preference. If a woman enjoys being knocked around a little bit on the assumption that she may also do some knocking around of her own or if she simply wants to test the limits of experience, she should be free to do as she pleases, and the responsibility should fall on her head. And if sex were truly analogous to speech, their case would be even stronger than it is.

The case is strong enough, provided we agree that the proliferation of codes and kangaroo courts constitutes the only alternative. But suppose we do not? Suppose we assume that sexual mores are of a different order of concern to a civilized community than freedom of speech? Campus speech codes, "political correctness," and a decade of experimentation have shown the regulation of speech to be more destructive to the purposes of education and, especially to academic freedom, than the defense of free speech, with all the possible abuses it entails. Sexual mores present a different problem—albeit one we have apparently lost the ability to talk sensibly about.

For example, most of us do know from common experience that young women and men tend to develop differently during adolescence. The recognition of those differences says nothing—puritan egalitarians to the contrary notwithstanding—about the adult capabilities of either, which common experience suggests may be remarkably similar. But the recognition of some developmental differences reminds us that young men's preferred sexual stories tend to focus on casual adventures, even conquests, while young women's tend to focus on relationships. For all of the progress in gender equality, young women are still more likely than young men to want an evening of sexual exchange to end in a meaningful conversation over breakfast. And although it flies in the face of contemporary fashion, it remains possible that young women's preferences for "relationships" have some lingering relation to their biological ability to bear children. Notwithstanding the staggering advances in young women's freedom and self-possession, not to mention contraception, sex still puts women at higher risk than it puts men.

The widespread recognition of the risks to which sex exposes young women helps to account for the widespread tendency of very different kinds of societies to protect or circumscribe young women's sexuality. Both new puritan and do me feminists have rejected that kind of protection on the grounds that women should be as free as men to take their sexual pleasure where they find it. The two groups differ only in the new puritan feminists' punitive claims that women must always be able to define the terms of sexual encounters. But neither has been willing to propose that the terrain of possible sexual encounter be circumscribed, even by young women's own internalized conventions. The do me feminists would be happy to see all vestiges of protection, including those in women's own minds, eradicated. Most puritan feminists want to restore protection at the level of the most powerful available central authority, and some would settle for the transformation of male sexuality—men's minds—as we have come to know it.

It is easy to mock manifestations of puritan feminism, like the Antioch sex code, that turn every sexual encounter between a young woman and a young man into an act of negotiation as if they were indeed engaged in a war. Thus at Antioch it is apparently necessary to ask permission before bestowing a kiss and again before unbuttoning a blouse and again before removing the blouse and so on. What, under these conditions, the delighted doubters cry, becomes of spontaneity, passion, or the mysterious chemistry of sex? What becomes of the sheer fun of it? They have a point. Those of us who grew up in a more innocent world will find it difficult to imagine consultations about every sexual move, but we may be too swift to assume that we understand the world our young people are dealing with.

In the more innocent and arguably safer world of my youth, it was entirely possible for a young woman to say no to a young man and mean simply "I don't do that." Depending upon the case, that reply might apply to intercourse on a first date, casual intercourse, or intercourse period. For those were days in which nice girls could rely upon conventions to protect young men from the full brunt of their refusal. In effect they could say, don't take my refusal personally. Today, it is difficult for young men not to take any refusal personally. For with the collapse of conventions have gone the polite fictions—the manners—that ease any social interaction. From the young man's point of view, a no means the naked rejection of "I don't want to do it with you." And if he may safely assume that the one who is refusing him probably does not refuse countless others, he may indeed be tempted to take the refusal personally.

Sex codes do nothing to ease this situation and may aggravate it. For sex codes rest on the premise of a radical individualism—a norm of individual freedom according to which the only relevant criterion is whether the young woman wants it with him tonight. As a result, they perpetuate the idea that sex pits women and men against one another in fearful combat. Worse, they perpetuate the notion that since men are likely to enjoy the greater power, women, as victims of that power, should be entitled to define the offense. Sex codes thus promote the idea that the world of sex is a lawless jungle in which hunters and their prey struggle for advantage. The puritanism of sex codes, accordingly, has nothing to do with conventions of restraint, much less internalized norms, but everything to do with the illegitimate imposition of sanctions upon independent behavior. Hawthorne and Miller were attempting to expose the diluted puritanism of their time as a dangerous farce, but the reinvigorated puritanism of our time is altogether more sinister, for it rests upon the assumption that all meaningful sanctions must be external to the individual conscience.

The socialist puritanisms which have come under most general attack during the twentieth century have been noted for the punitive sanctions they imposed upon those whom they defined as deviant, but also for their attempt to control individual behavior and thought. Notwithstanding abuses, most have been fiercely egalitarian and enforced severe limits upon the freedom of sexuality. Not for nothing have the new and postmodern leftwing movements in the Western world condemned the sexual and cultural attitudes of socialist régimes as hopelessly *passé*—not to mention fundamentally bourgeois. In contrast, the new puritanism of our time has absorbed a good measure of the most radical postmodern individualism, including the repudiation of basic standards of sexual decency. After all, to recall MacKinnon, have not standards of decency and obscenity been fashioned and imposed by men for their own advantage?

The new puritanism has, in this perspective, emerged not as an attempt to restore some sense of accepted and internalized sexual norms but as a determination to wrestle men to the floor. And since we know that women are rarely as strong as men, we have called upon the state to do our job. Heaven forefend that we should in any way curtail individual expression by the suggestion that some forms of behavior tend not to promote the harmony of social groups. That would limit our collective commitment to individual freedom. Instead we prefer to encourage people to act as dangerously as they choose, happy in the knowledge that should they offend our sensibilities we will be able to call the police. This scenario turns the definition of criminal behavior over to individuals who are party to the case. And that does fly directly in the face of our inherited notions of justice. Lorena Bobbitt may have been a heroine to many, but had she been a white southern male of the first half of the twentieth century, taking revenge against a black male who raped a white woman, her action would have been denounced as a form of maiming that lay beyond the pale of any civilized society.

Thus do our standards change. Maiming is only maiming if the bad guys do it. If the good guys do it, it becomes righteous retribution or an understandable outburst of indignation that temporarily clouded the mind of the perpetrator. There is an undeniable appeal to the notion that we, ourselves, know with certainty who is right and who is wrong. But such certainties have been known to deceive. Meanwhile, we recoil from the prospect of censoring the least expression of sexuality out of fear of abridging the liberty of single individuals, and, in order to defend that freedom, we embrace forms of judgment that defy every tradition of collective freedom and individual responsibility for which American democracy has stood. For, however paradoxical it may seem, the new puritanism has little to do with the internalization of a sense of responsibility.

More than a decade ago, Jean Bethke Elshtain and others attacked the puritan feminists for promoting a sense of women's victimization and, thereby, returning women to a position of passivity and dependence. [16] The do me feminists have followed suit, but in a more problematic way. In any case, the new puritanism is open to an even more serious charge. For the traditional protection of women was part of a social system grounded in a sense of reciprocal rights and responsibilities, and it articulated collective norms. True, as the do me feminists insist, it "protected" women from all kinds of fun as well as possible danger. But it also expected women to take some fundamental responsibility for themselves through the internalization of conventions. The new puritanism has broken decisively with that sense of individual responsibility, effectively arguing that women should be free to live on the edge if they choose without having to assume the risks. Some women, like the do me feminists, doubtless do want to live at the edge and are prepared to accept the risks. But what of the many women who may find that prospect daunting? What of the possibility that a young woman, alone at a singles bar, dressed in little more than a nightgown, unsure of herself and the rules, may send mixed signals? Her uncertainty assuredly does not exonerate young men from responsibility, but does it exonerate her? In the end the new puritanism ominously translates narcissism into a social norm for individuals and thereby undermines the very basis for the laws that protected individual freedom. For if we assume that our laws are grounded in the experience of incompetent individuals, we will inevitably transfer to the state a range of powers that would better rest with individuals who accept responsibility for their actions and understand that they have responsibilities toward others.

Notes

[1] Christopher Lasch, *The Culture of Narcissism* (New York: Norton, 1979).

[2] Gilbert T. Sewall, "Triumph of Textbook Trendiness," *The Wall Street Journal* (1 March 1994): A14.

[3] Dalma Heyn, *The Erotic Silence of the American Wife* (New York: 1993).

[4] Sigmund Freud, *Civilization and Its Discontents,* trans. James Strachey, *Collected Works* 21 (London: 1961).

[5] Richard Posner, *Sex and Reason* (Cambridge, Mass., 1992); Elizabeth Fox-Genovese, "Beyond Transgression: Toward a Free Market in Morals," *Yale Journal of Law and the Humanities* (1993).

[6] See, e.g., Ramsey Colloquium, "Morality and Homosexuality," *The Wall Street Journal* (24 February 1994), excerpted from a longer version in *First Things*.

[7] Catharine A. MacKinnon, "Complicity: An Introduction to Andrea Dworkin, 'Abortion,' Chapter 3, Right-Wing Women," *Law and Inequality* 1, no. 1 (June 1983): 89-93.

[8] Catharine A. MacKinnon, *Toward a Feminist Theory of the State* (Cambridge, Mass.: 1989), 197.

[9] Emily Buchwald, Pamela Fletcher, Martha Roth, ed., *Transforming a Rape Culture* (Minneapolis: 1993).

[10] Buchwald, Fletcher, Roth, ed., *Transforming a Rape Culture*, 18-19.

[11] Elizabeth Powell, "I Thought You Didn't Mind," in Buchwald, Fletcher, Roth, ed., *Transforming a Rape Culture*, 121.

[12] Emily Buchwald, "Raising Girls for the 21st Century," in Buchwald, Fletcher, Roth, ed., *Transforming a Rape Culture*, 196.

[13] Tad Friend, "Yes," *Esquire: The Magazine for Men* (February 1994): 48-56.

[14] Katie Roiphe, *The Morning After: Sex, Fear, and Feminism on Campus* (New York,: 1994).

[15] Naomi Wolf, *Fire With Fire: The New Female Power and How It Will Change the 21st Century* (New York: 1994).

[16] Jean Bethke Elshtain, "The Victim Syndrome: A Troubling Turn in Feminism," *Progressive*, 46, no.6 (June 1982),42-47.

What is the Politically Correct?

BY DANIEL HARRIS

When the San Francisco AIDS Foundation recently launched a refreshingly brash safe-sex campaign targeted at young gay men, they received as much flak from the Left as the Right for a series of posters displayed at bus stops around the city featuring two androgynous men, draped in an American flag, who smiled directly out at us, naked, life-size, and in sensuous color. While most of those ruffled by these innocuous, if blatantly homoerotic, images objected to the desecration of the flag by "pervert[s]. . .[who] do not deserve the great privilege of being Americans," as one irate San Francisco resident put it, an entirely unexpected criticism arose from within the gay community itself, as excerpts from the following letter, published in the local gay newspaper, *The Bay Area Reporter*, suggest:

> My outrage does not arise from the moralistic sensibilities of Jesse Helms, but from the disenfranchisement I feel and been [sic] subjected to as a woman, an Asian American and a lesbian. I am no longer willing to be the "silent majority" in any of these categories nor am I willing to be silent when I see other peoples being subjected to the same racism and sexism I have experienced. . . the [San Francisco AIDS Foundation] uses the American flag and two stereotypical White All-American looking males. . . The Asian gay man, Black gay man, Hispanic gay man, substance user of any color and heterosexual female of any color are also at risk. . . Where are the Black men wrapped in an American flag? Where are the Hispanic men wrapped in an American flag? Where are the Asian men wrapped in the American flag? Where is the heterosexual couple wrapped in the American flag? This new safe-sex campaign is dangerous to gay men of color, substance users of any color, and to heterosexual couples of any color.

In the flurry of vitriolic responses printed in the issue of the following week (which referred to the author of the above as everything from a "moralistic pig" to just plain "scum"), the photographer of the series himself wrote in to lambaste her for an unforgivable racial oversight on *her* part: that one of the men included was actually a light-skinned Hispanic. Another respondent diligently rooted out her heresies and the crypto-fascism implicit in her accusations when, beating her at her own game, he excoriated her for sexism and homophobia directed against a disenfranchised minority that she herself neglected, "Gay White Males," who, as he pointed out, still comprise 90% of the cases in San Francisco. To complicate the racial and sexual dynamics of the controversy even further, his attack fell short of its mark when one of the models in the poster, presumably aghast at the disquieting possibility that the AIDS Foundation's campaign could inflict irrecoverable damage on future modeling prospects, leaked to the press that, even though he looked gay in the photograph, he was in actuality a heterosexual. If there's a lesson to be learned from this troubling instance of in-house skirmishing, it's that no one group will ever prevail in its attempt to claim exclusive squatter's rights on prime property in the treacherous and ever-shifting terrain of the politically correct until we call a truce in the fashionable game of minority one-upmanship.

Although the politically correct is almost impossible to avoid, it is difficult to define, perhaps because we are somewhat unfairly predisposed against it from the outset. In a society that is not only apolitical but vigorously anti-political, activism as a whole is often denigrated as a ridiculous charade performed by a self-serving group of purists who, like the Princess Casamassima, are in it for the illicit thrill of self-negation. Our contempt for the reigning bickering about the oppressed is in fact something intrinsically ridiculous in ourselves—our ineffectuality and our inability to take political initiative in a world in which we have relinquished power to a special class of bureaucrats. Before I go on to examine the purpose and utility of this relatively recent strain of censoriousness, I offer for the sake of clarity one further example of what it is, of its occasionally alarming zealotry, and then two contrasting examples of what it is not.

First, an instance of the way the activism inspired by unquestioning allegiance to the "pc," as it is often derisively abbreviated, leads to extremism. Several months ago, an upscale San Francisco card shop called Does Your Mother Know stocked a birthday card that represented a shambling group of barefoot, antebellum black children above a caption reading "If You Get Somethin' for Your Birthday, Can I Have It?" Posters of this image, with a text accusing the store of racism, began appearing around town on lamp posts. If the card was indeed racist (and certainly it tacitly exploited the iconography of the pickaninny), its use of these children, with their beseeching faces, raggedy clothes, and gangly, prepubescent bodies, was probably intended to be endearing rather than satiric or patronizing. But however virulent and offensive the bigotry it unconsciously betrayed, it surely didn't merit the boycotting, leafletting, and, ultimately, *picketing* held outside of the shop until the bewildered owner and his disgusted black clerk, who scoffed at the protests as shameless grandstanding, relented, apologized, and, within a week, removed it from the racks.

Two instances of the politically *in*correct provide an illuminating foil to these examples of pedantry and priggishness that often link both the tactics and the objectives of various sectors of the Left with fanatics on the Right, Andrea Dworkin with Phyllis Schlafly, the Reverend Al Sharpton with Jesse Helms. Deliberately organized as a vicious broadside against the perceived humorlessness of the pc, the student-curated "Straight White Male Show" held at the San Francisco Art Institute elicited a barrage of angry criticism from the "Coalition of Degenerate Artists," which denounced it with hilarious solemnity for its jeering disrespect for "multi-cultural, gay, lesbian and women's concerns." The sole criterion for admission into the harmless burlesque of exclusionary politics, which the Right Wing are constantly reviling as an unconscionable form of racism in reverse, was that the artist had to be a Caucasian heterosexual male—in the eyes of many, the consummate martyr of the contemporary art agenda.

Virtually at the same time this controversy flared up and then just as quickly fizzled out, Saturday Night Live threw itself into a much more disturbing fray when it announced that it had invited the scurrilous stand-up comedian Andrew Dice Clay to host one of its up-coming shows. Like Eddie Murphy's savage and gratuitously sadistic humor, Clay's truly objectionable taunting of homosexuals, women, fat people, and the handicapped is fixated on the pc, whose linguistic taboos it dismantles with as much sacrilegious carnage as it can. In the course of his routine, we are forced to watch a kind of ideological cannibalism, as if he were chewing with his mouth open all of the forbidden words and prejudices that only a licensed buffoon can utter with impunity. Naturally disaffected members of the cast refused to appear on the show and many others protested (with good reason in this instance) but that evening's ratings soared so high that they surpassed the bast that the program had even received.

Why are these sudden eruptions of the politically incorrect (which usually boil over in an off-color remark but which occasionally seize an entire community like Bensonhurst or Howard Beach) in one sense inevitable and, in another, necessary? At least part of the answer lies in the inadequate ways in which the majority of Americans, including the Left, have dealt psychologically with integration. Providing a salve instead of a solution for social complexities, the agenda of the pc is rooted in a typically middle-class response to the disorienting phenomenon of ethnic diversity: the innocuous panacea of reducing the relations between various antagonistic groups to a simple matter of etiquette, to saying, rather than thinking, the right thing and thinking, rather than doing, the wrong. If the examples I have given of how fractious we can be about such red herrings as a poster and a birthday card are any indication, all that feminism, gay liberation, and the civil rights movement have taught us is to watch what we say, to curb our tongues, and to cringe before a new and distinctly menacing sense of decorum, of what we can air in public without trampling on the feelings of the minorities we welcome among us, not with genuine acceptance, but with a frozen smile that masks a discomfort with racial differences that we must never openly reveal.

In a culture that substitutes politeness for tolerance, silence and repression are our answer to the stress of ethnic pluralism. Our daily lives have become so constrained with anxieties about potential tribal faux pas that it has become almost impolite to mention someone's color or sexual

orientation in his presence, with the result that the only political achievement we have made at the most fundamental level of the American
consciousness is the institutionalization of distrust and caution. The
discussion of ethnic issues has thus been fractured between the public
forum (which we have painstakingly depoliticized in order to avoid
insulting others) and the private forum of our own homes (in which we
escape the stranglehold of these new social prohibitions in the presence
of members of our race and class). In other words, the contemporary
focus on semantics and protocol guarantees the introversion as opposed
to the control and eventual elimination of xenophobia. We internalize and
quarantine our prejudices in the private circle in which they are acceptable
and in the process create the ideologically antiseptic no-man's land of the
business world, an eerie, intellectually inert neutral zone, in which the
races coexist in a fragile detente that we have achieved through etiquette
rather than understanding, through silence rather than debate, through
repression rather than dialogue.

And thus the necessity for these cathartic purges in which the politically incorrect is released amidst all of the brittle taboos that we have
introduced into public discourse. Even if unconsciously, we despise the
hair shirt of timidity and reticence that we are forced to wear as part of a
new disingenuous social code, the retrograde and superficial accommodation we have made to three decades of minority rights movements—an
accommodation that serves only to heighten, not diminish, our resentment of cultural differences. Just as obsessive dieting makes us hate our
bodies so that we are constantly in danger of binging, so excessive
sensitivity about offending minorities creates, not respect or understanding, but the hostility and bitterness that culminate in bigoted scatologists
like Andrew Dice Clay rushing into the depoliticized public forum to
shriek out all of the bad words on which we have imposed such an
inhibiting moratorium. In that incendiary moment when the satirist
heaves all of our prejudices onto the pyre he has raised in a forum in which
they have been previously outlawed, we delight in gutting the artificial
divisions we make between our public personas and our private beliefs.
In this sense, the politically correct provokes and unleashes, rather than
monitors or contains, the politically incorrect.

An entire subculture, the pc itself, has grown up around this rigidly enforced closeting of racial and sexual phobias, this rictus grin of anxiously conciliatory professionalism. The extraordinary irony about run-of-the-mill liberal attitudes towards minorities is that, far from being an expression of an advanced and forward-looking counterculture, they rise out of, and are nourished by, the culture of repression that they ostensibly oppose. The pedantic politics implicit in the more exotic antics of contemporary activists are the concentrated essence of the new etiquette we have instituted out of our fear and intolerance of social differences. The pc is best understood as the body of rules and civilities that one small faction of the Left has codified into Holy Writ and then implemented with the proselytizing fervor of an evangelical sect for the sake of minimizing (or at least camouflaging) conflict and achieving specious harmony with various destabilizing components of the population by scrupulously adhering to a "correct" and socially inoffensive form of behavior. Just as etiquette teaches us to use the "correct" fork, so the pc teaches us to use the "correct" phraseology—"Asian" rather than "Oriental," "Afro-American" rather than "black."

In an era that has taken the easy way out and driven our insecurities about diversity inward, the duties of the pc are essentially janitorial and cosmetic in that its whole purpose is to sanitize discourse and to sweep under the carpet all visible traces of racism, sexism, and homophobia. Not coincidentally, of the four examples noted above, three of them involved controversies about images: a poster, a birthday card, and an art show. This compulsive and at times implacable caviling about what we can see—and, occasionally, as in the case of Andrew Dice Clay, what we hear—in public often reduces the efforts of even the most well-intentioned liberal groups to a trivialized form of pictorial and linguistic activism mired in the token politics of words and images. Although the radical posturing of members of the pc would lead us to believe that they are part of a visionary movement, a dissident underground which subverts the bigotries of the status quo, they actually march in lockstep with most Americans, whose concerns they share and interests they ultimately promote as the unwitting agents of a conservative ethnic agenda. As a self-appointed brigade of samaritans who follow after us disinfecting our terminology and tidying up our images, these ecologists of the verbal and visual euphemism serve a vital function as the custodians of a new and stifling sense of propriety.

That the pc is a manifestation of the dominant response of mainstream culture to ethnic tensions, as opposed to a manifestation of the irrelevant extremism of a subversive counterculture, is also apparent in the way that its adherents glamorize oppression. For many middle-class Americans, ethnic culture has become a colorful vacation spot in which the political tourist takes diverting ideological sprees of self-negation. The politics of the pc are essentially the politics of the "other" in that they aestheticize, sentimentalize, and, by necessity, *trivialize* the plight of disenfranchised groups by converting it into a form of chic. Only a member of the educated bourgeoisie can take such a radically external and non-implicated view of oppression which turns it into the opposite, a form of privilege and emancipation, as if quaint and bucolic minorities grazed peacefully in a pastoral idyll, at one with themselves, free of the burden of affluence and guilt whose onus their captivated admirers seek to relieve by exalting, and thus exploiting, ethnicity as an antidote to their own sense of culpability. For many of us, the minority represents freedom from ourselves, a means of pacifying our shame about our economic and social good fortune (without, nonetheless, requiring us to relinquish the opportunities, luxuries, and mobility our class provides). Given that marginality and oppression are never glamorous for those who are indeed marginal and oppressed, our romance of life at the fringes of American society is by definition a fiction that the majoritarian outsider, saddled with the deadweight of his own self-incriminations, has created at the expense of the politically and economically disadvantaged.

At their most doctrinaire, the excited attempts of the radical chic to deify the downtrodden often take us on a kind of safari in which members of the white majority, rigged out in populist khaki, hunt down the sacred cow of the most marginalized person, the ethnic group with most strikes against it—The Ultimate Minority: the crippled Jewish lesbian of color; the hearing-impaired, bisexual, substance-using Native American; the handicapped Asian gay indigent cross-dresser. Oppression has become so glamorous and such an enviable condition (at least for those who are immune to its direct effects) that a spirit of competition even prevails among educated members of minorities who scrimmage acrimoniously to rack up points on the "oppression count," that conversational tournament so frequently held among members of the Left for the undisputed title of the most victimized minority of all—the heterosexual woman vs. the gay man, the gay man vs. the lesbian, the lesbian vs. the Afro-American, the Afro-American vs. the Native American, and on and on with one group jousting with another for the privilege of being the most pitiably subjugated and "disempowered."

We have aestheticized marginality to such an extent that the whole concept of the minority has in itself been robbed of its specificity and become an engulfing and inclusive paradigm that is now applied to groups of peoples whose misfortune have virtually no social or political ramifications: fat people, alcoholics, the uncircumcised, smokers, incest victims, love addicts. In our minoritizing of the world, we have essentially become ethnic lepidopterists in that we chase after minorities like butterflies, which we add to our collections as a tangible confirmation of our own righteousness. Yet another irony thus emerges from the pride we take in our vast portfolio of oppressions. Just as the censoriousness of the pc derives from a conservative response to social tensions, so it must be acknowledged that the link between the politically correct and the politically incorrect implicit in the sentimentalizing of ethnic disadvantages is once again disturbingly direct: the bigot's desire to legislate segregation emerges from the same culture that glamorizes exclusion. In other words, in a way similar to that in which prejudice dehumanizes the group towards which its antipathy is directed, so the pc dehumanizes the object of its idolatry.

What psychological need does the aestheticizing of oppression fulfill for the majority of Americans and what is the reason for this anxious, almost imperialistic search to colonize new minorities, new groups that have been persecuted in new unsuspected ways? As mentioned above, the transformation of social disadvantage into a form of chic alleviates guilt among the middle class by refurbishing oppression into a privilege, an enviable condition with its own particular cachet. But perhaps the most important function that the cult of the minority serves for the mainstream is self-flattery. Since the '60s, we have cast ourselves over and over again in the heroic role of the rescuer of the downtrodden in order to play out a self-adulating fantasy that we are knights in shining armor swooping down through the classes for the dramatic deliverance of the minority in distress. We have become so infatuated with an alluringly narcissistic scenario, this basic Rapunzel myth of scaling up the tower in order to emancipate the imprisoned ethnic damsel, that we have actually begun to invent minorities for the sole purpose of rescuing them. In light of our quixotic attempts to stake out, define, and then rehabilitate new forms of ethnicity, it often seems that we build these dilapidated social hovels to enkennel the latest disenfranchised group in order to set them ablaze for the sheer pleasure of putting out the fire.

Although it is often difficult to say exactly what it is, the pc is clearly not just an agenda. Instead, it is a subculture, an ecompassing lifestyle which is far more than just the sum of its issues but rather a way of living and consuming that has built up an entire economy which sustains a number of flourishing cottage industries. We deride the pc not only because its members are puritanical, humorless, doctrinaire, censorious, and predictable but also because they wear the same Birekenstocks, eat the same granola, go to the same Shiatsu masseur, buy the same organi-cally-grown produce, read the same leftist magazines, boycott the same products, wash their clothes with the same non-phosphate detergents, and pursue the same kinds of liberating relationships. As a fully-contained and protective ideological ghetto which offers its cloistered denizens the amenities of a complete social life, the pc at once creates the conditions for its own insularity and ensures minimum contact with the mainstream culture that it has demonized. Residing in the hermetic isolation of the internal squabbles of their own leadership, its adherents retreat further and further into their test-tube utopianism—their divisive, academic politics that seem so irrelevant to the racial and ethnic issues plaguing society at large.

Given that the pc smothers its proponents in edicts about everything from where to eat to what to wear, there is something distinctly problem-atic about the incessant attempts of activist groups to achieve in their own ranks the inclusiveness, democracy, and parity of power which society at large has failed to achieve on such a demoralizingly grand scale. Are activist groups themselves as pluralistic and tolerant of cultural differences as their stated goals of multifariousness and equity suggest that they should be? Certainly the comprehensive lifestyle that has grown up around contemporary politics is anything but heterogeneous but rather is far more uniform and monolithic than mainstream capitalist culture itself. Moreover, the actual membership of the pc, while often multi-cultural in a superficial sense (in that it includes educated members of many races and ethnic groups), is based on a fundamentally flawed and illusory kind of pluralism: a pluralism of sameness that flourished on the affinities shared only by the educated and articulate representatives of minorities who are unified by the most leveling force of all in our culture, education. The composition of the pc is thus a paradox, an ethnic mirage, because it is essentially a coalition of unanimity, of the ideologically synonymous.

Despite this fact, the pc persists in believing in its own respect for social differences, when in fact it would be truly pluralistic only if it included in its membership the poor and the uneducated which by necessity it excludes: the crack dealer from the inner-city ghetto, the Hispanic gang member, the ancient Chinese street vendor who speaks no English, or the Filipino drag queen prostitute (none of whom could ever be classified—nor would they ever think of classifying themselves—as politically correct). In the confines of their own culturally monotonous vacuum, the tightly serried ranks of the educated elite have the luxury of nitpicking over minute technicalities of racial politesse (like the absence of Hispanics and heterosexuals from a safe-sex poster for gay men or the presence of patronizing stereotypes in a birthday card sold in a chichi boutique), while out there in the real world we see the resurgence of the widescale ethnic tensions of the '60s in Bensonhurst, Boston, and Howard Beach.

Which brings me to my final concern about a fashion in politics whose tactics I repudiate but whose social positions I subscribe to. As a writer and gay activist, my contact with the pc over the years has led me again and again to the disturbing realization, not only that its cliquishness demands rigid, totalitarian conformity of opinion, but that it is fundamentally *disrespectful* of cultural differences within society at large. It is a mistake to take literally its claims for pluralism and rainbow-coalition building, its anxious and often outlandish attempts to be uncompromisingly inclusive, swallowing up new minorities as fast as it can invent them, when it is clear how prescriptive the conditions for being admitted into its fold of the sanctimoniously like-minded really are. In fact, given the oppressive completeness of its lifestyle, the process of becoming politically correct for the member of an ethnic group essentially involves an act of minority self-suicide, an act of obliteration and submersion in a culture intolerant of differences of opinion and education, so that one is forced to slough off the habits one has been accustomed to since childhood in order to pledge fealty to the established political orthodoxies. What's more, the kind of assimilation involved in a minority entering the radical chic is in every way as strict and self-annihilating as the assimilation that racial and ethnic groups are understandably afraid of experiencing as they are integrated into society in general. For all of its championing of the underdog, its punctilious taxonomy of the myriad flora and fauna of oppression, the pc is an undifferentiatedly monolithic political group which mandates, not the preservation, but the wholesale cooptation of minorities. In the very act of testifying to the value and, in some extreme instances, to the hallowedness of ethnic diversity, the pc wipes it out among its own ranks. The defenders and apologists of social disparities themselves thus inadvertently offer appalling proof of how intolerant American culture is of heterogeneity and "otherness": the self-appointed guardians of ethnic differences, who have adopted multi-cultural politics as their platform, insist on creating for themselves a social enclave that is irreducibly, irretrievably uniform.

VIII
Varieties

Dealing with What's Dealt

BY NANCY HUSTON

I'm beautiful. I've never written about this before, so I thought I'd try to write about it. It's lasted quite a long time, this beauty of mine, but it won't be lasting much longer because I'm forty now, as I'm writing this, forty now and probably by the time you read it forty-one, and so on and so forth, and we all know it ends up as worms or ashes, but for the time being I'm still beautiful. More or less. Less than I used to be, despite the regular application of henna to my graying hair and concealer to the rings beneath my eyes. Less than Benazir Bhutto of Pakistan, who is precisely my age. Less than many of my students now—but still, perhaps, a little more than my eleven-year-old daughter. For another year or two ("Mirror, mirror . . .")

I'm also intelligent. Less so than Simone Weil. My intelligence, too, is already going downhill—though differently from my beauty—and it, too, will end up as worms or ashes. But still. For the time being I'm quite intelligent.

When I say I'm beautiful and intelligent, I'm not boasting. All I've done is take reasonable care of the beauty and intelligence programmed into me by the dice-toss of my parents' chromosomes. (They were both beautiful and intelligent, too, when they were young; they're considerably less so now, but that probably doesn't interest you as much as the rest of what I have to say.) How is it possible to boast about things for which one is not responsible ?

We are dealt a hand at birth: some of the cards are genetic (skin color, musicality, bunions), others are cultural (religion, language, nationality), but all are given rather than chosen. Later, as adults, we can make a conscious decision to change a few of the cards in our hands—by converting from Catholicism to Judaism, for example, or by moving to another country, or even by having a sex change operation—but the original deal inevitably leaves its deep and indelible imprint on us.

I've never quite understood people's boasting about their destiny-dealt hand, though it's certainly a ubiquitous phenomenon. Perhaps my own origins are too bland to have instilled in me this sort of pride: it's never occurred to me to derive self-esteem from the fact that I was born in Calgary, Alberta or that I was raised a Protestant or that I have white skin or that I am female. Likewise, I'm responsible for neither my beauty nor my intelligence, which have been two incredibly salient features of the forty years I've spent on this earth so far—and which, until today, I've never had the courage to write about.

My beauty has gotten me many places, to some of which I very badly wanted to go, and to some of which I did not want to go at all. Over the years, I've watched it attack and corrode borders, then take me with it into foreign territories. Borders are ideas erected between age groups, social classes, all sorts of hierarchical entities, in order that society may function as predictably and as decently as possible. They are not solid brick walls. Beauty eats them away. This is the truth; we've all seen it happen, though it happens differently in different places (I'll be coming back to this).

I was not particularly beautiful as a child. I started getting that way at around age fifteen, when I was a junior in high school (I'd skipped a grade—much earlier, because my intelligence was manifest long before my beauty), and as soon as it happened I seduced and/or was seduced by my creative writing teacher. He was ten years older than I (though younger than the man to whom I'm now married), and, shortly before the end of the school year, he took whatever virginity childhood sex games with my brother had left me. I was thrilled, flattered, crazily in love, and, for a long time, proud—yes, proud, for this was something in which my responsibility was implicated. The love affair was a serious one. It culminated in engagement—an engagement I broke off at age eighteen, when I fell in love with someone else. For nearly three years, then, my life revolved around this man. There was no sexual harassment involved.

Ah, but was he not taking advantage of his position? Of his superior education? Of the intellectual awe in which I held him? He certainly was, just as I was taking advantage of my youth, beauty, and whatever innocence I still appeared to possess. We wanted the same thing, which was to be in love with each other. Were we equals? Were Socrates and the young men whom he instructed and sodomized. . . equals? American society, it seems, would in all likelihood condemn Socrates to death just as Athens did, though for different reasons.

Let us be careful. Let us be subtle. Let us not be polemical and deliciously angry and righteously indignant. The subject is a messy one, as messy and contradictory as the species to which we belong, so let us not pretend to tie up all its loose ends and get it straight and iron it flat. Would I like the idea of my daughter sleeping with one of her teachers? No, not at age eleven. At what age, then? At an age when she has acquired a will of her own, a desire of her own, and an intellect capable of critical discernment. In other words, at an age when (and IF, for not all young girls have the same weird penchant for brainy older men as I) she wants it. I tend to think that in her case that might mean something like never, but naturally I don't know.

Listen. Last spring I was at a literary cocktail party in Montreal, standing in a corner drinking wine with my brother and an eminent elderly Québecois writer, and the conversation came around to the cases, currently hitting the headlines, of young boys who'd been sexually abused by priests in Quebec's Catholic schools. "The problem with this whole outcry," my brother said suddenly, "is that it'll make it impossible for actual love affairs ever to take place in those situations again." I saw the older man do a double take and then—to my utter astonishment—heard him say, "Yes, you're right. I had that experience myself. Of course, I wasn't ten or eleven years old, I was sixteen. But still. . ."

The man was now in his seventies. It had probably been several decades since he'd dared allude to this experience, his teen-age love for one of his teachers, but the memory of it was still vivid enough to make his voice tremble with emotion. Clearly, he had loved that teacher, just as I had loved the one to whom I later became engaged. And because we loved them, we also learned a great deal from these seductive teachers.

They fed our intelligence, brought our bodies and our minds to life. I read a thousand books because of mine.

Again, the child's age makes an important difference—and also his or her psychological vulnerability. I am by no means challenging the fact that students have been, can be, are being sexually manipulated or abused by their teachers, I am only asking that we not leap from this fact to the grotesque conclusion that bodiliness should be radically eliminated from all pedagogical situations. In my own teaching experience over the years, though it so happens I've never flirted with students let alone slept with them, I'm fairly sure my beauty has contributed positively to the transmission of knowledge and ideas, the stimulation of their brains.

Other borders eaten away by my beauty I would definitely have rather seen preserved. For example, I could have done without having my thighs stroked by the grey-haired doctor who performed my first gynecological examination, or my eyes longingly stared into by the bespectacled young dentist who removed my impacted wisdom teeth. Probably since the Stone Age, beautiful (and less beautiful) girls have needed to learn to defend themselves—whether through sarcasm, cool rejection or karate chops—against these annoying infringements on their integrity. They can come from almost anyone—including, unexceptionally, women. Again, the only criterion for whether this behavior is oppressive or not is whether or not one is made uncomfortable by it—that is, whether or not there is space and desire for response, interaction.

Still other experiences with borders strike me, so to speak, as borderline. After I finished high school and before I entered college (indeed, in order to earn money to attend college, because the gifts and advantages bestowed on me at birth had not included wealth), I worked full-time as a medical secretary in the psychiatric clinic of an august educational institution. By this time, I was seventeen and really quite beautiful, in my WASPish sort of way. I was also extraordinarily depressed. My depression may indeed have contributed to my beauty (as Bob Dylan pointed out, there is something irresistible about sad-eyed ladies). I was depressed partly because my fiancé was far away, partly because typing psychiatric records was one hell of a lousy initiation into adulthood, and partly because my superior intelligence made it painful and humiliating for me to be working full-time as a secretary. After a few months I was so suicidal that I myself entered therapy with one of my bosses. This is not a joke. The therapy was free, part of my health benefits as an employee of the august institution. The shrink whom I chose to see—regularly, alone, in his office, once or twice a week—was, naturally, the one I had come to like and respect the most, after months of transcribing his Dictaphone summaries of sessions with his patients. Indeed we had become rather chummy. He was forty, as I am now, and, like myself, not badly endowed in body and in mind—and I, as I have said, was seventeen. By the time I began lying down on his couch, I had already sat for his children a couple of times, attended some of his lectures at the august institution, and received from him as a Christmas present a wonderful pair of running-shoes (like millions of other Americans then and now, he jogged to work off his calories and his anger).

I entered therapy with him, and more borders were eaten away. No, he did not rape or maul me; he did not even crush me on the couch with the frightening weight of his body. As a matter of fact, his was a small and unprepossessing body; there was nothing frightening about it whatsoever. He kissed me, standing up, at the end of every session. I kissed him back. We mostly kissed on the lips. Sometimes on the cheeks or the neck. No tongue work, as I recall. Never the least constraint. I found the kisses comforting, and flattering, though not arousing. Perhaps he was aroused—but if he was, he never pressed it upon me. That border, at least, was preserved.

Was this a traumatizing experience? In my case, I think not. It seems to me that other acts performed by irresponsible or immature authority figures have left far deeper scars on my psyche. My first-grade teacher, for instance, who—before I skipped into second grade—slashed her red pen across my imperfect copy-book so hard that the page was torn. I'd rather be kissed than slashed any day.

Still, the question is, why did this shrink feel compelled to kiss me? As I saw it (fairly lucidly) at the time, it was partly because of my beauty and intelligence, and partly because the state of extreme fragility I was in had stimulated his protective male instincts. I say this with no irony whatsoever. In fact, I know it to be the truth because I had dinner last month with this man. I'd returned to teach for a semester at the same old august institution, we hadn't seen each other in twenty-three years, he is now nearing retirement, we still got along famously, and in the course of this dinner he told me that in 1971, when I was his patient and his secretary and his babysitter and his friend, he had longed to cast an invisible mantle of protection over my shoulders as I went out into the world.

And I believed him.

Also in the course of our dinner, he complimented me on having pulled through so well. I could see him casting about for laudative adjectives to describe me, body and soul, and for intensifying adverbs to describe the adjectives. The compliments he came up with were perfectly delightful, but it was hard for me to relish them to the full, as they were almost invariably prefaced by the demurral, "I hope you won't think I'm being patronizing." "Oh, no!" I encouraged him, in my very warmest voice. "More, more!" But deep down I was dismayed. What has been going on in this country? I wondered. Can it really have grown as dangerous as that to tell a woman she is beautiful and intelligent?

But I've gotten much too far ahead of my story.

After a year of working as a secretary, I had set aside enough money to be able to attend college, with the help of a scholarship and a loan. It was an excellent college—thanks, presumably, this time, not to my superior beauty but to my superior intelligence. By now I was eighteen and—due to the free-love ambiance in which all of us were floating in those post-Pill, pre-AIDs years—no longer innocent at all. I had slept with a frightening number of men (men could no longer frighten me—only their number). I was living with the one for whom I'd left my creative-writing-teacher-fiancé. And I had decided to study, among other things, creative writing.

Although the writer-professor with whom I studied at this college was not then, as he is now, world famous, he definitely had charisma. There were about twelve students in his class—ten women and two men, if I remember correctly. The men can be dismissed at once. The ten women were all, by definition, exceptionally intelligent. For some unfathomable reason, most of them were also exceptionally beautiful. From the beginning of September until the end of June, all of us competed frantically to please the teacher.

Now, what does "competed frantically to please the teacher" mean? Well, it means that we used our minds and bodies to gain his approval, just as he used his to gain ours. We dressed in a certain way, talked in a certain way, wrote our short stories in a certain way, and walked into his office for our bi-monthly individual "conferences" in a certain way, each of us hoping against hope he'd recognize us as that very special person whose body and mind he could appreciate, admire, cherish and caress.

I won.

But then, I may not have been the only winner. Perhaps there were ten winners, and he was just prodigiously gifted at juggling his time schedule to include all of us.

At college as in high school, I was an active subject rather than a passive object in my love affairs with professors. This time, though, I knew the person was not a crucial element in my destiny. Both of us felt fairly rotten about betraying our partners, and found the hotel rooms we resorted to at once expensive and shoddy. We soon phased out the erotic aspect of our friendship—and fortunately so, for had the other students become aware of it, the atmosphere in the classroom would probably have been affected. We stayed in touch, however, for a number of years afterward.

But now my story switches directions.

At the age of twenty, under the auspices of my excellent college, I came to Paris for my "junior year abroad," then went on to spend my senior year abroad, and to do a Master's degree abroad, and now, twenty years and two French children later, I have hit upon the perfect inscription for my tombstone: "Once abroad, always abroad."

Oddly enough, despite Frenchmen's worldwide reputation for being sexually obsessed, my dealings in France with professors, employers, gynecologists, dentists and shrinks have all been relatively maul-free. Since I did not become ugly overnight upon moving to Paris, I have gradually come to wonder whether my borderline erotic experiences as a young woman were not, at least partially, determined by cultural factors—i.e., whether there was not something specifically American (rather than, say, "modern" or "Western") about them. It seems to me that as a general rule (and with all the usual caveats regarding this sort of generalisation), the French accept the fact that they have and are bodies. The prevailing social decorum is not as all-or-nothing as it is in the States, where the alternative seems to be: either overt sexual contact or feigned indifference to all physical characteristics. In France there is an intermediary level of communication based on the constant exchange of glances, witty remarks, hand gestures and the like. Both men and women take part in this exchange. As the French do not attempt to radically rid social existence of physicality, they are not in such a state of patent contradiction and frustration as are the Americans (I think I am mainly speaking of white Americans here). In a word, they tend to value the art of sublimation.

Americans, it would seem—again, these are the humble clumsy observations of a former insider and current outsider who has just spent a few perplexed months back on the "inside"—are taught less to love or enjoy their bodies than to take care of them. As a people, they seem to conceive physicality essentially in terms of health, exercise, self-defense, autonomy, anatomy, and how-to sex manuals. When one roams the aisles of the supermarkets from which they feed themselves, one essentially has the choice between health food and junk food; plain ordinary wonderful unprocessed unimproved unadulterated food is virtually impossible to find. Americans are becoming phobic about what they put into their bodies—no other country in the world diets so much or suffers from so many eating disorders. In the realm of eroticism, analogous extremes are represented by pornography and The Joy of Sex. It is as though the American people required that everything erotic and gastronomic be quantified, verbalized, exhaustively described and dissected and discussed.

As a result, they often seem genuinely (or disingenuously?) convinced that the whole aesthetic, interactive dimension of their bodies is non-existent. Taking this dimension into account can imply concealing as much as revealing, modesty as much as brazenness; it is the opposite of "letting it all hang out." I once had a beautiful young long-blonde-haired

American female student who came close to getting herself lynched in Morocco by sauntering across a field wearing nothing but short shorts and a halter-top. A group of Arab peasants tore after her waving pitchforks – and she was not only terrified but totally nonplussed at the aggressiveness of their reaction to her body. She was just being natural! By European standards, beautiful young long-blond-haired American girls who stare men straight in the face are not natural, they are come-ons. By North African standards, they are prostitutes if not witches. No, I'm not defending the veil; I'm simply marvelling at American lack of sensitivity to the fact that—and the manner in which—other people, other peoples, might respond to their bodies.

Sexual harassment, on the job and elsewhere, definitely exists in France, but that is not quite what I'm talking about here. I am talking, rather, about the way in which a certain degree of eroticism is not only tolerated on the social scene but considered to be a normal part of it. Like my own American students of today, I was enraged and humiliated, when I first came to Paris, by the stares, whistles and muttered remarks of men I passed in the streets. My first attempts to take pensive solitary walks in the cities of Southern Italy invariably ended in fits of hysteria and tears. But the native women in these countries know perfectly well how to handle their men. And the rape rates are far, far higher in the United States, where playful, tacit, intangible erotic exchange in public is increasingly taboo. (I still squirm whenever I recall the time, on a French TV-show with a number of other women writers, I was the only one who claimed she resented these unsolicited displays of male approval. The other guests were overtly nostalgic about the "good old days" when men used to whistle at them in the streets, though it wasn't quite clear whether these days had vanished because they had aged or because feminism had cowed men into silence.)

Admittedly, there have been occasions in France on which I've felt my beauty to be a handicap. Once or twice I've narrowly escaped rape; more than once or twice I've had devastating doubts about whether a person's enthusiasm for one of my books or articles might not be rightfully due to my big blue eyes. This has tended to make me insecure—and even, sporadically, miserable. But I refuse to exaggerate. These are small dramas. My beauty has never made me nearly as miserable as an assembly-line worker, or a crack addict, or a black mother on welfare.

I have also—calmly, naturally, as every beautiful woman knows how to do—allowed my beauty to bring me minor favors and advantages: faster service in restaurants, increased courtesy in libraries, more humorous and less expensive exchanges with policemen. . . The occasions have literally been countless. They have also been unavoidable—to avoid them, I should have had to disguise myself as an ugly person (as did Simone Weil) by wearing thick black glasses and dressing in frumpy clothes, or indulging in some extreme "eating disorder."

Listen, I would like for once to lay all my cards on the table (I might as well—I'm a novelist now, which means I can be neither hired nor fired; in many important ways I have nothing to lose). Every human being on this earth is a combination of a mind and a body, an intelligence and a beauty, greater or lesser, now greater, now lesser, forever in flux and forever in interaction. But it is quite rare that one and the same person should experience both extremes, being treated alternately as all-body and as all-mind. Having exercised such wildly disparate professions as masseuse and feminist journalist, nude model and English professor, bar "hostess" and guest lecturer in prestigious universities, I am probably in a better position than most to revolt against the bad faith so prevalent in the United States today (since it cannot possibly be a question of naïveté), which pretends that our minds do not live in bodies, and that we respond to each other's minds independently of each other's bodies, and that what we love in each other when we make love to each other's bodies is not also, in large part, each other's minds, and that professors can teach and students study without their bodies ever being present in the classroom, and that bosses and employees and colleagues and work-mates can interact professionally without their bodies ever being present in the office or factory—and that, moreover, it is possible for bodies to miraculously burst into existence when, in private darkened bedrooms enclosing one or two or more consenting adults, all systems are suddenly said to be "go," whereas they have been forced to "stop" "stop" "stop" and "stop" all day long in every other situation in which they have found themselves.

These American bodies are no longer allowed to smoke, they are no longer allowed to joke, they are no longer allowed to smell; all of their sexy ambiguities have been banished to oblivion, war has been declared on their capacity for innuendo; flirting has been outlawed because it presupposes inequality (and this is true, or, more accurately, flirting underlines, renders flagrant and therefore undeniable, the inequality that in fact exists between the beautiful and the less beautiful, the intelligent and the less intelligent, the funny and the less funny)—oh at all costs let us not recognize these sorts of inequality, let us cover our eyes and pinch our noses and plug our ears in front of them; the work place is for getting work done and schools and universities are for getting an education and restaurants are for eating and bars are for drinking and streets are for striding purposefully from one place to another and none of these places no no no is an appropriate place for bodies, for sensuality, for sidelong glances, for flirting, ah ah ah, flirting leads to rape, the eyes and words of a man on a woman's body are already a miniature version of rape, and all forms of physical exchange between human bodies must be as predictable and safe and contractual as the sale of a house.

Again, let me attempt to be clear and discerning and calm. People who study well and write good papers, whether they are beautiful or ugly, brown or yellow, tall or short, should receive good marks; and people who have appropriate credentials or working records should never need to consent to being sodomized by the powers-that-be to get a job or a degree or a promotion. The role of beauty—and every other culturally or genetically inherited factor—in such situations as legal trials, political elections, thesis defenses and tenure hearings should be as close to zero as possible. (Thus, it is outrageous that Californians should currently be discussing the length of a judge's skirt: if judges and lawyers in many countries wear long black robes, it is precisely in order to annul or at least neutralize the particularities of their bodies.)

In public life, in other words, modern democratic institutions are rightly required to be blind to physical traits. At the opposite end of the spectrum there is love-making, in which physicality attains extremes of intensity. But in between the two there is social existence—life on the job, in the neighborhood, at school, in the subway—a fascinating, shimmering, shifting mix of public and private, physical and spiritual, proximity and distance, conformity with code and spontaneous invention. What I am saying is that this crucial middle ground (of which, of course, physicality is but one of numerous aspects) is currently being eroded to nothingness, in the United States, by maniacal verbalization and ludicrous legalism. And that the compulsion to aberrant sexual behavior is worsened, not attenuated, when sociality is thus unnaturally invaded by moral imperatives and declarations and calculations.

What I am not saying (I insist, politely banging my fist on the table) is, "Hey, Men! Hunting Season Open All Year!" All forms of sexual coercion are repulsive. But we must be careful or, under pretext of policing them, we shall lose a vast and rich dimension of human existence, namely the language of bodies, the hundred silent languages of bodies, which vary from country to country, social class to social class and milieu to milieu—yes, the complex, moving languages through which, wordlessly, endlessly, men and women ask and answer questions about each other, move, suggest, demur, wiggle, giggle, arch eyebrows, light cigarettes, graze a hand, a cheek, a shoulderblade, manifest wonder, admiration, tenderness, arousal, delight, defiance. . . (Is it because these languages are being silenced in America that gays and Lesbians so often resort to grotesquely obvious codes to get their messages of desire across ?) But—ah ah ah and then, but then, what if desire becomes aggression? What if it becomes manipulation and threat and blackmail? What if it becomes forcing and pushing, shoving and battering, angry hell? Well then then then, if it becomes that, well then, there are already laws against that. But if it does not become that, then it becomes life. And the very definition of life is "you win a few, you lose a few." Since when does one go running to a lawyer or a journalist every time there is a loss?

What we have a right to in this life, as even the American constitution acknowledges, is not happiness; it is, rather, the pursuit of happiness, which is a very different thing indeed. In the same way, the concept of equal rights in no way implies we are or must pretend to be identical to one another. If a deck of cards contains fifty-two fours of diamonds, what sort of passionate poker game will anyone be able to play?

* * *

My daughter is also turning out to be beautiful and intelligent—which means that, in addition to teaching her to eschew boasting about it, I shall need to teach her a certain number of things about what sort of treatment she can expect at the hands of the world, just as parents have always prepared their children for the (positive and negative) effects of being Ukrainian, Tasmanian, Jewish, Catholic, dwarves, white, black, haemophilic, red-haired, skinny, knock-kneed, and so on and so forth, including all the possible combinations of these traits.

Though they will have more or less weighty consequences depending on the geographical, historical, political and social context in which one grows up, all these factors are part of the hand one is dealt at life's outset. There is no fatalism here; I don't mean that once you get your cards the game is tantamount to over. I simply mean that all of us play the game according to the cards we have in our hand—bluffing and feinting, discarding and drawing, trying to influence the other players, winning and losing. . . The progressive / liberal / revolutionary / existential philosophies we have espoused over the past couple of hundred years have tended to blind us to this simple truth, universally recognized by novelists and children: one deals with what is dealt.

To Feel These Things

BY LEONARD MICHAELS

I

My mother was seventeen when she married and said goodbye to her parents in Brest Litovsk. She then sailed the Atlantic to New York and settled in an apartment in Coney Island. Soon afterwards, the year Hitler came to power, I was born. Roosevelt had been elected president a bit earlier. These two names, intoned throughout my childhood, belonged to mythical deities. One was evil. The other was the other.

My mother's family expected to follow her to America, but the day her father went to get their emigration papers he was attacked in the streets by a vicious mob. They left him for dead. He didn't recover quickly and then it was too late to get out of Poland. In photos he is pale and thin. The skin pulls tight across sharp facial bones. He looks ill-nourished, but sits posing in the old style, as if a photo is serious business. My mother says they threw his unconscious body into a cellar. I heard the story around the time children hear fairy tales, as if it too were make-believe. Once upon a time my grandfather. . . .

The beating occurred during a pogrom, before the official beginning of the Holocaust, when it was still possible to know what was happening in Poland. I heard about pogroms from my mother who had been a witness. Years later I would hear that organized terrorism had been reported for centuries in Europe, Russia, and the Middle East; and that rabbinical commentaries engaged questions as to whether the community should surrender a few to save the rest, die with the few, or resist. Rabbis consulted the commentaries while the SS prepared gas chambers and worked out train schedules. When the Nazis seized Brest Litovsk, my grandfather, his wife, and youngest daughter were buried in a pit with others. My mother thought she had lost her whole family in Poland. I was all she had left of close blood. As she sat in the living room waiting for my father to come home from work, she sometimes cried. This was my personal experience of the Holocaust, though only the effects of it thousands of miles away, in a small apartment, amid claw footed furniture covered by plastic to protect the fabric. I saw her crying, but mainly I imagined things. To understand, I was obliged to imagine, to dream up the world from little clues, the story about my grandfather, my mother crying.

I came to understand that it was always bad for the Jews, the way "it" is said to be raining. I didn't know what it was, but I was sure it was more than a man called Hitler. He was the leader of the Nazis, the latest manifestation, but it was far greater than he, infinitely more pervasive, and much older. It was cruel, unreasonable, strong, able to fix the plumbing and paint the walls. It didn't speak Yiddish. It was like animals and trees more than a person, though it appeared in persons, anywhere, anytime. It lived for pleasure and murder, especially the murder of Jews because they were everything it wasn't. No other reason.

I came to understand all this because my mother, an adolescent without her own parents, siblings, or friends, was very intimidated by her surroundings in America, even fearful of going out alone in the streets. She had long black hair and grey blue eyes. Strange men wanted to approach and talk to her. She kept me close. We were constantly together, and I was constantly sick with respiratory diseases and ear infections; many colds, bronchitis, pleurisy, and pneumonia twice. She sat at my bedside saying "Meir fa deir," again and again, which meant let me die rather than you. I never thought I was going to die, only that I'd be weak and feverish forever, unable to compete in playground games with other boys, always skinny, timid, badly co-ordinated, burdened by sweaters and scarves and winter coats buttoned to the neck. If I loosened my scarf or undid a coat button, my mother would fly into a state of panic as though millions of germs were shooting through the gap I'd made in my clothing.

My mother was beautiful and hysterical. She told me about pogroms.

After we moved from Coney Island to the Lower East Side of Manhattan, my mother and I were separated for the first time. I began going to school. There I was quickly singled out as an exceptional child and subjected to intelligence tests. They were to determine whether I was a moron. I, too, was intimidated by everything. During the war I began to change.

I put a large map of Europe on my bedroom wall. When I read about Allied bombing raids in Germany, Poland, Italy or elsewhere, I would find the city and stick a red pin in it. I imagined myself as a pilot or a bombardier in a B17. When I saw in the movies the doors of the bomb bay swing open and the long bombs with tails and the sticklike incendiaries fall away toward factories and railroad tracks, or whole cities, I felt satisfaction and enormous relief. The great work was being done. Ordinary Americans, plain folks, regular guys from Brooklyn and Kansas were winning the war. I saw it in the movies.

My mother took me to the movies on Friday afternoons when school let out. I waited all day through math, history, reading, drawing, and assembly with bombers and fighter planes raging in my head toward Germany, and the minutes passed slowly, so slowly they didn't seem to pass at all, but then, suddenly, school ended and I was free to run home. Before we left for the movies, I had to drink a glass of milk. I hated its whiteness, the whiteness of its taste, and the idea of it as good for me. "Finish the whole glass. It's good for you." She watched until the whole glass, like a column of liquified teeth, went down into me. To the last nauseating drop. But then came the B17, a big dark bird struck with machine guns in its ribs, nose, belly, and tail. It was a primordially winged reptile dragging long flaps and lugubrious claws for landing gear, lumbering up into the gray dawn among its thousand brothers, each of them bearing a great load of bombs. It was my image of the good, love's fierce answer to evil. The B17 was the best thing I had with which to hit back hard. An image. Almost an action; almost my action. I carried it about for years in my head and heart, the feeling of that clumsy mass of aluminum sculpture called the "flying fortress." It was how I avenged my mother's grief, how I did something to ease my sense of responsibility, my need to act, be effective.

After the war, her brother's name appeared in the Yiddish newspaper, *The Forward*, which was published a few blocks from where we lived, in a tall white building opposite the Seward Park Library. It seemed miraculous that my uncles' names had come from Europe to the *Forward* building, which I'd passed many times going to the library or to my father's barber shop around the corner on Henry Street. But the distant, the exotic, the unimaginable was in these streets, even in the Garden cafeteria near the foot of the *Forward* building where I sometimes sat with my father and ate white fish on black bread with onion, and stared at the dark Jewish faces of taxi drivers, pickle salesmen, dry goods merchants, journalists, and other urban beings who sipped coffee or borscht, and smoked cigarettes and argued, joked, or complained in Yiddish or in such English as had been mutilated into the nuances of sense and feeling required by Yiddish, grammatical niceties flung aside so that meaning could walk on the earth.

The names of my uncles, Yussel and Srulke Czeskies, had appeared among the names of survivors who had been gathered in camps for displaced persons, in Italy and elsewhere, and who now sought relatives in America. One uncle had been in the Russian army, the other in the Polish army.

I was happy. I was also worried. My mother would bring them to America, but would she be held guilty for what they had endured? She hadn't been with them. She hadn't been able to save the family. But they hadn't seen how she cried, and they couldn't know what it was like to live amidst American greatness and be unable to do anything for them, or even to know what had happened to them. When they came to America, says my mother, my character changed. I became a "cold boy."

There is injustice, more imagined than real, against which nothing can be said. We'd done nothing bad and yet I felt a weight of blame and had an early notion of guilt as fundamental to life. It was wonderful to see her brothers in our apartment, but I retreated to corners, looking cold and sullen, as if absorbed in private shadowy thought, like a neighborhood cat. A strange mechanism of feelings drew me away from simple happiness into inward complications, like one who is depressed by holidays.

My parents didn't disclaim our religion, and nothing strange or skeptical entered their orthodoxy, but the father of a friend of mine, as a result of the Holocaust, began to detest all organized religious expression. He developed his own interpretations and religious practices, as if he were the only Jew who really understood what was on God's mind. His life reduced to secret study and his tuxedo renting business. To his mind the Jews had been punished for some grotesque mistake. He sacrificed himself to put things right, and spent no time with his children or, if he had any, friends. Nothing but God and the wretched distraction of business.

Maybe he wasn't exceptional. Even as a child, I thought we were obsessed with meaning. We didn't just eat, sleep, work, study, play, but wanted the meaning of these things and everything. Meaning as such, as if it had inherent practical value, like wood or gold. We sought it with brain fingers, loved how it feels in the elaborations of talk. At the heart of talk and all meaning was religion, the law, forever established, yet open to analysis and explanation. My parents sent me to Hebrew school and I was Bar Mitzvahed, and I made a speech though I had nothing to say. A rabbi wrote it for me. I only demonstrated that I could talk, make the sound of meaning.

I went to Hebrew school in the late afternoon every weekday, every weather. It was in a low ceilinged room of dull yellowish light, reflected off thickly varnished wood desks and panelled walls. The room was in the bottom of a tenement on East Broadway. To sing in public, in the synagogue, was a frightening prospect, since I couldn't carry a tune, but I entered a delirium of Hebrew prayer, as if I'd acquired an ear and became a true believer. The idea of sacrifice works for Christians; the Holocaust worked for me. I believed if you flip a coin and it comes down heads, Hitler murders Jews. If it comes down tails, nobody cares that he murders Jews.

I could tell one Jew from another according to whether they believed as I did. They were lucky or frivolous if they didn't; or, in their indifference to plain truth, they were self-annihilating. Believe it, I thought. Your life is at stake. If it isn't true about the endless murdering, who knows? So believe it anyway. Feel Jewish. Improve your chances against being murdered. Thus, I advanced to a higher level of thought.

Seeing my mother alone and helpless in her grief, I'd also felt alone, strangely invisible. It was as if we'd been abandoned, like her family and the others, to the nature of things, wherein there is a general complicity with murder. It was in the concrete sidewalks, the grass, the weather, and the human heart, not to mention all the fish in the sea, a need to murder, a need for the pleasure in it. I remember pictures of President Roosevelt, his long handsome face, with its insouciant smile, his cigarette holder aloft in a white aristocratic hand, perhaps in the manner of SS officers outside the windows of the gas chambers, chatting and smoking as we died in agony visible to them. Of course I wasn't there. I had nothing to fear. I only had a sense of ubiquitous savagery, the inchoate nightmarish apprehensions of a child, much like the insanity or the ominousness of a religious vision where ideas have the force of presence, over-riding logic. I heard Yiddish-speaking relatives discuss the president's tepid reaction to Kristallnacht and his decision to turn away a ship of Jewish refugees from American shores. From those who could make a difference, I figured, came indifference. Knowing nothing about immigration laws or the isolationist politics of America, I understood only an aesthetics of power, the weird mixture of comfort and sadism in the president's smile. In the very capacity to do something, lived the frisson of doing nothing, of not caring. I could not have articulated this understanding any more than I could have said how I tied my shoelaces. It was up to the Jews, then, to take care of themselves, and there were two ways to do it, learn to use guns, or, like the father of my friend, analyze God, get at the meaning of things and put them right.

"Take care," writes Primo Levi, "not to suffer in your own homes what is inflicted upon us here." He means don't let his experience of Auschwitz become yours. Don't let it happen again. He is very clear, but I had to read the sentence repeatedly before I understood that is all he means, and that he doesn't mean : NOT TO FEEL THESE THINGS IN THE DAILINESS OF YOUR LIFE OR IT WILL POISON EVERYTHING ELSE.

Thus, misreading a few words, I discover primitive ego-centric apprehensions in myself long after the Holocaust. Levi isn't talking about feelings. He doesn't mean what I thought. Still, not to have felt these things in my own home wasn't and isn't easy. A governor of feelings would have had to be screwed into my head. But I confess to misgivings. I must literally remind myself that nothing happened to me. I wasn't with my grandparents and other relatives in Poland, or with the children in the trains to the death camps. Local citizens didn't hear my screams. My childhood was touched by the horror, nothing more. I cannot claim too little.

II

In the early sixties I lived on 104th Street, near Riverside Drive, a short walk to Columbia University where, one afternoon, Hannah Arendt was to make a personal appearance and talk about her book on Eichmann, which had caused dismay and outrage in Jewish literary circles. I couldn't imagine what an impersonal appearance might be, but this one would be quite personal. Arendt would surrender authorial invisibility and come forward, testify. With her physical presence she would take responsibility for her book, as if to say, "Here I am. I really mean what I wrote. Jews conspired in their own destruction, etc." In this New York setting, to say it was more courageous than to write it, since the audience was likely to be hostile. She'd already been abused in print. Some said her book was ill-informed; others said worse. Maybe she would offer a few more words on what she called "the banality of evil," but I was less interested in her ideas than the drama of the occasion, and I wondered if she would find a way, within the scope of her dignity, to apologize for the book. To me, it issued from a kind of snobbery, suggested by her use of the word "banality." For the sake of an off-rhyme jingle, she'd written "banality of evil" instead of a less surprising, but adequate, less clever, less self-regarding qualifier.

Snobbery, if that's what it was, seemed an odd response to Holocaust matters, like a refusal to feel common things or to identify with the grief and rage of survivors. I suppose every Jew felt grief. It seemed inevitable, but I was eventually to learn there are more ways not to feel things, common and otherwise, than to feel even what seemed inevitable. To me, that is. To me, whatever it's worth, being told that Eichmann is a dull, ordinary fellow was like being told Nazi murderers took pleasure in Mozart. In the light of their crimes, neither dullness nor refined taste seemed a fascinating perplexity. I'd heard people say that the Nazis had undermined western civilization, and brought meaning itself into question. If so, I hadn't noticed. Too big; an idea like the sky; too vague. Western civilization was a course in universities, a hypothetical construction invented by professors. Grief and rage were real ; beyond question. Then came the Eichmann book, its ironical tone, the word "banality" ; Nazis were merely contemptible. The snobbish air certainly wasn't unique to Arendt, but part of a familiar tone, something like a protective coloration, that is often discovered in the prose of intellectuals, and it is typically associated with irony.

Along with other colors of rhetoric, irony derives from the camouflage techniques of animals. To hide or kill, they become indistinguishable from their environment. A twig is a snake. A light streaked bush is a tiger. A rock is a lizard. An innocuous comment is a deadly cut. Irony feeds on doubleness, separating you from your subject, your outside from your inside. It can be hilarious or chilling. It shades easily into snobbery. Even Socrates, original master of irony, if he applied his manner to the Holocaust, would seem insufferable, especially if he carried on about allegiance to the state, the necessity of obeying orders.

Arendt described the effects of terror as unimaginably awesome in a previous book. In this book about Eichmann, the agent of terror, it was an ordinary, shabby, boring business. Perhaps, in the talk, she would insist on distinctions. What she seemed to say as opposed to what she said in fact. All this gave interest to seeing and hearing her. I had another interest, too, that was entirely emotional. It had to do with my marriage to Sylvia Bloch, a brilliant German Jew whom I considered crazy. She had refused to go with me to the talk, but then she couldn't read more than a few pages of Arendt without having a fit and railing at me for bringing the book into the apartment, for calling it to her attention, for thinking about huge evils when we had so much else to think about of far greater immediate importance, like our relationship, the source of daily trouble, violence, and gloom. In a way, then, against Sylvia, I went to the talk.

It was a beautiful sunny day, like an open mind, and I looked forward to the drama of Arendt's appearance, even to be edified, though my life was a mess and I was confused and unhappy about everything. Recently, in a doctor's waiting room, I'd read a magazine article about Patagonia and I'd begun to dream of going there, living in a bleak lovely place that was incessantly cleansed by fierce winds and the corrosive air of the tumultuous Pacific. Then I remembered that Nazis fled to Argentina after the war, establishing pockets of poison in even the remotest areas.

The auditorium was nearly full when I arrived, and soon it became over-crowded with people sitting on the floor and window ledges, mostly students, young, nicely dressed, respectful of the occasion, long trained to listen to authorities, or whoever happened to be standing in the front of the room. A few years later, during the war in Vietnam, this would change.

Arendt paced the stage, and, with her arms crossed on her chest, she stopped to face her questioners. Her posture was defiant and defensive at once. It became apparent that she was a strong proud woman who intended nothing like an apology, and that the event would be only serious and too polite. Academic. It could have been conducted by telephone. I began to lose interest and to drift away on my interior cloud of personal anxieties. There was no drama to hold me, no agon. Then, toward the end, in response to some question, I think she said, "We must wait for the poets." I sat right up, tried to focus, to recreate the context, but hands were already in the air with new questions, new remarks.

It was a long time ago. I didn't take notes. If indeed she said "We must wait for the poets," perhaps she meant they would teach us how to speak about the Holocaust without exploiting the subject, without assimilating it to advertisements of our sensibility, without bad rhetoric, without risk of any other obscenity. The poets would transform what isn't even anybody's subject—except for victims and scholars—into a language free of all narcissism. They will speak with correct impersonality, which is by no means unfeeling, of the hideous abomination. In this future speaking, we will rediscover our humanity. If indeed she said "We must wait for the poets," it might count as an apology, a good thing to say. Whatever she said, I carried that phrase back down Riverside Drive and into the small hell of my three room apartment on 104th Street and I've thought about it many times over the years while waiting for the poets.

Baby Talk

BY DANIEL HARRIS

Although I can't remember where she said it (or indeed *if* she said it), I attribute to Mary McCarthy a withering blast against baby talk between lovers that had haunted my own intense and fetishistic practice as a fugitive baby talker of the highest magnitude ever since. It was a contemptuous and dismissive comment that is forever lurking in the peripheral vision of my love life where it keeps grim and disapproving company with another bitter appraisal by a friend: "You really know that things have gone to hell when you find yourself lapsing into baby talk with your lover." At the time he said this, I enthusiastically (and disingenuously) agreed, all the while fully aware of both the importance of baby talk in my own mating rituals and my complete and utter unwillingness to discontinue it in the face of the fact that it has fallen into such disfavor in contemporary sexual politics. I offer the following remarks on this humiliating romantic taboo neither to appease my own critics, who insist that lovers should court and woo as adults, nor to exorcise my own demons, but simply to draw attention to the paramount importance of baby talk in the modern relationship and the vital if insipid role it plays in sustaining intimacy.

In an age in which people feel free to air every vice and personal failing before perfect strangers in casual and public situations, baby talk remains something about which the most immodest nurturer of intrapersonal relationships is ashamed. It tests the mettle of even those who pride themselves on their candor and leads even those of us inured to the habit of baby talk to live in terror of the eavesdropper, of the ubiquitous ear of the smirking neighbor flattened against the other side of the bedroom wall. Only in the most intimate situations in the most well-guarded whispers will we relax our injunctions against this last and most persistent of sexual prohibitions, so tenacious for an era in which secrets seem to exist for the purpose of their disclosure and in which everything from alcoholism to incest has found its own public forum where the transgressor can confess and be shrived. Intense, titillating shame accompanies it, so that it is easier to admit to any other sort of fetishism—sadomasochism, coprophilia, transvestism—than it is to take a forthright stance on one's own self-abasing activities as a baby talker.

The emotional background of this embarrassment is, of course, the evolving Realpolitik of contemporary relationships, the new emphasis on maturity, equality, and independence nurtured by both feminism and the human potential and self-help movements. The latter in particular has launched a vigorous critique of that faddish syndrome, co-dependence, whether it be on drugs, alcohol, romance, or, as the culture of self-helplessness would have it, on all three simultaneously. In the midst of these reassessments of sexual intimacy, baby talk is a flat contradiction of theory by practice, an unwelcome testament to the stability and stamina of old romantic habits, which ultimately thwart our efforts to modify our behavior in accordance with new ideas about the "correct" style of deportment in love. Even those of us who have taken the lessons of the sexual revolution, feminism, and gay liberation to heart are troubled by this stark reminder in our own behavior of a less sexually mature age, this lingering vestige of a callow period before the "Enlightenment" in which lovers brought to their relationships little guilt, less intelligence, and none of the ideology that we presently bring to bear on our romantic fantasies.

Protected from the new political thought about independence and adulthood, baby talk is a repository of reactionary beliefs about love—the place into which we have swept all of our sentimental fondness for dependence and helplessness. It is one of the last strongholds of our culture's view of relationships as utterly disarming and preemptive emotional experiences, of such stormy irrationality that they reduce us to children. As we perform the rituals of baby talk—its personification and subsequent naming of parts of the body (penises, vaginas, feetsies, piggies), its narratives involving imaginary characters, its ingenious if esoteric scripting and plotting—we live out fantasies of total helplessness and likewise of total parental control, for baby talk almost invariably presumes not two children but an adult and a child, two mutually exclusive but interchangeable roles. This paradigm is especially convenient for the heterosexual couple whose regressive foreplay—to the understandable horror of feminists—eroticizes the inequalities of power implicit in gender, with the woman cast as the querulous child pouting her way seductively to the mink stole or the new car and the man as the forbearing Daddy-cum-Santa Claus, or, vice versa, with the man as the petulant Naughty Boy pampered and cajoled by his nanny-cum-Mom. Given the intense pleasure we take from these roles, it is even fair to wonder if some sort of dialectic hasn't been established in our culture between these closet costume dramas (in which we use childishness to intensify intimacy) and the new mandate for maturity and independence. The more we are told that the ecstatic helplessness we have come to expect from love and the innocuous theater we use to dramatize this helplessness are both a violation of taste and politically in bad form, the more exciting they become, the more illicit, the jealously protected from exposure to the judgmental modern world, and therefore the more pleasurable and intimate.

Aside from giving free reign to conservative notions of submission, surrender, and obedience, baby talk embodies our culture's complex attitude towards children. For many (certainly not all) practitioners, it is, strangely enough, an aphrodisiac, a prelude to sex, a form of foreplay at once banal and bizarre, that seems natural, even cozy to lovers when the heat is on but that is nonetheless almost indecent—if we stop to think about it (which we never do)—in light of society's sensitivity to the molestation of children. The somewhat imbecilic infantilism we lapse in and out of as the occasion requires is the domestic pornography that comes directly out of our efforts as a culture to hide sex from children, drawing such clear demarcations between the erotic world of adults and the antiseptic, non-sexual world of minors that we balk at even the most elementary forms of sex ed. A culture that protects children from sex is almost by definition a kiddie porn culture because with repression comes shame and with shame comes guilt and with guilt comes intense arousal, since we are most turned on by that which is outlawed and untouchable. It is one of the odd paradoxes of this most housebroken form of lovemaking that its buttercup and dumpling endearments are linked inextricably to some of our most illicit and unresolved obsessions with children and sex.

So much is being made these days of the concept of private life and the way it has evolved historically: from the largely pejorative view of it in ancient Greece and Rome, where privacy was the domain of second-class citizens like women and slaves, to the modern celebratory view of it as the source of our deepest personal satisfactions, the place to which we withdraw for vacations, to relax, to get away from it all. Within the context of the relentlessly public lives of the ancients, on the one hand, and the secretive and isolated lives of the moderns, on the other, baby talk stands, along with the diary and the billet-doux, as one of the most extreme developments in the history of privacy. It thrives on the rigidly exclusive distinctions we make between the public and private spheres. Our hermetic attempts to use language, allusions, and in-jokes to rope off a furtive space in which to make love reveal a number of things about our understanding of sex and intimacy. For the most part, we view love as an intensely subjective and isolating experience that requires total immersion in a clandestine world cut off from other men and women not only physically with our bedroom doors or emotionally with our jealousies and obsessions but linguistically with our baby talk as well.

And yet in the last few decades, there has been a significant erosion of our strict separation of the public from the private—an erosion that has the potential to change the whole course of the history of private life and undermine the introversion and exclusivity on which baby talk is based. The human potential movement, as well as the New Age and self-help industries, have encouraged a growing intolerance of private life, an impatience for those who can't "express themselves" before others, who can't relate their feelings, be honest, be real. As our culture becomes saturated with the slogans and mannerisms of psychotherapy, we are increasingly seeking out new forums—the workshop, the AA meeting— for encounters we once reserved for the confessional and the bedroom. As a result, the whole concept of privacy is gradually changing in the face of our attempts to be more forthcoming in social situations where we were previously more guarded, so that we can now "express our feelings" before colleagues, acquaintances, and large anonymous groups. In order to be fully satisfied in our personal lives, there is less of a need for either intense isolation or its linguistic equivalent, baby talk, for the private sphere is becoming more public and the public sphere in turn more private, owing to its widescale annexation by a culture now accustomed to bringing its emotions almost exhibitionistically to the attention of others. As the hard and fast distinction between the manner one assumes at work and at home, before one's family and one's colleagues, an acquaintance and a best friend is weakened by the new imperative for self expression, baby talk may lose some of its surreptitious and fetishistic appeal and be retired (an antique like chivalry and courtly love) as a form of foreplay based on a largely archaic notion of the intense seclusion, physically and linguistically, that relationships require.

Baby talk also embodies a concept central to our culture's view of the self and how love functions to preserve and release that self. Some of our most oppressive fantasies about relationships are those that involve the idea that love is a solvent that first strips away the social mask and all of the artificial mannerisms we cultivate to shield our "inner being" and then "sets us free" in order to reveal the True Self, the person that we really are "underneath" the false show of politicking and bonhomie. The pleasure of baby talk thus derives not only from conservative beliefs about the paralyzing and preemptive nature of love, which reduces us to semi-articulate children desperate for autocratic parental control, but also from conservative beliefs about the self, the Real Self that exists in bewitched captivity somewhere "within." Baby talk ultimately serves as a form of linguistic pastoral, a way of playing out our shepherd and shepherdess convictions that love emancipates a childlike creature, natural, spontaneous, free of inhibitions, a creature we can only be when we are in love. Just as more literary forms of pastoral involve simulated ideas about spontaneity and naturalness (which we experience by travelling to a special place—a forest, a desert island), the pastoral of infantilism involves artificial ideas about the Real Us which we can experience only by using the special voices of children and by speaking a special pastoralized language.

The danger of what might be called the utopianism of baby talk is that it encourages us to believe that we are "real" only insofar as we are in love, that we are somehow incomplete, dishonest, and not fully ourselves when we are not in a relationship. Our ideal of romance as the custodian or midwife of the authentic "Us" thus contributes to our sense of deficiency when we are living alone. (It is also interesting to note in passing that the notion of authenticity and the ideal of selfhood that baby talk suggests draws on our culture's contempt for reason, logic, control, and intelligence, since the Real You turns out to be a dependent child, imbecilic, petulant, demanding, needy, inarticulate.)

Discussions of art and the history of ideas have revolved around the rise and fall of various sensibilities—the naturalism of Zola; the romanticism of Byron; the decadence of Huysman and Wilde (which was in turn refurbished by Firbank in accordance with another sensibility, camp); or even the futuristic aesthetic of Art Deco whose proponents attempted to outstrip the artistic sensibility of the future through streamlined forms with bold outlines in new materials like plastic. Little attention has been given, however, to an aesthetic as pervasive and, in the long run, as prepossessing as all of these various sensibilities taken as a whole: the aesthetic of the cute, a romantic or Victorian invention that continues to exert a profound influence on the basic choices that the least sophisticated and also the largest sector of our population makes in matters of fashion, interior decoration, art for the walls, bric-a-brac, and even the manner in which they make love and address each other to express this love.

What are some of the things that we think of as "cute"? Pets, stuffed animals, children, dolls, or miniatures of things that are not in themselves necessarily cute, like the plates, tables, and chairs that we find in a doll's house. A five-year-old boy is cute when he swaggers around imitating a man, or a five-year-old girl when she rocks her doll in imitation of her mother. A doll in itself is cute as an imitation of a child, and a monkey in a cage is cute when it embraces its offspring like a human mother embracing *her* child. A dress is cute when it seems to allude to the sense of fashion of someone younger than the woman who wears it (although the same dress is grotesque, not cute, when the discrepancy between the age of the dress and the woman who wears it is too noticeable; a dress that is vampish or ultra-stylish, by the same token, is *not* cute because it is not meant to evoke the style of someone younger). In short, the aesthetic of the cute is an aesthetic of the small, the young, the adorable, the defenseless, the inarticulate, the mute, and, perhaps most importantly, the human*oid* as opposed to the human: the child who imitates us, the monkey that looks like us, the doll's house that resembles our own. The cute is an aesthetic that induces benevolent condescension on the part of the viewer, with the characteristic posture associated with the experience of seeing something cute being a figurative bend at the waist, a slight mental dip to the level on which the cute thing exists in all of its adorable vulnerability. The cute presents an image of the adult world in fanciful miniature, with all of the basic ingredients of our daily lives transposed into another context where we see them with new eyes, aestheticized by the aura of innocence and defenselessness that the cute is intended to radiate.

The cute is also what people turn themselves into for the purpose of seducing or charming their lovers. Baby talk is the most esoteric and artificial form of cuteness, an attempt by adults, often well past their prime, to approximate the same endearing cuddliness of a teddy bear or a kitty cat on a calendar. To any witness other than the person for whom it is intended, baby talk is not cute but grotesque, because the attempt to imitate a child (who is, in light of the imitative nature of cuteness, imitating us) can be charming only to the indulgent audience of one's lover who is willing to overlook the obvious poetic license involved in the transformation of an emphatically large and uncute thing into a kissable and cuddlesome miniature. For the eye at the keyhole or the ear on the other side of the bedroom wall, on the other hand, the effect of this strange attempt to transform oneself in accordance with a vastly inappropriate aesthetic has some of the same winsomeness as Bette Davis dressed up like Shirley Temple singing "I've Written a Letter to Daddy" in *Whatever Happened to Baby Jane?*

Cuteness, and therefore by extension baby talk, are like most aesthetics, highly ideological. It is an aesthetic with an agenda, which serves a large cohesive social and political function and whose influence extends far beyond art or fashion, having a determinative effect on how we look at a number of disparate things in the world: from which calendars we buy and how we dress our children to how we perceive our lovers. What at first sight seems to be the most innocent and unpolitical of aesthetics is not only ideological but propagandistic in that cuteness aestheticizes images of powerlessness, vulnerability, and innocence. Cuteness thus serves to aestheticize all emotions associated with control and parenthood, calling forth with Pavlovian infallibility our maternal and paternal instincts to take care of something, to nurture and raise it. Cuteness, as the aesthetic of the family, makes the fundamental units that structure our society not just necessary but attractive and endearing and thus perpetuates all of the institutions that are in any way associated with procreation and the strengthening of social bonds, whether that be by making our children or our lovers adorable. Baby talk shows how invasive and adaptable the aesthetic of cuteness can be inasmuch as it allows us to aestheticize our spouses, our children, our pets, and the emotions of pity and condescension that are invariably involved when one person exercises a proprietary right over another.

Laziness

BY NATALIA GINZBURG

(TRANSLATED BY LYNNE SHARON SCHWARTZ)

In October of 1944 I came to Rome to find work. My husband had died the previous winter. In Rome there was a publishing house where he had worked for years. The publisher was away in Switzerland at the time, but the firm had resumed business right after the liberation of Rome, and I though that if I asked, they would give me a job. The prospect of asking was burdensome, however, because I thought they would be hiring me out of pity, as I was a widow with children to support. I would have liked someone to give me a job without knowing me, on the basis of my skills. The trouble was that I had no skills.

I had brooded over all this during the months of the German occupation, which I spent in the country, in Tuscany, with my children. The war had passed through there, followed by the usual silent aftermath, until finally, in the quiet countryside and the villages thrown into turmoil, the Americans arrived. We moved to Florence, where I left the children with my parents and went on to Rome.

I wanted to work because I had no money. True, if I had remained with my parents I could have managed. But the idea of being supported by my parents was also very burdensome, and besides, I wanted to make a home for myself and my children again. We hadn't had a place of our own for a long time. During those last months of the war we lived with relatives and friends, or in convents and hotels. Driving to Rome in a car that stalled every half-hour, I had lovely fantasies of adventurous jobs, such as being a governess or covering crime for a newspaper. The major obstacle to my career plans was the fact that I didn't know how to do anything. I had never taken a degree, having dropped out when I failed Latin (a subject no one ever failed, back then). I didn't know any languages except a little French, and I didn't know how to type. Aside from caring for my children, doing housework very slowly and ineptly, and writing novels, I had never done a thing in my life. Moreover, I was very lazy.

My laziness didn't run to sleeping late in the morning—I have always awakened at dawn, so that getting up was no problem—but to losing an infinite amount of time idling and fantasizing. As a result I had never been able to complete any studies or projects. I told myself the time had come to uproot this weakness. Applying for work at the publishing house, where they would take me on out of pity and understanding, suddenly seemed the most logical, practical idea, even though their motives would be painful to me. Just around that time I had read a beautiful book called *Jeunesse sans Dieu*, by Aden di Norvath, an author I knew nothing about except that he died young, hit by a falling tree while leaving a movie house in Paris. I thought that as soon as I began work in the publishing house I would translate this book which I loved and have them bring it out.

In Rome, I took a room in a pensione near the church of Santa Maria Maggiore. The pensione's particular virtue was that it cost next to nothing. I knew from experience that during the war and right after, such pensiones tended to turn into something like barracks or encampments. This one was a cross between a pensione and a boarding school. There were students, refugees, homeless old people. Every now and then a gong with a deep hollow ring would resound up and down the stairs, summoning people to the telephone. In the dining room, frugal communal meals were taken—Roman cheese, boiled chestnuts, broccoli. In the course of these meals, a little bell would ring from time to time and the manager of the pensione would read aloud some of her thoughts, which were exhortations to simplicity.

I spoke to a friend who was running the firm in the publisher's absence. This friend was short and fat, as round and bouncy as a ball. When he smiled, thousands of tiny wrinkles rippled across his pale, shrewd, sweet Chinese-baby face. Besides running the publishing firm, he was involved in countless other activities. He said he would take me on part-time, by the hour, and when the publisher returned my position would be defined more clearly. He told me to come to the office the next morning, and also said that in my very pensione lived a girl from the firm who had an administrative job: she and I could walk to work together.

Back at the pensione, I climbed upstairs to knock at the door of a room two floors above mine. A pretty girl with curly brown hair and red cheeks appeared and I asked if we might walk to work together the next day. She said she had to go to some bank or other and so would be taking another route. She was polite enough, but cold and reserved. I went back down feeling embarrassed and depressed, overcome by a fatal sense of inadequacy. That girl must have been working for years, maybe forever; her work was administrative and therefore well-defined, necessary, and indestructible. In addition, she had a nine-year-old brother with her, whom she was supporting, while I wasn't sure if I would be able to support my own children.

I was restless all night, full of agonizing thoughts. I was convinced that the moment I entered the office everyone would discover the great sea of ignorance and laziness inside me. I thought of the friend who had hired me, and of the publisher, far off, but perhaps on his way back. I had tried to explain to my friend that I had no degree of any kind, I didn't know English, and couldn't do anything, and he had replied that it didn't matter, I would find something or other to do. But I hadn't told him about my laziness, my vice of slipping into a state of inertia and dreaminess as soon as I was faced with a specific task. I had never before been properly horrified by this vice, but that night I confronted it, with fear and profound horror. I had always been a poor student. Everything I had ever begun just remained hanging. Villon's famous lines echoed in my ears: "Ah, God! If only I had studied in the days of my mad youth, and learned good habits, now I'd have a house and soft bed, but look! I fled from school like a bad boy. . ."

Actually my French wasn't even very good. Nor had my youth been especially "mad," only idle and confused.

In the morning I arrived at what would be my office: the ground floor of a small house, surrounded by a garden. There was my friend, along with the girl with the red cheeks, seated in front of a calculator, and two typists. My friend had me sit at a table and handed me a sheet of paper that said, "typographic rules." And thus I learned that "perché" and "affinché" had acute accents, but "tè" and "caffè" and "lacchè" had grave accents. He then gave me a manuscript: a translation of *Gosta Berling*. I was to proofread it and put in the accent marks. As he bounced around the room like a ball, he informed me that I needn't worry about my lack of a degree—our mutual boss could hardly scorn me on that account since he didn't have one himself. When I asked what my next assignment would be, after *Gosta Berling*, I realized with some horror that he hadn't any idea.

I had such dread of falling into laziness that I threw myself into the revision and finished in three days. My friend proceeded to give me a copy of Lenin's wife's memoirs, in French. I hastily translated about thirty pages, at which point he said he had changed his mind, they wouldn't be doing that book after all. He gave me a translation of *Homo Ludens*.

One day, just at the entrance to the office, I found myself face to face with the publisher. Though I had known him for quite a while, we had barely exchanged more than two words. Now so much had happened since we had last been face to face that it was like meeting him for the first time. I felt as if he were at once a friend and a total stranger. And mingled with these feelings was the fact that he was now my boss, that is, someone who could turn me out of the office at any moment. He embraced me and blushed, because he was shy; he seemed pleased and not too amazed to find me working there, and said he looked forward to hearing my ideas and suggestions. Choked with emotion and timidity, I said perhaps they might translate and bring out *Jeunesse sans Dieu*. He didn't know the book, so I hurriedly told him the story of the movie house and the falling tree. He was very busy and dashed off. I didn't see him again over the next few days, but the girl with the red cheeks came to tell me that I had been hired full-time. She and I never spoke, but when we met in the corridor we smiled, linked by common memories and expectations of bells ringing and broccoli.

One day I learned that we were moving our offices. That was too bad, for I had grown fond of the office, especially of the mandarin orange tree outside my window. The new office was downtown and had huge rooms with rugs and armchairs. I chose a small room at the end of the hall, where I would be alone and could learn to work, for I was still obsessed by feelings of inadequacy. My friend also took refuge in a room of his own. Gradually the larger rooms filled up with new typists and other staff, who would pace feverishly back and forth across the rugs, dictating endless pages to the typists. I would overhear snatches in passing, but understood none of it. Or they would hold lengthy, mysterious meetings with visitors in the conference room. My friend said that he found all these new employees and new typists quite pointless. He found the rugs, the visitors and the meetings pointless as well. I grasped that the new people's politics were different from his own. He seemed depressed and didn't bounce any more, but sat separate and inert at his desk, his face sad and wan, like the moon. And seeing him grow so discouraged and flabby, I realized in a flash that he might be just like me and maybe even more so—sick with a boundless passivity.

I felt very alone in that office. I never said a word to anyone, and I worried constantly about being found out: my vast ignorance and laziness, my absolute dearth of ideas. By the time I managed to ask about the rights to *Jeunesse sans Dieu*, they had already been bought by another firm. That was my only idea and it vanished into thin air. To guard against my laziness I worked furiously, dizzily, immersed in total isolation and utter silence. Yet I couldn't help but wonder, all the while, how and if my work was connected to the intense and, to me, incomprehensible life swarming and filling the other rooms. I had a key made and went to work at the office even on Sundays.

On Christopher Lasch:
An Editor's Notebook

BY ROBERT BOYERS

I first met Christopher Lasch at Skidmore College in 1973. He'd come to deliver a *Salmagundi* lecture on "Bourgeois Marriage." From the first he was uneasy about the paper he had prepared, almost apologetic, as if he had contracted to do one thing and turned up with another. At dinner he characterized the paper as not really the right sort of piece for a magazine like ours. It was too entirely preoccupied with the past. It contained too many scholarly citations. Many people in our readership would be likely to find it dull. He himself thought it a little dull. We would see. And when we understood what he was uneasy about, we'd also understand why he fully intended to send us something else for the magazine. Our "live" audience at Skidmore would make of the oral presentation what it would. But *Salmagundi* readers would want something else.

In fact, Lasch's lecture stimulated heated discussion, and we had no misgivings whatever about publishing it in the magazine. If it did not quite have the bite of the pieces he often published in *The New York Review of Books* in the late sixties and early seventies—or later on in *Salmagundi*—, it was nonetheless full of fresh ideas on a subject not then inspiring very much more than easy polemic. But what struck me quite as much as the content of Lasch's talk on that first evening was his way of handling audience questions. He was unfailingly forthright and courteous, though now and then visibly irritated by what he took to be idiotic questions. He was reluctant to challenge people who would be unlikely to do well defending themselves, but he was also unwilling to offer a merely perfunctory or dismissive response. He wanted to treat each question as though it contained—or might have contained—something important, and he was exasperated by how hard some people made it for him to take them seriously.

My sense of Kit Lasch never changed throughout the course of twenty years in which he often visited us in Saratoga Springs and contributed to *Salmagundi* dozens of articles and columns. Occasionally playful, unfailingly generous to those he liked, he was passionate about ideas, and he had no patience for obfuscation or pretentiousness. He knew how to praise, and enjoyed writing for us about thinkers he admired, from Lewis Mumford and Hannah Arendt to Dwight MacDonald and Jacques Ellul. But many of my most vivid memories of him are associated with the criticism he directed at those whose influence exceeded their merit. There was no bloodlust in his criticism, no appetite for bringing down the easy prey. When he quarreled, there was nothing personal in his tone, no trace of a desire to obliterate the opposition. He was frequently sharp and contentious, often went out of his way to point up a difference or to expose a folly. Once I heard him use the word "stupid" to characterize the remarks of an eminent American political theorist—seated next to him—who had told thirty people at a Skidmore round-table that religious sentiments inevitably incapacitated moral thinking. But he was rarely confrontational or uncivil, and those who thought him cranky usually discovered that he welcomed debate and was eager to find common ground with those he criticized.

When he wrote the "Introduction" to the tenth anniversary issue of *Salmagundi* in 1975, he stressed the importance of our often criticizing "leftist cliches. . . . from a point of view sympathetic to the underlying objectives of the left," and of course we had admired in his brilliant work precisely that disposition. He liked our tendency to celebrate the "iconoclastic" and the unpredictable, our interest in the writings of people as diverse as Norman O. Brown and Paul Goodman, Philip Rieff and Simone Weil—and of course we were always struck by the range of Lasch's enthusiasms, his ability to entertain seriously, say, Rieff's critique of "the therapeutic" (or "psychological man") at a time when most of our colleagues on the left dismissed Rieff with epithets like "reactionary" or "pessimistic." Though he was especially grateful for *Salmagundi's* deep commitment to the theoretical perspectives opened up by Adorno and Benjamin and Marcuse, he was also eager to see us take on "politics as such," and often made common cause with other *Salmagundi* writers who lamented the "fake radicalism" of literary academics whose ideological posturing concealed a distaste for real politics.

Like everyone else who came of age in the fifties and sixties, Lasch was disappointed by much that happened on the left in recent years, and he was not sanguine about our collective grasp of problems that seemed to grow worse with every passing decade. Increasingly he reminded us about "limits," about the consequences of a self-indulgence which included not only the will to consume but the will to project our own most extravagant wishes onto the field of social reality. He wrote often about the excesses of the utopian imagination when it sought to translate its hopes into political programs without sufficiently considering the actual needs and living conditions of those apt to be most affected by those programs. Some accused him of capitulating to the "despair" he had warned against in earlier critics of liberalism, just as others had accused him of "nostalgia" when he invoked the past to help us confront the present. But he never supposed that it was possible to go back to an earlier time, or indeed that "the true and only heaven" aimed at by generations of American progressives had ever previously existed. Nostalgia, as he often indicated, was simply "an abdication of memory," and as such had little to recommend it. As to despair, well, there was surely much to warrant, if not to recommend it, and the best way to deal with it was to understand how nineteenth century writers like Carlyle and Emerson and William James achieved "grateful acceptance of a world that was not made solely for human enjoyment." Lasch struggled for many years to develop a portrait of "the good life" in which the principal pleasures included "the self-forgetfulness that comes with immersion in some all-absorbing piece of work", the sense of responsibilities routinely acknowledged and addressed, the self-respect that can only be sustained in the absence of "envy, resentment and servility." That these pleasures, so conceived, would seem to many of his contemporaries paltry Lasch fully understood, and it was a part of his project to explain the roots, and the consequences, of that resistance.

I was never entirely comfortable with Kit's growing absorption in the society and ethos of the lower middle class, a class in which he found several of the qualities he wished to recommend. It was not that I did not admire those qualities. Like Kit, I had long been drawn not only to the sometimes austere utopianism of Frankfurt school theorists but to Adorno's "philosophical defense of the contingent, suffering, empirical subject"— the words are taken from Martin Jay's *Adorno*, but comparable formulations are to be found in Lasch, who also deplored Adorno's investment in the idea of a "cultural vanguard" alone equipped to realize the essential virtues. Like Kit, I had a feeling for writers—utterly inimical to the Frankfurt School theorists—who helped us to appreciate the virtues of patience, restraint, and modesty, who themselves exemplified an unspectacular probity of mind and an unfailing candor of expression. But I couldn't help feeling that Kit's attempt to ground his examination of the moderate or contingent virtues by situating them in a lower middle class culture "organized around the family, church, and neighborhood" would unnecessarily invite misreading and dismissal. Even if Kit was right— and I didn't think he was—in asserting that members of the lower middle class were typically more apt than others to exhibit "fortitude" in the face of adversity, or "honor" in the face of opportunities to "lie and cheat" and "get ahead," the fact was that such persons were also apt to exhibit unmistakable signs of provinciality, anti-intellectuality, obdurate resistance to change, racism and so on. Kit knew all of this, of course, and carefully addressed these very aspects of those whom he nonetheless— for other reasons—admired. He had no intention, he said, "of minimizing the narrowness and provincialism" or any of the other unlovely qualities he found. But because it was characteristic of progressive intellectuals to dismiss altogether the views and the outlook of persons they had never tried to understand, he would see what could be done to make a case for them. When I pointed out to him at lunch one afternoon in Saratoga Springs that this effort would cost him dearly, he responded that he couldn't get on with his work by calculating the effectiveness of this or that "strategy" for achieving good will.

The result of this determination is Kit's magnificent 1991 book on "progress and its critics," entitled *The True and Only Heaven*. As I predicted, and as Kit surely anticipated, the book was bitterly attacked for its "populism," often by reviewers who pretended that Kit was unaware of the "difficulties" anatomized in the very work they criticized. But Kit had long attracted more than his fair share of detractors, and he was surely right to believe that his latest work would survive, quite as several of his earlier books had done in spite of their sometimes hostile reception. More than once—most memorably in a 1979 symposium on his book *The Culture of Narcissism*—Kit had used the pages of *Salmagundi* to answer not only the critics we had assembled to address his book but other critics as well. More recently, in a 1992 "reply" to critics (*Salmagundi*, no. 93), Kit had noted that reviewers for leftist publications increasingly scorned him as a convert to the political right, while reviewers for *The New Criterion* and *National Review* expressed only scorn for his "eco-angst," his relentless attack on the ethos of capitalism, his "fixation on wage slavery" and his lamentable concern with questions of "social justice." So much was to be expected. "What I did not foresee," Kit wrote, "is the general reluctance. . . to explore the historical interpretations" at the heart of a work, the tendency among educated reviewers to read a work of political criticism and dense historical analysis "as if it were itself an ideological manifesto." This tendency seemed to Kit to point up the impoverished condition of political discourse in the United States, its domination by slogans and positions and accusations, and he was surprised that now and again a powerful new voice might nonetheless emerge.

Kit wrote on these and other matters for *Salmagundi*, and though he was a severe critic, he often wrote in praise, or in an attempt to extend an idea that had been cogently developed by an admirably independent thinker. When I wrote him in 1992 about an article on "Inequality" by Mickey Kaus of *The New Republic* and told him how much trouble I'd been having formulating a response to it for one of my Editor's Notebooks, he sent me a letter explaining what he took to be the root of the trouble I was having. Then, a few months later, I received a new installment of his *Salmagundi* column, this one focussed on Kaus and

"Inequality" and carefully engaging—as I'd requested in my letter—not only the very important ideas Kaus had raised but the framework of the larger "discussion" to which Kaus had contributed. The column appeared in issue No. 98-99.

In fact it always seemed to me extraordinary that Kit was ever willing to take up my proposals for various projects. When I asked him to write on Lewis Mumford, or on Hannah Arendt or George Orwell, he did. When I hoped he'd contribute to a symposium on "The Politics of Anti-Realism" or on nationalism, he did not disappoint me. At a three-day *Salmagundi* meeting on "Intellectuals" in 1985 he feared that things would go off in too many directions, and so proposed on the evening things began that he try to pull things together each day by summarizing the ground we'd traversed, identifying common themes and suggesting what would be the most fruitful directions we might take in subsequent sessions. To accomplish this he retired to his room immediately after dinner and lunch each day, emerging with freshly filled pages of cunning observation and commentary, to be delivered throughout the proceedings as recapitulation and instigation. The published results of this extraordinary intervention appear in *Salmagundi*, No. 70-71(1986).

Often, as we planned a special issue or a public conference, I'd ask Kit for suggestions. Most recently he helped us to select the participants for a three-day meeting on race and racism in America, at the end of which he characteristically apologized—this time for being so taken with much that others had said that he spoke less often than he expected he would. Last year I wrote to him about our hope to bring out an issue of the magazine on "The New Puritanism," and though he was rightly skeptical about the term itself, he was predictably enthusiastic and full of ideas about the direction such an issue might take. He recommended contributors, and agreed to write a lengthy introductory essay for the volume. But by the fall of 1993, having been told that he had no hope against the cancer he had been struggling against for about a year, he wrote to withdraw from the project. When Peg Boyers and I visited with him and Nell Commager Lasch in Rochester in November, he was wonderfully and vividly himself, if clearly weakened by the progress of the disease and by the weekly treatments he was taking to give himself a little more time. He was very excited about the work he had been doing to ready two volumes of previously uncollected papers for book publication. In the year previous to our visit he had written a substantial introduction to one of the volumes and prepared other kinds of connective tissue to bind together what might otherwise have seemed disparate materials. It gave him obvious pleasure to show us pieces of the assembled manuscript. Off and on in the afternoon he spoke eagerly on the phone with close friends like Jean Elshtain and Rochelle Gurstein. We talked about politics and children, about music and house construction. We reminisced a little about close and bristling encounters at *Salmagundi* conferences. He was interested in everything, unillusioned, uncomplaining, fiercely lucid.

It will take a long time for those of us who knew him, and for others who were stirred and chastened by his writing, to accept that he is gone.